LAW, RELIGION, CONSTITUTION

Law, Religion, Constitution

Freedom of Religion, Equal Treatment, and the Law

Edited by

W. COLE DURHAM, JR.
Brigham Young University, USA

SILVIO FERRARI
University of Milan, Italy

CRISTIANA CIANITTO
University of Milan, Italy

DONLU THAYER
Brigham Young University, USA

Routledge
Taylor & Francis Group
LONDON AND NEW YORK

First published 2013 by Ashgate Publishing

2 Park Square, Milton Park, Abingdon, Oxfordshire OX14 4RN
52 Vanderbilt Avenue, New York, NY 10017

Routledge is an imprint of the Taylor & Francis Group, an informa business

First issued in paperback 2020

British Library Cataloguing in Publication Data
A catalogue record for this book is available from the British Library

The Library of Congress has cataloged the printed edition as follows:
Ferrari, Silvio.
Law, religion, constitution: freedom of religion, equal treatment, and the law/by Silvio Ferrari, W. Cole Durham, Jr., Cristiana Cianitto, and Donlu D. Thayer.
pages cm
Includes bibliographical references and index.
ISBN 978-1-4724-1613-1 (hardback: alk. paper)
1. Freedom of religion. 2. Religion and law. 3. Constitutional law—Religious aspects.
4. Church and state. 5. Religious pluralism. I. Durham, W. Cole, Jr., 1948-
II. Cianitto, Cristiana. III. Thayer, Donlu D. IV. Title.
K3258.F47 2013

342.08'52—dc23

2013011978

ISBN 978-1-4724-1613-1 (hbk)
ISBN 978-0-367-60147-8 (pbk)

Contents

List of Contributors

Carmen Asiaín Pereira, University of Montevideo, Montevideo, Paraguay

Zachary R. Calo, Valparaiso University, Valparaiso, United States of America

Santiago Cañamares Arribas, Complutense University, Madrid, Spain

Pauline Capdevielle, National University of Mexico, Mexico City, Mexico.

Cristiana Cianitto, University of Milan, Milan, Italy

W. Cole Durham, Jr., Brigham Young University, Provo, Utah, United States of America

Nassima Ferchiche, University of Aix-Marseille, Aix-en-Provence, France

Silvio Ferrari, University of Milan, Milan, Italy

Alain Garay, Lawyer, Advisor of the Organization for Security and Cooperation in Europe (OSCE), Paris, France

Carl Hollan, Brigham Young University, Provo, Utah, United States of America

Iván C. Ibán, Complutense University, Madrid, Spain

Natan Lerner, Interdisciplinary Center (IDC), Herzliya, Israel

Ofrit Liviatan, Harward University, Cambridge, United States of America

Rafael Palomino Lozano, Complutense University, Madrid, Spain

Gianluca P. Parolin, American University, Cairo, Egypt

Liu Peng, China Academy of Social Sciences, Beijing, China

Jorge Precht Pizarro, Catholic University of Santiago, Santiago, Chile

Kofi Quashigah, University of Ghana, Accra, Ghana

Julian Rivers, University of Bristol, Bristol, United Kingdom

Gerhard Robbers, University of Trier, Trier, Germany

Brett G. Scharffs, Brigham Young University, Provo, Utah, United States of America

Pamela Slotte, University of Helsinki, Helsinki, Finland

Emma Svensson, Uppsala University, Uppsala, Sweden

Kanak Bikram Thapa, Tribhuvan University, Kathmandu, Nepal

Donlu Thayer, International Center for Law and Religion Studies, Brigham Young University, Provo, Utah, United States of America

Helena van Coller, Rhodes University, Grahamstown, South Africa

Johan D. van der Vyver, Emory University, Atlanta, United States of America

Preface

W. Cole Durham, Jr.

With this volume, the International Consortium for Law and Religion Studies ('ICLARS') continues its tradition of providing important contributions to current understanding of the necessarily interdisciplinary field of law and religion. ICLARS was founded in 2007 based on the vision, energy and committed scholarship of Professor Silvio Ferrari of the University of Milan. Now embracing roughly 300 members from more than 40 countries, ICLARS serves as an umbrella organization for scholars and experts around the world engaged in academic research regarding the field of law and religion. While the primary focus of this research is on law, this center of gravity necessarily draws into its orbit work from a variety of other disciplines.

Like *Law and Religion in the 21st Century: Relations between States and Religious Communities*,[1] the volume issued after the first ICLARS conference, held in Milan in 2009, the present volume contains a selection of the chapters presented at the second ICLARS conference held at the Faculty of Law of the Pontifical Catholic University of Chile in Santiago, Chile from 8–10 September 2011.

One of the major themes running through the Santiago conference was voiced by Gerhard Robbers: 'Religion is on the rise again.'[2] The view of history as a progressive process of secularization is giving way to the recognition that for sizeable portions of the world's populations, the religious factor is here to stay, and while it is being manifested in new ways, it continues to play a significant role 'either individually or in community with others and in public and in private', to use the operative phrase from Article 18 of the International Covenant on Civil and Political Rights. This is evident at the level of constitutional texts in numerous constitutions around the world, as described comprehensively by Iván Ibán in his Chapter on 'God in Constitutions and Godless Constitutions'.[3] But it is evident as well in more substantive ways as countries everywhere wrestle with continuing questions about the nature of the modern state and its relationship to religious institutions and to religious life.[4] Questions about religious symbols, from Muslim headcoverings

---

1 S. Ferrari and R.Cristofori (eds.), *Law and Religion in the21st Century: Relations between States and Religious Communities* (London: Ashgate, 2010).

2 G. Robbers, 'Church and State Relations in the Constitutions', Chapter 3. (Note that all references to chapters in these notes are to chapters in this volume.)

3 I. C. Ibán, 'God in Constitutions and Godless Constitutions', Chapter 2.

4 J. Martínez-Torrón and W. C. Durham, Jr., *Religion and the Secular State/La Religion et l'*État *laïque*, Interim National Reports Issued for the Occasion of the XVIIIth

to Italian crucifixes in public schools, raise recurrent sensitivities. Debates about 'defamation of religions'[5] have been prominent in UN circles and elsewhere.[6] Questions about the extent of cooperation of church and state in the form of funding of religious instruction, religiously affiliated institutions, faith-based initiatives that assist in carrying out public tasks, recur everywhere. Cases in both the European Court of Human Rights and the United States Supreme Court have focused great attention on the scope of religious autonomy, particularly with respect to the hiring, supervising, disciplining, and termination of religious personnel.[7]

Several chapters in the volume address the constitutions of a widely dispersed and representative set of countries (e.g., China,[8] England,[9] Israel,[10] Mexico,[11] Nepal,[12] Spain, [13] South Africa[14]) while others provide coverage that is regional

International Congress of Comparative Law (Provo: International Center for Law and Religion Studies, 2010), 3–5, available at http://www.iclrs.org/index.php?pageId=3&contentId=20&blurbId=975.

5 For a collection of UN documents treating this issue see *'Defamation of Religions' – UN Documents Relating to the Topic*, at http://www.religlaw.org/index.php?pageId=19&linkId=188&contentId=1626&blurbId=778.

6 See R. C. Blitt, 'The Bottom-up Journey of "Defamation of Religion" from Muslim States to the United Nations: A Case Study of the Migration of Anti-Constitutional Ideas', in A. Sarat (ed.), *Human Rights: New Possibilities/New Problems: Studies in Law, Politics, and Society* (2011) 56:1, 212–211; R. C. Blitt, 'Should New Bills of Rights Address Emerging International Human Rights Norms? The Challenge of 'Defamation of Religion', *Northwestern Journal of International Human Rights* (2010) 9:1-26.

7 See, e.g., *Hosanna-Tabor Evangelical Lutheran Church and School v. EEOC*, 132 S.Ct. 694 (2012); *Obst v. Germany*, App. No. 425/03, 23 September 2010; *Schüth v. Germany*, App. No. 1620/03, 23 September 2010; *Siebenhaar v. Germany*, App. No. 18136/02, 3 February 2011. The religious autonomy theme is discussed extensively in W. C. Durham, Jr., 'Religion and the World's Constitutions,' Chapter 1; J. D. van der Vyver, 'Constitutional Protections and Limits to Religious Freedom', Chapter 6; and H. van Coller, 'Religioius Institutions and Fundamental Rights: Applicability, Interaction and Limitations of South Africa', Chapter 11.

8 Liu Peng, B. G. Scharffs, and C. Hollan, 'Constitutional, Legislative and Regulatory Change Regarding Religion in China', Chapter 14.

9 J. Rivers, 'The Right to Religious Liberty in English Law', Chapter 16.

10 N. Lerner, 'Religion and Basic Laws in Israel', Chapter 12.

11 P. Capdevielle, 'The Constitutional principle of Separation between Church and State in Mexico', Chapter 8.

12 K. B. Thapa, 'Religion and Equal Treatment in the Nepalese Constitution', Chapter 13.

13 S. Cañamares Arribas, 'Religious Equality in the Spanish Constitutional System', Chapter 17.

14 Van Coller, Chapter 11.

in nature (e.g., Latin America,[15] the Maghreb,[16] Sub-Saharan Africa,[17] and Islamic countries more generally.[18]) The chapters that focus on particular states each shed significant light on the specific legal systems involved. In the China chapter, for example, the authors situate the current regulatory scheme in its historical context, drawing on Yang Fenggang's three-market explanation that describes current practical realities.[19] In this picture, as adapted by the authors, there are a small number of red market (approved) religions, a substantial number of black market (forbidden) religions, and a gray market of religious groups that are allowed to function without legal protection. The authors argue in favor of better implementation of the rule of law in the religious domain in China. The chapter on the English system laments that there is an 'increasing intolerance of the public presence and status of religion' and that 'the law seems to be trivializing the claims of religions and instead exalting its own secular ethos as a fundamental constitutional good.'[20] The Israeli and Nepali chapters highlight challenges in countries where prevailing religions continue to exert considerable power. The Mexican chapter traces the place of religion in a country that has been highly laicized for over a century, identifying practical problems for religious communities within a separationist context. Finally, the chapter on South Africa,[21] flanked by considerable discussion of South Africa in Johan van der Vyver's chapter,[22] describes how religious autonomy protections work out in a constitution with a strong equalitarian and dignitarian bent.

While several of the country-specific and regional chapters focus on specific constitutional texts, several recognize that in the contemporary constitutional setting, it is important to go beyond the text and focus on the so-called 'block of constitutionality'—i.e., the combination of constitutional text, relevant norms drawn from international law, constitutional jurisprudence and principles which together mold contemporary constitutional outcomes. The chapter by Jorge Precht[23] explores this notion in particular detail. He first identifies relevant international norms bearing on the religion-state interface, noting constitutions that have been explicitly updated to take international norms into account, but

15 C. Asiaín Pereira, 'Religion and Religions in the Latin American Constitutional Framework', Chapter 7.

16 N. Ferchiche, 'Religious Freedom in the Constitutions of the Maghreb', Chapter 10.

17 K. Quashigah, 'Constitutional Protection of Religious and Cultural Minorities in Sub-Saharan Africa', Chapter 9.

18 G. P. Parolin, 'Religion and the Sources of Law: *Sharî'ah* in Constitutions', Chapter 5.

19 See F. Yang, 'The Red, Black, and Gray Markets of Religion in China', *The Sociological Quarterly* (2006) 47:93.

20 Rivers, Chapter 16, concluding paragraph.

21 Van Coller, Chapter 11.

22 Van der Vyver, Chapter 6.

23 J. Precht Pizarro, 'Constitutional Reception of International Law Provisions on Religious Freedom', Chapter 4.

also observing that many have not kept up with the latest developments. He contends that the shortfalls may not be as serious as they first appear, because international norms may be received directly into domestic legal systems, and ultimate outcomes are shaped by the whole 'block of constitutionality'. Also, what have been called 'laws in constitutional orbit'[24] may raise standards by legislation, thereby curing constitutional shortfalls. Carmen Asiaìn also draws attention to the fact that, increasingly, constitutional analysis has to take this richer 'block of constitutionality' into account.

Emma Svensson views the fusion of multiple layers of constitutional law or constitution-like norms from another perspective: that of constitutionalization of religious freedom within the evolving context of the European Union.[25] She provides a detailed examination of the way that religious freedom norms of the Lisbon Treaty's Charter of Fundamental Rights can be expected to interact with, supplement, and cohere with the more detailed picture of freedom of religion or belief emerging from the burgeoning jurisprudence of the European Court of Human Rights.[26] While in general she anticipates that EU law as developed by the European Court of Justice will be consistent with the jurisprudence of the Strasbourg Court, there are ways that the ECJ's focus on issues such as right to travel, free movement of capital, and right to establishment may strengthen some religiously significant aspects of these rights.

For those following developments in the Muslim world, several of the contributions in this volume will be of particular interest. Gianluca Parolin's essay provides a very insightful overview of the way Islamic law (*Sharî'ah*) is conceptualized in a variety of contemporary states. He surveys the evolution of key constitutional phrases that grapple with this issue (e.g., *Sharî'ah* as 'a'/'the' [chief/sole] source of [legislation/law]), and how these ideas have migrated from constitution to constitution in recent years. He then describes how the varying formal constitutional language is dealt with as a matter of interpretation and explains shifting paradigms concerning the relationship of *Sharî'ah* to the other portions of national legal systems resulting from the move from pre-modern to modern legal systems.[27] Nassima Ferchiche provides an in-depth picture of post-Arab awakening in Maghreb countries against the background of historical religion-state relations, thereby providing very helpful insight into still unfolding developments.[28] A still

24 I. C. Lupu, 'Statutes Revolving in Constitutional Law Orbits', *Virginial Law Review* (1993) 79:1.

25 E. Svensson, 'The Constitutionalization of Freedom of Religion in the European Union: What Changes Are the Charter of Fundamental Rights Expected to Bring About?', Chapter 15.

26 For convenient access to this jurisprudence, consult www.strasbourgconsortium.org

27 Parolin, Chapter 5.

28 Ferchiche, Chapter 10.

different slant emerges in Kofi Quashigah's chapter, where he contrasts treatment of Christianity, Islam, and traditional religions in Sub-Saharan Africa.[29]

The final section of the book deals with a number of forefront issues that reflect permanent underlying tensions in the religion-state domain. Alain Garay explores ways that media and hate speech law collide with religious freedom protections, emphasizing problems in the concrete context of France, including complications added by the Internet age.[30] Pamela Slotte and Rafael Palomino address different aspects of the perennial and perennially difficult problems of religion in educational settings. Slotte's chapter studies the results of significant religious freedom reforms in Finnish schools that have been in place for about a decade. She analyzes the legislative changes that were made and how education professionals, NGOs, and faith communities have experienced the changes, including reactions to the introduction of a compulsory ethics class, and at a deeper level, the challenge of being neutral in a world with rival perceptions of what constitutes neutral treatment. She concludes, drawing on Emmanuel Levinas, with the notion that 'freedom should not be understood as "the reduction of the other to the same".'[31] Palomino describes various models of religious education extant in Europe, and then analyzes approaches of Council of Europe and European Court pronouncements on religious education, identifying assumptions in the approaches they propound. In the end, he concludes that where denominational education continues, 'maximum optionality' is essential. More can be required when teaching *about* religion is involved. But problems will inevitably remain.[32] Ofrit Liviatan provides a fascinating perspective on the comparative social role of law in American and European constitutional conflicts.[33] Zachary Calo rounds things out with a philosophical exploration of tensions between secular human rights and religious pluralism, taking the British debate about the place of Islam in British society as a starting point.[34]

Running through all the contributions are major themes that make law and religion an enduring and perpetually relevant topic: the tensions between secular rules and conscientious beliefs that are as old as Antigone; the ontological divide between spiritual and temporal, and how that is understood, interpreted, policed,

---

29 Quashigah, Chapter 9.

30 A. Garay, 'Freedom of Religion and Freedom of Speech in the French Case Law: A Constitutional Dilemma', Chapter 18.

31 P. Slotte, 'Freedom of Religion, Freedom of Conscience and Education—A Nordic Example', Chapter 19, quoting E. Lévinas, 'Philosophy and the Idea of Infinity', in *Collected Philosophical Papers by Emmanuel Lévinas* (A. Lingis, trans.) (Dordrecht: Martinus Nijhoff Publishers, 1987), 48.

32 R. Palomino Lozano, 'Religion and Education in the Council of Europe: Toward a "Soft" Constitutionalization of a Model of Religious Teaching?', Chapter 20.

33 O. Liviatan, 'Comparing Law's Social Role in American and Western European Constitutional Conflicts over Abortion', Chapter 21.

34 Z. R. Calo, 'Secular Human Rights, and Religious Pluralism: The British Debate', Chapter 22.

and structured in from varying religious perspectives and in different state systems; the extent to which religious institutions and persons are allowed autonomy in religious matters; how legitimate limitations on freedom of religion or belief are analyzed and implemented, and so on. The richness of the contributions of this volume portends a fruitful future for the International Consortium of Law and Religion Studies, which played a key role in bringing them together.

Acknowledgments

This volume could not have been completed without valuable input on many sides. We necessarily begin by acknowledging the important role played by the International Consortium for Law and Religion Studies ('ICLARS') and its Steering Committee and general membership. We are grateful for their support in encouraging contributions to the necessarily interdisciplinary field of law and religion. ICLARS was founded in 2007 and now embraces roughly 300 members from more than 40 countries. It serves as an umbrella organization for scholars and experts around the world engaged in academic research regarding law and religion. We appreciate the impetus from this organization which has already done much to foster scholarship in this field. We also express gratitude to the Latin American Consortium for Religious Liberty, which joined with ICLARS in holding the conference on 'Religion and Constitution' in Santiago, Chile, from 8–10 September 2011. That conference provided the initial context for the chapters in this volume.

For support that made the Santiago Conference a success, we owe major thanks to the Faculty of Law of the Catholic Pontifical University of Chile and its Center for Religious Liberty Law, the General Secretariat of the Presidency of the National Government of Chile, and the International Center for Law and Religion Studies at Brigham Young University ('ICLRS'), as well as to Banco Santander, CCU, Banco Security, PUROCOBRE, and Pérez de Arce Abogados Limitada. Several professors played a critical role in the overall organization and work of the conference: Ana María Celis Brunet, María Elena Pimstein Scroggie, René Cortínez Castro S.J., Sebastián Zárate, and Maurizio Sovino. At Brigham Young University, Professor Gary Doxey and Robert Smith provided important support. We are also grateful for the work performed by Paulina Eyzaguirre and Anita Rivera, staff members of the Center for Religious Liberty, and by Deborah Wright at ICLRS. Thanks also to Chilean law students Vicente Allende, Constanza Garrido, Tomás Greene, Javier Hernández, Francisco Marin, Rodrigo Pérez de Arce, Joaquín Santuber, and Valentina Venegas, as well as other volunteers, including Pilar Celis Brunet, Isabel Bilbao, Pilar Lioi, Benjamín Echeverria, and Nicole Figari in Chile and Eimi Priddis at BYU. We are of course particularly grateful for the authors of the many chapters in this volume.

A final word of thanks goes to the editorial staff at Ashgate for encouraging the work, with particular gratitude to Bethan Dixon and Sarah Horsley for their efforts in design and editing, and for their patience in expediting publication of the volume.

PART I
Religion and Constitution: Main Themes

Chapter 1
Religion and the World's Constitutions

W. Cole Durham, Jr.[1]

Introduction

At the outset of these reflections on 'Religion and the World's Constitutions', it is appropriate that I express appreciation for the foundational work of Professor Silvio Ferrari in organizing the International Consortium for Law and Religion Studies ('ICLARS').

As I thought about the extensive work that Silvio has done over the years, my mind went back to one of my early experiences with him. We were in Romania. It was the conclusion of a long day at a conference on religious freedom issues. Because relevant legislation was pending in the Romanian parliament, a small group of us were invited to meet with a group of senators responsible for clearing all legislation that might have impact on Romania's accession to the European Union. We expected only a short courtesy visit, because the senators had just finished a lengthy meeting on other matters. In fact, they spent over an hour with us. It fell to me to introduce the group and make some introductory remarks about religious freedom principles relevant to the legislation. I could see their eyes glazing over, and the unstated thoughts: 'One more irrelevant American.' At that point, Silvio came to my rescue, indicating that while there are significant differences between United States and European approaches, there are in fact core principles that we all share as a common heritage, and the principles I had been addressing were among those on which strong consensus exists.

That was Silvio at his best: recognizing what had to be said; saying it effectively and concisely; and identifying the consensus ideas that tie all of us together. I thank him for that late afternoon, and for countless other moments over the past two decades I have known him when he has been the leader quietly and precisely identifying common principles and finding the way we could go forward together.

---

1 The author wishes to thank Donlu Thayer for assistance in the preparation of this chapter. The current version is based on the keynote address delivered at the Second Conference of the International Consortium for Law and Religion Studies held in Santiago, Chile from 8–10 September 2011. The chapter has been adapted from the original speech format and has been updated to take into account decisions in key cases decided since the address was originally delivered and to take into account additional research conducted in the interim.

I hope that in a small way, I can continue that tradition in this chapter, which is intended to serve in part as an introduction of the general theme running through this volume. As I have reflected on the topic of religion and the world's constitutions, I have been conscious of the many ways that ICLARS, with its focus on law and religion studies, contributes to understanding of this impossibly broad theme. I realize that my experience with Silvio has been replicated many times over through collaboration with the wonderful people working in the law and religion field. Few fields are blessed with so many experts committed to working together to optimize contributions for the common good.

Law and religion embraces several sub-disciplines: (1) comparative law study of the relationship of religion and state institutions; (2) defense of human and constitutional rights to freedom of religion or belief; (3) exploration of the relationship between religious and secular legal systems, both from the side of law and from the side of theology; (4) empirical research on the place of religion in society; and (5) other salient areas where law and religion interact (e.g. law and theology, legal history, sociology of law, legal philosophy). No one is capable of mastering all of these sub-fields. My hope in this chapter is to raise issues urgently needing the best work that each of us, and others we know, can provide.

The Constitutional Setting

The basic constitutional and international human rights setting is familiar. By the middle of the twentieth century, freedom of religion or belief came to be recognized as a fundamental human right—at least in theory, if not always in practice. By the time that international human rights were being codified in the aftermath of World War II, freedom of religion or belief emerged as an axiomatic feature of the international human rights regime, memorialized in Article 18 of the Universal Declaration of Human Rights,[2] Article 18 of the International Covenant on Civil and Political Rights (ICCPR),[3] in the 1981 United Nations Declaration on the Elimination of All Forms of Intolerance and of Discrimination Based on Religion or Belief,[4] and in a variety of other international instruments.[5]

Most modern constitutions have provisions affirming the right to freedom of religion or belief. This right is recognized in the overwhelming majority of the

2 GA Res. 217 (A(III), December 10, 1948, UN Doc. A/810 at 71 (1948)).

3 GA Res. 2200A, UN GAOR, 21st Sess., Supp. no. 16 at 52, 55, UN Doc A/6316 (1966), 999 U.N.T.S. 171 (1976) (Art. 18).

4 Adopted 18 Jan. 1982, GA Res 55, 36 UN GAOR Supp. (No. 51), UN Doc. A/RES/36/55 (1982).

5 American Declaration of the Rights and Duties of Man, art. III, OAS Res. XXX, adopted by the Ninth International Conference of American States, Bogota (1948): Novena Conferencia Internacional Americana, *6 Actas y Documentos* (1953), 297–302.

world's constitutions,[6] including virtually every European constitution and the constitution of every independent country in the Western Hemisphere.

While there are of course disputes about the universality of human rights norms, freedom of religion or belief has come to be recognized by most nations of the world (and by most religions) as a principle that has universal validity.[7] Constitutions and laws should be construed in ways that respect this fundamental principle, recognizing that although it is universal, it can and should be implemented in diverse ways in different cultural and historical settings. Comparative constitutional analysis can expand horizons, but in itself, it has no intrinsic authority,[8] except to

---

6 For a summary analysis of the relevant provisions, see 'Religion in World Constitutions' at http://www.religlaw.org/index.php?contentId=1926&linkId=188&pageId=19.

7 A sign of its universality is that the right to freedom of religion or belief has been broadly recognized along with other key human rights as having acquired the status of customary international law. See, e.g. (arguing that the 1981 Universal Declaration is customary law): P. Alston, 'The Universal Declaration at 35: Western and Passé or Alive and Universal', 30 *The Review of the International Commission of Jurists* (1983), 69; R. Bilder, 'The Status of International Human Rights Law: An Overview', in J. Tuttle (ed.), *International Human Rights Law and Practice* (Chicago: American Bar Association, 1978), 8; D. Davis, 'The Evolution of Religious Freedom as a Universal Human Right: Examining the Role of the 1981 United Nations Declaration on the Elimination of all Forms of Intolerance and of Discrimination Based on Religion or Belief, *Brigham Young University Law Review* (2002), 230; Louis Henkin, *The Age of Rights*, (New York: Columbia University Press, 1990), 19; J. Humphrey, *No Distant Millennium: The International Law of Human Rights* (Paris: UNESCO, 1989), 155 and 'The International Bill of Rights: Scope and Implementation', 17 *William and Mary Law Review* (1976), 529; R. B. Lillich, 'Civil Rights', in T. Meron (ed.), *Human Rights in International Law: Legal and Policy Issues* (Oxford: Clarendon Press, 1984), 116; A.H. Robertson and J.G. Merrills, *Human Rights in the World*, 3d edn., (Manchester: Manchester University Press, 1989), 96; L.B. Sohn, 'The Human Rights Law of the Charter', 12 *Texas International Law Journal* (1977), 133; B.G.Tahzib, *Freedom of Religion or Belief: Ensuring Effective International Legal Protection* (Boston: Martinus Nijhoff, 1996), 184–85; Patrick Thornberry, *International Law and the Rights of Minorities* (Oxford: Clarendon Press, 1991), 237–38; Humphrey Waldcock, 'Human Rights in Contemporary International Law and the Significance of the European Convention', *The European Convention of Human Rights, Series No. 5* (London: British Institute of International & Comparative Law, 1965), 15 (arguing that the Universal Declaration is customary law). But see C. Evans, 'Time for a Treaty? The Legal Sufficiency of the Declaration on the Elimination of All Forms of Intolerance and Discrimination', *Brigham Young University Law Review* (2007), 631–32 (contending that while the 'long, slow, and on-going process of generating consensus around the fundamental need to protect religious freedom' is 'strengthening', as of yet they 'have generally not achieved the status of customary law').

8 For debates on the extent to which comparative law should influence U.S. jurisprudence, see *Atkins v. Virginia*, 536 U.S. 304, 316 n. 21, 347–48 (2002) (Stevens, J., for the Court and Scalia, J., dissenting); *Lawrence v. Texas*, 539 U.S. 558, 576–77, 598 (2003) (Kennedy, J., for the Court and Scalia, J., dissenting); *Printz v. United States*, 521 U.S. 898, 976–78 (1997) (Breyer, J., dissenting); R.B. Ginsburg, 'Foreword to the Third Edition', in D. P. Kommers and R. A. Miller (eds.), *The Constitutional Jurisprudence of the Federal*

the extent it yields insights that are genuinely persuasive to those charged with interpreting their own legal system—i.e., except to the extent it is persuasive to the judges and other officials responsible for interpreting constitutional norms, and to the people (the individuals and the communities) who ultimately judge the judges, constitute the constitutions, and choose their own freedom by deciding how they will rule and be ruled.[9]

The Right to Religious Autonomy

My aim in this chapter is not to describe in detail precisely how religion figures in the array of the world's constitutions, but to take one issue I regard as both particularly central and particularly urgent, and discuss how several of our related disciplines may make relevant contributions. The issue is religious autonomy. Religious autonomy as I am using it here is not a synonym for religious liberty in a more general sense, but is a competence of religious communities to decide upon and administer their own affairs without governmental interference. It is in effect a right of self-determination for religious groups.[10]

Republic of Germany, 3d rev. edn. (Durham, N.C.: Duke University Press, 2012), xi-xii ('Foreign opinions, of course, are not authoritative; they set no binding precedent for the U.S. judiciary. But they can add to the store of knowledge relevant to the solution of trying questions.'); G. L. Neuman, 'The Uses of International Law in Constitutional Interpretation', 98 *American Journal of International Law* (2004), 82; M. D. Ramsey, 'International Materials and Domestic Rights: Reflections on *Atkins* and *Lawrence*', 98 *American Journal of International Law* (2004), 69; M. Tushnet, 'The Possibilities of Comparative Constitutional Law', 108 *Yale Law Journal* (1999), 1225 and 'When is Knowing Less Better Than Knowing More? Unpacking the Controversy over Supreme Court Reference to Non-U.S. Law', *Minnesota Law Review* (2006) 90:1275; G. Sitaraman, 'The Use and Abuse of Foreign Law in Constitutional Interpretation', 32 *Harvard Journal of Law and Public Policy* (2009), 653. Other jurisdictions are often much more receptive to comparative constitutional law. This is inevitable in the European Court of Human Rights, given its multinational jurisdiction, and is formally sanctioned by the South African Constitution para. 39(1)(c) ('When interpreting the Bill of Rights, a court, tribunal or forum … may consider foreign law').

9 Parts of the foregoing are drawn from J. Martínez-Torrón and W. C. Durham, Jr., 'Religion and the Secular State', General Report prepared for the XVIIIth World Congress of Comparative Law (Provo, Utah: The International Center for Law and Religion Studies, July 2010), available at http://www.iclrs.org/content/blurb/files/General%20Report.pdf.

10 Among the excellent comparative collections on this topic are: G. Robbers (ed.), *Church Autonomy: A Comparative Survey* (Frankfurt: Peter Lang, 2002); H. Warnink (ed.), *Legal Position of Churches and Church Autonomy* (Leuven: Uitgerverij Peeters, 2001).

The issue is timely in light of a set of particularly significant decisions in the European Court of Human Rights[11] and in the the United States Supreme Court.[12] Each of these cases (as many like them in courts around the world) raises the question of the extent to which states may intervene in disputes between religious communities and their religious personnel. The U.S. case is representative. It involved a challenge to the existence and scope of the so-called 'ministerial exception', which protects the right of religious communities to select, supervise, discipline and terminate religious leaders without government interference. Precisely because this exception raises issues going to the core of religious autonomy doctrine, it has been characterized as the 'most important religious freedom case in 20 years'.[13] The case involved a fourth grade teacher, Cheryl Perich, who had served as a 'commissioned minister' at a religious school. Along with the Equal Employment Opportunity Commission (EEOC), she challenged her termination for insubordination and disruptive conduct, claiming that she had been discriminated against because of a disability. Nearly one hundred amici, representing most religions in the United States, filed briefs opposing Perich's claim.[14] In the lower federal courts, Perich and the EEOC accepted the general validity of the ministerial exception, but claimed it did not apply in her case because although she was serving as a 'called minister' and had some religious duties, she was only marginally involved in religious matters.

The stakes in the case were raised considerably by the decision made by lawyers for Perich and the EEOC at the Supreme Court level to switch tactics and mounta frontal attack on the validity of the ministerial exception, even though it had been unanimously approved by all the federal appellate courts for a period going back forty years.[15] This shift in strategy sought to extend the holding in an

---

11 *Obst v. Germany*, App. No. 425/03, 23 September 2010; *Schüth v. Germany*, App. No. 1620/03, 23 September 2010; *Siebenhaar v. Germany*, App. No. 18136/02, 3 February 2011; *Sindicatul 'Păstorul cel Bun' v. Romania*, App. No. 2330/09, 31 January 2012) (Third Section Judgment; Grand Chamber decision is pending).

12 Hosanna-Tabor Evangelical Lutheran Church and School v. EEOC, 132 S.Ct. 694 (2012).

13 R. Garnett, 'Here we go! The Court grants cert. in the ministerial-exception case', *Mirror of Justice Blog*, 28 March 2011, available at http://mirrorofjustice.blogs.com/mirrorofjustice/2011/03/here-we-go-the-court-grants-cert-in-the-ministerial-exception-case.html .

14 See 'The Becket Fund Files Final Supreme Court Brief in Church Employment Case, http://www.becketfund.org/the-becket-fund-files-final-supreme-court-brief-in-groundbreaking-church-employment-case/ .

15 *Natal* v. *Christian and Missionary Alliance*, 878 F.2d 1575 (1st Cir. 1989); *Rweyemamu* v. *Cote*, 520 F.3d 198, 204–10 (2d Cir. 2008); *Petruska* v. *Gannon University*, 462 F.3d 294, 303–07 (3d Cir. 2006); *EEOC* v. *Roman Catholic Diocese*, 213 F.3d 795, 800–05 (4th Cir. 2000); *Combs* v. *Central Texas Annual Conference*, 173 F.3d 343, 347–50 (5th Cir. 1999); *Hollins* v. *Methodist Healthcare, Inc.*, 474 F.3d 223, 225–27 (6th Cir. 2007); *Schleicher* v. *Salvation Army*, 518 F.3d 472, 475 (7th Cir. 2008); *Scharon* v.*St. Luke's*

earlier landmark decision, *Employment Division v. Smith*,[16] which held that neutral and generally applicable laws trump religious liberty claims. The *Smith* decision had noted an exception for an established line of religious autonomy cases,[17] but the government lawyers in *Hosanna-Tabor* sought to narrow or eliminate that exception. This line of attack on religious autonomy doctrine was unanimously rejected by the Supreme Court in its resolution of the case, but the full implications of this precedent will necessarily await elaboration in future cases. It is safe to say that this is an issue that Professor Ferrari (and many others in ICLARS) could easily help to resolve; this is not a problem limited to the United States.[18]

The Topography of Religious Autonomy

The right to religious autonomy raises issues of profound importance that are located at the heart of religion-state relations. At the same time, it is a problem that is richly layered. Working from the ground level to issues of progressively greater abstraction, the initial challenge is coming to terms with what can be described as the factual topography of the autonomy problem. This topography has at least four dimensions.

The first is the horizontal dimension, which begins with the core religious community—the church, synagogue, mosque, the core religious polity—and extends horizontally to controlled or affiliated entities such as integrated auxiliaries, religious schools, print and other media facilities, health care organizations, counseling services, humanitarian aid organizations, and other charitable entities. The horizontal dimension extends from the non-profit into the for-profit domain, since religious communities may choose to organize some profit-making activities to support their organizational missions or aims.

The second dimension involves the vertical array of types of personnel positions, ranging from religious leaders at the top (e.g., those who are understood as having the mantle of religious authority and leadership with the community,

---

Episcopal Presbyterian Hospitals, 929 F.2d 360, 362–63 (8th Cir. 1991); *Werft* v. *Desert Southwest Annual Conference*, 377 F.3d 1099, 1100–04 (9th Cir. 2004); *Bryce* v. *Episcopal Church*, 289 F.3d 648, 655–57 (10th Cir. 2002); *Gellington* v. *Christian Methodist Episcopal Church, Inc.*, 203 F.3d 1299, 1301–04 (11th Cir. 2000); *EEOC* v. *Catholic University*, 83 F.3d 455, 460–63 (DC Cir. 1996). The ministerial exceptions traces back to the decision of the Fifth Circuit in McClure v. Salvation Army, 460 F.2d 553 (5th Cir. 1972).

16 Employment Division, Department of Human Resources of Oregon v. Smith, 494 U.S. 872 (1990).

17 See *Smith* at 876–77, 887.

18 The *Hosanna-Tabor* case was in fact one in which many from ICLARS rendered assistance by providing input used in the amicus brief filed by the International Center for Law and Religion Studies, which I direct. Brief of Amicus Curiae International Center for Law and Religion Studies at Brigham Young University in Support of Petitioner (hereinafter 'Brief of Amicus Curiae ICLRS'), available at http://www.religlaw.org/document.php?DocumentID=5577. See 'Other Authorities' at viii–xvi for a list of those whose contributions were referenced in the brief.

such as hierarchical leaders—bishops, priests, pastors, ministers and the like) down through those who are charged with carrying out various other significant religiously significant functions (e.g., teachers, counselors, those who represent the community to the broader public, missionaries, and so forth) and including others who work or volunteer at religious institutions, with varying levels of engagement in religious tasks. The question along the vertical continuum is at what point personnel functions become so secular or so distinct from religious affairs that religious autonomy protections no longer apply.

The third or depth dimension is a reflection of the fact that different religious communities, whether as a matter of religious belief, administrative efficiency, or a combination of the two, configure the various aspects of the horizontal and religious dimensions of religious autonomy in different ways. This variation could be thought of as the pluralistic depth of types of autonomous structures that a society allows, nurtures and protects.

A final dimension is temporal: the nature of the autonomous institutions permitted and protected in various societies varies over time in accordance with a variety of higher level considerations. In all of these dimensions, the issue is how far the obligation of the state to defer to religious autonomy extends, and how this obligation of deference is to be understood.

The Substantive Scope of Religious Autonomy

For purposes of thischapter, I will be focusing on the issue of autonomy in matters of religious employment. But it is significant to note that this is only one of a wide range of issues covered by autonomy claims. The scope of religious autonomy issues is much broader, and it will be helpful to sketch the full range of this topography before proceeding further.[19] The substantive scope of religious autonomy covers a range of characteristics and activities of religious communities. Most fundamentally, it includes the ability to determine fundamental beliefs, including basic notions of doctrine, dogma and teachings. Among the key beliefs thus covered are beliefs about the structure of the religious polity of the community and the principles of its governance. In this sense, the ability to determine fundamental beliefs extends to formulating the norms by which the community is governed and administered, whether this takes the form of canon-law, informal rules of governance, or some other normative structure.

The substantive scope of religious autonomy also includes a range of issues that belong to the core ministry of the community. These include matters of worship, ritual and liturgy; establishing places of worship; confidential counseling and confession; teaching the faith to members, clergy, and to non-members; and humanitarian care for members and others. The religious employment cases I am

19 For an extended treatment of these issues, see W. C. Durham, Jr., 'The Right to Autonomy in Religious Affairs: A Comparative View', in G. Robbers (ed.), *Church Autonomy: A Comparative Survey* (Frankfurt am Main: Peter Lang, 2001), 683.

focusing on in this chapter fit in here. They are particularly significant for the life of any community because they involve the selection, supervision, disciplining and termination of the individuals who shape, represent and in a very real sense constitute and personify the religious community as it structures itself internally and as it relates to the world. Personnel issues include religious or ministerial personnel, employees and volunteers who contribute directly to the religious mission of the community, as well as other employees and volunteers who perform support services within and on behalf of the community.

Religious autonomy also determines church membership: requirements for entrance into, participation in, and withdrawal or expulsion from the community. The determination of the nature, governance and territorial arrangements of substructures, linkages to other religious communities, and so forth, are also very significant. Matters of finance are critical to the functioning of the organization, and the methods of acquiring, using, and disposing of funds and other church property are central issues for church administration.

Religious communities necessarily interact with the world and with surrounding legal systems in a variety of ways. In this regard, the right to acquire legal entity status is of immense practical importance.[20] The right to conduct religious life without such status is one way in which religious autonomy can be used, but most communities have come to prefer the convenience and the enabling power of liberal legal entity rules. Religious autonomy presupposes that access to entity status should be easy, and that the status acquired should be sufficient to carry out the full range of religious activities. Religious autonomy also includes the right to create sub-entities and to have them recognized as decided by the religious community. There are a range of spheres including cultural, educational, humanitarian aid, health care, and the like, where the activities of religious communities encounter state regulation. Religious communities should also have broad latitude and strong cooperation with respect to access to the military, hospitals, prisons, and chaplaincies.

The foregoing gives a quick sketch of the topography of the dimensions and scope of the religious autonomy issue. Study of this topography is itself one of the significant areas of within the field of law and religion studies. But the issues at stake go beyond describing the landscape to determining the nature of the protections available in this complex domain. This depends on the resolution of a number of higher level issues. These also engage the various sub-disciplines of law and religion in a variety of ways that are even more critical.

20 For an extended discussion of these issues, see W. C. Durham, Jr., 'Legal Status of Religious Organizations: A Comparative Overview', 8:2 *The Review of Faith & International Affairs* (2010), 3–14, available at http://www.informaworld.com/smpp/section?content=a923076944&fulltext=713240928.

Levels of Discourse Bearing on Religious Autonomy

Religious Autonomy and Legislation

In what follows, I first provide a catalogue of the successive levels of inquiry in which the religious personnel issues are nested, and then comment on how the evolution of discourse at each of these levels is being eroded, so that the fundamental protections of religious autonomy in concrete cases are being weakened. The initial level consists of normal labor and anti-discrimination law as it applies to the domain of religious personnel. This includes both concrete legislation imposing normal labor law and anti-discrimination rules that should defer to or accommodate religious autonomy, and more general laws structuring broad sectors of social life that impinge on religious communities and their personnel. Ultimately, the autonomy question is about how religious autonomy shapes the contours of state-imposed norms that determine the extent of permissible state encroachment in this sphere, and how reciprocally those state-imposed norms shape the structures of religious autonomy.

Specialized Legal Disciplines

I will not say much about this domain, except to note that it is typically a specialized field of legal practice, and in many countries, the politics of labor law is highly secularized and often associated with fairly anti-religious ideologies. My underlying contention is that it is too easy in our time to see issues of religious employment through the filter of standard specialized practice—as just one more anti-discrimination case, with just one more insensitive employer. In this respect, employment law is one of many increasingly isolated specialty areas in contemporary societies characterized by burgeoning state regulation. It is all to easy to see the interface of with religion in each of these areas from the perspective of the relevant specialty disciplines, which tend to filter out or overlook the constitutional religious freedom values at stake.

In the leading German case regarding religious personnel, for example, lower labor courts invalidated dismissals of personnel in religiously affiliated institutions, failing to take into account the unique religious autonomy issues involved. It was only when the cases reached the German Constitutional Court that constitutional values of religious autonomy were taken into account and vindicated.[21] Narrow bureaucratic vision that fails to look beyond the horizon of typical labor law cases can easily overlook much deeper constitutional issues that are vital to the protection not only of authentic religious diversity, but to the broader values associated with rich and genuine pluralism. More generally, the recurrent difficulty is that too often, the domains of specialty disciplines are experienced as autonomous legal realms, seldom penetrated by more fundamental constitutional norms.

---

21 Federal Constitutional Court of Germany, BVerfGE 70, 138 (1985).

Constitutional Analysis

This leads to analysis of the place of religious autonomy at the level of constitutional analysis. In the United States this raises questions about the nature of the doctrinal grounding of religious autonomy: is it derived from free exercise, non-establishment, freedom of expression, freedom of association, some combination of these, or is it an independent constitutional principle, reflecting or based upon some more fundamental principle? The *Hosanna-Tabor* decision has clearly held that the ministerial exception is grounded in the Free Exercise and Establishment Clauses, and implicitly recognized that it is protected by freedom of association as well.[22] Whether it should be thought of as a structural feature of the constitution or as a more standard right subject to interest balancing remains open.[23] Similar questions arise in other constitutional and human rights regimes, depending on the texts and the existing jurisprudence in the relevant systems. For example, religious autonomy doctrine in the European Court of Human Rights is predicated on rights to freedom of religion and freedom of association, read in light of each other.[24]

The way that religious autonomy is conceptualized at the constitutional level may lead to significant variation in analysis. For example, about a third of the constitutions of the world have provisions taking a strictly secular approach to religion-state affairs, whether by calling for separation of religious and state institutions,[25] for non-establishment (i.e., not allowing formal creation or

22 *Hosanna-Tabor*, 132 S.Ct. at 706.

23 Compare M. A. Helfand, 'Religion's Footnote Four: Church Autonomy as Arbitration' (forthcoming, *Minnesota Law Review*) (contending that the *Hosanna-Tabor* Court's treatment of the ministerial exception as an affirmative defense rather than as a jurisdictional matter signals movement away from a structural approach to religious autonomy doctrine) with C. H. Esbeck, 'A Religious Organization's Autonomy in Matters of Self-Governance: Hosanna-Tabor and the First Amendment', available at *http://papers.ssrn.com/sol3/papers.cfm?abstract_id=2016930##* (maintaining that *Hosanna-Tabor* sets a 'structural limit on the scope of the government's authority').

24 See, e.g., *Svyato-Mykhaylivska Parafiya v. Ukraine*, App. No. 77703/01, 14 September 2007, para. 112 (Article 9 (freedom of religion) must be interpreted in light of Article 12 (freedom of association)); *Religionsgemeinschaft der Zeugen Jehovas and Others v. Austria*, App. No. 40825/98, 31 July 2008, paras. 61, 63 (same); *Hasan and Chaush v. Bulgaria* (Grand Chamber), App. No. 30985/96, 26 October 2000, para. 62 (same).

25 Angola art. 8; Armenia art. 8.1; Azerbaijan art. 18 cl. 1; Bhutan art. 3 cl. 3; Bolivia art. 4 ('The state is independent of religion'); Bulgaria art. 13 cl. 2; Cameroon pmbl. ¶ 5 cl. 14 ('neutrality and independence of the State'); Cape Verde arts. 2 cl. 2, 48 cl. 3, 102 cl. 3; Chad art. 1; Croatia art. 41 cl. 1; Cuba art. 8; Ethiopia art. 11; Gabon arts. 2, 6 cl. 1; Guinea-Bissau art. 6 cl. 1; Hungary art. 60 cl. 3; Kyrgyzstan art. 8 cl. 3; Hungary art. 60 cl. 3; Italy art. 7 ('The state and the Catholic Church are independent and sovereign, each within its own sphere.'); Japan art. 20 cl.1 ('No religious organization shall receive any privileges from the State, nor exercise any political authority;'); South Korea art. 20 cl. 2; Latvia art. 99; Liberia art. 14; Macedonia art. 19 cl. 3; Mexico art. 130; Mongolia art. 9 cl. 2; Montenegro art. 14; Mozambique arts. 12, 292; Niger arts. 4, 152; Peru art. 50 ('framework

recognition of a state religion),[26] or for maintenance of the secularity of the state.[27] (Of course, there is some overlap in these categories.) In separationist regimes, it is easier to make the case that religious autonomy should be understood as a jurisdictional or structural issue—as a domain lying beyond (or separate from) the competence of the state in an absolute, jurisdictional sense. Where the issue of religious autonomy is approached through a regime protecting freedom of religion or belief without a separation clause, it is more natural to see religious autonomy as an extension of individual religious freedom rights, and to use various balancing or proportionality techniques to weigh autonomy claims against other regulatory interests of the state.

Structural features of constitutional orders that are not overtly focused on the place of religion in society can also have significant ramifications for religious autonomy. For example, with the emergence of massive modern states, there is a tendency to presume that states are omnicompetent and that their authority extends to all domains. The idea of limited government has suffered substantial erosion, and the notion that there are domains to which the state's authority does not extend has slipped to the back of legal consciousness. Yet theories of limited government are related in critical ways to the idea religious autonomy.[28] Indeed, ensuring

---

of independence and autonomy'; Philippines art. 2 cl. 6; Portugal art. 41 cl. 4; Russia art. 14, cl. 2; Serbia art. 11; Slovenia art. 7 cl. 1; Tajikistan art. 8; Turkmenistan art. 12; Ukraine art. 25; Uzbekistan art. 61.

26 See, e.g., Australia art. 116; Brazil art. 19; Czech Republic Charter of Fundamental Rights and Basic Freedoms art. 2, cl. 1 ('it may not be bound either by an exclusive ideology or by a particular religious faith); Ethiopia art. 11 cl. 2; Gambia art. 200 cl. 2; Germany Basic Law art. 140, incorporating Weimar art. 137 cl. 1; Ireland art. 44 cl. 2 (no 'endowment' of any religion); South Korea art. 20 cl. 2; Kyrgyzstan art. 8 cl.1; Liberia art. 14; Lithuania art. 43 cl. 7; Micronesia art. 4 §2; Nicaragua art. 14; Nigeria art. 10; Palau art. 4 § 1; Paraguay art. 24; Philippines art. 3 § 5; Russia art. 14 cl. 1; Serbia art. 11; Seychelles art. 11 cl. 6; Spain art. 16 cl. 3; Tajikistan art. 8; Uganda art. 7; Ukraine art. 35; United States amend. 1; Uruguay art. 5.

27 Angola art. 8, cl. 1, Azerbaijan pmbl., art. 7 cl. 1; Benin arts. 2, 23; Burkina Faso art. 31; Burundi arts. 1, 61, 299; Cameroon pmbl. para. 5, art. 1 cl. 2; Central African Republic arts. 18, 20; Chad Const. arts. 1, 128. 225; Congo arts. 1, 189; Democratic Republic of Congo art. 1; Cote d'Ivoire arts. 30, 127; Ecuador arts. 1, 3; France art. 1; Gabon art. 2, 7; Guinea art. 1, 91; Guinea-Bissau arts. 1, 130; India pmbl.; Kazakhstan art. 1, cl. 1; Kyrgyzstan art. 1, cl. 1; Lithuania art. 40; Madagascar art. 1 cl. 1; Mali pmbl., arts. 25, 118; Mexico art. 3 cl. 1; Mozambique art. 12 cl. 1; Namibia pmbl., art. 1 cl. 1; Nepal art. 4 cl. 1; Nicaragua art. 124; Russia art. 14 cl. 1; Rwanda art. 1; Senegal art. 1; Serbia Const. art. 11; Tajikistan arts. 1, 100; Tanzania pmbl., art. 3 cl. 1; Togo arts. 1, 25, 144; Turkey pmbl., arts. 2, 4, 13, 14, 81, 103, 174; Turkmenistan art. 1. Cf. Czech Republic Charter of Human Rights and Freedoms art. 2(1) ('The State … must not be tied either to an exclusive ideology or to a particular religion.'); Slovak Republic art. 1 ('The Slovak Republic … is not bound by any ideology or religion.').

28 See, e.g., R. Garnett, 4 *Catholic Journal of Social Thought* (2007), 59, 59; H. Berman, *Law and Revolution: The Formation of the Western Legal Tradition* (Cambridge:

respect for religious autonomy has long been a principle reason for making certain that state power remains bounded.

Beyond broad structural features of constitutions that shape the way religious autonomy questions are perceived, there are inevitably more practical questions about how state institutions (especially the courts) apply these doctrines. One set of questions has to do with how deferential the judiciary should be to legislative enactments that encroach on religious autonomy. Another has to do with the types of deference that should be applied in connection with religious autonomy claims. There are a variety of possibilities, ranging from absolute refusal to take jurisdiction over religious disputes, through jurisdictional adjudicative abstention (refusal to interpret the locus of religious authority in a religious community) to substantive interpretive abstention (refusal to engage in interpretation of substantive religious doctrines), and finally to procedural interpretive abstention (refusal to examine whether a religious community has followed its own procedural rules).[29]

Still a third set of questions has to do with the judicial standards of review that should be applied in assessing these cases. Courts in the United States analyze religious freedom claims using various levels of scrutiny: rational basis scrutiny that is very deferential to legislation; strict scrutiny that allows constrains on religious freedom claims only if there is a compelling state interest that cannot be achieved in some less burdensome way, or possibly some form of heightened or intermediate scrutiny. Elsewhere, German-style 'proportionality analysis' has won acceptance in a remarkable number of jurisdictions worldwide, including in such prestigious tribunals as the European Court of Human Rights.[30] In general, constitutional discourse is inevitably mediated through judicial constructs which can clarify, amplify or distort religious autonomy doctrine.

Trans-Constitutional Considerations: Theory and Paradigms of Thought

At a still higher level of abstraction, religious autonomy protections are affected by shifts in dominant legal paradigms. In this regard, an important aspect of the relationship of religion and the world's constitutions has to do with what stands behind or above constitutional orders. What is the ultimate axiology of constitutional systems, and what role do religions (or competing world views) play in shaping those ultimate axiological considerations? For many if not most national constitutions, religion or belief systems hold an important place in the constellation of values behind constitutional commitments. A 'higher law

---

Harvard University Press, 1983), 94.

29 P. Dane, 'The Varieties of Religious Autonomy', in Robbers, *Church Autonomy*, supra note 9, text accompanying notes 35–43. Dane actually describes eight varieties of deference evident in the way various courts have approached the issue of religious autonomy.

30 A.S. Sweet and J. Matthews, 'Proportionality Balancing and Global Constitutionalism', 47 *Columbia Journal of Transnational Law* (2008), 73, 73–74.

background' is a significant feature of many constitutions, or at least of specific constitutional provisions.[31] Many constitutions invoke Deity or the significance of religious traditions directly.[32]

Religious values provide important sources of value that shape specific constitutional values. The Preamble to the Treaty of Lisbon draws 'inspiration from the cultural, religious and humanist inheritance of Europe, from which have developed the universal values of the inviolable and inalienable rights of the human person, freedom, democracy, equality and the rule of law'.[33] Many Islamic regimes reference Shari'a as an ultimate source of or constraint on legislation.[34] Constitutions and human rights instruments also acknowledge the significance of religion and belief in the lives of their people. Provisions protecting freedom of religion or belief and proscribing discrimination on this basis are the clearest evidence of this.

At the other end of the spectrum, secular constitutionalism avoids grounding of constitutional norms in specific religious traditions and appeals instead to notions of 'public reason' or other bases of secular consensus.[35] In extreme cases, this can take forms that are aggressively hostile toward religion, as in a number of former communist regimes. Holders of beliefs in particular religious or secular traditions may find themselves in disagreement with some of the core values held by others, but it remains clear as a matter of fact that the belief systems of country's citizenry have a strong impact on the shaping of constitutional orders.

Religious beliefs play important roles not only at constitutional moments when constitutions are drafted and ratified, but also at times of important constitutional change. Thus, religion played a critical role in the United States in the anti-slavery movement in 19th century and in the civil rights movement of the 20th century.[36] Religion was also a significant factor in the collapse of communism in Eastern

31 See, e.g., E.S. Corwin, 'The Higher Law Background of American Constitutional Law', 42 *Harvard Law Review* (1928), 149. But see 'Coke, Corwin and the Constitution: The 'Higher Law Background' Reconsidered', 55 *Review of Politics* (1993), 393.

32 See, e.g., I.C. Ibán, 'God in Constitutions and Godless Constitutions', Chapter 2 of this volume.

33 Treaty of Lisbon, Second Recital, *Official Journal of the European Union* 83, 30 March 2010.

34 See generally T. Stahnke and R.C. Blitt, 'The Religion-State Relationship and the Right to Freedom of Religion or Belief: A Comparative Textual Analysis of the Constitutions of Predominantly Muslim Countries', 36 *Georgetown Journal of International Law* (2005), 947.

35 See, e.g., J. Rawls, *The Law of Peoples: with 'The Idea of Public Reason Revisited'* (Cambridge: Harvard University Press, 1999).

36 See A. Koppelman, *Defending American Religious Neutrality* (Cambridge: Harvard University Press, 2013), ch. 4, text accompanying nn.14–15.

Europe in the 1990s,[37] and in the abolition of apartheid in South Africa.[38] Religion is important in less dramatic ways in the quiet steady processes that cultivate the virtues of a law-abiding citizenry and the patterns of voluntary compliance with law upon which every legal system ultimately depends.[39] Constitutional provisions that establish secular state structures that accommodate, facilitate and respect the belief systems of their citizens (whether religious or non-religious) play important roles in this regard.

Religious autonomy is part of the deep history of constitutionalism. The institutional background against which this idea emerged was Caesaro-Papism, which subjected the spiritual authority of the Church to the power of the secular emperor and allowed little room for religious autonomy. This arrangement was typical of the Byzantine Church, and continued in Russia, where the church organization (the Patriarchate) was dominated by the czar.[40] It re-emerged in many of the Protestant countries after the reformation, where established churches were subordinated to secular states.

The idea of 'freedom of the church' (*libertas ecclesiae*)—a key fountainhead of religious autonomy—was a revolt against dominance by the secular ruler, and traces back at least to the Papal Revolution launched Gregory VII in the 11th century. This was a critical turning point in the development of Western constitutionalism.[41] In many ways it embodies at least in idea if not always in practice the strongest conception of religious autonomy: the idea of a church as an independent sovereign, related to the state on a basis of legal equality.[42] This conception has echoes in models of autonomy represented by nonconformist churches. In countries allowing toleration, these bodies set up religious organizations that either had substantial freedom from state control, or certainly argued that they were entitled to such freedom. They were not conceived as co-equal sovereigns, and remained subject to some general state regulation, but they had (or sought) substantial autonomy.[43]

The evolution of stronger separation of church and state in the United States represents still a third model.[44] Many of the key notions of the American constitutional experiment first forged by Jefferson and Madison ultimately trace

37 See, e.g., W. Echikson, *Lighting the Night: Revolution in Eastern Europe* (New York: William Morrow and Co, Inc., 1990).

38 See, e.g., L. Thompson, *A History of South Africa*, rev. ed. (New Haven & London: Yale University Press, 1995), 243–44.

39 The classic text on this issue is Alexis de Tocqueville, *Democracy in America* (J.P. Mayer, trans., Garden City, New York: Anchor Books, 1969) (notably chapters 5, 15, and 17).

40 R. Minnerath, 'The Right to Autonomy in Religious Affairs', in T. Lindholm, W. C. Durham, Jr., and B.G. Tahzib-Lie (eds.), *Facilitating Freedom of Religion or Belief: A Deskbook* (Leiden: Koninklijke Brill NV, 2004), 291, 294.

41 Garnett, supra note 27.

42 Minnerath, supra note 39 at 295–96.

43 See Minnerath at 296.

44 Minnerath at 296–300.

back to this formative period.[45] John Courtney Murray regarded the principle of *libertas ecclesiae* as a great idea marking the 'entrance into history marked the beginning of a new constitutional era'.[46] He perceived continuities between this idea and the Religion Clause of the U.S. Constitution.[47] In fact, one can discern a number of broad structural approaches to religious autonomy, of which the U.S. separation model is but one. Subsequent constitutional history around the world reflects varying elaborations and refinements of these fundamental alternatives.[48] Whether given strong protection or short shrift in particular national regimes, the idea of religious autonomy has come to be understood as a core structural feature in the provision of effective religious freedom protections.

Even where the protections are strong, the place of religious autonomy within constitutions is subject to shifts in the general paradigms affecting legal thought and practice. This is perhaps most obvious in the shift from a view of constitutional governance that focused on limiting government powers to the much heavier contemporary emphasis on rights. Where state powers are strictly limited, constitutional space left for religious autonomy is general expansive.

Even if one focuses only on contemporary rights-oriented systems, however, it is clear that paradigm shifts can have significant implications for religious autonomy. With the growth of powerful judiciaries, particularly since World War II, it has become more typical to rely on courts to protect rights and freedom.[49] Also, in part because courts work by comparing cases, but also because of more general political trends, this tendency toward judicialization has contributed to the ascendancy of an equality paradigm by granting subtle and often not-so-subtle priority to equality over freedom claims.[50] Discrimination rather than infringement of freedom becomes the archetypal offense. Religious freedom is reconceptualized as an equality norm. For example, in the United States, the holding in *Employment Division v. Smith* that courts should defer to neutral and generally applicable legislative rules except where targeting of particular religious groups or individuals

45 See J. Witte Jr., *Religion and the American Constitutional Experiment: Essential Rights and Liberties* (Boulder, Colorado: Westview Press, 2000), 13.

46 J.C. Murray, *We Hold These Truths: Catholic Reflections on the American Proposition* (Kansas City: Sheed and Ward, 1960), 202.

47 Murray at 204–5.

48 See generally Minnerath at 299–319.

49 W. C. Durham, Jr.,'Das Grundgesetz—eine grundsätzliche Bewertung aus amerikanischer Sicht', in P. Kirchhof and D.P. Kommers, *Deutschland und sein Grundgesetz: Themen einer deutsch-amerikanischen Konferenz* (Baden-Baden: Nomos Verlagsgesellschaft, 1993), 41, 45–49 (describing the subjectivization and judicialization of rights in post-World War II constitutionalism).

50 W. C. Durham, Jr. and B. G. Scharffs, 'State and Religious Communities in the United States: The Tension between Freedom and Equality', in *Church and State Towards Protection for Freedom of Religion* (Japanese Association of Comparative Constitutional Law, Proceedings of the International Conference on Comparative Constitutional Law, 2–4 September 2005), 362.

is involved[51] shifted the emphasis in free exercise analysis from freedom to equalitarian concerns. At the international level, while both freedom and equality norms are protected, the pronounced emphasis in many international instruments on proscribing discrimination on the basis of religion reflects the strength of the equality paradigm. Obviously, both freedom and equality are fundamental values, but where equality is overemphasized, the hazard is an equally reduced range of religious freedom for all.

All of the foregoing considerations shape answers to the deeper question about whether religious autonomy should be analyzed primarily as a matter of rights, in accordance with currently prevalent practice, or whether it needs to be thought of as a structural or jurisdictional matter that defines limits of state sovereignty, in accordance with deeper and often older constitutional conceptions linked to notions of limited government. Again, these are questions that scholars with a law and religion background are uniquely well suited to address.

Tensions at the Level of Theory

The question of the appropriate constitutional strategy to use in protecting religious autonomy raises still higher-level questions about the nature and justification for religious institutions in free societies, and indeed, about the justification for free societies in general. This leads to questions about the nature and role of religious institutions, and what distinctive needs they have if they are to be protected and to flourish. This in turn raises questions about group rights, about how the autonomy of groups can be reconciled or balanced with the rights of individuals, and how religious autonomy can be squared with classic liberal theory.

Specifically, during much of the history of civilization, the existence of independent sources of normative authority was perceived to be profoundly threatening to state institutions. Why should the state ever tolerate rival sources of legitimate authority? On the surface, this appears to make no logical sense, and there is a type of Hobbesian/positivist view of sovereignty that results, holding not only that the state holds the competence of normative competences, but that it should hold the monopoly of all valid legal authority, including authority over religious institutions. But this approach forgets the most fundamental insights that made modernity and modern pluralism possible—the recognition that within broad limits, society is both more stable and culturally enriched if it protects a wide array of different communities of belief—both religious and secular.

Modern constitutionalism emerged precisely by learning the very hard lesson that interference with the complex and delicate structures of religious communities is far more threatening to social peace than allowing diversity and respect for different groups. Some of the greatest contributions to thought in the field of

---

51 See *Smith*, supra note 15 at 894 (1990) (O'Connor, J., concurring) (noting that only laws that target particular religious practices retain heightened scrutiny under *Smith*); *Church of the Lukumi Babalu Aye, Inc., v. City of Hialeah*, 508 U.S. 520, 533–34 (1993).

law and religion, as in political, legal, and social theory more generally, have underscored precisely this axiom concerning the value of free, open and pluralistic societies.[52] These insights continue to find validation in the empirical studies of those working in our field.[53] In the phrase recurrently quoted in the decisions of the European Court of Human Rights,

> As enshrined in Article 9 (art. 9), freedom of thought, conscience and religion is one of the foundations of a 'democratic society' within the meaning of the Convention. It is, in its religious dimension, one of the most vital elements that go to make up the identity of believers and their conception of life, but it is also a precious asset for atheists, agnostics, sceptics and the unconcerned. The pluralism indissociable from a democratic society, which has been dearly won over the centuries, depends on it.[54]

It is of course impossible to replicate here the vast range of arguments supporting this position, but this discourse lies at the heart of the work of the various sub-disciplines of law and religion.

At a still higher level, there are questions about how religious autonomy relates to basic conceptions of law and transformations in our understanding of key jurisprudential notions. At one level, these are general questions of jurisprudence about the nature of law. But they cannot help implicating still higher questions about relation of human beings to what they sense as transcendent, and how state institutions should be structured to protect the sensitive domain of conscience, and the institutions that help cultivate and protect it.

In short, to summarize the argument to this point, concrete issues of religious autonomy such as those that arise in employment cases, are nested in a richly layered set of progressively more abstract considerations, all of which have a bearing on the resolution of concrete religious autonomy questions. Because resolution of more concrete issues of religious autonomy in the domain of the employment cases depends on resolution of more abstract issues, I will start at the top and work back down to the concrete cases.

---

52 See, e.g., J. Locke, *A Letter Concerning Toleration* [1689] (Indianapolis: Liberal Arts Press, 1955), 55; A. Smith, An Inquiry into the Nature and Causes of the Wealth of Nations [1776] (Chicago: University of Chicago Press, 1976) 314–15.

53 See, e.g., B. J. Grim and R. Finke, *The Price of Freedom Denied* (Cambridge: Cambridge University Press, 2011) (providing both philosophical and empirical validation for the notion the religious freedom promotes stability and countless other social goods).

54 *Kokkinakis v. Greece*, App. No. 14307/88, 25 May 1993, para. 31.

Erosion of the Layered Protections of Religious Autonomy Doctrine

At each of the levels described above—statutory law, constitutional analysis, and trans-constitutional theory—one senses an unraveling of some of the deepest insights into the relationship of religion and constitutional order. In this regard, we are facing a crisis—a crisis in the place of religion within, behind and above constitutions, and a crisis in the protection of religious institutions. In some ways, the crisis—at least as experienced in strong constitutional democracies—is an odd one. It is not a crisis that takes the form of a frontal attack on religious freedom norms or their status as fundamental human rights. No one is suggesting repeal of Article 18 of the International Covenant on Civil and Political Rights, or that the guarantees of religious freedom in most constitutions on earth should be withdrawn. Rather, there is a tipping point phenomenon and a pattern of erosion by exception—exceptions in the name of other rights and other state interests, exceptions in the name of transformed equality norms, and exceptions deriving in the end from lost perspective concerning the importance of freedom of religion. In what follows, I examine the types of erosion evident in the various layers of the constitutional and jurisprudential setting in which the doctrine of religious autonomy is nested, and then conclude with reflections on the cumulative effect these patterns of erosion have on practical protection of religious autonomy rights.

Erosion at the Level of Theory

At the highest jurisprudential level, much depends on profound differences in basic conceptions of the legal order. The corresponding erosion can be described as the loss of an integralist conception of law. Where religion comes into conflict with the state and conscientious objections are asserted against compliance with state law, there are at least two broad ways that conscientious objection can be conceptualized. The first could be described as the legalist or positivist view: the legal system is understood fundamentally as legislation. Legislation is the paradigmatic form of law, and all law is legislation. Granting exceptions for conscientious objection under this view undermines the authority of law, makes individuals or groups a law unto themselves, and would 'pulverize' the law and lead to anarchy.[55]

The alternative is an integralist view: the legal system includes legislation as adjusted to take constitutional norms into account. Conscientious objection in this view is not a tolerated exception to a general rule. It is an integral part of the rule structure itself. Conscientious conflicts do not pose a confrontation of private and public, but a resolution of two public interests. The law is not legislation subject to exceptions, but legislation as contoured by the requirements of constitutional and

55 This is essentially Justice Scalia's view in *Employment Division v. Smith*, which held that religion-based exemptions to neutral and generally applicable laws would lead to an anarchic system 'in which each conscience is a law unto itself … .', supra note 15 at 890.

international human rights law.[56] The integralist view has obvious affinities to natural law, in the sense that the underlying conception of law might assume that there are deeper principles that ground constitutional axiology than the 'positive' norms of constitutions and laws alone. But one could be committed to an integralist view of law without necessarily being committed to the existence of transpositive (in the sense of trans-constitutional) norms. Exploration of these issues has long been a key focus for the jurisprudential and philosophical sub-disciplines of law and religion.

The fading of the integralist conception of legal order and the tendency to see conscientious objection through the legalist filter connects with a second and more general shift in equalitarian jurisprudence. Instead of being seen as a legitimate distinguishing factor justifying differential treatment, religious considerations are gradually demoted, until they become a ground for discrimination. Religious beliefs and conduct once thought to deserve the highest forms of constitutional protection increasingly come under censure from those administering a new orthodoxy in equalitarianism. In this framework, conscientious objection comes to be seen not as an expression emanating from the core of human dignity, but as a potentially anarchic and dangerous anomaly in the legal system.

This erosion takes the following form.[57] The first stage emerges as an equalitarian questioning of the constitutional privileging of freedom of religion or belief. The fact that this protection of freedom of religion is constitutional bedrock in most legal systems, including the international human rights system, is ignored, and seemingly benign questions are asked: Why is religion special? Why should the conscientious objector to working on his or her Sabbath receive special deference? Why should special care be taken to avoid discrimination in religious land use decisions? Why should religious belief serve as the ground of a special exemption from otherwise applicable law?

In principle, these are fair enough questions. People should be treated equally. Their dignity should be respected. But the questions are too quick. They ignore the fact that at profound historical and constitutional moments, some of the best constitutional minds in human history thought there were sound answers to these questions—answers that explain why religion and religious institutions deserve special respect and special protection. These reasons include the fact that religious members of religious communities might not have agreed to the general social contract if joining the political community exposed them to the risk of violating their even deeper religious principles. They include recognition that religious communities are unlikely to be maximally productive members of society if their belief system

56 R. Navarro-Valls and J. Martíinez-Torrón, *Conflictos entre conciencia y ley. Las objeciones de conciencia* (2d ed., Madrid: Iustel 2012), 41–47, 62–80. See also R. Bertolino, *L'obiezione di coscienza 'moderna'. Per una fondazione costituzionale del diritto di obiezione* (Torino: Giappicchelli, 1994), 63 ff, 87 ff.

57 The idea for the threefold erosion described here was stimulated by an address given by Michael K. Young, then President of the University of Utah, at Brigham Young University on 4 April 2011. Copy on file with the author.

is threatened. The questions elicit rhetorical but misleadingly superficial answers. They forget that equality is not the only value in social equations. Achievement of equal non-freedom of religion for all would be a tragic social failure.

Moreover, while the 'why is religion different' questions reflect a legitimate call for equality, as a practical matter they have an unforeseen effect. They place a virtually infinite and costly ongoing justificatory load on religious groups. Ironically, while maintaining that all beliefs should be treated neutrally and equally, the effect of the ostensibly benign question is to place the burden on religious groups in case after case of constantly re-demonstrating their social value. There is no finality, but only endless re-justification. And because religion touches virtually every area of life, the re-justification burden is far more extensive than other entities might bear. It is faced repeatedly in every subdiscipline of law. Moreover, what the questions pose are not merely interesting thought experiments, but burdensome litigation.

There is also a tendency in determining whether some secular concern outweighs a religious belief to weight the scale in favor of secular interests. More accurately, because secular and spiritual values are incommensurable, the tendency is to create presumptions in favor of the secular.

A second stage of the erosion is embedded in the claim that 'religion is a private affair'—that it is fine for religion to have its freedom, so long as it stays in the private sphere. A corollary is that religious premises may not be invoked in public arguments. Religion is fine when it is doing charitable work, but it should stay out of politics altogether. The erosion goes a step further when it comes to decision of the constitutionality of legislation that has been supported in the political process by religious advocates. In recent cases involving same-sex marriage[58] and the Defense of Marriage Act (DOMA),[59] analysis has focused on whether a 'rational basis' test should be used to assess constitutionality of the relevant legal provisions. The rational basis test is designed to be very deferential to the legislative branch, and holds that if there is any conceivable rational basis for a law, it should be sustained. Judges in the same-sex marriage cases have held that religious arguments do not rise to the level of a rational basis for the laws and constitutional provisions in question.[60] In this setting, the religious beliefs citizens

---

58 *Perry v. Schwarzenegger*, 704 F.Supp. 2d 921 (N.D. Cal. 2010), affirmed sub nom. Perry v. Brown, 671 F.3d 1052 (9th Cir. 2012), cert. granted sub nom. Hollingsworth v. Perry, 133 S.Ct. 786 (2012). The transcript and audio recording of the oral argument in the this case, heard before the U.S. Supreme Court on 26 March 2013, may be found at http://www.oyez.org/cases/2010-2019/2012/2012_12_144#argument.

59 See *Windsor v. United States*, 833 F. Supp.2d 394, affirmed, 699 F.3d 169 (2d Cir. 2012), cert. granted, 133 S.Ct. 786 (2012) (holding that heightened scrutiny should be used in analyzing the constitutionality of DOMA). The transcript and audio recording of the oral argument in this case, heard before the U.S. Supreme Court on 27 March 2013, may be found at http://www.oyez.org/cases/2010-2019/2012/2012_12_307.

60 *Perry*, supra note 57 at 995–1003.

hold are demoted to second-class status in the marketplace of ideas, and the effect is to marginalize religious freedom protections.

That leads to yet a third stage in the erosion of protections. Instead of being seen as a presumptively beneficial factor in society, religion comes to be seen as a predominantly negative force. The dark side of the 'ambivalence of the sacred'[61] is seen as more representative; positive contributions are overlooked. Such judgments are never scientific, and in the nature of things, probably never can be. Moreover, there is an inevitable skewing factor. Bad or scandalous conduct attracts media coverage; positive contributions are routine and thus little noticed. These and related processes result in profound attrition of social memory and understanding of the importance of religion and religious freedom.

In the end, the three-fold process just described results in a movement starting with special protections for religion, then questioning whether any privileging is justified, then suggesting that religious speech should have second-class status, and finally ending at a point with religion being seen as an essentially negative factor that at best needs to be limited to the private sphere and at worst warrants presumptively negative reactions by the state and society. The result that appears to emerge is one in which no discrimination is possible on the grounds of any life-stance preferences, except if the life-stance preferences are religious. Viewed from a different vantage point, a conception of equality that initially recognizes conscientious objection as an appropriate ground for differential treatment gives way to a conception of non-discrimination which abstracts from and ignores religious differences. That is in turn equated with the neutrality of the state, which is linked to secularism, which is all too prone to neutralize religion, or at least drive it from public space.[62]

Shifts such as the foregoing have profound implications for the notion of religious autonomy, particularly where that notion collides with equalitarian concerns, as in the current religious employment cases. This became evident in a dramatic way in the *Hosanna-Tabor* litigation. At a critical juncture in the oral argument of the case,[63] Chief Justice Roberts asked the lawyer representing the government whether the administration thought there was anything 'special about

61 R.S. Appleby, *The Ambivalence of the Sacred* (Lanham, Maryland: Rowman & Littlefield Publishers, 2000).

62 See M. Cartabia, 'The Challenges of 'New Rights' and Militant Secularism', in M. A. Glendon and H. Zacher (eds.), *Universal Human Rights in a World of Diversity: The Case of Religious Freedom* (Vatican City: Pontificia Academia Scientiarum Socialium, 2012), 428, 436–51.

63 The oral argument in *Hosanna-Tabor* can heard online at http://www.supremecourt.gov/oral_arguments/argument_audio_detail.aspx?argument=10-553. The description of the colloquy at oral argument that follows is drawn from an account posted on one of the leading academic blogs dealing with law and religion issues: I. Somin, 'Oral Argument in the Hosanna-Tabor Religious Freedom Case', The Volokh Conspiracy, 7 October 2011, http://www.volokh.com/2011/10/07/oral-argument-in-the-hosanna-tabor-religious-freedom-case/.

the fact that the people involved in this case are part of a religious organization'. The government lawyer responded that 'there was no difference whether the group was a religious group, a labor group, or any other association of individuals.' Justice Scalia responded by exclaiming, 'That's extraordinary. That is extraordinary. We are talking here about the free exercise clause and about the establishment clause and you say they have no special application?' Even former Obama Solicitor General Elena Kagan was 'amazed' by the Administration's opinion. The Court's formal opinion in the case echoed this colloquy. Writing for a unanimous Court, Justice Roberts stated, 'We cannot accept the remarkable view that the Religion Clauses have nothing to say about a religious organization's freedom to select its own ministers.'[64] Despite the firmness of this statement, the position advocated by the government, that religious autonomy deserves no special protection beyond what is afforded by freedom of association continues to find support in academia and wider circles, and threatens to erode religious autonomy rights.

Religious Autonomy: Limiting State Jurisdiction

Turning from philosophy to history, one of the most striking changes in thinking about the protection of religious freedom is the shift from a jurisdictional to a rights-based approach. Over much of the past millennium, a key struggle has been to protect the freedom of the church.[65] This was at the heart of the investiture controversy of the 11th and 12th centuries.[66] The assertion of royal authority to appoint bishops was a significant source of the conflict between King Henry II and Archbishop Thomas Becket.[67] The institutional history of the West is rife with struggles between political and ecclesiastical powers to shore up their respective powers. In retrospect, one of the distinctive features of this history is that while each side managed to prevail in its own domain, neither the political nor the religious powers were able to achieve wholesale hegemony over the other. Over time, this accident of historical struggles evolved into a sense that the opposed jurisdictions were rooted in a profound ontological divide separating spiritual and temporal, and that constitutional ordering ought to take the difference between these two jurisdictions seriously.

Distinguishing the spiritual and temporal sphere was a principal focus of John Locke's *Letter Concerning Toleration.*[68] Distinctive histories in different religious traditions gave birth to different theologies on this point. Abraham

64 *Hosanna-Tabor*, 32 S.Ct. at 706.

65 For excellent overviews, see Minnerath, supra note 39 at 291–319; Garnett, supra note 27.

66 See B. Tierney, *The Crisis of Church and State 1050-1300* (Englewood Cliffs, N.J.: Prentice-Hall, 1964).

67 See L. Pfeffer, *Church, State & Freedom*, rev. ed. (Boston: Beacon Press, 1967), 18.

68 Locke, supra note 51.

Kuyper's notion of 'sphere sovereignty' is one example from the Calvinist tradition,[69] and there are, of course, countless others. This complex and intricate history is a significant focus of a number of the sub-disciplines of law and religion. I can only brush by this vast field of historical work.

What I want to highlight on this front is a debate about the implications of this jurisdictional dimension of church-state history for constitutional argumentation. We have moved from a constitutional paradigm in which rights were in fact protected by limiting state power to a paradigm in which the only limits to state power are rights, and rights can be overcome all too easily by powerful state interests. In the United States, scholars such as Carl Esbeck and Richard Garnett have argued that the Establishment Clause must be understood against this jurisdictional background and that non-establishment is to be understood as a structural limitation on the scope of state power.[70] This has profound practical implications, for if separation of religion and state is to be understood jurisdictionally, religious autonomy (at least at its core) is not a matter of balancing collective autonomy rights against state and individual interests, but is a matter lying wholly beyond the jurisdictional competence of the state. The deeper question for law and religion specialists is whether indeed religious autonomy can and should be understood in this jurisdictional way, and what part of its complex topography accordingly lies beyond state authority.

Religious Autonomy and the Protection of Group Rights

Liberal theory has an ambivalent attitude toward the role of groups in society. On the one hand, liberal theory is fundamentally a theory of individual rights, and the existence of groups poses an inevitable but inconvenient reality for the theory. From this standpoint, groups pose a fundamental paradox: they both enhance and subvert individual autonomy by challenging the sovereign power of the liberal state.

If the government can act to eliminate groups that it believes threaten majoritarian social policies and values merely because such groups are anti-majoritarian, then the power of the government over groups and individuals is unlimited.[71]

---

69 For a useful overview of Kuyper's theory, see P. Horwitz, 'Churches as First Amendment Institutions: Of Sovereignty and Spheres', *Harvard Civil Rights-Civil Liberties Law Review* (2009) 79.

70 C.H. Esbeck, 'The Establishment Clause as a Structural Restraint on Governmental Power', 84 *Iowa Law Review* (1998) 1 and 'The Establishment Clause as a Structural Restraint: Validations and Ramifications',18 *Journal of Law and Politics* (2002), 445; Garnett, supra note 27.

71 F. M. Gedicks, 'Toward a Theory of Group Rights', *Wisconsin Law Review* (1989) 99, 168. I am particularly indebted to Gedicks' views in this chapter, but note that Gedicks has now distanced himself from some of the views expressed in his *Wisconsin Law Review* article.

The result would be that the social basis of pluralism would be subverted. With respect to anti-discrimination norms, the liberal perspective would be that a religious group's interest in autonomy and self-definition is overshadowed by individual and government interests in non-discrimination. From a group rights perspective, in contrast, group autonomy is necessary to preserve pluralism and the individualism at the heart of liberalism. Government intervention threatens authenticity (and the authentic existence) of groups as well as the number and diversity of groups.

This is particularly problematic with respect to religious groups. Religious groups contribute to society in at least three critical ways. First, they serve a buffering value. That is, they help protect individuals from the state. Second, they have an identity-forming value. Religious groups provide a context for the development of individual personality that is important for those significantly committed to religious groups. Third, they perform an envisioning function. In the context of a neutral state, religious groups are part of a larger collection of necessary social institutions that create, advocate, refine, nurture and maintain values.

Vigorous group pluralism, including strong protection of religious autonomy, has costs. At the extreme, it threatens government stability and legitimacy. Moreover, it poses threats to the autonomy of those who do not conform to the norms of the relevant group. On the other hand, groups are a social necessity. Human beings would not exist without family groups, and in fact, numerous other groups are necessary and valuable to the functioning of society. The continued existence of diverse and vigorous non-governmental groups is valuable for safeguarding individual autonomy and the values that diverse individuals may choose to incorporate in their life plans. In this sense, constraints or variations associated with religious autonomy may enhance long-term freedom. State intervention may protect the autonomy and values of non-discrimination with respect to dissenters, but this also narrows the autonomy of those who support the group (by coercing changes in the group structure and changing the group in ways that are not consistent with the views of others in the group).

As a practical matter, there are a limited number of ways that a state may resolve the trade-offs inevitably involved in group right situations. The state can engage in ad hoc balancing of state, group, and individual interests.[72] This constantly runs the risk of striking the wrong balance, or at any rate of allowing excessive discretion to government officials, who may resolve questions in arbitrary or biased ways. It has the added detriment that it risks the constant reassessment by the state of government, group, and dissenting interests, which from the standpoint of the group is costly and has a chilling effect on taking otherwise legitimate action. Moreover, this balancing fails to take into account the freedom of the group to freely interpret its own norms. A second approach is for the state to engage in abstract or definitional balancing, defining the balance in advance.[73] This avoids case-by-case assessment, and can be applied in subsequent

72 See Gedicks at 139–47.

73 See Gedicks at 147–148.

cases without constantly reweighing the interests involved. Thus, for example, there are cases in the United States that appear to reflect an abstract assessment according to which the value of religious groups to both individuals and society is thought as a general matter to outweigh anti-discrimination and other government interests.[74] In a pluralistic society, where there are genuine rights to exit from the religious community, it is difficult to see why dissenters or the outside community should coerce a group, particularly a religious group, to be something that is not in harmony with its beliefs. A third approach is to reach a categorical assessment, based not on a comparison of state, group and individual interests, but on the intrinsic value of protecting (in this case) religious groups because they are 'a locus for certain of the constitutive, foundational activities by which Americans define and determine who and what they are'.[75]

Subject to genuine voluntariness in joining and leaving the religious community, a strong case can be made for a categorical approach to protection of religious autonomy. To the extent that freedom of religion is a fundamental right, it is difficult to understand how it can be adequately guaranteed if the religions in which people believe are not allowed to be authentically themselves. Social contract theories have understood that they can gain no traction with believers if the social contract itself does not have a 'reservation clause' for protection of religious freedom. A religiously sincere person would not enter into an actual[76] or hypothetical[77] social contract if it was clear *ab initio* that this could entail a requirement to compromise an individual's religious values. In such cases, individuals (and religious groups) would either refrain from entering into or accepting the obligations of civil society rather than ignore their religious beliefs, or the integrity required to make civil obligations meaningful would be lacking from the start. Another line of support for categorical protection can be seen in recent writings on First Amendment institutionalism in the United States, which have underscored the importance of protecting not just individual expressive rights, but the institutions that that serve as the seedbeds of pluralism.[78]

---

74 Justice Brennan's concurrence in *Corporation of the Presiding Bishop v. Amos,* 483 U.S. 327, 340–46 (1987), may be an example of this type of definitional balancing. See Gedicks at 148.

75 Gedicks at 158.

76 See, e.g., J. Madison, 'Memorial and Remonstrance Against Religious Assessments', in G. Hunt (ed.), 2 *The Writings of James Madison* (New York: G.P. Putnam's Sons, 1901) ('Religion … must be left to the conviction and conscience of every man; and it is the right of every man to exercise it as these may dictate … . This duty is precedent both in order of time and in degree of obligation, to the claims of Civil Society.'). The *Memorial and Remonstrance* is also printed as an appendix to Justice Rutledge's dissenting opinion in *Everson v. Board of Education*, 330 U.S. 1, 28 app. at 63 (1947) (Rutledge, J. dissenting).

77 See, e.g., J. Rawls, *A Theory of Justice*, rev. edn. (Cambridge: The Belknap Press of Harvard University Press, 1999), sec. 33 (Equal Liberty of Conscience).

78 See, e.g., P. Horwitz, supra note 68; F. Schauer, 'Principles, Institutions, and the First Amendment', 112 *Harvard Law Review* (1998), 84.

A categorical approach to religious autonomy aligns with the jurisdictional and sovereignty based approach to religious autonomy that has been a critical feature of that doctrine throughout most of its long history. The arguments advanced here on that point are admittedly sketchy and need much more in the way of full articulation. My main point here is that there is much need for further work in this area from collaborators in the law and religion field.

Autonomy and Standards of Review

A key step in the movement toward concrete resolution of religious autonomy claims involves analysis of the applicable standards of judicial review. Unfortunately, this is one of the most dramatic areas of erosion or threatened erosion of religious freedom protection: shifts in or manipulations of the standards in constitutional and human rights law that are used to assess the viability of religious freedom claims. Erosion occurs in this area both through reformulation of the applicable standards themselves and through less obvious changes in the starting calibrations of the balancing mechanisms used by judges (the baseline assumptions of what constitutes neutrality) and through changing the weights assigned to other values thrown into the balance against religious freedom.

The struggle concerning the standard of review has been the central drama regarding religious freedom for the past two decades in the United States, and is also vital in other legal systems where religious freedom claims wend their way into courts. Prior to 1990, Supreme Court decisions in the United States held that burdens on religious liberty could only be justified by narrowly tailored compelling state interests. That is, they had to withstand 'strict scrutiny'—a difficult though not insurmountable challenge. In 1990, in *Employment Division v. Smith*,[79] the Supreme Court jettisoned that test, and held that subject to certain exceptions, any general and neutral law would override religious freedom claims. This unleashed a series of efforts in Congress and state legislatures to reinstate strict or at least heightened scrutiny, thereby providing stronger protection of religious freedom than had been established by the Supreme Court as the minimum constitutional standard. Free exercise rights have shown remarkable resilience in this drama, but the result is a patchwork that provides less comprehensive protection of religious freedom than had previously been in place.[80]

Similar risks of erosion are present in international settings, such as in the case law of the United Nations Human Rights Committee or the European Court

79 *Smith*, supra note 15.

80 For a more extensive treatment of these issues, see W. W. Bassett, W. C. Durham Jr. and R.T. Smith, *Religious Organizations and the Law* 2.64 (New York: Thomson Reuters /West, 2012); W. C. Durham Jr. and R.T. Smith, 'Religion and State in the United States at the Turn of the Twenty-First Century', in Silvio Ferrari and Rinaldo Cristofori (eds.), *Law and Religion in the 21st Century* (Farnham, Surrey, United Kingdom: Ashgate, 2010).

of Human Rights. These bodies apply virtually identical treaty language in assessing permissible limitations on manifestations of religion.[81] Limitations on manifestations must pass three tests. First, they must be prescribed by law. This requirement has a formal element (requiring that the interference in question is legally authorized) and a qualitative element (requiring that fundamental rule of law constraints such as non-retroactivity, clarity of the legal provisions, absence of arbitrary enforcement and the like be observed). Note that as a practical matter this is the minimum floor established by the *Smith* decision in the United States, which implicitly assumes that rule of law constraints alone provide a sufficient protection of religious freedom.

International standards go further and prescribe a restricted set of permissible or legitimating grounds for limitations. As enunciated in the European Convention for the Protection of Human Rights and Fundamental Freedoms, these legitimating grounds are restricted to those which are necessary 'in the interests of public safety, for the protection of public order, health or morals, or for the protection of the rights and freedoms of others'.[82] While the legitimating grounds are quite broad and in most cases at least one is available to support the particular limitations being challenged, it is quite clear that only the enumerated legitimating grounds may be invoked to justify a limitation.[83] Note the U.S. 'compelling state interest' test is arguably broader, in the sense that anything a court thinks is 'compelling' may meet the standard.

The real core of the ICCPR/ECHR test lies in assessing whether the particular limitation is 'necessary' or 'necessary in a democratic society'. The European Court of Human Rights has construed this to require a 'pressing social need' that is 'proportionate to the legitimate aim pursued'.[84] Clearly, when analyzed in these terms, the issue of necessity must be assessed on a case-by-case basis. However, certain general conclusions have emerged.

First, in assessing which limitations are 'proportionate', it is vital to remember that 'freedom of thought, conscience and religion is one of the foundations of a 'democratic society'.[85] State interests must be weighty indeed to justify abrogating a right that is this significant. Second, limitations cannot pass the necessity test

81 Compare ICCPR art.18(3) with ECHR art. 9(2).

82 ECHR art. 9(2).

83 See UN Human Rights Committee, General Comment 22 (48), adopted by the UN Human Rights Committee on 20 July 1993. UN Doc. CCPR/C/21/Rev.1/Add.4 (1993), reprinted in UN Doc. HRI/GEN/1/ Rev.1 at 35 (1994); *Nolan and K v. Russia*, App. No. 2512/04, 12 February 2009, para. 73.

84 See, e.g., *Kokkinakis v. Greece*, App. No. 14307/88, 25 May 1993, para. 49; *Wingrove v. United Kingdom*, App. No. 17419/90 25 November 1996, para. 53; *Manoussakis and Others v. Greece*, App. No. 18748/91, 26 September 1996, paras. 43–53; *Serif v. Greece*, App. No. 38178/97, 14 December 1999), para. 49; *Metropolitan Church of Bessarabia v. Moldova*, App. No. 45701/99, 13 December 2001), para. 119.

85 Metropolitan Church of Bessarabia, para. 114.

if they reflect state conduct that is not neutral and impartial,[86] or that imposes arbitrary constraints on the right to manifest religion.[87] Discriminatory and arbitrary government conduct is not 'necessary'—especially not in a democratic society. In particular, state regulations that impose excessive and arbitrary burdens on the right to associate and worship in community with others are impermissible.[88] In general, where laws are not narrowly tailored to further one of the permissible legitimating grounds for limitation, or where religious groups can point to alternative ways that a particular state objective can be achieved that would be less burdensome for the religious group and would substantially accomplish the state's objective, it is difficult to claim that the more burdensome alternative is genuinely necessary. Further, counterproductive measures are obviously not necessary. Finally, the UN Human Rights Committee has noted that limitations 'must not be applied in a manner that would vitiate the rights guaranteed in article 18',[89] and the European Court would no doubt take a similar position. Finally, restrictions on religious freedom 'must not impair the very essence of the right in question'.[90]

In addition to the foregoing, both the United States strict scrutiny and the ICCPR/ECHR approaches impose threshold requirements below which religious liberty claims are not cognizable. In the United States there must be a 'substantial burden' on free exercise before the burden shifts to the state to establish that there is a compelling state interest that cannot be accomplished in some less restrictive manner. In Europe, there must be an 'interference' with a manifestation of religion. Unfortunately, as cases proliferate, it is becoming evident that some courts will find ways to set this threshold unreasonably high, so that they can dismiss a case without further balancing of the rights and interests at stake. One of the most striking cases in this regard was *Jewish Liturgical Association Cha'are Shalom ve Tsedek v. France.*[91] There the European Court of Human Rights held that denial of independent authority to an ultra-Orthodox Jewish group to slaughter meat in compliance with their religious requirements did not constitute an interference with manifestation of religion of the group in France, because they could obtain conforming meat from Belgium. These cases are fact-sensitive, and time does not allow exploring them in depth here, but in the future, efforts are needed to prevent setting the burden/interference threshold too high, as I believe it was in the ritual slaughter case. Some of the cases seem to suggest that even massive

---

86 *Metropolitan Church of Bessarabia*, para. 116.

87 *Metropolitan Church of Bessarabia*, para. 118; *Manoussakis*, paras. 43–53.

88 *Metropolitan Church of Bessarabia*, para. 118.

89 United Nations Human Rights Committee General Comment No. 22 (48) (Article 18) Adopted by the UN Human Rights Committee on 20 July 1993. UN Doc. CCPR/C/21/Rev.1/Add.4 (1993), reprinted in UN Doc. HRI/GEN/1/ Rev.1 at 35 (1994), ¶ 8.

90 Decision, Republic of Korea [2007] UNHRC 5; CCPR/C/88/D/1321-1322/2004 (23 January 2007) (UN HRC).

91 *Cha'are Shalom ve Tsedek v. France*, App. No. 27417/95 (Grand Chamber), 27 June 2000.

monetary burdens are not sufficient to cross the threshold because they are 'merely financial'. In some cases, this has allowed imposition of significant burdens on individual claimants.[92]

There are a variety of ways that religious freedom rights can be eroded under the various tests examined here. Relying solely on rule of law constraints (as opposed to insisting on proportionality tests in addition) places religious groups at the mercy of legislative majorities. More significantly, it drastically shifts the likelihood of success for religious claimants at the grass roots level. When a religious claimant meets with an official requesting an accommodation with respect to a religious claim, the official is more likely to seek a solution if his solution will be subjected to strict scrutiny.[93] In contrast, if the laws authorizing the official's activity are reviewed under a deferential standard of review according to which any neutral or general law can trump religious freedom, the official has virtually no legal incentive to cooperate and an accommodation depends on his or her good graces. This is particularly problematic for unpopular or less well-known groups.

More significantly, both American compelling state interest and proportionality analysis confer significant discretion on judges in weighing religious freedom claims. A primary issue here is that cultural shifts associated with the process of secularization lead many judges to assign greater weight to secular state interests and less to religious concerns. This can occur because religion is no longer seen to deserve special protection, because there is a sense that religious activities and religious views should be consigned exclusively to the private sector, because religion has become more suspect as a locus of social danger, or for any of a variety of other reasons.

Even if judicial biases are not skewed in this way, there is a risk that the characterization of the values being balanced can be manipulated so that they system wide interests of the state are balanced against the individualized concerns of the religious freedom claimant. A more reasonable approach balances the marginal burden faced by the state in the particular interest against the actual burden of the claimant.

Religious Autonomy and the Religious Employment Cases

At the outset, I drew attention to the many layers of religious autonomy issues in which the religious employment cases are nested. Let me now return to the cases

92 See, e.g., *Braunfeld v. Brown*, 366. U.S. 599 (1961) (fact that Sunday Closing Laws caused observant Jew to close his retail establishment on both Saturday and Sunday imposed mere financial burden). This case was implicitly overruled by *Sherbert v. Verner*, 374 U.S. 398 (1963), but is still thought to support the notion that mere financial impact does not count as a substantial burden for free exercise purposes.

93 See D. Laycock, 'Interpreting the Religious Freedom Restoration Act', 73 *Texas Law Review* (1994), 209, 244.

themselves. I have tried to suggest how erosion is occurring within each of the 'layers', and that if this is not effectively countered, there is a substantial risk that we will see an unfortunate narrowing of protections for religious autonomy. For the present, however, strong protections are likely to continue.

On the basis of research conducted in preparing our 'comparative law' *amicus* brief[94] in the *Hosanna-Tabor* case, I can confirm the widespread global recognition of the principles of religious autonomy that apply in that case and countless others. In our brief we noted that while 'church-state law in the United States varies significantly from that of many countries around the world, in large part because of the Establishment Clause', it was striking that 'European and other democratic societies broadly recognize the importance of the [religious autonomy] principles underlying the ministerial exception.'[95] The fact that ministerial personnel play a vital and indeed a constitutive role in the life of religious communities is clearly understood, and laws are contoured to take this into account.

The unanimous decision of the United States Supreme Court in *Hosanna-Tabor*[96] has sent a very strong signal and provides powerful reinforcement for a vital bulwark of religious freedom. It confirms that there is strong constitutional protection, grounded in both the Free Exercise and the Establishment Clause of the First Amendment, for religious autonomy, and that this is a special protection that goes beyond what freedom of association covers. The decision also made it clear that the earlier holding in *Employment Division v. Smith*,[97] that neutral and general laws trump individual religious freedom claims, does not apply in the context of the core religious autonomy domain protected by the ministerial exception. The Court cited pages of history, beginning with the first clause of Magna Carta and continuing through centuries of bitter experience with an established church, to emphasize the importance of religious autonomy, particularly with respect to religious personnel, concluding that '[t]he contention that *Smith* forecloses recognition of a ministerial exception rooted in the Religion Clauses has no merit.'[98]

The *Hosanna-Tabor* decision necessarily implies that the religious autonomy strand of cases in United States jurisprudence has unquestioned constitutional validity, and that the doctrine has sufficient scope to ground a ministerial exception that covers teachers in religiously affiliated schools who are viewed by their religious community as having religious responsibilities. The decision implies *a fortiori* that religious autonomy in determining matters of doctrine and belief are protected, since these are even more central than matters of personnel and governance.

As strong as the *Hosanna-Tabor* judgment was, however, it leaves important questions open. In the end, it didn't really answer the question that took the case

94 Brief of Amicus Curiae ICLRS, supra note 17 at 2–3.
95 Brief of Amicus Curiae ICLRS at 2.
96 *Hosanna-Tabor*, supra note 11.
97 *Smith*, supra note 15.
98 *Hosanna-Tabor* at 707.

to the Supreme Court: Exactly who counts as a minister? The Court achieved unanimity by leaving the outer boundaries of the autonomy doctrine uncertain in this respect. The doctrine clearly protects classic ministers in their churches, and extends horizontally to religious institutions with a teaching mission such as schools, but it is not clear how much further the doctrine reaches. What of religious hospitals, thrift stores, religiously owned (but commercial) media outlets? It also clearly extends vertically down the hierarchy of religious personnel from pastors to teachers in religious schools, but what of media spokesmen, choir leaders and other musicians, secretaries, cooks, gardeners, and janitors?

Even more difficult are questions about the extent to which courts can assess the bona fides of religious personnel decisions. The Court's opinion makes it clear that the ministerial exception is designed to protect not only employment decisions made for religious reasons. Instead, it 'ensures the authority to select and control who will minister to the faithful'. But this doesn't really answer the extent to which courts are free to assess the authenticity of the reasons a religious body gives for its employment decisions. Justice Alito's concurrence points out that 'In order to probe the *real reason* for [an employee's] firing, a civil court—and perhaps a jury—would be required to make a judgment about church doctrine.'[99] In short, the Court gave strong support for religious autonomy in the employment area, but also gave little latitude for judicial monitoring (and second-guessing) the bona fides of exercises of that autonomy.

The European cases paint a similar picture, although European Courts are more likely to retain jurisdiction to control for abuses of religious autonomy. *Siebenhaar v. Germany*[100] involved a woman who served as child care assistant in a Protestant day care center and later in the management of a Protestant kindergarten. Her contract obligated her to be loyal to the church and provided that she was not allowed to be a member of or work for organizations whose views or activities were in contradiction to the church's mandate. The fact that Ms. Siebenhaar was Catholic had apparently caused no problems, but when her employers learned that she had become involved with a group called the Universal Church/Brotherhood of Humanity and she had taught lessons for the group, she was dismissed. The European Court found that there was no violation of Article 9. Thus, autonomy protections extend to people with teaching and administrative functions in religious educational facilities. Moreover, the religious school obviously has some latitude in determining how much deviation is permissible from its own teachings. Being Catholic was acceptable, but involvement in the obscure religious group went too far.

Obst v. Germany[101] extended the picture in a slightly different direction. Obst was in charge of public affairs for The Church of Jesus Christ of Latter-day Saints for all of Europe. While not in an ecclesiastical position per se, he clearly was in

99 *Hosanna-Tabor* at 715 (Alito, J., concurring).

100 *Siebenhaar v. Germany*, App. No. 18136/02, 3 February 2011.

101 *Obst v. Germany*, App. No. 425/03, 23 September 2010.

an important representational role for the Church. After learning that Obst had committed adultery, the Church promptly fired him on the basis of clear Church policy guidelines known to Obst. After balancing Obst's privacy interests with the autonomy interests of the Church, the Court found no violation of Obst's privacy rights under Article 8 of the European Convention. Sensitive employment decisions involving high level and highly visible church leaders with responsibility to represent a religious community are thus also covered by religious autonomy.

The same day the European Court decided *Obst*, it handed down its decision in *Schüth v. Germany*,[102] holding that religious autonomy rights were not sufficient to withstand an Article 8 claim brought by the organist and choirmaster of his Catholic parish. Like Obst, Schüth was terminated when the Church learned he was guilty of adultery. The Church found this situation particularly troubling because it meant that someone guilty of a serious offense against Church moral standards was integrally involved in liturgical activities. Nonetheless, the Court ruled in Schüth's favor. However, the long term implications of the case are not clear, because the Court's reasoning turned on the fact that the German courts had not taken all the factors relevant to his case into account. Only Schüth's interest in maintaining his employment had been explicitly weighed. German courts had not taken into account the length of Schüth's service, or the difficulty he would have getting new employment, especially given the prominence of his employer in the relevant work sector. Implicitly, the Court left open the possibility that if a German court in a similar case did weigh all the factors, it might be able to conclude that religious autonomy should prevail.

However, a number of the factors mentioned by the European Court in *Schüth* as deserving consideration are troubling. For example, the Court criticized the fact that the German Labor courts made no mention of Schüth's family life, although in fact Schüth's living with a woman without benefit of marriage was precisely what was offensive to the Church and was inconsistent with his contractual obligations. The Court acknowledged that by signing his employment contract, Schüth had limited his right of privacy 'to some degree', but seemed to discount the seriousness of this problem. The Court pointed out that the applicant did not seek to publicize his case, and indeed, the Church found out about the non-compliant lifestyle only because of notifications that came through the state's payroll system. Of course, it would have been more difficult if Schüth's conduct was more flagrant, but that did not make his conduct acceptable to the Church. What is troubling in this regard is the extent to which the European Court seems to expect lower courts to second guess what is religiously important to the church, which is exactly what secular courts should not be doing. In effect, the Court requires the church to send messages that it condones conduct, even when it has sought contractually to avoid being put in that position, and even when the church may believe some of its most sacred rituals are being tainted as a result. It is one thing to take the position that

102 *Schüth v. Germany*, App. No. 1620/03, 23 September 2010.

this is none of the business of an ordinary commercial establishment, but quite another to suggest that it is not a legitimate concern of a church.

Despite the questions raised by *Schüth*, it remains clear that the core of what is covered by the United States ministerial exception is recognized elsewhere, though the breadth of the penumbra surrounding that core remains uncertain. Among other things, as a practical matter, where religious communities enter into contracts with employees that clearly explain why a particular position has religious significance and explicitly articulate religiously-based standards of conduct that are part of the terms and conditions of employment, religious autonomy principles call for strong deference to the determinations of the religious community. I believe one of the major challenges is to provide better understanding of the importance of autonomy protections across a broader range of the relevant topography.

This is a challenge that law and religion experts are uniquely qualified to address. We need a richer and deeper understanding of why it is that religious organizations have distinctive requirements in this area. It is more than self-interest that explains why virtually all the religious organizations in the United States (and in other countries) care so deeply about this principle, and it is certainly not that they are seeking to cloak some form of invidious discrimination. What religious communities understand is that ministerial personnel in particular, but often other personnel as well, play a vital role in their religious life. State interference with that role, even for reasons as otherwise laudable as promoting equality and non-discrimination, sacrifices the dignity of pluralism to coerced equalitarianism.

As attractive as such equality may appear in the short run, and as important as the ideal of equality is in most contexts, requiring sameness of religious communities undercuts one of their deepest values: their capacity to envision and implement better ways of life than current majorities, current governments and current bureaucracies imagine. Interfering with the exercise of religious autonomy in selecting, supervising, disciplining and removing religious personnel strikes at the heart of religious communities' ability to achieve this value. It interferes with religion's ability to envision and achieve their best. It also interferes, and this is too easily forgotten, with the ability of religious communities to recognize and restrain what otherwise might be their worst. If anything, courts have been too hesitant in protecting autonomy in this domain.

The *Hosanna-Tabor* decision will provide strong protection at least for the core domain of religious autonomy for years to come in the United States. But one of the principal contentions raised by the case remains a threat in other jurisdictions. That is, other jurisdictions might accept the argument that neutral and general laws can prevail over religious autonomy rights without any specially compelling justification. It was a sad day just over twenty years ago when the U.S. Supreme Court held that any neutral and general laws can override individual claims to conscientious objection. One of the few comforts at that time was that the long chain of cases protecting religious autonomy was left intact. But if the central citadel of religious autonomy is rendered open to legislative attack—particularly at the key leverage point of managing religious employment—the consequences could be devastating. Allowing general and neutral laws to override individual conscientious objection claims without compelling justification is profoundly objectionable, but in the end has affected relatively unusual claims. Religious autonomy is different. It is critical to every religion that seeks to pursue and implement its distinctive vision with authenticity. To lose the battle for religious autonomy is ultimately to lose the battle for religious freedom itself. But that battle can only be won if we engage at all the levels I have described, from abstract theory, through various levels of constitutional analysis, to concrete case law.

One of the hallmarks of the West is its recognition of the ontological divide between temporal and spiritual matters. If religious autonomy is compromised, other religious freedom rights are inevitably eroded. And where religious liberty is weakened, other liberties also suffer. Failure to render unto God the things that are God's ultimately impoverishes the aspects of the world that are left to render unto Caesar—even the broader world of other human rights. This helps to explain why religion and religious freedom in general, and religious autonomy in particular, are such an enduringly significant feature in the world's constitutions.

Chapter 2

God in Constitutions and Godless Constitutions

Iván C. Ibán

God in Constitutions

God is referred to in more than one hundred of the world's constitutions.[1] To this list could be added the Greek Constitution, given its reference to the 'Holy and consubstantial and indivisible Trinity' (Preamble and 33.2).[2] We should also include the Constitution of Andorra, with its allusion to the Virgin Mary (First Transitional Provision).[3] The Constitution of Bhutan is unique for its use of a polytheistic reference: 'our guardian deities' (Preamble). In North Korea, in reference to Kim Il Sung, the constitution recalls his maxim that 'the people are my God' (Preamble).

There is no rule that could be established to explain the presence of an express reference to God in the texts studied here. In general terms, such references

---

1 Afghanistan, Albania, Algeria, Argentina, Bahamas, Bahrain, Bangladesh, Barbados, Belize, Benin, Bolivia, Brazil, Brunei, Canada, Colombia, Comoros, Costa Rica, Democratic Republic of the Congo, Denmark, Dominica, Dominican Republic, Ecuador, Egypt, El Salvador, Equatorial Guinea, Fiji, Gabon, Gambia, Germany, Georgia, Granada, Guatemala, Haiti, Honduras, India, Indonesia, Iran, Iraq, Ireland, Jamaica, Jordan, Kenya, Kiribati, Kuwait, Lebanon, Lesotho, Liberia, Liechtenstein, Madagascar, Malawi, Maldives, Mali, Malta, Marshall Islands, Mauritania, Monaco, Morocco, Namibia, Nauru, Netherlands, New Zealand, Nicaragua, Niger, Nigeria, Norway, Oman, Pakistan, Palau, Panama, Papua New Guinea, Paraguay, Peru, Philippines, Poland, Qatar, Romania, Syria, Rwanda, Saint Kitts and Nevis, Samoa, Saint Lucia, Saint Vincent, San Marino, Saudi Arabia, Senegal, Seychelles, Sierra Leone, Solomon Islands, Somalia, South Africa, Sudan, Sweden (Act of Succession), Switzerland, Suriname, Swaziland, East Timor, Togo, Tonga, Trinidad and Tobago, Tunisia, Tuvalu, Uganda, United Arab Emirates, Vanuatu, Venezuela, Yemen and Zimbabwe. For the purposes of this study I have considered any state that was a member of the United Nations 'in December 2010, and have made the fictitious assumption that all of them (except the Central African Republic) have a constitution.

2 Reference is also made to the 'Most Holy Trinity' in the preamble to the Constitution of Ireland, and it is also likely that in the name of the country Trinidad and Tobago, the first word is a reference to the same concept.

3 We can also find a reference to the Virgin Mary in the Constitution of Peru (Twelfth Final and Transitory Provision).

appear in the constitutions of Muslim countries, and of those that were formerly part of the British Empire. This is more common in Protestant countries than in Catholic countries.

There is never a definition in the constitutions of what God is, but there are often references to God's attributes. The most common of these is the epithet 'Almighty'.[4] The supremacy of God is recognized in various constitutions.[5] It is significant that all such cases are in countries that were formerly part of the British Empire. In Muslim countries, God is 'merciful' and 'compassionate'.[6] God's oneness is another characteristic recognized in several Muslim nations.[7] His status as creator is mentioned in a few texts.[8] He is identified as eternal in two constitutions,[9] in another as the Father,[10] and in yet another as omniscient.[11] Such attributes of God do not constitute a definition, but they may allow us to form a general idea if we analyze some of the authority and actions attributed to God.

In some constitutions,[12] those who have the authority to enact a constitutional text consider that in doing so they have a responsibility to God. Others[13] appear

4 God is thus characterized in the constitutions of Afghanistan (Preamble and 63), Bahrain (33a and 78), Bangladesh (Preamble), United Arab Emirates (Preamble and 73), the Philippines (Preamble), Gambia (Preamble), Ireland (12.8 and 34.5.1), Jordan (43), Kenya (Preamble), Kiribati (Preamble), Lebanon (50), the Maldives (Schedule 1), Mauritania (Preamble), Nauru (Preamble), Norway (44.1), Oman (7 and 50), the Netherlands (11), Pakistan (Preamble), Peru (Preamble), Qatar (10, 74, 92 and 119), Syria (7), Rwanda (Preamble, 41, 56.2 and 60.2), Saint Kitts and Nevis (Preamble), Samoa (Preamble and Third Schedule), Saint Lucia, Seychelles (Preamble), Sudan (Preamble, 56, 71 and 89), Sweden (Act of Succession: Preamble), Switzerland (Preamble), Suriname (Preamble and 65), Swaziland (Preamble), Tonga (34), Tuvalu (Preamble), Uganda (Fourth Schedule) and Yemen (160).

5 Bahamas (Preamble), Belize (Preamble), Brunei (Preamble and Final Part; the terms used are 'Lord of the Universe' and 'King of Kings'), Dominica (Preamble), United Arab Emirates (Preamble), Granada (Preamble), Kenya (Preamble), Lebanon (9; the phrase I believe is equivalent to 'Most High'), Pakistan (Preamble: 'Sovereignty over the Universe belongs to'), Samoa (Preamble: same expression as that used in Pakistan), Saint Lucia (Preamble), Saint Vincent (Preamble) and Trinidad and Tobago (Preamble).

6 Afghanistan (63), Saudi Arabia (Preamble), Algeria (Preamble), Brunei (Preamble). Comoros (13), Iran (67.1), Iraq (Preamble), Kuwait (Preamble), Pakistan (Third Schedule), Somalia (Preamble) and Tunisia (Preamble).

7 Afghanistan (19.4), Saudi Arabia (3), Indonesia (Preamble) and Iran (2.1).

8 Dominica (Preamble), United Arab Emirates (Preamble), Granada (Preamble), Madagascar (Preamble) and Trinidad y Tobago (Preamble).

9 Nauru (Preamble) and Tuvalu (Preamble).

10 Kiribati (Preamble).

11 Norway (9.1).

12 Germany (Preamble), Equatorial Guinea (Preamble), Iran (1.6), Poland (Preamble), Democratic Republic of the Congo (Preamble) and Gabon (Preamble).

13 Algeria (Preamble), Bahrain (Preamble), Brunei (Preamble), Egypt (Preamble), Gambia (Preamble), Greece (Preamble), Iraq (Preamble), Kuwait (Preamble) and Switzerland (Preamble).

to have received a mandate of divine origin for the purposes of drafting the constitution, as it is enacted in His name. In yet other cases,[14] there is no mention of such 'empowerment' by God, who is limited merely to supporting the task of drafting the constitution. In a number of countries that were formerly part of the British Empire,[15] it seems that God has a much more 'legal-technical' function, as it is the deity who has conferred certain rights upon men.

Greater detail is given when possession of a particular power is justified on divine grounds. The predecessors of three reigning European monarchs held their power by divine right, and it seems reasonable to assume that this continues to be the justification for the legal position of the current monarchs.[16] Such is also the case of the monarch of Brunei (Preamble) and the members of Tunisia's Constituent Assembly (Preamble).

But God has not only legitimated certain dynasties; He has also protected the Fiji Islands through the ages (Preamble), supported the Irish for centuries (Preamble), turned the Seychelles into one of the most beautiful countries in the world (Preamble) and contributed to the happiness and wellbeing of the inhabitants of Tuvalu (Preamble).

Moreover, the deity has not been above performing other more political and technical tasks, such as assigning ownership of the country's natural resources to the Saudi Arabian State (6), contributing (together with Pachamama) to the founding of a new Bolivia (Preamble), granting Liberia its status as a Free, Sovereign and Independent State (Preamble), and allowing a peace agreement to be reached in Sudan (Preamble).

There can be no doubt that many of these affirmations are merely rhetorical, with no practical effect in legal terms. The fact that the German people believe they have a responsibility to God, or that the Constitution is proclaimed in His name, may perhaps allow us to classify such constitutional texts as theist, but I do not believe that any consequence follows from this. However, in other cases, I would argue that practical effects do indeed exist. The theist notion of natural law used to justify fundamental rights has an obvious practical application, and to some degree brings with it a limitation on the legal system. Such is the case of the divine origin of the power held by the reigning dynasties in Brunei, Liechtenstein and Monaco, as this means that sovereignty does not lie with the people.[17] And it is impossible to ignore the fact that state ownership of the natural resources in Saudi Arabia has some specific consequences on the national economy and income distribution.

---

14 Bhutan (Preamble), Brazil (Preamble) and Solomon Islands (Preamble).

15 Belize (Preamble), Dominica (Preamble), Granada (Preamble), Marshall Islands (Preamble), Saint Lucia (Preamble) and Trinidad and Tobago (Preamble).

16 Liechtenstein (Preamble), Monaco (Preamble) and Sweden (Act of Succession: Preamble).

17 The 'ordinary' functioning of these states makes this situation clear.

Human Conceptualizations of God: Religions

The concept of religion is employed profusely by the authors of constitutions. There is only one constitution for which religion is an irrelevant phenomenon: the Czech Constitution.[18] But I will begin this section by examining the cases in which there is a generic reference to religion.

In Vietnam, it is acknowledged that religions are among the forces that have contributed to the formation of what appears to perform the function of a single party, the Vietnam Fatherland Front (9. 1). The Queen of Cambodia is required to protect religious interests (16.2). This duty also falls upon the Irish State (44.1) and the government of the Dominican Republic (7), as well as upon all Thai (66) and Yemeni citizens (60). Sacred sites must be protected in Israel (Basic Law: Jerusalem, Capital of Israel: 3). Religion is even a reason for protecting the spreading of certain languages in South Africa,[19] and for exemption from paying taxes in Uruguay (297.7). And a religious affiliation will result in a different treatment from that stipulated in common law for questions such as applicable legislation in the declaration of a state of emergency in Singapore (150.5.iii), or in Swedish broadcasting regulations (Fundamental Law on Freedom of Expression: 1.8).

Religious persecution in any country calling for extradition is sufficient grounds for establishing a right of asylum for foreigners.[20] It is also sufficient grounds for claiming exemption from military duty in Brazil (143.1), Slovenia (123.2), Estonia (124.2), Montenegro (48), Poland (85.3), Serbia (45.1) and Ukraine (35).

Religion is sometimes used as grounds for unfavorable treatment. It is not uncommon to find bans on the establishment of political parties with a religious basis or name,[21] or unions of a similar nature.[22] Although it may be risky to generalize, such countries seem to fall into two categories: either they are sociologically Christian, or they are recently independent and run the risk of being 'Islamized'. In some countries there is a generic ban on using religion for

18 Neither the word religion nor any other related term appears in the Constitution of the Czech Republic. It could thus be argued that it is the only truly secular constitution, as the religious phenomenon is irrelevant.

19 'A Pan South African Language Board established by national legislation must... promote ... Arabic, Hebrew, Sanskrit and other languages used for religious purposes' (6.5.a.ii).

20 Cape Verde (35.2), Ivory Coast (12), Hungary (65.1), Mali (12), Montenegro (44) and Peru (37).

21 This is the case in Bulgaria (11.4), Cape Verde (125.2), Djibouti (6), Gambia (60.2), Ghana (55.4 y 7.c), Guinea (3), Equatorial Guinea (9), Kazakhstan (5.4), Kenya (91.2.a), Kirghistan (8.5), Liberia (79), Niger (9), Nigeria (222.e), Panama (181), Portugal (51.3), Nepal (142.4; actually, in this case the ban is against parties 'that would disturb the religious ... harmony'), Tanzania (20.2.a.i), Senegal (4), Sierra Leone (35.5), Turkmenistan (30) and Uzbekistan (57).

22 Guinea Bissau (45.3) and Portugal (55.4).

political ends.[23] In North Korea it is stipulated that 'religion must not be used as a pretext for drawing in foreign forces or for harming the State or social order' (68.2). In other cases, such as the United States (VI.3) or the Philippines (III.5), religion should not be taken into account for political purposes.

However, references to a specific religion are much more common.[24] In some cases, reference is made to a religion merely with the aim of indicating the applicable calendar, such as the use of the Buddhist calendar in the Thai Constitution (Preamble), or the Bruneian, which is dated using the Christian calendar and indicates this fact expressly (*in fine*). There is also a reference to Buddhism in the Constitution of Laos.[25]

What follows is a list of some generic references to religious organizations. Churches are exempt from taxation in Brazil (150 VI) and in Chile (19). The establishment of private schools in the Philippines is prohibited, unless they established by a religious organization (XIV.4.2.). In Ghana, religious organizations must be represented on the Prisons Service Council (206 h) In Lithuania the constitution recognizes the 'traditional Lithuanian churches' (43.1). One third of the Senate of Madagascar must be appointed by the President from among representatives of different social groups, including religious organizations (77.1). The Governor General of Saint Lucia may appoint senators after meeting with religious bodies (24.2 c). Minority faiths must receive state support in Montenegro (79.6), and public funding in the Netherlands (Additional Article 4). And there must be representatives of religious bodies on a Commission for the Protection of Minorities in South Africa (186.2 a).

Some constitutions express a fear of foreign intervention through religious organizations; thus, certain restrictions are imposed on them in Belarus (16.2), China (36.4) and Kazakhstan (5.5). Meanwhile, certain conditions are imposed on their access to property in Mexico (27.II) and Tonga (108).

The Roman Catholic Church is the most oft-cited religious body in the world's constitutions. In Andorra, the constitution guarantees 'the preservation of [a] relationship of special cooperation' with this church (11.3). In Argentina 'the federal government upholds the apostolic and Roman Catholic faith' (2) and implicitly establishes a concordat system (72.22). Such a system also appears to be established in the constitutions of Luxembourg (22) and Poland (25.4). In Spain, the constitution guarantees 'relations of cooperation with the Catholic Church' (16.3). Its legal status is recognized in Guatemala (37), and

---

23 Costa Rica (28), Honduras (77), Myanmar (156.c) and Turkey (24.5).

24 The identification of religion with 'religious denomination' I believe is implicit in numerous constitutional texts, but is explicitly stated in many of the countries that once formed part of the British Empire, for example: Barbados (19.7), Solomon Islands (11.8), Lesotho (13.3.7), Papua New Guinea (45.5), Saint Kitts and Nevis (11.6), Saint Lucia (9.6), Saint Vincent (9.6), Tuvalu (23.9) and Zimbabwe (19.6).

25 'L'Etat respecte et protège les activités légales des pratiquants de la religión bouddhique et des autres religions' (9).

the constitution of Uruguay also makes reference to its control over its places of worship. It is mentioned in the Italian Constitution in order to establish its independence from the state (7.1). The recognition of 'parochial' schools in Palau appears to be restricted exclusively to Catholic schools (IV.1). Independence, cooperation and autonomy are the foundations of the relationship between the state and the Catholic Church in Paraguay (24). The Peruvian State 'recognizes the Catholic Church as an important element in the historical, cultural and moral formation of Peru, and lends it its cooperation' (50). In East Timor, 'the State acknowledges and values the participation of the Catholic Church in the process of national liberation' (11).

Other Christian churches are mentioned in the constitutions of the following countries: in Armenia, where 'the Republic ... recognizes the exclusive historical mission of the Armenian Apostolic Holy Church' (8.1); in Bulgaria, where 'Eastern Orthodox Christianity is considered the traditional religion' (13.3); in Cyprus, where special status is recognized for the Orthodox Church (110.1); the Orthodox Church is permitted to establish schools in Macedonia (19.3); in the Constitution of Finland mention is made of the Evangelical Lutheran Church (76.1); in Georgia, the state 'shall recognize the special role of the Apostle Autocephalus Orthodox Church of Georgia' (9.1); the Protestant churches have the right to appoint a member of the Electoral Council of Haiti (289.8); and the Church of Sweden is appointed depositary of certain official documents (Freedom of the Press Act: 2.17).

Men of Religion and Religious Officials: Religious Affiliation and 'Ministers of Worship'

I will begin this section with the cases in which it is necessary to profess a particular religion to be eligible to hold a specific public office. In most such cases, it is the Islam faith that must be professed: Afghanistan,[26] Algeria,[27] Brunei,[28] Jordan,[29] Kuwait,[30] the Maldives,[31] Mauritania,[32] Oman,[33] Pakistan,[34]

26 Candidates for president (62.1) or vice president (62.3).

27 Candidate for president (73.1).

28 The prime minister (4.5).

29 The king, whose parents must also be Muslims (28.e).

30 The crown prince, whose parents must also be Muslims (4.5).

31 Members of parliament (73.a.3), the president (109.b), ministers (130.a.3) and judges (149.b.1). Specifically, the constitution stipulates that a candidate for the Maldivian legislature must be 'a follower of a Sunni school of Islam'.

32 The president (23).

33 The Sultan, whose parents must also be Muslims (5).

34 The president (41.2) and prime minister (91.3). It is worth noting that in this case some posts are reserved for non-Muslims: ten seats in the National Assembly (51.4), four in the Senate (59.1.f) and various in the provincial assemblies (106.1). It would

Syria,[35] Tunisia,[36] and Yemen.[37] In the Christian world, similar requirements are imposed on the King of Denmark,[38] the King of Norway,[39] and the king and heir to the throne in Sweden.[40]

The unique case of Cyprus deserves separate mention. The division of public posts between the Greek and Turkish communities is strict and precise (46; 48.a; 49.a; 7.1). The division is ethnic, but also religious, as to one community belong the faithful of the Orthodox Church (2.1) while the other is entirely Muslim (2.2).

Outside the Christian and Muslim world, I have found only one case where the profession of a specific religion is required to occupy a public post: the Head of State of Bhutan (Drug Gyalpo), who must be a Buddhist (2.2).

Being a Muslim is a requirement for citizenship in the Maldives (109), while the defense of Islam is an obligation for all Saudi citizens (34). Adherence to this religion gives citizens the right to bring cases before specific courts in Gambia (137.4), Kenya (24.4), Nigeria (262.2.e), Somalia (30.2) and other countries.

But nowhere are the 'political' and the 'religious' more clearly fused than when, by virtue of their position, political authorities exercise political functions, or vice versa. For example, one of the two co-princes of Andorra is also the Bishop of Urgel (43.2), while the King of Saudi Arabia is 'the guardian of the two mosques' (Preamble). The King of Bahrain is the 'loyal protector of the [Muslim] religion' (33.a). Iran's religious leaders are also the most senior political authorities in Iran (*passim*), and Malaysia's Head of State is also the head of the Muslim religion (3.3). In Morocco, the king is commander of the believers (19.1). Bhutan is a unique case, as its Head of State is deemed protector of 'all religions' (3.2); similarly, the monarch of Thailand is the 'upholder of religions' (9).

---

probably be reasonable to assume that the rest are all to be occupied by Muslims. With the characteristic fondness of constitutional texts of British origin for definitions, one is offered in the Pakistani constitution for 'non-Muslim': '"non Muslim" means a person who is not a Muslim and includes a person belonging to the Christian, Hindu, Sikh, Buddhist or Parsi community, a person of the Quadiani Group or the Lahori Group who call themselves Ahamadis or by any other name or a Bahai, and a person belonging to any of the Scheduled Castes.' Non-theist options are, quite simply, non-existent.

35 The president (3.1).

36 The president (38) and presidential candidates (40.1).

37 Candidates for member of parliament (64.2.d) and the president (107.d). In both cases, they are also required to fulfill their religious obligations.

38 Must be a member of the Evangelical Lutheran Church (6).

39 Must profess the Evangelical Lutheran faith (4), and more than half of the members of a Royal Council appointed by the monarch must also profess this faith.

40 Specifically, the King must be of 'the pure evangelical faith, as adopted and explained in the unaltered Confession of Ausburg and in the Resolution of the Uppsala Meeting of the year 1593' (Act of Succession: 4).

I will now turn to cases where holding a qualified position in a religious organization entails a restriction on political rights. In Argentina, the 'regular clergy cannot be members of the Congress … or governors' (73). It is reasonable to assume that the ban on 'religious men' entering the Parliament of Azerbaijan also refers to ministers of worship (85.2). The same is true in Barbados for those who have taken holy orders or are ministers of religion (44.1). In Bolivia, 'the ministers of any religious faith … are not eligible for any elected public office' (238.5). Clergy cannot be president or vice president (131.2), members of parliament (115), cabinet ministers (142.3) or magistrates (159.3) in Costa Rica. In Dominica, ministers of worship are prohibited from being senators (32.1). In El Salvador, 'ministers of any religious faith … may not belong to political parties or run for elected office, nor may they engage in political propaganda of any kind' (82), and for various offices[41] it is specifically required that candidates must be of 'secular status'. The president and vice president (186.f), cabinet ministers (197.e), magistrates and judges (207) in Guatemala may not be ministers of worship either. In Honduras (77) we find a ban similar to the general prohibition established in El Salvador with specific reference to the necessarily 'secular' status of members of congress (198.4), the president and vice president (238.4). A prohibition against ministers of worship from entering Parliament is also found in Israel (Basic Law: The Knesste: 7.7). The situation in Mexico is very similar to the cases described above in El Salvador and Honduras[42]. Restrictions on members of religious orders are more extensive in Myanmar, where they are not even permitted to vote (178.a). In Nicaragua, ministers of worship may not be candidates for the congress (134.2.b), or for president or vice president (147.e). The restriction is not so broad in Panama, where they 'may only hold public offices related to social assistance, education or scientific research' (45). In Paraguay, they may not run for parliament (197.5) or for president or vice president (235.5). The prohibition against running for parliament also appears in the constitutions of Saint Kitts and Nevis (28.1), Saint Lucia (26.1.b y 32.1.b) and Saint Vincent (26.1.b). In Thailand, any person who is a 'Buddhist priest, novice, monk or clergy' is not permitted to vote in general elections (106).

In the Muslim world the tendency to identify the state with religion appears obvious: the requirement to profess the Muslim faith in order to exercise one's political rights is evidence of the fact. In Christian countries with a colonial past,

41 The president (151) and vice president (153), Supreme Court, appellant court or trial court judges (176; 177; 179), justices of the peace (180), the attorney general, the public prosecutor (192) and governors (201).

42 Ministers of worship may not be members of Mexico's lower house (55.VI), president or vice president (82.IV), or 'hold political offices. As citizens they have the right to vote, but not to be voted for …. They may not join any association with political purposes or engage in proselytism for or against any political candidate, party or association' (130.d and e).

there is a clear tendency to separate the two powers. The prohibition against 'ministers of worship' holding public office is a reaction against the intense political presence of ecclesiastical hierarchies during colonial times. The separation between 'church' and state is an element of national self-affirmation.

Among other references to ministers of worship is this declaration in the constitution of Laos: 'l'Etat ... mobilise et encourage les bonzes, bonzillons ainsi que les prêtes des autres religions à participer aux activités servant a les intérêts de la Patrie et du peuple' (9). The attitude is similarly favorable in Haiti,[43] Lebanon,[44] and Malawi.[45] In Tonga, 'ministers of religion shall be exempt from serving on juries' (28). They are permitted to receive government stipends both in the Netherlands (Additional Article 4) and in Luxembourg (106). However, in the Philippines such funding is prohibited (V1.29.2). The Belgian Constitution establishes that the state shall not intervene in the appointment of 'ministers of worship' (21.2), while in Luxembourg it falls upon the ordinary legislator to regulate such appointments (22). In Kazakhstan, the 'appointment of heads of religious associations ... by foreign religious centers shall be carried out in coordination with ... the Republic' (5.5).

God as Legislator

The underlying question throughout this section is very specific: Do some constitutions assume the existence of a regulatory system of a higher order than the system they establish?

There are references to so-called 'Natural Law' in the constitutions of Burundi (30) and Chad (38), which proclaim that the right of parents to educate their children is a 'natural right', but this would appear to me to be a law with no practical application. Nor do I believe that there is any practical significance in the affirmation that 'secular ethics ... [is] the basis of the ... legal system' in Ecuador (3.4), or in the declaration in Bolivia that the indigenous peoples would have a legal system beyond the system of the state.[46] But it is not merely in the realm of 'indigenism' that we find restrictions imposed on the application of the state legal system by other regulatory systems. On educational matters, the constitution of Liechtenstein proclaims the 'inviolability of the doctrine of the [Catholic] church' (16.1).

43 The Electoral Board must include a representative of the Episcopal Conference and other '*cultes reformés*' (289.2 and 8).

44 The 'officially recognized heads of religious communities' are entitled to consult directly with the Constitutional Council on certain matters (19).

45 Members of the Senate are required to nominate another series of senators, which must include 'representatives of the major religious faiths in Malawi' (68.2).

46 The 'indigenous nations and peoples...enjoy [the right] ... to exercise their own ... legal ... systems' (30.II.14). A reading of the rest of the Constitution leads to the conclusion that this is not a regulatory proclamation in the strict sense.

In two Orthodox countries there are suggestions of a belief in the existence of 'religious law', distinct from and recognized by the law of the state. The constitution of Cyprus establishes that certain questions related to property, monasteries and mosques, among others, shall be regulated by religious laws (110); this also includes questions of family law (111). In Greece, the same is true of the regime of the Aghion Oros.[47]

Another case in which religious stipulations are recognized to have legal force is in Tonga, whose constitution establishes the absolute nullity of any agreement signed on the Sabbath (6). In some cases there appears to be an admission of the possibility of deference to religious systems,[48] or of the establishment of religious courts.[49] But the most obvious examples of this are found in Muslim countries.

In Saudi Arabia, the 'constitution is Almighty God's Book, The Holy Qur'an, and the Sunna (Traditions) of the Prophet' (1). This use here of the term 'constitution', which in our times has a very precise legal application, leaves no room for doubt.[50]

The hierarchical superiority of religious law appears clearly in the constitutions of Afghanistan,[51] Pakistan,[52] Iraq,[53] the Maldives,[54] Yemen,[55]

---

47 'The determination in detail of regimes of the Aghion Oros entities and the manner of operation thereof is effected by the Charter of Aghion Oros which, with the cooperation of the State representative, shall be drawn up and voted by the twenty Holy Monasteries and ratified by the Ecumenical Patriarchate and the Parliament of the Hellenes' (105.3).

48 Thus, in South Africa: 'This section does not prevent legislation recognizing … systems of personal and family law under any tradition, or adhered to by persons professing a particular religion' (15.3.a.ii).

49 Ethiopia (34.5 and 78.5), Indonesia (24.2), Israel (Basic Law: The Judiciary: 1.b.1 and 15.c.4) and Sri Lanka (105.4).

50 In a certain sense it may be considered a theoretical proclamation, as the same law stipulates that the authority of the Government is derived from this book and these traditions, which are 'the ultimate source of reference for this Law and the other laws' (7); the courts must apply Sharia law (48); and the king must reign in accordance therewith (55), as he and his ministers are responsible for its implementation (57).

51 'No law can be contrary to the beliefs and provisions of the sacred religion of Islam' (3). Consistent with this principle, the educational curriculum must be based on this religion (45), the State must ensure that any family traditions contrary to Muslim tradition are eliminated (54.2), the President must safeguard the provisions of Islam (63), etc.

52 'All existing laws shall be brought in comformity with the Injunctions of Islam as laid down in the Holy Quran and Sunnah … and no law shall be enacted which is repugnant to such Injunctions' (227.1). A court and procedure are even established to decree the 'unconstitutionality' of any laws that fail to respect this requirement (203.D).

53 'No law may be enacted that contradicts the established provisions of Islam' (2.1.A).

54 'No law contrary to any tenet of Islam shall be enacted' (10.b and 70.b.2). And a curious situation is created whereby Muslim precepts are simultaneously 'constitutional' and supplementary laws: 'When deciding matters on which the Constitution or the law is silent, Judges must consider Islamic Shari'ah' (142).

55 'Islamic Shari'ah is the source of all legislation' (3). The economy is to be based on these principles (7), the State is to collect a religious tax (21), and inheritances are to

Mauritania,[56] Bahrain,[57] Egypt,[58] Kuwait,[59] Oman,[60] Qatar,[61] Somalia,[62] and, on a shared footing, in Sudan.[63]

Warranting separate mention is the case of Iran, whose constitution is not limited to declaring the superiority of a religion over the legal system of the state, as it also establishes the superiority of religious hierarchies over political ones. Its preamble alone leaves this clear enough: 'The Constitution provides for the establishment of leadership by a holy person possessing the necessary qualifications ... such leadership will prevent any deviation by the various organs of State from their essential Islamic duties'.

In view of the above, the legal systems of some Muslim countries hardly seem secular. For example, with regard to inheritance law the Libyan Constitution states only that it shall be regulated by Sharia (8). Gambia's constitution stipulates the application of Islamic law to Muslims in family and inheritance matters (173.4), as is the case in Jordan (105),[64] Kenya (24.4 y 170.5), and Nigeria (240, 244.1, 260.1, 261.1, 2621 and 2.e and 275). In Brunei, the constitution exempts Muslim taxes from certain auditing procedures (69).

The conclusion is simple. There are some countries with a Christian tradition where reference is made to religious values, but this does not mean that any regulatory systems that may derive therefrom constitute a legal framework to which the state must defer. However, in many of the Muslim systems, Islamic law is positioned as a hierarchically superior system to that of the state.

---

be regulated by the Islamic system (23), as are women's rights (31) and criminal law (47).

56 'Precepts of Islam, the sole source of law' (Preamble).

57 In the case of Bahrain there is a qualification, as Islamic law is only 'one' main source: 'The Islamic Shari'a is a principal source of legislation' (2). Nevertheless, laws related to women and inheritance (5.b and d) and property, capital and labor (9.a) must adhere to that source.

58 'Principal source of legislation is Islamic jurisprudence (Sharia)' (2).

59 In Kuwait it is also qualified: 'Islamic Sharia shall be a main source of legislation' (2).

60 'The Islamic Shariah is the basis of legislation' (2). Specifically, it is to regulate inheritance law (11).

61 In Qatar it is also qualified: 'Shari'a law shall be a main source of its legislation' (1). It is also to regulate inheritance law (51).

62 'The doctrine of Islam shall be the main source of the laws of the State' (50). Along the same lines, 302.2 and 98.1.

63 'Sudan shall have as its sources of legislation Islamic Sharia and the consensus of the people' (5.1).

64 I am unaware of its practical application, but it is important to note that Jordan's constitution admits the possibility of establishing courts of other religions to decide matters related to personal status (99, 108 and 109.i).

States that Believe in a Specific God: The Nationalization of Religion

To profess a religious belief is an intellectual activity unique to human beings. For a state to profess a religion is a conceptual absurdity. Nevertheless, it is common in constitutional texts for a religion to be proclaimed the state religion.

In some case, the deity seems to be attributed the character of the nation's founder. Thus, 'the people of the Fiji Islands acknowledge that worship and reverence of God are the source of good government and leadership' (5). In Indonesia, 'the State shall be based upon the belief in the One and Only God' (29.1). In Saint Vincent, 'the Nation is founded on the belief in the supremacy of God' (Preamble). But these simple references to God mention no specific human conceptualization of God, which means that no particular religious belief is accorded a privileged position.

In other cases, there are references that include the consideration of a particular religion but that could not be deemed to constitute the nationalization of that religion. This is the case of the Catholic faith in Andorra,[65] Argentina,[66] Panama,[67] and East Timor,[68] among others, while for the Orthodox Church, an example would be Bulgaria.[69] Bhutan would be an example for Buddhism,[70] and the United Arab Emirates for Islam.[71] But I will now turn to clear, express proclamations of a national religion.

The case of Israel is problematic: it is proclaimed a Jewish State (Basic Law: Human Dignity and Liberty: 1 and Basic Law: Freedom of Occupation: 3). But is the reference to Judaism a reference to religion or race?

---

65 'The Constitution guarantees the Catholic Church … the preservation of … a special relationship of cooperation with the State' (11.3).

66 'The Federal Government upholds the apostolic, Roman Catholic faith' (2).

67 'The Catholic religion is recognized to be the faith of the majority of Panamanians' (35). The establishment of a statistic as a (supposed) legal rule is nothing short of shocking. What is the legal consequence? What happens if the statistics no longer reflect the constitutional proclamation?

68 'The State acknowledges and values the participation of the Catholic Church in the process of national liberation' (11). *Mutatis mutandis*, the same comments apply as in the previous case.

69 'Eastern Orthodox Christianity is considered the traditional religion' (13.2).

70 'Buddhism is the spiritual heritage of Bhutan' (3.1).

71 The Emirate Constitution employs a unique tactic of evading a proclamation of Islam as the state religion, while making reference to its importance in a manner that is not merely ornamental: 'The foreign policy of the Union shall be directed towards support for … Islamic causes and interests' (12).

Three countries declare themselves Buddhist. Cambodia does so very clearly.[72] Less obvious are the declarations of Sri Lanka[73] and Thailand.[74]

Catholicism is the official religion in Costa Rica,[75] Liechtenstein,[76] Malta,[77] and Monaco.[78]

In Armenia, 'the Republic ... recognizes the ... Armenian Apostolic Holy Church as a national church'.[79] Meanwhile, in Greece, 'the prevailing religion ... is that of the Eastern Orthodox Church of Christ' (3.1).

Only three Protestant countries establish national churches: Denmark,[80] Iceland,[81] and Norway.[82]

However, an established state religion is an almost universal rule in the Muslim world: Afghanistan (2.1), Saudi Arabia (1),[83] Algeria (2),[84] Bahrain (1.a and 2), Bangladesh (5),[85] Brunei (3.1), Egypt (2), Iran (12 and *passim*),[86] Iraq

---

72 'Buddhism is the State religion' (43.3). In addition, the State is committed to promoting a Buddhist education system (68.2).

73 'The Republic ... shall give to Buddhism the foremost place' (9). Protection mechanisms have also been established for the amendment of this precept (83.a).

74 The declaration is highly qualified by virtue of its extension to all religions: 'The State shall patronize and protect Buddhism and other religions' (73).

75 'The Roman Catholic, Apostolic Religion is the religion of the State' (75).

76 'The Roman Catholic Church is the State Church' (37.2). I am unsure as to whether it is a question of a translation problem, but if not, this affirmation is conceptually meaningless. In the Christian world, the idea of a state church is unique to Protestantism. Regalist attempts to nationalize the Church in the 18th century, when they came close to succeeding, brought it to the very brink of rupture (Gallicanism). Of course, although some remnants of regalism remain in some legal systems, the doctrine did not survive.

77 'The religion of Malta is the Roman Catholic Apostolic religion' (2.1).

78 'La religion cattholique, apostolique et romaine est religión d'Etat' (9).

79 This affirmation is extraordinarily qualified however by the fact that in the same paragraph (8.1) is the stipulation that 'the church shall be separate from the state' (8.1).

80 'The Evangelical Lutheran Church shall be the Established Church ..., and, as such, it shall be supported by the State' (4).

81 'The Evangelical Lutheran Church shall be the State Church ... and, as such, it shall be supported and protected by the State' (62). A specific mechanism for amendment is also established (79).

82 'The Evangelical-Lutheran religion shall remain the official religion of the State'. In the same article, the following surprising (for Europe) prescription is added: 'The inhabitants professing it are bound to bring up their children in the same' (2.2).

83 In addition, the State shall promote Islamic values (10), education is to have the same objective (13), it must spread Islam (23) and its civilization (29) and it falls upon the Armed Forces to defend its principles (33).

84 Moreover, on this point the Constitution cannot be altered (178.3).

85 A protection mechanism has also been established for the amendment this precept (142).

86 In addition, one of the objectives of the Government is the expansion and strengthening of Islam (3.15), including in its foreign policy (3.16), its Armed Forces shall

(2.1), Libya (2), Jordan (2), Kuwait (2), Malaysia (3.1),[87] the Maldives (2),[88] Morocco (6),[89] Mauritania (5), Oman (2), Pakistan (2), Qatar (1), Somalia (1.3),[90] Tunisia (1), and Yemen (2).

Godless Constitutions: The Secular State

Parallel to the above category is the group of states that proclaim themselves secular: Angola (8.1),[91] Azerbaijan (7.1),[92] Benin (2,)[93] Burundi (1), Cameroon (Preamble and 1.2), Chad (1),[94] Congo (1),[95] Ivory Coast (30),[96] Ecuador (1),[97] Russia (14.1),[98] France (2.1), Gabon (2),[99] Guinea (1),[100] Guinea Bissau (1), Guyana (1), India (Preamble),[101] Kazakhstan (1.1), Madagascar (1.1),[102] Mali (25),[103] Mozambique

be Islamic (144), the requirements to become a judge shall be established using religious criteria (163) and, of course, all these precepts are unalterable (177.5).

87 Moreover, in certain territories religious proselytism among Muslims may be prohibited (11.4) and all regulations on religious matters are unalterable (161.e.2.d).

88 In addition, education shall have the objective of fostering obedience to Islam (35 c) and it is an obligation of every citizen to preserve and protect the religion (67.g).

89 Moreover, all constitutional stipulations on religious matters are unalterable (100).

90 All non-Islamic religious proselytism is also prohibited (29).

91 Moreover, 'political parties shall ... contribute to ... the defense of ... the secular nature of the State' (4.2) and a protection mechanism is established for amendment of this precept (159.e).

92 In addition, 'the State educational system is secular' (18.1), and the secular nature of the State may not be subject to amendment by means of a referendum (155).

93 Moreover, no constitutional reform is permitted on this point (156).

94 Moreover, no constitutional reform is permitted on this point (225).

95 Moreover, no constitutional reform is permitted on this point (178.5).

96 Moreover, no constitutional reform is permitted on this point (127).

97 In addition, it is the duty of the State to 'guarantee secular ethics as the foundation of government activity and the legal system' (3.4), whatever that may mean, and education shall be secular (28).

98 A protection mechanism is also established for amendment of this precept (135.1).

99 Additionally, 'tout acte portant atiente à la...laïcité de l'État...constitue un crime de haute trahison' (7).

100 Moreover, no constitutional reform is permitted on this point (91).

101 However, this stipulation in the Preamble is not applicable to the state of Jammu and Kashmir (Appendix II.1.a).

102 However, in contradiction of this proclamation, the Constitution's Preamble declares that the people believe in God the Creator.

103 Moreover, 'le Peuple ... s'engage solennellement à defendre...la laïcité de l'Etat' (Preamble), the parties must respect the secular principle (28) and no constitutional reform on this point is permitted (118).

(120), Namibia (Preamble y 1.1), Democratic Republic of the Congo (1),[104] Nepal (4.1), Sao Tomé (8),[105] Serbia (11.1), Togo (1),[106] Turkmenistan (Preamble and 1),[107] and Turkey (Preamble and 2).[108]

Most of these countries either belong to the French legal-cultural realm or are former members of the Soviet Union.

Negative Definitions

A negative definition is by its nature imprecise. Yet there are numerous constitutional texts that opt for this solution. Underlying this point is the fact that positive definitions are not a model of precision either. I will begin with the countries that proclaim that no religion shall have official status: Albania (10.1), Australia (116), Slovakia (1), the United States (Amendment 1), Ethiopia (11.2),[109] the Philippines (III.5),[110] Gambia (100.2.b), Ghana,[111] Kenya (8), Kirghistan (8.1), Liberia (14),[112] Lithuania (43.7), Mexico (24), Micronesia (IV.2), Nicaragua (14), Nigeria (10), Palau (IV.1), South Korea (20.2),[113] Seychelles (21.6), Tajikistan (8),[114] Ukraine (35),[115] Uganda (7), and Uruguay.[116]

104 However, the Preamble includes the affirmation: 'Conscients de nos responsabilités devant Dieu.'

105 Moreover, no constitutional reform is permitted on this point (154.b).

106 Moreover, no constitutional reform is permitted on this point (144); nevertheless, in the Preamble the people are defined as 'sous la protection de Dieu'.

107 In addition, the public education system shall be secular (12).

108 Moreover, no constitutional reform is permitted on this point (4), any restrictions on rights and freedoms in specific cases cannot affect the secular nature of the State (13) and the programs of political parties may not oppose this nature (68.4).

109 However, the Ethiopian Constitution also adopts a positive definition, of the kind I will analyze later in this article: 'State and religion are separate' (11.1).

110 As in the Ethiopian case, a positive definition is also offered (II.6).

111 In a complex prescription: 'Parliament shall have no power to enact a law to establish or authorize the establishment of a body or movement with the right or power to impose on the people of Ghana a common program or a set of objectives of a religious or political nature' (56).

112 The same article also makes reference to the separation of Church and State.

113 The same article also establishes that 'church and state are to be separated'.

114 The same article also sets forth the separation between 'religious organizations' and the State.

115 The same article stipulates the separation between 'the Church and religious organizations' and the State.

116 The formula is distinct in this case, and may perhaps have a different application: 'The State does not uphold any religion' (5).

In other countries, the point of reference for the negative definition is not religion, but a religious organization (church, denomination, etc.): Germany,[117] Brazil,[118] Spain,[119] Estonia,[120] Japan,[121] Paraguay,[122] and Romania.[123]

A unique case meriting separate mention is that of Lebanon, where Christians and Muslims must have equal representation in Parliament (24.1.a and b). This system is not considered desirable, and so the Constitution also sets forth that 'the abolition of political confessionalism is a Basic national goal and shall be achieved according to a gradual plan' (Preamble h).

The State Seeks No Relationship with Religion or Religious Organizations: Separatism

'Separatism' is a doctrinal formula developed to define a type of (non-)relationship between religious organizations and the state. The number of constitutions that explicitly admit this formula are few: Bolivia (4), Cape Verde (48.3),[124] Croatia (41.1), Cuba (8), Slovenia (7.1), Hungary (60.3), Latvia (99), Montenegro (14), Niger (4),[125] and Uzbekistan (61). We find a similar affirmation in the Bulgarian Constitution (13.2), although it is qualified by a reference to a specific religion.[126] Something analogous is found in the Constitution of Fiji.[127]

Although they do not use the exact term 'separation', I believe that the constitutions of Portugal,[128] Moldova,[129] and Venezuela[130] could also be included in this category.

A different case is that of countries whose constitutions proclaim independence from a specific church. That they refer to a single church highlights the fact that

117 'There is no state church' (137.1 of the Weimar Constitution, still in effect by virtue of Article 140).

118 The reference is to 'sects or churches' (19).

119 The reference is to 'denominations' (16.3).

120 The reference is to the 'church'.

121 The reference is to 'religious organizations' (20.2), and there is also a ban on public funding of such organizations (89).

122 The reference is to 'denominations' (24).

123 The reference is to 'religious sects' (29.5),

124 Moreover, this precept cannot be amended by referendum (108.3).

125 Moreover, no constitutional reform is permitted on this point.

126 'Eastern Orthodox Christianity is considered the traditional religion' (13.3).

127 'Although religion and the State are separate, the people of the Fiji Islands acknowledge that worship and reverence of God are the source of good government and leadership' (5).

128 'Churches and religious communities are independent of the State' (41.4).

129 'Religious groups shall be…independent from the State' (31.4).

130 'The State shall guarantee... the independence and autonomy of the churches and religious denominations' (59).

the separation is not total. This is the case of the Catholic Church in Italy[131] and Peru[132] and the Orthodox Church in Georgia.[133]

Inconclusive Conclusions, or How Constitutional Provisions Are Not Necessarily Law and the Preferable Nature, in this Field, of Not Being Too Specific

When legal doctrine makes mention of constitutional values, constitutional principles, etc., what it does is introduce a range of technical categories that ultimately hinder comprehension of what a constitutional text is.

A constitution performs three functions. It is intended to be the organizing legal framework for a state. To fulfill this function, it is replete with regulatory orders in the literal sense (without doubt, these are laws). When it establishes that there will be a bicameral parliament, sets forth the means of appointment of its members and so forth, it is providing a catalog of legal provisions with very little emotive value. Generally, the majority of the people to whom it applies are not even remotely familiar with this content.

At the other end of the spectrum is its symbolic function. It may be the symbol of independence from a colonizing metropolis, of the establishment of a democratic system, etc. Constitutions are replete with proclamations of this kind which do not exactly constitute legal rules. When they declare that the authorities shall promote the common good, that the citizens shall be free, etc., they are making affirmations empty of content, unless they are given real application with specific legal stipulations. These proclamations are often well-known by the nation's citizens.

At the midway point between these two extremes, I believe there is a third function: the proclamation of fundamental rights. 'Fundamental Rights' comprise a precise technical category, but at the same time they exercise a symbolic function, and they are often included in constitutional texts.

The above findings are the result of the examination that has been the focus of this study. The 'fundamental right of religious freedom' is contained in numerous constitutional texts, but this is beyond the scope of this analysis. So I will focus here on the other two functions: the strictly legal and the symbolic.

There is no doubt that the Argentine Constitution's ban on regular clergy from becoming members of congress is a case of a legal rule in the strict sense. Nor is there any question of the legal application of the requirement that the Prime Minister of Brunei must be Muslim. On the other hand, I doubt that there is any

131 'State and Catholic Church are… independent' (7.1).

132 'Within a system of independence… the State recognizes the Catholic Church as an important element in the historical, cultural and moral formation of Peru' (50).

133 'The State…shall recognize the special role of the Apostle Autocephalous Orthodox Church of Georgia in the history of Georgia and its independence from the state' (9.1).

legal effect in the recognition that the religions have contributed to the formation of the 'Vietnam Fatherland Front', or any real legal significance in the stipulation that ministers may include a religious expression in the oath they take upon accepting an Austrian government post.

I will now attempt a simplified assessment of all the constitutional precepts related to religion that have immediate legal significance, and then conclude with a brief reflection on the application of the solemn generic proclamations of 'secularism', 'state religion', and so on.

Two situations may be classified under the first category: When a religious qualification entails an alteration of the rights of an individual; or when a religious legal system is placed above the legal system of the state. It would seem necessary to note a point here that is obvious: the two religions that operate on these levels are Christianity and Islam.

Insofar as the individual is concerned, it could be said that there are two significant issues. The first is the requirement to profess a particular religion for the purposes of being able to hold a particular public office. With a few exceptions in the Christian world (King of Norway, King of Sweden, etc.), all of the cases in this category are found in the Muslim world. Behind this is a whole conception of the function of religion and the submission of the individual to it. The second category on the individual plane is the ban on people with a particular religious status from holding public office. This situation appears to be almost exclusive to Christian countries with a colonial past and those where the colonizing power promoted a specific Christian denomination, although it also includes countries that were formerly French colonies. History explains all, but explanations are not necessarily justifications. The fact that there was once a church that collaborated with the metropolis should no longer be relevant.

Once case where exceptions are practically nonexistent is in the positioning of religious precepts (religious law) on a legal footing above the law of the state: this is clearly a Muslim phenomenon. Behind this is a conception of the function of religion and the submission of the state to that religion.

To conclude, I cannot help but offer a reflection on the constitutional proclamations that attempt to define the position of the state on religious matters, without such proclamations appearing to have any direct legal application.

Such proclamations have no real legal significance; action at other legal levels is necessary for them to be vested with content. For example, France is a state that is constitutionally proclaimed to be 'secular'; indeed, it is considered by some to be a prototype for this way of conceiving the religious phenomenon. On the other hand, Italy, although not a religious state, gives special consideration to the Catholic Church, as the Italian Constitution not only expressly mentions it, but also makes reference to some specific instruments (7.2) regulating the relationship with that church, which were in force at the time the Constitution was enacted (the Lateran Pacts). There are few issues more sensitive on the religion-state question than those related to religious education; given the fact that the French model of public funding for Catholic religious education is more generous than the Italian, it would seem that 'secularism' is not an obstacle to such support.

Nevertheless, proclamations of 'secularism', 'state religion', and such are not merely rhetorical proclamations; they have a practical legal function which is not automatic but potential. For example, the only reference to religion in the French Constitution is the proclamation of the secular state. However, legislation has now been introduced into the French legal system that has an obvious religious application: the ban on women wearing a particular garment which their religion requires them to wear in certain places. The ultimate constitutional justification is none other than the principle of secularism. A different example can be found in Switzerland, where, in recent years, the biggest legal debate related to religion has been over the constitutional ban on the construction of certain religious buildings: minarets.[134] Beyond the problems associated with defining the application of the law, its existence introduces a rigidity in the system that will create considerable difficulties in practice: any adaptation of the law to a changing reality will require the application of the complex systems for amending the Swiss Constitution. The French solution constitutes a more flexible approach to resolving a problem. The Swiss solution is more precise and clear, but this is not necessarily a virtue when such sensitive matters need to be regulated. In short, proclamations of 'values' or 'principles' in religious matters serve one basic function: to provide constitutional support to legal solutions proposed by the ordinary legislator or by the courts.

There is nothing further to add. I am unable to draw any conclusion other than one that is obvious: In questions of legal regulation, everything is explained on the basis of two coordinates: history, and what is understood should be the function of the state. The topic examined here is no exception.

134 'The construction of minarets is prohibited' (72.3).

Chapter 3

Church and State Relations in the Constitutions

Gerhard Robbers

A Preliminary Observation

Religion is on the rise again. This is evident on many fronts. To the surprise of those who had assumed that history was destined to follow a unilinear path toward increasing secularization, we are witnessing what has been called 'the desecularization of the world'.[1] There is an unmistakable resurgence of religion, especially in the public sector.[2] A major reawakening of religion is evident in Latin America,[3] across Africa[4] and throughout the Muslim world.[5] Even in China, with its more restrictive policies on religion, religiosity appears to be on the rise among many sectors of the population.[6]

Religion is also on the rise again at the level of constitutions. Religion is finding new places in national constitutions. The relationship between religion and the law is newly defined in a number of these basic laws. For some time, religion tended to be set aside in human rights catalogues. One could take this as – at least by tendency – indicating that religion is a merely individual matter, an individual

---

1 P. L. Berger, *The Desecularization of the World: Resurgent Religion and World Politics* (Washington, DC: Ethics and Public Policy Center, 1999).

2 J. Casanova, *Public Religions in the Modern World* (Chicago: University of Chicago Press, 1994).

3 P. E. Sigmund (ed.), 'Introduction', in *Religious Freedom and Evangelization in Latin America: The Challenge of Religious Pluralism* (Maryknoll, New York: Orbis Books, 1999), 1–2; D. Martin, *Tongues of Fire: The Explosion of Protestantism in Latin America* (Oxford: Blackwell, 1990).

4 M. C. Green and J. van der Vyver, 'Law, Religion and Human Rights in Africa: Introduction', 8 *Africa Human Rights Law Journal* (2008), 337–356.

5 See, e.g., P. Marshall (ed.), *Radical Islam's Rules: The Worldwide Spread of Extreme Shari'a Law* (Lanham, Boulder, New York, Toronto and Oxford: Rowman & Littlefield Publishers, Inc., 2005).

6 X. Zhuo, 'Religion and Rule of Law in China Today', *Brigham Young University Law Review* (2009), 519; W. C. Durham, Jr., 'Religious Freedom in a Worldwide Setting: Comparative Reflections', in M. A. Glendon and H. F. Zacher (eds.), *Universal Rights in a World of Diversity: The Case of Religious Freedom* (Vatican City: Pontificia Academia Scientiarum Socialium, 2012), 359, 362.

freedom among other individual freedoms, and only as such – if at all – part of the public sphere. Today, religion is again placed somewhat explicitly into the public sphere by constitutional law. Examples of this are found not only in Islam-based constitutions, where specific religious rules are situated on the same legal level as the constitution or even above it, and in the framework of the constitutions of the Americas, which consider 'religion as a transcendent human phenomenon'[7], but also in the debate about the constitution of the European Union, when Christianity and Judaism were explicitly advanced as a basis of the constitution.

Introduction

Constitutions represent the legal basics of a country. They contain the rules that are fundamental for governing the community. Today, most countries of the world have one central document in which all or most of these rules are laid down. In a few countries, such as Austria, Israel or the United Kingdom, several documents taken together form the constitution. Sometimes, constitutional documents, be they one or more, are combined with other sources of constitutional law such as custom or even religious rules. In any case, the idea that a country should have a constitution has been adopted throughout the world. Whatever differences or similarities between constitutions there may be it is obvious that some common ideas govern at least constitutional law. There is hardly a country in the world that does not explicitly claim to be a democracy and assert that it should respect the rule of law and fundamental rights. At least in theory, these ideas have been accepted throughout the world.

Constitutions differ. They are long or short, stable or easily changed. Government institutions as established by the constitutions vary in structure and powers. Mostly, however, constitutions give an idea of the very identity of a country. Usually, no other law of a given legal system may contradict the constitution of that specific country. All other laws and legal rules must then comply with what the constitution says.

Constitutions are meant to rule reality. As all law intends to do, constitutions should direct the facts of life, the actions of governments. They do not always do that. In some countries, constitutions are strong and they are implemented in fact. In other countries, respect for the constitution is weak. In such cases there may well be a convincing constitution, nicely worded, and in perfect harmony with what can be regarded as being good and just. Nevertheless, the factual situation in that country may well be intolerable. Constitutions can be misused as mere propaganda, but constitutions then can serve as yardsticks to insist on improvement.

---

7 C. Asiaín Pereira, 'A Consideration of Religion and Religions in the Latin American Constitutional Framework', in p. 127 of her chapter, in this volume.

Constitutions develop. Most constitutions contain explicit provisions providing for amendment. Usually, these provisions differ from the normal process of legislation and make changing the constitution more difficult than other legislative change. On the other hand, no wording of a constitution can escape interpretation. Even if the words remain the same, the understanding of what these words mean develops over time. The text of a constitution can be interpreted narrowly or broadly, and what equality or freedom means differs from generation to generation, from country to country, and from culture to culture.

Constitutions relate to religion. Religion is a central topic of constitutions throughout the world. Some sort of separation between churches or other religious communities and the state is predominant. Separation may be radical or moderate. It can be hostile, serving to push religion away, or it can be friendly, permitting religion the freedom to flourish. Naturally, much depends on practice. There are a number of constitutions declaring a certain religion or confession to be the religion of the state, the predominant religion or a church to be the people's church. Others define themselves explicitly as Islamic republics or refer to a particular form of Christianity. These explicit identities as secular or religious do not necessarily lead to unequal treatment of other religions or even to a loss of religious freedom.

Peter Häberle, the famous German constitutionalist, has said that a constitution 'is not only a legal text or a normative system of rules, but also an expression of a state of cultural development, a means of the cultural self-portrayal of a people, mirror of its cultural heritage and fundament of its hopes'.[8] One may add that this is the case when a constitution succeeds, when it is in fact an expression of the identity of a people, not just a mere octroi, an alien aspect of law imposed on the people. A constitution needs to be accepted in order to be alive; a people must live their constitution to make it happen. This means also that the constitutional provisions should represent the will of the people, so that people can identify with them.

This also indicates that constitutional interpretation is primarily an endeavor that should be done from the inside for the inside, something that only those who share the history, the feeling, and the spirit of a country can adequately do. It is especially difficult to interpret a foreign constitution. Constitutional law carries so much of implicit national experience, cultural characteristics, historical preconditions, battles, wounds, feeling, controversy, and comradeship, thus carrying so much unwritten presupposition that a foreigner will not be able to fully understand its meaning. The lack of awareness of social context necessarily results in a lack of understanding.

Different countries have different cultures of legal interpretation. The United States of America, to take but one example, seems to be somewhat resistant to legal comparison. Absent a need to integrate into something like the European Union, integrative interpretation does not seem important.

---

8 Quoted in M. Kotzur and L. Michael (eds.), *Peter Häberle, Verfassungsvergleichung in Europa- und weltbürgerlicher Absicht: Späte Schriften* (Berlin: Duncker & Humblot, 2009), Vorwort at vii.

Institutional Provisions or Fundamental Rights Provisions

Most constitutions speak of religion in terms of individual human rights, sometimes understood as also having a corporative meaning – such as Article 9 of the European Convention of Human Rights as interpreted by the European Court of Human Rights. An equivalent approach is taken by Kenya in Article 78 of its constitution: '(1) Except with his own consent, no person shall be hindered in the enjoyment of his freedom of conscience. And for the purposes of this section that freedom includes freedom of thought and of religion, freedom to change his religion or belief, and freedom, either alone or in community with others, and both in public and in private, to manifest and propagate his religion or belief in worship, teaching, practice and observance.'

A number of constitutions add specific provisions viewing religions as institutions, a special institutional approach (the United Kingdom, Germany, and Italy, but also in the United States of America in a rejecting way by prohibiting the establishment of any religion). This may be viewed as a somewhat ancient approach, outdated by individual human rights. However, the meaning of such an approach is broader and deeper than just a reflection of legal history. Such an approach accepts other institutions than the state as having institutional relevance – perhaps on the same level of legitimacy as the state though in different fields. Article 7 of the Italian constitution is a remarkable example of this notion: 'The State and the Catholic Church are independent and sovereign, each within its own sphere.' Such an approach can be taken as denying the supremacy and exclusiveness of the state. It may be an anti-totalitarian approach, at least an anti-etatistic approach.

In terms of language – 'state and church in constitutions', but also in terms of the topic 'Religion and Constitution' – this topic seems to be a basically Christian approach. It asks for the relation of institutions: state and church. The question I want to raise is this: Has only Christianity developed institutions that can be seen at the same level as states? The relationship described in constitutions of state and church is a relationship of two competing institutions. Those religions that do not form institutions, communities, do not raise the issue.

To go into more detail: This concept is a basically Roman Catholic approach – if not of today after Vatican II, then of historical import. Protestantism has from the very beginning emerged as intertwined with statehood, Lutheran churches being subject to the secular monarch. We may see here some parallels with Islam beyond existing parallels of theology in a more immediate sense. Christian orthodoxy again is somewhat different: In its concept of 'symphonía' the church is separated, distinguished from statehood, not competing but rather seeking harmony.

Identification and Separation of State and Religions or Identification and Separation of State and Religion

It is often argued that states should be separate from religion. I wonder whether that is realistic or even legitimate. Is it realistic to separate the state from religion? It is possible for the state to refrain from identifying with a specific religious creed (while Malta's constitution says that its religion is the Roman Catholic faith, many states today call themselves an Islamic Republic; others identify as atheistic). It may also be understood as a specific religious approach when a state calls itself secular or laic.

However, a state cannot refrain from incorporating religious characteristics in its law and life. It starts with days of rest, the structure of a week, counting of the years (the French Revolution introduced new names for months and a new system of reckoning years – a (negative) religious act in itself). Human rights have roots in religion; marriage and family law is intrinsically religiously based. People will rely on their religious convictions in (democratic) elections. Religion is just there – no one, no state can ignore it or evade it. The state cannot separate from religion as it cannot separate from culture, cannot separate from values, cannot separate from history, cannot separate from economy, cannot separate from people. Religion is unique in that it pervades all parts of life; religious people will live their lives in all aspects from a religious point of view.

Is it legitimate to separate the state from religion? This would mean that people would have to depart from their religious convictions when deciding state matters, when taking part in elections or referenda, when acting as representatives and office holders. It would require that for each and every decision they take in that respect they would have to find a non-religious 'secular' reason – whatever that may mean – in place of or at least in addition to the religious one. Thinking and decision-making that was exclusively religious would be prohibited. This would not be consistent with democracy, and this would not be consistent with a human rights approach that guarantees freedom of religion.

What is possible and what is legitimate, however, is that the state does not identify with a specific religious teaching, an elaborate set of ideas, a construction of religious statements. A state can be neutral in that respect. It is possible to separate the state from a religious institution, to separate state and church. This does not per se render illegitimate any identification with a religious set of teachings. Many states do identify in this way with religion. This can be an expression of historical development, of cultural adherence and identity. The question to be raised is whether such identification in fact violates human rights of people who live in such a state. Full freedom of religion must be guaranteed for everyone. The same applies to equal treatment. Any state identification with religion or belief must comply with the requirements of legitimate limitations to such freedoms and rights.

It seems to be quite apparent that in the UK the position of the Church of England does not as such necessarily violate freedom of religion within the country nor does the identification of Malta with the Roman Catholic faith. The same can be true when a state calls itself an Islamic Republic. On the other hand, faith minorities may feel less accepted in the legal order of a country. This may also occur for majorities when the religious identification of the state is that of a minority. This may amount to an interference with equality rights, but this interference can be (though not necessarily is) justified by legitimate reasons such as historic development, national identity or cultural characteristics.

It is not the correct approach to impose models from abroad onto a people. This does not exclude voluntary reception of model constitutions, and, of course, the same wording in a different people's setting will have a different meaning.

Rather, I would suggest developing criteria for a good relationship between religions and state constitutions. Some points may be mentioned here, some of which may be debatable at least in their scope. A constitution should

- Provide for the full scope of all human rights.
- Provide for equal treatment: meaning to treat equal what is equal and what is unequal to treat appropriately unequal – equality is not identical treatment.
- Permit participation in the (democratic) political process for all religions.
- Recognize the special status of religious existence.
- Promote respect for the cultural tradition of the country.

However, no constitution will succeed, if there is no

- Factual acceptance by the people of the relationship between state and religious communities.
- Factual acceptance of the relationship between religious communities and state by the believers, those who belong to the religious organizations (this requires religions to make statements on what they expect from the constitutions).

The Secular State and the Notion of Neutrality

While religion is on the rise again, public debate in many parts of the world still centers on the concept of a secular state. Also, a number of states explicitly call themselves secular states as a matter of constitutional law.

We can understand the notion of a secular state in a political, philosophical, sociological, historical, also theological way, and we can view it as an issue of constitutional law. Several states in the world explicitly provide in their constitutions that they are a secular state.

Concepts of Secularization

Secularization can be understood as 'the people turning away from religion'. But if ever such a development should have taken place, we see now that people are turning to religion again. Religion matters again. Secularization seen as retreat of or from religion has come to an end. People need religion. The question 'why is there something and why is there not nothing' is a question that calls for answers. The question of 'why' – not the mere 'how' – can be fully answered only in religious contexts. Religion belongs to the human being in the same way as love and hate or truth and error. All attempts in history to do away with religion have failed. Secularization understood as extinguishing religion would be an anti-human concept.

Secularization could mean that sacred things are stripped of their dignity; they become only secular. However, this notion would turn against itself: making sacred things secular necessarily entails a religious decision, a decision about what is sacred and what is not. The secular itself would become religious. In this sense we could interpret what mostly is described as a modern history of secularization in a different way: We have witnessed not a secularization of the sacred but a sacralization of the secular. This is an abuse. Dictatorships have made extensive use of such a process, and as a German I am thinking of the history of my own country.

As a positive concept, secularization means the distinction between the sacred and the secular. At the heart of this view is the primarily, but in no way exclusively, Christian perspective of 'Give to Caesar what is Caesar's and give to God what is God's'. The secular state is a state of separation between the two spheres, with the state on the secular side and religion on the side of the sacred.

This enables the state to concentrate on what the state can do properly. And it enables the religions to concentrate on what they can do properly. For a Christian church: The church can concentrate on its task of a spiritual way of life. The church is rid of the burden of worldly, secular power, all too tempting and all too often compromising to the religious teaching.

Secularization and World Legal Structures

Some constitutions in the world explicitly provide that the state is secular. A number of states have this:

> Azerbaijan (art. 7); the Gambia (ch. 1); Guinea-Bissau (art. 1); Guyana (art. 1); Kazakhstan (art. 1); Mali (art. 25); Namibia (Preamble); Russia (art. 14); Serbia (art. 11); Tajikistan (art. 1); Turkmenistan (art. 1); [India until 1976].

Some other states call themselves laicist, mostly from the French tradition:

> France (art. 1); Angola (art. 10); Benin (art. 156); Burkina Faso (art. 31); Gabon (art. 2); Cameron (art. 1); Togo (art. 1); Turkey (art. 2).

Immediately, problems of translation arise. Very often, the term 'laicist' or 'laic' is translated by the word 'secular'. The Turkish constitution uses in the original Turkish version the term 'lâik'. The official translation into English is 'secular', not laic.

A very large amount of law in the world owes its existence to reception. States copy laws of other states, often changing them somewhat to make them fit for their own country. Reception of Roman law in Central Europe over the centuries is the basis of today's Central European law; Turkey has adopted the Swiss Civil Code; Meiji-Japan in 1889 has taken over much of the Prussian 1851 Constitution and later the German civil code; US legal rules on leasing or factoring have spread around the world as have human rights documents from England, France, the US and other countries; the basic international law on diplomatic relations owes its existence to Muslim law; and many other examples can easily be added. The French system of laïcité has had much influence on other states, predominantly in former French colonies, but also elsewhere.

Turkey is an example of reception of the term 'laic' into constitutional law. However, the term 'lâik' – or in its official translation 'secular' – in Turkey means something quite different than it does in France. Another course of reception may well be the notion of secular in the Russian constitution, found in Azerbaijan, Kazakhstan, and Tajikistan or in Turkmenistan. It is probably not wrong to assume that in Russia today the Russian Orthodox Church has quite a substantial position, quite a special meaning for the Russian state. And it is probably equally accurate to assume that in Azerbaijan, Kazakhstan, Tajikistan, and Turkmenistan, specific forms of Islam have predominant influence and a special position. With the changes and developments of the factual situation, the law also changes its meaning; the specific circumstances in a country will alter the meaning of law that arises from reception. The same specific legal rule, the same specific legal term, means something different in Russia than in Turkmenistan; it means something different in France than in Turkey.

And yet, keeping this in mind, legal interpretation can draw inspiration from the system and from the doctrine from which a legal term originates. It is not for nothing that a legal provision has been adopted and taken from another system; it will not hide or negate its origins.

Religion and State Neutrality

Neutrality has become another way of structuring the relationship between state law and religion. It seems to be a concept first or at least most intensively used in Germany. It is in fact very near to the notion of secularity understood in a positive sense.

The German constitution does not say that the state is secular. Secularity is not a constitutional term in Germany. The Federal Constitutional Court takes from the constitution that the German state has to be 'neutral' in view of religion and world views.

Neutrality requires the state not to identify with a church; there is to be no Established Church (Article 137 section 1 WRV in conjunction with Article 140 GG). The state is not allowed to have any special inclination towards a particular religious community or to judge such an organization's particular merits or ideologies to be true. Ideological institutions are to be on equal footing with religious institutions; this deals with organizations that have a humanistic ideology or a position without reference to the question of a God or gods; they might also be called worldview communities. On the other hand, religious institutions must not be placed in a more disadvantageous position than societal groups; anti-religious state policies would be incompatible with a neutral approach, because these would discriminate against religion. This prohibits a decision in favor of state atheism. Neutrality, furthermore, means non-intervention; that is, the state is not allowed to take decisive action in the affairs of religious communities. This is made particularly clear by the constitution: 'Religious societies shall regulate and administer their affairs independently within the limits of the law that applies to all.'[9]

Neutrality does not mean neutrality in respect of specific values. It is quite clear that the Basic Law and with it the entire legal system is based on strong values such as human dignity, freedom, and equality. However, neutrality means not to identify with a specific religious or philosophical concept, teaching, or institution. State neutrality is not violated when the state adopts values and concepts that have been developed in the religious sphere.

Neutrality also means positive neutrality. This concept obligates the state to actively support religion and to provide for the space religion needs to flourish. This makes possible and requires, for example, that the state include religious needs in planning law: State authorities have to provide for real estate in their urban development plans on which religious communities can construct places of worship according to the needs of the population. This concept of positive neutrality is predominant in the official discourses and not only in the law. It is actively supported and implemented by the courts and state authorities.

While neither the constitution itself nor the Federal Constitutional Court speak of a secular state, the notion of secular state has become strong in Germany in constitutional theory; it has almost become a principle of constitutional law doctrine. While the Federal Constitutional Court does not explicitly use it, many scholars, including constitutional court judges, have turned to it. A very prominent one of them, Prof. Ernst-Wolfgang Böckenförde, in fact has introduced the term into constitutional law thinking.[10] Here, in short, it means that the state does not justify itself in the sacred sphere. The secular state leaves the sacred sphere to the people, to religion.

---

9 Article 137 section 3 Constitution of Weimar in conjunction with Article 140 Basic Law.

10 See e.g. and as a conclusion E.-W. Böckenförde, *Der säkularisierte Staat. Sein Charakter, seine Rechtfertigung und seine Probleme im 21. Jahrhundert. Themenband 86 der Carl Friedrich von Siemens Stiftung* (München: Carl Friedrich von Siemens Stiftung, 2007).

Consequences for Constitutions

A state with a constitution of freedom must provide forms of organization fit for the self-understanding of the religious that are appropriate in view of religion's social relevance. To take laicist France as an example: In order to meet these requirements of freedom, France has a highly complex system of association law. Religious communities as such do not have legal personality, but they can form special associations, *associations cultuelles*, which have legal personality for them. For the Roman Catholic Church there is another special form of association, the diocesan association, *association diocésaine*. This special type of association exists only for the Catholic Church and guarantees that the bishop has the right of final decision in the association, a right that is necessary in Catholic theological teaching. There also is a great variety of forms of associations for other religious communities that provide a lesser degree of financial and tax benefits.

Religious organizations must be allowed in the public sphere, and impact of religion in social issues is more than acceptable. This is something normal in an open, democratic state based on human rights. Public statements of church authorities or of individual priests in social issues, legislation or other actual problems such as birth rates, abortion, homosexuality, drug abuse is not clerical and illegal, and is not in opposition to secularism. Public statements by churches and religious communities contribute to the development of a pluralist, democratic state as do public statements by trade unions, by associations of writers, journalists and artists, or by representatives of economic enterprises.

Finally and most importantly, full freedom of religion must be guaranteed as well as equal treatment of religions. This will make religion as such flourish as well as the states and communities that provide this full freedom.

Chapter 4
Constitutional Reception of International Law Provisions on Religious Freedom

Jorge Precht Pizarro

It is an established fact that the International Human Rights Covenants have enriched the concept of religious freedom, while the different national constitutions of the world remain in earlier stages of the development of that freedom.

Of course, although this is the general rule, there are exceptions.

In the global system of human rights protection, the Universal Declaration of Human Rights of 1948[1] and the International Covenants on Human Rights of 1996

1 The legal value of the Universal Declaration has been disputed. Personally, I believe that it is legally binding insofar as it contains general principles of international law, which also form part of *jus cogens*. See A. Truyol Serra, *Los Derechos Humanos*, 2nd edn. (Madrid: Editorial Tecnos, 1977), 31. On the same question, see L. Martín-Retortillo Baquer, 'La efectiva aplicabilidad de la Declaración Universal de Derechos Humanos en el sistema jurídico español', in 153 *Revista de Administración Pública* (September-December 2000), 41 et seq. The Declaration on the Elimination of all Forms of Intolerance and of Discrimination Based on Religion or Belief was proclaimed by the UN Assembly on 25 November 1981. I also believe that it is a binding declaration for the reasons put forward by Truyol. On the same question, see J. Castañeda, *Valor jurídico de las resoluciones de las Naciones Unidas* (México DF: El Colegio de México, 1967), especially Chapter VII, 'Resoluciones que contienen declaraciones de otros pronunciamientos de carácter general y más recientemente'; see also E. S. Galvan, *El reconocimiento de la libertad religiosa en Naciones Unidas* (Madrid: Marcial Pons, Ediciones Jurídicas y Sociales, 2000). I subscribe to the view expressed by the Dutch government in a memo dated 18 August 1950, regarding the Draft Declaration on Rights and Duties of States prepared by the United Nations International Law Commission: 'It could not be denied that General Assembly resolutions constitute to some extent a source of law. Indeed, in the event of any uncertainty on the point of whether a rule already belongs to the domain of international law or whether it belongs to *jus constituendum*, a formal statement from the General Assembly could bring the rule at issue into the recognized domain of Positive International Law.' Nevertheless, the Declaration of 1981 contains programmatic statements, as well as a few flaws, such as the fact it makes no reference to churches, denominations or religious bodies. Article 4 is clearly programmatic. In any event, religious freedom – the first of the freedoms – is, without doubt, a general principle of international law.

guarantee religious freedom.[2] Other international protection agreements could also be added to the list.[3]

In the Pan-American system, the covenants in effect are the American Declaration of the Rights and Duties of Man (Bogotá, 2 May 1948) and the American Convention on Human Rights (Pact of San José, Costa Rica, 22 November 1969).

There are countries in the Latin American region whose constitutions have notably modern stipulations on religious freedom. One example can be found in the Brazilian Constitution, in Article 5, numbers 6, 7 and 8.[4]

However, the constitutions of other Latin American countries contain provisions that are conceptually anchored in the nineteenth or early twentieth century. This may be for historical reasons or because constitutional amendments are restricted by rigid protection mechanisms.

Such is the case of Chile, whose constitution contains a stipulation on freedom of conscience, expression of beliefs and free exercise of worship that is taken verbatim from Article 10, number 2 of the Constitution of 1925 (now Article 19, number 6 of the Constitution of 1980), the wording of which only makes sense in the context of the official status that the Catholic Church had enjoyed until 1925.[5] Thus, if we compare the Chilean text with the wording of the Covenant on Civil and Political Rights (Article 18), the stipulation in the Chilean constitution is clearly obsolete.[6]

2 International Covenant on Civil and Political Rights (ICCPR), art. 18.

3 For example, the Convention on the Rights of the Child (20 November 1984), arts. 14 and 30; the International Covenant on Economic, Social and Cultural Rights, arts, 13.1 and 13.2; the Convention on the Prevention and Punishment of the Crime of Genocide, art. 11.

4 '6. Freedom of conscience and of belief is inviolable, the free exercise of religious worship being ensured and, under the terms of the law, the protection of places of worship and their rites being guaranteed; 7. Under the terms of the law, the rendering of religious assistance in civil and military establishments of collective confinement is ensured; 8. No one shall be deprived of any rights by reason of religious belief or philosophical or political conviction, unless he invokes it to exempt himself from a legal obligation required of all and refuses to perform an alternative obligation established by law'.

5 It should be added, however, that Chile includes the Covenants on Human Rights among its constitutional documents by virtue of Article 5, paragraph 2 of its constitution following the constitutional amendments of 1989. Law 19.638 of 1999 includes statements copied almost word-for-word from the Covenants, via Spain's Organic Law of Religious Freedom of 1980.

6 See J. Precht, 'Vino nuevo en odres viejos: Derecho Internacionales convencional y derecho interno chileno', 2 *Ius et Praxis* (1997), 121–154.

J. Precht, *Derecho Eclesiástico del Estado de Chile: Análisis históricos y doctrinales* (Ediciones Universidad Católica de Chile, 2001).

J. Precht, 'Laity and Laicism: Are These Catholic Categories of Any Use in Analyzing Chilean Church – State Relations?' *Brigham Young University Law Review* (2009), 697–704.

Turning to Europe, we find that Article 9 of the European Convention for the Protection of Human Rights and Fundamental Freedoms (1950) guarantees religious freedom, as does Article 10 of the Charter of Fundamental Rights of the European Union, adopted on 12 December 2007, whose legally binding nature ('which shall have the same legal value as the treaties') was established by the Treaty of Lisbon on 13 December 2007. But if we examine an extreme case, the Greek Constitution has yet to be adapted to the parameters of the International and EU Covenants on Human Rights (Article 13, number 2).[7]

Yet one may well ask just how many countries in the European Union actually have brought their constitutions into line with Article 10, number 2, of the Charter recognizing the right of conscientious objection.[8]

In the case of the African system of human rights protection, the same lack of correlation between the Covenants and the constitutions is evident. Article 8 of the African Charter on Human and Peoples' Rights (Banjul, 27 June 1981) guarantees religious freedom, as does the Treaty of Human Rights of the African Union signed on 27 June 1981. Both texts support the elimination of Zionism (arts. 2, 8 and 12).

However, outdated constitutional articles on religious freedom remain in place. For example, in the Congo-Brazzaville Constitution of 15 March 1991, although the Preamble includes a declaration of adherence to the principles of the UN, the Organization of African Unity and various human rights covenants, conscientious objection is expressly excluded in Article 26: '(3) No one shall be relieved from fulfilling a civic duty because of religious opinion'; on the other

J. Precht, 'Laïcité et constitutions latino-américaines', in J. Lagrée and P. Portier (eds.), *La modernité contra la religión? Pour une nouvelle approche de la laïcité* (Rennes: Presses Universitaires, 2010), 181–192.

7 The Greek Constitutional reform in the spring of 2001 and the amendment of 2008 evaded the question of religious freedom, along with the relationship between church and state. This was also a consequence of the outcome of the European Court of Human Rights case of *Kokkinakis v. Greece* (App No. 14307/88, 25 May 1993). Although numeral 1 of Article 13 of the Greek Constitution asserts that freedom of conscience is inviolable, numeral 2 sets forth that: 'All known religions shall be free and their rites of worship shall be performed unhindered and under the protection of the law; however, the practice of rites of worship may not offend public order or common decency, and *proselytism is prohibited.*' I subscribe to the opinion submitted by Judge Pettiti: 'Freedom of religion and of conscience certainly entails accepting proselytism, even where it is not respectable. Believers and agnostic philosophers have a right to expound their beliefs, to try to get other people to share them and even to try to convert those whom they are addressing'. In reality, Greece should not have been condemned only because the conduct of *Kokkinakis* was correct, but because the mere fact of punishing proselytism with a prison sentence is contrary to Article 9 of the European Convention on Human Rights of 1950.

8 Nevertheless, many European countries have previously resorted to laws or decrees to deal with this issue, at least insofar as military service is concerned. See L. Vannicelli, 'Obiezione di coscienza militare negli ordinamenti europei ed extraeuropei: un confrotto aggiornato', *Mucchi Editore* 2003.

hand, it accepts sects as a legitimate expression of freedom of belief: '(2) The free exercise of religious sects shall be guaranteed within the limits compatible with public order and good mores.'

In spite of such discrepancies between covenants and constitutions, there are constitutional texts that have been updated to reflect the wording of the Covenants. In the Transitional Constitution of South Sudan, 2011, not only is the text in keeping with the International Covenants on Human Rights (Preamble), but there is also a clause on implicit human rights (9.3: 'All rights and freedoms enshrined in international human right treaties, covenants and instruments ratified or acceded to by the Republic of South Sudan shall be an integral part of this Bill'), which are established as irrevocable ('no derogation from the rights and freedoms established in this Bill shall be made'); moreover, the rights contained in the Bill must be defended, protected and applied by the Supreme Court and other competent courts, and the 'Human Rights Commission shall monitor its application in accordance with this Constitution and the law' (art. 10).

Article 8.1 proclaims the separation of religion and the state, while 8.2 declares that '[a]ll religions shall be treated equally and religion or religious beliefs shall not be used for divisive purposes.'

On the other hand, Article 23 identifies the following rights as guaranteed by the Constitution:

a. the right to worship or assemble in connection with any religion or belief and to establish and maintain places for these purposes;
b. the right to establish and maintain appropriate faith-based, charitable or humanitarian institutions;
c. the right to acquire, possess and own movable and/or immovable property and make, acquire and use the necessary articles and materials related to the rites or customs of religion or belief;
d. the right to write, issue and disseminate religious publications;
e. the right to teach religion or beliefs in places suitable for these purposes;
f. the right to solicit and receive voluntary financial and other contributions from individuals, private and public institutions;
g. the right to train, appoint, elect or designate by succession appropriate religious leaders called for by the requirements and standards of any religion or belief;
h. the right to observe days of rest, celebrate holidays and ceremonies in accordance with the precepts of religious beliefs; and
i. the right to communicate with individuals and communities in matters of religion and beliefs at national and international levels.

Turning to the Bolivian Constitution, the intention of which is to 're-found' Bolivia, and which makes express mention of the goddess Pachamama,[9] we find in Article 4: 'The State respects and guarantees freedom of religion and spiritual beliefs, in accordance with their world views. The State is independent of religion.' This article does not go beyond the precepts set forth in the American Convention on Human Rights of 1969,[10] nor does the reference to religious freedom in Article 21.3. However, Article 30.II does indeed go further, with its recognition of the right of indigenous nations and peoples of rural origin 'to their cultural identity, religious belief, spiritualities, practices and customs, and to their own world view' (number 2); 'to the protection of their sacred sites' (number 7); and 'to the valuing, respect and promotion of their traditional knowledge and understanding, their traditional medicine, their languages, their rituals and their symbols and manner of dress' (number 9). And in Article 30.III the State 'guarantees, respects and protects the rights of indigenous nations and peoples of rural origin enshrined in this Constitution and the law.'[11]

---

9 The Preamble speaks of 'this Sacred Mother Earth' and declares that, 'fulfilling the mandate of our peoples, with the strength of our Pachamama and thanks to God, we refound Bolivia' (Final compatibilized text, Official Version, October 2008).

10 See the Inter-American System: American Declaration of the Rights and Duties of Man, Bogotá, 2 May 1948, and the American Convention on Human Rights, 22 November 1969. However, Article 13, numeral IV of the Bolivian Constitution is highly significant: 'The international treaties and conventions ratified by the Plurinational Legislative Assembly, which recognize human rights and prohibit their restriction in states of emergency, *shall prevail in domestic law*. The rights and duties enshrined in this Constitution shall be interpreted in accordance with international human rights treaties ratified by Bolivia.' Moreover, Article 410.II states: 'The Constitution is the supreme law of Bolivian legislation and takes precedence over any other legal provision. The nation's constitutional documents include international treaties and conventions on human rights and provisions of community law ratified by the country.' See also the Constitution of Peru, whose fourth transitional provision states: 'The provisions related to rights and freedoms recognized by the Constitution shall be interpreted in accordance with the Universal Declaration of Human Rights and with the international treaties and agreements on such matters ratified by Peru.'

G. García-Montúfar and D. Alegre Porras, 'The Long Road to Religious Freedom in Perú', in *Brigham Young University Law Review* (2009), 597–650. See also S. González Sandoval, 'The Colombian Experience in the Area of Protection of the Freedom of Religion', *Brigham Young University Review* (2009), 651–672.

11 The Ecuadorian Constitution of 2008 contains similar articles. The Preamble reads: 'Celebrating nature, the Pacha Mama, of which we are a part and which is vital to our existence; Invoking the name of God and recognizing our diverse forms of religion and spirituality [...], [we] determine to build: A new form of public coexistence, in diversity and harmony with nature, to achieve the good way of living, the *sumak kawsay*.' Article 3, paragraph 4, sets forth that it is a primordial duty of the state 'to guarantee secular ethics as the basis for public affairs and the legal system.' Article 10, paragraph 1, declares that 'persons, communities, peoples, nations and communities are bearers of rights and

It is evident that in this case Bolivia has taken a step forward in constitutionally recognized religious freedom, and no doubt in the future the Inter-American system of human rights protection will introduce similar declarations. Clearly, the ruling classes are coming to acknowledge that Latin America is the product of interracial mixing and that it is made up of easily identifiable nations, peoples and multicultural communities.[12]

On the other hand, it is worth noting that the Bolivian and Ecuadorian references to Pachamama have been accused of opportunism and ideological manipulation.[13]

In spite of the lack of direct correlation between the International Covenants and the constitutions of their signatory states, and that constitutions usually contain articles that are less protective of religious freedom than the Covenants, it should be noted that such discrepancies may not be as serious as they first appear, for the following reasons (some of which have already been touched on):

---

shall enjoy the rights guaranteed in the Constitution and in international instruments.' See also art. 10, no. 7; art. 11, no. 3 and Chapter 4, arts. 56, 57 and 58. In particular, art. 57: 'Indigenous communes, communities, peoples and nations are recognized and guaranteed, in accordance with the Constitution and human rights covenants, conventions, declarations and other international instruments, the following collective rights: 1. To freely uphold, develop and strengthen their identity, sense of belonging, ancestral traditions and forms of social organization. […]'

12 See, for example, this noteworthy article: '31.I. Indigenous nations and peoples of rural origin who are in danger of extinction, in a situation of voluntary isolation and not in contact, shall be protected and respected with respect to their forms of individual and collective life'; '31.II. Indigenous nations and peoples living in isolation and out of contact shall enjoy the right to remain in this condition, and to the delimitation and legal consolidation of the territory they occupy and inhabit.' The Afro-Bolivian people are recognized in Article 32. Bolivia's constitutional evolution is even more remarkable for the debate that went on for many years over Article 3 of the Political Constitution of 1967: 'The State recognizes and upholds the apostolic Roman Catholic religion. It guarantees the public practice of all other forms of worship. Relations with the Catholic Church shall be governed by means of concordats and agreements between the State and the Holy See.' See T. A. López Aparcicio, *Iglesia, Estado y bien común. el polémico artículo 3 de la Constitución Política del Estado Boliviano* (Santa Cruz: SEAPAS, 1995); R. Querejazu Calvo, *Historia de la Iglesia Católica en Charcas (Bolivia)* (La Paz, Bolivia: [s.n.], 1995); R. Valda Palma, *Historia de la Iglesia de Bolivia en la República* (La Paz, Bolivia : [s.n.], 1995). See also G. J. Aguilar Cavallo, *Dinámica internacional de la cuestión indígena* (Centro de Estudios de Derecho Constitucional de Chile: Librotecnia, 2007). For a complete compilation of international and constitutional regulations on religious freedom and regarding religious freedom and indigenous peoples, see M. González Sánchez and A. Sánchez-Bayon, *Regulación Iberoamericana de Derecho Eclesiástico* (Madrid: Delta Publicaciones, 2011), 277–380.

13 R. Lambert, 'El fantasma del pachamamismo', *Le Monde Diplomatique* (March 2011, edición chilena), 36–37.

1. The Covenants on Human Rights may be received into domestic law by order of the constitution itself, and this may also be true of the protocols and resolutions of international bodies.
2. It is not only the Constitution that needs to be considered, but the whole 'block of constitutionality'.
3. In the event of an outdated constitutional stipulation on religious freedom, laws or decrees may raise the legal system as a whole to the level of protection given by international agreements.
4. The mere fact of a stipulation on religious freedom may give rise to political action to ensure greater protection of that freedom, and even to new constitutional provisions that lead to future international covenants.
5. Even with obsolete constitutional stipulations, international human rights courts can make significant advances.
6. Domestic courts may also achieve similar advances.
7. It is important to consider the phenomenon of 'dialogue between jurisdictions', which is significant on questions of religious freedom.
8. In treaties dealing with economic and financial matters, loans and development aid, although apparently unrelated to questions of religious freedom, significant advances can be made through 'conditionality clauses'.

I will now consider each of the above points in more detail:

1) Reception into domestic law of the International Covenants on Human Rights, including provisions on religious freedom, with their protocols and resolutions.

Constitutions themselves often contain provisions that do this.[14]

Since the right of religious freedom is a human right, and human rights are general principles of law and form part of *jus cogens*, it may be considered an element of general international law.

Several constitutions refer to general international law and stipulate that this international law is fully and automatically received into domestic law. Such

14 See M. Diez de Velasco, *Instituciones de Derecho Internacional público (Biblioteca Universitaria)*, 17th edn. (Madrid: Editorial Tecnos, 2009), 247–267. Article 10.2 of the Spanish Constitution stipulates that 'laws related to fundamental rights and freedoms recognized by the Constitution shall be interpreted in accordance with the Universal Declaration on Human Rights and the international treaties and agreements on the same matters ratified by Spain.' Recently, Mexico (in the Official Decree of 10 June 2011) amended Article 1 of its Constitution to establish the 'pro persona' principle as the criterion for interpretation, thereby giving the Universal Declaration, the International Covenant on Civil and Political Rights and the American Convention on Human Rights constitutional status. It remains to be seen how the courts will interpret the restrictions of Article 130 and whether it will be necessary to amend Article 24 of the Constitution. J. D. González Campos, *Curso de Derecho Internacional Público* (Madrid: Editorial Civitas S.A., 1998), 257–280. C. Gutiérrez Espada, *Derecho Internacional Público* (Madrid: Editorial Trotta, 1995), 623–666.

is the case of the German Constitution, the Italian Constitution and the French Constitution of 1958, whose Preamble upholds the terms previously contained in the French Constitution of 27 October 1946.[15]

But it is also important to consider conventional international law, with regard to which nations take either a monist position (precedence of international law) or a dualist position (precedence of domestic law). Examples of the monist position are Spain and France, while an example of the dualist position is Italy.[16] But whatever the case may be, national constitutions or domestic laws cannot oppose treaties, and even less so the Covenants on Human Rights, according to the stipulations of case law and the Vienna Convention on the Law of Treaties of 1969 (arts. 26 and 27).

2) An outdated or flawed constitutional provision is not necessarily a problem, because nations must adhere to what constitutionalists call their 'block of constitutionality'.[17]

The 'block of constitutionality', according to French legal doctrine, refers to all of the 'rules of reference' against which the Constitutional Council contrasts the stipulations with the force of law whose legitimacy must be accepted.[18] For

15 See Article 25 of the German Constitution: 'The general rules of public international law constitute an integral part of federal law. They take precedence over statutes and directly create rights and duties for the inhabitants of the federal territory'; and Article 10 of the Italian Constitution: 'the legal system of Italy conforms to the generally recognized principles of international law'; and the Preamble to the French Constitution: 'the Republic, true to its traditions, adheres to the rules of international law.'

16 Article 55 of the French Constitution of 28 September 1958 sets forth that 'duly ratified or approved treaties or agreements do, upon their publication, override laws, subject, for each agreement or treaty, to its application by the other party.' The Italian Constitution requires the transformation of the treaty into a domestic law, by either an act or a decree, depending on whether it falls under the jurisdiction of the Parliament or the Executive (*adattamento*). This creates the problem of its possible repeal or modification by domestic laws subsequent to the signing of the Covenant. In Latin America, many constitutions incorporate the Covenants on Human Rights (Argentine constitutional reform of 1994, art. 75, numeral 22; Brazilian Constitution of 1988, art. 4; art. 5, no. 1; Colombian Constitution of 1991, art. 93; Constitution of Costa Rica, art. 48, introduced by the reform of August 18, 1989; Ecuadorian Constitution of 1998, art. 18; Guatemalan Constitution of 1985; Nicaraguan Constitution of 1987, art. 46; Venezuelan Constitution of 1999, art. 23, Mexico: Constitutional Reform 2011, art. 1.

17 For the Latin American context, see especially H. Nogueira Alcalá, *Lineamentos de interpretación constitucional y del bloque constitucional de derechos* (Santiago de Chile: Librotecnia, July 2006).

18 F. Rubio Llorente, 'Voz "bloque de constitucionalidad"', in *Enciclopedia Jurídica Básica* I (Madrid: Civitas, 1995), 818. See also T.R. Fernández, *Las leyes orgánicas y el bloque de constitucionalidad*' (Madrid: Cuadernos Civitas, 1981), and L. Favoreu and F. Rubio Llorente, *El bloque de constitucionalidad* (Madrid: Civitas Ediciones, S.L.,1991).

example, it is obvious that when the Cuban Constitution stipulates that 'the law regulates the relations of the State with religious institutions' (art. 55, para. 2), that law becomes part of the 'block of constitutionality'. The same occurs in the Constitution of Haiti: 'The law establishes the conditions for recognition and practice of religions and faiths' (art. 30.2).

This means that even if the constitutional text is inadequate, it could be improved not only by the Covenants incorporated therein, but also, for example, through Article 29 c) of the American Convention on Human Rights: 'Article 29. Restrictions regarding Interpretation No provision of this Convention shall be interpreted as: [...] c) precluding other rights or guarantees that are inherent in the human personality or derived from representative democracy as a form of government.'[19]

An interesting problem is posed by so-called 'implicit rights', i.e. rights that are not contained in the enumerations of explicit constitutional freedoms, but derive from the human person and human dignity or from the republican form of government. These also form part of the 'block of constitutionality'. An example of these implicit rights related to freedom of conscience is the right to conscientious objection, which was incorporated into the European Charter on Human Rights in 2007. Another example might be the right of a person not to be discriminated against on the basis of homosexuality, also incorporated into the European Charter.[20]

---

19 See wording of Article 23 of the Venezuelan Constitution of 1999: 'The treaties, pacts and conventions relating to human rights which have been executed and ratified by Venezuela have a constitutional rank, and prevail over internal legislation, insofar as they contain provisions concerning the enjoyment and exercise of such rights that are more favorable than those established by this Constitution arid the laws of the Republic, and shall be immediately and directly applied by the courts and other organs of the Public Power.' See A.R. Brewer-Carías, 'La Constitución de 1999', *Derecho Constitucional Venezolano* 4th edn., augmented and annotated with the case law of the Supreme Court of Justice up to March 2004 (Caracas, Venezuela: Editorial Jurídica, 2004).

20 Examples of European constitutions that include 'implicit human rights' are the Basic Law of Germany, art. 1, para. 1 and 2; constitutions of Spain, art. 10; Italy, art. 2; Spain, art. 10.1; and Portugal art. 16. Examples of Latin American constitutions include Colombia, art. 94; Ecuador (1998), art. 19; Uruguay, art. 72; Venezuela, art. 22; Chile, art. 5, para. 2; Bolivia, art. 35; Brazil, art. 5, no. 2; Costa Rica, art.. 74; Guatemala, art. 4; and Paraguay, art. 80.

O. Lo Prete, 'The Protection of Religious Freedom by the National Constitution and by Human Rights Treaties in the Republic of Argentina', *Brigham Young University Review* (2009), 697–705.

Humberto Nogueira points out that Argentina, in its constitutional reform of 1860, introduced Article 33: 'The declarations, rights and guarantees which the Constitution enumerates shall not be construed as a denial of other rights and guarantees not enumerated, but rising from the principle of sovereignty of the people and from the republican form of government' (supra note 17 at 234).

Last of all, the resolutions or declarations by international bodies (e.g. committees created by the Covenants or by ILO or UNESCO resolutions) pose another problem: do these also form part of the 'block of constitutionality'?

Consider the following examples: a) The interpretation given by the UN Human Rights Committee to Article 18 of the Covenant on Civil and Political Rights[21]; b) the interpretation given by the CEDAW Committee to its Optional Protocol and reports on the legalization of abortion.

a. The Human Rights Committee, in its comment on Article 18 of the International Covenant on Civil and Political Rights, adopts a broad definition of religious belief: 'Article 18 is not limited in its application to traditional religious or to religions and beliefs with institutional characteristics or practices analogous to those of traditional religions.'

For this reason, the Committee 'views with concern any tendency to discriminate against any religion or belief for any reason, including the fact that they are newly established, or represent religious minorities that may be the subject of hostility on the part of a predominant religious community'.[22]

This concept will clash with French legislation, legal doctrine and practices in relation to 'sects' and measures for dealing with the sectarian phenomenon.

b. On December 18, 1979, the UN General Assembly adopted the Convention Eliminating All Forms of Discrimination Against Women (CEDAW). Articles 12 and 14 of the Convention ensure 'access to health care services, including those related to family planning.' The Report of the Committee on the Elimination of Discrimination against Women, point 11 (New York 1999) states: 'It is discriminatory for a party State to refuse to provide legally for the performance of certain reproductive health services for women.' With regard to Chile, the Committee expresses its concern about

---

As early as 1946, Brazil established the right to conscientious objection in its constitution (art. 141, para. 8): 'No one shall be deprived of any rights by reason of religious belief or philosophical or political conviction, unless he invokes it to exempt himself from a legal obligation, duty or service required of all Brazilians, and refuses to perform an alternative to such duties as established by law, on the pretext of catering to conscience.'

Noteworthy in Latin American law is the pioneering work of the priest Fernando Retamal Fuentes, known as the Chilean canonist, who died in 2010: 'La libertad de conciencia y la libertad de las religiones en los grandes sistemas contemporáneos – America Latina', paper presented at the IX Congreso Internacional de Derecho Canónico, Universidad Nacional Autónoma de México, Ciudad de Méjico, September 1995, published in *Teología y Vida* XXVII (1996), 307–339.

21 See E. S. Galvan, *El reconocimiento de la libertad religiosa en Naciones Unidas* (Madrid: Editorial Marcial Pons, 2000).

22 United Nations Human Rights Committee: Comment on Article 18 of the Covenant on Civil and Political Rights, 20 July 1993.

> 'the inadequate recognition and protection of the reproductive rights of women', and especially about 'the laws prohibiting and punishing any form of abortion.' The Committee 'considers these provisions to violate the human rights of all women' (point 228) and recommends that the laws related to abortion be amended, 'in particular to provide safe abortion and to permit termination of pregnancy for therapeutic reasons,' including mental health, and it also asks the government to 'strengthen its actions and efforts aimed at the prevention of unwanted pregnancies' (point 229).

The above recommendations clash with Chilean legislation (and, according to some, with the Chilean Constitution and the American Convention on Human Rights itself). As a result, Chile refused to sign the Optional Protocol of the CEDAW Committee.

These examples do not carry the same legal force as what is known in legal circles as 'soft law', the increasing importance of which is a growing concern.

As shown in the example above, soft law does not necessarily deal directly with religious freedom, but it may deal with moral questions associated with religious freedom, i.e. freedom of conscience (especially in relation to bioethics, marriage and family).

The Venezuelan Constitution of 1999, which I have cited above twice in relation to the incorporation of international agreements into domestic law (art. 23) and in relation to implicit rights or 'open clauses'[23], is also clear in not confusing 'soft law' with the 'hard law' of the international covenants.

In other words, it incorporates the covenants but not the reports or opinions of international bodies that seek to interpret the scope of the provisions of international instruments.[24]

At the 28th Extraordinary Sessions Period, the General Assembly of the Organization of American States approved the so-called Inter-American Democratic Charter, which in Article 9 calls for the elimination of discrimination not based on sex, but on 'gender' (sex is not mentioned). This article is used by Chilean gay rights groups to argue that the Chilean state is under obligation to institute 'homosexual

---

23 'Article 22: The recitation of rights and guarantees contained in this Constitution and in international instruments concerning human rights are not to be understood as negating others inherent to individuals, not expressly mentioned in such recitation. The absence of a law regulating these rights shall not adversely affect the exercise thereof.' Open clauses will permit – wherever they exist – the establishment of rights of religious bodies when there are no provisions in the Covenants regarding them (for example, the right of religious bodies to create legal entities or to be governed by their own legal system).

E. X. Gomes: 'The Implementation of Inter-American Norms on Freedom of Religion in the National Legislation of OAS Member States', *Brigham Young University Law Review* (2009), 575–596.

24 See the Venezuelan Supreme Court's noteworthy judgment N° 1942 of 15 July 2003: Case challenging various articles of the Criminal Code.

marriage' and child adoption rights for homosexuals. Another declaration used in the same way is the 'Resolution on Human Rights, Sexual Orientation and Gender Identity' adopted by the Organization of American States on 3 June 2008.

The legal status and scope of 'soft law' has been widely disputed. Personally, I would leave aside questions related to human rights declarations, which in my view are legally binding, except for their programmatic precepts; but I would call attention to the importance of reports, principles, codes of conduct and communiques by bodies created by international covenants or in relation to human rights agreements, such as the European Commissions in the case of Europe, the Human Rights Committee in the case of the Inter-American Pacts, and the CEDAW Committee, which are not legally binding, but which are often invoked in matters that border on the religious, such as homosexuality, euthanasia, palliative care, genetic research, cloning, etc., as well as the diverse principles on bioethics determined by UNESCO.

Often these decisions assume that 'it is expected that the nations signing soft-law documents will make the effort necessary to implement them and that such efforts will be based on good faith.'[25]

In any event, soft law is frequently used in the area of human rights.[26]

3) In the event of a very brief and even outdated constitutional stipulation, laws or decrees may bring the domestic legal system as a whole up to the level of protection of the Covenants.

As already noted above, this is the case of Chile Law 19.638 of 1999 and the regulations implementing it greatly enriched the legislation on religious freedom, at least in relation to minority religious bodies.[27]

---

25 A. Mazuelos Bellido, 'Soft Law: ¿Mucho ruido y pocas nueces?', *Revista Electrónica de Estudios Internacionales* (2004); R.R. Baxter, 'International Law in "her infinite variety"', 29 *International Comparative Law Quarterly* (1980), 549–566; A.E. Boyle, 'Some Reflections on the Relationship of Treaties and Soft Law', 48 *International Comparative Law Quarterly* (1999), 901–913; H. Hillgenberg, 'A fresh look at Soft Law', 10 *European Journal of International Law* (1999), 499–515; D. Shelton, 'Introduction: Law, Non Law and the problem of "Soft Law"', in S. Shelton (ed.), *Commitment and Compliance: The Role of Non-binding Norms in the International Legal System* (New York City: Oxford University Press USA, 2000); L. G. Colín Villavicencio: 'El Soft Law; una fuente formal más del Derecho Internacional?', available at http://www.tuobra.unam.mx/publicadas/030330120008.html (accessed 31 January 2013).

26 The Holy See is particularly sensitive to 'soft law' related to life, marriage and family-bioethics. Consider, for example, the Beijing and Cairo Conferences, where it aligned itself with Muslim nations. For an understanding of the importance of the issue, see R. Andorno, 'The Invaluable Role of Soft Law in the Development of Universal Norms in Bioethics', Deutsche UNESCO-Kommission e. V., available at http://www.unesco.de/1507.html (accessed 31 January 2013).

27 Law No. 19.638 of 22 September 1999 was regulated by Decree No. 303 of the Ministry of Justice on 21 March 2000, on the registration of religious bodies under public

Throughout the Latin American region, laws and bills on religious freedom are beginning to proliferate, as are projects to compile the domestic legislation.[28] In each country, it is important to analyze whether or not these laws form part of the 'block of constitutionality'.

The process was led by Mexico's Religious Association and Public Worship Act, passed on 15 July 1992.[29]

In Europe, compilations are common and provide a demonstration of the contribution that sub-constitutional legislation can make to religious freedom,[30] especially laws that may be deemed part of the 'block of constitutionality'.

---

law. Ministry of Defense Supreme Decree 115 of 18 July 2007 regulated religious assistance in armed forces, law enforcement and public security institutions. A detailed compilation of Chilean legislation can be found in R. Cortínez, A.M. Celis Brunet, and M.E. Pimstein Scroggie (eds.), *Derecho Eclesiástico chileno: Normas concordadas y comentadas* (Santiago: Universidad Católica de Chile, Centro de Libertad Religiosa, August 2010).

28 Argentina: See Draft Bill 2005 for the Ministry of Worship's Registration of Religious Organizations Act, amending Law 21.745 of 1978 and the 1995 law, No. 24.483, on civilian life in institutes of consecrated life. The Ministry of Worship published *Digesto de Derecho Eclesiástico Argentino* (Buenos Aires, 2001), which compiles the country's ecclesiastical law, and R. Bosca and J. Navarro Floria edited *La Libertad religiosa en el Derecho argentino*, published by Centro Argentino para la Libertad Religiosa (Konrad Adenauer Stiftung, 2007). Perú: Ley 29.635 (Diciembre 2010) – DS 010 – 2011 – Justicia – 27 Julio 2011. Bolivia: Bill on worship ('Proyecto de Ley de Culto de 2001'). Venezuela: Draft bill on religion and worship ('Anteproyecto de ley de religión y culto de 2003'). Ecuador: Law on worship (Ley de Cultos DS 212 R.O. 547) on July 23, 1937. Colombia: Law 133 of 23 May 1994; see also the recent book by V. Prieto, *Estado Laico y libertad religiosa: Antecedentes y desarrollos de la Constitución colombiana de 1991* (Medellín: Biblioteca Jurídica Dike, 2011). Useful for understanding the Inter-American context is the compilation by M. González Sánchez and A. Sánchez-Bayon, *El derecho Eclesiástico de las Américas: Fundamentos socio jurídicos y notas comparadas*, Instituto Metodológico del Derecho Eclesiástico del Estado (Madrid: Delta Publicaciones, 2009). A clear enhancement of the aforementioned book can be found in the recent work by the same authors, *Regulación Iberoamericana de Derecho Eclesiástico* (Madrid: Delta Publicaciones, 2011).

29 The bibliography is extensive. See M.C. Medina González (ed.): 'Una puerta abierta a la libertad religiosa' (México a quince años de las reformas constitucionales en materia religiosa 1992–2007) (México DF: Subsecretaría de Población, Migración y Asuntos Religiosos, 2007). R.M. Martínez de Codes, 'La modernización de las relaciones Iglesia-Estado en México en el curso del siglo', XX *Anuario de Derecho Eclesiástico del Estado* XXIII (2007), 445–454. A. Patiño Reyes, *Libertad religiosa y principio de cooperación en Hispanoamerica* (Universidad Complutense de Madrid, 2011).

30 For example, in France, B. Jeuffroy and F. Tricard (eds.): *Liberté relidieuse et régimes des cultes en droit francais: texts, pratique administrative, jurisprudence* (Paris: Les Éditions Cerf, 1996). F. Curtit and F. Messner, *Droit des religions en France et en Europe: Recueil de textes* (Brussels: Bruylant, 2008). In Spain, I. Martín Sanchez (ed.), *Legislación Básica de Derecho Eclesiástico del Estado*, 1st edn., (Madrid: Editorial Colex, 2000 and successive editions); A. Molina and M.E. Olmos (eds.), *Legislación Eclesiástica*,

4) The mere fact of a stipulation on religious freedom in international documents may give rise to political action to ensure greater protection of religious freedom, and even to new constitutional provisions and more International Covenants in the future.

The clearest example of this is the Helsinki Final Act in 1975. In the countries of Eastern Europe, dissidents used the articles on religious freedom (among others) to promote domestic liberalization[31] and to pressure the Soviet Union and the governments of the 'people's democracies' so that the increase in exchanges with the West might lead to emancipation.[32]

In this way, a merely declarative international agreement unleashed a process which, without constitutional changes, resulted in greater religious freedom.[33] It is highly likely that the current Hungarian Constitution, enacted in 2011, with a

---

4th edn. (Madrid: Editorial Civitas, 1992). In Italy, P. Moneta (ed.), *Il Codice di Diritto Ecclesiastico* (I codici vigenti e le leggi speciali 2001) (Piacenza: Casa Editrice La Tribuna, 2001 and successive editions).

31 The articles on religious freedom in the Final Act of the Conference on Security and Cooperation in Europe read as follows: 'VII. The participating States will respect human rights and fundamental freedoms, including the freedom of thought, conscience, religion or belief, for all without distinction as to race, sex, language or religion [...] Within this framework the participating States will recognize and respect the freedom of the individual to profess and practice, alone or in community with others, [his] religion or belief acting in accordance with the dictates of his own conscience.'

32 The religious situation was criticized by dissidents. In Czechoslovakia, Catholics and Protestants joined with others to sign the Charter 77. In Poland, intellectuals created the Workers' Defense Committee (KOR). In both cases, Catholic bishops supported them publicly. The intellectuals in turn supported the bishops to call an end to discrimination and persecution against Catholics. Cardinal Wyzsyński protested against a Polish constitutional reform that extolled the 'leading role' of the Communist Party and the irreversible nature of the alliance with the Soviet Union. In August 1976, Eastern Europe's Protestant communities were shocked by the self-immolation of Pastor Brüsewitz in the German Democratic Republic. See F. Fejtö, *Histoire démocraties populaires, Tome 2: Après Staline (1953–1979)* (Paris: Éditions du Seuil, 1969), 373–374.

33 The Holy See played an important role. From 1967, Cardinal Casaroli, with the support of Pope Paul VI, launched a diplomatic offensive on the East. In 1971, the Holy See deposited the official document of accession to the Treaty on the Non-Proliferation of Nuclear Weapons in Moscow. In 1975, Monsignor Casaroli led a Vatican delegation at the Helsinki Conference on Security and Co-operation in Europe. It was the first time since 1815 that the Holy See had participated in such an important international conference as a full party and not a mere observer. See M. Merle, *Le Saint-Siège dans les relations internationales* (Paris: Editions de Cerf-Cujas, 1989), 109.

Preamble that reads as if it were written by Cardinal Mindszenty himself,[34] never would have existed[35] without Helsinki 1975.

5) Even with very general constitutional precepts, international human rights courts can foster domestic processes in different countries in the area of protection of religious freedom.

It is clear that this progress is achieved '*ad casum*', but an atmosphere favorable to religious freedom is gradually developing. If the jurisdiction of an international court is recognized by domestic law, especially constitutional law, its judgments have a huge domestic impact.

This is not the case of the Inter-American Human Rights Court ('IACHR'), which to date has never issued a single judgment directly based on a violation of religious freedom, nor has the Inter-American Commission issued a single consultative opinion on the question.

The case of *The Last Temptation of Christ*[36] could have been judged as a violation of this freedom, but it was judged as a violation of freedom of expression. But this case is significant as the first one in which an international court led a signatory state to amend its constitution, as duly noted by Giuseppe de Vergottini.[37]

---

34 National Avowal: 'We are proud that our King Saint Stephen built the Hungarian State on solid ground and made our country a part of Christian Europe one thousand years ago'[…] 'We believe that our national culture is a rich contribution to the diversity of European unity' […] 'We hold that the family and the nation constitute the principal framework of our coexistence, and that our fundamental cohesive values are fidelity, faith and love'[…] 'We honor the achievements of our historical constitution and we honor the Holy Crown, which embodies the constitutional continuity of Hungary's statehood and the unity of the nation' […] 'We hold that after the decades of the twentieth century which led to a state of moral decay, we have an abiding need for spiritual and intellectual renewal.'

35 Cardinal József Mindszenty is well remembered for his famous radio speech of 3 November 1956: 'I have always said bluntly what I have considered right and just. […] I would like to stress that, beyond our borders, the whole civilized world is helping us and unanimously backing us. […] After the reign of our first sovereign, Saint Stephen, we became a great nation. Our present situation depends on the answer to this question: what do the Russian people of two hundred million people, with their military forces stationed on the territory of our border, intend to do? We have not attacked Russia, and we have, for that reason, the hope that it will withdraw its armed forces from our country as soon as possible.' *Memorias del Cardenal Mindszenty* (Madrid: Ediciones Palabra, 2009), 472–479. [editor's translation]

36 *Olmedo Bustos et al. v. Chile*, IACHR, 5 February 2001, Ser. 6, No. 73, 74.

37 G. De Vergottini, *Más allá del diálogo entre tribunales. Comparación y relación entre jurisdicciones,* 1st edn. (Madrid: Cuadernos Civitas, 2010), 163–164:'The Inter-American Court noted the incompatibility of a provision in the Chilean Constitution with the Convention due to its restriction on freedom of expression of thought, and determined that Chile had to amend its own domestic legal system, eliminating the institution of prior

There have also been judgments that have obliquely touched on the religious freedom of indigenous peoples.[38]

The influence of the European Court of Human Rights ('ECtHR') has not been reflected in the constitutional impact of its judgments, but it has been highly significant in the area of religious freedom,[39] even if it has used (sometimes questionably) the margin of discretion granted to it by the states.[40]

Lorenzo Martín-Retortillo, for example, analyzes 44 judgments by the ECtHR on questions of religious freedom from December 1976 to 2006, followed by 36 more between 2006 and December 2009, on questions as diverse as conscientious objection, conflicts between the state and religious groups, autonomy of religious groups in their internal organization, clothing with religious significance and religious symbols in public activities and spaces.[41]

The influence of the international courts at the domestic level of jurisdictional authorities on religious matters varies from country to country.[42] But a significant

---

censorship and thus permitting the screening of a film banned by the judicial authority [...] Moreover, the case is noted as the only occasion to date in which the Court has ordered an amendment to a national constitution, which was carried out by the affected State.' [editor's translation]

38 *The Mayagna (Sumo) Awas Tingni Community v. Nicaragua*, IACHR., 32 August 2001 (Ser. C, No. 79); *Masacre Plan de Sánchez v. Guatemala*, IACHR, 29 April 2004 (Ser. C, No.105, No. 116); *Moiwana Community v. Suriname*, IACHR, 15 June 2005 (Ser. C, No. 142).

39 The bibliography is very extensive. I have consulted the following: T. Massisa and C. Pettiti (eds.), *La liberté religieuse et la Convention Européenne des droits de l'homme* (Brussels: Bruylant, 2004); P. M. Taylor, *Freedom of Religion: UN and European Human Rights Law and Practice* (New York: Cambridge University Press, 2005); J. García Roca and P. Santolayal (eds.), *La Europa de los Derechos. El Convenio Europeo de Derechos Humanos, Centro de Estudios Políticos y Constitucionales*, 2nd edn. (Madrid: Centro de Estudios Políticos y Constitucionales, 2009). I have also used the collective volume J. Martínez-Torrón and W.C. Durham, Jr. (general reporters), *Religion and the Secular State: Interim Reports*, prepared for and issued upon the occasion of The XVIIIth International Congress of Comparative Law, held 25–31 July 2010 in Washington, DC (Provo, Utah: International Center for Law and Religion Studies, 2010). I have also studied the comments on judgments by L. Martín-Retortillo Baquer in the *Anuario de Derecho Eclesiástico del Estado*, and in his work *La afirmación de la libertad religiosa en Europa: de guerras de religión a meras cuestiones administrativas* (Madrid: Thomson Civitas, 2007).

40 For example, *Otto-Preminger-Institut v. Austria*, App. No. 13470/87(ECtHR, 20 September 1994) and *Lautsi and Others v. Italy*, App No. 30814/06 (ECtHR Grand Chamber, 18 March 2011); cf. *Lautsi v. Italy* Second Section Judgment of 3 November 2009. See also the case of *A, B and C v. Ireland*, App. No. 25579/05 (ECtHR Grand Chamber, 16 December 2010), on abortion as a right.

41 See L. Martín-Retortillo Baquer, supra note 39.

42 Apparently, one of the first cases in which a US judge cited the Universal Declaration of Human Rights was in the California District Court of Appeal (*Fujii v. the State of California,* 38 Cal. 2d 718, 242 P.2d 617 (1952)), in which, according to the

number of international treaties, national constitutions and laws, and both national and international decisions after the Universal Declaration of Human Rights have invoked the Declaration, as can be seen from the list compiled early on by Nehemiah Robinson.[43]

6) Domestic courts, their constitutional rulings and the influence of the Covenants on their decisions.

It is clear that domestic courts, both Supreme and Constitutional, use the Covenants on Human Rights to interpret the Constitution.

For example, Professor Marcos González Sánchez conducted a research project to demonstrate that international human rights agreements have influenced the case law of the Spanish Constitutional Court, either to justify their judgments or simply by way of example.[44]

It is worth recalling of course that in Spain there is a constitutional order to use the Covenants on Human Rights as criteria for interpretation, contained in Article 10.2 of the Constitution.

The aforementioned author quotes, by way of example, Constitutional Court Judgment 21/1981, dated 15 June 1981 (FJ 10)[45] and Constitutional Court Judgment STC 245/1991.[46]

Alien Land Law, foreigners who were not eligible for citizenship were prohibited from purchasing agricultural land. The judge cited Article 17 of the Declaration, 'the right to own property' and used it not as a legally binding treaty (hard law) but because it 'emphasized the purposes and guarantees of the [United Nations] Charter.' See Q. Wright, 'National Courts and Human Rights – The Fujii Case', 45 *The American Journal of International Law* 1 (January 1951), 70–77.

43 N. Robinson, *Universal Declaration of Human Rights: Its Origins, Significance and Interpretation* (New York: Institute of Jewish Affairs, 1958).

44 M. González Sánchez, *La incidencia de los acuerdos internacionales sobre derechos fundamentales en la jurisprudencia de Derecho Eclesiástico del Tribunal Constitucional* (Madrid: Thomson Civitas, 2008). González highlights case law dealing with principles of ecclesiastical law, law on religious freedom and its content, teaching, marriage and conscientious objection.

45 By virtue of Article 10.2 of the Constitution, 'the authors of the constitution introduced an international legal corpus that would permit the Constitutional Court to accede directly to current human rights developments existing in our immediate legal environment, as was the case of the Council of Europe [...];' 'Article 10.2 has allowed Spain to salvage something most notably lacking since the establishment of the democratic system, to wit, the lack of criteria for interpretation of rights and fundamental freedoms that had been dropped like a dead weight by the dictatorship.'

46 'The laws related to fundamental rights and public freedoms contained in the Spanish Constitution shall be interpreted in accordance with the international treaties and agreements on the same matters ratified by Spain (art. 10.2 CE). The European Court of Human Rights is the qualified body entrusted with the mission to interpret the Convention

The Constitutional Court of Peru issued a ruling on the withdrawal of Catholic religious symbols from court rooms and chambers (Causa 06111-2009) on 7 March 2011.

The Colombian Constitutional Court has been very active on the question of religious freedom. One need only recall its famous judgment of 5 February 1993 (C-027), which declared the 'supervening unconstitutionality' of various articles of the Concordat of 12 July 1973 (*Ley aprobatoria 20 de 1974*).[47] Professor Prieto notes a total of 93 Constitutional Court judgments between 1992 and 2007.

The activity of Argentina's domestic courts is also worthy of note. One example of this is the recognition of canon law as an applicable legal system, which established not only in relation to the Concordat of 1966, but to rules of the Code of Canon Law itself, applying the three criteria set forth by Antonio Boggiano.[48] For example, in 1992 the ecclesiastical authority imposed penalties on a member of the clergy who had violated the rule of celibacy. The offender appealed to the courts and challenged the constitutionality of priestly celibacy, alleging that it contravened constitutional and legal guarantees. While most members of the Court declared lack of jurisdiction and competence (non-justiciability), the votes cast indicate that there is recognition of jurisdiction of ecclesiastical courts and that the most applicable criterion pointed to canon law as the applicable legal system, given the fact the appellant had consented to ordination.

From this it may be inferred that Argentine legal doctrine recognizes the right of each faith to be governed by its own legal system, provided that it is not contrary to public order and the other limitations on religious freedom enshrined in the Covenants. A right of religious bodies – in this case the Catholic Church – which is not made explicit in the International Covenants but which is clearly one of the rights associated with religious freedom, is enshrined in case law and legal doctrine,[49] with a similar result to Article 20 of Chile's Law 19.638 and the case law of the Chilean courts, which accept the application of Canon Law.[50]

---

and its decisions are furthermore mandatory and binding upon Spain whenever it is the defendant state' (STC 245, December 16, 1991, FJ 3).

47 See V. Prieto, *Libertad religiosa y confesiones: Derecho eclesiástico del Estado Colombiano* (Bogotá: Editorial Tenis S.A., Universidad de La Sabana, 2008), 80–86; see also Prieto, *Estado Laico y libertad religiosa*, supra note 28.

48 See A. Boggiano, *Derecho internacional: derecho de las relaciones entre ordenamientos jurídicos y derechos humanos* (Buenos Aires: La Ley, 2001), 64–66. These criteria are precedence, closest connection, and diverse spheres of jurisdiction. See *Juan Lastra c. Obispo de Venado Tuerto* (Fallos 314: 1342 of 22 October 1991), and High Court of Córdoba, Civil and Commercial Chamber, *Arzobispado de Córdoba c. Edmundo Rodriguez* Álvarez *y otro*, judgment of 15 November 2001.

49 'Antonio Rybar v. Rómulo García' (Fallos 315: 1294, 16 June 1992).

50 The case of Father Aguirre, in which compensation for damages was claimed from the Archbishopric of Santiago (Rol No. 3.636-s002-F) and a claim for legal protection against the Vicar of Education of the Diocese of San Bernardo brought by a lesbian professor whose authorization to teach Catholic religion was revoked. Homosexual groups

Chile's Constitutional Court has not to my knowledge issued a single judgment on religious freedom, but it has issued rulings on related moral issues, such as the case of the morning-after pill, and its judgment on marriage as defined in Article 102 of the Civil Code, which homosexual groups have alleged is unconstitutional, is currently pending.

In the Chilean courts there is a case currently in process against the Adventist Church, which expelled a member who alleges violation of constitutional guarantees in the unlawful application of the restraining rules contained in the internal regulations of the church in question.[51] This is in spite of a surprising decision by the Chilean Courts that asserted that the right of religious freedom does not cover appeals for legal protection.

Therefore, by interpreting the Constitution in accordance with the Covenants because of an explicit constitutional stipulation, because the Covenants are incorporated by the Constitution, or because the Covenants are mentioned in the Preamble, national courts are contributing decisively to the relationship between international and domestic law.

7) 'Conditionality clauses' and religious freedom

Another of the elements that contribute to linking international agreements and constitutions is the so-called 'conditionality clause'. For example, the former European Economic Community inserted a democratic (or human rights and democracy) clause into the Framework Agreement for Commercial and Economic Cooperation with Argentina. I will leave aside the fact that since the 1970s the World Bank has added the concept of 'good governance' to these clauses, and focus on the point that the fundamental right to religious freedom is included among human rights.

As a result, the reference to human rights – which includes religious freedom – brings the Covenants into agreements on free trade, assistance and cooperation, financial affairs and humanitarian aid, and even on military cooperation.

Thus, for example, Article 1 of the Framework Agreement on Cooperation between the European Economic Community and the Republic of Chile contains the following conditionality clause: 'Cooperation ties between the Community and Chile and all the provisions of this Agreement are based on respect for the democratic principles and human rights which inspire the domestic and external

are seeking to take the case to the Inter-American Court. On Father Aguirre's judgment see M.E Pimstein Scroggie, Responsalidad civil de la Iglesia por delictos cometidos por clérigos in Chile, Boletín Jurídico–Centro de Libertad Religiosa, Publica Universidad Catholica de Chile, 8 (June 2010), 44–48.

51 Judgment date 29 November 2010 (Rol No. 7112-2010), delivered by the Third Chamber of the Court of Appeals of Santiago. See J. Precht, 'Comentario a una sentencia sobre libertad religiosa', 38 *Revista Chilena de Derecho* 2 (2011), 389–390.

policies of both the Community and Chile'.[52] The Preamble also makes reference to adherence to the principles of the UN Charter.

Violation of this clause may result in positive or negative sanctions. Compliance may even be emphasized with a so-called 'non-execution' clause, which predetermines the possible consequences of non-compliance.[53]

In the Treaty of Lisbon, Article 51 No. 1 includes such a clause: 'The provisions of this Charter are addressed to the institutions, bodies, offices and agencies of the Union with due regard for the principle of subsidiarity and to the Member States only when they are implementing Union law. They shall therefore respect the rights, observe the principles and promote the application thereof in accordance with their respective powers and respecting the limits of the powers of the Union as conferred on it in the Treaties.'

And Article 52 No. 2: 'Rights recognized by this Charter for which provision is made in the Treaties shall be exercised under the conditions and within the limits defined by those Treaties.'

'Conditionality clauses' are also common practice today in trade agreements between developed and developing countries.

The United States will also operate through the International Religious Freedom Act of 1998, which 'has channeled this priority (of religious freedom) through the State Department, entrusting it with a series of activities ranging from the preparation and presentation of reports by a special office established for the purpose, to the creation of a website on religious freedom, the training of diplomatic personnel, the establishment of contacts with non-governmental organizations, the

52 Framework Agreement for Cooperation between the European Economic Community and the Republic of Chile, signed on 20 December 1990 (DOCE L 79, 1991, 3). If we examine other Agreements we will find references to the Universal Declaration of Human Rights and sometimes to the Helsinki Final Act or the Charter of Paris for a New Europe. See M. del Carmen Muñoz Rodríguez, *Democracia y derechos humanos en la acción exterior de la Unión Europea*, 1st edn. (Madrid: Editorial Reus, 2009).

53 The Resolution of 28 November 1991 makes reference to the actions taken to support the Rule of Law: institutional reforms, independence of the judiciary, improvement of the prison system, good governance, actions to support the democratic transition process, especially for elections (sending observers, purchasing material, preparing electoral codes, registering voters), and actions to strengthen the role of NGOs and other institutions that ensure the pluralist nature of civil society. The resolution itself establishes a range of measures for possible implementation, observing a criterion of proportionality between de facto assumption and reaction to adopt a range of measures of greater or lesser severity: maintenance of confidentiality or public disclosure; modification of the content of cultural, scientific and technical cooperation programs; postponement of the meeting of a Joint Commission; suspension of bilateral contacts at the highest level; the postponement of new projects; refusal to respond to weapons initiatives; interruption of military cooperation and suspension or termination of cooperation. The resolution allows for the exception of humanitarian and emergency aid to disadvantaged populations through non-governmental channels, such as non-governmental organizations.

preparation of programs and allocation of funds, and the compilation of lists of people imprisoned on religious grounds.'[54]

The IRFA defines its understanding of the right to religious freedom, the violation thereof, and particularly serious violations.[55]

A body created by the Act (Office on International Religious Freedom) has among its various functions the preparation of an Annual Report, which identifies states guilty of serious violations of religious freedom rights (Countries of Particular Concern) and the situation in countries where religious freedom is of special interest (Country-Specific Conditions of International Religious Freedom).

The Act authorizes the application of economic sanctions at the discretion of the President. For example, Burma (Myanmar) suffered a ban on exports or transfers of defense articles in 2007, while China faced only a restriction on exports of safety tools and equipment.[56]

For the purposes of this study, any actions taken through conditionality/non-execution clauses will influence the application of the International Covenants on Human Rights and encourage the interpretation of domestic legislation (including the Constitution) through the prism of the provisions of general international law and conventional international law.[57]

Conclusions

An analysis of the constitutional reception of provisions in international law referring to religious freedom poses various complex legal problems:

1. A simple comparison of texts in four human rights protection systems (the Universal, Inter-American, European Union and African systems)

54 See J. Ignacio Rubio, 'La Defensa y Promoción de la libertad religiosa por la Administración Norteamericana (2000–2007). Parte II United States Department of State (USDS)', 48 *Ius Cononicum* 96 (2008), 493–536, quotation here from 499, 500.

55 Sec. 3, def. 13 ('Violations of religious freedom') and sec. 3, def. 11 ('Particularly severe violations of religious freedom').

56 In 2006, Condoleezza Rice designated Burma, China, Eritrea, Iran, North Korea, Saudi Arabia, Sudan and Uzbekistan as countries guilty of serious violations of religious freedom, to which Pakistan and Turkmenistan were subsequently added at the request of the independent agency USCIRF (United States Commission on International Religious Freedom), also created by the International Religious Freedom Act.

57 On this question, see the contribution of The Hon Michael Kirby, 'International Law – The Impact on National Constitutions,' 21 *American Society of International Law* 3 (2006), 327–364, and the commentary of Professor A. Mark Weisburd of the University of North Carolina at Chapel Hill, 'Using International Law to Interpret National Constitutions–Conceptual Problems: Reflections on Justice Kirby's Advocay of International Law in Domestic Constitutional Jurisprudence', 21 *American Society of International Law* 3 (2006), 356–377.

reveals that the stipulations on religious freedom contained in conventional international law are more extensive than those contained in national constitutions. However, although this is the general rule, there are exceptions, such as the constitutions of Bolivia and Ecuador, both enacted in 2008, which refer to indigenous religions and their protection, which in this respect go further than the Covenants, as does the Constitution of South Sudan with regard to the rights included under religious freedom.

2. Nevertheless, regardless of the existence of a particularly superficial or outdated constitutional stipulation, it is important to consider the systems with which domestic legal systems receive and interpret the Covenants, whether in provisions of the constitutions themselves or in the respective 'block of constitutionality'.
3. A particular problem is posed by'soft law', that is, the diverse range of resolutions issued by different international bodies created by the Covenants or in relation with the Covenants, which in principle are not legally binding, but which in current international law have acquired great importance, especially in matters related to morality, most of which are also linked to religious beliefs.
4. It is important to examine the scope that the constitutions allow for the creation of sub-constitutional legislation on religious freedom, as through such legislation the constitutional provisions can be complemented and taken to higher levels of protection not evident from a simple reading of the constitutional text.
5. Even with flawed constitutional texts, the degree to which the national constitutions accept the decisions of international human rights courts needs to be examined. While these decisions are ad casum, they may contribute to the development of domestic trends in court decisions and legal doctrine, which may even lead to constitutional amendments. Domestic courts, insofar as they cite or support their judgments with the Covenants, contribute to the creation of a corpus of interpretation or application that complements the Constitution through judicial decisions. However, it is necessary to determine the real significance of the so-called 'dialogue between jurisdictions'.
6. Lastly, the Covenants are introduced into domestic law by means of 'conditionality' and 'execution' clauses contained in international agreements on trade, aid and assistance and even for humanitarian interventions through foreign policy agreements between developed and developing countries.

In short, to measure the impact of the International Covenants on the constitutions on matters of religious freedom, it is not enough to analyze the wording of the constitutional text; it is also necessary to examine what the constitution allows or does not allow its domestic agencies to do in relation to the Human Rights Covenants, including religious freedom.

Chapter 5

Religion and the Sources of Law: *Sharî'ah* in Constitutions

Gianluca P. Parolin

On 22 August 2011, in the aftermath of the takeover of Qaddâfî's stronghold of Bâb al-'Azîziyyah in Tripoli, the Transitional National Council released an interim draft constitution which, in its Article 1, read: Libya is an independent, democratic state wherein the people are the source of powers. The city of Tripoli shall be the capital of the state. Islam is the religion of the state and the chief source of legislation is Islamic law (*sharî'ah*). [...][1]

The provision that Islam is the religion of the state in the new Libya and that Islamic law is the chief source of its legislation caught many by surprise and generated a heated debate in the media and among intellectuals. It shouldn't have.

I was asked to deliver a chapter addressing precisely the issue of how constitutions in the region regulate the sources of law and the position of Islamic law therein. Quite a daunting task.[2]

The Kuwaiti constituent assembly repeatedly asked this very question to its constitutional law expert in the early 1960s. 'Uthmân Khalîl 'Uthmân, the Egyptian constitutional law consultant to the Assembly, answered by pointing at the distinction between declaring *sharî'ah* 'a' chief source of legislation rather than 'the' chief source of legislation. 'Uthmân advised the members to adopt the softer 'a' version, if the assembly wanted to mark its attachment to Islam while avoiding being forced to comply with all its commands and prohibitions.[3]

---

1 After Qaddâfî's assassination, the statement was reiterated by the president of the National Transitional Council Mustafà 'abd al-Jalîl at the dawn of the liberation during a rally in Benghâzî on 23 October 2011. References in Mustafà 'abd al-Jalîl's liberation speech to the need to bring in conformity with *sharî'ah* provisions on bank interests and lift the old regime's restrictions on polygyny were considered untimely and at best inappropriate by large sections of Libyan society, while part of 'abd al-Jalîl's Islamist supporters rallied in favor.

2 In the last two decades, a significant number of remarkable studies on constitutional provisions on *sharî'ah* have been published (generally with a national focus). It is beyond the scope of this chapter, however, to engage with all such contributions, even if the author feels highly indebted to this mass of outstanding literature.

3 Minutes of the 19th session of the Constituent Assembly meeting, held on 11 September 1962, 4-8. The a/the controversy was repeatedly tabled until a unanimous decision in favor of the 'a'-version during the 24th session, held on 24 October 1962, 3.

Kuwait in 1962 heralded the countries that would declare in their constitutions Islamic law (*sharî'ah*) 'a' chief source of legislation. Such a middle ground was fully in line with the other provisions of the Kuwaiti Constitution, a Constitution commonly regarded as one of the most liberal, but also as a model compromise between the dynamics of traditional governance and the requirements of modern constitutionalism.

A provision stipulating Islamic law (*sharî'ah*) as 'a'/'the' chief source of legislation became increasingly popular to the point that almost all new constitutions that establish Islam, also include it.

Constitutional Provisions on Islam

Most constitutions of countries with a significant Muslim population include references to Islam. Such references have been traditionally classified under four headings: (1) generic references in preambles, (2) religion of the state/ establishment clauses, (3) principle of conformity of legislation to *sharî'ah*, and (4) requirements of the Head of State[4]. References to Islam in preambles, just as provisions establishing Islam as the religion of the state, and the eligibility requirement of being Muslim in order to serve as Head of State are but Islamic steel in a liberal mold. Formulations of liberal constitutionalism are reproduced verbatim and generally interpreted along its traditional canons of construction.

Does this apply to the principle of conformity of legislation to *sharî'ah* as well? Constitutional provisions on the incorporation of international law into municipal law might be the closest mold of liberal constitutionalism. The relations of international law to municipal law—just as those of *sharî'ah* to positive law—can be variably construed and gave rise to a number of constitutional provisions regulating them. Behind every constitutional provision regulating the relations between *sharî'ah* and positive law lies a certain conception of the legal order that is seldom mirrored in the provision itself.

After giving a brief overview of the provisions, I will therefore advance some preliminary suggestions for moving beyond the provisions themselves in order to grasp the peculiar conceptions of the legal order and their development, especially with the advent of modernity and its modes of legal production—conceptions that, I argue, offer the key to interpreting constitutional provisions on *sharî'ah*.

Constitutional Provisions on *Sharî'ah*

Provisions on *sharî'ah* started appearing in constitutions in the 1950s, well after establishment clauses. The two forerunners were Syria (1950) and Pakistan (1956).

4 J.-F. Rycx and G. Blanchi, 'Références à l'Islam dans le Droit Public Positif en Pays Arabes,' 12 *Pouvoirs* (1980), 57–70.

The Syrian constitution phrased it in the affirmative ('Islamic jurisprudence (*fiqh*) is the chief source of legislation,' art. 3)[5], whereas the Pakistani phrasing was in the negative ('No law shall be enacted which is repugnant to the Injunctions of Islam (*islâmî ahkâm*) as laid down in the Holy Quran and Sunnah, hereinafter referred to as Injunctions of Islam, and existing law shall be brought into conformity with such Injunctions,' art. 198(1)).

The two approaches seem to have had primarily a geographical diffusion along linguistic lines. The Syrian provision in the affirmative spread mainly in the Arabic-speaking region, while the Pakistani repugnancy clause spread mainly in the non-Arabic-speaking Muslim world. Somalia in 1960 followed the Syrian example in the section on the National Assembly, but declared Islamic jurisprudence (*fiqh*) 'a fundamental source of the laws of the state' (art. 50).[6] Indonesia in the late 1950s was about to follow the Pakistani example,[7] but the Constituent Assembly was dissolved in 1959 by Sukarno, who reinstated the 1945 Constitution. Before dissolution, a repugnancy clause had been included in the draft proposed by the largest coalition in the Indonesian Constituent Assembly, the Islamic Bloc (holding 274 seats out of 514 total), alongside with strong references to Islam in the Preamble[8] and Article 1.[9]

In the 1960s the Northern Gulf witnessed remarkable shifts in the constitutional provisions on *sharî'ah*. While the 1958 Provisional Constitution of Iraq included only an establishment clause, Iraq's neighbor Kuwait, the first Gulf Emirate to become independent, declared in 1962 Islamic law (*sharî'ah*) 'a chief source of legislation'[10]. Iraq responded in 1964 in the new Provisional Constitution with an even stronger provision, declaring Islam 'the basic foundation of the Constitution'[11], but the only explicit reference to the application of Islamic law in the Iraqi legal system was to inheritance (art. 12).

The number of constitutions regulating the position of Islamic law (*sharî'ah*) within the sources of law has steadily increased ever since the 1970s and 1980s, with a peak in the 1990s and the new millennium.

A seminal role was certainly played by Egypt under the auspices of Anwar al-Sâdât. The self-proclaimed 'believing President' (*al-ra'îs al-mu'min*) issued in 1971 a Constitution that declared 'the principles of Islamic law (*sharî'ah*) a chief

5 *al-fiqh al-islâmiyy huwa al-masdar al-ra'îsiyy li-l-tashrî'.*

6 *al-fiqh al-islâmiyy masdar asâsiyy li-qawânîn al-dawlah..*

7 Art. 118(a).

8 *manba' a'là li-l-hukm huwa kitâb allâh wa-sunnat rasûlih al-bayyinah.*

9 *kitâb allâh wa-sunnat rasûlih al-karîm humâ al-marja' al-awwal wa-l-a'là li-nizâm al-jumhûriyyah al-indûnîsiyyah.*

10 *al-sharî'ah al-islâmiyyah masdar ra'îsiyy li-l-tashrî'* (art. 2).

11 *al-islâm dîn al-dawlah wa-l-qa'îdah al-asâsiyyah li-dustûrihâ* (art. 3). Formulation maintained in the 1986 Provisional Constitution (art. 4), but not included in the 1970 one.

source of legislation,'[12] and later amended it in 1980 to be 'the' chief source of legislation.[13]

In the same decade, the Fundamental Law of the Islamic Republic of Iran in its articulate structure of institutions and jurisdictions declared that 'all civil, penal, financial, economic, administrative, cultural, military, political, and other laws and regulations must be based on Islamic criteria (*bar asâs mawâzîn islâmî*). This principle applies absolutely and generally to all articles of the Constitution as well as to all other laws and regulations, and the wise persons of the Council of Guardians are judges in this matter.'[14]

Formulations, more varied in the 1970s and 1980s, have become progressively more standardized. Just as we have heard from the draft Libyan interim constitution, Islamic law (*sharî'ah*) is generally declared 'a'/'the' chief source of legislation,[15] or

---

12 *Mabâdi' al-sharî'ah al-islâmiyyah masdar ra'îsiyy li-l-tashrî'* (art. 2).

13 *Mabâdi' al-sharî'ah al-islâmiyyah al-masdar al-ra'îsiyy li-l-tashrî'* (art. 2, as amended in 1980).

14 Art. 4.

15 Kuwait (1961, art. 2: 'Islamic *sharî'ah* shall be a chief source of legislation (*al-sharî'ah al-islâmiyyah masdar ra'isiyy li-l-tashrî'*)'); United Arab Emirates (1971, art. 7: 'Islamic *sharî'ah* shall be a chief source of legislation [in the Union] (*al-sharî'ah al-islâmiyyah masdar ra'isiyy li-l-tashrî' fîh*)'); Pakistan (1973, art. 227(1) : 'all existing laws shall be brought in conformity with the injunctions of Islam (*islâmî ahkâm*) as laid down in the holy Qur'ân and Sunnah'); Syria (1973, art. 3: 'Islamic jurisprudence is a main source of legislation (*al-fiqh al-islâmiyy masdar ra'isiyy li-l-tashrî'*)'); Iran (1979, art. 4: 'All civil, penal financial, economic, administrative, cultural, military, political, and other laws and regulations must be based on Islamic criteria. (*bar asâs mawâzîn islâmî*)'); Egypt (1980, art. 2: 'the principles of Islamic law (*sharî'ah*) are the chief source of legislation (*Mabâdi' al-sharî'ah al-islâmiyyah al-masdar al-ra'îsiyy li-l-tashrî'*)'); Mauritania (1991, art. 5: 'precepts of Islam, the sole source of law, (*ahkâm al-dîn al-islâmiyy, al-masdar al-wahîd li-l-qânûn*)'); Yemen (1994, art. 3: 'Islamic *sharî'ah* is the source of all legislation (*al-sharî'ah al-islâmiyyah masdar jamî' al-tashrî'ât*)'); Oman (1996, art. 2: 'Islamic *sharî'ah* is the basis of legislation (wa-*l-sharî'ah al-islâmiyyah hiya asâs al-tashrî'*"); Comoros (2001, preamble: 'The Comorian people solemnly proclaim their aspiration to draw from Islam, religion of the state, the permanent inspiration of the principles and laws that shall govern the State and its institutions (*an yustamadd min al-islâm, masdar al-ilhâm al-dâ'im, al-mabâdi' wa-l-qawâ'id allatî tahkum al-ittihâd*)'); Bahrain (2002, art. 2: 'Islamic *sharî'ah* shall be a chief source of legislation (*al-sharî'ah al-islâmiyyah masdar ra'isiyy li-l-tashrî'*)'); Qatar (2003; art. 1: 'Islamic *sharî'ah* shall be a chief source of its legislation (*al-sharî'ah al-islâmiyyah masdar ra'isiyy li-tashrî'âtihâ*)'); Iraq (2005, art. 2 : 'Islam is the official religion of the State and is a foundation source of legislation (*wa-huwa masdar asâs li-l-tashrî'*)'); Sudan (interim 2005, art. 5(1) : 'Nationally enacted legislation having effect only in respect of the Northern states of the Sudan shall have as its sources of legislation Islamic Sharia and the consensus of the people (*takûn al-sharî'ah al-islâmiyyah wa-l-ijmâ' masdaran li-l-tashrî'ât allatî tusann 'alà al-mustawà al-qawmiyy wa-tutabbaq 'alà wilâyât shamâl al-Sûdân*)');.

it is asserted that no piece of legislation can be contrary to it.[16] Significant exceptions can be found in the Arab West,[17] the Central Asian Republics,[18] and Far East Asia.[19]

Defective Canons of Construction

Defining the scope and assessing the impact of constitutional provisions on *sharî'ah* is a challenge faced by municipal lawyers, who are confronted with questions that are not too dissimilar from those raised by constitutional provisions on incorporation of international law. Unsurprisingly, a high degree of ideological polarization governs the recourse to alternative canons of constitutional construction. Yet, the first compelling remark is that alternatives are sought within the realm of traditional canons inspired by a statist, monist, positivist approach to law. The uninspiring and unimaginative debate over the supremacy of the constitution or *sharî'ah* over the other is but a reminiscent of weary disputes among supporters of dualist and monist theories in international law. The one and only datum that can be drawn from this debate is that traditional canons of constructions do not offer adequate solutions.[20]

What municipal lawyers seem to hold dearest is the principle of internal consistency of the system, even if the exercise proves more complex than expected. Scholars insist that provisions on *sharî'ah* are not set in a vacuum and need to be coordinated with other constitutional provisions. In Egypt, for instance, jurists argue that *sharî'ah* as the chief source of legislation (art. 2) must be construed together and in accordance with the principle of citizenship on which the democratic system is declared to be based on according to the Constitution (art. 1, as amended in 2007). In Iraq, likewise, the *sharî'ah*-repugnancy clause is construed together with the other two repugnancy clauses contained in the same sub-section and related to the principle of democracy and constitutional rights and

16 Afghanistan (2004, art. 3: 'no law can be contrary to the beliefs and provisions of the sacred religion of Islam (*mu'taqadât wa-ahkâm al-islâm*)'), Iraq (2005, art. 2(A): 'no law may be enacted that contradicts the established provisions of Islam (*lâ yajûz sann qânûn yata'ârad ma'a thawâbit ahkâm al-islâm*)'); Maldives (2008, art. 10: 'no law contrary to any principle of Islam can be applied'); Pakistan (1973, art. 227(1): 'no law shall be enacted which is repugnant to such injunctions (*islâmî ahkâm*)').

17 Morocco, Algeria, Tunisia, all with an establishment clause; whereas other West African constitutions do not even establish Islam (Mali, Senegal, Gambia, Guinea, Niger, Sierra Leone, Burkina Faso).

18 Kazakhstan, Kyrgyzstan, Tajikistan, Turkmenistan, Uzbekistan.

19 Bangladesh, Brunei and Malaysia with an establishment clause, Indonesia only endorsing the belief in the one and only God within the state doctrine of Pancasila.

20 Western scholars fall in the same trap as they try and explain such provisions as sheer forms of recognition of unconsequential supremacy (Rycx and Blanchi, 'Références à l'Islam Dans Le Droit Public Positif En Pays Arabes,' 59.), often based on textual canons alone (P. Rondot, *L'Islam Et Les Musulmans D'aujoud'hui* (Paris: Editions de L'Orante, 1958), 262.).

basic freedoms (art. 2(1)).[21] These constructions are rarely put to the test, but even their conceptual shortcomings are not fully addressed.[22]

Construction of *sharî'ah*-provisions encounters a further element of complexity in systems of multi-level government. In Malaysia, for instance, Islam is declared the religion of the federation (art. 3), but religion falls within state jurisdiction (sched. 9) yet it is the federal constitution that sets limitations to *sharî'ah*-compliant state legislation.[23] Religion is treated as any other area of jurisdiction, and the Supreme Court is called to determine its boundaries in settling conflicts of jurisdictions between federal and state authorities.[24] In Indonesia, *sharî'ah*-compliant local legislation is enacted under a constitution that carries no reference to *sharî'ah* or Islam, but within an institutional framework of differentiated levels of decentralisation that include specific provisions and limitations on local jurisdiction over *sharî'ah*.[25] In Nigeria, the federal Constitution only provides for a non-establishment clause at all levels of government (art. 10) and for Shariat Courts of Appeal of the federal capital territory (art. 260–4) and of 'any State that requires it' (art. 275–9). State jurisdiction over *sharî'ah* should be determined according to the general rules set out in the federal Constitution, but the Constitution seems to be often overruled by the dynamics between states and federation in a number of areas, including criminal law, evidence, *zakat*, and *hisbah* police.[26] The Constitution of the United Arab Emirates is the only federal constitution that declares *shari'ah* to be a chief source of legislation at the federal level (art. 7).

A case that reflects at once the difficult coordination with the principle of internal consistency and multi-level government is the 2005 Interim Constitution for Sudan, which read that 'nationally enacted legislation having effect only with

21 'First: Islam is the official religion of the State and is a foundation source of legislation: A. No law may be enacted that contradicts the established provisions of Islam; B. No law may be enacted that contradicts the principles of democracy; C. No law may be enacted that contradicts the rights and basic freedoms stipulated in this constitution.' (art. 2(1), 2005 Constitution).

22 B. Botiveau, *Loi Islamique et Droit dans les Sociétés Arabes: Mutations des Systèmes Juridiques du Moyen-Orient* (Paris: Karthala, 1993), 286.

23 See, for instance, the Syariah Courts (Criminal Jurisdiction) Act 1963.

24 The leading ruling in the field is probably the 1988 *Mamat bin Daud* case on an intricate question touching on religion and the penal code. See A. Harding, 'Sharia and National Law in Malaysia', in *Sharia and National Law: Comparing the Legal Systems of Twelve Islamic Countries*, ed. J.M. Otto, 1st edn. (Cairo: The American University in Cairo Press, 2010), 513.

25 See J. M. Otto, 'Sharia and National Law in Indonesia', in *Sharia and National Law: Comparing the Legal Systems of Twelve Islamic Countries*, 461–2.

26 See P. Ostien and A. Dekker, 'Sharia and National Law in Nigeria', in *Sharia and National Law: Comparing the Legal Systems of Twelve Islamic Countries*, 581–4.

respect to the Northern states of the Sudan shall have as its sources of legislation Islamic *sharî'ah* and the consensus of the people' (art. 5).[27]

The Wider Setting

Municipal lawyers and foreign scholars struggle to expound the constitutional provisions on *sharî'ah* with the traditional canons of construction. Excessive emphasis is placed on the provisions and their textual formulation. As virtually every compromise arrangement, constitutional provisions on *sharî'ah* cannot be fully comprehended on textual arguments alone. Could one appreciate the complexities of the social function of property on the basis of the constitutional provisions contained in European and Latin American constitutions alone?

Constitutional provisions on *sharî'ah* point to a complex system of legal sources, but if we intend to ascertain the authority of *sharî'ah* and its relation to other sources of law, I argue that we need to shift our attention from the mid-game score (the provision itself) and widen the focus of our analysis to the playing ground, the players, their techniques, and the referee. I further suggest considering the encounter with modernity as one of the most significant moments of the game, after which two major paradigm shifts can be identified.

The Pre-Modern Tradition[28]

In the pre-modern tradition, the playing field is defined by the fundamentally plural conception of Islamic scholars that law is partly derived from God's commands and prohibitions (*fiqh*), and partly produced by the political authority (*siyâsah*). God's commands and prohibitions (*al-shar'*) are the cornerstone of the system; *fiqh* encompasses both interpretation and extension, while all that is left unregulated by *fiqh* can be validly regulated by the political authority as *siyâsah*. Historically, *sharî'ah*'s playing field can therefore be rendered as a system of twin organs: a domain regulated by confessional law (*fiqh*) and one by positive law (*siyâsah*)—organs with a semipermeable membrane between them that allowed a certain osmosis.

---

27 While the second clause read: 'Nationally enacted legislation applicable to Southern Sudan or states of Southern Sudan shall have as its sources of legislation popular consensus, the values and the customs of the people of the Sudan, including their traditions and religious beliefs, having regard to Sudan's diversity.' See O. Koendgen, 'Sharia and National Law in the Sudan,' in *Sharia and National Law: Comparing the Legal Systems of Twelve Islamic Countries*, 202–3.

28 I use the definition of 'pre-modern tradition' and 'modernity' adopted by W.B. Hallaq, *Sharī`a: Theory, Practice, Transformations* (Cambridge, UK: Cambridge University Press, 2009).

The players wear their team colors and are confined to their respective fields. Scholars (*fuqahâ'*) receive a religious education where the study of law (*fiqh*) epitomizes the Islamic curriculum, and later contribute to the development of *fiqh* alone, whereas the political authority must keep within the limits of what is left unregulated by scholars (*siyâsah*). Even when the political authority possesses the qualifications to operate in the field of *fiqh*, it can do so according to *fiqh*'s methodology, and its view has no higher standing than that of any other scholar. The authority can wear both colors, but it does not have a free hand in *fiqh* as it does in *siyâsah*.

The techniques employed in the two fields mark their distinctive characters. On the one hand, *fiqh* elaborates a complex methodology that requires proficiency in a number of disciplines included in the Islamic curriculum, from grammar to logic. The technique becomes so crucial after the formative period of *fiqh* that the validity of the operation of the *faqîh* is evaluated primarily on the correctness of the methodology employed. On the other hand, *siyâsah* is considered unworthy of scientific interest and left—almost entirely unregulated—in the province of the authority.

Rather than to a referee, one should look to the linemen in the pre-modern context. But linemen are team players, not third parties. The line of scrimmage is determined and patrolled chiefly by *fuqahâ'*, who wish to preserve their domain and prevent incursions by the political authority. This arrangement can be considered as one of the main cornerstones of Islamic constitutionalism insofar as it serves as a legal limitation to government, with an equivalent function to that of the common law in McIlwain's reading of Anglo-Saxon constitutionalism.[29]

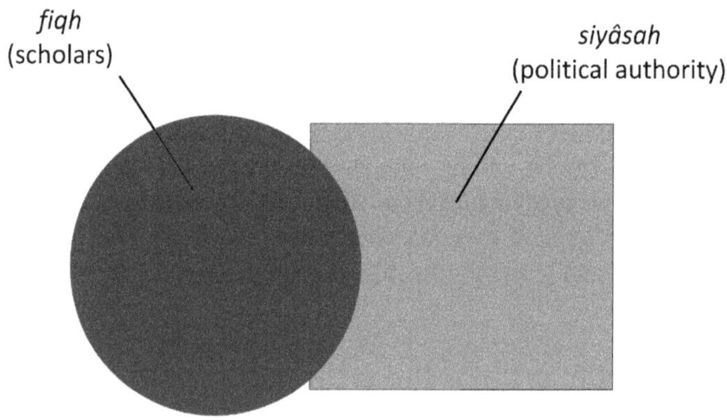

Figure 5.1 Pre-modern Tradition

29 C.H. McIlwain, *Constitutionalism, Ancient and Modern* (Ithaca, N.Y: Cornell University Press, 1940).

Modernity and the First Paradigm Shift

The emergence of the modern state propelled an abrupt paradigm shift in the pre-modern configuration of law. Change operated at all the levels considered, and we can label it as paradigmatic because of the fundamental shifts in the underlying structures of law. It is against this backdrop that the constitutional provisions on *sharî'ah* need to be considered.

The 'modern' playing field is characterized by a redefinition of the domain of *fiqh* and an enfeeblement of the membrane between *fiqh* and *siyâsah* to the detriment of the former. The operation was conducted in two steps. At first the camp of *fiqh* was redefined by subtracting areas of jurisdiction from the *qâdî* (the judge who resorts to *fiqh* to decide on cases brought before him) and reallocating them to courts that adjudicate on the basis of rules set by government as *siyâsah*. The redefinition of the domain of *fiqh* can be read as a concession by *fuqahâ'* to government on contracts and torts in view of retention of full authority over a broad area of subject-matters of secondary interest to government and relabeled collectively as 'personal status' (including capacity, marriage, filiation, divorce, maintenance, inheritance, wills).[30] Later on, government started an initially timid series of incursions into the stronghold of personal status that in certain countries culminated with a codification. The degree of legitimacy of these *siyâsah* incursions into *fiqh* has been of concern to governments that often tried to ground their 'reforms' in the Islamic tradition in one way or the other.[31]

The playing field has therefore been redefined, with a significant expansion of *siyâsah* at the expense of *fiqh*, and along a line set with the conventional instruments of *siyâsah*: orders (*nizâm*), decrees (*marsûm*), statutes (*qânûn*) and constitutions (*dustûr*). With the advent of modernity we also witness a terminological shift from the dichotomy *fiqh/siyâsah* to *sharî'ah/qânûn*.

Modern states tried to bring all the players under their control. The operation was particularly problematic for the *fuqahâ'*, but their displacement and subjugation was accomplished as a result of the reforms introduced in the administration of religious endowments (*waqf*), the traditional source of income and hence of independence of the *fuqahâ'*. The state seizing control over religious endowments (even where it did not reach the level of nationalizations) transformed the *fuqahâ'* from independent scholars in salaried employees of the state. Later, states also extended their control over the very institutions of religious learning that were traditionally licensing *fuqahâ'*; the nationalization of al-Azhar al-sharîf in 1961 in Egypt is a typical example of this latter phenomenon.

30 D. Crecelius, 'The Course of Secularization in Modern Egypt', in D.E. Smith (ed.), *Religion and Political Modernization* (New Haven: Yale University Press, 1974).

31 B. Johansen, 'The Constitution and the Principles of Islamic Normativity Against the Rules of Fiqh: A Judgment of the Supreme Constitutional Court of Egypt', in M.K. Masud, R. Peters, and D. S. Powers (eds.), *Dispensing Justice in Islam: Qadis and Their Judgements*, ed., *Studies in Islamic Law and Society* 22 (Leiden ; Boston: Brill, 2006), 169–193.

Modernity also brought dramatic transformations to the techniques of *fiqh* (*sharî'ah*) and *siyâsa* (*qânûn*), both internally and in their reciprocal relations. Not only did *siyâsah* become worthy of study, but its techniques turned into the axis of higher education and they eventually supplanted those of *fiqh* as the reference system of what is 'law'. A modern, European-style law (identified at first as *siyâsah* and later as *qânûn*) was seen as the lever to an efficient administration, fundamental for an efficient state. Law schools were generally the first schools of newly established European-style universities, and the law taught in these institutions of higher education was primarily a continental brand of positivism, with no room for *fiqh*. States would also recruit graduates from these universities, rather than licensees of traditional institutions of Islamic learning. The phenomenon further intensified with colonialism and independence to the point that concepts and terminology of positive law became the standard reference also for Islamic modernists working on *fiqh*. *Fiqh* on the other hand witnessed a collapse of its traditional methodology and hermeneutics. The friendly fire of Islamic modernists (often educated in the new curricula) dealt a fatal blow to the classical system of methods (*madhhab*) of legal production, dividing the now state-salaried traditional scholars of *fiqh* between those deferential to the classical *madhâhib* and those embracing modernity. The bodies on the ground were unquestionably *fiqh*'s plurality, and a consensus on what *fiqh* in the modern world is and its methodology.

In the persistent absence of a referee, modern states brought linemen within their lines with the displacement of the *fuqahâ'* and the use of *siyâsah* (*qânûn*) as the determinant of the line of scrimmage. It is no longer Islamic scholars, but rather state law and its apparatus that set and define the domain of *fiqh* (*sharî'ah*) and that of *siyâsah* (*qânûn*), claiming the state's monopoly of law in line with the positivist creed of the time.

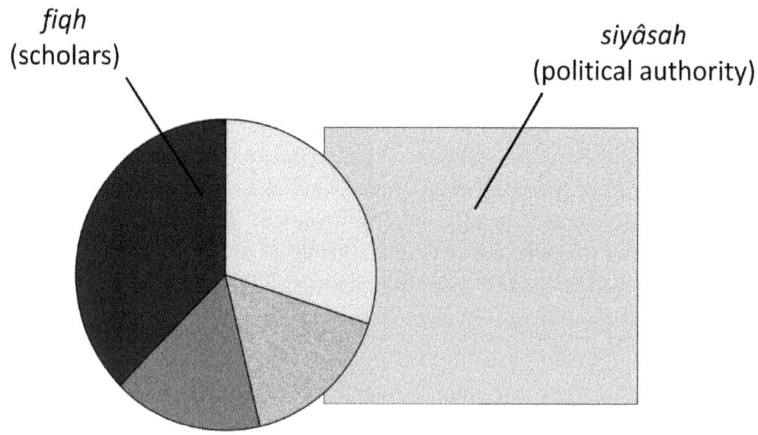

Figure 5.2 First Paradigm Shift

The Second Paradigm Shift

Constitutional provisions on *sharî'ah* and their justiciability by courts are the most significant aspects of the paradigm shift in the structure of the sources of law in the post-modern context. Where provisions on *sharî'ah* have been introduced in constitutions, states have generally mandated that their higher courts interpret such provisions and review legislation deemed in conflict with them. Besides considerations on the state of judicial review in the region,[32] one could argue that higher courts are but organs of the state and their neutrality on the *sharî'ah/qânûn* relations can be questioned, as they can act as state-law patrollers according to their positivist premises.

Due consideration should be given to the legal background of the justices sitting on the bench of the higher courts called to review legislation in conflict with *sharî'ah*. Are all or some of them required to have been trained in the classical Islamic curriculum? Where justices are not required to have a special training in Islamic law, do courts outsource *sharî'ah* briefs or do they decide all in-house? On what bases? Similar questions could be profitably addressed also to other branches of government when they look into questions related to *fiqh/sharî'ah*.

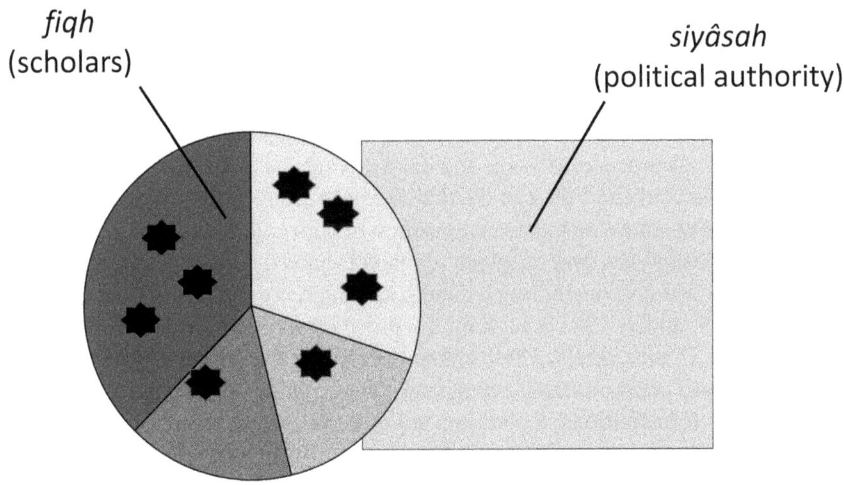

5.3 Second Paradigm Shift

32 For the Arab region, see N. J. Brown, *Constitutions in a Nonconstitutional World*, SUNY Series in Near Eastern Studies (State University of New York Press, 2002), 145ff.

Outer Divergence and Inner Convergence

The wider setting briefly outlined above helps us assess the impact of constitutional provisions on *sharî'ah* in two systems that apparently have opted for fairly divergent solutions: Egypt and Pakistan. Both Egypt and Pakistan adopted *sharî'ah* provisions, yet with a significant difference in the degree of intensity. Both Egypt and Pakistan mandated their high courts' review of legislation in violation of such provisions, yet with a significant difference in the structure and staffing of the respective courts. Both Egypt and Pakistan initiated plans to Islamicize their laws, yet with a significant difference in outcomes. Upon a closer look on the interpretation and implementation of constitutional provisions on *sharî'ah*, however, signs of convergence of the two systems appear.

In Pakistan, a stringent provision including a repugnancy clause and a duty to bring all existing law in conformity with the injunctions of Islam (*islâmî ahkâm*) was included in the very first constitution after independence (1956)[33] and maintained with a slight inversion of clauses ever since (1962 and 1973).[34] In Egypt, the first constitutional provision on *sharî'ah* was introduced only in 1971, and read that 'the principles of Islamic law be the [added in 1980] chief source of legislation'.[35]

Until 1980 in Pakistan all constitutional *sharî'ah*-provisions were unenforceable; there was no judicial review for the repugnancy clause, and instead a mere advisory body was charged with reporting to parliament on both repugnant laws and areas in which legislative intervention was required to comply with the injunctions of Islam. In 1980, however, a constitutional amendment created the Federal Shariat Court but subtracted from its jurisdiction the constitution, Muslim personal law, all procedural laws, and for ten years also all fiscal and banking laws.[36] Decisions of the FSC can be challenged in front of the Shariat Appellate Bench of the Supreme Court. The composition of both courts is mixed, with judges trained in Pakistani law and religious scholars (*ulamâ'*) sitting on the bench, but with the latter always constituting a minority. A Supreme Court was established in Egypt in 1969, and in 1971 it took up the jurisdiction on the *sharî'ah* provision. The Supreme Court exercised full judicial review, but interpreted Article 2 as a non-retroactive, programmatic, repugnancy clause addressed to the legislator.[37] The Supreme Constitutional Court, created in 1979, is following the approach of the Supreme Court, and just as its predecessor it is staffed only by judges trained in Egyptian law.

In Pakistan, the politics of Islamicization of law has accompanied and somehow inspired the creation of the state, but reached its apex in the late 1970s under

33 Art. 198(1), 1956 Constitution.

34 Art. 227(1), 1973 Constitution.

35 Art. 2, 1971 Constitution (as amended in 1980).

36 Art. 203B-C, 1973 Constitution.

37 'Ā. 'U. Sharīf, *Qadâ' al-dustūrīyah: al-Qadâ' al-dustūrī fī Misr* ([Cairo: s.n.], 1988), 207.

general Zia'-ul-haqq's regime. Driving motives and employed methodology, however, seem not to be immediately connected to the constitutional provisions, which allowed for evident policy oscillations ever since the Constitution of 1956. The creation of an *ad hoc* court, the Federal Shariat Court, even followed the highest wave of Islamicization of law. In Egypt, the introduction of a *sharî'ah*-provision into the constitution in 1971, and its reinforcement in 1980, was followed by a comprehensive plan to assess conformity of existing legislation with the principles of Islamic law, but in the mid-1980s the plan was shelved and the Supreme Constitutional Court did not censure the legislature for its inertia, but rather encouraged it with its jurisprudence of no review of legislation passed before the 1980 amendment.

Differences in provisions, court structure and composition, and plans of Islamicization, however, often hide convergences or unexpected outcomes that point to a picture that requires fuller consideration of the wider setting to be evaluated. One such convergence may be the similar reasoning behind the decision of both Pakistani and Egyptian courts to wave the procedural burdens on unilateral divorce introduced by the legislature to curb the phenomenon, whereas unexpected outcomes arise when considering the jurisprudence of the courts on state-driven reforms on such *sharî'ah*-relevant matters as the inheritance of orphaned grandchildren.

Recourse to unilateral divorce (*talâq*) is a phenomenon that modern states tried to limit, aware that classical *sharî'ah* allows for it and frames it as a right of the husband. Strategies of reform have therefore been procedural, fundamentally requiring registration. Since the requirement of registration does not affect the validity of the *talâq* according to *sharî'ah*, both Egypt and Pakistan decided to couple the requirement with the prohibition of the courts' considering unregistered *talâq*s, thus indirectly affecting the validity of *talâq* according to state law (*qânûn*). A procedural reform eased by the full state control over jurisdiction in matters of personal status. In Pakistan the registration requirement was combined with the notification to the wife,[38] whereas in Egypt it was ancillary to an attempt to reconciliation mandatory for the completion of the registration procedure.[39]

The interplay of the registration requirement with other provisions prompted both the Pakistani and Egyptian courts to decide on the conflict of laws revolving around the validity of the unregistered *talâq*. In Pakistan, a number of adultery (*zinâ*) lawsuits were filed against remarried wives of former husbands who had failed to register their *talâq*, and the Federal Shariat Court managed to wave the prohibition on lower courts' considering unregistered *talâq*s when looking at adultery cases, yet maintained the validity of the principle that all *talâq*s must be registered. The Pakistani court thus admitted the superiority of *sharî'ah* by dismissing the requirements of state law while leaving the text of the Ordinance

38 Sec. 7(1) of the 1961 Muslim Family Laws Ordinance.

39 Art. 21 of Law 1/2000.

untouched.[40] In Egypt, the Supreme Constitutional Court was called upon to decide a combined set of lawsuits, one filed by a woman petitioning the court to certify her status of divorcee, and the other filed by her former husband to enjoin her to fulfill conjugal duties. According to Egyptian law, evidence of a denied unilateral divorce (*talâq 'ind al-inkâr*) could only be its registration (*al-ishhâd wa-l-tawthîq*), but the Court recognized that the divorce had taken place according to Islamic law (*shar'an*) and declared the restriction of evidentiary rules unconstitutional. Both courts navigated the porous boundary between *fiqh* and *siyâsah*, *sharî'ah* and *qânûn*, and both tried to retain in principle the registration requirement while acknowledging that classical Islamic law is the ultimate authority on the validity of *talâq*, not state legislation.[41]

The societal shift from the extended family model of classical *fiqh* to the conjugal family of modern *qânûn* can be considered the root of the thorny reforms of inheritance law in both Egypt and Pakistan. Legislatures, however, employed different strategies to address the issue of the inheritance of the children of the predeceased child of the propositus. Survival of a male child of the propositus bars all orphaned grandchildren from inheriting according to classical (Sunni) Islamic law. Egypt disposed by law an automatic bequest in favor of the orphaned grandchildren (*al-wasiyyah al-wâjibah*), while Pakistan established that predeceased children be considered alive at the death of the predecessor for inheritance purposes.

On the one hand, the Egyptian solution has the limit of the disposable third and severely restricting the liberty of the propositus to dispose of the assets, yet it has the advantage of never having been considered against *sharî'ah* as even in a number of *fiqh* treatises the bequest in favor of the orphaned grandchild is qualified as recommended; the Egyptian legislature simply changed the qualification of such a bequest from recommended to obligatory (obligatory *qânûnan*, however, not *shar'an*, obviously), and many other countries in the region followed suit. On the other hand, the Pakistani solution introducing the principle of representation—a principle alien to classical Islamic law—affected the allotment of shares to other heirs, thus generating a host of extravagant interpretations and the accusation of affecting the right to the fixed share, one of the pillars of the Islamic inheritance system according to *fiqh*. The Federal Shariat Court[42] declared the provision

40 W. Menski, *Comparative Law in a Global Context: The Legal Systems of Asia and Africa* (New York: Cambridge University Press, 2006), 376–8.

41 G. P. Parolin, 'La sharî'a nella giurisprudenza della Corte costituzionale suprema egiziana. La sentenza del 15 gennaio 2006, n. 113/XXVI,' in M. Papa, G.M. Piccinelli, and D. Scolart (eds.), *Il libro e la bilancia : studi in memoria di Francesco Castro* 2 (Naples: Edizioni Scientifiche Italiane, 2011), 929–48.

42 The jurisdiction of the Federal Shariat Court was established by a reversal of the earlier strict interpretation of the constitutional provision by the Shariat Bench of the Supreme Court. Supreme Court (Shariat Bench) (Pakistan) of 13 June 1993 in *Dr. Mahmood-ur-Rahman Faisal v. Government of Pakistan.* See L. Carroll, 'Orphaned Grandchildren

contrary to Islamic regulations, and allowed the government a deadline to take action.[43] By doing so, the Court did not settle a dispute in favor of *sharî'ah*; rather it recognized that the state is the legitimate intermediary between *sharî'ah* and society, and that law (*qânûn*) is its proper instrument. The same surprising approach was maintained in late 2010 when the Court struck down the abrogation by the 2006 Women's Protection Act of the overriding clauses of the *zinâ* and *qadhf* Ordinances of 1979.[44]

Despite the remarkable differences in provisions, court structure and composition, and plans of Islamicization, convergence of the Egyptian and Pakistani experiences coupled with counterintuitive divergent solutions suggests that an assessment of the position of *sharî'ah* within the legal sources of modern states needs to be based on a 'formula' that is not necessarily the constitutional provision. As experiences at the ends of the spectrum seem to indicate, the 'formula' might lie in a certain trajectory of the relations between *fiqh* and *siyâsah*, *sharî'ah* and *qânûn*.

A Dynamic Formula?

Constitutional provisions on *sharî'ah* need to be situated in the context of the post-modern development of religious/secular law dynamics. The trajectory is clear. In the pre-modern setting, religious law (*fiqh*) defined the areas it regulated and left the rest to secular law (*siyâsah*). Modernity redefined the boundaries, with secular law (*qânûn*) appropriating significant areas of religious law (*sharî'ah*), but recognizing the latter's primacy in the area of personal status. An ensuing development witnessed a further penetration of secular law (*qânûn*) into the stronghold of religious law (*sharî'ah*), regulating elements that did not touch the 'essentials' of *sharî'ah*, thus introducing a hierarchy within *sharî'ah* provisions. The distinction between 'essentials' and 'particulars' of *sharî'ah* redefined the boundaries for a third time, representing the second major paradigm shift after modernity; secular law advances in the modern domain of *sharî'ah* in the presence of 'particulars', but in the presence of 'essentials' secular law needs to retreat from the domain it had claimed with the advent of modernity.

---

in Islamic Law of Succession: Reform and Islamization in Pakistan,' 5 *Islamic Law and Society* 3 (1 January 1998). 409–447.

43 Federal Shariat Court (Pakistan) of 5 January 2000 in *Rehmat Khan v. Federation of Pakistan* (S.P. No.32/I/1993). For an analysis of the FSC decision, see Carroll, 'The Pakistan Federal Shariat Court, Section 4 of the Muslim Family Laws Ordinance, and the Orphaned Grandchild,' 9 *Islamic Law and Society* 1 (1 January 2002), 70–82.

44 Federal Shariat Court (Pakistan) of 22 December 2010 in *Mian Abdul Razzaq Amer v. Federation of Pakistan* (Sh.P. No.1/I/2007). It allowed the government six months to take action.

The introduction of constitutional provisions on *sharî'ah* (as interpreted by higher courts), rather than a limitation to state powers, enabled the latter powers to significantly extend their reach in the heart of *sharî'ah* while potentially withdrawing only from a very limited number of areas. Moreover, these provisions empowered state institutions (primarily higher courts) to define what is 'essential' and what 'particular' in *sharî'ah*, and thus freely regulate the latter. Rather than a 'constitutional Islamization,' the introduction of such provisions served as a legitimization strategy for state authorities. Even where Islamicization of laws had been planned and implemented, it did not depend on the constitutional provision and was carried out by state authorities.

Scenarios

As mentioned earlier, the ambiguities of the constitutional provisions on *sharî'ah* are a key element of their success. In systems where personal status is determined by the confessional affiliation of the citizen, a provision on *sharî'ah* is deemed necessary to avoid constitutional challenges for violation of the principle of equality before the law. Would not a clause establishing Islam be sufficient to guarantee the application of different confessional laws to citizens? If that indeed is the case, constitutional provisions on *sharî'ah* need to be interpreted as defining a certain combination of secular and confessional law relations.

Based on the current interpretation given by higher courts, the provisions are enabling rather than restricting state authorities in their regulation of *sharî'ah*-relevant sectors. The same provisions, however, could also allow for an unlikely extension of the principles of *sharî'ah* beyond the scope of *fiqh* and into *siyâsah*, along the lines of the theory of *siyâsah shar'iyyah* – an interpretation now unwarranted by the observation of the trajectory of secular/confessional law, but yet admissible on the basis of the text of the constitutional provisions on *sharî'ah*.

Broader elements of the setting need to be considered in order to assess possible variations of the current constructions of the provisions. Particularly significant are considerations of whether swelling identity politics will be satisfied by the sheer presence of the provisions, or if a re-drawing of the borders of the playing field based on a different compromise than the one reached with the advent of modernity will be required; if religious elites will stage a come-back reacquiring their lost independence and authority; whether the classical methodology of *fiqh* will be rejuvenated, a new methodology developed, or rather the field left to the intervention of state authorities through *siyâsah*; and if requirements to sit on the benches of higher courts when adjudicating on *sharî'ah* provisions will be modified.

Chapter 6
Constitutional Protections and Limits to Religious Freedom

Johan D. van der Vyver

Religious freedom in the broad sense includes four basic principles:

1. freedom of religion or belief, which is an individual right and includes (a) the right to believe, and (b) the right to manifest one's religion or belief in teaching, practice, worship and observance;
2. freedom from discrimination based on religion or belief, which is an individual right and includes (a) an obligation of the state to display in its laws and practices neutrality toward all religions, and (b) an obligation of the state to outlaw unfair discrimination and to take action against persons who discriminates in the public sphere against persons on grounds of religion;
3. the right to self-determination of religious communities, which is a collective group right (it vests in individuals as members of the religious community) and includes (a) the right to practice one's religion, in association with other members of the religious community, and (b) the right to form, join and maintain religious associations;
4. sphere sovereignty of religious institutions, which is an institutional group right (the right vests in a religious institution as such) and which requires of the state not to interfere in the internal affairs of religious institutions.

Every one of these components of freedom of religion, except the right to believe, is subject to limitations. For example the manifestation of religion or belief may be subjected to limitations in the interest of public safety, for the protection of public order, or for the protection of the rights and freedoms of other persons; freedom from discrimination does not implicate differentiations in law based on religion or belief in cases where the religious base of the differentiation is truly relevant to the purpose to be served by the differentiation; the right to self-determination does not protect religious rituals or practices of religious communities that threaten the life or bodily integrity of any member of the religious community, such as female genital mutilation, the killing of persons believed to be witches, or ritual murders.

I propose, for purposes of 'this discussion, to deal in some detail with the constitutional limitations that attach to the sphere sovereignty of religious institutions; I shall confine my analysis to the constitutional systems of Germany and South Africa. First, though, a few introductory comments for the sake of conceptual clarity.

Conceptual Specificity

Freedom of religion, belief and opinion is by its very nature an individual right that can be exercised by 'everyone', either individually or in community with other (individual) members of a religious community. Freedom of religion can also take on the form of a collective group right; that is to say, a right that vests in an individual in the capacity of belonging to a particular category of persons, such as the rights of a child (the repository of such a right is an individual, but one that falls within the category of persons under the age of 18 years).[1] The right to self-determination of a religious community is a typical example of a collective group right within the range of religious freedom.[2]

These freedoms must be clearly distinguished from the competence of a group entity, such as a church institution, to regulate and administer its internal affairs without interference by outside forces, including the agencies of state authority. The entitlement of private educational institutions or religious organizations to determine whom to admit within their ranks, whom to employ for the exercise of their calling, or what conditions to apply for the rendering of their services, vests in the institution or organization as such. It is by its very nature an institutional group right.[3]

A distinction should be made between the exercise of power by an organization in virtue of a concession granted to it by another organization on the one hand, and the exercise of internal authority by an organization as of right on the other. Contemporary Calvinism refers to the first instance of domestic authority as a matter of autonomy, and the second as a matter of internal sphere sovereignty.[4] Autonomy in this sense is confined to instances where the organization granting the power of domestic governance, and the recipient of such a grant, function within the enclave of a single social structure. The institution entrusted with autonomous power invariably forms part of an overarching organization that grants the power and is essentially structured as a subordinate part of that overarching organization.

1 See J. D. van der Vyver, *Leuven Lectures on Religious Institutions, Religious Communities and Rights* (Leuven: Peeters, 2004), 72 (defining the concept of collective group rights).

2 Van der Vyver, *Leuven Lectures*, 77.

3 Van der Vyver, *Leuven Lectures* (defining the concept of institutional group rights).

4 Van der Vyver, *Leuven Lectures*, 43–45; and see also J.D. van der Vyver, 'Sphere Sovereignty of Religious Institutions: A Contemporary Calvinistic Theory of Church-State Relations', in G. Robbers (ed.), *Church Autonomy: A Contemporary Survey* (Frankfurt am Main: Peter Lang, 2001), 645, 656; J.D. van der Vyver, 'The Jurisprudential Legacy of Abraham Kuyper and Leo XIII', 5 *Markets & Morality* (2002), 211, 220–221; J.D. van der Vyver, 'Book Review: Culture and Equality: An Egalitarian Critique of Multiculturalism by Brian Barry', 17 *Connecticut Journal of International Law* (2002), 323, 329–30.

Autonomous powers may thus be afforded by a central governmental institution to regional and local political authorities within the domain of a single body politic. Autonomous powers may similarly be entrusted by the central power base of a church institution to subordinate local congregations.

Sphere sovereignty, on the other hand, implies the relationship between two or more structurally distinct social entities, such as church and state.[5] Here the internal sphere of competencies of the respective institutions is not dependent on a concession of the other but belongs to each one in its own right and is founded on its existence and functioning as an independent component of human society. Quite often, constitutional provisions relating to freedom of religion or belief seem to suggest that the entitlements of religious institutions is a matter of autonomy while these entitlements ought to be treated as instances of sphere sovereignty.

The Status of Religious Organizations in Germany

The status of churches and other religious institutions in Germany is governed by the Church Clauses (*die Kirchenartikel*) in the Weimar Constitution of 11 August 1919,[6] which were incorporated into the German Constitution by Article 140 of the *Grundgesetz für die Bundesrepublik* Deutschland of 1949.[7] Article 137(3) of the Weimar Constitution provides as follows:'Religious societies shall regulate and administer their affairs independently within the limits of the law that applies to all. They shall confer their offices without the participation of the state or the civil community.'[8]

The principle embodied in this provision is commonly referred to as 'the right to self-determination of churches' (*das kirchlichen Selbstbestimmungsrechts*).[9] Its details were specified in a judgment of the *Bundesverfassungsgericht* of 1985[10]

5 Van der Vyver, *Leuven Lectures*, 32–33, 41–43; Van der Vyver, 'The Jurisprudential Legacy of Abraham Kuyper and Leo XIII', 217–218.

6 *Die Verfassung des Deutschen Rechts* (1919), arts. 137–141 [hereinafter 'Weimar Constitution'].

7 *Grundgesetz für die Bundesrepublik Deutschland*, art. 140 (entered into force on 23 May 1949) (incorporating the provisions of arts. 136–139 and 140 into the *Grundgesetz*).

8 Weimar Constitution, art. 137(3): 'Jede Religionsgesellschaft ordnet und verwaltet ihre Angelegenheiten selbständig innerhalb der Schranken des für alle geltenden Gesetzes. Sie verleiht ihre Ämter ohne Mittwirkung des Staates oder der bürgerlichen Gemeinschaft.'

9 *Selbstbestimmungsrecht* as exemplified by the Weimar Constitution must not be confused with the right to self-determination of contemporary international law. The right to self-determination of contemporary international law does include the right of members of religious communities to practice their religion, and to form, join, and maintain religious associations (see Constitution of the Republic of South Africa, 1996, sec. 31(1)(a) and (b)). It does not include the right of religious institutions to regulate and administer their own internal affairs. This is a matter of sphere sovereignty.

10 BVerfGE 70, 138 – Loyalitätspflicht (4 June 1985).

in an appeal against two decisions of the German Federal Labor Court relating to (a) the dismissal of a medical doctor in a Catholic hospital in Essen,[11] and (b) the dismissal of an accountant at a Catholic youth hostel in München.[12] The doctor was dismissed because he publicly testified to his personal view on abortions (which was in conflict with official church policy on the matter), and the accountant because he defected from the Catholic Church.

The *Bundesverfassungsgericht* decided that the provisions of Article 137(3) of the Weimar Constitution do not only apply to churches and their independent components, but also to other institutions, irrespective of their legal construction, which in view of their purpose and disposition, are self-evidently, according to perceptions of the church, associated with the church in a certain way and which can be required to undertake and to execute a component of the church's calling.[13] The constitutional guarantee of the right to self-determination remains of vital importance for purposes of specifying these labor relations, and includes the competence of churches to require of their employees to uphold the prevailing principles of the religious and ethical doctrines of the church.[14] Employees of churches are accordingly bound to uphold 'loyalty commitments' (*Loyalitätsobliegenheiten*) toward the church and the principles it stands for.[15]

Churches, like all other persons, must execute their freedom of contract subject to the labor laws of the state.[16] This does not mean, however, that the labor law of the state will necessarily in all instances trump the right to self-determination of a church.[17] It is therefore necessary to strike a balance between the conflicting interests inherent in obligatory labor practices and the demands of ecclesiastical autonomy, and in this process a special premium is to be placed on the personal image or self-esteem of churches (*Selbstverständnis der Kirchen*).[18]

---

11 2 AZR 591/80 and 2 AZR 628/80 (21 October 1982).

12 7 AZR 249/81 (23 March 1984).

13 BVerfGE70,138,para.B.II.1a):'DieseSelbstordnungs-undSelbstverwaltungsgarantie kommt nicht nur den verfaßten Kirchen und deren rechtlich selbständigen Teilen zugute, sondern allen der Kirche in bestimmter Weise zugeordneten Einrichtungen ohne Rücksicht auf ihre Rechtsform, wenn sie nach kirchlichem Selbstverständnis ihrem Zweck oder ihrer Aufgabe entsprechend berufen sind, ein Stück des Auftrags der Kirche wahrzunemen und zu erfüllen.'

14 BverfGE 70, 138, para. B.II.1d): 'Die Verfassungsgarantie des Selbstbestimmungsrechts bleibt für die Gestaltung dieser Arbeitsverhältnisse wesenlich … Dazu gehört weiter die Befugnis der Kirche, den ihr angehörenden Arbeitsnehmern die Beachtung jedenfalls der tragenden Grundsätze der kirchlichen Glaubens- und Sittenlehre aufzuerlegen …'

15 See, for example, BverfGE 70, 138, para. Apr, and A.2.

16 BverfGE 70, 138, para. B.II.1e).

17 BverfGE 70, 138.

18 BverfGE 70, 138: 'Dabei ist dem Selbstverständnis der Kirchen ein besonderes Gewicht beizumessen.'

It after all remains constitutional to leave it up the church itself to take binding decisions as to what 'the credibility of the Church and the advocacy thereof' requires, what constitutes 'specific ecclesiastical matters', what the 'closeness' of such matters entails, what is included in the 'essential principles of faith-related and ethical doctrine', and what should be regarded as — at times, serious — violations of these doctrines.[19]

The Impact of the European Convention of Human Rights on Church 'Autonomy' in Germany

On September 23, 2010, the European Court of Human Rights (ECtHR) handed down judgments in two distinct cases based on similar facts but which came to opposite conclusions. The applicants in both cases were employees of church institutions and were dismissed, again in both instances, because they were involved in extra-marital relations.[20] The complaint against their dismissal was essentially based on Article 8 of the European Convention for the Protection of Human Rights and Fundamental Freedoms, which protects the right of everyone 'to respect for his private and family life, his home and his correspondence.'[21]

The dismissal of Michael Heinz Obst, Director for Europe in the Department of Public Relations of The Church of Jesus Christ of Latter-day Saints (the Mormon Church), was upheld by the ECtHR on the basis that the labor courts of Germany, in reviewing the legality of his dismissal, adequately considered the impact of the applicant's discharge on his personal and family life.[22] The ECtHR noted that the effect on the personal and family life of the applicant would be minimal, given the fact that Mr. Obst was still relatively young and should be able to find alternative employment without too much hassle.[23] The ECtHR also noted that Mr. Obst, upon accepting the position of Director for Europe was, or should have been, aware of the special premium placed by the Mormon Church on marital fidelity.[24] His dismissal by the Mormon Church could therefore not be faulted.

---

19 BverfGE 70, 138, para. B.2a): 'Es bleibt danach grundsätzlich den verfaßten Kirchen überlassen, verbindlich zu bestimmen, was 'die Glaubwürdigkeit der Kirche und ihrer Verkündigung erfordert', was 'spezifisch kirchliche Aufgaben' sind, was 'Nähe' zu ihnen bedeutet, welches die 'wesentlichen Grundsätze der Glaubens- und Sittenlehre' sind und was als — gegebenenfalls schwerer — Verstoß gegen diese anzusehen ist.'

20 *Obst c. Allemagne*, App. No. 4205/03, 23 September 2010; *Schüth c. Allemagne*, App. No.1620/03, 23 September 2010.

21 European Convention for the Protection of Human Rights and Fundamental Freedoms, art. 8, 213 U.N.T.S 222, entered into force on 3 September 1953 [hereinafter 'European Convention'].

22 *Obst*, para. 49.

23 *Obst*, para. 48.

24 *Obst*, para. 50.

In the case of Bernhard Josef Schüth, organist and choir master of the Catholic congregation of St. Lambert in Essen, Germany, the ECtHR came to the opposite conclusion. The marriage of Mr. Schüth had broken down in 1995; he subsequently lived with another woman in an extra-marital relationship, and at the time of his dismissal by the church, that other woman expected his baby. The ECtHR paid special attention to the question whether or not the labor courts of Germany considered the impact of his dismissal on his personal and family life, and noted that the legal protection afforded to the rights of the applicant by the European Convention was never mentioned in proceedings before the labor courts.[25] The labor courts consequently failed to strike a balance between the interests of the Catholic Church and the rights of the applicant.[26] The signature of Mr. Schüth on his contract of employment cannot be interpreted as an indisputable undertaking to lead a life of abstinence following the break-up of his marriage or in the event of a divorce.[27] The fact that the applicant would only have limited opportunities to find alternative employment received special emphasis in the opinion of the ECtHR (at the time, he had a temporary job at a Protestant congregation).[28] Since the labor court neglected to strike a balance between the rights of the applicant in respect of his private and family life and the interests of the church, the ECtHR decided that respect for the private and family life of Mr. Schüth, as protected by Article 8 of the European Convention, had been violated. His discharge consequently constituted a violation of the European Convention.

More recently, in *Siebenhaar v. Germany*, the ECtHR reiterated the principles outlined in *Obst* and *Schüth*.[29] In this instance, though, the applicant's rights in contention were based on the freedom of thought, conscience and religion guaranteed by Article 9 of the European Convention. Astrid Siebenhaar was employed by a day-care center of a congregation in Pforzheim of the Evangelical (Lutheran) Church, and she was discharged by church authorities when they were alerted to the fact that she was a member of the Universal Church of Humanism and in fact also conducted primary education classes within that religious sect. The ECtHR, following the same reasoning as in *Obst*, decided that her dismissal did not amount to a violation of the freedom of religion provisions of the European Convention.

It must be emphasized that the ECtHR does not have jurisdiction over either the Mormon Church or the Roman Catholic Church or the Lutheran Church. It can only adjudicate compliance by High Contracting Parties (Member States of the Council of Europe) with their obligations under the European Convention.

However, the ECtHR has developed the 'doctrine of positive obligation', based on Article 1 of the European Convention, which provides: 'The High Contracting

25 *Schüth*, para. 67.
26 *Schüth*, para. 74.
27 *Schüth*, para. 71.
28 *Schüth*, para. 73.
29 *Siebenhaar c. Allemagne*, App. No. 18136/02, 3 February 2011.

Parties shall secure to everyone within their jurisdiction the rights and freedoms defined in ... this Convention.'[30] In virtue of this provision, High Contracting Parties are not only obliged to refrain from human rights violations through state action, they must also put laws and procedures in place that will protect the rights and freedoms of their nationals against infringement by non-state actors.[31] In *Obst*, the ECtHR referred to the principle of positive obligation as 'the adoption of measures aimed at respect for the private life, even in mutual relations between individuals,'[32] and it added that 'it is required of the State, as a component of its positive obligation under Article 8, to recognize the complainant's right to respect for his private and family life as against measures enforced by the Mormon Church for his dismissal.'[33] Germany complied with its positive obligation by establishing labor courts and by making provision for the review of judgments of those courts by the Federal Constitutional Court (*das Bundesverfassungsgericht*),[34] and further by affording to the applicant the opportunity to take his case to a labor court in order to contest the legality of his dismissal in view of the rights associated with his ecclesiastical duties and by balancing his competing interests up against those of the church.[35] In *Obst*, the ECtHR decided that Germany, through its labor courts, complied with its positive obligation by taking into account the right of the applicant to his private and family life and violation thereof by the Mormon Church; and in *Siebenhaar* the ECtHR came to a similar conclusion, holding that the German labor courts adequately considered the effect of the applicant's dismissal in relation to her freedom of religion.

In *Schüth*, the ECtHR came to the opposite conclusion. The labor court did not balance the entire scope of the conflicting interests that were in issue. It made no mention of the family life of the applicant,[36] and 'the interests of the ecclesiastical employer was not weighed up against the right of the applicant to respect for his private and family life as guaranteed by Article 8 of the European Convention, but [the labor court] only considered his interests of remaining in the employ

30 European Convention, art 1.

31 See, for example, *HLR v. France*, App. No. 24573/94 , 29 April 1997, para. 40; *A v. The United Kingdom*, App. No. 25599/94, 23 September 1998, para. 22. Many years ago, an American court also seemed to subscribe to the same idea by proclaiming: 'Denying includes inaction as well as action, ... the omission to protect, as well as the omission to pass laws for protection.' *United States v. Hall*, 26 F.Cas. 79, 81 (C.C.S.D. Ala. 1871). However, the principle of state action was the one that prevailed in the United States.

32 *Obst*, para. 41 ('l'adoption de mesures visant au respect de la vie privée jusque dans les relations des individus entre eux.'); and see also *Schüth*, para. 55; *Siebenhaar*, para. 38.

33 *Obst*, para. 43 ('l'Etat était tenu, dans le cadre de ses obligations positives découlant de l'article 8, de reconnaître au requérant le droit au respect de sa vie privée contre la mesure de licenciement prononcée par l'Eglise mormone.'); and see also *Schüth*, para. 57; *Siebenhaar*, para. 40.

34 *Obst*, para. 45; *Schüth*, para. 59; *Siebenhaar*, para. 42.

35 *Obst*, para. 45; *Schüth*, para. 59; *Siebenhaar*, para. 42.

36 *Schüth*, para. 67.

of the Church.'[37] Therefore, the protection afforded to him did not comply with the positive obligation of Germany as a High Contracting Party to the European Convention.

The question that had to be decided by the ECtHR was therefore not primarily whether or not the Mormon or Catholic or Lutheran Churches violated the Convention provisions relating to the right of everyone to respect for their private and family life,[38] or with a view to freedom of religion,[39] but whether Germany adequately secured that right and freedom from infringement by the churches concerned. Proceedings in the German labor courts, and not the discriminatory practices of the concerned churches, were therefore in issue.

The judgment of the ECtHR in *Obst*, *Schüth* and *Siebenhaar* added a particular dimension to the principles which Germany is required to demand of its labor courts: the effects of dismissal of an employee, for whatever reason, on the personal and family life, or on religious freedom, of the employee. This particular constraint on the constitutional right of church institutions to require loyalty of its workers with regard to the principles and practices upheld by the church as part of its confession of faith seems to place a special burden on the 'right to self-determination' of religious institutions. It might happen that church institution are constrained, in view of human rights standards deriving from the European Convention, to put up with the services of someone who commits marital infidelity (*Obst* and *Schüth*), who turns out to be an active member of a sect whose beliefs and practices are at odds with those of the employer church (*Siebenhaar*), who publicly contradict established dogma of the church (2 AZR 591/80 and 2 AZR 628/80), or who terminates his or her membership of the church (7 AZR 249/81). On the other hand, though, labor courts are only required to take account of the effect of the dismissal of an employee on his or her personal and family life, or on his or her freedom of religion, and to ask themselves whether the consequences of the employee's conduct with regard to the spiritual calling of the church was really of such a nature as to justify the negative effects his or her dismissal would have on his or her personal and family life or religious freedom. It might turn out that the game was after all not worth the candle.

The judgments of the ECtHR will clearly have an impact on future proceedings in the German labor courts. On 8 September 2011, a Labor Court was perhaps over cautious when called upon to evaluate the dismissal oh a medical superintendant at a Catholic hospital who was dismissed following his civil divorce (which was not recognized by the church) and his re-marriage (regarded by the church as invalid).[40] The doctor was indeed required by his contract of employment to

37 *Schüth*, para. 67 ('Les intérèts de l'Eglise employeur n'ont ainsi pas été mis en balance avec le droit du requérent au respect de sa vie privée et familiale, garanti par l'article 8 de la Convention, mais uniquement avec son intérêt d'être maintenu dans son emploi.')

38 European Convention, art. 8.

39 European Convention, art. 9.

40 2 AZR 543/10.

accept and to uphold the basic principles embodied in the religious and moral doctrines of the church. However, the Labor Court decided that the doctor's dismissal would only be justified if, upon balancing the conflicting interests of both parties to the dispute, violation of the loyalty commitment that went with his office and implicated by the Catholic verdict pronouncing his second marriage to be null and void was found to carry sufficient weight ('[hat] ein hinreichend schweres Gewicht'). The Labor Court decided that the dismissal of the doctor was unjustified and upheld his complaint.

Freedom of Religion or Belief in South Africa

The current South African Constitution can in general be described, as far as religion and religious diversity are concerned, as one of profound toleration and accommodation. It in general allocates to church institutions the rights in the Bill of Rights to the extent required by the nature of the right and the nature of the church as a legal person;[41] it guarantees the free exercise of religion;[42] it sanctions freedom of assembly[43] and freedom of association[44] of '[e]veryone'; it guarantees the right to self-determination of religious communities,[45] and makes provision for a Commission for the Promotion and Protection of the Rights of Cultural, Religious and Linguistic Communities;[46] it envisions the establishment, by means of national legislation, of a Pan South African Language Board charged, *inter alia,* with promoting and ensuring respect for 'Arabic, Hebrew, Sanskrit and other languages used for religious purposes in South Africa.'[47]

The Constitutional Court on several occasions emphasized the vital importance *for the state* of religion as a component of South Africa's constitutional democracy. In a case instructing the legislature to amend a provision in the Marriage Act that was based on the common-law definition of a marriage as 'a union of one man with one woman, to the exclusion, while it lasts, of all others,' in order to make allowance for same-sex marriages,[48] the Constitutional Court was confronted with *amicus* briefs claiming, with reference to texts from the Old and the New Testament, that from a religious perspective 'the institution of marriage simply

41 Constitution of the Republic of South Africa, 1996, sec. 8(4) [hereinafter 'SA Constitution'].

42 SA Constitution, sec. 15(1).

43 SA Constitution, sec. 17.

44 SA Constitution, sec. 18.

45 SA Constitution, sec. 31.

46 SA Constitution, secs. 181(1)(c) and 185-86; and see Commission for the Promotion and Protection of the Rights of Cultural, Religious and Linguistic Communities Act 19 of 2002.

47 SA Constitution, sec. 6(5)(b)(ii).

48 *Minister of Home Affairs v. Fourie; Lesbian and Gay Equality Project v. Minister of Home Affairs*, 2006 (1) SA 524; 2006 (3) BCLR 355 (CC) (South Africa).

cannot sustain the intrusion of same-sex unions.'[49] Justice Albie Sachs, delivering the unanimous decision of the Court, noted the many difficulties attending 'the relationship foreshadowed by the Constitution between the sacred and the secular.'[50] He went on to say:

> Religious bodies play a large and important part in public life, through schools, hospitals and poverty relief programmes. They command ethical behaviour from their members and bear witness to the exercise of power by State and private agencies; they promote music, art and theatre; they provide halls for community activities, and conduct a great variety of social activities for their members and the general public. They are part of the fabric of public life, and constitute active elements of the diverse and pluralistic nation contemplated by the Constitution. Religion is not just a question of belief or doctrine. It is part of the people's temper and culture, and for many believers a significant part of their way of life. Religious organizations constitute important sectors of national life and accordingly have a right to express themselves to government and the courts on the great issues of the day. They are active participants in public affairs fully entitled to have their say with regard to the way law is made and applied.[51]

The state of affairs relating to the sovereignty of religious institutions, as regulated by the Constitution of the Republic of South Africa, 1996, offers a commendable comparison with the comparable situation in Germany. In the South African constitutional dispensation, equality is a preferred right.

Comparative analyses should be sensitive to distinct foundational predilections that permeate the human rights regime of the different jurisdictions being surveyed. Every system of human rights protection is founded on, or affords special prominence to, a particular basic norm – *die Grundnorm* – of the entire rights regime: in the United States, the First Amendment freedoms with special prominence being afforded to freedom of speech; in Germany, human dignity; in Canada, perhaps, the principle of equal protection.[52]

Equal protection and the proscription of discrimination is without doubt the *Grundnorm* of the South African constitutional dispensation. Given the history of racial discrimination in that country, this stands to reason. The Constitution defines the 'new South Arica' as 'an open and democratic society based on human dignity, equality and freedom.'[53] In a recent judgment of the Constitutional Court, Justice

---

49 *Fourie*, para. 88.

50 *Fourie*, para. 89.

51 *Fourie*, para. 93.

52 J.D. van der Vyver, 'Constitutional Protection of Children and Young Persons', in J.A. Robinson (ed.), *The Law of Children and Young Persons* (Durban: Butterworths, 1997), 265, 282; J.D. van der Vyver, 'Limitations of Freedom of Religion or Belief: International Law Perspectives', 19 *Emory International Law Review* (2005), 499, 508.

53 SA Constitution, sec. 39(1)(a), and see also secs. 1(a), 7(1), 36(1).

Froneman stated, with a view to this provision: 'Equality, together with dignity and freedom, lie at the heart of the Constitution.'[54] The Constitution accordingly protects the equality of everyone before the law and 'the right to equal protection and benefit of the law,'[55] subject, though, to remedial action 'to protect or advance persons, or categories of persons, disadvantaged by unfair discrimination' of the past.[56] It prohibits unfair discrimination, directly or indirectly, by the state and by other persons based on 'race, gender, sex, pregnancy, marital status, ethnic or social origin, colour, sexual orientation, age, disability, religion, conscience, belief, culture, language and birth,' or on other similar grounds.[57] The constitutional right to equality is therefore 'foundational to the open and democratic society envisaged by the Constitution.'[58] It is 'a core and fundamental value; a standard that must inform all law and against which all law must be tested for constitutional consonance.'[59]

The special significance of the basic norm emerges when different constitutionally protected rights and freedoms come into conflict with one another. One should in such cases always try to reconcile the conflicting rights and freedoms, but where that becomes too challenging the provision that is most supportive of the basic norm will prevail. In our discussions today, the question is exactly how to construe a fair balance between the dictates of sphere sovereignty and equality.

The constitutional proscription of unfair discrimination in South Africa is, for purposes of the present survey, quite unique in two special respects: (a) sexual orientation is included as one of the grounds that would render differentiations for legal purposes a matter of unfair discrimination (unless it can be proven that the differentiation 'is reasonable and justifiable in an open and democratic society based on human dignity, equality and freedom'[60]); and (b) the Constitution also makes provision for the proscription of discrimination by persons and institutions other than the state. To this latter end, the Promotion of Equality and Prevention of Unfair Discrimination Act was enacted in 2002.[61] Since the Act 'binds the State and

54 *Bengwenyana Minerals (Pty.) Ltd. & others v. Genorah Resources (Pty.) Ltd.*, Case No. CCT 39/10 [2010] ZACC 26 930 (November 2010) (South Africa).

55 SA Constitution, sec. 9(1).

56 SA Constitution, sec. 9(2).

57 SA Constitution, secs. 9(3) and (4); and see also the Promotion of Equality and Prevention of Unfair Discrimination Act 4 of 2000, sec. 1(xxii) 'prohibited grounds' para. (a) [hereinafter 'Act 4 of 2000'].

58 *Strydom v. Nederduitse Gereformeerde Gemeente, Moreleta Park*, 2009 (4) SA 510, para. 14 (Equality Court, TPA) (South Africa); and see also *Prince v. President, Cape Law Society & others*, 2002 (2) SA 794; 2002 (3) BCLR 231, para. 49 (CC) (South Africa).

59 *Minister of Finance & another v. Van Heerden*, 2004 (6) SA 121, para. 22 (CC) (South Africa); and see also *Minister of Education & another v. Syfert Trust Ltd. & another*, 2006 (4) SA 205, para. 31 (CC) (South Africa); *Strydom* 2009 (4) SA, para. 10.

60 SA Constitution, sec. 36(1).

61 Act 4 of 2000, supra note 57.

all persons'[62] and proclaims that '[n]either the State nor any person may unfairly discriminate against any person,' one might expect that discrimination by religious organizations based on gender or sexual orientation has been outlawed for all ends and purposes in South Africa. And let it not pass unnoticed that persons under an obligation to uphold the provisions of the Bill of Rights, including the dictates of equality and non-discrimination, include 'a natural or a juristic person if, and to the extent that, it is applicable, taking into account the nature of the right and the nature of the duty imposed by the right.'[63]

The prohibition of unfair discriminatory practices by the state, as well as by private individuals and group entities (legal persons other than the state), is included in the constitutional proscription of discrimination. Drafters of the 1996 Constitution instructed the legislature to enact a law to afford substance to the prohibition of unfair discrimination by non-state perpetrators. The Promotion of Equality and Prevention of Unfair Discrimination Acts was enacted in 2000 to give effect to this instruction.

The Act singled out unfair discrimination based on race, gender, and disability for special scrutiny, but applies broadly to discrimination by the state and by non-state perpetrators. It thus deviated from the constitutional legislative intent in at least three respects:

1. It should be clear to everyone that the drafters' instruction only applied to unfair discrimination by non-state perpetrators,[64] yet the legislature included unfair discrimination by the state in its provisions.[65]
2. Drafters of the Constitution was sensitive to the fact that discrimination in the private sphere should be made subject to less, or other, limitations than those applying to discrimination by the state, but the legislature saw fit not to make that distinction.[66]
3. The proscription of unfair discrimination by the state and in the private sphere based on race, gender and disability were singled out by the legislature for special scrutiny and was subjected to limitations that do not apply to unfair discrimination on any of the other grounds specified in the Constitution.[67]

---

62 Act 4 of 2000, sec. 5(1).

63 SA Constitution, sec. 8(2).

64 The instruction that '[n]ational legislation *must be* enacted' (emphasis added) is part of Section 9(4) of the 1996 SA Constitution, which deals exclusively with unfair discrimination in the private sphere.

65 Act 4 of 2000, sec. 6 ('Neither the State nor any person may unfairly discriminate against any person').

66 Act 4 of 2000.

67 Act 4 of 2000, secs. 7-9.

In terms of the Act, discrimination based on gender includes 'any ... religious practice, which impairs the dignity of women and undermines equality between women and men'.[68] This provision clearly implicates the exclusion of women from ecclesiastical offices. Since gender is included in the list of grounds that *prima facie* renders differentiations for legal purposes to be a matter of unfair discrimination,[69] the burden of proof would be on a church institution to show that exclusion of women from ecclesiastical offices is in fact not 'unfair'.[70] The Act contains a long list of circumstances that may be considered in this regard, for example 'whether the discrimination reasonably and justifiably differentiates between persons according to objectively determinable criteria, intrinsic to the activity concerned',[71] 'the impact or likely impact of the discrimination on the complainant',[72] and 'whether the discrimination has a legitimate purpose'.[73] It does not seem as though these considerations would contribute to alleviate the burden of proof resting on a church institution in any way.

Imposing the constitutional proscription of unfair discrimination on, for example, religious institutions, was in a sense unfortunate. Many mainline churches still uphold age-old practices that amount to gender discriminate against women, and does one really want to entrust the state with the power and obligation to compel the Roman Catholic Church, the Greek Orthodox Church, or Jewish religious institutions, to ordain women as part of their clergy? Surely, that would amount to political totalitarianism, which 'becomes evident when State authority extends into the private enclave of non-State societal circles, such as family life, academic institutions and the sovereign sphere of the churches'.[74]

Implementation of the Equality Directive in Actual Practice

In spite of the Act, South African authorities have remained particularly sensitive to the internal sphere sovereignty of religious institutions.

Discrimination based on sexual orientation by a church institution was in issue in the case of *Strydom v. Dutch Reformed Congregation, Moreleta Park*, decided by the Equality Court, Transvaal Provincial Division on 27 August 2006.[75] Johan Daniel Strydom was employed by the Moreleta Park congregation as a music

68 Act 4 of 2000, sec. 8.

69 Act 4 of 2000, sec. 1(xxii).

70 Act 4 of 2000, sec. 13(2)(b)(ii).

71 Act 4 of 2000, sec. 14(2)(c).

72 Act 4 of 2000, sec. 14(3)(b).

73 Act 4 of 2000, sec. 14(3)(f).

74 J.D. van der Vyver, 'The Function of Legislation as an Instrument of Social Reform', 93 *South African Law Journal* (1976), 56, 66; and see also J.D. Van der Vyver, *Gelykberegtiging*, 61 *Journal of Contemporary Roman-Dutch Law* (1998) 367, 395.

75 *Strydom v. Dutch Reformed Congregation, Moreleta Park*, 2009 (4) SA.

instructor (organ teacher) in its Arts Academy. He was fired by the church authorities because he became involved in a same-sex relationship. Mr. Strydom challenged his dismissal before the Equality Court and was awarded compensation in the amount of R 75,000 for pain and suffering and a further R 11,000 for loss of income. The Reverent Dirkie van der Spuy of the Moreleta Park congregation testified that elders and deacons of the church may be gay but are not allowed to practice homosexuality. The dismissal of Mr. Strydom, according to the Equality Court, amounted to unbecoming discrimination under the Promotion of Equality and Prevention of Unfair Discrimination Act. The church did not take the matter on appeal.

The Equality Court based its decision mainly on the fact that Mr. Strydom (a) served as an independent contractor,[76] (b) was in no way involved in the spiritual activities of the church, and (c) was not even a member of the particular Dutch Reformed Church which brought suit in the matter.[77] The Equality Court made it abundantly clear that it would not have ruled against the church if Mr. Strydom's contractual obligations included functions that were part of the spiritual mission of the church. It referred in this regard to the exposition by a leading analyst of the religion clauses in the South African Constitution, Paul Farlam, of instances where the state ought not to interfere in the internal affairs of religious institutions, and cited (with approval) the following passage from the Farlam article:

> The first scenario involves discrimination against a person with *spiritual responsibilities* (such as a priest or a candidate for ordination). Few exercises are more central to religious freedom than the right of a church to choose its own spiritual leaders. If a court were to hold that churches could not deem sexual orientation, or any of the other enumerated ground in the equality clause, a disqualifying factor for the priesthood, the effect on many churches could be devastating. Consequently, although the value of equality is foundational to the new constitutional dispensation, it is unlikely that equality considerations could outweigh the enormous impact of failing to give churches an exemption in relation to their spiritual leaders. Where the appointment, dismissal and employment conditions of religious leaders (such as priests, imams, rabbis,

---

76 In South African labor law a distinction is made between an employee (someone who works for an employer and executes his or her contractual obligations under the constant command and control of the employer) and an independent contractor (someone who is hired to produce a certain service or deliver an end product without being under the command and control of the employer as to the manner in which he or she executes the contractual obligation).

77 The Churches denoted in English as Dutch Reformed actually comprise three quite distinct denominations (two distinct words in the Afrikaans language that are used to distinguish the three churches — 'Gereformeerd' and 'Hervormd' — can only be translated into English as 'Reformed'). The Plaintiff in this case was a congregation of the 'Nederduitse Gereformeerde Kerk' and Mr. Strydom was a member of the 'Nederduitsch Hervormde Kerk'.

> and so forth) are concerned, religious bodies are likely to be exempted from compliance with legislation prohibiting unfair discrimination.[78]

The substance of this citation – although it was included in the judgment merely as an *obiter dictum* – must be commended. It reflects the spirit thus far maintained in practices and court judgments dealing with domestic affairs of religious institutions.

For example, public benefit activities that are exempt from income tax include 'the promotion or practice of religion which encompasses acts of worship, witness, teaching and community service based on a belief in a deity,' as well as 'the promotion and/or practice of a belief,' and 'the promotion of, or engaging in, philosophical activities.'[79] There are many racially exclusive churches in South Africa,[80] but, to the best of my knowledge, no one of those has been denied tax exemptions.

The law that was enacted in 2006 to afford legal sanction to same-sex marriages (referred to in the Act as 'civil unions') contains a provision that affords the right to a marriage officers to inform the Minister of Home Affairs that they objects on grounds of conscience, religion and belief to solemnizing a civil union between persons of the same sex, whereupon the marriage officer cannot be compelled to solemnize such civil unions.[81]

In South Africa, courts of law will not 'embark upon an evaluation of the acceptability, logic, consistency or comprehensibility of … [religious] belief.'[82] However, should a conflict arise as to the legal rights and duties of parties to a dispute, a court will not decline to give a judgment in the matter by reason of doctrinal issues that might have a bearing on those rights and duties.[83] South African courts have thus entertained jurisdiction, following a schism, to decide

---

78 *Strydom*, para. 15, referring to P. Farlam, 'Freedom of Religion, Belief and Opinion', in S. Woolman et al. (eds.), 3 *Constitutional Law of South Africa* 41 (2nd edn., Revised Service, 2009), 47.

79 Income Tax Act 58 of 1962, Ninth Schedule, pt. I, para. 5.

80 Leaving aside adherents to Traditional African Religions and the many Independent Christian Churches in the African community (of which there are about 7000 varieties in South Africa), mention can be made of the *Afrikaanse Protestantse Kerk* (Afrikaans Protestant Church) which expressly reserves membership of the Church to whites only.

81 Civil Union Act 17 of 2006, sec. 6.

82 *Christian Education SA v. Minister of Education of the Government of the RSA*, 1999 (4) SA 1092, 1100; 1999 (9) BCLR 951 (SE) 958 (South Africa), upheld on appeal in *Christian Education v. Minister of Education*, 2000 (4) SA 757 (CC) (South Africa); and see *Taylor v. Kurtstag NO & Others*, 2005 (1) SA 362; 2005 (7) BCLR 705 (W), para. 61 (South Africa).

83 *Allen & Others NNO v. Gibbs & Others*, 1977 (3) SA 212 (SEC) 218 (South Africa).

which one of two religious factions was entitled to the use of a particular name,[84] or could lay claim to church property;[85] and they have taken decisions of an internal ecclesiastical tribunal on review.[86]

Religious institutions are particularly sensitive to the exercise of review powers by secular courts in regard to disciplinary proceedings of an ecclesiastical tribunal.[87] In South Africa, decisions of an ecclesiastical tribunal cannot be taken on appeal to a secular court, but such decisions are subject to review by a court of law.[88] The court exercising review powers will not interfere in the domestic affairs of the ecclesiastical institution duly constituted and operating in terms of its own rules, but will intervene if an ecclesiastical tribunal has failed to follow the internally prescribed procedural rules or acted *ultra vires*.[89] The tribunal must apply its mind to the matter and not take arbitrary decisions; it must remain within the confines of its authority and not act *ultra vires*; it must maintain good faith and not be motivated by malice, ill-will or spite; and it must act reasonably.[90]

In conducting disciplinary hearings, an ecclesiastical tribunal must uphold the 'elementary rules of justice.'[91] Emphasis is often placed on the right of a person under investigation to be heard in his or her own defense *(audi alteram partem),* but even then, the ultimate test is not *audi alteram partem* as such but 'the fairness of the process' in light of the nature of the proceedings.[92] The *audi alteram partem*

---

84 *Old Apostolic Church of Africa v. Non-White Old Apostolic Church of Africa*, 1975 (2) SA 684 (C) (South Africa).

85 *The Nederduitsche Hervormde Church v. The Nederduitsche Hervormde of Gereformeerde Church*, 10 Cape L.J. 327 (1893) (South Africa).

86 *Jamile v. African Congregational Church*, 1971 (3) SA 836 (D) (South Africa); *Theron v. Ring van Wellington van die NG Kerk in SA*, 1976 (2) SA 1 (A) (South Africa); *Taylor* 2005 (1) SA.

87 See M.J. Broyd, 'Forming Religious Communities and Respecting Dissenter's Rights: A Jewish Tradition for a Modern Society', in J. Witte Jr. & J.D. van der Vyver (eds.), *Religious Human Rights in Global Perspective: Religious Perspectives* (The Hague: Martinus Nijhoff, 1996), 203, 224 (noting that 'the question of membership in the colony of the Church should be beyond review of a secular court'), cited with approval in *Taylor* 2005 (1) SA, para. 43.

88 *Du Plessis v. Synod of the Dutch Reformed Church*, 1930 CPD 403, 420-21 (South Africa); *Taylor* 2005 (1) SA, para. 42.

89 *Odendaal v. Loggerenberg NNO (1)*, 1961 (1) SA 712 (0) 719 (South Africa); *Yiba & others v. African Gospel Church*, 1999 (2) SA 949 (CPD) 961 (South Africa); and see also *NGK in Afrika (OVS) v. Verenigde Geref. Kerk in Suider-Afrika*, 1999 (2) SA 156 (SCA) 170 (South Africa) (noting that the General Synod must comply with the internal rules of church law).

90 J.D. van der Vyver, 'Religion', in W.A. Joubert & T.J. Scott (eds.), *The Law of South Africa* 23 (1st edn., 1986), para. 299.

91 *Theron v. Ring van Wellington van die NG Kerk*, 1976 (2) SA 1 (A) 10 (South Africa); *Odendaal* 1961 (1) SA, para. 719.

92 *Taylor* 2005 (1) SA, para. 63.

rule in any event does not apply if the person wanting to be heard lays claim to a privilege to which he or she will normally not be entitled.[93]

Upholding the basic principles of justice and other constitutional rights of members of a religious institution has become critical in South Africa due to, and to the extent of, applying the Bill of Rights obligations to juristic persons. In *Taylor v. Kurtstag,* the Witwatersrand Local Division of the High Court was confronted by exactly that dilemma.[94] The Plaintiff in the matter had been served a notice of excommunication (*cherem*) from the Orthodox Jewish Faith by a Jewish ecclesiastical court (*Beth Din*) and applied for the *cherem* to be set aside on the grounds that it violated his constitutional right to freedom of religion (Section 15(1) of the Constitution) and, as a component of the right to self-determination, the entitlement to practice his religion and maintain religious associations with fellow members of his faith (Section 31(1)(b) of the Constitution). That indeed was found to be the case, but the Court went on to consider the legality of those violations in view of the limitations provisions of the Constitution (Section 36). The Court noted that '[a] religious tribunal is subject to the discipline of the Constitution, but its being a religious body giving effect to the associational rights of its members, must be accounted for.'[95] Having noted that 'the reluctance to interfere in matters of faith, whether it be procedural or otherwise, cannot be discarded,' and in the absence of evidence of bias or bad faith on the part of the *Beth Din*,[96] the Court upheld the constitutionality of its *cherem*.

In December 2009, the Reverend Ecclesia de Lange, a minister in the Methodist Church of Southern Africa in Rondebosch, Cape Town entered into a same-sex union with Amanda van Aswegen. The church, which does not condone same-sex marriages, suspended her in January 2010 from her post. De Lange contested her suspension through internal church arbitration cannels. In a statement on Facebook and other websites, De Lange proclaimed: 'I desire to serve Jesus. I desire to be true to myself. I desire to minister within the Methodist Church of Southern Africa with integrity and be faithful to God's call on my life.

I have reached the point where I can no longer be silent. I have come to see that it is better to be rejected for who I am than to be accepted for who I am not.'[97]

Following a hearing behind closed doors in January, 2011, a disciplinary committee of the church recommended that De Lange 'continue under suspension

---

93 *Mankatshu v. Old Apostolic Church of Africa & others*, 1994 (2) SA 458 (Tk AD) 463–64 (South Africa). See also *Jacobs v. Old Apostolic Church of Africa & another*, 1992 (4) SA 172 (Tk GD) (South Africa) (holding that a member of a Church cannot insist on inspecting the books and financial records of the Church where no such right has been vested in him by the Constitution of the Church).

94 *Taylor* 2005 (1) SA 82.

95 *Taylor* 2005 (1) SA, para. 63.

96 *Taylor* 2005 (1) SA, para. 62.

97 'Minister's Allies Talk of Court Action', *Sunday Times* (Johannesburg), 6 February 2011.

until such time as the Methodist Church of Southern Africa makes a binding decision on ministers in same-sex unions'. She was eventually defrocked because of her gay marriage. She has not pursued the matter further, and perhaps wisely so. It is highly unlikely that a civil court will overrule the church's decision, provided only that the proper internal procedures were applied by the church.

Concluding Observations

Traditionally, both Germany and South Africa were quite meticulous in upholding the sphere sovereignty/self-determination/autonomy of religious institutions, which among other things placed considerable constraints upon state interference in the domestic affairs of churches. In recent years, the sphere sovereignty of religious institutions have come under stress in both Germany and South Africa: in Germany, because of its obligations as a Member State of the Council of Europe to protect the rights and freedoms of individuals enunciated in the *European Convention of Human Rights and Fundamental Freedoms* against infringements by private individuals and non-state institutions, including religious organizations; in the case of South Africa, because its Constitution has placed individuals and non-state institutions, including religious institutions, under an obligation to uphold the constitutional prohibition of discrimination based on, for example, gender and sexual orientation.

German labor courts have now been informed of their obligation to find an appropriate balance between the protected rights of church employees under threat of dismissal against their expected loyalty towards the internal doctrinal and morally based predilections of the concerned religious institution; and should South African courts of law question church practices that discriminate on basis of gender or sexual orientation, it would be open to the church to show that those practices are 'reasonable and justifiable in an open and democratic society based on human dignity, equality and freedom, taking into account … the importance of the purpose of [such practices]'.[98] However, as this writer observed before, '[t]he mere fact that a church may be compelled to justify its internal legal provisions before a secular tribunal, amounts to totalitarianism of the worst kind.'[99]

---

98 SA Constitution, sec. 36(1)(b).

99 J.D. van der Vyver, 'Constitutional Perspective of Church-State Relations in South Africa', *Brigham Young University Law Review* (1999), 635, 664–67; and see also Van der Vyver, *Gelykberegtiging*, supra note 74 at 397 (author's translation from the original Afrikaans).

PART II
National Experiences and Cases

Chapter 7

Religion and Religions in the Latin American Constitutional Framework

Carmen Asiaín Pereira

Preliminary Observations

Due to the breadth and complexity of the topic, this chapter will highlight only certain aspects of Latin American constitutions and constitutional law, contributing only with selected perceptions and reflections, primarily concerning Spanish-speaking states, notwithstanding some remarkable characteristics of the remaining countries geographically comprised within the Americas. We will be specifically concerned with member countries of the Inter-American System (Organization of American States), either signatories to the American Convention of Human Rights or not.

The chapter will focus on the text of the constitutions in force, dealing only with historical references that may be necessary to explain the origins of some inequalities. Latin American constitutions refer to international human rights law – particularly regional – as part of a constitutional or human rights 'block' (*Bloque de Constitucionalidad o Bloque de los Derechos Humanos*).[1] Human rights law, therefore, will be considered here as a source of constitutional law, together with general principles of law, international mandatory law or *ius cogens*, implicit rights, and international customary law.

We intend to analyze how the Latin American constitutional framework considers religion as a transcendent human phenomenon, and then turn to the different religions that form Latin American spiritual pluralism. We will approach the analysis from the perspective of the principle of equality, considering basically how constitutional provisions have acknowledged religion and religious groups in relation to each other, that is, in terms of inequality, discrimination, disregard (*prescindencia*[2]), even hostility. With this background in mind, we may arrive at greater definition of how Latin American constitutional law (meaning constitutional

---

1 M. J. Risso Ferrand, *Derecho Constitucional* T I, 2ª edn (Montevideo: Fundacion de Cultura Universitaria, 2006), 369ff.

2 *Prescindencia* is very strong expression, which has no exact English equivalent; it connotes a state attitude that dispenses with, abstains from dealing with, or utterly disregards the subject of religion, meaning that the state does not take religion into account at all, overlooks the religious factor in society, believes it is unworthy of consideration.

texts and also the law incorporated within the broader context of constitutionality or of human rights) has considered human beings and their dignity, as persons who are the subject, the object, the very beginning and end of the rights and freedoms declared by law – in other words, placing the human person at the very center of the entire legal system.

What Latin American States Have in Common

Latin American Constitutionalism

The 'New World' was born in the 15th century as a result of the 'discovery' of America by Europeans, a process which allowed the territories of North and South America to enter into universal history and develop under the influence of a certain European 'weltanschauung'.[3] After a painful and traumatic process that lasted three centuries, the New World gave birth to a group of new states coming to independent life after revolutionary cycles of peoples' rights vindication, when the concepts of 'constitution' and 'democracy' where just beginning to be thought of and defined by political philosophy and the history of the moment.

Thus, the term 'constitution' receives this meaning in the American Hemisphere from the end of the 18th century. The 1787 United States Constitution and succeeding documents adopted after the 1776 independence are inspired by the same concept of a supreme, written regulatory framework that organizes the powers of government, which is present in the original Latin American constitutionalism following the Revolution.

Far from being a strictly American conception, the idea of constitution also pays tribute to French constitutionalism (1789 French Declaration of the Rights of Man and the Citizen and the 1791 Constitution), as well as to the 1808 Bayonne Constitution and the 1812 Cadiz Constitution from Spain and the 1822 Constitution of Portugal; these all had great influence in Latin American constitutions in their respective areas of influence.

From the beginning, then, a common conception of the term *constitution* is held – juridical as well as political – all throughout the Americas, from the United States to Chile and the River Plate.

Thus, Latin American constitutionalism is the unavoidable and necessary consequence of the juridical process of the post-Independence – approximately from 1810 to 1830 – producing liberal politically oriented constitutions. All of them, either explicitly or implicitly, affirm that the human being has inalienable rights prior to the political formation of the state, and that the state's principle aim is to guarantee the plenary exercise of these inalienable rights of the human being. Its formulas are based upon liberalism, republican representative systems

3 H. Gros Espiell, 'Constitución y Democracia en el Nuevo Mundo', *Estudios Constitucionales* (Montevideo: Ingranusi Ltda, 1998), 187–193 (author's translation).

and rising democracies,[4] models often criticized for being too perfectly enunciated but far from reality, with juridical force but lack of effectiveness, notwithstanding the undeniable educational effect of the constitutional provision.

As for the reception of freedom of religion or belief, all constitutions have acknowledged such a right as fundamental. This inclusion is crucial in countries in which effectiveness of rights fails to comply with the letter of the constitution, not only due to the educational effect of the constitution, but also because of the self-executing nature of constitutional provisions in the frame of the Latin American constitutional and human rights system. This leads us to the conclusion that freedom of religion is specially protected by the Latin American constitutions, which promote its respect in compliance with the principle of equality.

International Human Rights Law as Part of the 'Constitutionality Block'

International human rights law, together with general principles of law explicitly or implicitly acknowledged, along with international customary law and mandatory or peremptory law (*ius cogens*) comprise what is considered a human rights or constitutionality 'block'[5] that rules every Latin American state, either by express incorporation or tacitly, but either way binding the state according to the Vienna Convention on the Law of Treaties.[6]

Many constitutions provide, if not supra-constitutional validity, 'at least constitutional validity[7] to human rights treaties and conventions, including them as part of the constitution or charter itself[8] or granting them precedence over national law[9] or acknowledging their supra legal force.[10] Some establish that interpretation of national law must be made in accordance with international human rights law[11] and others adhere to the treaties according to principles of non-alignment.[12] Moreover, human rights law provisions are self-executing in national legal systems,[13] having been increasingly invoked and quoted by national judges in their rulings.

4 Gros Espiell, supra note 4 at 321–328.

5 See supra note 2 and accompanying text.

6 Arts. 26, 27, 53, 1969 Vienna Convention on the Law of Treaties (*pacta sunt servanda, ius cogens).*

7 Argentina, art. 75; Venezuela, arts. 19 & 23; Dominican Republic, art. 74 3.

8 Chile, art. 5.2; Colombia, art. 93; Honduras, arts. 15, 17 & 18; Mexico (2011 reform) art. 1.

9 Brazil, art. 4; Guatemala, art. 46; Paraguay, art. 141, 137 & 143.

10 Costa Rica, art. 7.

11 Haiti, Preamble.

12 Nicaragua, art. 5.

13 Paraguay, art. 45; Venezuela, art. 22; Brazil, art. 5.1; Colombia, art. 85; Ecuador, art. 11; Uruguay, art. 332.

As for implicit rights, respect for them is called for in Article 29c of the American Convention on Human Rights,[14] and almost all constitutions acknowledge them,[15] revealing that besides provisions on rights, there are rights without provisions.[16] Several constitutions mandate that the provision which best protects a given right must be chosen, regardless of the hierarchy of its source;[17] and many constitutions recognize the principle of the 'progressiveness' of economic, social, and cultural rights.[18]

This constitutional block limits the states' sovereignty, as well as the exercise of power in government, including the constituent power.[19]

The comparative Latin American legal framework imposes the consideration of constitutional law and human rights international law as sources of a unique human rights protection system based on human dignity. The national and the international sources reinforce each other.[20]

Since freedom of religion has been included in the core of this mandatory law, as the origin of all liberties, as a development derived from the acknowledgement of the dignity of the human being, respect and effective enjoyment of this freedom stand as imperatives for every state, regardless of whether they have subscribed to a convention, or omitted the acknowledgement of freedom of religion rights in domestic law or even restricted some liberties. This law rules *erga omnes* for all Latin American states, limiting the power of states.

---

14 The American Convention on Human Rights, issued by the Inter-American Commission of Human Rights of the Organization of American States, was adopted at the Inter-American Specialized Conference on Human Rights, in San José, Costa Rica, on 22 November 1969; the Convention entered into force, in accordance with its Article 74.2, on 18 July 1978. Article 29, Restrictions Regarding Interpretation: 'No provision of this Convention shall be interpreted as: … c. precluding other rights or guarantees that are inherent in the human personality or derived from representative democracy as a form of government.' The Conventon is available in English at http://www.cidh.oas.org/basicos/english/basic3.american%20convention.htm (last consulted 20 January 2013) and in Spanish at http://www.oas.org/Juridico/spanish/firmas/b-32.html.

15 Argentina, art. 33; Brazil, art. 5; Colombia, art. 94; Paraguay, art. 45; Perú, art. 3, Uruguay, art. 72.

16 H. Nogueira de Alcalá, *Dignidad de la persona, derechos fundamentales y bloque constitucional de derechos: una aproximación desde Chile y América Latina,* in *Revista de Derecho 2010, 05,* Universidad Católica del Uruguay D.A. Larrañaga (Montevideo: K. Adenauer, 2010), 99.

17 Venezuela, art. 23; Ecuador, art. 11; Dominican Republic, art. 74.4.

18 E.g., Ecuador, art. 11, s. 8: 'The contents of rights shall be developed progressively by means of standards, case law, and public policies.'

19 Nogueira de Alcalá, supra note 17at 93–94 and 109–110.

20 G. Bidart Campos, *La interpretación de los derechos humanos* (Buenos Aires: Ediar, 1994), 30–31.

The Contents of Human Rights Regional Conventions

Human rights law stands on the acknowledgement of human dignity as a premise prior to written law and to the state, perceiving the spiritual and transcendent nature of the human personality, thus recognizing what is basic to human nature: religious freedom, the religious dimension of mankind, and religions as having value in themselves.

The American Declaration of the Rights and Duties of Man ('the Declaration'),[21] prior and very similar in its contents to the United Nations' Universal Declaration of Human Rights,[22] was the world's first international human rights instrument. The Declaration opens by asserting that

> The American peoples have acknowledged the dignity of the individual, and their national constitutions recognize that juridical and political institutions, which regulate life in human society, have as their principal aim the protection of the essential rights of man and the creation of circumstances that will permit him to achieve spiritual and material progress and attain happiness;
> The American States have on repeated occasions recognized that the essential rights of man are not derived from the fact that he is a national of a certain state, but are based upon attributes of his human personality; ...[23]

The Preamble and provisions of the Declaration further reveal its connection to natural law. It is not the citizen of the state, but the human being in his own right who is entitled to essential rights.

These notions of freedom and equality in dignity and the rights of man stand as milestones, acknowledging 'reason and conscience' as natural dimensions of man, expressed in the axiom, 'While rights exalt individual liberty, duties express the dignity of that liberty.' The Declaration's Preamble holds that 'Duties of a juridical nature presuppose others of a moral nature which support them in principle and constitute their basis', recognizing an axiological order. 'Inasmuch as spiritual development is the supreme end of human existence and the highest expression thereof, it is the duty of man to serve that end with all his strength and resources.'

The principle of equality before the law for all individuals is proclaimed in Article I, followed by the protection of freedom of religion in Article III, which includes 'the right freely to profess a religious faith, and to manifest and practice it both in public and in private'.

---

21 OAS, Res. XXX, 9th International Conference of American States, April1948, Bogotá, Colombia, available at http://www.cidh.oas.org/Basicos/English/Basic2.american%20Declaration.htm.

22 Adopted by the General Assembly on 10 December 1948; text at http://www.un.org/en/documents/udhr/.

23 OAS, Res. XXX, Preamble.

Sharing the American Declaration's axiology, the American Convention on Human Rights, adopted at San José, Costa Rica in November 1969,[24] binds a majority of countries in the Americas: Argentina (09/05/84); Barbados (11/27/82), Bolivia (07/19/79), Brazil (09/25/92), Chile (08/21/90), Colombia (07/31/73), Costa Rica (04/08/70), Dominica (06/11/93), Ecuador (12/28/77), El Salvador (06/23/78), Grenada (07/18/78), Guatemala (05/25/78), Haiti (09/27/77), Honduras (09/08/77), Jamaica (08/07/78), Mexico (03/24/81), Nicaragua (09/25/79), Panama (06/22/78), Paraguay (08/24/89), Peru (07/28/78), Dominican Republic (04/19/78), Suriname (11/12/87), Trinidad and Tobago (05/28/91), Uruguay (04/19/85) and Venezuela (08/09/77).

The Convention's purpose, enunciated in its Preamble, is to consolidate a system of personal liberty and social justice based on respect for the essential rights of man. The protection granted is not innovative but 'reinforcing or complementing the protection provided by the domestic law of the American states'.

Thus, member states agree to respect the acknowledged rights, under the principle of equality (art. 24), with a special reference to religion: 'without any discrimination for reasons of … religion …' (art. 1).

Spiritual liberties are dealt with in Article 12. Freedom of Conscience and Religion:

1. Everyone has the right to freedom of conscience and of religion. This right includes freedom to maintain or to change one's religion or beliefs, and freedom to profess or disseminate one's religion or beliefs, either individually or together with others, in public or in private.
2. No one shall be subject to restrictions that might impair his freedom to maintain or to change his religion or beliefs.
3. Freedom to manifest one's religion and beliefs may be subject only to the limitations prescribed by law that are necessary to protect public safety, order, health, or morals, or the rights or freedoms of others.
4. Parents or guardians, as the case may be, have the right to provide for the religious and moral education of their children or wards that is in accord with their own convictions.

Some of the verbs in Article 12 stand out as novel if compared to those in other international instruments: maintain, change, profess, and disseminate one's religion, as limits imposed even upon states themselves.

The Convention enlists member states in human rights promotion, urging them to 'adopt legislative or other measures as may be necessary to give effect to those rights or freedoms' (art. 2). Thus states are obliged to accommodate their domestic legal systems in order to make rights, including freedom of religion or belief, effective. Suspension of guarantees of freedom of religion is forbidden (art. 27.2).

24 See supra note 15.

The 1988 Additional Protocol to the American Convention on Human Rights in the Area of Economic, Social and Cultural Rights ('Protocol of San Salvador')[25] was subscribed to or ratified by Argentina, Bolivia, Brazil, Chile, Colombia, Costa Rica, Ecuador, El Salvador, Guatemala, Haiti, Mexico, Nicaragua, Panama, Paraguay, Peru, Dominican Republic, Suriname, Uruguay and Venezuela. The Preamble to the Protocol introduces the principle that human rights are indivisible, *interdependent*, and interrelated: 'When one of these rights is affected, the whole group is impaired; just as pathology in biology disturbs – and even may conclude – life itself of the unitary entity that man is.'[26]

Perhaps the Protocol's most innovative contribution is its attention to the principle of progressiveness, foreseeing the 'inclusion of other rights and expansion of those recognized' (art. 22).

In the area of freedom of religion, the Protocol underlines the obligation of nondiscrimination on the basis of religion (art. 3) and promotes 'ideological pluralism in education, fostering understanding, tolerance and friendship among all nations and all racial, ethnic or religious groups' (art. 13).

The idea that peace and peaceful coexistence among groups can only be achieved by means of a pluralistic education that allows pupils to acquire knowledge and understanding of other religious groups is held as an inspiring juridical principle; it is also a valued principle from educational science.[27]

This regional human rights law, nourished by domestic and international sources, applies to all of Latin America, functioning as a limit to national sovereignty, both to derived constituent power, and to legislative, administrative and jurisdictional powers, which must comply according to the principles of progressiveness and irreversibility, as well as to the principle of '*pro homine*' (according to which all law is created for the benefit of human beings). The principles are unavoidably part of the constitutionality control parameter. In this context, national judges and courts have a duty to ensure compliance, in order to assure a minimum level of respect of the fundamental rights. This implies the preferential application of the American Convention over infraconstitutional norms, which completes the constitutionality control every state undertakes.[28]

---

25 The Additonal Protocol was adopted in San Salvador, El Salvador on 17 November 1988. The text is available in English at http://www.oas.org/juridico/english/treaties/a-52.html (accessed 12 January 2012). A Table of Ratifications in Spanish is available at: http://www.oas.org/juridico/spanish/firmas/a-52.html.

26 M.R. Brito, *Derecho Administrativo: Su Permanencia – Contemporaneidad – Prospectiva* (Montevideo: Editorial Universidad de Montevideo, 2004), 11 [author's translation].

27 C. Asiaín Pereira, 'Religión en la Educación Pública: Deberes del Estado Uruguayo a la luz del Derecho Humanitario Internacional', in C. Asiaín (ed.), *Religión en la Educación Pública. Análisis comparativo de su regulación jurídica en las Américas, Europa e Israel* (Madrid: Fundación Universitaria Española, 2010).

28 Nogueira de Alcalá, supra note 17 at 138–139 [author's translation].

The Preferential Treatment of Religion as a Common Denominator in Latin American Constitutions

Both international and domestic law highly esteem religion as a phenomenon and provide special protection of it, compared to how other human dimensions are treated. Neither conventions nor constitutions omit considering religion as a fact. Our first conclusion, then, and also first premise, is that Latin American constitutional law holds religion and religions themselves in high regard, granting them a special status, revealing a primary inequality in comparison to other dimensions and groups.

The Value of Preambles in Invoking the Transcendent

In the preambles of their constitutions, nations take the opportunity to set out the founding principles of their legal systems, sealing axiology and teleology, marking the way in which provisions should be interpreted, standing as an unavoidable matrix to understanding the core spirit of a legal system. No system is aseptic in terms of values held. The preamble is where we find adherence to a given set of values: this is what we are, in this we believe, this is where we are going.

If 'the Constitution is one State's navigation chart',[29] then we may say that its preamble is the marked destination for which the ship is bound. It demonstrates the human urge to provide institutions with some meaning, to relate them to something that transcends the political association.

Even those constitutions that exclude the *invocatio dei* from their preambles have replaced it with other absolutes occupying the place of the deity, since '[m]an is a religious animal. Even his atheisms have something religious.'[30] An example is the 2003 Cuban Constitution, embodying a socialist and Marxist-Leninist profession of faith in its preamble, speaking of human dignity as 'the cult of Cubans'.

Mexico's and Uruguay's omission of the preamble occurred not because the concept of a preamble was rejected but for historical reasons involving confrontation between the state and the Catholic Church. Omitting the preamble circumvented the necessary reference to the transcendent, resolving to some degree the church-state conflict.

In the remainder of the Latin American countries, sound preambles precede and preside over their constitutions; regardless of secularization, genuine neutrality, or establishment of a church, they invoke God Almighty before legislating.

Examples are Argentina, invoking the protection of God, source of all reason and justice; Barbados, Bolivia, with compliments to the 'Pachamama' and giving thanks to God; Brazil, Chile, Colombia, Costa Rica, Dominica, Ecuador, El

29 P. Serna and F. Toller, *La interpretación constitucional de los Derechos Fundamentales. Una alternativa a los conflictos de derechos* (Buenos Aires: La Ley, 2000), 102, quoting Juan Bautista Alberdi (quote 307).

30 J. Guitton, *Mi Testamento Filosófico* (Buenos Aires: Editorial Sudamericana, 1999), 26–29.

Salvador, Grenada, Guatemala, Honduras, Nicaragua, Panama, Paraguay, Peru, Dominican Republic, Venezuela, Saint Kitts and Nevis, Santa Lucia, St. Vincent and the Grenadines, Antigua and Barbuda, The Bahamas (Commonwealth of), Belize, and Suriname.

Religion as a Main Character in the Dogmatic Section of Constitutions

When addressing rights and liberties in the dogmatic section, every constitution contains a special and priority reference to religion and religious rights, with different doses of equality between religious groups. Generally these provisions are contained in the first chapters, designed to give priority to religion in the definition of the nation's identity.

For example, Argentina, as early as Article 2 provides that the 'federal Government supports the Roman Catholic apostolic religion', and later (art. 14) that 'All the inhabitants of the Nation are entitled ... to profess freely their religion ....' Article 19 of the Constitution of Chile guarantees to all persons 'freedom of conscience, manifestation of all creeds and the free exercise of all cults which are not opposed to morals, good customs or public order' (art. 19.6). Colombia includes among the essential goals of the state (art. 2), and as realization of its instrumental nature, that 'The authorities of the Republic are established in order to protect all persons residing in Colombia, their life, dignity, property, beliefs, and other rights and freedoms, and in order to ensure the fulfilment of the social duties of the state and individuals', consecrating explicit guarantees for freedom of conscience (art. 18) and religion (art. 19): 'Freedom of religion is guaranteed. Every individual has the right to freely profess his/her religion and to disseminate it individually or collectively. All religious faiths and churches are equally free before the law.'[31]

Thus, Latin American constitutions distinguish religion in a positive manner, particularly esteeming it, regardless of the support provided to a given church or religion. Even when some charters discriminate in a negative manner, they are revealing that the state, far from being neutral in terms of religion (in the sense of indifferent), takes religion into account, one way or another.

Religion in the Name of Countries and in National Symbols

When compared to other continents, the names of Latin American countries, capitals, and general geography stand out because of their religious nature.

31 For further analysis, see: Bolivia, arts. 4 & 21.3; Brazil, art. 5.6; Costa Rica, art. 75; Cuba, arts. 8 & 55; Ecuador, art. 66; El Salvador, art. 25; Guatemala, art. 36; Haití, art. 30; Honduras, art. 77; México, arts. 130 & 24; Nicaragua, arts. 14, 29 & 69; Panamá, art. 35; Paraguay, art. 24; Perú, arts. 2 & 50; Dominican Republic, art. 45; Suriname, art. 18; Trinidad and Tobago, art. 4; Uruguay, art. 5; Venezuela, art. 59. Commonwealth countries have a similar regulation, rephrasing art. 18 of the UDHR: Barbados, art. 19, Belize, art. 11; Dominica; Grenada, art. 1.b; Guyana, art. 145.1; Jamaica, arts. 13 & 21; Saint Kitts and Nevis; Santa Lucia; St. Vincent and the Grenadines; Antigua and Barbuda, The Bahamas (Commonwealth of).

Countries such as Dominica, Dominican Republic,[32] El Salvador, Trinidad and Tobago, as well as Commonwealth countries are named in remembrance of saints. Many capitals have Christian names: Santa María de los Buenos Aires, Santiago de Chile, San José de Costa Rica, Nuestra Señora de La Paz (Bolivia), Asunción de Paraguay, Santo Domingo (Dominican Republic), San Salvador (El Salvador), San Cristóbal de La Habana (Cuba), San Felipe y Santiago de Montevideo (Uruguay), Santiago de Quito (Ecuador), La Leal Villa de Santiago de Managua (Nicaragua). Religion thus becomes an identity factor.

As for national symbols, apart from those exhibited by several coats of arms and flags, Dominican Republic has the issue sealed in the Constitution (art. 31): the coat of arms will have a Bible opened in St. John's Gospel at Chapter 8, verse 32,[33] with a cross above it, crowned by a ribbon bearing the motto 'God, Nation and Freedom'.

Differences in the Treatment of Religion by Latin American States

We will attempt to identify three categories, according to the different ways in which Latin American States deal with religion: a first division responds to historical causes; a second group separates countries according to their religious definition: denominational or secular; and a third classification focuses on the level of equal or unequal treatment, privilege or support dispensed to religious groups.

Historical Genesis of Differences in Dealing with Religious Pluralism

When the West 'discovered' the New World in 1492, it encountered a huge multicultural, multilingual, multireligious continent inhabited by diverse nations, showing pronounced differences in terms of historical evolution and cultural development, political, social and economic organization, and of course, religion. This diversity of preexisting native peoples was partly driven to formal uniformity in the sphere of religion through the evangelization undertaken fundamentally by the Spanish Crown as a divine mission,[34] as opposed to Portugal's attitude when facing colonization, producing two different manners of coexistence with religious pluralism.

The monarchs Isabella and Ferdinand of Spain obtained the discovered lands as a donation from Pope Alexander VI in a succession of bulls, which established

32 Dominic, from Latin, *dominĭcus [dies]*, 'Of Our Lord' or 'Belonging to God'.

33 John 8:32, 'And you will know the truth, and the truth will set you free.'

34 C. Asiaín Pereira, 'Law and Religion in Latin America: General Aspects of Law and Current Concerns', 162 *Law and Justice: The Christian Law Review* (Hilary/Easter 2009), 62–78, abstract available at http://www.lawandjustice.org.uk/LJabstracts.htm#168_3.

the obligation to instruct the inhabitants in the faith.[35] Thus, the Spanish monarchs were juridically bound to evangelize the native inhabitants, a burden not imposed upon the Portuguese.

This legal obligation imposed upon the Spanish Crown gave rise to what is known as patronage, which took a variety of forms historically, but which in each case effectively resulted in a *missionary state*. The Portuguese Crown, on the other hand, notwithstanding its compromise with the Catholic faith, was not entrusted with the duty to evangelize the 'unfaithful'. There was no legal binding as a counterpart of royal privileges.

These differences were projected into the new nations after independence from both crowns. After emancipation, constituents of the Spanish-speaking nations accepted inheritance of former patronage systems that had been instituted in favor of the Spanish Crown and embedded these sets of prerogatives in their constitutions in favor of the new rulers, together with the mission of evangelization and protection of Catholic faith, with or without a Concordat to legitimize them. Consequently, independence of Latin American countries from Spain led them to passionately embrace constitutionalism, adding the establishment of the Roman Catholic Church to its two classic elements – separation of powers and individual guarantees.[36]

Brazil, however, was born free from the legal imposition to exercise patronage powers. This different genesis may explain the development of a policy of tolerance and peaceful coexistence with the multiplicity of cults present in the former Portuguese territory, notwithstanding its first constitution's denominational definition (1824). Moreover, going back to the monarchy established after independence of Brazil from Portugal in 1822, one of the government's objectives consisted in 'consecrating and widening, to the maximum extent, freedom of religion within the Empire, a requisite considered essential for increasing European immigration towards Brazil, and therefore, for the economic and technological development of the country'.[37]

This explains why the present Brazilian Constitution is based on the principle of equalitarian treatment of all beliefs, openly pluralistic, yet addressing every manifestation of religion and protecting it, showing more liberty than other Latin American constitutions in the design of its charter:

35 G. González Merlano, *El Conflicto Eclesiástico (1861-1962): Aspectos jurídicos de la discusión acerca del Patronato Nacional* (Montevideo: Ed. Tierra Adentro, Universidad Católica del Uruguay D.A. Larrañaga, 2010), 17–42, 99–100.

36 C. Salinas Araneda, *Las relaciones Iglesia-Estado en la América Indiana: Patronato, Vicariato, Regalismo,* in J.G. Navarro Floria (ed.), *Estado, Derecho y Religión en América Latina* (Buenos Aires: Editorial Marcial Pons, 2009), 51–52.

37 E.D. Callioli, *Religión y Derecho en Brasil,* in J.G. Navarro Floria (ed.), *Estado, Derecho y Religión en América Latina* (Buenos Aires: Editorial Marcial Pons, 2009), 92.

> Art. 3. The fundamental objectives of the Federative Republic of Brazil are: … IV – to promote the well-being of all, without prejudice as to origin, race, sex, colour, age and any other forms of discrimination. …
>
> Art. 5. All persons are equal before the law, without any distinction whatsoever, Brazilians and foreigners residing in the country being ensured of inviolability of the right to life, to liberty, to equality, to security and to property, on the following terms: … VI – freedom of conscience and of belief is inviolable, the free exercise of religious cults being ensured and, under the terms of the law, the protection of places of worship and their rites being guaranteed.

The Brazilian constitution pays special attention to noncoercion, spiritual assistance, conscientious objection, religious education in public schools, ideological pluralism, civil effects of religious marriage, rights of native peoples, tax exemption to churches, guaranteeing the free exercise of religion in boundaries unexplored by other states.

The former Spanish colonies, on the other hand, have tended to grant some formal privileges to the Roman Catholic Church, giving rise to an inequality before the law. As examples: The Argentine Constitution announces that the 'Federal Government supports the Roman Catholic Apostolic religion' (art. 2); Paraguay recognizes the role of the Catholic Church in the historical and cultural formation of the nation (art. 82); Panamá, setting Christian morality as a legitimate limit to freedom of religion, recognizes it as the majority religion (art. 35); and in Peru, the state recognizes, within a system of independence and autonomy, the Catholic Church as an important element in the historical, cultural and moral formation of the state, and grants it collaboration (art. 50).

Other examples only grant the Church legal status, in acknowledgment of the fact that it preexisted the national states, or as the terms of agreement in the process of secularization. Examples are found in El Salvador (art. 26), Guatemala (art. 37), Paraguay (art. 24), and Uruguay (art. 5). Other constitutions expressly refer to the Church, for example Panamá, which recognizes that 'most Panamanians' are of the Catholic religion but declares free profession and exercise of all religions with no limitation 'other than respect for Christian morality and public order' (art. 35).

Differences in How the States View Religion

As for how the legal systems of Latin American states define and respond to religion, we can identify three basic groups: denominational, nondenominational with recognition of one church in particular, and genuinely neutral, nondenominational legal systems.

Denominational States

Catholic denominational states

The Constitution of Costa Rica (1949, with reforms till 2002) stands out for officially establishing the Church in Article 75: 'The Roman Catholic and Apostolic Religion is the religion of the State, the State contributes to its maintenance, without preventing the free exercise in the Republic of other forms of worship that are not opposed to universal morality or good customs.' Notwithstanding this stance, freedom of association is guaranteed to religious groups (art. 25), forbidding compulsory membership to any association whatsoever.

A religious oath is required in order to assume public service, by a comprehensive formula referring to God (art. 194). In contrast, political propaganda alluding to religion is forbidden to both clergymen and lay persons (art. 28). The formal inequality in favor of the Church, however, is undeniable.

Denominational states of a different type?

Given the fact that authentic neutrality does not exist[38], we may posit that when some constitutions hold a given ideology, they are also making a profession of faith, although not religious but of a different type.

The Cuban Constitution, after stating the final objective of building the communist society, explicitly adheres to a given faith in its early Article 5: 'The Communist Party of Cuba, a follower of Martí's ideas and of Marxism-Leninism, and the organized vanguard of the Cuban nation, is the highest leading force of society and of the state, which organizes and guides the common effort toward the goals of the construction of socialism and the progress toward a communist society.'

The state makes a profession of Marxist-Leninist faith, an ideology inspiring the whole legal system to the extent that rights and guarantees will find in it its limit, and should be interpreted in accordance to it (art. 62). This posture is extended to 'education and cultural policy' (art. 39), which is based upon principles including 'the ideology of Marx and Martí'. Moreover, 'the state promotes the patriotic and communist education of the new generations'. In accordance to these objectives, 'parents have the duty to … contribute actively to [the] education [of their children and their] integral development as useful and well-prepared citizens for life in a socialist society' (art. 38).

This clear auto definition leads us to include this system as denominational, primarily if we take into account the posture of Marxism-Leninism in regard to religion. Nevertheless, freedom of religion is proclaimed in the letter of the Cuban Constitution in Articles 8 and 55.

Nondenominational States

This category contains four subgroups under the auspices of the principle of equality: those who privilege a given religion, basically the Roman Catholic Church,

38 Guitton, *Mi Testamento Filosófico*, supra note 30 at 26–29.

notwithstanding secularity; genuinely neutral states; states whose constitutions imply discrimination against the religious phenomenon itself, without implying inequality among religions; and states involved in cooperation and promotion of religions in general, or of underprivileged groups by means of affirmative action. Note that any attempt to classify tends to incur simplification, and that neither is this classification rigid, nor are the groups and subgroups compact or hermetic.

Nondenominational states that privilege the Roman Catholic Church or Christianity
The set of privileges granted on behalf of a given religion does not automatically make the state denominational, as there is still no confusion between religious and juridical or political fields; the state remains unattached to a given religion, offering protection to all religions on an equal basis.

What then does the privilege entail? It mainly consists of a special status acknowledged to the Church, explained for historical, cultural and traditional reasons, consistent with the Church's contribution to the identity of the nation and with its pre-existence.

In a descending scale, we may start with Peru, its constitution invoking God in its Preamble and recognizing the Catholic Church as an important element in the historical, cultural and moral formation, with which Peru cooperates (art. 50), besides respecting other creeds. Christian morality and ethics are omnipresent throughout all its provisions, as for instance, protecting the unborn (art. 2.1). Peru has signed a Concordat with the Holy See (1980) regulating several church-State issues.

Paraguay, after the *invocatio dei*, and a proclamation that no religion is official (art. 24), deliberately mentions the Catholic Church to define the state's relations with her, which are based upon independence, cooperation, and autonomy. There is a special recognition of the Catholic Church as protagonist in the historical and cultural formation of the nation (art. 82), which is projected to several fields. Its 1960 Covenant with the Holy See regulates spiritual assistance to armed forces, among other aspects.

Argentina, as already mentioned, invokes the protection of God, the source of all reason and justice, and supports the Catholic faith in its early Article 2. The 1966 Agreement between the Republic of Argentina and the Holy See details the principles of autonomy and cooperation between Church and the State, followed by covenants concerning spiritual assistance to armed forces (1992 after 1957). Despite the fact that some of its provinces may be catalogued as quasi-denominational (Santa Fe and Catamarca),[39] and notwithstanding the Church's constitutional pre-eminence, the term 'support' in Article 2 of the constitution does not qualify Argentina as a denominational state, understanding it either as

39 Santa Fe proclaims the Catholic faith as official and Catamarca requires the governor to be Catholic. J.G. Navarro Floria, *Derecho Eclesiástico y libertad religiosa en la República Argentina,* in Navarro Floria (ed.), *Estado, Derecho y Religión en América Latina,* supra note 37 at 56.

economic support or as moral support, but either way denying that the Catholic Church constitutes a political power within the Argentine regime,[40] especially after the 1966 Agreement and the 1994 constitutional reform.[41]

Panama establishes that Catholic faith is to be taught in public schools, but participation in such instruction and in religious worship is not compulsory when parents or tutors request otherwise (art. 107). Legal personality of the Catholic Church is implicit.

Other States grant legal personality to the Catholic Church. El Salvador begins by entrusting its confidence to God and recognizing legal personality for the Catholic Church (art. 26), with other churches being able to obtain it as well, according to law.

Guatemala grants legal personality to the Catholic Church (art. 37), and grants the other churches, cults, and religious entities and associations the possibility of obtaining recognition according to rules of the institution, which process the government shall not deny unless for reasons of public order. Likewise, the state will hand over the title deeds of the real estate presently and peacefully possessed by the Catholic Church for its own aims, as long as they have belonged to the assets of the Catholic Church in the past.

Uruguay recognizes the Catholic Church's ownership of all temples that have been partially or completely built with funds from the national treasury, with the exception of chapels that have been designated to serve as shelters, hospitals, jails, or other public settlements (art. 5). Legal personality is derived from recognition of dominion rights.

Assessment: Recognition of legal personality for the Catholic Church (i) is originary and constitutional, and therefore can only be abrogated after constitutional reform, which will be limited by acquired rights; (ii) is automatic, recognized *per se;* (iii) does not require approval of its statutes, its legal status being recognized as including all guidelines, authorities, and regulations set forth by the religious entity, without the government requiring them to be presented for approval[42]; (iv) the usual

---

40 H.R. Bermúdez, *La libertad religiosa en la Constitución Nacional,* in R. Bosca and J.G. Navarro Floria (eds.), *La libertad religiosa en el Derecho argentino* (Buenos Aires: Konrad Adenuaer Stiftung / CALIR, 2007), 94–98, quoting jurisprudence and academic opinions as Bidart Campos. '*The Supreme Court has repeatedly sustained that the Roman Catholic religion is not the Argentine State's official religion, in spite of the prefferent status acknowledged by art. 2 of the National Constitution.*' [author's translation]

41 O. Lo Prete, *Consideraciones sobre la Libertad Religiosa en la Argentina* (publicado en Anuario Argentino de Derecho Canónico, AADC XII (2005) 379–393), available at http://www.libertadreligiosa.net/ articulos/Consideraciones_LR_Argentina_2005.pdf.

42 C. Asiaín Pereira, 'El gran desafío del Derecho Eclesiástico del Estado en el Uruguay: Su Existencia misma como Rama del Derecho' (Secretaría de Gobernación, México, D.F., 2006) and C. Asiaín Pereira, 'Religion and the Secular State, Uruguayan Report', in J. Martínez-Torrón and W.C. Durham, Jr. (general reporters), *Interim Reports, XVIIIth International Congress of Comparative Law,* Washington D.C., July 2010 (Provo, Utah: The International Center for Law and Religion Studies, Brigham Young University, 2010), 780.

legal requisites –worship objective, historical rooting, religious nature- for applying for state benefits such as tax exemption, are proved beforehand. As a final point (v), the Holy See as subject of Public International Law is another peculiarity for state–church relations. Inequality, though not reprehensible, is undeniable.

Other constitutions grant a special treatment to Christianity in general: Nicaragua's Preamble invocation is in the name of Christians, who from their faith in God have committed and inserted themselves in the fight for liberation of the oppressed; Panamá, as mentioned above, sets Christian morality as an admissible limit to freedom of religion.

Nondenominational states that grant equal treatment to religious groups within a coordination/cooperation scheme

1. Freedom of association of religious entities
    a. States granting some scope of protection to religious entities from the generic freedom of association, such as Argentina, Bolivia (art. 14.3), Brazil, (art. 5.17 & 18), Costa Rica (arts. 7, 33 & 75), Honduras (arts. 77–78), Peru (art. 2.13), Dominican Republic (art. 47) and Uruguay (art. 39).
    b. States that specifically protect religious entities in their right to legal personality include Chile (art. 19.6): 'Religious communities may erect and maintain churches and their facilities in accordance with the conditions of safety and hygiene as established by the laws and ordinances. With respect to assets, the churches and religious communities and institutions representing any cult shall enjoy the rights granted and acknowledged by the laws currently in force. Churches and their facilities assigned exclusively for religious activities shall be exempt from all taxes.'
    Other examples include Colombia (arts. 19 & 38), Ecuador (arts. 10, 11& 66), Guatemala (art. 37), Jamaica (arts. 13 & 21.1 & 3, establishing a safeguard clause for religious entities' autonomy), and Nicaragua (arts. 49 & 69). Panamá recognizes *ex professo* religious autonomy (art. 36); Paraguay also secures autonomy (art. 24, 42 & 88); Venezuela (art. 53), binds the state to facilitate the exercise of this right as well as religious autonomy.
    c. States that in spite of protecting, exhibit hostile provisions: The prototype example is Mexico: 'All religious associations organized according to article 130 and its derived legislation, shall be authorized to acquire, possess or manage, just the necessary assets to achieve their objectives' (art. 27.2). Article 130 proclaims the guiding principle that 'the State and the churches are separated entities from each other'. According to this provision, religious ministers are forbidden from performing any governmental employment, from political associations or taking part in political campaigns. Political parties shall neither invoke nor evoke a given religion. Confiscation of temples (occurred in 1917) is ratified by transitory Article 17°.
    In El Salvador ownership by religious entities is granted under the condition that assets are immediately and directly assigned to the institution (arts. 26

& 108). In Cuba restrictions come from the accomplishment of the socialist ideal (art. 7).

2. Religion in the public schools
   a. With no specific provision: Several constitutions omit the reference to religious education or even instruction on beliefs in schools, either public or private. Neither Argentina, nor Chile, nor Haiti, nor Dominican Republic, nor Uruguay foresee this issue, although they all follow the general principle of freedom of education and the rights of parents or tutors to choose it. Honduras defines education as secular, matching this same category.[43]
   b. With specific provisions for religious education in public schools on equal religious basis: Brazil serves as a model in setting the principle of pluralism as a guideline in education (art. 206.3 & 210.1): 'The teaching of religion is optional and shall be offered during the regular school hours of public elementary schools.' For others, Bolivia guarantees religious education also for native peoples (art. 86). Other provisions are found in Colombia (art. 68), Jamaica (art. 21(2)), Ecuador (arts. 27-28), Venezuela (art. 59), Guatemala (art. 73), Paraguay (art. 74), Peru (art. 14), El Salvador (arts. 55–60).
   c. States that offer denominational religious education, without imposition: Costa Rica (art. 79) and Panamá (art. 107).
   d. States that exclude *ex professo* religion from public education, and other hostilities: Nicaragua, which allows religiously-oriented private schools to impart religious education as an extracurricular subject (art. 124), while the case of Mexico is very interesting, because it reveals the constituent's need to justify proscription of religion from public schools: as guaranteed under Article 24, 'education shall be secular and therefore, free from any religious orientation'.[44] As for Cuba, we had outlined that education is ideologically oriented towards Marxist and 'Martian' (from José Martí) thinking in order to promote the communist training of new generations, imposing upon parents the duty to prepare their children for life on the socialist society (arts. 38–39).

43 The IX Colloquium of the Latin American Consortium for Freedom of Religion or Belief on 'Religion in Public Schools', 2009, Universidad de Montevideo, Uruguay, published in Asiaín Pereira (ed.), *Religión en la Educación Pública*, supra note 27, established that the vast majority of the 27 countries establish some form of religious education in public schools, with the exception only of Uruguay.

44 After the 2011 constitutional reform, which incorporated International Human Rights Law, this issue is actually under revision.

3. State financial support of religion
   a. Without specific provisions: Bolivia, Colombia,[45] Cuba, Ecuador, Honduras, Nicaragua, Panama, Dominican Republic and Venezuela.
   b. With generic provisions for all religions: Brazil includes among the limitations to the powers of taxation, 'collecting tributes from: ... 8. Temples of any cult' (art. 150.3). Chile (art. 19.6), El Salvador (art. 231), Guatemala (art. 37) and Uruguay (art. 5) contain similar exemptions.
   c. For a given religion in particular: Argentina, as was previously mentioned, supports Roman Catholic religion (art. 2), a provision which was never fully accomplished, the state paying only insignificant subsidies.[46] Paraguay (arts. 24 & 83) and Peru (art. 50) seem to open the way to state cooperation with the Catholic Church.
   d. Constitutions that forbid the state to contribute to religion, and other hostilities: Mexico, far from financing religions, institutes special restrictions on their institutional life, such as the religious associations and its members' incapacity to inherit by will (art. 130). Probably the outstanding hostility is confiscation of temples and assets that belonged to the Catholic Church.
   e. Assessment: Most Latin American States establish some form financial support of religions in general, revealing a positive valuation of religion as a phenomenon and of religions in general deserving state promotion.

4. Civil effects of religious marriage and other acts
   a. With generic provisions for all religions: Brazil (art. 226.2: 'Religious marriage has civil effects, in accordance with the law') and Colombia are the best examples, the latter also extending civil effects to judgments of nullity (art. 42). Guatemala (art. 49), and Dominican Republic (art. 55) also grant it.
   b. With specific provision for one religion in particular: Costa Rica would be the case.
   c. States that *ex professo* deprive religious marriage of civil effects, and other hostilities: As a result of secularization, civil marriage is exclusively recognized as officially valid. This happens in Peru (art. 4), El Salvador (art. 25, referring to religious acts in general, thus including birth, death and ecclesial condition), Honduras (art. 112, reserving marriage for the union of man and woman), and, of course, Mexico, as a consequence of the principle of secularization (art. 130, making it clear that marital status exclusively belongs to administrative jurisdiction).

---

45 Note the Concordat with the Holy See, and Statutory Law on Freedom of Religion 133/94, allowing the conceción of tax exemption on equal basis for all religions.

46 Navarro Floria, *Derecho Eclesiástico y libertad religiosa,* supra note 39 at 62 (noting that subsidies are granted to other religions by law).

5. Spiritual assistance to confined persons
   a. Without specific provision: these are the vast majority.
   b. With generic provision for all religions: once again, Brazil stands out for its tradition of contemplating diverse fields of religious freedom on an equal and plural basis, establishing in Article 5.7 that 'the rendering of religious assistance in civil and military establishments of collective confinement is ensured'. Guatemala provides it as a right of the imprisoned (art. 19.c).
   c. With specific provision for one religion in particular: apart from Costa Rica, this would be the case of countries which have subscribed Concordats with the Holy See and other religious entities, or have established it by law.

6. Conscientious objection protection
   a. With no specific provision: as most Constitutions proclaim freedom of conscience as a fundamental right, we may affirm that, at least in the letter of its norms, all Latin American States protect freedom of conscience, and hence its manifestations, such as conscientious objection. In practical terms, however, regulation by law has been necessary to realize actual respect of this right in fields of expansive applicability, such as bioethics.
   b. With generic provision for all regions: Brazil is to be praised for providing protection to conscientious objection, and foreseeing the fulfilment of an alternative service: 'No one shall be deprived of any rights by reason of religious belief or philosophical or political conviction, unless he invokes it to exempt himself from a legal obligation required of all and refuses to perform an alternative obligation established by law' (art. 5.8 & 143.1 & 2, exempting women and clergymen from military service). Approaching complete protection are Colombia (art. 18), Ecuador (arts. 20 & 66), Paraguay (arts. 37 & 129) and Suriname (art. 180.5), some with special provisions for military service.
   c. Constitutions that deny the right to conscientious objection: Nicaragua incurs a logical contradiction, since it denies objection, after having proclaimed the right as a premise, together with the principle of noncoercion (art. 29 & 69), establishing that 'No one shall elude the observance of law nor refrain others from exercising their rights and fulfilment of their duties invoking religious beliefs or dispositions.' Venezuela involves the same paradox (arts. 59 & 61).

7. Privacy in relation to religious affiliation

Colombia proclaims that no person shall be compelled to reveal his beliefs (art 18), Ecuador (art. 66), Nicaragua (art. 29), Paraguay (art. 24) and Peru (art. 2.18) likewise.

8. Religion in the public sphere

Guatemala explicitly allows religious mass meeting outside temples (art. 33). Bolivia specially protects native peoples' sacred places (art. 304.I. 10). The utmost opposite example is that of Mexico, whose Constitution limits public cult to the inside of temples, submitting to regulation by law those 'extraordinarily celebrated outside of these' (art. 24).

Haiti surprisingly and categorically forbids the cult of the personality (art. 7),[47] as well as images and names of individuals in currency, stamps, public premises and works of art, a measure with eventual repercussions on freedom of expression related to religion.

9. Religious oaths. A form of inequality?

The oath has religious connotations in itself, meaning 'A solemn promise, often invoking a divine witness, regarding one's future action or behavior.'[48] The constitution itself is established by oath, as a commitment with supreme values requested of public officers. Some generic formulas privilege faith in God – comprehensive of many faiths – while others offer a secular alternative, respecting pluralism. When a secularist formula is imposed, excluding the possibility of transcendent invocation, then freedom of religion suffers as much as it suffers when religious oath is imposed.

a. Oath with no specified formula: In the cases of Bolivia (art. 161), Brazil (art. 78), Chile (art. 27), Ecuador (art. 144), Peru (art. 166), El Salvador (art. 235), and Guatemala (arts. 154 & 165), the public officer takes an oath to defend the Constitution and the well-being of the people, or makes a promise. Also Nicaragua, (arts. 137, 148, 165, 174), Paraguay (arts. 183, 188, 202, 232, 250, 271), and Venezuela (arts. 231 & 255).
b. With specific provision to respect pluralism of religion or belief: Argentina in its last constitutional reform has incorporated the possibility for the President and Vice-president to choose a formula that suits his or her beliefs (art. 93). Jamaica (art. 21.5), Panamá (art. 181), and Suriname (arts. 93 & 125) offer alternatives in view of religious and ideological pluralism.
c. Religious oaths: Colombia requires swearing to God, with no specification of a given religion (art. 192), as well as Costa Rica (art.194), Haiti (arts. 135.1 & 187), and Dominican Republic (art. 127), somehow conditioning access to public office to religious belief.
d. States that impose a non-religious formula: Honduras (arts. 322 & 244) and Uruguay (art. 158) prefix formulas, and even substitute the term 'oath' for 'promise' or 'declaration' and compromising for 'honor'. Mexico is the utmost example because the banning of religious oath is made explicit in art. 130.e): 'The simple promise to tell the truth and to comply with legal obligations is binding ....'

47 The historical explanation may be the cult of the personality developed by former President François Duvalier.

48 This is clear in Spanish, according to Diccionario de la Real Academia Española, 22ª ed. 'Afirmación o negación de algo, poniendo por testigo a Dios, o en sí mismo o en sus criaturas.'

Nondenominational states whose constitutions imply discrimination against religion and religions in general

Some constitutions imply discrimination against the religious phenomenon in itself, without also implying inequality among religions. Such discrimination appears most notably in the political sphere.

1. Ineligibility of clergy to run for public office or access public service
    a. With no limitation: Most of the constitutions refrain from limiting access.
    b. General prohibition for clergymen: Guatemala (arts. 186.f, 197.e & 207). Some constitutions allow clergymen to run for office, but only after a term of having resigned from ministry: Bolivia (art. 238.5); Honduras (art. 77), Panama (art. 45), Nicaragua (arts. 134.2.b & 147.e), Paraguay (arts. 197.5 & 235.5)[49], and Mexico, establishing ineligibility for any public service (art. 130.d). Argentina bans regular 'ecclesiastics' (art. 73 & 89), which poses the question whether the prohibition may be extended to those religious ministers who are not called 'ecclesiastics'.
    c. *Ex professo* inclusion of religious hierarchies in government: Haiti foresees in transitory provision (art. 289) a body of 9 members, integrated by a representative to the Episcopal Conference and one for the protestant churches, among others, revealing the unquestionable reliance these hierarchies provide.

2. Limitation of political activity
    a. In most constitutions political activity may be engaged in freely.
    b. Restriction of freedom of expression, assembly, and association to all religious groups: Costa Rica, as a counterbalance of the establishment of the Catholic Church, proscribes religion from politics (art. 28). Similarly, Honduras (art. 77) and Panama (art. 139) ban religious arguments and agenda. In Cuba restrictions to religious groups are shared by other ideological groups (art. 53).
    Of course, Mexican regulation is the most restrictive (art. 130 e):

> Religious ministers shall neither form political associations among them nor incur in proselytism in favor or against any candidate, political party or association whatsoever. They shall abstain themselves from opposing the country's laws or its institutions in any public gathering, religious ceremonies or propaganda or publishing, nor offend national symbols whatsoever. The formation of political groups under the name or making reference to religious groups is strictly forbidden. Political meetings shall never take place inside

49 A former Catholic Bishop, Fernando Lugo abandoned priesthood before running for President.

temples. This provision is in plain force and has been recently applied to outcast a political group because of its candidate's allusion to religion.[50]

However, the incorporation of Human Rights International Law to the Constitution (2011 reform) forces an unavoidable revision.

c. The *ratio legis* of these restrictions? Various explanations have been made for these political freedom and religious freedom restraints: that Canon Law forbids Catholic priests to access public office; that religious doctrine and hierarchies may have powerful influence in politics; that permitting ecclesiasts in public office would interfere with state neutrality or would undermine equality, representativity and democracy or threaten the law of the state, due to the pledge of obedience rendered to religious doctrine. Actually, what is revealed is the recognition of the power of religion, which states attempt to control in the sphere of politics.

Nondenominational states that cooperate with underprivileged groups

A final type of nondenominational response to religion is found in the Latin American constitutional movement sometimes called 21st-century Latin American Socialism,[51] which abandons the typical features of the traditional scheme of privileges and special consideration granted to the Roman Catholic Church while providing special protection to native religions by means of public policies, in an attempt to compensate for past marginalization. Thus, indigenous peoples' traditions, culture, and religion are recognized and supported.

Bolivia's 2009 Constitution is the most illustrative example. Its Preamble starts by emphasizing native peoples' beliefs in a mythical story of Bolivia, which is being refounded: 'With different faces we inhabited this sacred Mother Earth and from the beginning we understood the living pluralism of all matter and our diversity as beings and cultures … with the strength of our *Pachamama*[52] and thanks to God, we refound Bolivia.' Consequently, when freedom of religion is proclaimed, spiritual beliefs, according to 'cosmovisions', are expressly included (art. 4).

What is most outstanding in the new Bolivian Constitution, due to its novelty, is that while 'the State is independent from religion' (art. 4), it assumes and promotes as ethical and moral principles of a pluralistic society, a number of rules written in the native language, which are true religious commandments converted into legal binding obligations, incorporating their axiology as juridical governing principles (e.g., art. 8.I: 'do not lie, do not steal').

50 Case related by A. Patiño Reyes, 'Religion and the Secular State: Comparative Perspectives', Conference, Columbus School of Law, Catholic University of America, 30–31 July 2010, session on *Religious Symbols in Public Space*.

51 E. Esteva Gallicchio, Constitutional Law Professor, Universidad de Montevideo.

52 *Pachamama o Mama Pacha*, 'Mother Earth', great deity, protecting and provider, personifying land and nature, and more recently, the world and the cosmos, related to fertility, venerated by several indigenous peoples (from the Andes and other locations).

Provisions protecting native culture and rights abound: arts. 10.1, 30.I 98–100, 304.I, include such religious aspects as 'protection of sacred places, cosmovisions and myths as cultural heritage, rituals, symbols and dress, language and education, promoting cultural diversity and religious education as well as the native peoples' spirituality' (art. 86).

The 2008 Ecuador Constitution also evokes Pachamama and God in its Preamble and renders tribute to diverse forms of religiousness, sanctioning religious commandments in a form of legal syncretism. Besides defining itself as a secular state (art. 1), 'The State adopts affirmative action to promote actual equality' (art. 11). Forms of protection similar to those of Bolivia are endowed (arts. 21, 23, 57, 27, 29, 66). As a correlative to recognition of rights to individuals, groups and Nature or Pachamama (who is entitled with rights, art. 10 & 71), ethical duties written in native language (*Ama killa, ama llulla, ama shwa* [to not be lazy, not lie, not steal]) are imposed on inhabitants (art. 83).

Nicaragua (1987 Constitution with 2007 reforms) takes a similar posture (arts. 5, 8, 11 & 180), as does as Venezuela (1999 Constitution, Preamble and arts. 9, 100, 119, 21.2).

Other constitutions, though not classifying in this category, also consider native peoples' religious rights, such as Paraguay (arts. 62, 63, 66 & 77), Brazil (arts. 231 & 210.2), and Colombia (arts. 1, 7, 13, 10, 63, 72, 68).

Is 21st-century Latin American neoconstitutionalism: a form of neodenominationalism? Very accurately, Professor Silvio Ferrari has noted that 'the crux of the separation between State and religion, which constitutes one of the fundamental features of Western constitutionalism, lies in [the] statement of the independence of the constituent power from every religious law that claims to limit the State's right to make laws.' This concept, says Professor Ferrari, 'substantially triumphed, with differences that are not determinant, throughout the West: both in Europe and in the Americas and in the other countries that have adopted the Western model', where constitutions did not accept 'that the norms of a religion represent the basis on which the laws of the State must be founded or the limit that it must respect'. Religious law, according to this concept, does not constitute a source of law, and all this, 'by sovereign decision of the State', results in the 'monopoly of the State over the production of law'.[53]

This description applies to the vast majority of Western constitutions, including those in Latin American ambit. However, 21st-century Latin American neoconstitutionalism seems to have moved contrary to this tendency, introducing native peoples' religious commandments, moral precepts, and ethical principles as a source of law, and establishing that the whole legal order shall be interpreted accordingly. As a result, religious commandments rule with constitutional value and force.

---

53 S. Ferrari, 'Religion and Constitution: Towards the Second ICLARS Conference', ICLARS Newsletter, July 2011, N° 1 – 2011.

Freedom and Religion, Three Concluding Observations

Many Latin American Constitutions Privilege the Catholic Church

As noted at the outset, the privileging of the Catholic Church in Latin America may find justification in the fact that the Church pre-existed nations, was discoverer, conqueror, colonizer, and evangelizer, forger of identity and culture, inspiring legislation, customs, and education, and is even now the majority religion. In fact, almost half of the world's Catholics live in America.[54]

It may be asserted that in privileging the historical majority, states are merely complying with the principle of cooperation and peaceful coexistence with religions, recognizing what is due in view of objective, reasonable facts, with balanced and harmless results in relation to other religious groups. And in any event, privilege is circumscribed to legal personality recognition in most cases.

Some Latin American Constitutions Treat Religious Groups Unequally

Apart from the already acknowledged inequality, we should analyze neodenominationalism with regard to the preferential treatment of native religions as a form of inequality. Affirmative action undertaken by 21st-century Latin American neoconstitutionalism (Bolivia, Ecuador, Nicaragua, Venezuela) implies application of the principle of equality as a leveling mechanism, what is called 'unequally equalitarian equality', intended to 'level out differences and reduce inequalities'.[55] The focus is set upon the final aim, which is equity.

One may wonder why these promotion measures cannot benefit other religious groups as well, in recognition of their contributions to history, culture, and tradition.

Before making our last observation, let us state some fundamental presuppositions: equality is not a goal in itself. Equality is a means, an instrument for realizing the ideal of justice. It is a value that allows reaching another value: freedom.

Equality is a juridical presupposition fundamental to attaining freedom. Equality between individuals and groups is not real; reality is – fortunately – diverse. Given the fact of difference, the juridical presumption that individuals are equal in rights is proposed, in order to achieve recognition of rights allowing access to equitable conditions.

Equality and freedom: their juridical status. Law exhibits nuances in the reception of both equality and freedom. The American Convention on Human Rights, for instance, proclaims the 'intention to consolidate a system of personal liberty and social justice based on respect for the essential rights of man' (Preamble), and asserts that this ideal can only be achieved under certain created

---

54 *ACI Prensa*, 19 February 2011: 49.4 percent of Catholics live in North and South America.

55 L. Ferrajoli, *El Principio de Igualdad* (Montevideo: Fundacion de Cultura Universitaria, 2008), Chapter 1.

conditions, among which is equal treatment before the law (arts. 1, 3 to 23 and 24). So equality is a means to reach for the supreme values of freedom and justice, and therefore is subordinated to them, in the sense that it serves them.

What is equality for then, if it is not an end in itself in religion? Equality serves the actual exercise of freedom of religion, not the reverse. So the meaningful question we may pose is: How is freedom of religion facilitated by the principle of equality?

The rule of proportionality, 'giving each what is due' will frequently give rise to differences. However, the main underlying value, *equity*, will still be served, since the principal imperative for the defense of diversity and pluralism is to begin by granting their existence.

When application of law results in impairment, are we dealing with exceptions to the principle of equality, or just with harmonization of equality with freedom and justice in order to comply with the latter?

Religion in Itself Is Manifest by Constitutions

As a final, undeniable assertion, religion is a main character in the government of nations; God is the protagonist of all Latin American constitutions. Their writers invoke the Creator and commend to God the destinies of the nation, instituting the powers of government as primary warrants of religious rights, revealing the state's instrumental nature for the wellbeing of individuals.[56]

One way or another, the consideration of religion in the Latin American constitutional framework has inherited qualities of the divine: such consideration is eternal (present since its origins), omnipresent, good (as valued by its writers), almighty (limiting law and state sovereignty), and transcendent (going beyond written law).

56 M. Brito, supra note 26.

Chapter 8
The Constitutional Principle of Separation between Church and State in Mexico

Pauline Capdevielle

Topic Analysis

No one model of church-state relations has a monopoly on recognizing and guaranteeing religious freedom. The European experience clearly demonstrates this: its diverse national situations—confessional states, cooperative systems, recognized religious denominations, and secularist regimes—all commonly accept certain fundamental principles, which provide ample recognition of the right to religious freedom. Therefore, respect for liberty within democratic states can result in diverse forms, whether through consensus or subtle equilibrium, in number directly proportional to the different visions of the religious phenomena that have been created in national histories and cultures.[1]

However, in practice, it is undeniable that all of these different systems affect some aspect of the exercise of religious freedom, whether it be subjection to a religious cult, religious teaching, conscientious objection, convictional manifestations in the public sphere, or equal treatment. From this perspective, the separatist model appears especially attractive in guaranteeing the autonomy of individuals, such as those who are members of religious groups. It creates a neutral state that does not undertake religious-based discrimination.[2]

Separation is a political-judicial principle that creates a strict autonomy between the state and different religious confessions, affirming the existence of their individual influential spheres and actions. The state is aconfessional and does not take any part in the different religious confessions and groups present in society. Generally, the concept of separation is associated with the idea of secularism, even though perhaps it is broader and still carries closely the principles of religious freedom and equality and additionally postulates the autonomy of the civil and religious circles.[3] From different perspectives, it is possible to consider that the separation principle constitutes the concrete judicial regimen of secularism

---

1 C. Proeschel, *L'idée de laïcité: une comparaison franco-espagnole* (Paris: L'Harmattan, 2005), 16.

2 Cf. J.P. Willaime, *Europe et religions : les enjeux du XXIe siècle* (Paris: Fayard, 2004), 9.

3 Cf. Universal Declaration on Laicity in the 21st Century.

at an institutional level, although the diverse national situations prevent one from generalizing the correspondence of the notions, in particular, when referring to 'empirical secularities'[4] or informal ones. Here, 'separation' is understood to be a principle, involving an explicit bestowal of rights, which establishes formal independence between the civic sphere and the spiritual realm, and which excludes collaboration or institutional cooperation between them, under the rules of a democratic state.

On the other hand, religious freedom is also understood to be an extensive and expansive concept that extends to more than just the recognition of freedom of conscience or the freedom of a religious organization to shelter all the aspects of the believer's life. It is supported by other fundamental rights in order that it might have content and efficacy, in particular by the freedom of expression, of the press, of association, of assembly, of possession of belongings, of education, etc.[5] Likewise, religious freedom is experienced in a variety of settings: in families with children; in communities with their magistrates; and in church buildings, scholarly establishments, and hospitals. Moreover, it is as prevalent in the private sphere as in the public, in the individual sphere as in association with others. In this manner, if religious liberty relates to the most intimate thoughts of the people, then it also presents a collective and institutional aspect that must be recognized by the states, as organized groups that pursue personal gains in society. In addition, as explained by Professor Isaacson, the constitution, or a law's declaration of religious liberty, is ineffective when the institutional and judicial practices fail to recognize the capacity of individual religious groups to form legal entities and practice all aspects of their religion.[6]

In Mexico, freedom of religion is established by Article 24 of the Constitution, which guarantees the right to 'profess the religious beliefs one may please and to practice all ceremonies, devotions, or the acts of respective cults, only if they do not constitute an infraction or crime punishable by the law'. In accordance with the jurisprudence of the Supreme Court, this right implies the liberty to believe or not, to change religions, to practice the rites and ceremonies of the religion, and in a general manner, to 'act in conformance with a particular world vision in which the relation between man and the divine is defined'.[7]

On the other hand, though the principle of religious freedom constitutes the pillar of ecclesiastical rights in the Mexican State, the results are impossible to

---

4 Willaime, *Europe et religions : les enjeux du XXIe siècle*, 349.

5 S. E. Isaacson, 'Reconocimiento jurídico de las asociaciones religiosas o iglesias y su relación con el Estado: el caso de Estados Unidos', in Varios, *V Coloquio del Consorcio Latinoamericano de Libertad Religiosa: Actualidad y Retos del Derecho Eclesiástico del Estado en Latinoamérica* (México DF: CNDH-SEGOB-CLLR-2005), 270.

6 Isaacson, 'Reconocimiento jurídico ', 270–271.

7 Suprema Corte de Justicia de la Nación, 1a. Sala, Tesis aislada, 9a. Época, Tesis LX/2007 Libertad Religiosa sus Diferentes Facetas, Amparo en revisión 1595/2006, *Stephen Orla Searfoss*, 29 November 2006, S.J.F. y su Gaceta, t. XXV, February 2007, 654.

analyze in an isolated manner, because the freedom is regulated by a secular benchmark, which is supported, at a constitutional level, in the 'historic' principle of separation of the state and of the churches, established in Article 130 of the Fundamental Law. This article affirms that, 'The historic principle of the separation between churches and State influenced the norms contained in the present article. Churches and religious groups shall be organized under the law. This corresponds exclusively to the legislation of the Congress on the subject of outward ecclesiastical forms, churches, and religious groups.' Likewise, Article 130 develops a series of more specific rules, which include:

a. The recognition of the judicial personality of church and religious groups once they are registered with the Secretary of Governance.
b. The principle of no intervention from authorities in the internal life of religious associations.
c. The freedom of Mexicans and foreigners to exercise the ministry of any religious organization, always respecting all regulation the law imposes.
d. The prohibition against religious ministers performing any governmental employment, or being elected to public office, until such time as they are no longer engaged in the ministry.
e. The interdiction of religious ministers from associating with political interests or from promoting or attacking any candidate, party, or any political association, or opposing the country's laws or its institutions or attacking its symbols in any public gathering or through religious activity or religious publications.
f. The prohibition of conducting meetings of a political character in places of worship.
g. The exclusive competence of administrative authorities in civil state acts.
h. The exclusion of religious oaths from the civil sphere.

In a similar sense, the Constitution's first article prohibits religious-based discrimination, while the third article establishes secular education in the country's public schools and affirms the liberty of teaching 'in all their types and modalities'.[8] Finally, the separatist organization of the Mexican State is reinforced by the third article of the Law of Religious Associations and Public Cults of 15 July 1992, which affirms the laic character of the Mexican State, emphasizing that it is strictly neutral toward the different confessions, and that its actions in religious matters are limited to 'the observance of the laws, conservation of order and public moral and the tutelage of third party rights'.[9]

8 Art. 3-VI of the Constitution.

9 Literally, the article third of the *Ley de Asociaciones Religiosas y Culto Público* says: 'El Estado mexicano es laico. El mismo ejercerá su autoridad sobre toda manifestación religiosa, individual o colectiva, sólo en lo relativo a la observancia de las leyes, conservación del orden y la moral públicos y la tutela de derechos de terceros. El Estado no podrá

The articulation of the contrast between the principle of separation and the principle of religious liberty is not always evident, especially in Mexico, where the subject of religion continues to be highly emotionally charged, and where an important contrast between the anticlericalism of the elites and the strong religious tradition of the communities has existed for so many years. In this sense, the principle of separation is presented from a theoretical perspective and is used as a tool for favoring robust religious liberty. The principle also has a darker side, however, that has been used in the history of the country as a way of subordinating the churches under state authoritarianism.

Separation: Guaranteed Religious Freedom

The modern idea of separating the religious and political spheres is rooted in the question of the liberty of conscience, the recognition of which became indispensable to restoring social peace in the context of the violent conflicts that tormented Europe in the second half of the sixteenth century. More than a simple organization of the state, the separation proclaimed by Locke strove to guarantee a regime of peace and freedom, while recognizing the natural right to freedom of conscience, making the state a limited human society for the satisfaction of the internal interests, and the church, a free and voluntary association.[10] From this perspective, the ideas of separation and the freedom of religious associations takes form in the disassociation of citizenship and religious affiliation, and in the displacement of the legitimacy of the state in religious realms, rather leaving it to focus on popular sovereignty.[11] The separation of the state and the churches was considered by its proponents—besides Locke, also Voltaire, Roger William, and Thomas Jefferson—as a political organization capable of permitting the coexistence of the different groups of individuals that make up society through the neutrality of the state in matters of faith.

Currently, the regimen of separation as an instrument to guarantee religious freedom in all societies that are characterized by a plurality of growing confessions has not lost its pertinence. Instead, it solidifies the autonomy of individuals before a state that is incompetent in the matter of religion, causing the state to decline

---

establecer ningún tipo de preferencia o privilegio en favor de religión alguna. Tampoco a favor o en contra de ninguna iglesia ni agrupación religiosa. Los documentos oficiales de identificación no contendrán mención sobre las creencias religiosas del individuo.'

10 Cf. J. Baubérot and M. Milot, *Laïcité sans frontières* (Paris : Editions du Seuil, 2011), 50, and J. Locke, *Carta sobre la Tolerancia*, translation of *A Letter Concerning Toleration* (originally published 1689), 2d edn., 11th printing (Indianapolis: Bobbs-Merrill, 1977), available at http://www.hacer.org/pdf/Locke01.pdf (accessed 29 January 2013).

11 Locke, *Carta sobre la Tolerancia* at 21. Cf. also, R. Blancarte, 'El por qué de un Estado laico', in R. Blancarte, *Los retos de la laicidad y de la secularización en el mundo contemporáneo* (México: El Colegio de México, 2008), 30.

to pronounce itself superior to the legitimacy of different beliefs and obligations that are implicated for believers. The separatist organization of the state leaves space for all particular convictions and philosophies, by not subjecting the people to a positive social link through the dominant religion, but rather uniting them through freedom, as a negative link, a value shared by everyone and a pillar of democratic legitimacy.[12] Furthermore, the strict neutrality of the states derives from its incompetence in matters of faith and, therefore, it restrains a nation's identification with a particular religion and the creation of second-class citizens, excluded from the dominant culture, who can only exercise their religious freedom with the authorization of the majority.[13]

In schools, for example, the secularism of the Mexican public system permits all students to preserve their convictions through the abstention of authorities in matters of faith. People are not excluded from classes of religion nor are there people who feel they are in nonconformity with religious symbols in the classrooms. Such neutrality does not signify ignorance or a lack of awareness of religious phenomenon, whose role in civilization cannot be negated. Rather, religious analysis is possible when it is realized in a neutral manner with respect to the truths diffused by confessions, and also in conformity with a desire to foster—paraphrasing Article 3 of the Constitution—democracy, human rights, the respect of a human person's dignity, and the ideals of fraternity and equality without religious-based privileges and discrimination. Concerning oaths, a matter that creates severe difficulties for confessional traditions in some states, the Mexican separation prohibits religious declarations, replacing oaths with simple promises of telling the truth, liberating the non-believer from professing something they do not accept, and the believer from mixing the spiritual with the profane.[14] In the end, this seems to be a better form for preserving the freedom of conscience for everyone.

Nevertheless, the constitutional principle of separation does not imply abstention or immobility of the state in confessional situations. On the contrary, the state can and should have an active role when the civil consequences of convictions are susceptible to disturbing the public order or the freedom of others. In this sense, the public religious association has a regulated freedom, since public manifestations are subject to surveillance by competent authorities, which cannot be helped because of public order and funding motives.[15] Also, if the state does

---

12 H. Pena-Ruiz, *Dieu et Marianne : philosophie de la laïcité* (Paris: Presse Universitaires de France, 1999), 19.

13 M. Nussbaum, *Libertad de conciencia: contra los fanatismos* (México: Tusquets Editores, 2010), 17.

14 J. L. Soberanes Fernández, *El derecho de libertad religiosa en México: un ensayo* (México DF: Editorial Porrúa, 2001), 57.

15 Since the constitutional reforms of 1992, Mexican legislation accepts manifestations of worship outside of church buildings exclusively, based on a declarative system. This system is developed by Articles 21 to 24 of the *Ley de Asociaciones Religiosas y Culto Público* of 15 June 1992.

not actively promote religion, it has the obligation of guaranteeing religious freedom as a fundamental right, assuring the existence of effective conditions for its exercise. Therefore, in Mexican legislation, the principle of separation does not hinder the state's ability to facilitate access to religious assistance for people who are in a state of subjection, namely, those in the hospitals, centers of social assistance, jails, and migrant detainee stations, as according to the Regulation of the Law of Religious Associations and Public Worship of 6 November 2003.[16]

From the approach of the churches and religious groups, the constitutionalization of the principle of separation in 1992 permitted an apparent paradox, a greater recognition of the churches and religious groups through the creation of a structure adapted to their organization and operation: the 'religious association'. Contrary to the legislation previous to 1992, the state now recognizes the existence, judicial personality, and capacity to act in society of confessional groups, and prohibits public authorities from intervening in their internal issues. Likewise, the Mexican State recognizes the institutional freedom of religious associations: the freedom of organization in matters of dogma, discipline, religious organization, and ministry designations; the liberty to celebrate all types of judicial acts and to act in their own name; and patrimonial freedom in accordance with Article 27-II of the Constitution, which affirms the possibility for religious associations regularly constituted to possess personal property and real-estate necessary for the realization of their objectives.

Therefore, separation gives extensive liberty not only to the institutions but also to the individuals, as it forbids the state to interfere with the internal affairs of religious associations and in fine guarantees, the religious life of the citizens.[17] From this perspective, separation and religious freedom no longer intertwine, as quoted in Miguel Carbonell's terms: 'It wouldn't be possible to understand the individual right to choose a religious belief, if it were not for the existence of a collective decision to maintain both religious and political power separate.'[18]

On the other hand, religious freedom and equality have a very complex relationship, as the former is much more controversial if the latter does not guarantee the benefit of fundamental freedoms for all individuals and confessions.[19] This relationship is based on the principles of separation, secularism, and

---

16 Article 6 of *Reglamento de la Ley de Asociaciones Religiosas y Culto Público* states, 'Los responsables de los centros de salud e instituciones de asistencia social, del sector público o privado, así como las autoridades de los centros de readaptación social y de estancias o estaciones migratorias, de conformidad con sus atribuciones, proveerán las medidas conducentes para que a sus internos o usuarios, a petición expresa de los mismos, reciban asistencia espiritual de las asociaciones religiosas y los ministros del culto.'

17 Nussbaum, *Libertad de conciencia: contra los fanatismos*, supra note 13 at 231.

18 M. Carbonell, 'De la libertad de conciencia a la libertad religiosa', available at http://www.juridicas.unam.mx/publica/librev/rev/jurid/cont/33/pr/pr7.pdf, 17 (accessed 14 December 2012).

19 Baubérot and Milot, *Laïcité sans frontières*, surpra note 10 at 77.

non-discrimination, those which, mutually reinforced, prohibit the state from discriminating and categorizing citizens based on their religious orientation. These principles should be translated to practice, in order to establish vigilance for rights of institutional life, whether at the legislative, judicial, or administrative level.[20]

However, equality is not uniformity, and the point is not to give everyone the same treatment. On the contrary, it is to give everyone their respective share, while respecting similarities and differences among them.[21] On the other hand, equality signifies judicial patrimony for all.[22] In other words, people are just as capable of being convicted as they are of exercising their rights. From the perspective of religious associations, the egalitarian nature of the principle of separation is yet more clear, because the Mexican State cannot distinguish between majority or minority religion, or even more between true religions and supposed 'cults', meaning religions that are considered evil, strange, or dangerous. According to the principle of separation, and in accordance with the opinion of Professor Martínez-Torrón, illegal religions exist only if they act anti-judicially, and this would justify the state's intervention only to guarantee public safety and order.[23]

Ultimately, the separation of church and state, in a democratic society, is used as an instrument to uphold liberty and equality on the basis of religious freedom for all.[24] In this sense, it should not be analyzed as an ultimate and definite end, but as a means to guarantee and encourage the most freedom possible.[25]

The Other Side of the Coin: A Restrictive Principle

The precedential developments that emphasized the virtues of the principle of separation as a universal and abstract idea did not take into consideration the complex situations of certain socio-judicial realities. In Mexico, the separation of the state and the churches, inaugurated in 1859 in the context of the Reform laws, acquired an openly anticlerical slant after the Revolution, with the promulgation of the Constitution of 1917. The problem was that the constituency was trying to solve a conflict that had dominated a great part of the nineteenth century by means of the minimal reduction of the possibility of action by the Catholic Church in society.[26] More than a separation of the state and the churches, the

---

20 Article 3 of the Universal Declaration on Laicity in the 21st Century.

21 A. Molina Meliá, 'El Estado moderno y la libertad religiosa', in J. Ruiz de Santiago, E. González Morfín, A. Molina Meliá et al., *Libertad religiosa, derecho humano fundamental* (México: Instituto de Doctrina Social, 1999), 67.

22 Molina Meliá, 'El Estado moderno y la libertad religiosa' at 68.

23 J. Martínez-Torrón, *Religión, derecho y sociedad* (Granada: Comares, 1994), 179.

24 Molina Meliá, 'El Estado moderno y la libertad religiosa' at 73.

25 Baubérot and Milot, *Laïcités sans frontières*, supra note 10 at 75.

26 J. A. González Fernández, J. F. Ruiz Massieu, and J. L. Soberanes Fernández, *Derecho eclesiástico mexicano* (México DF: Universidad Nacional Autónoma de México -

Constitution mandated the subordination of the confessions to the arbitrariness of political powers. The prohibition of confessional schools and congregations; the limitation of the religious worship to church buildings and particular locations; the prohibition of ministers of a religious organization criticizing the laws of the country or commenting on national matters in confessional newspapers, such as the competency of local legislatures to establish a maximum number of ministries of religious associations in federal entities,[27] would make the regimen of Mexican ecclesiastical rights among the most severe of the occidental world. Following upon the religious conflict of 1923–1926, coinciding with the 'Cristiada' (popular counter-revolution of 1926–1929), constitutional dispositions are objects of informal negotiations between the government and the Catholic hierarchy that gave space to an extra-constitutional pragmatism: in exchange for its support in public political matters, the state allowed the Church to lead an institutional and cultural life with relatively little government interference.[28]

In 1992, national legislation took a radical turn in religious matters, with the reform of Articles 3, 5, 24, 27, and 130 of the Constitution, which permitted the country to enter into modernity in religious matters. Article 130 underwent a profound modification of its provisions, in particular, the recognition of the legal personality of the churches. For that reason, because the other measures were amply accommodated, the government continued, in essence, translating the will of the legislators to prescind religious influences in the public sphere.

So, the principle of separation of the state and the churches did not present itself as neutrality of the state, but rather as an ideological principle that postulated an extreme privatization of religious convictions, with a basis in a negative conception of religious acts. In this context, the provisions in force appear to be remnants of the revolutionary anticlericalism.[29] This is especially true of the prohibition against ministers occupying political positions, of being selected within the frame of popular elections, of associating in political matters, of activism in favor of or against political candidates and parties, of organizing political meetings in religious buildings, and of opposing the laws of the country and its institutions in public meetings, acts exercised by the religious group or in publications of a confessional character. The principle therefore has an ambiguous

---

Instituto de Investigaciones Jurídicas – Editorial Porrúa, 1992), 15.

27 The Mexican Constitution of 1917 in its original version is available at http://www.bicentenario.gob.mx/PDF/MemoriaPolitica/1917COF.pdf (accessed 14 December 2012).

28 About the idea of *Modus Vivendi*, cf. R. Blancarte, *Historia de la Iglesia católica en México (1929-1982)* (Zinacantepec: El Colegio mexiquense, Fondo de Cultura Económica, 1992).

29 F. J. Acuña Llamas, 'El contenido esencial de las normas referentes a derechos humanos en la Constitución mexicana: Consideraciones en torno a las limitaciones para asegurar su debido respeto y protección', in M Carbonell (ed.), *Derechos fundamentales y Estado: Memoria del VII Congreso Iberoamericano de Derecho Constitucional* (México DF: Universidad Nacional Autónoma de México - Instituto de Investigaciones Jurídicas, 2002), 29.

character, protecting the freedom of conscience of individuals before the state and religious denominations, but limiting in great measure the freedom of expression of confessional institutions.

In this sense, the issue of the legitimacy of such restrictions creates a doctrinal division. For some authors, these dispositions are justified by their base in the particular circumstances of the country, which demands strong measures so the religious sentiments of the people will not be manipulated.[30] Similarly, the prohibition against political proselytism, meaning giving consignments of votes to the loyal, obeys the will to preserve the freedom of conscience of the voters, under the frame of electoral processes free of religious references. In this way, the prohibition against the passive vote of ministers of the religious associations is justified because 'the moral and psychological [influence] that in fact, the ministers of the cult exercise over a great majority of the people, would give them a superiority and prepotency contrary to the equality that should exist in all tenured positions of political rights'.[31] Likewise, the restrictive status of the religious ministry would simply present incompatibilities,[32] justified by the existence of similar norms in the canon law.[33] There would be little seriousness in the measure that abandoning the priest function reestablishes the political and civil rights of the ministries in their completeness.[34]

However, the other part of the doctrine denounces 'violence to the condition of the citizen'[35] based on the right of every citizen, recognized by the American Convention of 1969, 'of voting and being selected in authentic periodic elections'. So, a clear ethical incompatibility exists between the activity of religious ministry and political activity. Some authors support such a prohibition based on internal

---

30 Soberanes Fernández, *El derecho de libertad religiosa en México*, supra note 14 at 58.

31 R. Sánchez Medal, 'Régimen jurídico de los ministros de culto religioso', in *Estudios jurídicos en torno a la Ley de asociaciones religiosas y culto público* (México DF: Universidad Nacional Autónoma de México Secretaría de Gobernación, 1994), 96.

32 Sánchez Medal, 'Régimen jurídico de los ministros de culto religioso' at 97.

33 Cf. Código de Derecho Canónico, edición bilingüe comentada (Madrid: Biblioteca de autores cristianos, MCMLXXXIII, cánones 277, 285–3, 286, 287), 168, 172–173.

34 The article fourth of *Ley de Asociaciones Religiosas y Culto Público* specifies that the clerymen 'no podrán ser votados para puestos de elección popular, ni podrán desempeñar cargos públicos superiores, a menos que se separen formal, material y definitivamente de su ministerio cuando menos cinco años en el primero de los casos, y tres en el segundo, antes del día de la elección de que se trate o de la aceptación del cargo respectivo. Por lo que toca a los demás cargos, bastarán seis meses.' In addtion, la 'separación de los ministros de culto deberá comunicarse por la asociación religiosa o por los ministros separados, a la Secretaría de Gobernación dentro de los treinta días siguientes al de su fecha. En caso de renuncia el ministro podrá acreditarla, demostrando que el documento en que conste fue recibido por un representante legal de la asociación religiosa respectiva.'

35 R. González Schmal, *Programa de derecho constitucional* (México DF: Universidad Iberoamericana-Editorial Limusa-Grupo Noriega Editores, 2003), 436.

regulations of the churches, and in no such case on the Constitution, the principal mission of which is always to preserve the freedom and equality of its citizens.[36] In this same sense, Benito Juárez, the liberal leader and father of the separation in 1859, observed: 'With respect to the clergy, [...], it does not seem just to deprive from one of the most important rights of citizenship. Moreover, the fact that they might exercise undue influence to make themselves be named representatives did not seem a sufficient rationale, since is the legitimacy of the election must necessarily trust in the name of freedom and the prudence and discretion of the electorate [...].'[37]

Summarizing Miguel Carbonell's analysis, the exclusion of the churches from the political sphere will be acceptable only if it is interpreted in a restrictive manner, meaning, from the electoral perspective.[38] In no case should this allowable area of exclusion be confused with the area of having and sustaining ideas about the social reality and its problems, which is a fundamental liberty for all in the democratic regimen. Even when understood like that, in practice, the tensions are frequent in the Mexican public setting. In particular, there are tensions involving sensible subjects like those that put the values of Mexican – such as the interruption of a pregnancy, matrimony between or possibility to adopt for people of the same sex, or euthanasia – to judgment. These are very delicate subjects that necessitate difficult discussions about the legitimacy of the influence of religious discourse in the public sphere and about the question of the freedoms enjoyed by everyone, believers and non-believers alike, within the framework of a secular state that has an obligation to elaborate norms for everyone, independent from all particular beliefs. The state, representative of everyone and not just one dominant culture, needs to maintain a distinction between the common values that govern the life of all and those that apply only to those who voluntarily follow a religious confession.

From this perspective, as Habermas mentions, the liberal state can legitimately expect all citizens to accept the neutrality of power over different world visions,[39] and defend this principle, in different cases, against the intrusion of religious groups searching to impose their doctrines and behaviors on all society. However, the defense of the secular principle should not imply restrictions to the peoples'

---

36 A. M. Prida Peón del Valle, 'El derecho eclesiástico del Estado mexicano, desde las perspectivas del ideario de Benito Juárez y del derecho internacional de los derechos humanos', 31 *Revista de Investigaciones Jurídicas* 31 (2007), 765.

37 Cited by González Schmal, *Programa de derecho constitucional* at 437. ("Respecto de los eclesiásticos, [...], no parecía justo privarlos de uno de los más importantes derechos de ciudadanía. Además, no parecía razón suficiente para privarlos de él, la presunción de que ejercieran una influencia ilegítima para hacerse nombrar diputados; ya porque necesariamente debe confiarse el acierto del nombramiento a la libertad y discreción de los electores [...]".)

38 M. Carbonell, 'La libertad religiosa en la Constitución mexicana artículos 24 y 130', *Documento de Trabajo* (México DF: Universidad Nacional Autónoma de México - Instituto de Investigaciones Jurídicas, 2003), 13.

39 Cited by Baubérot and Milot, *Laïcités sans frontières*, supra note 10 at 148.

liberties. Rather, religious visibility and expression should be accepted in the public space, especially when it includes themes relative to human dignity and fundamental rights,[40] and, in a general manner, sensible forms of human coexistence. In reality, despite the necessity of separating religious and civil circles, the spheres have areas of shared influence, which the state must recognize,[41] as a representation of social diversity.

Conclusion

The regimen of the separation of church and state, framed as a principle for preserving religious freedom as demanded by the state's guarantee of democratic rights, raises questions regarding the relationship between the state, religious groups, society, and the individual. In all countries, the articulation of this relationship is presented as the result of historic processes, influenced by circumstances and by the contemporary resolution of problems.[42] In this context, institutional agreements are not always presented as rational choices, but as pragmatic solutions in determined contexts as well. Thus, the church-state relationship cannot simply be analyzed through theoretic models. Instead, it demands to be examined through the concrete screening of the socio-cultural conditions of every society.

In Mexico, the question of separation as a positive or negative factor for the recognition of religious freedom has two different facets. From an individual focus, it is presented as a mechanism capable of assuring liberty of conscience to a majority, liberty from the state as well as from the influence of religious groups throughout the country. However, from an institutional perspective, the situation is much more delicate, because the constitution, beginning in 1992, permitted the recognition of religious institutions as guardians of equal rights. Article 130 of the Constitution creates a severe separation between the public and religious spheres that strictly limits expressions used in public debate, as well as the liberty and fundamental rights of religious leaders. From this perspective, 'Mexican style' separation needs to include a balance between the traditional secularism that seeks to preserve individual liberty of conscience and the necessary respect for religious institutions as relevant social actors that have the same rights to express their opinions as those holding secular viewpoints. Ultimately, it is about finding a more extensive liberty for all, believers or non-believers, and to renounce the paternalistic vision of a society that is becoming more secularized[43] and creating

40 Cf. J. M. Setién Alberro, 'La misión de la Iglesia y la comunidad política', in C. de la Torre Martínez (ed.), *Memoria del Primer Congreso Internacional sobre Iglesias, Estado laico y sociedad* (México DF: Comisión Nacional de los Derechos Humanos, 2006), 22–50.

41 Setién Alberro, 'La misión de la Iglesia y la comunidad política' at 36.

42 Proeschel, *L'idée de laïcité : une comparaison franco-espagnole*, supra note 1 at 13.

43 According to Roberto Blancarte, 90 percent of the population is in favor of separation between state and churches as an organizational principle of social life.

distinctions between believers and non-believers. In addition, the Mexican State must assume the risks of freedom[44] and of giving responsibility to its citizens. That is the only path towards a democratic development of the country.

44 González Schmal, *Programa de derecho constitucional*, supra note 35 at 436.

Chapter 9
Constitutional Protection of Religious and Cultural Minorities in Sub-Saharan Africa

Kofi Quashigah

Introduction

Religion is an integral part of the African way of life; religion played and continues to play an important role in the lives of Africans; all aspects of the life of the average African have religious connotations; almost every segment of the lifestyle of traditional societies is a religious practice – birth, childhood, marriage, economic activities, death and burial are all heavily steeped in religious rites.

Among traditional African societies religious beliefs and manifestations were personal matters. Religion served the group and the beliefs and manner of worship add to promote group identity. Religion served the kinship system which was the social system of the traditional African societies. It was rare for one group to seek to compel another to abandon its religious belief and practice and to adopt that which the first group subscribed to. Proselytism was virtually unknown in these societies, and therefore the possibility of religious conflicts emerging was rare.

With the intrusion of Christianity and Islam the stage was set for religious differences coming to the fore.

Types of Constitutional Guarantee of Religious Rights

The significance of religion in the personal and public lives of a people is well known and has taken central stage in the constitutional affairs of almost all countries. Religious considerations have increasingly become one of the essential factors in the determination of control of political power in many African countries. Constitutions have therefore become instruments used either to clearly determine the religious preference of the nation or to indicate the degree of distance that should exist between the political enclave and the religious lives of the people.

In terms of the relationship between state and religion in Africa, a few have constitutionally declared a preference for one religion as the state religion. Some also specifically describe the state as secular, while others simply guarantee religious liberty. Mauritania is an example of a state with an open declaration of a state religion, thus giving virtually no legal recognition to other faiths. By the Constitution of the Islamic Republic of Mauritania the country is declared as an Islamic Republic[1] with Islam as the religion of the people and state.[2] The constitution by Article 10 guarantees the following freedoms to all individuals:

- freedom to move and settle in all parts of the territory of the Republic;
- freedom to enter and leave the country;
- freedom of opinion and thought;
- freedom of expression;
- freedom of assembly;
- freedom of association and freedom to join any political organization or union of their choice;
- freedom of trade and industry;
- freedom of intellectual, artistic and scientific fields;

Significantly no mention is made of freedom of belief and worship.

Further, Article 23 of the Mauritania Constitution declares that to qualify as President of the Republic, the aspirant must be a Muslim.

While Mauritania in no uncertain terms declares Islam as the state religion, Zambia declares in the Preamble to its constitution that, Zambia is 'a Christian nation while upholding the right of every person to enjoy the person's freedom of conscience and religion'.[3] The preamble has been held as non-justiciable;[4] and unlike the Mauritanian Constitution the Zambian Constitution provides an elaborate guarantee for religious freedom.

In contrast is The Gambian Constitution,[5] which by Article 1 declares the country as a Sovereign Secular Republic. Article 25 further guarantees the right to freedom of thought, conscience and belief and freedom to practise any religion and to manifest such practice.

On the other hand the Constitution of Sierra Leone like that of many other African countries guarantees the right to religious liberty in rather simple terms; examples are the Constitution of Senegal[6] and that of Ghana, the latter which for instance simply provides: 'All persons shall have the right to – (c) freedom to practice any religion and to manifest such practice.'[7]

Although many African countries purport to be constitutionally secular, the practice of their national affairs tends to reflect influence of the dominant religious community more than being truly a-religious. The example has been given of

1 Constitution of the Islamic Republic of Mauritania, art. 1.

2 Constitution of the Islamic Republic of Mauritania, art. 5.

3 Constitution of Zambia 1991 (as amended 1996).

4 *Zambia Democratic Congress v. Attorney* – General SCZ Judgment 37 of 1999, referred to in A. Mwansa, 'Law, religion and human rights in Zambia: The past, present and the practice', 8 AHRLJ (2008), 546, 558.

5 Constitution of the Republic of The Gambia, 1997.

6 Art. 8.

7 1992 Constitution of Ghana, art. 21(1)(c).

Liberia, where the 1984 Constitution, Article 14 provides: 'All persons shall be entitled to freedom of thought, conscience and religion and no person shall be hindered in the enjoyment .... The Republic shall establish no state religion.'

In addition there is the statutory prohibition of religious education in public schools to the effect that 'No special or sectarian religious instruction shall be given in the public schools of this Republic other than such general instructions in morals and ethics as the Ministry of Education shall by regulation require.'[8]

It is reported that, this injunction notwithstanding, the Bible is taught 'as a major subject in all government schools from primary school to high school and is on the national curriculum as a required course'.[9] Muslim students lacked the legal support to opt out of it.[10] It is further observed that the Christian religion predominates in all aspects of public life in Liberia and that it 'enjoys evident preference and, historically, the Christian religion has shaped much of the culture, law, government and practices of modern Liberia'.[11] The same observation has been made in respect of Botswana, where the constitution does not recognize any state religion; nevertheless, it is claimed that there is some evidence of 'Christian preference by the statutory observance of Christian events as public holidays'.[12] The same could be made as a general observation for other African countries such as Ghana. In Nigeria the effort has been made to a large extent to accommodate the sensitivities of the two dominant religious groups – Christians and Muslims.

Generally the degree to which religion serves as a national issue varies from country to country depending upon the dynamics of colonial history and the role that history might have played in affecting the aspirations of the dominant groups. Brief case studies of selected countries may help in this discourse. The examples of Nigeria, South Africa, and Benin are worth exploring: Nigeria because of the endemic issue of Sharia and the upsurge of religious intolerance highlighted by the *Boko Haram* violence; South Africa because of its large number of varying religious faiths and the conscious efforts being made to accommodate them all in a post-apartheid system; Benin because of the rare influence of traditional religion within the country.

The Case of Nigeria

Nigeria is a highly pluralistic society with more than 250 tribes. Demographically Nigeria presents a rare example of a nation in which the populations of Christians

8 Liberian Codes Revised, vol. III, ch. XIV, 94, 216, quoted in G. Heaner, 'Religion, law and human rights in post-conflict Liberia', 8 AHRLJ (2008), 458, 478.

9 Heaner, 8 AHRLJ at 478.

10 Heaner, 8 AHRLJ at 478.

11 Heaner, 8 AHRLJ at 477.

12 E. K. Quansah, 'Law, religion and human rights in Botswana', 8 AHRLJ (2008), 486, 494, n. 49.

and Muslims are almost matched, with an equally large number of traditional religionists throughout the country,[13] and where the religious issue often becomes a platform on which political elections are fought. It also has the additional feature of the Southern part of the country having a majority of Christians while the North has a majority of Muslims. In the Northern part of the country, Islamic law is very endemic side by side with the pro-English common law legal system.[14] The British colonial administration in Nigeria had sought to achieve a compromise by the creation of a Penal Code for the Northern territories and a Criminal Code for the Southern groups. This compromise became necessary because it is the case that for the Muslims, as Nigerian scholar Nmehielle discovered, 'there is no distinction between the religious and the secular, between legal, ethical, and moral questions, or between the public and private aspects of a Muslim's life. The Sharia regulates different aspects of a Muslim's life whether secular or otherwise, such as prayer, dietary regulations, wills and contacts.'[15]

Under these circumstances the various constitutions of Nigeria have endeavoured to maintain a balance without allowing the country to be dragged down the slippery slope of religious antagonism. Sections 10 and 38 of the 1999 Constitution of Nigeria therefore seek to guarantee freedom of religion to all Nigerians:

> 10. The Government of the Federation or of a State shall not adopt any religion as State Religion. … 38. (1) Every person shall be entitled to freedom of thought, conscience and religion, including freedom to change his religion or belief, and freedom (either alone or in community with others, and in public or in private) to manifest and propagate his religion or belief in worship, teaching, practice and observance.
>
> (2) No person attending any place of education shall be required to receive religious instruction or to take part in or attend any religious ceremony or observance if such instruction ceremony or observance relates to a religion other than his own, or religion not approved by his parent or guardian.
>
> (3) No religious community or denomination shall be prevented from providing religious instruction for pupils of that community or denomination in any place of education maintained wholly by that community or denomination.

13 See A. A. Oba, 'The Sharia Court of Appeal in Northern Nigeria: The Continuing Crises of Jurisdiction', 52 *The American Journal of Comparative Law* 4 (Autumn 2004), 859.

14 Oba at 859.

15 V.O.O. Nmehielle, 'Sharia Law in the Northern States of Nigeria: To Implement or Not to Implement, the Constitutionality is the Question', 26 *Human Rights Quarterly* 3 (August 2004), 730, 737.

As is provided in Section 10 of the 1999 Constitution of Nigeria one would have thought, as ascribed to by Nmehielle,[16] that the secularity of the State is thereby assured. However, Yadudu, another Nigerian writer, argues that the absence of the phrase 'secular state' from Section 10 is an indication that the constitution does not declare Nigeria as a secular state.[17] From Yadudu's perspective a justification for the establishment of Sharia courts in the Northern states could be found even in the constitution itself.

Indeed a number of Nigerian scholars have surmised that the declaration and establishment of Sharia courts together with the formalization of state machinery and policy along the tenets of Islam is clearly an adoption of a state religion.[18] The Governor of Zamfara State which was the first to introduce the Sharia Courts was quoted as having declared that, "the introduction of Sharia courts and of Islamic criminal justice in general will be quickly followed by sustained efforts to align all official functions of government and indeed all socio-economic activities in his state to the tenets of Islam."[19] The Civil Liberties Organization, an NGO, was quoted as confirming this:

> What obtains in Zamfara State is the adoption of Islam as State Religion … Though the governor of the State argues that Islam was not adopted as a State Religion, the establishment of a Ministry of Religious Affairs and the creation of a Preacher's Council, which has the responsibility of mobilizing support for Islam, clearly indicates that Islam is the official religion of the State.[20]

In all these the Federal Government remained tactically silent, obviously not intending to get itself embroiled in a controversy that could cascade into a conflict between Christians and Muslims in an already uncomfortably frail and conflict-prone environment. Kolawole Akinwande described the reaction of former President Obasanjo on the issue of the Sharia courts:

> He was actually tempted into reacting to the contrary and had he countered the moves made (overtly and covertly) by the Sharia mongers, the country would have been thrown into a state of anarchy. But, by act of providence, he kept his cool only to later come out with a verdict that allayed the fears of Nigerians by declaring the hullabaloo a "political issue.[21]

16 Nmehielle at 741.

17 Nmehielle at 741. Being a comment and disagreement by Nmehielle on Yadudu's opinions in his paper *Sharia Implementation in a Democratic Nigeria: Between Deference to Popular Will and Libertarian Challenges* (unpublished).

18 Nmehielle in addition to himself mentioned others such as Chukkol and Nwauche.

19 Nmehielle at 745.

20 Nmehielle at 745.

21 K. Akinwande, 'The *Boko Haram* Backers', *Sunday Tribune* (4 September 2011).

The push for *sharinization* is now being blamed for the increasing threat posed by the group known as the *Boko Haram*, which has claimed responsibility for a number of recent violent attacks in Northern Nigeria, including an attack on the UN Building in Abuja, the national capital.[22] It is asserted that *Boko Haram* was initially established in 2002 as a peaceful organization but staged a short-lived violent armed uprising in June 2009 and has since then gone underground and continued with its violent attacks on the populace.

The *Boko Haram* is believed to be a tool of those who have touted the idea of *sharianization*. According to Kolawole Akinwande,

> *Boko Haram* has now come out with an addition to its agenda in its fight to spread Islam in this country. Its clamour for 'sharianisation' of Nigeria is not a new demand in that it is an age-long desire by some Muslim religious leaders in the North. The change in nomenclature does not matter but the forces behind it. It is now Sharia or destruction in all forms—an irreconcilable issue.[23]

However, a researcher on *Boko Haram*, Abdulkarim Mohammed, has been quoted as saying that

> *Boko Haram* is essentially the fallout of frustration with corruption and the attendant social malaise of poverty and unemployment … The young generation see how [the nation's resources] are squandered by a small bunch of self-serving elite which breeds animosity and frustration, and such anger is ultimately translated into violent outbursts.[24]

Thus the Nigerian state finds itself confronted with a socio-political problem that is clothed in religious garb.

In response to a string of bombings carried out by the group, the President of Nigeria came out to declare that the military option which had been adopted against the group has done more harm than good and therefore set up a committee to negotiate with the group and to report back before the 16th of August 2011.[25] Obviously not much has been achieved along these lines yet. It has been reported that while the military option continues, secret talks have been going on, including

---

22 On Friday 26 August 2011 *Boko Haram* claimed responsibility for a devastating bomb attack on the UN building in Abuja, the National Capital.

23 Akinwande, supra note 21.

24 'Analysis: Understanding Nigeria's Boko Haram radical', *IRIN, Humanitarian News and Analysis* (18 July 2011), http://www.irinnews.org/printreport.aspx?reportid=93250 (accessed 7 December 2012).

25 Aljazera Report, 31 July 2011.

one in August 2012 held in Saudi Arabia between Nigeria's Vice President Namadi Sambo and *Boko Haram's* deputy leader Abu Mohammed.[26]

It is obvious that irrespective of Nigeria's constitutional guarantee of the right to religious freedom, practical socio-economic factors have operated to create a state of uncertainty, and religious tension, and conflict leading to loss of lives, particularly between Christians and Muslims. Between 2000 and August 2011 not fewer than 24 violent religion-based clashes occurred in Nigeria,[27] resulting in the deaths of thousands of people.[28]

The case of Nigeria suggests that it takes more than just the guarantee of religious rights in a constitution to secure respect for religious tolerance and therefore peace. The Nigerian situation may be summed up with the observation of Isizoh:

> It is true that most of these conflicts have many sources, which include poor, corrupt, and inept leadership; exaggerated ethnic affiliation, religious extremism, etc. In itself religion does not generate conflicts. It is often the manipulation of religion and religious sentiments that lead to tension and could degenerate into violent conflicts.[29]

The problem in Nigeria is the perception by Muslims of the 'relatively marginal status of Islamic law within the Western oriented constitutional architecture of the Nigerian state'.[30] It is, however, the case that the Nigerian constitutional system has endeavoured to level the field for Christians and Muslims.

The Case of Benin

Benin provides a rare situation where traditional religions not only have held sway but also have been accorded extensive national recognition in the political scheme of things. The country has been known for its deep-rooted traditional religious background, which revolves around the voodoo religion, which recognizes the existence of *Mawu*, the one God, who is supreme but who must be accessed

26 See A. E. Olojo, 'Engaging Boko Haram: Militarization, Mediation or Both?', *Global Observatory*, http/www.theglobalobservatory.org/analysis (accessed 4 January 2013).

27 Including the attack on the UN building at Abuja.

28 See Aljazeera.net, http:/English.aljazeera.net/news/Africa/2010/01/20101234108187505.html.

29 C. D. Isizoh, 'Religions in sub-Saharan Africa: Working and Walking Together – A Christian Reflection', http://www.africaworld.net/afrel/religions-in-africa.htm (accessed 13 August 2011).

30 Centre for Research on Inequality, Human Security and Ethnicity (CRISE) Management of Horizontal inequalities in Cote d'Ivoire, Ghana and Nigeria Issues and policies, www.Crise.ox.ac.uk.

through the medium of other smaller gods or spirits. According to Mezzane, the voodoo practice suffered just as other religious faiths during the 17-year period of the Marxist-Leninist regime between 1972 and 1989.[31] It however bounced back with renewed vigour with the restoration of democracy in 1990, which culminated in the declaration of a national holiday for adherents on the 10th of January for its celebration just like other mainstream religions.

The Constitution of Benin guarantees religious liberty to all; Article 23 of the constitution for example provides:

> Every person has the right to freedom of thought, of conscience, of religion, of creed, of opinion and of expression with respect for the public order established by law and regulations. The exercise of a creed and the expression of beliefs shall take place with respect for the secularity of the state. The institutions and the religious or philosophical communities shall have the right to develop without hindrances. They shall not be subject to the guardianship of the state. They shall regulate and administer their affairs in an autonomous manner.

Unlike other countries where traditional African religion is viewed with some degree of amusement and mostly derided by the often dominant Christian groups, the case of Benin provides us with a dramatic example to the contrary. The fate of traditional religion in Benin presents a peculiar example of a country in Africa that openly promotes the traditional religion even to the discomfiture of the Christian and Islamic religions.

The Case of South Africa

Among the constitutions of African countries that of South Africa stands out in view of the depth of the guarantees in respect of religious liberty and cultural rights. Possibly guided by the country's immediate past history of apartheid, the South African Constitution contains a most elaborate provision on the protection of group rights, including religious freedom. In addition is the establishment of the Commission for the Promotion and Protection of the Rights of Cultural, Religious and Linguistic Communities.

For our purposes and in a numerical order the South African Constitution commenced with the creation of an institution for the promotion of and respect for specific languages that are of some religious value, as recorded in Section 6(5):

> S. 6(5) A Pan South African Language Board is to be established by national legislation to
> *(b)* promote and ensure respect for

31 D. Mezzane, 'African Traditional Religions and Modernity', *AfikaWorld.net*, http://www.afrikaworld.net/afrel/religionitrad.htm (accessed 13 August 2011).

> (ii) Arabic, Hebrew, Sanskrit and other languages used for religious purposes in South Africa.

The specific mention of these three languages is made because they not only have religious relevance for specific religious groups but are by reason of their not being mainstream languages at risk of being sidelined and possibly lost.

Next in line of the constitutional provisions is the guarantee of equality of all and the prohibition of discrimination. Both the state and individuals are specifically prohibited from discriminating on various grounds including religion, conscience, belief, culture, language and birth:

> S. 9(3) The state may not unfairly discriminate directly or indirectly against anyone on one or more grounds, including race, gender, sex, pregnancy, marital status, ethnic or social origin, colour, sexual orientation, age, disability, religion, conscience, belief, culture, language and birth.
> (4) No person may unfairly discriminate directly or indirectly against anyone on one or more grounds in terms of subsection (3). National legislation must be enacted to preventor prohibit unfair discrimination.
> (5) Discrimination on one or more of the grounds listed in subsection (3) is unfair unless it is established that the discrimination is fair.

The next provision which makes interesting reading is Section 15, which is devoted exclusively to the freedom of religion, belief and opinion:

> S. 15(1) Everyone has the right to freedom of conscience, religion, thought, belief and opinion.
> (2) Religious observances may be conducted at state or state-aided institutions, provided that
> *(a)* those observances follow rules made by the appropriate public authorities;
> *(b)* they are conducted on an equitable basis; and
> *(c)* attendance at them is free and voluntary.
> (3) *(a)* This section does not prevent legislation recognising-
> (i) marriages concluded under any tradition, or a system of religious, personal or family law; or
> (ii) systems of personal and family law under any tradition, or adhered to by persons professing a particular religion.
> *(b)* Recognition in terms of paragraph *(a)* must be consistent with this section and the other provisions of the Constitution.

By this provision the state or state institutions may observe religious practices provided they are carried out in an equitable manner to the satisfaction of adherents of other faiths. The provision also guarantees recognition for family relationships as governed by traditional systems and various religions.

Section 16 guarantees the right to freedom of expression but prohibits advocacy of hatred based on race, ethnicity, gender or religion.

Of further significance is Section 31, which complements Section 9 by specifically re-emphasizing the equal treatment for cultural, religious or linguistic groups:

> S. 31 (1) Persons belonging to a cultural, religious or linguistic community may not be denied the right, with other members of that community-
> *(a)* to enjoy their culture, practise their religion and use their language; and
> *(b)* to form, join and maintain cultural, religious and linguistic associations and other organs of civil society.
> (2) The rights in subsection (1) may not be exercised in a manner inconsistent with any provision of the Bill of Rights.

The right to maintain relationships with co-religionists is carried to the extent that Section 35(2)(f)(iii) even guarantees to the detainee the right to communicate with his or her chosen religious counselor.

Unlike in many other countries, and to ensure a monitoring process of the religious and cultural rights, there is a constitutionally mandated Commission under Section 181(1)(c) – The Commission for the Promotion and Protection of the Rights of Cultural, Religious and Linguistic Communities. The detailed functions of the Commission provide an insight into the specific degrees to which South Africans intend cultural and religious rights to be protected. Section 85 sets out the functions:

> S. 85 (1) The primary objects of the Commission for the Promotion and Protection of the Rights of Cultural, Religious and Linguistic Communities are-
> *(a)* to promote respect for the rights of cultural, religious and linguistic communities;
> *(b)* to promote and develop peace, friendship, humanity, tolerance and national unity among cultural, religious and linguistic communities, on the basis of equality, non-discrimination and free association; and
> *(c)* to recommend the establishment or recognition, in accordance with national legislation, of a cultural or other council or councils for a community or communities in South Africa.
> (2) The Commission has the power, as regulated by national legislation, necessary to achieve its primary objects, including the power to monitor, investigate, research, educate, lobby, advise and report on issues concerning the rights of cultural, religious and linguistic communities.
> (3) The Commission may report any matter which falls within its powers and functions to the South African Human Rights Commission for investigation.
> (4) The Commission has the additional powers and functions prescribed by national legislation.

In its totality the provisions in the South African Constitution appear unsurpassed by any others on the continent. This must definitely have been influenced by the apartheid experience and therefore is driven by the strong desire to protect both major and minor cultural and religious communities from abuse either by the state or by fellow citizens.

Nevertheless, Amoah and Bennett, writing of the situation in South Africa, bemoan the comparatively scant attention that is accorded traditional religions in comparison to the others, particularly Christianity and Islam.[32] The same is true of Ghana, where the 1992 Constitution openly assigned constitutional space to the Christian and Islamic religious groups without a similar recognition of the traditional and other smaller religious groups.[33]

It is nevertheless worthy of note that the African Traditional Religions were not left out of the recently launched South African Charter of Religious Rights and Freedoms. The Charter has as its objective the promotion and protection of religious rights and freedoms in South Africa. On the whole the Charter represents a concerted effort by the various religious groups in South Africa – the Jewish religion, Christians, the Muslim faith, the Hindu Religion, the National Council of the Bahá'ís in South Africa, African Traditional Religions, and African Independent Churches – to support the promotion and protection of religious rights and freedoms in South Africa. There is also established a South African Council for the Promotion and Protection of Religious Rights and Freedoms, which has been mandated to find ways and means to bring the Charter before Parliament to be accepted as the law of the land.

The African Charter Provisions and the African Commission Applications

The value of religion to the life of the African is recognized in the African Charter on Human and People's Rights (ACHPR), particularly the Preamble and Articles 8 and 17(2), (3).

In the Preamble, African states give consideration to the virtues, historical traditions, and values of African civilization. The Preamble further acknowledges that civil and political rights cannot be dissociated from economic, social, and cultural rights, and also that the satisfaction of economic, social, and cultural rights is a guarantee for the enjoyment of civil and political rights.

32 J. Amoah and T. Bennett, 'The Freedoms of Religion and Culture under the South African Constitution: Do Traditional African Religions Enjoy Equal Treatment?', 24 *Journal of Law and Religion* (2008), 10.

33 1992 Constitution, Article 166 mandates representation of the following religious groups on membership of the National Media Commission: Christian group (The National Catholic Secretariat, the Christian Council and the Ghana Pentecostal Council), the Federation of Muslim Councils, and Ahmadiyya Mission.

Thus African virtues and values which embody considerations and respect for the spiritual life of the individual and of the community, as well as the importance of the cultural heritage to the overall quality of life of the human being, are acknowledged in the Preamble.

With respect to the substantive provisions, the ACHPR guarantees the right to equality of all in Article 2, which provides that, 'Every individual shall be entitled to the enjoyment of the rights and freedoms recognized and guaranteed in the present Charter without distinction of any kind such as race, ethnic group, colour ....'

In the case of *Malawi Africa Association and Others v. Mauritania*[34] the African Commission interpreted Article 2 of the ACHPR as having as one of its goals the elimination of all forms of discrimination and the guarantee of the equality of all. The African Commission quoted with approval Article 1(1) of the Declaration of the Rights of People Belonging to National, Ethnic, Religious or Linguistic Minorities[35] and re-emphasized the concerted effort under international human rights law and the comity of states to 'accord a certain importance to the eradication of discrimination in all its guises'.[36]

Specifically, Article 8 provides for the substantive guarantee of the right to religious freedom, that 'freedom of conscience, the profession and free practice of religion shall be guaranteed. No one may, subject to law and order, be submitted to measures restricting the exercise of these freedoms.'[37]

On a more general note is the guarantee of cultural rights in Article 17(2) and (3), which provides that '(2) Every individual may freely take part in the cultural life of his community', and that '(3) The promotion and protection of works and traditional values recognized by the community shall be the duty of the state.'

Article 17(2) vests the rights in the individual, while Article 17(3) imposes duties on the state. These two provisions may be read together with Article 19 of the ACHPR, which recognizes the equality and respect of all. Article 19 reads: 'All peoples shall be equal; they shall enjoy the same respect and shall have the same rights. Nothing shall justify the domination of a people by another.'

These various provisions taken together justify the view that religious and cultural liberties are guaranteed in the African Charter on Human and People's Rights.

The African Commission on Human and Peoples' Rights (African Commission) has endeavoured to give detailed meaning to this assertion in a number of its thematic works and series of decisions.

---

34 54/91-61/91-98/93-164/97-196/97-210/98.

35 Adopted by the General Assembly of the United Nations in Resolution 47/135 of 18 December 1992.

36 *Malawi Africa Association and Others v. Mauritania*, African Commission on Human and Peoples' Rights Comm. Nos. 54/91, 61/91, 98/93, 164/97 à 196/97 and 210/98 (2000), available at http://www.escr-net.org/docs/i/401108 (accessed 7 December 2012).

37 It is important to indicate that the permitted derogations cannot be interpreted as at large; see the decision of the African Commission in the *Endorois Case*, infra note 41.

In the Report of the African Commission's Working Group on the Indigenous Populations/Communities (2005)[38] it was observed that the issue of dispossession of land and its resources is a major human rights problem for indigenous peoples,[39] and further that the dispossession threatens the economic, social, and cultural survival of indigenous pastoralist and hunter-gatherer communities.[40]

Of relevance is the Report of the Special Rapporteur on the situation of Human Rights and Fundamental Freedoms of Indigenous People in Kenya wherein it was observed that the livelihoods and cultures the indigenous peoples have been traditionally discriminated against, and their lack of legal recognition and empowerment reflects their social, political, and economic marginalization.

The importance accorded these rights is further captured in the African Commission's Guidelines for National Periodic Reports[41] wherein the Commission directs that 'Article 17(2) should be understood as requiring governments to take measures aimed at the conservation, development and diffusion of culture, such as promoting cultural identity as a factor of mutual appreciation among individuals, groups, nations and regions ... promoting awareness and enjoyment of cultural heritage of national ethnic and minorities and indigenous sectors of the population.'

The African Commission was presented with the opportunity to make determinative pronouncements on Articles 8, 17 and 19 in a number of cases in which complaints were filed seeking the protection of religious and cultural rights of indigenous peoples; prominent among them was the case of *Centre for Minority Rights Development (Kenya) and Minority Rights Group (on behalf of the Endorois Welfare Council) v. Kenya (the Endorois Case)*.[42]

In this case the complainants filed a complaint with the African Commission on behalf of the Endorois people, an indigenous people that inhabit the lands around Lake Bogonia within the Rift Valley Province of Kenya. The complaint alleged that the Government of Kenya forcibly removed the Endorois from their ancestral lands to make way for the creation of a game reserve. It is the case of the complainants that the area surrounding Lake Bogonia is fertile land that provides green pasture and medicinal salt licks for their cattle, an environment

38 Available at http://pro169.org/res/materials/en/identification/ACHPR%20Report%20on%20indigenous%20populations-communities.pdf (accessed 7 December 2012).

39 Ibid.

40 Ibid.

41 See Second Annual Activity Report of the African Commission on Human and People's Rights 1988-1989, ACHPR/RPT/2nd Annex XII. Article 62 of the ACHPR requires each state party to submit every two years, a report on the legislative or other measures taken with a view to giving effect to the rights and freedoms recognized and guaranteed by the Charter.

42 *Centre for Minority Rights Development (Kenya) and Minority Rights Group International on behalf of Endorois Welfare Council v. Kenya*, 276/2003, African Commission on Human and Peoples' Rights, 4 February 2010, available at http://www.unhcr.org/refworld/docid/4b8275a12.html (accessed 8 December 2012).

that supports their pastoral way of life. It was further alleged that Lake Bogonia is central to Endorois' religious practices and encompasses their historical prayer sites, places for circumcision rituals and other cultural ceremonies. The Endorois people believe that the spirits of all Endorois, no matter where they are buried, live on the lake. Weekly, monthly, and annual festivals are held at the lake. In effect, the complaint of the Endorois can be summed up as being that their health, livelihood, religion, and culture are all intimately connected with their traditional land, as grazing lands, sacred religious sites, and plants for traditional medicine are all situated around the shores of Lake Bogonia.[43]

The complainants alleged that the Republic of Kenya had violated Articles 8, 14, 17, 21 and 22 of the African Charter on Human and People's Rights and therefore sought a restitution of their land with legal title and clear demarcation and compensation for the loss of their property, development, and natural resources and also the freedom to practice their religion and culture.[44] The Commission upheld these claims, thereby supporting the religious and cultural rights of the minority Endoris.

There have been some other circumstances in which the African Commission has endeavoured to protect freedom of thought, religion, and belief. One such instance was the Commission's decision to declare admissible the case of *INTERIGH and the Egyptian Initiate for Personal Rights v. Egypt*.[45] In this case the alleged victim was arrested and detained for his widely distributed but unpublished religious research work that purported to refute 'the often held opinions of the "duty of Muslims to kill converts from Islam to other religions" and "prohibition on Muslim women marrying non-Muslim men"'. The petition was brought to seek protection of the right to personal liberty and also to assert that rights under Article 8 of the ACHPR were violated because the victim was discriminated against in his enjoyment of the Charter right on the basis of his religious beliefs. In the end, the African Commission could not proceed with the matter because the complainant withdrew the case because the victim had been released.

The African Commission has gradually demonstrated a strong desire to protect the guaranteed rights to freedom of religion, thought, and belief.

The Endorios case demonstrates the degree of scant respect that is often accorded minority groups by African governments. If the Endorois were a dominant religious group, the Kenyan Government would have been more circumspect in how it treated the members.

43 African Commission on Human and Peoples' Rights, 4 February 2010.

44 African Commission on Human and Peoples' Rights, 4 February 2010

45 African Commission 312/05.

The Case of Rastafarians

The two separate issues of Rastafarian use of the herb known as cannabis and same-sex relationships have become recurrent in sub-Saharan Africa with little sympathy for these minorities.

Reactions differ from country to country on the issue of same-sex relationships; while the South African official system accords some legal recognition to same-sex relationships the general populace abhors it, with even violent attacks on individuals alleged to be involved in such relationships; in Uganda, both officialdom and the generality of the populace are up in arms against it; in Ghana the Government has been cautious in its pronouncements on the issue, with human rights NGOs being sympathetic while religious groups are vehemently opposed to it. It is viewed as a cultural issue, and its acceptance will require a gradual re-orientation of the cultural sensitivities of the people.

The particular issues of the religious practice of the Rastafarian sect in the wearing of the hair style known as dreadlocks and the use of the herb cannabis for religious purposes have received judicial consideration in a number of countries, in South Africa and Zimbabwe for example. In the case of *In re Chikweche*[46] the applicant, a citizen of Zimbabwe and a devout follower of the Rastafari movement, upon obtaining the necessary qualifications prescribed by law lodged an application in the High Court for registration as a legal practitioner, notary public and conveyancer. He wore his hair in dreadlocks as is the practice of Rastafarians. When the applicant appeared in person before the High Court for the purpose of taking the oath, the learned Judge considered him to be 'unkempt' and not 'properly dressed', principally because of his hair style. In the Supreme Court it was contended on behalf of the applicant that the attitude of the learned Judge was an infringement of the applicant's rights under the Constitution of Zimbabwe to freedom of conscience (Section 19(1)), freedom of expression (Section 20(1)) and protection from discriminatory treatment (Section 23(1)(b)). The Court held for the applicant, and Chief Justice Gubbay in the lead judgment expressed his opinion that the applicant's manifestation of his religion by the wearing of dreadlocks fell within the protection afforded by section 19(1) of the constitution. He quoted with approval Justice Wilson in the Canadian case of *Morgentaler and Others v. R*[47] that 'in a free and democratic society 'freedom of conscience and religion' should be broadly construed to extend to conscientiously-held beliefs, whether grounded in religion or secular morality'.[48]

---

46 *In re Chikweche*, Case No. CA 626/93, Zimbabwe: Supreme Court, 27 March 1995, available at http://www.unhcr.org/refworld/docid/3ae6b6914.html (accessed 7 December 2012).

47 *R. v. Morgentaler*, [1988] 1 SCR 30, available at CanLII, http://www.canlii.org/en/ca/scc/doc/1988/1988canlii90/1988canlii90.html (accessed 7 December 2012).

48 [1988] 1 SCR 30, at 179.

In the case of *Prince v. South Africa*, where the issue was the use of the herb cannabis for religious rituals, the Court was not prepared to accede to the applicant's claim of entitlement to exemption from legal prohibition of its use. The facts of the case were that the Law Society of the Cape of Good Hope in South Africa refused to admit the applicant as an attorney because of his disclosure of two previous convictions for possession of cannabis. According to the complainant his use of cannabis was inspired and required by his Rastafari religion. It was his claim that reasoning and meditation are essential elements of the religion and that cannabis is key to these practices. He alleged that 'the use of cannabis was believed to open one's mind and helped Rastafari gain access to the inspiration provided by Jah Rastafari, the Living God.'[49] The applicant further disclosed that he intended to continue using cannabis 'as inspired and required by his Rastafarian religion'.[50]

Obviously there were strong faith-based reasons for the applicant's commitment to the use of the prohibited herb; nevertheless the African Commission found no violation of the applicant's rights and held specifically that the African Charter's protection of freedom of religion is not absolute and that the limitations visited on the applicant and his fellow Rastafarians fall within the ambit of the law.

Derogations from the Guaranteed Religious and Cultural Rights

Irrespective of the exhibited strong desires in the various constitutions and the ACHPR to guarantee the religious and cultural rights of all segments of their societies, steps have been taken to derogate from the rights guaranteed but essentially for the interest of the generality of the whole society. The South African provision under which the rights in the Bill of Rights, which include the religious and cultural rights, could be derogated from in Section 36 is couched in rather general terms:

> S. 36 (1) The rights in the Bill of Rights may be limited only in terms of law of general application to the extent that the limitation is reasonable and justifiable in an open and
> democratic society based on human dignity, equality and freedom, taking into account all relevant factors, including-
> *(a)* the nature of the right;
> *(b)* the importance of the purpose of the limitation;
> *(c)* the nature and extent of the limitation;
> *(d)* the relation between the limitation and its purpose; and
> *(e)* less restrictive means to achieve the purpose.
> (2) Except as provided in subsection (1) or in any other provision of the Constitution, no law may limit any right entrenched in the Bill of Rights.

49 *Prince v. South Africa* (2004) AHRLR 105.
50 *Prince* at 106.

In the case of *Christian Education South Africa v. Minister of Education*[51] the Constitutional Court of South Africa was called upon to consider the constitutionality of Section 10 of the South African Schools Act 1996, which sought to prohibit resorting to corporal punishment at a school. The Christian Education South Africa is a voluntary association that is dedicated to the promotion of evangelical Christian education. It was their claim that corporal punishment is an integral part of their religious belief and training and that the blanket prohibition of its use in its schools invades their individual rights to freely practise their religion. The appellant based its position on a number of provisions of the South African Constitution. These include Section 14, which guarantees to everyone the right to privacy; Section 15, which protects the right to freedom of conscience, religion, thought, belief and opinion; Section 29, which supports the right of everyone to establish and maintain at their own expense, independent educational institutions; Section 30, which protects the use of language and participation in the cultural life of choice; Section 31 which prohibits denial to persons belonging to a cultural religious or linguistic community the right with other members of that community, to enjoy their culture, practise their religion and use their language and also to form, join and maintain cultural, religious and linguistic associations and other organs of civil society. The Court held that by Section 31 (2) these rights may not be exercised in a manner inconsistent with any provision of the Bill of Rights.

The constitutions of other countries show similarities in the derogations from the religious and cultural rights.[52] Equally the African Commission expressed the opinion in the case of *Prince v. South Africa*[53] that the right to participation in one's culture should not be at the expense of the overall good of the society and therefore that minorities like the Rastafari may freely choose to exercise their culture but not to the extent that they be granted unfettered power to violate the norms that keep the whole nation together.

Conclusion

The issues of religious and cultural rights are central to life in Africa. In most of Sub-Saharan Africa the state prefers to guarantee religious and cultural rights but subject to limitations that take into account the interests of the generality. This general fact notwithstanding, the influence of the dominant religions still pervade and permeate political life in almost all the countries. In most situations traditional religion becomes the main loser. Also at the losing end are minorities whose beliefs and practices run contrary to the beliefs of the dominant groups; the fate of same-sex minorities therefore does not seem to be very good in most of Africa. Cultural sensitivities of many African states have yet to accommodate the

51 Case CCT 4/00.

52 See for example the Constitution of Sierra Leone, sec. 25(4).

53 (2004) AHRLR 105.

interests of this group of minorities. Generally therefore although religious liberty and its protection in Africa is an important consideration the actual practice has left some blemishes. The constitutional protection of religious liberty needs to be supplemented with an attitude of tolerance if the right to religious liberty is to be fully realized by all.

Chapter 10
Religious Freedom in the Constitutions of the Maghreb

Nassima Ferchiche

Introduction

Until 2011, the Arab regimes were living in a fictitious world, characterized by varying degrees of despotism. In January of that year, the uprising began in Tunisia, followed by Egypt, and then spread throughout Northern Africa, and to the Persian Gulf, Syria and Lebanon. We are bearing witness to an era of changes in the Arab world, particularly in the Maghreb. In Morocco, the social system and the distribution of wealth, seriously unequal but more transparent than in Algeria, continue to pose problems. In the last ten years, the monarchy of Mohammed VI has initiated a few reforms, designed and agreed on publicly. Nevertheless, the demonstrations in February reveal that the Moroccan monarchy needs to make some fast and profound changes. This is the intention behind the adoption of the new constitution. The same is about to happen in Tunisia, following the social uprising that spread throughout the country and degenerated into revolution.

The Maghreb, which in the Arab world means 'the West country', is easily defined by its geography. 'It refers to that massif of highlands, highly compartmentalized and relatively well irrigated, which extends between the Mediterranean, the Atlantic and the desert, and which houses within its folds a Berber population that is less and less Arabized the further west we travel.'[1] The Muslims of the three largest countries – Tunisia, Morocco and Algeria – represent approximately 95 percent of the total population of this region.[2] None of these countries recognizes secularism. Yet this principle would seem to be the one that would best 'preserve the integrity of religion and spiritual values, safeguarding them from the manipulations of politicians in competition for power, while preserving the integrity of the state from the manipulations of religious leaders.'[3]

1 P. Rondot, 'L'Islam dans la politique des États du Maghreb', 1 *Politique étrangère* (1973 – 38th year), 41.

2 'Mapping the Global Muslim Population: A Report on the Size and Distribution of the World's Muslim Population', October 2009, http://pewforum.org/uploadedfiles/Orphan_Migrated_Content/Muslimpopulation.pdf, 16 (accessed 13 December 2012).

3 G. Corm, 'Globalisation et communautarisation du monde: quel futur pour la laïcité ?' Cycle of Lectures: *Masques et figures de la guerre*, 3 April 2008, Marseille.

Far from enshrining the separation of church and state, the public authorities of the Maghreb interrelate the two closely, elevating Islam to the level of official religion in their constitutions.

In the Maghreb, this affirmation has given Islam a special importance that is the product of historical and cultural circumstances prior to independence.[4] Indeed, the influence of the Muslim religion is evident in legal frameworks, such as in family law, which draws heavily from *Sharia* (Islamic law based on the Koran).[5] However, these countries are home to different religious minorities (Christians, Jews) who have a right to their religious freedom, which includes 'the freedom to have or adopt the religion or belief of [their] choice, and freedom, either individually or in community with others and in public or private, to manifest [their] religion or belief in worship, observance, practice and teaching'.[6] On the other hand, we may well ask the question: how can the individual and collective religious freedom of these people be respected, while at the same recognizing the superiority of a particular religion, i.e. Islam? How is this right defined in the countries of the Maghreb?

To answer this question, which is far from simple, it is necessary to go back to the origins of the constitutionalization of Islam as state religion, before analyzing the legal consequences of the constitutional provisions related to religion on the respect for the religious practices of the faithful.

The Constitutional Status of Islam and Constitutional Protection of Religious Freedom

To analyze religious freedom in the constitutions of the Maghreb, we need to identify the legal bases, in domestic law, for the protection of this essential right. Religious freedom will be assumed here to be a fundamental right, although this concept may seem vague,[7] since it forms part of the 'set of rights and freedoms afforded to individuals and organizations (both private and public) under the constitution, but also under international agreements, and protected from both

4 Tunisia and Morocco won independence in 1956; Algeria in1962.

5 Le Code de la famille algérien, available at http://20ansbarakat.free.fr/codedelafamille.htm (accessed 13 December 2012). The National Commission to revise the 1984 code set up at the end of 2003 (shortly after completion of the revision of Morocco's *Moudawana*) led to the adoption of a slightly modified version of the same code, on 27 February 2005.

6 Article 18 sec. 1 of the International Covenant on Civil and Political Rights, adopted on 16 December 1966, available at http://www2.ohchr.org/english/law/ccpr.htm (accessed 13 December 2012).

7 J. Rivero, 'La protection des droits fondamentaux par les juridictions constitutionnelles en Europe', *Revue internationale de droit comparé* (1981), 659.

executive and judiciary infringement by constitutional and international courts'.[8] Indeed, such rights cannot be neatly classified within a formal legal category, as a right may prove fundamental without endorsement by the constitutional or international court, and conversely, the textual guarantee of a freedom does not predetermine its fundamental nature.[9] Moreover, constitutional affirmations of religious freedom appear everywhere today, yet they are not necessarily applied in practice. Is the affirmation of religious freedom in the constitutions of the Maghrebi nations one of the elements of a democratic facade to present an irreproachable image of the system of governance on the international stage? Or is it in fact a guarantee that this principle will be enforced, conditioning the existence of a true Rule of Law in the Maghreb (or in Arabic, *siyyadat-al-Qanun*, literally, 'the sovereignty of the law'[10])? To answer these questions, is essential to examine the value of the constitutional status given to religious freedom in the Maghreb, analyzing the degree to which the constitutional tradition has taken root, and the circumstances that led to the constitutionalization of this freedom, before interpreting the constitutional provisions on religious freedom.

The Origins and Content of this Constitutionalization

The Ambition of the Authorities to Regulate Religion

An analysis and comparison of the constitutions of Morocco, Algeria and Tunisia reveals many similarities and a few notable differences. All three were the product of an independence won either peacefully[11] or violently[12] from colonial France.[13] Tunisia was the first in 1959, followed by Morocco in 1962 (the year after the arrival to the throne of Hassan II), and, finally, Algeria in 1963. Constitutionalism has a long history in the region; the first constitution in the Arab world was adopted

---

8 L. Favoreu, 'L'élargissement de la saisine du Conseil constitutionnel aux juridictions administratives et judiciaires', 4 *Revue française de droit constitutionnel* (1990), 581.

9 Abdelfattah Amor goes further than this, as he argues that the identification of fundamental rights with constitutionally protected and sanctioned rights 'can be full of consequences in the countries that do not fully guarantee it'. Their constitutional enshrinement cannot constitute anything more than a presumption of their fundamental nature. See S. Hamrouni, 'Les droits fondamentaux et les constitutions maghrébines', in *Mélanges offerts au doyen Abdelfattah Amor* (Centre de Publications Universitaires Tunis, 2005), 548.

10 Freedom of thought, conscience and religion 'is one of the foundations of a democratic society', *Leyla Şahin v. Turkey*, App. No. 44774/98 (ECtHR), 29 June 2004, para. 66.

11 Morocco and Tunisia, in 1956, after having been French protectorates since 1912 and 1882, respectively.

12 War of Independence in Algeria from 1954 to 1962.

13 T. Le Roy, 'Le constitutionnalisme : quelle réalité dans les pays du Maghreb ?', 79 *Revue française de droit constitutionnel* (2009/3), 544.

on 26 April 1861 on the initiative of Sadok Pacha Bey,[14] ruler of Tunisia, and a constitutionalist movement emerged in Morocco as early as 1906.

In general terms, the purpose of these first constitutions had more to do with the need to legitimate their governments (for example, Bourguiba as opposed to the Bey) than with the affirmation of a democratic legislature (which would be replaced by the Ulamas, for example). It was thus an effort to galvanize a young state (for example, Mohammed V's kingdom, through the appearance of a constitutional monarchy) rather than affirm the rights of the citizens in relation to their governments. In all cases, the role of the constitution was more symbolic or pragmatic than legal.

However, the heritage of colonization is obvious, especially in the case of Algeria, as the constitutional text, which affirms the sovereignty of the new state, is dedicated to the victory of the national revolution and includes references to socialism in the organization and operation of the new Algerian institutions. Yet the break is not total, because, although liberated from French colonization by a socialist revolution, Algeria gave itself the same legal instrument that France had after the bourgeois revolution of 1789 to establish and operate its institutions. There is thus a certain formal connection between the new Algerian state and the former colonizer, particularly with regard to the reclaiming of liberal ideals.[15]

The circumstances of the constitutionalization of religious freedom in Algeria are also closely linked to the fight for independence, the international context and the activity within the country of protest movements pushing for effective democratization and greater respect for individual rights and freedoms. By any hypothesis, lying behind the general, constant and verifiable intention throughout the constitutional processes in the Maghreb is the fact that the independent governments, in spite of the latent threat it posed to their power, could not ignore the protection of such fundamental rights after having fought to win them back.[16]

---

14 One particular catalyst for Tunisia's modernization process was the promulgation of the *Pacte fundamental* on 10 September 1857, which guaranteed freedom and equality of Tunisian subjects. The new Bey, continuing the work of his predecessors, issued a Constitution on 26 April 1861. However, the deterioration of public finances resulted in increasing interference from the European powers, and in 1881 France made Tunisia a protectorate. The 1861 text clearly recognized freedom of worship for foreigners (Article 105: 'Full freedom is guaranteed to all foreigners settled in the Tunisian States with regard to the practice of their religious beliefs') and implicitly for Tunisians (Article 94: 'Non-Muslim Tunisians who change religion shall continue to be Tunisian subjects and subject to the jurisdiction of the country.').

15 See B. Stora, *Histoire de l'Algérie coloniale (1830–1954)* (Paris: Éditions La Découvert, 2004), 110: 'From then on, to say "1789" meant to call for an end to colonial status' in the context of the events of May 1945.

16 Although the fight for independence only took the form of a war of liberation in Algeria, the Moroccans and Tunisians also took part in the battle for decolonization. On this question, see M.R. de Madariaga, *En el barranco del lobo. Las guerras de marruecos* (Madrid: Alianza Editorial, 2005).

They thus opted to qualify the recognition of these rights with precautions that would confine them within an increasingly narrow framework.

The other limitation, common to all three countries, originated from the international political context that compelled the authorities to consider all definitions of civil liberties, and recognize both the 'collective rights' advocated by communist or socialist nations and the 'classical' or 'formal freedoms' defended by the other side, as well as the principles emanating from the Muslim religion. The challenge thus involved 'reconciling the construction of a modern state, inspired by a Western perspective born out of colonization, with an adherence to Muslim values'.[17]

From that time on, a unique relationship emerged between religion and politics, whereby the political authorities appropriated the regulation of Islam. This phenomenon has become clearer still since the victory of the Islamist-leaning parties in the last legislative elections in Morocco and Tunisia and the good position now held by the Islamist party in the Algerian government.[18]

Three Different Relationships between Religion and Politics with Islam Always Appearing as the Foundation of Public Morality and Social Progress

1) The 'Unitary Obsession' in Algeria

In Algeria, the liberation struggle, beginning in 1954 in the name of popular nationalism and fed by modern revolutionary ideas, had at least the psychological and sociological (if not theological) quality of a jihad.[19] From June 1965, Colonel Houari Boumédienne sought constantly to strengthen the regime through references to Islam. Muslim values were invoked in moral, social and cultural terms, underpinned by the 'Arab-Islamic' socialism of the state, and its development was fostered in the reformist direction advocated by Sheikh Abdelhamid ben Badis (who had died in 1940).

---

17 A. Derradji, *Le droit de la presse et la liberté d'information et d'opinion dans les pays arabes* (Éditions Publisud, 1995), 48; M. Flroy, *Les régimes politiques arabes* (Paris: Presses universitaires de France, 1990), 84–85: 'The inspiration behind the Arab political systems is a combination of a sentimentally justified desire to return to their roots and the need to build a modern State that could compete with the colonizers. These two poles would exert a force of attraction that varied from country to country and era to era. These contradictory influences would constitute a factor of ambiguity both in discourse and in constitutional texts. A double reading is nearly always possible. […] The Arab nations have always been searching for their political specificity.'

18 *En-nahda* in Tunisia in October 2011, the *Justice and Development Party (PJD)* in Morocco in November 2011, and the *Green Algeria Alliance*, made up of the *Movement of Society for Peace* (MSP) and other Islamic groups, which became the third biggest political force in Algeria in May 2012. T. Fattani, 'Après la Tunisie et la victoire des islamistes au Maroc. Vague verte sur le Maghreb', *L'Expression*, 27 November 2011.

19 Rondot, 'L'Islam dans la politique des États du Maghreb', supra note 1 at 41–50.

In Algeria, religion also constitutes one of the most solid foundations of 'the unitary obsession',[20] a basic characteristic of the Algerian nation. Effectively, since independence, the state, which chose not to be separate from religious matters, gave Islam a central role in the definition of its identity and as a symbol of national unity.[21] Rather than a private belief, Islam was made a rule for community life, covering family, social and political affairs, an official Islam[22] that induces the hostility of the state toward differing opinions and individuality on the one hand, and the division of the community of believers into parties, social classes or specific cultural groups (such as Berbers in an Algeria famous for being an Arab nation[23]) on the other. In this way, the traditional Arabic-Islamic values preached by the National Liberation Front (FLN) served to legitimate the claims to political power of the imams.[24]

Since the 1990s, which were marked by Islamic terrorism, relations between Islam and the state have evolved toward greater government control of the religion. This re-appraisal of relations has been accompanied by a strengthening of confessionalism in society and in the government, in the context of a state of emergency in effect until 2011[25] and an attempted national reconciliation that is still under construction.[26] In spite of the recurring debates in the Algerian press over the elimination of references to Islam as the state religion, the government

20 Expression used by L. Garon, *L'obsession unitaire et la Nation trompée/la fin de l'Algérie socialiste* (Québec: Presses universitaires de Laval, 1993), 278. The other expression Garon uses is '*l'arabité*' (lit. 'arabness').

21 Article 8, line 3 of the Constitution of 28 March 1996 defines one of the purposes of the institutions established by the people as 'the safeguarding and consolidation of national identity and unity.' The identity referred to is Sunni Islam.

22 The majority of Algerians observe the Sunni Malekite rite. There are also Amerites (Sunnis of Turkish origin), Ibadists (neither Sunni nor Shia) in the M'Zab, and brotherhoods mostly in the South. The state recruits theologians, appoints imams, regulates and coordinates their training, finances the construction of public mosques, publishes Islamic newspapers, broadcasts religious radio and television programs and prevents monopolies. Even the President of the Republic must be a Muslim, pursuant to Article 73, Section 2 of the Constitution of 28 November 1996, concerning the conditions for eligibility to be Head of State. Lise Garon describes this as a veritable 'nationalization of religious life', *L'obsession unitaire*, supra note 20 at 29.

23 This notion of the indivisibility of the Algerian nation is the justification for the single party formula.

24 M. Gadant, *Islam et nationalisme en Algérie d'après 'El Moudjahid', organe central du FLN de 1956 à 1962*, preface by B. Stora, Collection Histoire et perspectives méditerranéennes' collection (Paris: L'Harmattan, 1988). A reclaiming of Islamic values through the power provided by historical and ideological factors; this may be described as revolutionary Islam.

25 Presidential Order No. 11–01, of 23 February 2011, on lifting emergency rule (*JORA* No. 12, 23 February 2011, 4), which confirmed the official and formal end of a state of emergency that had lasted 19 years.

26 Order No. 06–01 of 27 February 2006 implementing the Charter for Peace and National Reconciliation, *JORA* No. 11, 28 February 2006, 3–7.

has not been able to eradicate Salafist tendencies. Indeed, it would be a mistake to believe that removing Islam from the constitution would further the secularization process. It might perhaps be better for the state to continue overseeing religious affairs rather than leaving them unregulated.

2) Tunisian Secularism or Gallicanism

In spite of the 'modernist audacity'[27] of Habib Bourguiba, who applied sweeping reforms based on a liberal interpretation of religious law, the Tunisian state has never been secular. His strategy consisted of implementing a secular political program while appealing to Islam.[28] However, this didn't last, and when Zine El-Abidine Ben Ali came to power in 1987, he launched a 'readjustment' of the political system in relation to the religious system in the form of a 're-Islamization' of society, the purpose of which was to neutralize Islamic contestation.

Instead of allowing an institutional separation between religion and the state, the policy initiated by Bourguiba (and continued by his successor) looks like a Tunisian version of the political Gallicanism that once existed in France.[29] Gallicanism, a doctrine on church-State relations implemented in France under the *Ancien Régime* (and under the Empire),was characterized by a union between the Church of France and the King, forged in order to limit the rights of the Holy See. Setting aside the French Catholic context, Gallicanism is an ideology and institutional practice aimed at establishing the primacy of the State over the religious sphere through systematic control of the latter. In most cases, this control includes the subjugation of religious leaders and the infiltration of senior religious positions by government officials, along with the financial subordination and monopolistic regulation of all activities involving the production and dissemination of religious symbolism. All these features can be found in the type of relations established by Bourguiba between the state and Islam. In this way, the nascent Tunisian state established a system of 'veritable regulation of worship'.[30]

Specifically, this management consisted of a department of religious affairs under the direction of the Secretary of State to the Presidency,[31] which would

27 F. Frégosi, 'La régulation institutionnelle de l'islam en Tunisie : entre audace moderniste et tutelle étatique', in F. Frégosi and M. Zenghai, *Religion et politique au Maghreb: les exemple tunisien et morocain,* Policy Paper No. 11 (Paris: Institut français des relations international, March 2005), 6, available at http://www.ifri.org/files/PP_11_kmf_fregosi_zeghal.pdf (accessed 31 January 2013).

28 Michel Camau describes this atypical situation very well in M. Camau (ed.), *Tunisie au présent. Une modernité au dessus de tout soupçon ?* (Paris: Éditions du CNRS, 1987), 11–49.

29 Frégosi, 'La régulation institutionnelle de l'islam en Tunisie', supra note 27.

30 Y. Ben Achour, 'Islam perdu, islam retrouvé', *Annuaire de l'Afrique du Nord* XVIII (Paris: Éditions du CNRS, 1979), 68.

31 Article 1 of Decree No. 67–345 of 5 October 1967, concerning the organization of the Office of the Secretary of State to the Presidency, *JORT* (*Journal Officiel de la République Tunisienne*) No. 43 (10 October 1967), 1252.

subsequently be attached to the Prime Minister's office, and then to the Ministry of the Interior from July 1986. This department was responsible for the coordination of government action in religious affairs (policy on construction and organization of religious centers), appointment and training of leaders of worship (imams and preachers) and their remuneration as government employees,[32] as well as the regulation of rites of worship and religious education programs.

At the same time, Bourguiba's government directly opposed the traditional religious apparatus,[33] especially with the dissolution of Sharia (and Jewish) courts, the nationalization of public and then private *habús*[34] and of the *zawiyas* (religious schools), and the abolition of the *habus*[35] category of land ownership. In this way, the financial resources of the religious apparatus became considerably limited and, from that time, it became financially dependent on the state. There were other measures defined as 'Bourguibi reformism with religious implications',[36] such as the prohibition of polygamy, the establishment of civil divorce, or the invitation to the people to refrain from fasting in the interests of the struggle against underdevelopment, depicted as a veritable jihad requiring the mobilization of all energies to ensure victory.

However, the reaction of religious leaders and the pressure they brought to bear, along with the liberalization of the country in the 1970s (which resulted in Bourguiba losing the support he had from leftists), provoked an inversion (or reversion) of the trend. This re-balancing would continue through the 1980s, while the sphere of Islamic influence moved gradually out of the shadows and gathered around the Movement of the Islamic Tendency (MTI). Nevertheless, the rapprochement between Islamists and the government would be limited to fact that the MTI shared an anti-Marxist agenda with the ruling PSD (Socialist Destourian[37] Party). But with the arrival to power of Ben Ali on 7 November 1987, the logic of repression against Islamists would be very quickly swept away, and Islam would be re-inscribed in the political practices and institutional activities of Tunisian society. According to this logic of strengthening the administrative structure of Islam beginning late in Bourguiba's rule, places of worship were subject to greater regulation and oversight by the state[38] for their construction (subject to a prior order from the Prime Minister), classification (also ordered by the Prime Minister),

32 Decree No. 66-151, of 8 April 1966, concerning the specific status of preachers of the Governorates and preachers of the delegations, *JORT* No. 17 (12 April 1966).

33 Decree of 29 March 1956, concerning the modernization of teaching in the Great Mosque and its annexes, *JORT* No. 27 (3 April 1956).

34 Also called *Waqf*: pious property or foundations.

35 Decrees of 18 July 1957, abolishing the *habus* property system.

36 M. E.-H. Cherif, 'Réformes et islam chez Bourguiba', in S. Ferchiou (ed.), *L'islam pluriel au Maghreb* (Paris: Éditions CNRS, 1996), 61.

37 From *destour*, which means 'constitution' in Arabic.

38 Law No. 88–34, of 3 May 1988, concerning mosques, *JORT* No. 31 (6 May 1988). State control was also extended to other religious buildings such as the *zawiyas* and tombs, whose construction is subject to tight control by the government.

maintenance (public domain system), and use (policy on worship implemented by the Ministry of Religious Affairs), as well as their closure outside prayer times, except for certain mosques of interest to tourists (Al-Zaytuna in Tunis, Mosque of Uqba in Kairouan, etc.).

3) The Moroccan Monarchy: The Only Legitimate Religious Institution?
In spite of the evolution of its elite class, Morocco has essentially remained very traditional; the structure of the state is based on a monarchy that for a long time held the title of Caliph; hence the continued use of terms like 'Sharifian dynasty' and 'Sharifian Empire'.[39] Although the monarchy has been extensively modernized (particularly the royal court), it continues to rely on its Caliphate origins for much of its prestige, which remains the essential factor behind its influence over the masses up to the present, in spite of public calls for greater democracy.[40]

Both Mohammed V and Hassan II attempted to build a Muslim community of royal subjects. Once independence had been won, the monarchy went to great lengths to appropriate the regulation of Islam. Hasan II wanted to maintain control over the religious sphere, which gave his power legitimacy, while at the same time weakening it so that it could not establish a competing forum in the country. Religious affairs were thus fragmented, which made them harder to control in the context of greater political openness.

In Morocco, except in developed urban society, the religious practices of adult Muslims are dominated by expressions of popular mystical piety; the brotherhoods, especially numerous and influential among the Berber communities, play an important social role. The country's youth are increasingly leaving behind these traditional ties, partially as a result of growing agnosticism. However, they seem to still be aware that they belong to the Muslim community, which is viewed as the normal context of civilization and society.

The Constitutional Provisions and Their Inherent Limitations

Islam, Religion Recognized by the State

While some commentators argue that the Algerian and Moroccan cases differ from the Tunisian due to the status its constitution confers on Islam,[41] it is fair to conclude

39 'Sharif' is an Arabic term meaning 'descendant of the prophet Mohammad'.

40 Exploited by the February 20 Movement. Béatrice Hibou offers an interesting analysis of this movement, examining it in its larger political context. See B. Hibou, 'Le mouvement du 20 février, le Makhzen et l'antipolitique. L'impensé des réformes au Maroc', *SciencesPo* | CERI/CNRS (May 2011), 9, available at (http://www.sciencespo.fr/ceri/sites/sciencespo.fr.ceri/files/art_bh2.pdf).

41 On the debate this question has aroused, see A. Amor, 'Constitution et religion dans les Etats musulmans', *Constitutions et religions*, Académie internationale de droit

that all three constitutions define it as the state religion. According to the Tunisian Constitution, 'Tunisia is a free, independent and sovereign state. Its religion is Islam, its language is Arabic and its type ofgovernment is the Republic.'[42] The declaration of 7 November 1987 includes the famous religious formula: 'In the name of God, the Clement, the Merciful.' Although this type of invocation has become a ritual formula in the Arab and Muslim world and its effective application is never really examined, it could only be viewed as surprising in the Tunisia of Bourguiba, who had always been sure to avoid such expressions in his official speeches. In contrast, the new Tunisian president, in addition to making use of such expressions during his speeches, would also end them with a sura from the Koran.

Beyond the formulaic expressions, the goal was to reaffirm Tunisia's Arab-Muslim identity. This would be stated forcefully in the National Pact of 1988 in the following terms: 'Tunisia, an integral part of the Arab world and the Islamic nation, is connected to its Arabness and its Islamness. The Arabic language spread throughout its whole population to become, centuries ago, the language of speech, writing and culture, and Islam spread to embrace all its inhabitants without sectarianism or clanism.'[43]

Moreover, at present and until its scheduled review by the political reforms commission, the Preamble to the Tunisian Constitution[44] proclaims 'the will of this people, who freed themselves from foreign domination thanks to their strong cohesion [...] to remain faithful to the teachings of Islam, to the unity of the Greater Maghreb, to its membership of the Arab community [...]'.

In addition, Articles 38 and 40 associate the role of president with the Muslim faith. Indeed, professing the Muslim faith is set forth explicitly in the Constitution as a condition for eligibility to hold the office of president. Furthermore, while Tunisian common law is totally secular, legislation on matters related to personal status, although progressive, continues to present elements of religious law, which have been confirmed by case law.

---

constitutionnel, 10th session, 1994 (Toulouse: Presses Universitaires de l'Université des Sciences Sociales de Toulouse), 55; Y. Ben Achour, 'Islam et constitution', *Revue tunisienne de droit* (1974), 114; C. Neifar, 'Constitution tunisienne et Islam', in *Assemblée nationale constituante*, Proceedings from the Colloquium of the Tunisian Association of Constitutional Law, 29–31 May 1986 (Tunis: CERP, 1996), 179 (in Arabic); B. Tekari, 'La place du droit musulman dans les constitutions des pays arabes', *Revue tunisienne de droit* (1982), 20 (in Arabic).

42 Article 1 of the Constitution of 1 June 1959.

43 Extract of the National Tunisian Pact, 7 May 1988, available in French from the Tunisian Association of Constitutional Law (ATDC) at http://www.atdc.org.tn.

44 Constitution of 1 June 1959, last amended by Constitutional Law No. 2008–52, 28 July 2008.

According to the Algerian Constitution, 'Islam is the religion of the State.'[45] This constitutional statute has been inviolable since 1976.[46] Moreover, the Preamble to the Constitution stipulates that 'the fundamental components of its [Algerian] identity are Islam, Arabity and Amazighity' and there is a clear tendency to identify Islam with the nation in the proclamation that 'Algeria, being a land of Islam, an integral part of the Great Maghreb, an Arab land, a Mediterranean and African country, is proud of the radiance of its 1st of November Revolution and is honored by the respect the country gained and knew how to preserve through its commitment to just causes in the world.'

References to religion can also be found in the national charters that formalize the ideological and political point of reference for the party and the state at all levels.[47] Thus, for example, describing the characteristics of Algerian society, the Charter of Algiers of 1964 asserts that 'Algeria is an Arab-Muslim country. However, this definition excludes any reference to ethnic criteria and is opposed to any underestimation of the contribution prior to Arab penetration. The division of the Arab world into individualized geographical or economic units could not relegate to the background the factors of unity forged by history, Islamic culture and a common language.'[48] A reference to Islam also appears in provisions of the constitution itself: 'The institutions are not allowed to [...] [engage in] practices that are contrary to Islamic ethics and to the values of the November Revolution';[49] the President of the Republic must be a Muslim;[50] and the oath taken by the President includes a promise to glorify Islam.[51]

Lastly, Islam constitutes one of the main sources of inspiration of Family Law in Algeria, as the predisposition of the Arab/Muslim elite toward referring to Sharia in legislation related to personal status and family law is illustrated perfectly in the Algerian case, as evident in the Algerian Family Code.[52] Thus, 'the reference to Sharia is often wielded by different agents in decision-making processes as a mythical reference, the ultimate representative of a supra-historical and non-effective authenticity. The Algerian case [...] is a patent illustration.'[53]

45 Article 2 of the Constitution of 28 March 1996, amended by Constitutional Law No. 08-19 on 15 November 2008 (*JORA* No. 63, 16 November 2008).

46 Article 178 (3) of the Constitution, 22 November 1976.

47 Article 6 of the Constitution of 22 November 1976.

48 Charter of Algiers, 1964, available in French at http://www.el-mouradia.dz/francais/symbole/textes/charte%20d'alger.htm (accessed 15 December 2012).

49 Article 9.

50 Article 73.

51 The text of the oath is contained in Article 76 of the Constitution.

52 The national commission to revise the 1984 code established at the end of 2003 (shortly after completion of the revision of Morocco's *Moudawana*) led to the adoption of a slightly modified version of the same code, on 27 February 2005, available (in French) at http://20ansbarakat.free.fr/codedelafamille.htm (accessed 15 December 2012).

53 S. Saad-Zoy, *Femmes, droit de la famille et système judiciaire en Algérie, au Maroc et en Tunisie*, Rabat, UNESCO, 2010, available at http://unesdoc.unesco.org/

Given the vital importance reserved for Islam in the Algerian Constitution, it would seem logical that debates over the elimination of the affirmation of Islam as state religion would prove fruitless.

In Morocco, the Preamble to the constitution originally described the Kingdom as an 'Islamic and fully sovereign state whose official language is Arabic, [... and] constitutes a part of the Great Arab Maghreb'. In the recent revision of the text, the wording of the Preamble was changed to the following, longer affirmation:

> A sovereign Muslim State, attached to its national unity and to its territorial integrity, the Kingdom of Morocco intends to preserve, in its plenitude and its diversity, its one and indivisible national identity. Its unity is forged by the convergence of its Arab-Islamist, Amazighe [Berber] and Saharan-Hassanic components, and enriched by its African, Andalusian, Hebraic and Mediterranean influences. The preeminence accorded to the Muslim religion on a national basis is evident in the adherence of the Moroccan people to the values of openness, of moderation, of tolerance and of dialogue for mutual understanding between all the cultures and civilizations of the world.

The expansion of the elements of national identity is notable, as is the affirmation of the essential unity of the kingdom.

The Moroccan Constitution still stipulates that 'Islam is the religion of the State, which guarantees to all the free practice of religious beliefs'[54] after emphasizing the 'moderate'[55] nature the Muslim religion practiced. It also affirms that

> 'the King, Amir Al Mouminine, sees to the respect for Islam. He is the Guarantor of the free practice of religious beliefs. He presides over the Superior Council of the Ulamas, charged with the examination of the questions that He submits thereto. The Council is the sole forum authorized to pronounce on the religious consultations (fatwas) that are officially accepted, on the questions brought before it, and in doing so it shall take as its basis the tolerant principles, precepts and designs of Islam. [...] The King exercises, by *dahirs*, the religious prerogatives inherent to the institution of the Imarat Al Mouminine conferred upon Him exclusively.[56]

Finally, Article 175 adds that 'no amendment may infringe on the provisions relative to the Muslim religion.'

The inviolable nature of the constitutional status of Islam is thus repeated, revealing that the political authorities responsible were visibly fearful of any deviations attributable to a fundamentalist conception of religion. All three nations

images/0018/001893/189399f.pdf (accessed 15 December 2012).

54 Article 3 of the Constitution of 1 July 2011.

55 Article 1, para. 2 of the Moroccan Constitution.

56 Article 41 of the Moroccan Constitution.

share this fear, and seek to appear open to the prevailing concerns of advanced democracies, which are considered to be under the influence of tolerance and the acceptance of religious pluralism. Moreover, all three constitutions guarantee the free practice of religious beliefs, or at least the inviolability of the freedoms of opinion and of conscience.

Religious Freedom through Constitutional Provisions

The Moroccan Constitution confers responsibility for guaranteeing the free practice of religious beliefs upon the state.[57] The Algerian text defines '*freedom of conscience*' as inviolable,[58] but says nothing in particular regarding the practice of other religious beliefs. However, inviolability is traditionally deemed the supreme guarantee, as it is associated with the idea of immunity.[59] The Constitution of 10 September 1963 stipulated only that: 'Islam is the religion of the State. The Republic guarantees to all respect for their opinions and beliefs, and the free practice of religious beliefs.'[60] The Tunisian Constitution is today the most complete, as it guarantees 'freedom of conscience, and defends the free practice of religious beliefs', although it adds the qualifier: 'provided this does not disturb public order'.[61]

With regard to the concept of this fundamental freedom, Pedro Juan Viladrich points out that a state adopts religious freedom when, in addition to prohibiting itself from any coercion or any substitution in this matter, also prohibits itself, as the state, from any public appearance together with its citizens as a participant in acts or attitudes with respect to faith and religion, whatever they may be.[62]

Freedom of worship should be understood as the right to profess any belief that an individual deems appropriate, and to express the fact of such profession, which includes the practice of one's own religion, in public or private. Freedom of conscience encompasses the right to subscribe to a religious belief, to change religious preference or to profess none at all, to express these beliefs or to remain

---

57 Article 41 of the Moroccan Constitution.

58 Article 36 of the Algerian Constitution.

59 The European Court of Human Rights explains that '[t]his inviolability is a public matter, which means that the judicial authorities have the obligation to to take judicial notice of this immunity and that acts that do not respect this rule are legally null . Moreover, the applicant cannot legally waive immunity, but may only request that it be lifted.' *Kart v. Turkey*, App. No. 8917/05 (ECtHR, 8 July 2008). However, the due protection of fundamental rights is characterized by various terms: inviolability (French '*intangibilité*', preferred in legal doctrine; see the thesis of Olivier de Frouville), intransgressibility (ICJ Advisory Opinion, 8 July 1996, *Legality of the threat or use of nuclear weapons*).

60 Article 4.

61 Article 5, para. 4.

62 J.L Soberanes Fernandez, 'El contenido de la libertad religiosa', *Memoria del primer congreso internacional sobre iglesias, estado laico y sociedad* (Mexico, Comisión nacional de los derechos humanos, November 2006), 139.

silent about them. Religious freedom covers the right to give and receive religious teaching, information and propaganda by any means of communication, and also guarantees parents the right to choose for their minor children a religious education in accordance with their beliefs. The International Covenants on Civil and Political Rights of 1966,[63] which impose a legal obligation upon the signatory states, require them to respect the possibility that individuals may practice a form of worship or hold meetings related to religion or beliefs and establish and maintain places for such purposes. On this question, the text of Article 18 of the Universal Declaration is perhaps more precise. Religious freedom also includes the right to establish and maintain charitable or humanitarian institutions, to make, acquire or use the necessary items and materials in adequate quantities for the rites and customs of a religion or belief; to write, issue and disseminate relevant publications in these areas; to teach a religion or belief in places suitable for these purposes; to solicit and receive voluntary contributions from individuals and institutions; to train, appoint, elect or designate leaders of any religion or belief; to observe days of rest and to celebrate the holidays and ceremonies of their religion or belief; and to establish and maintain communications with others in matters of religion or belief at both national and international levels.[64]

However, the right to religious freedom is expressed in each country in accordance with that country's social needs, its historical and cultural baggage, and, in general terms, with its other particular characteristics.

Moreover, although the Maghrebi affirmations seem obvious, reconciling them with the absolute prohibition against abandoning the Muslim religion poses a problem. The Koran and the Sunnah do not allow apostasy. This rule is hardly compatible with contemporary stipulations on religious freedom, as recognized under the international texts ratified by the three Maghrebi nations. I will now turn to how this question is addressed (or not) in practice.

Legal Enforcement and Social Consequences of the Constitutional Protection of Religious Freedom

Although they do so in very different ways, all three of the francophone constitutions of the Maghreb ostensibly appeal to Islam, almost from their very first lines. In Tunisia, President Bourguiba sought to position the religion in a context which, without explicitly stating it, appealed to a certain form of secularism. As a result,

63 It is worth recalling that Article 18 sec. 1 of the Covenant in effect guarantees 'the freedom to have or adopt the religion or belief of his choice, and freedom, either individually or in community with others and in public or private, to manifest his religion or belief in worship, observance, practice and teaching'.

64 Principles taken from the *Declaration on the Elimination of all Forms of Intolerance and of Discrimination Based on Religion or Belief*, submitted by the UN Economic and Social Council to the General Assembly, which approved it on 25 November 1981.

regardless of its form, the guarantee of freedom of worship in the constitution is of vital importance because it has both an obvious material quality and a formal aspect, being a legal text located at the top of the hierarchy of domestic laws.[65] However, to have effect, religious freedom (which derives from freedom of conscience as it is a freedom of belief) needs to be related to the exact conditions under which it is exercised. Indeed, religious freedom necessarily entails the free exercise of worship, which is an external manifestation of religious belief. The imposition of a legal text that specifies forms of worship is a reflection of the fact that these are nations that value the Muslim faith above other religious beliefs and practices.[66] Thus, in reality, the Maghrebi concept of religious freedom does not go further than freedom of conscience. To guarantee freedom of worship, which essentially depends on the state taking a passive stance in relation to religion, what is needed, paradoxically, is an attitude of promotion, of fostering by the state, as occurs with other fundamental rights and freedoms. How can Maghrebi legislators manage to implement the constitutional proclamations on religious freedom? And furthermore, how do their societies react?

The Application of the Constitutional Provisions

Algeria is the only one of the three nations to have adopted a specific law to guarantee religious freedom. This law is the Ordinance of 28 February 2006, concerning the practice of non-Muslim religions.[67] Unfortunately, this text, although apparently liberal, has numerous limitations. In the cases of Tunisia and Morocco, a few scattered provisions establish exceptions to freedom of worship.[68]

---

65 J. Andriantsimbazovina (ed.), *Dictionnaire des droits de l'homme* (Presses Universitaires de France, 2008), 447.

66 F. Frégosi, 'Les rapports entre l'islam et l'État en Algérie et en Tunisie : De leur revalorisation à leur contestation', in A. Mohiou, *L'État de droit dans le monde arabe* (Paris: Éditions du CNRS, 1999), 103–124; S. Lavorel, *Les Constitutions arabes et l'Islam. Les enjeux du pluralisme juridique* (Presses de l'Université du Québec, 2005), 202.

67 Ordinance No. 06-03, of 28 February 2006, establishing the conditions and rules for the practice of beliefs other than Islam, *JORA* No. 12 (1 March 2006), 23–25.

68 This was also the case in Algeria prior to 2006. Articles 3 and 4 of Law No. 63–278 of 26 July 1963, concerning holidays, recognize the right of both citizens and foreigners of the Jewish and Christian faiths to be given time off to celebrate their religious festivals. Article 160 sec. 3 of the Criminal Code establishes sentences for the defacement, destruction or desecration of 'places reserved for worship', while Article 160 sec. 4 criminalizes the mutilation, destruction or defacement of 'monuments, statues, works … which may be used for liturgical purposes.' Moreover, Article 77 of the Law of 3 April 1990, concerning information, criminalizes 'any offense in writing, sound, image, drawing or other direct or indirect medium, against Islam and the other heavenly religions'.

The Algerian Ordinance Concerning the Rules and Conditions for the Practice of Non-Muslim Worship and the Decrees that Implement It

1) The Ordinance of 2006

The Ordinance of 2006 sets forth the rules and conditions related to the practice of religious worship for non-Muslims, while recalling the constitutional status of Islam. This law makes religious freedom subject to a system of prior authorization, as the freedom to practice religious rites is conditioned by compliance with the Ordinance, the Constitution and other laws and regulations, as well as respect for public order, morality and the fundamental rights and freedoms of third parties.[69]

In practice, this ordinance allows the Algerian government to tighten up the procedures for registration of religious organizations, to intensify punishments against individuals accused of proselytism, to impose restrictions on imports of non-Muslim religious works and to ban public meetings in the context of the practice of non-Muslim beliefs. This legislation has been confirmed by two implementing decrees. Executive Decree No. 07-135 of 19 May 2007 which establishes the conditions and categories for the practice of religious expressions of beliefs other than Islam[70] and Executive Decree No. 07-158, of 27 May 2007, which stipulates the composition and categories for the operation of the national commission for beliefs other than Islam.[71]

It is not possible here to examine all the provisions of each of these texts in detail; however, it is worth highlighting a few notable stipulations. The ordinance begins by specifying that the practice of beliefs other than Islam shall occur within the context of religious associations[72] constituted in accordance with the laws and regulations that govern this area. However, Algerian legislation has not accorded a specific status to religious associations.[73] It is therefore necessary to refer to Algerian legislation concerning associations in general for the definition a religious association. Law No. 90-31 of 4 December 1990 concerning associations[74] establishes a liberal system based on a principle of freedom. Specifically, the law stipulates that '[a]n association is constituted freely by the will of its founding members, upon concluding a general constitutive assembly, at which at least fifteen founding members are present [...].'[75] This poses a problem for smaller groups seeking to establish religious associations. And what about the freedom of non-Muslim Algerian citizens to practice their religious beliefs individually?

---

69 Article 2 of the Ordinance.

70 *JORA* No. 33 (20 May 2007), 4.

71 *JORA* No. 36 (2 June 2007), 7.

72 Article 3 of the Ordinance.

73 Article 6 of the Ordinance.

74 *JORA* No. 53 (5 December 1990), 1438. This text generalizes the provisions of Law No. 89-11 of 5 July 1989, concerning political associations, a category that includes political parties. *JORA* No. 27 (5 July 1989), 604 ff.

75 Article 6; Article 7 specifies the existence of an obligation of prior declaration.

Article 7 of the ordinance also stipulates that 'collective expressions of worship shall take place only in buildings intended for this purpose, open to the public and externally identifiable.' What about a group of less than fifteen non-Muslim believers? Would they be allowed to practice their faith freely in a private space? Article 8 of the ordinance physically confines religious practices to buildings and makes them subject to public announcement and prior declaration; it is not clear whether this is a mere formality or involves an actual authorization and thus a form of control. Finally, strict supervision of these places of worship is imposed by the legislation, as 'buildings intended for the practice of worship shall be subject to census by the State, which shall ensure their protection.'

Among the criminal provisions, one of the most severe is the sentence established for anyone who 'produces, stores or distributes printed documents, audiovisual materials or in any other format or medium, with the intention of breaking the faith of a Muslim'.[76] This calls into question not only freedom of expression but also the right to change religion, which every Algerian should theoretically have, whether Muslim or not, under his constitutionally guaranteed freedoms of opinion and of conscience. In effect, the ordinance suggests that nothing may divert a Muslim from Islam. But the measure that without doubt delivers the hardest blow to non-Muslim religions present in Algeria is that which establishes a sentence for any person who 'incites, constrains or uses means of seduction tending to convert a Muslim to another religion, or by using to this end teaching, education, health, social or cultural establishments or training institutions, or any other establishment, or any financial means'.[77] In addition to condemning proselytism, this article confuses purely social or humanitarian activities with calculated actions and ulterior motives.

Similarly, Article 12, which sets forth that 'a sentence of one to three years' imprisonment and a fine of 100,000 dinars to 300,000 dinars shall apply to any person who collects or accepts donations without the authorization of the legally appointed authorities', needs to be reconciled with the aforementioned Law 90-31, of 4 December 1990, concerning associations, whose Articles 16 and 28, respectively, stipulate that a duly constituted association may 'acquire, free of charge or for good and valuable consideration, movable or immovable property for the performance of its activities as provided for in its bylaws', and receive donations from abroad, subject to state supervision. But the question of knowing how the National Commission will set the amount of the donations and the budgets that a community needs remains unanswered.

On the other hand, Article 14 establishes heavy penalties of fines and imprisonment for any breach of the prohibition imposed by Articles 5 and 7 of the Ordinance, respectively, against any activity contrary to the nature and objectives of worship in places intended for the practice thereof, and against any collective

76 Article 11 para. 2 of the Ordinance.

77 Article 11 para. 1 of the Ordinance establishes a sentence of two to five years' imprisonment and a fine of 500,000 Algerian dinars.

practice of worship outside the buildings intended for this purpose, open to the public and externally identifiable.

Finally, it is worth noting that these sentences, according to the wording used in the ordinance, are applicable 'without prejudice to more serious penalties'[78] that might be stipulated in other repressive provisions. While certain aspects of these provisions have raised questions, they have been regrettably dismissed by a narrow judicial interpretation that will be discussed below.

2) The decrees implementing the Ordinance of 2006

- Executive Decree No. 07-135 of May 19, 2007, establishing the conditions and categories of religious expressions of beliefs other than Islam[79]

This decree was adopted to explain the conditions for the application of Article 8 of the Ordinance of 2006. The decree begins by defining a religious expression as 'a brief gathering of people, organized in buildings accessible to the public, by associations of a religious nature',[80] subject to '*prior declaration before the Wali*',[81] i.e. the prefectural authority, at least five days before the date scheduled for the celebration of the gathering.

The decree goes on to stipulate that 'this receipt must be presented by the organizers upon demand by the authorities',[82] which clearly constitutes a measure for controlling such religious events. Moreover, the Wali (or prefect) has the power to request that the organizers, within 48 hours of submitting their declaration, change the place of the gathering,[83] and even to prohibit any gathering that might constitute a danger to the preservation of public order,[84] without first defining this notion or further explaining the circumstances whereby such an event would fall into this category.

- Executive Decree No. 07-158, of May 27, 2007, concerning the modes of operation of the National Commission for non-Muslim faiths[85]

With regard to the conditions for the practice of worship itself, Article 9 of the Ordinance, under the aegis of the Ministry of Religious Affairs and Wakfs, establishes a national commission for worship, responsible in particular for 'ensuring respect for the free practice of worship, dealing with matters and concerns related to the practice of worship, [and] giving prior notice to religious associations.' This forum, whose composition and modes of operation are regulated

78 Article 11 of the Ordinance.

79 *JORA* No. 33 (20 May 2007), 4.

80 Article 2 of the Decree.

81 Article 3 of the Decree. It is amusing to note that the official wording of the decree, as published in the *JORA*, requires the declaration 'of' and not 'to' the Wali! Is this a simple misprint or a genuine slip revealing an expectation of prior authorization by the prefecture?

82 Article 4 of the Decree.

83 Article 5 of the Decree.

84 Article 6 of the Decree.

85 *JORA* No. 36 (3 June 2007), 7–8.

by the Decree of 27 May 2007, thus renders the previously declared principle of freedom relative.

The composition of this Commission is problematic, since no representative of the non-Muslim communities occupies a seat on it: according to Article 4, section 1 of this decree: 'the Commission, presided over by the Minister of Religious Affairs and Wakfs or his representative, is comprised of representatives of the Minister of National Defense, the Minister of the Interior and local communities, the Minister of Foreign Affairs and Police Headquarters, the Command of the National Gendarmerie [and] the National Consultative Commission for the Promotion and Protection of Human Rights.' However, the second section does not preclude the possibility that 'representatives of each faith may be approached and their presence may be judged necessary.'

In this respect, apart from its flagrant lack of independence and the general and imprecise nature of the terms that establish its missions, replete with ambiguities (what is actually meant by dealing with matters and concerns related to the practice of worship?), the requirement of prior notice from this commission of approval of religious associations is particularly unsettling. This again imposes a prior authorization requirement upon the constitution of this type of association. Indeed, the urgent nature of such a consultation, mandatory *a priori*, is not specified, and could have serious consequences. Last of all, it is difficult to determine the criteria this commission will apply to decide whether it will grant its approval to communities interested in establishing an association. On this point, the Decree says nothing.[86]

Religious Freedom in Tunisia and Morocco[87]

The situation in Tunisia and in Morocco has been evolving since the adoption of the new Moroccan Constitution and the projects of Tunisia's commission for political reform. But it is fair to say that, in spite of the absence of general legislation aimed at governing freedom of worship for all citizens, there is some legislation that does refer to the matter. These provisions, unfortunately, appear to restrict religious freedom considerably.

In Tunisia, the protection of worship is guaranteed and the state is limited to regulating the Muslim faith. Articles 161 and 165 of the Tunisian Criminal Code establish imprisonment and a fine for people convicted of destroying, defacing or mutilating buildings, monuments or objects used for religious worship. A sentence

86 Article 9 indicates merely that '[...] the opinions of the Commission concerning the approval of religious associations and the allocation of buildings shall be notified to the appointed authority within a period of no more than one month after the establishment thereof.'

87 Most of the information analyzed here comes from international reports on freedom of religion in Tunisia and Morocco prepared by the US State Department, available at http://www.state.gov/j/drl/rls/irf/.

is also established for any person who disturbs the practice of worship or religious ceremonies, without prejudice to more severe sentences, when these are committed to offend, assault or threaten.

With regard to the Muslim faith, two government circulars in 1981[88] and 1986[89] banned the use of sectarian dress (which is generally interpreted to refer to the hijab) in government offices and discouraged women from wearing it in the street and at certain public gatherings.[90] The authorities declared that the hijab indicated membership of a fundamentalist group that hides behind religion to achieve its political objectives and that, according to the modern school of Muslim thought, the use of the hijab is not an obligation. The authorities claim that the hijab is a sectarian posture of foreign origin and justify the prohibition against wearing it in public institutions on the basis of the need to guarantee the neutrality and impartiality of government employees. School authorities have repeatedly penalized the use of the hijab, which also constitutes a deterrent measure. On 3 July 2008, local non-governmental organizations (NGOs) reported that the administration of the school Lycée novembre a Dar Chaabane El Fehri had asked female students to remove their hijabs before an awards presentation. According to a local NGO, on 13 September 2008, the Director of the Higher Institute of Technological Studies in Sidi Bouzid asked students who wore the hijab to sign declarations stating that from that time on they would stop wearing it, and acknowledging that they would be expelled if they failed to respect this commitment. In May 2009, national NGOs reported that directors of the Higher Institute of Biotechnology in Sfax suspended six students on 30 April and had made them sign a promise to stop wearing the hijab.

Following the rejection of this policy, not only by unrecognized Islamic movements but also by a significant proportion of the population, the response of the judicial system was quite tolerant. In 2006, an Administrative Court ruling declared the Decree of 1986 unconstitutional on the basis of its contravention of Article 5 of the Tunisian Constitution, which recognizes freedom of conscience.[91]

Although proselytism of Muslims may be deemed an act that disturbs public order in a country where the state religion is Islam, there is no provision in Tunisian legislation that prohibits Muslims from converting to another religion, and the authorities do not require any official declaration of conversions. However, there are cases of assault and discrimination against Muslim who have converted to other faiths, because public authorities resort to administrative harassment to discourage conversions. Moreover, through positive law government authorities control

88 Circular No. 108, 18 September 1981.

89 Circular No. 102, 29 October 1986.

90 S. Ben Achour, 'Convictions religieuses et la loi tunisienne', in *Convictions philosophiques et religieuses et droits positifs: Textes présentés au colloque international de Moncton (24-27 août 2008)* (Bruylant, 2010), 160, 161.

91 S. Ben Achour, 'Convictions religieuses et la loi tunisienne', 162. Tribunal administratif, 9 December 2006, No. 1/10976, decision unpublished.

religious belief by virtue of the guardianship they exercise over the pilgrimage to Mecca.[92] The state also controls the spreading of religious belief, specifically over the mosques[93] and koranic schools or Kouttabs.[94]

On the other hand, the authorities recognize all Christian and Jewish religious organizations established prior to independence in 1956. Although the authorities allow Christian churches to carry out their activities freely provided that they do not engage in proselytism, officially only the Catholic Church is recognized, by virtue of the Concordat with the Holy See in 1964. Occasionally, Catholic and Protestant groups organize services in private residences or other locations.

Religious groups are subject to the same restrictions on freedom of expression and the press as secular groups.[95] There is no law requiring the authorities to approve documentation printed locally prior to its publication or distribution. However, Christian groups have reported that the authorities generally would not authorize them to publish and distribute Christian texts in Arabic. These groups report that they can distribute previously approved religious publications written in European languages without trouble, but that only established churches are authorized to distribute religious publications to their congregations. The authorities deem the distribution of religious documents by other groups to be a 'danger to public order' and ultimately an illegal act.

The authorities allow the Jewish community to freely practice their religion and pay the salary of the Chief Rabbi. They also guarantee the safety of all synagogues and partially subsidize the restoration and maintenance of some of them. Government employees are responsible for the maintenance of the grass in the Jewish cemetery in Tunis.

The authorities consider the Baha'i faith a heretical sect of Islam and authorize its followers to practice their faith only in private. They allow the national council of the Baha'i to meet in private residences; three local spiritual assemblies, the local directive council, have been chosen since 2004.

Since the declaration of independence in 1956, the authorities have not authorized the legalization of Protestant Christian groups seeking to open new

92 Article 7 of Decree No. 94-597 of 22 March 1994, establishing the powers of the Minister of Religious Affairs, *JORT* No. 25 (1994), 541.

93 Law No. 88-34 of 3 May 1988 (Note No. 37).

94 Decree of 22 November 1956, concerning the nationalization of Koranic schools, *JORT* No. 95 (1956), 1574. Muslim religious education is compulsory in public schools, but in high schools the religious curriculum also includes the history of Judaism and of Christianity. The Zeitouna Qur'anic School, associated with the national university system, is secular.

95 The authorities have established a system of *de facto* prior authorization instead of the liberal *de jure* system stipulated in Law No. 59–154 of 7 November 1959, concerning associations, *JORT* No. 63 (1958), 1534. The revision of this text is one of the core matters to be addressed by the commission for political reforms. Law No. 75–32 of 28 April 1975, concerning the enactment of the Press Code, contains an excessive number of repressive provisions.

churches. Consequently, the vast majority of Christian groups no longer try to register with the authorities.

In Morocco, a few important points are worth noting. Article 220 of the Criminal Code establishes a criminal sentence for any person convicted of using 'means of seduction with the aim of breaking the faith of a Muslim', and establishes imprisonment and fines for such acts. In this way, Moroccan legislation effectively criminalizes proselytism. This can be understood in light of the Sharifian origin of the King. At the same time, Articles 221 to 223 outline the offenses related to the practice of religious worship. A sentence of six months to three years of imprisonment and a fine of 200 to 500 dirhams shall apply to 'any person who voluntarily obstructs the practice of worship or a religious ceremony, or voluntarily causes disorder of a kind that disturbs the peace'[96] and to 'any person who, voluntarily, destroys or defaces buildings, monuments or objects used for worship'.[97] Such a provision would effectively protect the practice of non-Muslim beliefs. Legislation has also established that 'anyone who, widely known to belong to the Muslim religion, ostensibly breaks his fast in a public place during the time of Ramadan, without a reason admitted by this religion, shall be sentenced to imprisonment of one to six months and a fine of 12 to 120 dirhams.'[98] This measure effectively imposes the practice of the Muslim faith upon all 'presumed' Muslims, which frankly contravenes their religious freedom.

Moreover, the law on public freedoms makes no mention of religious freedom. In addition, the Moroccan authorities have made use of Article 25 of the Immigration Law of 2003[99] which authorizes the government to summarily deport, without a fair trial, any foreign resident who in its judgment represents '*a threat to public order*', to deport foreign Christians.

The Visible Effects in Society

Morocco and Algeria have had to deal with the problem of real or supposed evangelism in their societies. In the case of Tunisia, however, it has been expressions of the Muslim faith that have suffered the authoritarianism of the state. In Tunisia, converts from Islam must deal with social ostracism and, after the events of the revolution, face the even more troubling problem of Salafism.

In the final analysis, Algeria appears to be the best place to examine the visible effects of attitudes toward the right to religious freedom in society. An examination of this right in practice reveals that, under the Ordinance of 2006 concerning the

96 Article 221.

97 Article 223.

98 Article 222.

99 Law No. 02-03, of 11 November 2003, concerning the entry and stay of foreigners in Morocco, and irregular emigration and immigration, Official Bulletin No. 5162 of 20 November 2003.

practice of beliefs other than Islam, it would clearly be impossible to welcome friends into your house or meet them in a public place to discuss matters related to the Christian faith with them, and that the provisions of Article 11, section 1 are intended to prevent a Muslim from changing his opinion or turning to another religion, even when this is his private conviction. An illustration of this fact is the case of Habiba Kouider, an Algerian convert to Christianity arrested in early April 2008 while on her way to Oran with a dozen copies of the Bible, who was charged with illegal (i.e. unauthorized) practice of a non-Muslim faith. Before the court in Tiaret, the prosecutor called for Kouider to be sentenced to three years' imprisonment, but in response to intense controversy, the court, at the hearing on May 27, requested supplementary information. Six other Algerians, converts to Protestantism, were brought before the Tiaret court on the same day for 'religious proselytism'.[100]

These examples also demonstrate that people who travel with the Bible or a few Christian texts are exposing themselves to criminal charges because they will be suspected of seeking to 'break the faith of a Muslim'. Such is the case of Rachid Mohammed Seghir, 40 years old, and Jamal Dahmani, 36, both computer programmers, who were sentenced in absentia in November 2007 to two years in prison and fines of 5,000 euros for 'proselytism and illegal practice of a non-Muslim faith', for which the verdict[101] was ultimately reduced to a deferred sentence of six months in prison and a 1,000 euro fine. Both computer programmers had been arrested in Tissemsilt, more than 300 kilometers to the southwest of Algiers, on 7 April 2007. A Bible and various religious CD-ROMs had been discovered when their vehicle was searched.[102] The processes established do not allow for a determination of the method to be used to estimate the quantity and nature of literature (and audiovisual material) possessed by a non-Muslim sufficient to 'break the faith of a Muslim'.[103]

Other cases have been heard by Algerian courts; a notable case is that of Father Wallez,[104] who during Christmas of 2008 in a neighborhood in Maghnia, had led a religious ceremony involving some sub-Saharan immigrants. He was assisted by a benevolent Algerian doctor, who was administering medical care to the foreigners.

---

100 'Algérie. Trois ans de prison ferme requis contre une chrétienne convertie', *Le Monde*, 23 May 2008.

101 Verdict delivered on 2 July 2008, by the Court of Tissemsilt, http://www.hrw.org/en/node/79166.

102 A. Akef, 'Algérie religions. Condamnation de deux algériens convertis au christianisme', *Le Monde*, 4 July 2008.

103 Artícle 11 sec. 2 of the Ordinance.

104 The conviction of Father Wallez was issued in a difficult climate in which, according to Monsignor Henri Teissier, Archbishop of Algiers, 'some groups want to reduce the presence of the Catholic Church and create difficulties for it.' For two years the Catholic community had considered itself 'under a pressure' verging on persecution. This feeling was accentuated in May 2007, when local authorities in 48 *wilayas* (provinces) of the country, in application of a directive from Algiers, invited Catholics to leave the country due to threats by Al-Qaeda in the Islamic Maghreb.

The trial resulted in a sentence of two years' imprisonment for illegal practice of non-Muslim worship and theft of medicine at a public health center.[105]

The previous year, some thirty sub-Saharan students, who had participated in a Bible study weekend in Tizi-Ouzou, had been served a notice of deportation from Algeria. Their deportation was prevented thanks only to the intervention of the ambassadors, particularly the Senegalese Ambassador, to revoke the measure. In November 2007, religious Catholic Brazilians of the Salam community, whose papers were in order, were ordered to leave the country within two weeks; the threat was withdrawn, once again, by virtue of the intervention of the Brazilian Ambassador. There was also a case of a citizen who was prosecuted for 'inciting Muslims to abjure their religion'; Abdelhamid B. was convicted in absentia in a trial court and sentenced to two years in prison, combined with a fine of 500,000 dinars. The police had questioned this 47-year-old family man while he was in the Jijel marketplace, where he worked as an itinerant merchant without a business registration. The investigation subsequently took a different turn after a thorough search of his vehicle and the discovery of copies of the Gospels from the Protestant Church in Constantine. The accused was condemned by the testimony of three citizens who claimed they had witnessed him proselytizing. An appeal for reversal should have been filed in response to this decision issued at the level of the lower court in Jijel.

On 8 November 2010, the prosecutor of the criminal court in Akbou called for a jail sentence of two to five years for eight 'non-fasters' from Ighzer Amokrane for 'offending the precepts of Islam'. The magistrate did not wish to pursue the charges and ordered their release. It was the third proceedings of this type in Aïn El Hammam, in the wilayas of Tizi Ouzou and Oum El Bouaghi (18 October 2010, in Oum El Bouaghi (East), two-year prison sentence for Farès Bouchouata, 27 years old, for the same reason after having broken the fast), which mobilized human rights organizations and all militants for the defense of individual and community freedoms to call for freedom of conscience as enshrined in the Constitution.

The youths charged of the same offenses in Ain El Hammam were swiftly and fully absolved by the court, which recognized that there was no legal provision in the organic law or in the Code of Criminal Procedure that criminalized the failure to observe the fast.[106] Similarly, four Kabyle youths from Ouadhia in Tizi Ouzou province were accused of offending the precepts of Islam and of offending the state religion and, for this crime, sentenced to three years' imprisonment, along with a 100,000-dinar fine, pursuant to Article 144 bis 2 of the Criminal Codel,[107] by the Court of Bir Mourad Raïs in Algiers province, on 30 September 2008. The four accused, who were workers on a construction site, had been charged with

105 A. Akef, 'Les inquiétudes de la Communauté catholique d'Algérie', Alger, Correspondance, *Le Monde*, 25 February 2008, available at www.algeria-watch.org/fr/article/div/inquietudes.htm (accessed 15 December 2012).

106 O. Berbiche, 'Clarification', *El Watan*, 9 November 2010, www.elwatan.com.

107 A legal basis traditionally reserved for offenses committed in the press.

failing to observe the Muslim fast.[108] The president of the jurisdiction specified that the detainees were not being sentenced for failure to observe Ramadan but for a public lack of respect toward Islam and Muslims.[109]

Just as practitioners of other faiths do not have the right to offend the religious sensibilities of the masses, those who do not observe fasting must also avoid public behavior that would run the risk of clashing with certain attitudes; this is the message that the verdict conveys. Indeed, it is pursuant to Article 144 bis 2 of the Criminal Code that they were prosecuted, but, according to their lawyers, the court, having established the absence of an offense and that the legal elements were lacking, determined that it could not convict citizens for not fasting, because this is a matter of personal belief.

On the other hand, Christian places of worship were closed for some time, which hindered the activities of several communities as they could no longer organize their weekly services due to notices of closure sent by the offices of the prefecture, sub-prefectures and local police. The last case was that of an order signed on 8 May by the Wali, serving notice of the 'permanent closure' of seven Protestant churches in the wilaya of Bejaïa in Kabylie region. The reason cited in a letter dated 22 May from the Chief of Security of the Wilay of Bejaïa, was the unlawful nature of 'any building consecrated or in the process of being dedicated to the practice of a non-Muslim faith without authorization'.

This measure, which provoked a public outcry, was lifted a few days later by the Wali, who met with the president of the Protestant Church of Algeria (who represents some 30 places of worship in the country). The discussions referred in particular to the abrogation of Article 2 of the Constitution, which proclaims Islam as the state religion, deemed offensive to other faiths. Another sign of appeasement was the invitation of the former Archbishop of Algiers, Monsignor Henri Teisser, by the advisory committee on political reform in Algeria.

The authorities were monitoring all non-Muslim communities closely. The church officials submitted the bylaws of their communities, which were given an 'authorization to exist' officially, but the government, in this case the regional administrative authorities, accepted the submission of the file only after continued perseverance on the part of the applicants, and even then engaged in delaying

108 Unfortunately, this is not an isolated case, as several similar examples have been reported in the press. One such case is the story of Mohamed R., who was almost fired for a report that he ate lunch in the month of Ramadan due to his insulin-dependent diabetes. After being called in by the head of the department to explain himself, he was required to present a medical report. This constituted a flagrant violation of his individual religious freedom. N. Afroun, 'La religion et les Algériens. La loi de 2006, les conservateurs et la conscience individuelle' and 'Après différents procès en inquisition. Laïcité, Kofr et Libertés religieuses', *Liberté*, 2 November 2008; M. Nadjah, 'Biskra: Six personnes condamnées pour non-respect du Ramadan', *El Watan*, 6 October 2008.

109 M. Aziri, 'La cour d'Alger a jugé hier 4 jeunes pour « atteinte à l'Islam ». Le « syndrome de Biskra » refait surface à Alger', *El Watan*, 12 November 2008.

tactics which they justified on the basis of the need to forward the documents to the Ministry of Religious Affairs in Algiers. Thus, the authorities ask the communities to cease their activities and regularize their status without providing clear information on the process they needed to follow. In addition, visitor visas are denied to priests, religious congregations and Protestant pastors, while Brazilian Catholic 'volunteers' are threatened with deportation. The declared objective is to 'put an end to the anarchic activities of associations and individuals in this area, as well as the enterprises of proselytism directed at Muslims in Algeria'. In response to the controversy and the deterioration of Algeria's international image, and to refute the accusation that they were carrying out a campaign of persecution against Christians, the authorities explain that it is merely the extension of a policy applied first of all to Muslim worship.

In Tunisia, since the fall of Ben Ali and the end of his control over the Islamists, with the state of emergency extended until March 2013 and the victory of the *En-nahda* Islamist party in the last legislative elections, the Salafist movement has gained strength in society. Several incidents have highlighted this fact. One such incident is the Nessma Affair, referring to the name of the television channel that dared to broadcast the French-Iranian film *Persepolis*, controversial for its critical description of Iran's Khomeini regime through the eyes of a young girl. One week before the first free elections in its history, on 7 October 2011, around 300 Salalfist-leaning Tunisians attempted to burn down the television station. The protest demonstrations spread throughout the country, forcing the president of the private TV network to issue an apology. A few months later, in June 2012, extremist groups stormed an art exhibition and destroyed some of the works which, according to the only law they respect, *Sharía* (Islamic law), were an offense to 'good conduct'.[110] In October, confrontations flared between the National Guard and Salafist youth. These incidents are multiplying to the point where it may well be wondered whether the Arab spring might not be turning now into an Islamist winter. All of these incidents seem to suggest that the end of the dictatorship has resulted in the liberation of the Salafist sphere of society.

In short, the overabundance of religious references in the Maghreb should not mislead us. While they do reflect the genuine adherence of the masses and the elite to Islam, they also aim, in the guise of religious fidelity, to delegitimize fundamentalist discourse. At the same time, they are associated with a liberal posture that reflects a general desire to move progressively toward the logic of secularization typical of modern democracies. Nevertheless, all these developments point to the conclusion that, in the sphere of religion, freedom of expression ends where there begins to be any threat or questioning, either real or supposed, of the principles of Islam, as clear as the boundary should be between freedom of conscience and offending the

110 However, since the events of the winter of 2011, there has been an observable reestablishment of the link between visual arts and social movements in the Arab world, according to Alexandre Kazerouni, researcher at the Center for International Studies and Research (CERI) and a specialist in the Arab art market.

religion, and the difference between punishable offense for disturbing public, social or economic order and an offense the public religious order. In light of the above, this palpable tension between the fundamentalist and liberal tendencies of Islam, which continues to be a driving force in the Arab world, should be watched closely.

Chapter 11
Religious Institutions and Fundamental Rights: Applicability, Interaction and Limitations in South Africa

Helena van Coller

Introduction

The South African society exhibits a growing multicultural character, which finds expression in a religious pluralism with much more diversity than in the past. It is becoming more and more important to recognize the need for religious diversity in a pluralistic society. Stuart Woolman is of the view that the Constitutional Court has not yet come to terms with the fact that there is a fundamental difference between 'largely ascriptive associations, like religious institutions, on the one hand, and voluntary associations, like sports and professional bodies on the other hand.[1]

It is an intolerable situation if religious institutions are expected 'to jettison a doctrine or two' in order to comply with broader social and political norms, whereas this can be expected of an association such as the cricket union or a political party, which operate to a greater degree in the public sphere. The court in both *Taylor v. Kurstag*[2] and *Wittman v. Deutscher Schulverein*[3] recognized the right of a religious institution 'to have one's life shaped in a manner that does not readily permit the alteration of either belief or act and that to be a member of a liberal society is to live in a state committed to not so readily dictating the ends of its citizens.'[4]

The state's interference in the internal affairs of an organization will depend to a large extent on the nature of the organization, the impact that it has on the public and in the public sphere, and the presence of a constitutional right that the organization promotes and protects. According to Justice Brennan in *Roberts v. United States Jaycees,*[5] the size, purpose, selectivity, policies, and a variety of other characteristics may be pertinent in determining the extent of state regulation. This chapter will therefore focus in more detail on religious institutions, the

---

1 S. Woolman, 'Association', in I. Currie and J. de Waal (eds.), *Bill of Rights Handbook* (2005), 442.

2 *Taylor v. Kurstag NO and others*, 2004 (4) All SA 317 (W).

3 *Wittman v. Deutscher Schulverein*, 1998 (4) SA 423 (T).

4 Woolman, 'Association', supra note 1 at 442.

5 *Roberts v. United States Jaycees*, 468 US 609 (1984).

right to freedom of association, whether this fundamental right allows religious organizations to discriminate, and if so, to what extent, with reference to the case of *Strydom v. Nederduits Gereformeerde Gemeente Moreleta Park.*[6]

Since a pluralistic religious society pre-supposes various definitions of 'religion' and 'religious organizations', the discussion will begin with a short overview of relevant concepts. In order to attain constitutional protection in the form of the right to freedom of religion, organizations require an appropriate definition and application of 'religion'. In a legal context, a functional and practical approach on the basis of a set of beliefs and characteristics is supported, rather than a formalistic, technical approach. Such a flexible approach ought to be followed to accommodate the multi-religious and multi-denominational South African society.

Conceptualization: A Short Overview of the Meaning of 'Religious Organization'

Most countries provide for a specific organizational structure for religious organizations, the so-called '*sui generis* religious organisation', whether referred to as a church, organization, association, or the like. Such an organization is not only regarded and observed as being of a religious nature, but according to Potz & Wieshaider, it can lay claim to 'the guaranteed autonomy to freely administer its internal affairs' and 'it is most likely linked with additional rights which are not necessarily considered to be the core of the exercise of religion, but very often go together as a result of co-operation between the State and the religious community in coping with societal challenges.'[7]

A religious community is described as 'a group of people who follow a particular system of belief, morality and worship, either in recognition of a divine being, or in the pursuit of spiritual development, or in the expression of a sense of belonging through social custom and ritual'.[8]

According to du Plessis,[9] this definition includes anti- and non-religious groups that will qualify in a similar way for protection. This induces the question of what

6 *Strydom v. Nederduits Gereformeerde Gemeente Moreleta Park*, 2009 (4) SA 510 (T).

7 R. Potz and W. Wieshaider, 'Religious Entities as Legal Persons – Parts of Western and Central Europe', in L. Friedner, *Churches and Other Religious Organisations as Legal Persons* (Höör: Peeters, 2007), 30.

8 A South African Declaration on Religious Rights and Responsibilities, accepted and assented to during a National Inter-religious Conference, held in November 1992 under the auspices of the South African Chapter of theWorld Conference on Religion and Peace (WCRP-SA). See further L.M. du Plessis, 'Current Problems Concerning Church and State Relationships and Religious Freedom in South Africa: The Viewpoint of a Constitutional Lawyer', in H. Warnink (ed.), *Legal Position of Churches and Church Autonomy* (Leuven: Peeters, 2001), 15 ff.

9 L.M. du Plessis, 'Grondwetlike Beskerming vir Godsdiensregte as Groepregte in Suid-Afrika', *Nederduitse Gereformeerde Teologiese Tydskrif* (2002), 216.

exactly is meant by 'religion'? In the case of *Christian Education South Africa v. Minister of Education,* Justice Sachs stated: 'Religion is not just a question of belief or doctrine. It is part of a way of life, of a people's temper and culture.'[10]

In a minority decision of the court in *Prince v. President Cape Law Society,* Justice Ngcobo stated as follows:

> Religion is a matter of faith and belief. The beliefs that believers hold sacred and thus central to their religious faith may strike non-believers as bizarre, illogical or irrational. Human beings may freely believe in what they cannot prove. Yet that their beliefs are bizarre, illogical or irrational to others, or are incapable of scientific proof, does not detract from the fact that these are religious beliefs for the purposes of enjoying the protection guaranteed by the right to freedom of religion. The believers should not be put to the proof of their beliefs or faith. For this reason it is undesirable for courts to enter into the debate whether a particular practice is central to a religion unless there is a genuine dispute as to the centrality of a practice.[11]

The meaning of 'religion' is also important for purposes of the collective right to freedom of religion in determining when an organization will be treated as 'religious' in order to qualify for the protection afforded by the Constitution.

Does 'religion' include 'atheism'? The court in *Wittman* was clear about the fact that it cannot.

> It [religion] cannot include the concepts of atheism or agnosticism which are the very antithesis of religion. The atheist and agnostic is afforded his protection under the freedom of thought, belief and opinion part of this section. There is conceptually no room for him under the freedom of religion part. Freedom of religion does not mean freedom from religion. Remarks in United States constitutional case law which tend to describe atheism or agnosticism as religion are in our context inapplicable.
>
> When therefore … s 15(2) of the Constitution permit[s] religious observances, this is a reference to the Jewish, Christian, Moslem, Buddhist and other faiths practising their religion at State and State-aided institutions. Religious observances (Afrikaans: 'godsdiens beoefening') does not mean a practice which neither Jew, Christian, Moslem, Buddhist, Hindu, nor other faiths recognise as such; where the Supreme Being is neither the God of Israel nor the Holy Trinity nor Allah the Merciful etc but a vague nonentity.[12]

10 *Christian Education South Africa v. Minister of Education*, 2000 (4) SA 757 (CC), para. 33.

11 *Prince v. President Cape Law Society,* 2002 (2) SA 794 (CC), para. 42.

12 *Wittman v. Deutscher Schulverein* 1998 (4) SA 423 (T) 449.

In Switzerland, a denomination is defined as 'a community for religious activities, of which an integral part is to arrange divine services'. This definition does not, therefore, include the Swiss Humanitarian Association, an association for atheists. According to Devenish,[13] the right to freedom of religion includes the right not to believe and the concept of 'religion' encompasses the notion of non-religion. The right to freedom of religion, therefore, often includes reference to freedom of conscience, thought and opinion, and includes reference to philosophical beliefs, convictions, or worldviews, without necessarily classifying these convictions as 'religious'.

Religious pluralism pre-supposes various definitions and interpretations of 'religion' and Choper states that 'the scope of religious pluralism ... alone has resulted in such a multiplicity and diversity of ideas about what is a 'religion' or a 'religious belief' that no simple formula seems able to accommodate them all.' [14]

For reasons of practicality and to empower the courts to efficiently deal with religious disputes, Van der Schyff[15] rightly proposes a functional approach, rather than a purely philosophical or theological approach. In a legal context, this functional approach will be followed throughout the discussion in terms of how a religious institution will be defined and qualified in accordance with certain qualities and characteristics.

According to Van der Schyff, the following characteristics must at least be present in order to qualify as 'religion': a belief in a supreme being, a belief in a transcendental reality, a moral code, a worldly view that describes the human role in the universe and in terms of which an individual organizes and manages his life, holy rituals and festivals, worship and prayers, holy scriptures and texts and the existence of a social organization that supports and develops the said beliefs system. [16] The latter is of great importance for religious institutions.

The Constitutional Court in *Taylor v. Kurtstag*[17] states with reference to Witte:

> [A]ctive religious rights require that individuals be allowed to exercise their religious beliefs privately and groups be allowed to engage in private worship assembly. More fully conceived, active religious rights embrace an individual's ability to engage in religious assembly, religious speech, religious worship, observance of religious laws and ritual, payment of religious taxes, and the like. They also embrace a religious institution's power to promulgate and enforce internal religious laws of order, organisation, and orthodoxy, to train, select, and

13 G. Devenish, 'Freedom of Religion, Belief and Opinion', *Obiter* 17 (1995).

14 Quoted from J.M.T. Labuschagne, 'Die Begrip "Godsdiens" in Godsdiensvryheid: 'n Bewussunsantropologiese Ekskursie na die Evolusiekern van die Reg', *De Jure Law Jounral* (1997), 118–119.

15 G. van der Schyff, 'The Legal Definition of Religion and its Application', 119 *South African Law Journal* (2002), 289.

16 Van der Schyff, 290.

17 *Taylor v. Kurtstag NO and Others*, 2005 (1) SA 362 (W), para. 37.

> discipline religious officials, to establish and maintain institutions of worship, charity, and education, to acquire, use, and dispose of property and literature used in worship and rituals, to communicate with co-believers and proselytes, and many other affirmative acts in manifestation of the beliefs of the institution.[18]

According to Justice Van Dijkhorst in *Wittman v. Deutscher Schulverein*,[19] 'religion' is not a neutral concept and encompasses a 'system of faith and worship [as] the human recognition of superhuman controlling power and especially of a personal God or gods entitled to obedience and worship.' Freedom of 'religion,' as interpreted in accordance with Section 9 of the European Convention, also applies to the individual or collective exercise of religion only if it forms part of an established religious practice.[20] The European Court of Human Rights in *Metropolitan Church of Bessarabia*,[21] however, emphasizes the view that 'in principle the right to freedom of religion [...] excludes assessment by the State of the legitimacy of religious beliefs or the ways in which those beliefs are expressed.'[22] This view will receive further attention later in the discussion.

In so far as a conceptualization goes, the concept of 'religious institution' is used in accordance with the (proposed) South African Charter of Religious Rights and Freedoms. Reference to 'every person' in the Charter thus includes a religious organization or institution and also includes any reference to church, religious entity, institution, and community.

This is also in line with the approach followed in Ireland, where all religious institutions and religious communities function as voluntary associations, and where the concept of 'religious denomination' refers to a 'generic term wide enough to cover the various churches, religious societies or religious congregations under whatever name they wished to describe themselves ... [and also] ... that each religious denomination should be respected when it says what its ethos is'.[23]

This approach is supported throughout the chapter. The courts will ultimately have to judge whether a specific religious institution qualifies as 'religious' for purposes of the right to freedom of religion, based on the nature of the institution, aims and objectives, functioning, and characteristics.

---

18 J. Witte Jr.,'The South African Experiment in Religious Human Rights: What Can Be Learned from the American Experience?', 18 *Journal of Juridical Science* 1 (1993), 24–25.

19 *Wittman v. Deutscher Schulverein*, 1998 (4 SA 423 (T) 449.

20 B.P. Vermeulen and M.J. Kanne, 'Kerk en Staat en de Mensenrechten', in L.C. van Drimmelen and T.J. van der Ploeg (eds.), *Kerk en Recht* (Utrecht: Lemma, 2004), 78.

21 *Metropolitan Church of Bessarabia and Others v. Moldova*, App. No. 45701/99, 13 December 2001.

22 Vermeulen and Kanne, supra note 20 at 79.

23 P. Colton, 'Religious Entities as Legal Persons – Ireland', in L. Friedner *Churches and Other Religious Organisations as Legal Persons*, supra note 7 at 128.

Religious Institutions and the Right to Freedom of Association and 'Non-Interference'

> 'Associational rights safeguard primordial religious and cultural attachments from undue state interference.' [24]

The right to freedom of association is one of the most fundamental rights in a democratic society and is described as a right that entails 'a general capacity for citizens to join, without interference by the state, in associations in order to attain various ends'.[25] The importance for religious organization, in particular, is that 'associations, such as religious communities, are integral to self-understanding, and that there can be no self without the host of associations that give the self content.'[26] It is often this element of 'voluntariness' that causes the right to freedom of association not to be taken seriously. This view is supported by Woolman, when he states: 'In 15 years, the Constitutional Court has never decided a case solely, or even largely, in terms of freedom of association. And that says quite a lot about where, in our hierarchy of rights, freedom of association is located.'[27]

An important aspect of the right to freedom of association is that it fosters diversity. Lenta uses the aspect of diversity to emphasize the importance of organizations and the right to freedom of association in society: 'Associations should not always be expected to conform to public principles, including non-discrimination, when those principles clash with the convictions of members, and the state should refrain as far as possible from interfering with the internal affairs of associations. *This is what the protection of diversity requires.*'[28][emphasis added]

The size, nature, and objectives of the organization will determine the degree of autonomy enjoyed by the organization for purposes of the performance of its functions, compliance with procedural requirements and formalities, limits of judicial review, and degree of interference by the state in the internal affairs of the association. The more an association performs a public function, the more interference from the side of the government can be expected.

The Australian Court in *Baldwin v. Everingham*[29] confirms this view:

---

24 Woolman, 'Association', supra note 1 at 421.

25 As quoted from H. Cheadle, D. Davis, and N. Haysom (eds.), *South African Constitutional Law: The Bill of Rights* (Families History Bound, 2002), 251.

26 S. Woolman, 'On the Fragility of Associational Life: A Constitutional Liberal's Response to Patrick Lenta', 25 *South African Journal on Human Rights* (2009), 286.

27 Woolman, 'On the Fragility of Associational Life', 296.

28 As quoted by Justice Brennan in *Roberts v. United States Jaycees*, 468 US 609 (1984), and referred to by P. Lenta, 'Taking Diversity Seriously: Religious Associations and Work-Related Discrimination', 126 *South African Law Journal* (2009), 832.

29 *Baldwin v. Everingham*, [1993] 1 Qd R 10 17.

> On general principles, where a voluntary association fulfils a substantial public function in our society, it may appear indefensible that questions of construction concerning its constitution should be beyond judicial resolution. It is one thing to say that a small voluntary association with limited assets, existing solely to serve the personal needs of members should be treated as beyond such supervision; it is another thing to say that a major national organisation with substantial assets, playing a central role in the determination of the affairs of the country should be so immune.[30]

Article 15 (freedom of religion),[31] Article 18 (freedom of association),[32] and Article 31 (right to associate in religious communities)[33] of the South African Constitution[34] play very important roles respecting religious institutions in relation to the degree of interference by the state in the internal affairs of the association (membership, activities, etc). Government interference can occur due to discriminatory practices by the organization, but only in accordance with Article 36[35] of the Constitution. Examples include activities or provisions in the organizations' constitutions that are in conflict with the principles of a society based on human dignity, equality, and freedom; where membership is declined on the basis of discriminatory practices; and where the internal affairs of the organization are not conducted in accordance with democratic principles. [36] In lieu of the fact that courts are prepared to scrutinize religious institutions' doctrines

30 Quoted from J.R.S. Forbes, *Justice in Tribunals*, 3rd revised edn. (Leichhardt NSW: Federation Press, 2010), 69.

31 '15. Freedom of religion, belief and opinion. (1) Everyone has the right to freedom of conscience, religion, thought, belief and opinion.'

32 '18. Freedom of association. Everyone has the right to freedom of association.'

33 '31. Cultural, religious and linguistic communities. (l) Persons belonging to a Cultural, religious or linguistic community may not be denied the right, with other members of that community

(a) to enjoy their culture, practise their religion and use their language; and

(h) to form, join and maintain cultural, religious and linguistic associations and other organs of civil society.'

34 The Constitution of the Republic of South Africa, 1996.

35 '36. Limitation of rights. (1) The rights in the Bill of Rights may be limited only in terms of law of general application to the extent that the limitation is reasonable and justifiable in an open and democratic society based on human dignity, equality and freedom, taking into account all relevant factors, including

(a) the nature of the right;

(b) the importance of the purpose of the limitation;

(c) the nature and extent of the limitation;

(d) the relation between the limitation and its purpose; and

(e) less restrictive means to achieve the purpose.'

36 G. Pienaar, 'Konstitusionele Voorskrifte rakende Regspersone', 60 *Tydskrif vir Hedendaagse Romeins-Hollandse Reg (THRHR)* [Journal of Contemporary Roman-Dutch Law] (1999), 576–577.

and inquire whether they form part of the specific religion in question, a huge responsibility rests on religious institutions to have clarity in their own religious doctrines and procedures. As the court correctly points out in *Minister of Home Affairs v. Fourie; Gay and Lesbian Equality Project v. Minister of Home Affairs*: 'Judges would be placed in an intolerable situation if they were called upon to construe religious texts and take side on issues which have caused deep schisms within religious bodies.' [37]

The *nature* of the religious institution together with the operation of Articles 15, 18, and 31 of the Constitution should limit state interference in the internal affairs of religious institutions and allow interference only in very exceptional cases. Religious institutions are afforded this privileged position for so long as and to the extent that their activities are of a *bona fide* religious nature.

Woolman and de Waal describe it as follows: 'The internal affairs of such associations are generally linked to some concrete vision of religious or community life. In a liberal society the state should have no role to play in the construction of these particular visions of the good life.' [38]

The opposite view also applies: 'The more public goods distributed by an association or the more public its function, the more likely it is to be subject to legitimate state intervention.'[39]

Where religious institutions are, therefore, pursuing purely economic or political objectives, 'state interference with the membership policies—and perhaps even the internal affairs—of the association may well pass constitutional muster.'[40] It has also been confirmed in several decisions 'that the intensity of review clearly depends on the subject matter in hand'.[41]

The threshold for interference with certain kinds of associations ought to be quite high. As Woolman correctly points out: 'With families, *religious groups* and traditional communities, the first inclination of a liberal state ought to be to allow the members to work out their voice on their own.' [42] [emphasis added]

This flows from the important premise that churches and religious association are not just ordinary associations; they are *religious* organizations. Therefore

37 *Minister of Home Affairs v. Fourie; Gay and Lesbian Equality Project v. Minister of Home Affairs*, [2006] (3) BCLR 355 (CC), para. 92.

38 S. Woolman and J. de Waal, 'Freedom of Association', in D. van Wyk et al. (eds.), *Rights and Constitutionalism: The New South African Legal Order* (New York: Oxford University Press USA, 1996), 384.

39 Woolman, 'Association', supra note 1 at 426.

40 Woolman, 'Association', 434.

41 See *R (Mahmood) v. Secretary of State for the Home Department*, [2001] 1 WLR 840 at [18] ('the intensity of review in a public law case will depend on the subject matter in hand'); *Sheffield City Council v. Smart*, [2002] EWCA Civ 14 [2002] HLR 639 at [42] ('There is now a good deal of modern authority to the effect that the intensity of judicial review varies with the subject-matter.').

42 S. Woolman, 'Freedom of Association', in S. Woolman (ed.), *Constitutional Law of South Africa*, 2nd edn. (JUTA, 2009), 44–20.

observance not only of the right to freedom of association, but also of the right to freedom of religion is required. As illustrated by Lenta:

> The right to freedom of religion incorporates the interest of churches in conducting the internal affairs, including labour relations, according to their perceived interests; that is, in keeping decision-making authority over operations within the church free of government interference. The argument that government should not regulate the way in which churches select their officers and workers is that to do so is an unacceptable encroachment on religious affairs: it is simply inappropriate for the state to insist that religious organisations carry on their internal affairs in a way that is inconsistent with settled religious convictions and practices. [43]

As noted above, the nature of an organization, and a religious institution in particular, plays an important role where fundamental rights come in conflict with each other. It has become necessary to appropriately balance the different rights entrenched in the Bill of Rights and engage in a process of balancing competing rights. This balancing exercise often requires the balancing of two distinct sets of rights. On the one hand are the fundamental rights of equality, dignity, and non-discrimination, and on the other hand we find the so-called community or associative rights, including the right to freedom of association, the right to freedom of religion, and the right to associate in cultural, religious, and linguistic communities.

The next section will focus on the interaction between the right to equality, the right to freedom of association, and the right to freedom of religion, with reference to the example of *Strydom v. Nederduits Gereformeerde Gemeente Moreleta Park.*[44]

Should Religious Organizations Be Allowed to Discriminate? The case of Johan Strydom

In *Strydom*, the court found that the Dutch Reformed Church unfairly discriminated against a gay music teacher, because the church could not prove that Mr. Strydom was involved in religious instruction. His contract was terminated on the basis that he was involved in a homosexual relationship. The decision was criticized in that religious freedom did not enjoy priority above the individual's right to equality.

The court in *Strydom* referred to the important and interesting American case of *Corporation of the Presiding Bishop of The Church of Jesus Christ of Latter-day*

43 Lenta, 'Taking Diversity Seriously', supra note 28 at 833.
44 *Strydom*, supra note 6.

Saints v. Amos.[45] In *Amos* certain provisions of the Civil Rights Act[46] were at stake, as understood to mean that religions institutions were allowed to discriminate on grounds of religion in their employment and labour relations, irrespective of whether an employee was in fact performing a religious function or not.[47]

This extended definition was challenged on the basis of the 'establishment clause' and the court affirms that the exception applies to all non-profit activities of the organization and emphasises the fact that 'it is a significant burden on a religious organization to require it, on pain of substantial liability, to predict which of its activities a secular court will consider religious.'[48] It is not that easy, however, to draw the line between 'religious' and 'secular,' and it would be understandable that a religious institution '[would] be concerned that a judge would not understand its religious tenets and sense of mission and possible liability might affect the way an organization carried out what it understood to be its religious mission'.[49]

Lenta is, however, of the opinion that it does not mean that 'religious associations should not be required to demonstrate to the court that the position related to the unfair discrimination is sufficiently closely connected to the doctrinal core of the church,' which the church had not sufficiently proved in the view of the court in *Strydom*.[50] He is further of the view that religious institutions should not be allowed to discriminate 'unless the job in question is sufficiently closely connected to the doctrinal core of the religion'. He therefore supports the view that the court's decision in *Amos* was incorrect.

This approach by the courts 'to delve (carefully) into questions of core tenets of belief – and decide which beliefs are trumped and which beliefs are not' is, however, not shared by Woolman,[51] who rather supports the view of Justice

---

45 *Corporation of the Presiding Bishop of The Church of Jesus Christ of Latter-day Saints v. Amos*, 483 US 327 (1987).

46 Chapter VII of the Civil Rights Act of 1964, 42 USC 2000e, makes it unlawful for an employer to appoint or fire an individual or to otherwise discriminate against any person on the basis of remuneration, conditions of employment or any benefit based on race, ethnicity, religion, or sexuality. It includes dismissals, promotion or any other conduct in the workplace. Section 702 creates an exception and reads as follows:

'§2000e–1. Applicability to foreign and religious employment

(a) Inapplicability of subchapter to certain aliens and employees of religious entities

This subchapter shall not apply to an employer with respect to the employment of aliens outside any State, or to a religious corporation, association, educational institution, or society with respect to the employment of individuals of a particular religion to perform work connected with the carrying on by such corporation, association, educational institution, or society of its activities.'

47 This exception only applies in respect of religion and not in the case of discrimination based on race, gender or sexuality.

48 *Amos*, 483 US at 336.

49 *Amos*, 483 US at 336.

50 Lenta, 'Taking Diversity Seriously', supra note 28 at 843.

51 Woolman, 'On the Fragility of Associational Life', supra note 26 at 298.

Brennan in *Amos* that 'religious organizations have an interest in autonomy in ordering their religious affairs.'[52] Justice Brennan upholds the constitutionality of Section 702, 'covering all types of church employee, no matter what the job, appropriately balances the right of employees to religious liberty and the autonomy of religious organizations'.[53] Mr. Strydom worked as an independent contractor in the so-called '*kunste-akademie*' of the church, teaching music to students. He was dismissed from his post as lecturer in the church's Arts Academy in July 2005, and instituted proceedings under the Promotion of Equality and Prevention of Unfair Discrimination Act, 4 of 2000 (PEPUDA). He argued that the church had infringed his constitutionally protected right to equality, dignity, privacy, and freedom to work in the profession of his choice, on the ground of his homosexual orientation.

The court had to decide if the church unfairly discriminated against Mr. Strydom on grounds of sexual orientation, and if a religious institution could be exempt from the provisions of PEPUDA dealing with discrimination based on sexual orientation in the workplace in relation to a music teacher. The court also had to decide whether a religious institution is allowed to discriminate beyond their spiritual leaders, to include a music teacher, not involved in religious instruction.

The church had strong views on the meaning of a 'spiritual leader': 'Just as the respondent would not allow its ministers, officials, *spiritual leaders* and lecturers to be alcoholics or to have active extra-marital affairs, it could not allow them to be involved in active homosexual practices.' [54] [emphasis added]

The court found that the church unfairly discriminated against Mr. Johan Strydom. The church was ordered to pay Strydom damages and to apologize unconditionally for its conduct. The court was of the opinion that the church had not proved that Strydom's job entailed religious instruction or that the discrimination against him had been fair or justified. In the words of Justice Basson: 'I am not convinced on the evidence presented by the church that on the facts of the matter at hand the complainant was in such a position of spiritual leadership.'[55]

De Vos is of the opinion that it would constitute a violation of the right to freedom of religion 'on churches, mosques or synagogues to force them to employ a gay dominee, imam, rabbi or priest or to force the Catholic Church to ordain woman priests. The same would be true for forcing them to employ someone giving religious instruction at that institution.' This approach, according to him, does however not apply to an individual in a non-religious capacity and he argues that the approach adopted by the court was a sensible compromise and

52 *Amos*, 483 US at 340.

53 Lenta, at 843.

54 'Gay lecturer sues Pta church', *News 24*, 11 August 2008, available at http://www.news24.com/SouthAfrica/News/Gay-lecturer-sues-Pta-church-20080811 (accessed 31 January 2013).

55 *Strydom*, supra note 6 at para. 17.

that '[t]o have held otherwise would have … created a situation in which religious institutions are in effect above the law …' [56]

In relation to 'spiritual leaders,' Woolman makes it clear that

> although the value of equality is foundational to the new constitutional dispensation, it is unlikely that equality considerations could outweigh the enormous impact of failing to give churches an exemption in relation to their *spiritual leaders*. Where appointment, dismissal and employment conditions of religious leaders (such as priests, imams, rabbis, and so forth) are concerned, religious bodies are likely to be exempted from compliance with legislation prohibiting unfair discrimination.[57] [emphasis added)

The church is in disagreement with the court's interpretation of 'spiritual leader'. According to them a spiritual leader encompasses much more than just ministers, deacons or elders. They are of the opinion that Mr. Strydom was in the position of a spiritual leader in that he acted as a role model for young students and was therefore subject to the church policy relating to spiritual leaders.[58]

According to De Vos:

> Where a religious group employs an individual in a non-religious capacity, for example, the Constitution demands that they do so without discriminating against anyone. A church that employs a secretary or a gardener cannot prohibit a gay man or a black woman from doing these jobs because that church happens to espouse homophobic or racist views.
>
> This is because these jobs are not directly linked to the religious nature of the institution. A person employed as a typist, a gardener (*or a music teacher for that matter)* does not give religious instruction and forcing a church to employ such a person in no way forces the church to espouse views or practices that its religion frowns upon or even abhor. The religious freedom of the church is therefore not affected while the rights of all citizens remain protected.
>
> This seems like a sensible compromise also adopted by the Pretoria High Court. To have held otherwise would have … created a situation in which religious institutions are in effect above the law …

56 P. de Vos ,'On freedom of religion and the gay music teacher', *Constitutionally Speaking Blog*, 3 September 2008, available at http://constitutionallyspeaking.co.za/?p=655 (accessed 4 December 2012).

57 *Strydom*at para. 15.

58 N. Jackson, 'Ekskuus…maar homoseksualiteit bly sonde', *Beeld*, 9 September 2008, available at http://www.beeld.com/Suid-Afrika/Nuus/Ekskuusmaar-homoseksualiteit-bly-sonde-20100617 (accessed 4 December 2012).

> So this judgment manages to balance the interest of the state against the interest of religious groups in a sensible and pragmatic fashion, refusing to sanction religious tyranny … In a country where we are building a culture of respect for diversity and difference churches can therefore not get a free pass.[59] [emphasis added)

It has been submitted that such an approach is not in line with the essence of the right to freedom of religion, which guarantees religious autonomy in so far as 'each religious denomination should be respected when it says what its ethos is.'[60] A court is hardly in a position to determine and interpret religious doctrines and to give content to something essentially religious in nature. Courts must show deference when religious institutions are of the view that, from a religious point of view, certain functions are of a religious nature, or as in this case, that a music teacher acts in the capacity of a spiritual leader within the church.

Lenta supports the view of De Vos, confirming the final decision by the court. He is however of the opinion that the decision 'fails to show sufficient respect for diversity'.[61] Woolman, on the other hand, takes a different view.[62] He is not convinced that the court came to the correct conclusion and submits that the court would have found in favour of the church had they presented a well-structured argument based on Article 15 (freedom of religion), Article 18 (freedom of association), and Article 31 (right to associate in religious communities) of the Constitution.

Discrimination in the workplace does occur often and Lenta is of the strong opinion that anti-discrimination legislation should not be used to prevent this type of discrimination, since 'religious associations have a right to manage their own affairs in accordance with the beliefs of members as expressed through their churches—freedom of religion and associational autonomy demands as much'.[63] This approach is, however, in strong contrast to his earlier view on the *Amos* case, where he did not support the view of Justice Brennan (who took a similar approach) and held the decision to be incorrect. If he takes this approach in his assessment of *Strydom*, he would support the view that allows the NG Kerk Moreletta Park 'to manage their own affairs in accordance with the beliefs of members as expressed through their churches' and he would respect their views and interpretation of the meaning of and role of a 'spiritual leader'. This is exactly what freedom of religion and associational autonomy demand!

In support of the decision in *Amos* and the view of Woolman, for instance, courts should display utmost restraint when deciding religious matters. This is a view that is not supported by Bilchitz, who rather supports a 'presumption of

59 De Vos, *Constitutionally Speaking Blog.*
60 Colton, 'Religious Entities as Legal Persons – Ireland', supra note 23 at 128.
61 Lenta, 'Taking Diversity Seriously', supra note 28 at 839.
62 Woolman, 'On the Fragility of Associational Life', supra note 26 at 283.
63 Lenta at 829.

equality' approach[64]: 'Courts thus are required to decide upon whose side they should intervene. Both the presumption of equality and the harmful nature of discrimination ... require the state to favour the group against which discrimination is being perpetrated.'[65]

Such a view does not give the necessary recognition to the right to freedom of religion and the right to freedom of association in a pluralistic society. In *Ryland v. Edros*[66] the court emphasized two important values entrenched in our Constitution: the value of equality, but also the value of 'tolerance and accommodation'. [67] Justice Farlam supports this view when he further emphasizes the importance of 'the values of equality *and tolerance of diversity and the recognition of the plural nature of our society* ...'.[68] [emphasis added]

The approach by Bilchitz further ignores the *sui generis* nature of religious organizations. Woolman correctly summarizes the *sui generis* character of religious institutions:

> Like it or not, religion is different. Time – sacred time – for religion is circular, not linear. Linear time – human time – is profane. Religion returns through holiday and ritual to the beginning: when God – of one stripe or another – made the world and laid down the law. Others – non-members – may find the religious beliefs and practices of a faith perverse. But rational distinctions – or the absence of rational distinctions – is hardly the point when an organised faith is put in the position of defending God's law – not their own. It is God's law that provides the setting for meaningful action for the members of the Nederduits Gereformeerde Gemeente Moreletta Park. The notion that they could alter God's law is akin to idolatry. It confuses the sacred and the profane. [69]

Lenta submits that the court in *Strydom* is creating the impression that the right to equality is a more fundamental right than the right to freedom of association and the right to freedom of religion.[70] Although the court gives recognition to the importance of the right to freedom of religion by referring to the view of the Constitutional Court in *Prins v. President, Cape Law Society and Others,*[71] Justice Basson goes further to state that the right to equality 'is viewed as foundational to

64 D. Bilchitz, 'Should Religious Associations be allowed to discriminate?', paper delivered at the Society of Law Teachers of South Africa(SLTSA) Conference, Stellenbosch, January 2011, unpublished Article 15.

65 Bilchitz, 'Should Religious Associations be allowed to discriminate?'

66 *Ryland v. Edros*, 1997 (2) SA 690 (CC).

67 See *Ryland* at 707H–708. I. Trengove refers to ten important constitutional principles as a manifestation of these two important values.

68 *Ryland* at 708, para. H.

69 Woolman at 294.

70 Lenta at 834–836.

71 *Prins v. President, Cape Law Society and Others*, 2002 (2) SA 794 (CC) in *Strydom*, supra note 6 at para. 9.

our constitutional order' and with reference to *Minister of Education & Another v. Syfrets Trust Ltd. NO & Another*[72]: 'As a cursory perusal of constitutional jurisprudence shows, equality is not merely a fundamental right; it is a core value of the Constitution. This is borne out by various provisions in the Constitution itself, which articulate the ideal of equality.'[73]

Such an approach and accompanying view are according to Lenta, false, and he is rather of the view that the right to freedom of religion is one of the most fundamental rights and that 'it would not be a huge exaggeration to suggest that this freedom is the grain of sand in the oyster of politics around which the pearl of liberalism gradually forms' and that the right to freedom of religion is 'not merely one of many rights, but the prototypical human right'.[74] This view is supported by Benson,[75] who correctly points out that 'equality is not more important than freedom of religion' and it is also a view supported by the author. This view does not support the 'egalitarian form of liberalism' approach taken by Blichitz[76] that requires 'a strong presumption in favour of equality and mitigates against effectively exempting religious associations from the provisions of the Constitution and PEPUDA relating to non-discrimination.'

No rights are absolute, including the rights entrenched in Sections 15, 18, and 31 of the Constitution. The court in *Christian Education SA v. Minister of Education* makes it clear that in accordance with Section 31(2), the rights in Section 31(1) may not be exercised in a manner inconsistent with any provision of the Bill of Rights:

> It should be observed, further, that special care has been taken expressly to acknowledge the supremacy of the Constitution and the Bill of Rights. Section 31(2) ensures that the concept of rights of members of communities that associate on the basis of language, culture and religion, cannot be used to shield practices which offend the Bill of Rights. These explicit qualifications may be seen as serving a double purpose. The first is to prevent protected associational rights of members of communities from being used to 'privatise' constitutionally offensive group practices and thereby immunize them from external legislative regulation or judicial control. This will be particularly important in relation to practices previously associated with the abuse of the notion of pluralism to achieve exclusivity, privilege and domination. The second relates to oppressive features of internal relationships primarily within the communities concerned,

---

72 *Minister of Education & Another v. Syfrets Trust Ltd. NO & Another*, 2006 (4) SA 25 (CC) in *Strydom*, supra note 6 at para. 10.

73 *Strydom* at para. 10.

74 Lenta at 836, and the view of K. Hasson, 'Religious Liberty and Human Dignity: A Tale of Two Declarations', 27 *Harvard Journal of Law & Public Policy* (2003), 88–89.

75 I. Benson 'The Freedom of Conscience and Religion in Canada: Challenges and Opportunities' 21 *Emory International Law Review* 148 (2007).

76 Bilchitz, supra note 64.

> where section 8, which regulates the horizontal application of the Bill of rights, might be specially relevant.[77]

Section 31(1) makes it clear that any exclusionary policies, actions, or procedures by voluntary associations, including religious entities, would not be allowed unconditionally and can be limited, but only in accordance with the requirements of the limitation clause and the test for proportionality. It is therefore not necessary to presume beforehand that any associational rights are subordinate and of lesser value than the right of equality and dignity.

Where does that leave religious institutions and presumably also the courts in relation to future decisions similar to *Strydom?* The view of Woolman is favourable, which he states in relatively strong words: 'So long as church rules clearly preclude openly gay and lesbian members of the church from participating in public practices in the church, neither our courts nor our state has any business using such blunt cudgels as the right to dignity to reinstate an openly lesbian organist so that she might teach in a faith-based school and be remunerated for her efforts.'[78]

Conclusion

This discussion has clearly emphasized the importance of the right to freedom of association for religious institutions and has indicated that 'With certain kinds of association the threshold for interference in determining the voice ought to be quite high. With families, *religious groups* and traditional communities, the first inclination of a liberal state ought to be to allow the members to work out their voice on their own.'[79] [emphasis added]

The example of *Strydom* and the court's approach has, however, proven the fact that these associational rights are not taken seriously, in particular when they stand in conflict with the right to equality and non-discrimination.

A discussion paper prepared by staff of the Human Rights Commission argues that there is a hierarchy of rights developed by the Constitutional Court and concludes that 'According to this hierarchy, the rights to human dignity and equality are superior to others. Therefore, when these core rights collide with other rights such as the right to freedom of association, the right to dignity and equality must prevail.'[80]

---

77 *Christian Education SA v. Minister of Education*, 2000 4 SA 757 (CC), para 26.

78 Woolman at 305.

79 Woolman at 44–20.

80 Discussion paper on Voluntary Associations prepared by SAHRC staff 7, as quoted from a report compiled by the Human Rights Commission, 2006 Report: 'Public Inquiry Exclusionary Policies of Voluntary Associations: Constitutional Considerations.

Such an approach is not in line with the view of Justice Sachs in *Christian Education SA v. Minister of Education* in relation to Section 31:

> 'There are a number of provisions designated to protect the rights of members of communities. They underlie the constitutional value of acknowledging diversity and pluralism in our society and give a particular texture to the broadly phrased right to freedom of association contained in s 18. Taken together they affirm the right of people to be who they are without being forced to subordinate themselves to the cultural and religious norms of other, and highlights the importance of individuals being able to enjoy what is called the 'right to be different'. In each case, space has to be found for members of the communities to depart from a general norm. These provisions collectively and separately acknowledge the rich tapestry constitute by civil society, indicating in particular that language, culture and religion constitute a strong weave in the overall pattern.'[81]

In a later report compiled by experts in the field of voluntary associations, this view is also rejected in favour of an approach that requires a 'more nuanced balancing of rights.' According to the report, 'a mere conflict between an associational right and the right to equality cannot always result, irrespective of circumstances, in the predominance of the right to equality. The consequence of this interpretation would be to emasculate associational rights and severely restrict cultural liberties.'[82]

There rests a duty on religious institutions to evaluate their exclusionary policies, rules, and conduct in accordance with the requirements set out in the Constitution. However, religious institutions, whose objectives are to achieve constitutionally legitimate goals, must be allowed to adopt exclusionary rules and policies in order to afford appropriate weight to associational rights aimed at developing and protecting religious liberties.

South African Human Rights Commission' 18, available at www.sahrc.org.za (accessed 4 December 2012).

81 *Christian Education SA* at para. 24.

82 HRC 2006 Exclusionary Policies 18, supra note 80.

Chapter 12
Religion and the Basic Legislation in Israel

Natan Lerner

Israel has no written, complete constitution. It has, however, a constitutional system based on a series of basic laws and jurisprudence that permitted the country to overcome its difficulties during the more than six stormy decades that followed its establishment. The state had to solve crucial problems, political and legal, in order to provide its heterogeneous population with a regime that was adequate to the twenty-first century and that was proper for a state young as an independent entity but representative of the aspirations of an ancient nation. This nation consolidated around a religion that had a seminal influence on Western thought.

I attempted to summarize that effort in an article published a few years ago.[1] Since the publication of this article, there have been few changes in the relationship between the state and religion in Israel.

The State of Israel and the Jewish People

On 14 May 1948, following the 1947 United Nations resolution on partition of the territory under the Mandate of Great Britain,[2] the State of Israel was established as a sovereign 'Jewish http://www.bbc.co.uk/news/uk-northern-ireland-21664403and democratic state',[3] fulfilling partially the program of the Zionist movement, created in 1987.[4] The 64-year-old state sees itself, in terms of history, as the successor of the Jewish State that existed two millennia earlier, on more or less the same geographic area. As such, Israel considers itself the national state of a globally-scattered community, the Jewish people, including the Jews of Israel—the large majority of the population of the state—and the Jews of the Diaspora, namely the Jewish communities living in different locations almost all over the world. This is explicitly stated in the Declaration of Independence, which refers to the recognition by the United Nations of the right of the Jewish people 'throughout the Diaspora'

1 N. Lerner, 'Religious Liberty in the State of Israel', 21 *Emory International Law Review* 1 (Spring 2007).

2 United Nations General Assembly Resolution 181(II).

3 See Declaration of the Establishment of the State of Israel, 1 LSI, 3–5.

4 For the Zionist program and development, see generally W. Laqueur, *A History of Zionism* (London: Weidenfeld and Nicolson, 1972).

to establish their own sovereign state.[5] It does not imply political ties between the state and the Jews of the Diaspora.

The history of the Jews is closely related to the role of religion. Not every Jew, in Israel or elsewhere, is religious. But, in collective terms, religion has been an essential ingredient in the self-definition and behavior of the Jews, believers or not, observant or not. Judaism 'conceived of itself not as a denomination but as the religious dimension of the life of a people. Hence, peoplehood is a religious fact in the Jewish universe of discourse. In its traditional self-understanding, Israel is related not to other denominations but to the 'nations of the world' ... Israel's ... body is the body politic of a nation.'[6] It is in that sense that, in reference to a Jewish state in all international texts, the term *Jewish* means 'pertaining to Jews'.

In legal terms, the State of Israel is a secular state. Its Parliament, the *Knesset*, makes its laws.[7] If a religious law should be applied, it would only be the consequence of a secular law giving it such force. Affirming that it is a secular state is, however, not enough to explain the role of religion in the state.

According to the official information of the Central Bureau of Statistics, Israel has a population of about 7,500,000 persons. About 75 percent of them are Jews, with different degrees and forms of identification with traditional Judaism or the Jewish religion; about 1,500,000 are Muslims; about 150,000 are Christians, belonging to the various denominations, including Arabs and non-Arabs; and about 122,000 are Druze.[8] This classification is obviously related to religion, beyond the personal beliefs of the members of each group.

How do state and religion relate to each other? How secular should the state, described in all official, national, and international documents as a 'Jewish state' be considered? What does the term *Jewish* mean? Is it an adjective indicating the religious character of the state? Or does it possess a sociological, anthropological, or demographic meaning applicable to the majority of the population, defining how members of that majority relate to Israeli society, culture, and way of life? Does 'Jewish state' mean something similar to 'French state' or 'German state' or 'Chilean state,' or does it mean something similar to 'Catholic state' or 'Muslim state'?

It seems reasonable to accept that the reference to Israel as a 'Jewish state' means that, in historical, political, and legal terms, it is the state of the Jewish people, a worldwide community of indisputable religious origin, scattered all over the world, although about 50 percent of it, more or less, is presently concentrated in the State of Israel, where about 25 percent of its present population does not belong to that worldwide community. The Balfour Declaration of 1917, addressed to the Zionist Organization by a spokesman of Great Britain; the British Mandate over Palestine of the League of Nations of 1922; and the 1947 United Nations'

5 See Declaration of the Establishment of the State of Israel, 1 LSI, 3-5.

6 R. J. Zwi Werblowsky, Jerusalem Colloquium on Religion, Peoplehood, Nation and Land, Proceedings, Jerusalem, 1972.

7 See H. Cohn, *Human Rights in Jewish Law* (New York: Ktav, 1984), 17.

8 Central Bureau of Statistics, *Statistical Abstract of Israel* 2009.

General Assembly Resolution 181 (II), on the partition of Palestine under the Mandate, all refer to a 'Jewish state.' *Jewish* means, in all of these documents, 'pertaining to Jews, namely, the individuals seeing themselves as the Jewish people, or nation, or community'.

While all point to a secular, not religious, use of the term '*Jewish*' in legal texts,[9] '[t]he precise meaning of Israel's self-definition as a Jewish State has never been clearly delineated and is a matter of controversy' with views varying 'from minimalist descriptive notions—which regard the Jewish majority as the only element that makes Israel the 'State of the Jews'—to Messianic visions of the state as an instrument in ushering in the millennium.'[10] In a draft Constitution proposed by a Knesset committee in 2006, the words 'a Jewish and Democratic State' seem to mean the State in which the Jewish people implement their right to self-determination,[11] 'the political framework in which the right of the Jewish people to self-determination materializes'.[12]

A Complicated State-Religion Relationship

An official report submitted by Israel to the Human Rights Committee in 1998,[13] combining the initial and first periodic report on the implementation of the International Covenant on Civil and Political Rights (ICCPR), describes very well the complicated character of the state-religion relationship in Israel. That relationship is 'quite labyrinthine': 'History, political expediency, party politics, the lack of a constitution which specifically deals with freedom of religion, and the broad power of the Knesset to legislate in religious matters have resulted in a patchwork of laws and practices that are not easily susceptible to generalization.'[14]

The Report adds:

> There is no established religion in Israel, properly so-called. Nor, however, does Israel maintain the principle of separation between matters of religion and the institutions of Government. Rather, the law and practice of Israel regarding religious freedom may best be understood as a sort of hybrid between non-

---

9 See generally, A. Shapira and K. C. DeWitt-Arar (eds.), *Introduction to the Law of Israel* (The Hague: Kluwer Law International, 1995).

10 D. Kretzmer, 'Constitutional Law', in *Introduction to the Law of Israel.*

11 *Proposals for a Constitution,* Constitution, Law and Justice Committee of the Sixteenth Knesset, 23 February 2006.

12 A. Rubinstein and B. Medina, *The Constitutional Law of the State of Israel*, 5th edn. 2005 (in Hebrew), 318–319.

13 UN Doc. CCPR/C/81/Add.13 (hereinafter 'Israel HRC Report').

14 Israel HRC Report. The report was prepared by the Ministries of Justice and Foreign Affairs and was preceded by a Foreword written by the general directors of both ministries.

> intervention in religious affairs, on the one hand, and on the other hand the interpenetration of religion and Government in several forms, most notably by legislation establishing the jurisdiction of religious courts of the different faiths in specified matters of 'personal status,' by government funding of authorities that provide religious services to several of the religious communities, and by a series of legal institutions and practices which apply Jewish religious norms to the Jewish population. While it may be said that Israel has been quite successful in guaranteeing the freedom of religious practice and the use of sites to the three monotheistic faiths, particularly for the non-Jewish communities, it is more difficult to claim that 'freedom from religion' is fully protected, particularly for the Jewish population.[15]

Still, as stated by Justice Sussman in a classic case,[16] 'there can be no freedom of religion if the citizen is not free not to belong to any religion,' a principle accepted in theory, that clashes sometimes with the system of recognized communities implying automatic membership for the majority of the population. Israel has been correctly described as 'a multi-religious state, where various religions are recognized, yet none enjoys the status of official state religion'.[17]

Israeli legislation reflects the Jewish historical continuity. Examples of this are the Law of Return, 1950, as modified, and such laws as the Flag and Emblem Law, 1949, adopting traditional Jewish symbols—the Jewish prayer shawl; the seven-branched candelabrum; and the national anthem, *Hatikva*. Also, there is the Days of Rest Ordinance, 1948, designating the Sabbath and Jewish holidays as official days of rest, with exceptions for non-Jews; the Martyrs' and Heroes' Remembrance Day Law, 1959, concerning the Holocaust; and the 1952 World Zionist Organization-Jewish Agency (Status) Law, granting special status to certain Jewish organizations.[18] Traditional Jewish law 'has legal standing and societal potency in Israel'[19] and the Legal Foundations Act, 1980, includes principles of the 'Jewish heritage' among the complementary sources of law.[20]

The fact that, six decades after its establishment, the State of Israel is still unable to enact a written, coherent Constitution is mainly due to the disagreements concerning religion, secularism, and the meaning of the term '*Jewish*'. The starting point of a constitutional process was the Declaration of Independence

15 Israel HRC Report, para.532.

16 *Segev v. Rabbinical Court,* High Court of Justice 130/66.

17 A. Maoz, 'Religious Human Rights in the State of Israel', in J. D.van der Vyver and J. Witte Jr. (eds.), *Religious Human Rights in Global Perspective: Legal Perspectives* (The Hague: Martinus Nijhoff, 1995), 349, 359.

18 See Lerner, 'Religious Liberty in the State of Israel'.

19 On the role of *Halakha* in Israeli legislation, A. Kirschenbaum, *An Introduction to Jewish Law* (Tel Aviv: Intedisciplinary Center, 2005), 133.

20 See Lerner at 247.

adopted in 1948,[21] which foresaw a swift adoption of a Constitution. It did not happen, despite the fact that the country became a functioning democracy, with institutions, according to international standards. A constitutional assembly early elected became the first regular Knesset (Parliament), and this body decided not to adopt an organic Constitution but to prepare a draft to be composed of separate chapters, each one having the character of a basic law. To amend them there is need for a special majority.

The most recent draft of a Constitution was prepared by the Constitution, Law, and Justice Committee of the Sixteenth Knesset, in 2006.[22] The draft engendered controversies. The drafters themselves acknowledged the shortcomings of the text, which avoided confronting the problems related to the so-called *status quo* concerning religious issues and family law and personal status. This situation has its origin in agreements concluded by the political parties in the early stages of the State, and kept, with some exceptions, during all these years.

The main issues of religion and religion-state relations are consequently not addressed in any organic basic text. The principles governing those issues are therefore to be found in legislative texts and case-law. On the whole, religious freedom is protected, although some limitations exist, mainly for the Jewish non-Orthodox sector of the population. There is no formally preferred or privileged religion, and the *Halakha* or Jewish law plays a minor role as a subsidiary source of law. There is no absolute equality between religions in fact, with the religion of the majority playing a role in public life, despite the overall respect for freedom of conscience and religion.

A major change introduced under the State of Israel related to the Jewish population. Jewish religious institutions became state bodies, exercising authority over all Jews of the country, without consideration to their self-definition and views on religion. This affects particularly marriage laws. Atheistic or non-religious Jews have to undergo a religious ceremony conducted by an Orthodox rabbi if they wish to marry in the country. A couple can marry abroad by a civilian authority or can sign a private marriage contract. Both acts will be recognized by the Israeli general courts and taken notice of by the Population Registry, but will be ignored by the rabbinical courts. In 2010, the Knesset passed a law permitting a civil union for people who do not belong to any religious community.[23] This law, that does not use the word 'marriage', has been praised by those who see in it a way of breaking Orthodox monopoly; others consider it an insufficient step that may be meaningful for a small portion of the population but is far from solving a major issue of principle.

---

21 For its text, 1 Laws of the State of Israel (LSI) 3, 4.

22 *Proposals for a Constitution,* Constitution, Law and Justice Committee of the Sixteenth Knesset.

23 The law was published on 22 March 2010. It was adopted by a majority of 56 Knesset members, less than a half of the house. For its text, see http://www.ynetviews.com/articles/0.7340.1.-3863253.00 html.

It is impossible to precisely identify the proportion of Jews which are non-observant. Many non-religious Jews observe some precepts, like circumcision, *bar mitzvah* celebrations, and religious weddings, although they may claim that no religious motivation is present in those acts and they are due to the desire to ensure recognition for the future generations. This may also be related to the overlapping of religion and nation in the long Jewish history.

The Recognized Communities System

For a general overview of the legal setting concerning state and religion in Israel, it is necessary to refer to the recognized communities system, developed under the two regimes that preceded the creation of the State, namely, the Ottoman Empire (1517–1917) and the British Mandate over Palestine (1918–1948). The Ottoman rule permitted non-Muslim communities to enjoy autonomy in their communal affairs, religion included.[24] Those communities, based on religion and called *millets,* had their own courts in matters of personal status, while the *Mejelle,* the Islamic civil law, governed the same issues for Muslims. Foreigners, under consular jurisdiction, were not subject to Ottoman law.

The British, during the Mandate established by the League of Nations, did not change the system. The principal provisions are contained in the Palestine Order in Council of 1922, art. 83, which recognized ten communities: Eastern Orthodox, Latin Catholic, Gregorian Armenian, Armenian Catholic, Syrian Catholic, Chaldean Uniate, Greek Catholic Melkite, Maronite, Syrian Orthodox, and Jewish (called *Knesset Israel*).[25] Muslims were not considered a 'recognized community' and but Muslim courts enjoyed jurisdiction over all matters of personal status regarding Muslims, even foreign nationals.

The State of Israel maintained the status quo, with some minor changes.[26] Religious law ruled in matters of personal status and the recognized communities have retained their jurisdiction. Additional religious communities, such as the Druze, the Evangelical Episcopal Church, and the Bahá'í were recognized. Other communities, such as the Lutherans, Baptists, Quakers, and others also operate in the country, despite not having been formally recognized.[27] One major change introduced under the State of Israel related to the Jewish population—Jewish

24 Y. Schachar, 'History and Sources of Israeli Law', in Shapira & DeWitt-Arar, *Introduction to the Law of Israel,* supra note 9; see also generally, A. Rubinstein, 'Law and religion in Israel', 2 *Israel Law Review* (1967), 380.

25 For the Palestine Order in Council, R. H. Drayton (ed.), 3 *The Laws of Palestine* (1936), 2569.

26 Lerner, 'Religious Liberty in the State of Israel', supra note 1 at 253.

27 Lerner at 253–55.

religious institutions became state bodies, exercising authority over all Jews of the country, without consideration to their self-definition and views on religion.[28]

The non-recognized communities also enjoy full religious freedom and rights, including the right to establish institutions, but they do not have their own courts with jurisdiction over their members. Although they enjoy certain tax benefits, they do not receive government funding, as do Jewish religious bodies and recognized non-Jewish communities. Some enjoy tax exemptions.[29] Relevant to this issue is also the Fundamental Agreement with the Holy See,[30] signed in 1993, dealing with the material rights of the Catholic Church.

A related issue is the situation of the non-Orthodox branches of the Jewish religion, not recognized as separate communities. Although they are totally free to practice Judaism the way they understand it, the rabbis of these communities—Conservative, Reform, and econstructionist—do not enjoy the status of the Orthodox rabbis and cannot authorize marriages. Also, non-religious Jews consider themselves discriminated against.[31]

The already mentioned Article 83 of the Palestine Order in Council, 1922,[32] is the starting point of Israeli legislation concerning state and religion. It proclaims that all persons 'shall enjoy full liberty of conscience, and the free exercise of their forms of worship subject only to the maintenance of public order and morals. Each religious community recognized by the Government shall enjoy autonomy for the internal affairs of the community.' The Order in Council nullified limitations on freedom of religion and worship and prohibited discrimination on religious grounds. After the creation of the State, the Order in Council remained in effect but does not prevail on the laws of the Knesset, which take precedence over all Mandate legislation, as declared by the Supreme Court when it denied to Jewish couples the right to perform private weddings. The Court referred the case to the Rabbinical Courts, which rule over questions of marriage and divorce.[33]

The Declaration of Independence proclaims that the State of Israel 'will guarantee freedom of religion and conscience, of language, education and culture' and will 'safeguard the Holy Places of all religions.' The Declaration is, of course, not a Constitution, but it was always considered a guideline for Israeli legislators and courts, and the principles it contains were extended in the Basic Law: Freedom of Occupation and in the Basic Law: Human Dignity and Liberty, as amended in 1994.[34]

---

28 Lerner at 253.

29 See Maoz, 'Religious Human Rights in the State of Israel', supra note 17 at 366–72.

30 Israel Ministry of Foreign Affairs, Fundamental Agreement between the Holy See and the State of Israel (30 December 1993), at http://www.mfa.gov.il/MFA/MFAArchive/1990_1999/1993/12/Fundamental+Agreement+-+Israel-Holy+See.htm.

31 Lerner at 255–56.

32 Order in Council, supra note 25.

33 See C.A. 450/70, *Rogozinsky v. State of Israel,* P.D. 26(I), 269.

34 See Basic Law: Human Dignity and Liberty, 1992, S.H. 90.

The official report submitted to the Human Rights Committee[35] summarizes 'the accommodation between Jewish religious law and the institutions of the secular state.' The State recognizes the jurisdiction of the Rabbinical courts over all Jewish inhabitants in matters of personal status, deciding these issues according to the *Halakha,* the Jewish religious law. A similar jurisdiction is granted to the other recognized communities over those belonging to them. The State confers powers upon the Chief Rabbinate, which is organized under law[36] and state-funded. It also confers powers on Religious Councils, similarly organized and funded.[37] The Knesset has enacted laws with a religious background regarding the Sabbath and Jewish holidays, dietary laws, and other matters related to religion.

The actions of all state institutions that act in the religious sphere are subject to review by the High Court of Justice, including matters related to the application of religious law. Religious courts exceed their jurisdiction if they issue judgments contrary to provisions of secular laws regarding equal rights for women, adoption, and spousal material relations.[38]

Public authorities do not intervene in the internal life or organization of religious communities and the law does not restrict the autonomy of the religious communities to govern themselves. Still, there have been some complaints about attempts of the authorities to influence internal affairs, such as, for instance, the appointment of religious personnel or the granting of admission visas to such personnel. No bilateral agreements between the State and religious communities have been concluded, except for the 1993 agreement with the Holy See, which led to the establishment of diplomatic relations beween the two states. No interference in doctrinal issues has been denounced. Religious communities are not represented as such in the legislature and no particular religion has been given power to control other religious communities. The geographic concentration of certain communities reflects itself obviously in policy matters and may lead to differences in treatment.

The regime of state-recognized communities has an impact on several issues and implies civil effects. Recognized communities have their own courts for subjects related to personal status and their officials may authorize acts affecting their status.[39]

Although freedom of religion and worship exists for every group claiming to be a legitimate religion, the problem of sects or cults has caused some concern and a parliamentary committee conducted a survey on this issue.

The religious communities are in charge of managing cemeteries.[40] There have been problems with persons not belonging to any community, or who did not want to be submitted to a religious burial ceremony, and such cases went to

35 Israel HRC Report, supra note 13.

36 See Chief Rabbinate Law of Israel, 1980, 34 L.S.I. 97 (1980).

37 See Lerner at 260.

38 Israel HRC Report at 231-232.

39 See Lerner at 246.

40 Lerner at 266.

court. Since 1996, the Right to Alternative Civil Burial Law permits the existence of alternative cemeteries respecting the desires of the deceased or his or her family. The Supreme Court denied the Orthodox Burial Society the right to limit the inscriptions on headstones in Jewish cemeteries. The High Court of Justice ordered the competent authorities to ensure equality in the allocation of funds for Jewish and Arab cemeteries.[41]

Israeli legislation in matters of religious human rights was negatively influenced by some external factors, such as the security situation, party politics, and above all the secular-orthodox conflict. Such shortcomings led the judiciary, particularly under the activist leadership of retired Chief Justice Aaron Barak, to play a constructive role in this area through a broad interpretation of the basic human rights laws. Some of the achievements of the courts were, however, frustrated by legislation playing to party interests. The final result, however, is that Israel is a country where the rule of law prevails and fundamental rights are respected and enforced.

Religious institutions—recognized communities and other legally constituted religious entities—enjoy various taxation benefits and exemptions.[42] The establishment of places of worship, the celebration of meetings, the distribution of literature, and other activities necessary to the work of religious associations are regulated by general principles proper to a democratic society. Some extremist religious groups have opposed what they deem to be missionary activities, in some cases violently, but, on the whole, the spread of religious ideas and convictions is being conducted freely and protected against religious intolerance.[43]

There have been some difficulties concerning the slaughtering of animals, *kashrut* (dietary laws), and the import and sale of pork and other non-*kosher* meat, all of which have reached the courts. Regulation, either legislative or jurisprudential, while cooperative with religion, is aimed at protecting basic individual rights. The Ministry of the Interior has records of the religious affiliation of individuals, and religious affiliation has legal consequences as a result of the recognized communities system. Problems of conscientious objection were raised in connection with the mandatory military service, but were not invoked with regard to laws or contractual clauses of general applicability.

Concerning financial support for religion, or rather for religious services, the HRC Report states bluntly that, in comparison with funding of Jewish religious institutions, 'the non-Jewish communities are rather severely undersupported by

---

41 There is abundant jurisprudence on this matter. See, e.g., S. Ct. 53/31, *Frederika Shavit v. Chevra Kadisha Rishon Letzion,* P.D. 53 (3) 600; S.Ct. 54/31, *Adalah v. Minister of Religious Affairs*, P.D. 52(2) 164.

42 See Israel HRC Report at 226.

43 There were incidents and activities particularly against a group called 'Messianic Jews' – Jews that believe in Jesus. The press denounced some cooperation between the Ministry of Interior and an ultra-Orthodox small organization engaged in persecuting the Messianic Jews. See *Haaretz Weekly Magazine* (2 October 2009), 21.

the Government.'[44] The state supports religious institutions, by direct funding and by tax exemptions. There are no clear-cut norms that might ensure equality between the various religions. The system has frequently been criticized by the Supreme Court. In 1995, following strong criticism by the State Comptroller, a public committee elaborated rules for the allocation of state subsidies. The taxation legislation exempts religious institutions from income tax. Christian churches and Baha'i have also received some preferential treatment.[45]

The Fundamental Agreement between the Holy See and the State of Israel contains provisions regarding property and fiscal matters. The Supreme Court declared in 1995 that the state engages in 'unlawful discrimination' when it allocates land on the basis of religion or nationality.[46] Clearly, the whole issue of state funding of religious institutions lacks appropriate regulation and is open to general criticism concerning its treatment of state-church relationships.

In Israel, the acts enacted by religious authorities have civil effects. The secular law recognizes the jurisdiction of religious courts and gives effect to their decisions adopted in accordance with law. Within the framework of the already mentioned status quo, various aspects of family law are regulated by religious law. Members of the different religious communities are subject to the respective religious laws of their communities, which differ between communities. The legal settlement of family law matters is split between religious and civil law. Matters such as child custody, including adoption, inheritance, and property relations between spouses are settled by civil, generally territorial, law.[47]

This same split exists in the judicial system. Religious courts decide matters in their competence on the basis of the positive religious law, except in those cases in which civil law is mandatory. The Rabbinical Courts Jurisdiction (Marriage and Divorce) Law of 1953 deals with Jewish matters; the Palestine Order in Council established the jurisdiction of the Muslim courts; the Druze Religious Courts Law, 1962, that of the Druze. The jurisdiction of the religious courts is exclusive in certain areas and concurrent in others. The Supreme Court determines the competence and jurisdiction of the courts when conflicts arise.

Religion and education are closely connected in Israel. There is a State Education Law[48] several times amended. The system, which existed in the pre-state period, consists of various educational trends. There is a general education system and an Arab education system. Within the Jewish majority there are various trends: non-religious public schools, with curricula including many religious elements,

44 Israel HRC Report at 228.

45 See Maoz, supra note 17 at 372.

46 H.C 6698/95, *Ka'adan v. The Israel Lands Authority,* P.D. 54(1) 258. The case dealt with a complaint of an Arab couple that was refused to build its home in a communal settlement that claimed that only Jews may belong to it.

47 See A. Rosen-Zvi, 'Family and Inheritance Law', in Shapira and K. C. DeWitt-Arar, *Introduction to the Law of Israel,* supra note note 9 at 75–76.

48 State Education Law, 1953, 7 L.S.I. 113.

such as Biblical studies; religious public schools under Orthodox control; and ultra-orthodox (*haredi*), non-Zionist oriented, including several sub-groups depending on religious affiliation. There is a core program, which is not always respected. Party politics strongly affects this area. Israel has adopted integrationist policies inspired by social and cultural considerations, but did not change the pluralist pattern of fragmented education, particularly within the Jewish majority. The integrationist efforts have lost intensity in recent years. All the schools enjoy financial support of the state, which also funds some non-Jewish religious schools, among them church schools not recognized formally by the state.

There are no restrictions on the use of religious symbols in public places, and there is no law governing the use of such symbols. *Kipot*, crosses, and head coverage are a normal part of the landscape. A Muslim girl was not accepted in a Christian private school and the Court abstained from interfering because of the private character of the school.

Israeli legislation contains many provisions intended to guarantee religious liberties. The Penal Law of 1977[49] punishes desecration of places of worship, disruption of funerals, or publication and uttering of offenses against religious feelings or beliefs of any person. The numerous holy places for the different religions are safeguarded by the Protection of Holy Places Law of 1967. The Basic Law: Jerusalem, Capital City of Israel, 1980, and the Antiquities Law, 1978, contain similar provisions. A well-known ongoing controversy relates to the Temple Mount, which has engendered many conflictive situations.

There is no legislation on blasphemy or defamation of religions. Limitations on hate speech are applied equally to all religions and beliefs.

Controversial Issues

The special character of the State of Israel, the tensions caused by political and security issues, the conflict with the Palestinians, demography, the recognized communities regime, the status quo arrangements concerning religious issues within the Jewish majority, and other issues have engendered many controversies and required judicial intervention. Several among them deserve special mention. The Sabbath and Jewish festivals are days of rest according to the Law and Administration Ordinance of 1948 and the Hours of Work and Rest Law of 1951. Non-Jews can choose their own day of weekly rest. The Sabbath issue has come several times before the courts. This is, of course, a matter affecting mainly the Jewish majority.

Cemeteries, burial, dietary laws, equality in the allocation of state land, state financing and support for religious and/or educational institutions, and holy places and access to them have all been the subjects of judicial settlement and have caused tensions and complaints. Another significant controversial matter concerns

49 4 L.S.I. 54, para. 323–27.

proselytism and conversion. The right to convert was clearly recognized in a well-known case, *Pessaro (Goldstein) v. Minister of Interior*.[50] In practice, there are difficulties relating to conversion into Judaism, a matter in which the Orthodox monopoly is being challenged by the other Jewish religious trends, and in which politics plays an indisputable role. A 1977 law, never applied, punishes material enticement to conversion.

Concluding Remarks

Israel is a democracy and generally respects religious liberties. Its legal system concerning religion is not, however, fully compatible with norms observed in Western democracies. The foundations for this situation can be found in history and in the complex character of the state established in 1948, which has developed into a modern but complex democracy during its six decades of existence. As indicated by a former UN Special Rapporteur on Freedom of Religion or Belief, Asma Jahangir, in her report on a mission to Israel in 2008,[51] religious minorities living in Israel acknowledge 'that there is no religious persecution by the state. Within the Israeli democracy, [Jahangir emphasized] the important role that the Supreme Court played in the past and can continue to play for safeguarding freedom of religion or belief.'

I have attempted to provide a general picture of the situation concerning the role of religion in a secular state such as Israel, without a formal Constitution. I believe it may help in understanding the peculiarities of this young state, influenced by history, politics, and a most complicated, but to a large degree successful, process of state-building in difficult conditions, launched and supported by an ancient community in which religion has played a major role.

50 H.C. 1031/93, *Pessaro (Goldstein) v. Minister of Interior*, P.D. 49(4) 661

51 Human Rights Council Report of the Special Rapporteur on Freedom of Religion or Belief, UN doc. A/HRC/10/8/Add.2 (2009).

Chapter 13
Religion and Equal Treatment in the Nepalese Constitution

Kanak Bikram Thapa

Country Context

Nepal is a pluralistic—multi-ethnic, multi-lingual, multi-religious, and multi-cultural—country. It is a country of highly diverse traditions and unique cultures and cosmologies. For example, the different cultures and languages number well over one hundred and all are pervasive. Consequently, the state is required to recognize and enforce norms and values embedded in many different religions, cultures, and traditions.

Nepal's faith systems include Sanatandharma (traditional), Prakritidharma (nature), Kiratdharma (Indigenous Peoples' religion), Hinduism, Buddhism, and other forms or manifestations of cultural ideologies. Hinduism, though, has become the dominant religion in Nepal. Hindus constitute 80.06 per cent of the population, as per the census of 2001.[1] It is said that Hinduism is the oldest of any systematic religious philosophy, and that it epitomizes the science of social order. That is because it incorporates all forms of belief and worship without necessitating the elimination of any.

The Nepalese social structure is still based on and guided by the age-old values, norms, customs, and practices of the Hindu religion and higher Hindu rituals. Some holy days, most of them Hindu, are recognized as national holidays, such as Mahashivaratri, Buddha Jayanti, Falgun Purnima, Krishna Asthami, Dasain, and Tihar. In addition, in the Vedic literature is found an explanation of the classifications of Brahmin, Kshatriya, Vaishya, and Shudra in society. However, the indigenous and aboriginal peoples of Nepal do not fall within the Hindu Varnasram Structure.[2] Some reports state that most of the indigenous and tribal peoples of Nepal espouse Buddhism, Bonism, or the Kirat religion, though some of them do espouse the Hindu religion.

Though the overwhelming majority of people in Nepal identify themselves as Hindus, the Country Code of 1963 abolished all kinds of discrimination and untouchability. The House of Representatives, on 4 June 2006, also declared Nepal

---

1 *Statistical Pocket Book Nepal* 2002, Central Bureau of Statistics, Thapathali, Kathmandu, Nepal, 6.

2 Constitution of the Nepal Federation of Nationalities (1991), art. 1(2)(c).

to be an untouchability- and discrimination-free Country. The Interim Constitution of Nepal, 2007, has named the right against discrimination and untouchability as a fundamental right. This constitution also states that all the Nepalese people collectively constitute the nation, having multi-ethnic, multi-lingual, multi-religious, and multi-cultural characteristics.[3] Likewise, it declares that Nepal is an independent, indivisible, sovereign, secular, inclusive, and fully democratic State.[4] Despite calling Nepal a secular state in the Interim Constitution, however, all other religious provisions have been kept intact.

Right to Religion and Equal Treatment in Nepal

Freedom of thought, conscience, and religion is one of the inalienable rights listed in the Universal Declaration of Human Rights of 1948 and in the International Covenant on Civil and Political Rights of 1966. From an ancient period until 1951, Nepalese laws were based on religion, local customs, usages, and royal edicts. The Hindu learned people (Shastrakaras) laid great importance on religion. Law was considered a branch of religion. The Country Code of 1963 (Muluki Ain) is based on the principle of equality before the law and doing away with castes. The 2007 Interim Constitution provides for freedom to practice one's religion and to preserve religious traditions handed down from ancient times, having due regard for the existing social and cultural practices. The Interim Constitution specifically denies the right to convert another person from one religion to another.[5]

Provision for Religion in Law

In ancient times in Nepal, there was no differentiation between law and religion, between law and customs. The legal and justice systems of the Kirati period, for instance, can be understood from the Kirati Veda (religious and legal texts of the kiratis, or indigenous peoples), namely the 'Kirat Mundhum'. The early sixth century B.C. has been taken as the initial period of Kirat reign in Nepal. In early Kirat society, the Mundhum was the only law of the state. Many of the rules were based on social customs, traditions, culture, values, and religion during the reign of Lichhavis (B.C. 300–600) as well.

Traditional concepts of fairness and impartiality under the law of religion were some of the basic rules of the justice system. The kings of subsequent dynasties began to promulgate laws after the advice of Dharmadhikara (the owner of justice) and the learned people (pundits). Laws during the Malla period (twelfth century) were Sruties (rules handed down by listening) and Smrities (rules handed down by

---

3 The Interim Constitution of Nepal (2007), arts. 3, 4 (1).

4 Interim Constitution, art. 4 (1).

5 Interim Constitution, art. 23.

memory). The Human Justice Text (Manab Nyaya Shastra), as well as the practice of ordeal (trial), were legalized in the administration of criminal justice.

Nepal, as a viable political entity as it exists today, came into being during the third quarter of the eighteenth century. King Prithvi Narayan Shah of Gorkha laid the foundation of a unified, modern Nepal in 1768. Before the unification of Nepal, the common feature among the principalities was the recognition of law based on religion. Where Dharmashastras (religious books), customs, or usages were silent to meet the needs of the situation, special royal proclamations were issued.[6] The laws before the codification of law were based on Hindu religious texts, and the practice of settling disputes was carried on by the village chieftains and local landlords.

Jung Bahadur Rana, the then-prime minister, visited England and France in the year 1849. After his return from those European countries, he started to review the laws and appointed a Law Council, which promulgated the Country Code (Muluki Ain) in 1854, under the red seal of King Surendra. It was the first code of modern Nepal based on Hindu Jurisprudence. It underwent thirteen minor and major amendments, but it continued as the main source of law in the country until 1963.

The New Country Code (Muluki Ain), which is based on the principle of equality before the law and doing away with caste and other religious considerations, was introduced in 1963. It has been serving as the common criminal code and the common civil code, and it is equally applicable to Hindus, Buddhists, Muslims, and others in matters such as marriage, adoption, inheritance, and succession. The New Code of 1963 codified all the laws of Nepal—civil, criminal, religious, and customary. The Code also abolished all kinds of discrimination and untouchability. The preamble of this Code mentions that scattered religious rules have been codified. In addition, Sections 8, 9, and 10 of the Court Management chapter recognize customary rules.

The 1963 Code prohibits converting a person from one religion to another religion. Section 1 of the Chapter on Etiquette (*Adal ko Mahal*) stipulates that no one shall carry on any activity causing any adverse effect to any other's religion, and no one shall initiate the religious conversion of others. If anybody attempts to convert another to his or her religion, that person shall be punished with three years imprisonment, and anybody who successfully converts somebody from one religion to another shall be punished with six years stringent imprisonment. If such a person is a foreign national, that person shall be expelled after completion of six years imprisonment. The chapter on Quadrupeds of the Country Code provides that no one shall be allowed to kill, ask others to kill, or attempt to kill a cow or an ox with the intention of killing it to take it to a foreign country for sale.[7] If anyone intentionally and knowingly kills any cow or ox, that person shall be punished

6 S.P. Gujurel, 'Nepalese Legal System: A Historical Perspective'; J.C. Regmi, 'A Historical Survey of Nepalese Legal System', *The Nepalese Legal System*, Souvenir, University of Delhi (29 December 1985), 147–163.

7 Country Code, Chapter on Quadruped, Number 1.

with twelve years, and the person who gave the order to kill such quadruped shall be punished with six years imprisonment. Therefore, these types of religious, social, customary, and traditional practices are incorporated in the law, which cannot be abrogated. All the Hindus, Buddhists, and Shamanists Adivasis Janajatis have been worshiping cows since time immemorial. If any Nepali citizen thinks of challenging this provision, he or she is required to submit a petition to the Supreme Court to declare any law or any part thereof void.

Provisions about Religion in the Constitutions of Nepal

A Constitution is legally binding on the state and all subjects within it. Since 1948 (2004 B.S.[8]), six Constitutions have been promulgated in Nepal: (1) The Government Act of 1948 provided to the citizens of Nepal certain fundamental rights, but it did not mention anything about a right to religion. (2) The Interim Government of Nepal Act 1951 was subservient to the democratic aspirations of the people. It contained directive principles about state policy, which suited the democratic urges of the people; it granted fundamental rights, and it assured the rule of law. However, the 1951 Act did not mention anything about religion. (3) The Constitution of the Kingdom of Nepal was prepared and enforced in the year 1959 (2015B.S). It guaranteed fundamental rights and their enjoyment, but it did not stipulate anything directly about the right of religion or anything regarding any religion. (4) The Constitution of Nepal 1962, Article 3(1), declared that Nepal is an independent, indivisible, sovereign, monarchical, Hindu kingdom. Religious freedom was granted, and religious conversion was prohibited. Article 14 of the 1962 Constitution provided fundamental rights to religion, according to which every person should have the freedom to profess and practice his own religion as handed down to him from ancient times, having due regard to traditional practices. It provided that no person should be entitled to convert another person from one religion to another religion. (5) The Constitution of the Kingdom of Nepal 1990, Article 4(1), formally recognized the Hindu kingdom, and declared: 'Nepal is a multiethnic, multilingual, democratic, independent, indivisible, sovereign Hindu and Constitutional Monarchical Kingdom.' This provision clearly stated that the Hindu religion occupied the paramount position in Nepal. Article 19(1) of the Constitution of the Kingdom of Nepal 1990 provided that every person should have the freedom to profess and practice his own religion as handed down to him from ancient times, having due regard to traditional practices. The proviso of this Article stated that no person should be entitled to convert another person from one religion to another. (6) The Constitution of the Kingdom of Nepal 1990 was repealed by The Interim Constitution of Nepal 2007, introduced on 15 January

8 Bikram Sambat (B.S.) or Vikram Samvat, is the official calendar of Nepal; it is also popular in India and elsewhere throughout southeast Asia. It is a lunar calendar based on ancient Hindu tradition and is 56.7 years ahead in count of the solar Gregorian calendar.

2007 by the outgoing House of Representatives. This constitution declares that all the Nepalese people collectively constitute the nation, having multiethnic, multilingual, multi-religious and multi-cultural characteristics.[9] The mono-cultural policy of the state had resulted in the enormous loss of the cultures of tribal and indigenous peoples and minorities. Taking this into account, the 2007 Interim Constitution declared Nepal to be an 'independent, indivisible, sovereign, secular, inclusive, and federal, democratic republican state'.[10] The Interim Constitution provides that every person shall have the right to profess, practice, and be protected in his or her own religion as handed down to him or her from ancient times, having due regard to the existing social and cultural practices.[11] It is provided, however, that no person shall be entitled to convert another person from one religion to another, and that no act or action shall be done in such a manner as to jeopardize the religion of another.[12]

The Interim Constitution of Nepal, 2007, makes provision for strengthening the national unity by maintaining the cultural diversity of the country. The cultural diversity is maintained by developing healthy and cordial social relations amongst various religions, cultures, tribes, communities, denominations, origins, and linguistic groups, based on equality and co-existence, and through the equal development of their languages, literatures, scripts, arts, and cultures by the state.[13] The state shall have the obligation to make an inclusive, democratic, and progressive restructuring of the state, by ending the existing centralized and unitary structure of the state, so as to address problems, including those of women, dalits, indigenous peoples, the oppressed, the excluded, minority communities, and backward regions, while at the same time doing away with discrimination based on class, caste, language, gender, culture, religion, and region.[14]

At present, Nepal is in the process of making a new constitution, and it is hoped that the new constitution will incorporate appropriate provisions relating to religion in Nepal.

Equal treatment for Religions by the Government of Nepal

The Government of Nepal treats all religions equally and fairly and takes positive steps with respect to religious freedom. The Government generally does not interfere with the practices of religious groups, and religious tolerance is broadly observed. However, there are some restrictions on conversion from one religion to another religion. There are no specific laws favoring the Hindu majority, nor does

---

9 Interim Constitution, art. 3.

10 Interim Constitution, art. 4 (1), amended by the Fourth Amendment.

11 Interim Constitution, art.23(1).

12 Interim Constitution, Proviso to art. 23(1)

13 Interim Constitution, art. 35(3)).

14 Interim Constitution, art. 33(d).

the Government control the expression of Hinduism. The President of Nepal and the Prime Ministers have been visiting myriad religious shrines, mosques, churches, stupas, pilgrimage sites, etc. and participating in religious activities organized not only by Hindus, but by religious minorities as well, such as Buddhists, Muslims, animists, by invitation. The Government of Nepal has occasionally provided aid, upon request and as per necessity, to Hindus, Buddhists, and Muslims for developing religious shrines, stupas, or mosques, even facilitating and providing some amount of monetary help to some Muslims who are desirous of attending Haj in Mecca and Medina. The aforementioned laws and government policies reveal that all religions are being treated equally in Nepal. Generally, adherents of the many religious groups in Nepal co-exist peacefully and harmoniously, and they revere places of worship.

Again, it may be mentioned that the Legislative-Parliament, through the Interim Constitution of Nepal, officially declared the country a secular state in January 2007. However, no laws specifically affecting freedom of religion were changed. A number of Christian and Muslim religious organizations, though, claimed that, unless registration requirements for religious groups were allowed, such organizations were restricted from owning land, which is an important step for establishing churches, mosques, synagogues, or burial sites. Proselytizing has also remained illegal. The Government of Nepal enforces the immigration laws, and if foreign workers are found to proselytize, they are expelled from the country. Still, some reports indicate that there are more than 170 Christian churches operating in Kathmandu and nearly 2500 madrassahs existing in Nepal.

Concluding Remarks

Although Nepal is declared to be a secular state, in the Nepalese context, secularism means to treat all the religions equally, not to separate religion from the state. The Nepalese Constitution guarantees every citizen the right to profess and practice his or her religion without any interference from either the state or any other community. However, a unique characteristic of this right to religion is that it totally prohibits conversion from one religion to another. Conversion is a criminal offense and punishable under the law of Nepal. Thus, it is apparent that the Nepalese law prevents the right to practice one's religion of choice because of the prohibition against conversion.

Besides the aforementioned constitutional and statutory provisions, Nepal is a party to various binding international instruments. The Nepal Treaty Act of 1991 explicitly provides the pre-eminence of international treaties over national laws. In pursuance of this, the government may be required to analyze some of the provisions of international instruments, such as the Universal Declaration of Human Rights of 1948 and the International Covenant on Civil and Political Rights of 1966. Article 27 of the International Covenant on Civil and Political Rights of 1966 states that in those States in which ethnic, religious, or linguistic minorities exist, persons belonging to such minorities shall not be denied the right, in community with the other members of their group, to enjoy their own culture, to profess and practice their own religion, or to use their own language. Thus, it is clear from this provision that every citizen has the right to choose the religion of his or her choice. In order to apply this provision in Nepal, someone shall have to file a case in the court to nullify the extant provision in the Nepalese Constitution regarding the conversion to another's religion.

Nepal is not a theocratic country because none of the essential characteristics of theocracy are found in Nepal. The Nepalese secularism is not anti-God or anti-religion; it recognizes that religion has relevance and validity in the lives of people. The Nepalese secularism does not create a partition or wall between state and religion. It accepts all religions and ensures that the state will support and treat all religious communities equally.

Chapter 14

Constitutional, Legislative and Regulatory Change Regarding Religion in China

Liu Peng, Brett G. Scharffs, Carl Hollan

Introduction

This purpose of this chapter is to provide a general overview of religion and the rule of law in China, focusing on history, contemporary reality, and the way forward. Sections of the chapter will provide first a brief introduction to religion and its regulation in Chinese history, then an overview of the regulation of religion since 1978, followed by a discussion of contemporary issues relating to religion and the rule of law in China, a brief description of models of constitutional, legislative, and regulatory change that are under consideration in China, and finally a brief conclusion.

To some extent Western perceptions of the religious situation in China are stuck in a time warp, based upon policies and realities that existed during the Cultural Revolution when Mao Zedong closed all places of worship and tried to extinguish religion altogether. While there is in the United States and elsewhere in the West quite a deep understanding and appreciation for the dramatic economic changes that have taken place in China over the past 25 years, there is less understanding of the ways in which laws and policies governing religion have also undergone significant transformation.

For example, while there are still only five officially recognized religions in China (Buddhism, Daoism, Islam, Catholic, and Protestant), and while there is ongoing concern about foreign domination of Christian religions in China, there has been a dramatic increase in the types and levels of interactions between Christians in China and their foreign counterparts. Ongoing tensions exist between the registered and unregistered churches of a single denomination. Unregistered religious groups, sometimes labeled 'evil cults',[1] can become targets for particular government concern.

Over the past 30 years there has been a dramatic growth in religious belief in China. The Chinese government estimates that there are more than 100 million religious believers in China today, a majority of whom are Buddhist. The growth has not been limited to officially recognized religious groups, but includes unofficial Buddhist organizations and Protestant 'house churches', which meet in small groups

1 Chinese: "邪教."

in believers' homes. For example, after 100 years of missionary efforts in China from the 1840s until the establishment of the People's Republic of China in 1949, there were approximately 700,000 Protestants in China. Even with the Communist government's official policy of atheism, and the harsh suppression of religion during the Cultural Revolution, since 1978 there has been a quiet resurgence of Protestantism in China. Official estimates place the number of registered Protestants in China at 15 million, while some church groups estimate that there are more than 50 million unregistered Protestants. While there are five million registered Catholics, the Vatican estimates that there are another seven million unregistered Catholics. These numbers will come as a surprise to many in the West, who remain under the impression that religion is absolutely suppressed in China.

If context is necessary for understanding any text, nowhere is this more clearly the case than in seeking to understand the relationship between law and religion in the People's Republic of China.

History

During their 2000-year history, the imperial governments of China sought supremacy over and have claimed a divine mandate for governance and oversight of religion. For most of its history (221 BC–1912 AD) Imperial China did not have a concept of the rule of law that paralleled the western idea of the rule of law. Rather, Confucianism, with its emphasis on hierarchical filial relationships, was the dominant paradigm for understanding the relationship between law and the state. 'Within family and society, all key relationships were those of superior to inferior with a general duty of obedience owed by the inferior to the superior and a reciprocal duty of caring, support, and guidance owed by the superior to the inferior.'[2]

The last imperial dynasties, the Ming Dynasty (1368–1644) and the Qing Dynasty (1644–1912), each viewed itself as a bridge between heaven and earth, so it was natural for these governments to view themselves as overseers and custodians of all religious groups. In the dynastic ministerial system it was taken for granted that religion was to be monitored and controlled in the service of state ends.

1840–1912

By the nineteenth century, the Qing dynasty was 'paralyzed by greed, ignorance and incompetence'.[3] Although the Qing dynasty pursued policies of isolationism, European powers sought greater access to Chinese markets. In the 1830s, England sought to resolve their trade imbalance with China by importing opium from India to China. When the Chinese resisted by destroying opium stocks in the southern

2 D.C.K. Chow, *The Legal System of the People's Republic of China* (St. Paul, MN: West Group, 2002), 43.

3 Chow at 4.

port city of Guangzhou, the result was the Opium War of 1839–1842. As described by Professor Daniel Chow, 'The antiquated and ill-equipped armies of the Qing were no match for the superior technology of the British gunboats. After a series of humiliating defeats, China capitulated in the unequal Treaty of Nanjing in 1842.'[4]

In the historiography of contemporary China, the period between the end of the First Opium War in 1842 and the establishment of the People's Republic in 1949 is viewed as a period of national humiliation and foreign domination, symbolized by the Treaty of Nanjing and the Treaties at Tianjin in 1858, and is often referred to as China's 'One-Hundred Years of Humiliation'. Among other provisions, these treaties exempted foreigners in more than eighty port cities from Chinese law, subjecting them instead to foreign consular jurisdiction under their own national law.

During this period, Protestant and Catholic churches engaged in extensive missionary work in China, which was closely identified with their sponsoring foreign governments. According to Ye Xiaowen, Consultant to the Chinese Association of Religious Studies, in an article widely disseminated in English, 'China entered the twentieth century with a deep sense of national humiliation. … At this time of national disaster and intensified clashes between indigenous and Western cultures and as the traditional Chinese religions struggled for survival, Protestantism and Catholicism made large-scale inroads into China. A religion that was supposed to spread the words of the Gospel had become the tool of the aggressors.'[5]

A series of quasi-religious domestic rebellions in the mid-nineteenth century, including the Taiping, Nian, Muslim, and smaller rebellions, further weakened the Qing dynasty. But it was conflicts with foreign powers that were the most damaging to the Qing dynasty, including the Sino-Japanese War of 1894–95. This was followed almost immediately by the Boxer Rebellion of 1898–1901, which in many ways was a religiously based uprising fueled by a fanatical hatred of foreigners. Several hundred foreigners were killed before the Boxer Rebellion was crushed by an alliance of eight national armies. In the early twentieth century, revolutionary forces led by Dr. Sun Yat-sen and his Nationalist Party began to plot the overthrow of the Qing dynasty. In 1911 an uprising in Wuhan triggered a series of provincial defections that resulted in the Qing emperor abdicating in 1912.

1912–1949

From 1912–1949, the Nationalist Party attempted but failed to set up a parliamentary system for the fledgling republic. The Nationalists, led by Dr. Sun's successor, Chiang Kai-shek engaged in a decade-long battle against various warlords, culminating the Northern Expedition in 1927, 'a military campaign led by Chiang that defeated or absorbed warlord forces into the Nationalist government'.[6] The Nationalists then

4 Chow at 5.

5 Ye Xiaowen, 'China's Religions: Retrospect and Prospect', *China News and Report* (7 October 2002), 3.

6 Chow at 10.

turned their attention to battling the Communists, who had collaborated with the Nationalists in the battles with the warlords. This campaign was interrupted in 1931 when Japan seized the northern region of Manchuria, and in 1937 Japan began an all-out invasion to conquer China. The Nationalists and Communists created a temporary truce while China battled the Japanese in a war that lasted from 1937–1945, and in which as many as 25 million Chinese lives were lost.

After World War II, all-out conflict erupted between the Nationalists and Communists, now under the leadership of Mao Zedong, and China was once again plunged into war. Although the Nationalists had the backing of the United States, the Communists eventually emerged victorious, and the Nationalists fled to the province of Taiwan where Chiang set up a government in exile. In 1949, Mao formally declared the founding of the People's Republic of China.

1950–1978

After the establishment of the People's Republic of China in 1949, the Communist Party established atheism as the official policy of the state. According to Wang Zuo'an, 'Only after the establishment of the People's Republic of China, when the Chinese nation became truly independent, were the Chinese Protestant and Catholic churches able to detach themselves from foreign control and the Chinese believers to manage their own affairs.'[7]

Reviving an old exit strategy drafted by several Western missionaries in 1892, and facing the certain dissolution of his church due to the Communists' stoppage of US funding coming into China, Wu Yaozong (commonly referred to by his 'Western' name of Y.T. Wu) began developing a solution to ensure the survival of Christianity in Communist China in 1948. In May 1950, Wu and several other Christian leaders met three separate times with the Premier of the newly formed People's Republic of China, Zhou Enlai, and discussed plans to organize what has come to be known as the 'Three-Self Patriotic Movement' (the 'TSPM'). This movement's name references its undergirding principles of Chinese religious independence, namely that Chinese religions should be self-governing, self-supporting, and self-promulgating. This total severance of Chinese churches from foreign ties would mean that Chinese believers could look only to Chinese nationals for religious authority. Chinese churches would deny any support or financial aid from foreign sources, and would promulgate itself themselves without the input or aid of foreign missionaries.

Wu's resulting popularity and his influence with CPC officials led to the emergence of the TSPM as the premier Protestant Christian ecclesiastical authority

---

7 Wang Zuo'an, 'China's Policy on Freedom of Religious Belief', paper presented at the 10th Annual Internatioanl Law and Religion Symposium, 5–8 October 2003, Provo, Utah, USA (on file with authors). Wang adds: '[The churches] affirm the "Principle of the Three 'Selfs'"(self-administration, self-support, and self-propagation of the gospel) and lead the believers to establish a truly self-administered religious enterprises.'

in China.[8] The TSPM's role in governing religion in China was solidified in 1958 when the CPC officially dissolved all other Protestant sects and unified all Protestant churches as a single faith in an attempt to collectivize religious organizations in the same way all other aspects of Chinese life would be collectivized.[9] During the 1950s, other religious organizations underwent similar changes. Ultimately, five religions were officially recognized, each of which was under the control of the Communist party, and were directed to 'eliminate from their ranks remnants and influence of imperialism.'[10]

In the 20-year period between 1956 and 1976, during which there were several Anti-Rightist campaigns and the Cultural Revolution, there were harsh crackdowns upon religious leaders and believers, and 'Mao closed all places of worship and tried to extinguish religion altogether.'[11] The Cultural Revolution ended with Mao's death in 1976, and after a period of political infighting in 1978, Deng Xiaoping emerged as China's new leader. Deng soon began to initiate a series of economic and other reforms that launched China on a path towards modernization.

Regulation of Religion Since 1978

It is important first to understand the structure of the religious regulatory system currently in place in China. These bodies of regulation exist within three major organizations: the Party, the state, and officially recognized religious organizations. In the Communist Party, the United Front Work Department is the main regulatory body for religious affairs. In the State PRC government, the State Administration for Religious Affairs exists at the national level as an executive agency charged with religious regulation. Within the state at levels below the national level, Religious Affairs Bureaus act as enforcing agencies. State regulatory agencies are subordinate to the Communist Party's United Front Work Department, as the United Front develops all religious policy and the state agencies exist only to enact that policy.

---

8 Wu has been strongly criticized by his contemporaries and modern day historians alike for his role in the creation of a Communist-controlled Christian church. In the words of his contemporary: "Wu has been branded by some a heretic or an anti-Christ, while others would question his intentions and integrity as a Christian and wonder if he has not betrayed his faith through the close alliance with the Communist government." Gao Wangzhi, *Christianity in China: From the Eighteenth Century to the Present* (Palo Alto: Stanford University Press, 1999), 338. His high position in the Communist-TSPM hierarchy serves as confirmation for some that his motives in leading the Chinese Christian revolution were less than pure.

9 See Gao Wangzhi at 347.

10 Ye Xiaowen, supra note 5 at 5.

11 P. Marshall (ed.), *Religious Freedom in the World: A Global Report on Freedom and Persecution,* Hudson Institute Center for Religious Freedom (Nashville, Tenn.: B&H Publishing Group, 2000), 101.

Officially recognized religious organizations are not part of the Party or state per se, but are subject to close oversight by both the Party and the state.

As for religious policy on religious affairs, Kim-Kwong Chan and Eric R. Carlson explain that '[t]he 1982 state constitution is theoretically the supreme document undergirding China's legal and governmental system. Promulgated by the National People's Congress, it sets forth the legal relationships between the government and the people, and in that process recognizes the existence of religion.'[12] Chapter II of the Constitution lists 'The Fundamental Rights and Duties of Citizens'. Article 36 of this chapter reads: 'Citizens of the People's Republic of China enjoy freedom of religious belief. No state organ, public organization or individual may compel citizens to believe in, or not to believe in, any religion.' The state protects normal religious activities. No one may make use of religion to engage in activities that disrupt public order, impair the health of citizens or interfere with the educational system of the state. Religious bodies and religious affairs are not subject to any foreign domination.[13]

In the same year as the passage of the Constitution, the Central Committee of the Chinese Communist Party issued Document 19: The Basic Viewpoint and Policy on the Religious Question During our Country's Socialist Period. This document illuminated Chinese policy on religious freedom, reading in part:

> Religion is a historical phenomenon pertaining to a definite period in the development of human society. It has its own cycle of emergence, development, and demise. Religious faith and religious sentiment, along with religious ceremonies and organizations consonant with this faith and sentiment, are all products of the history of society. Religion will eventually disappear from human history. But it will disappear naturally only through the long-term development of Socialism and Communism, when all objective requirements are met.

The basic policy the Party has adopted toward the religious question is that of respect for and protection of the freedom of religious belief. Communists are atheists and must unremittingly propagate atheism. Yet at the same time Communists must understand that it will be fruitless and extremely harmful to use simple coercion in dealing with the people's ideological and spiritual questions — and this includes religious questions.

The central authorities of Party and state emphasize once again that all Party members must clearly understand that the Party's religious policy is not just a temporary expedient, but a decisive strategy based on the scientific theoretical foundation of Marxism-Leninism and Mao Zedong Thought, which takes as its goal the national unification of the people for the common task of building a powerful,

---

12 Kim-Kwong Chan and E. R. Carlson, *Religious Freedom in China: Policy, Administration, and Regulations: A Research Handbook* (Institute for the Study of American Religion, 2005), 4.

13 Constitution of the People's Republic of China (1982), art. 36.

modernized Socialist state. Under Socialism, the only correct fundamental way to solve the religious question lies precisely in safeguarding freedom of religious belief. Only after the gradual development of the Socialist, economic, cultural, scientific, and technological enterprise and of a Socialist civilization with its own material and spiritual values, it is asserted, will the type of society and level of awareness that gave rise to the existence of religion gradually disappear.[14]

While theoretically the Communist Party's policy on religion has no legal effect, because state agencies only enact the policy which is disseminated by the United Front, and because the United Front is a part of the Communist Party structure, the policy implications of Document 19 are more informative as to the true circumstance of religious affairs. Chan and Carlson go on to explain:

> Theoretically, citizens enjoy unlimited freedom of belief or internal freedom of conscience. Further, the constitution protects against compulsion toward belief or nonbelief and protects against discrimination among believers and nonbelievers. In matters of religious practice and expression, however, the state grants itself broad regulatory powers, beginning with extending its protection only to what are considered 'normal' religious activities. Religious actives must not disrupt, impair, or interfere with state responsibilities. Finally, foreign domination or interference in religious affairs is prohibited.[15]

Moreover, the Chinese Constitution, at least currently, does not hold the same level of legal authority as some other constitutions. There are no constitutional courts in the PRC and the judiciary has no authority to interpret the Constitution or the constitutionality of actions taken by other branches, leaving those who believe their freedom of religious belief has been violated without a remedy. While Chinese courts have expressed that they may be more open to the possibility of 'judicialization of the Constitution',[16] in practice there have been no appreciable changes to these limitations.

China's policy and practice with respect to religious affairs since the end of the Cultural Revolution has been more tolerant of religious belief and believers. In 1978, the Communist Party announced that its focus would change from class

---

14 The People's Republic of China: Document 19: The Basic Viewpoint and Policy on the Religious Question During Our Country's Socialist Period (1982), selections available at http://www.religlaw.org/document.php?DocumentID=789 (accessed 4 February 2013). Translation reprinted with permission from D. E. MacInnis, *Religion in China Today: Policy and Practice* (Maryknoll, NY: Orbis Books, 1989), 8–26.

15 Chan and Carlson, supra note 12 at 4.

16 See '*Qi Yuling v. Chen Xiaoqi*, Case of Infringement of Citizen's Fundamental Rights of Receiving Education Under the Protection of the Constitution by Means of Infringing Right of Name', 5 *Zuigao Renmin Fayuan Gongbao* [Gazette of the Supreme People's Court of the People's Republic of China] (2001), 158; C. X. Lin, 'A Quiet Revolution: An Overview of China's Judicial Reform', 4 *Asian Pacific Law and Policy Journal* 180 (2003), 192–205.

struggle to economic development. Over time, some free markets have been allowed to develop, although in keeping with Marxist-Leninist ideology the state continues to own all real property and the means of production.

In the years since 1978, the five state-registered religions have been given increased latitude to operate within the Chinese religious regulatory structure under the oversight of SARA and the Religious Affairs Bureau, which, as stated above, are controlled by the CPC's United Front Work Department, which is itself controlled by the Central Committee of the Communist Party. The last twenty-five years have also seen a surge in activity by unregistered religious groups, and a series of government crackdowns against such groups. Wang Zuo'an, Director General of the State Administration for Religious Affairs (SARA), has stated that 'for an atheistic ruling party to handle religious affairs is a historic task, and a challenge of the party's capability in both leadership and governance.'[17] While embracing and advocating atheism, the Communist party has a stated policy of freedom of religious belief. According to Director Wang, 'The freedom of religious belief is a basic right that China's Constitution bestows on her citizens. It is also the basic policy of China's Communist Party on religion.'[18]

Director General Wang notes that today there are more than 100 million believers in various religions in China. 'If the Chinese Communist Party were to impose its atheism on everyone and persecute religious believers, that would only serve to drive 100 million people to an antagonistic position. Such hypothetical practice, which would virtually undermine its very own foundation of governance, is unimaginable.'[19] According to Ye Xiaowen, Consultant to the Chinese Association of Religious Studies, there has been an evolution of China's religious policies over the past 50 years. But, Ye maintains, 'two key policies remain constant – that of respect for freedom of religious belief and that of independent running of religious affairs.'[20]

In a widely distributed statement of China's policy towards religion in 2002, Ye Xiaowen stated: 'In China, the state treats all religions equally and the law protects the equal rights of all religions. While stressing the protection of the freedom to believe in religions, the law also provides for protection of the freedom not to believe in religions. All are equal before the law. Citizens enjoy the right to religious freedom.'[21] This statement would seem to be significantly different from many outsiders' views about the status of religious freedom in China.

There are several keys to understanding Mr. Ye's assertions. First, as noted above, there are only five 'religions' recognized in China – Buddhism, Taoism, Islam, Catholicism, and Protestantism – and there is an official, recognized structure for these religions. Most other churches or religions are not considered 'religions', but

17 Wang Zuo'an, supra note 7 at 1.
18 Wang Zuo'an, supra note 7 at 1.
19 Wang Zuo'an at 2.
20 Ye Xiaowen, supra note 5 at 9.
21 Ye Xiaowen at 9.

rather 'evil cults' that are not entitled to legal recognition or protection.[22] Second, the five recognized 'religions' are independent of their foreign counterpart organizations and subject to a degree of oversight and supervision by the Communist party. Thus so-called 'unregistered' or 'underground' churches are not considered to be religions at all, and equal treatment and equal rights apply only to the five officially recognized religious groups.

On 30 November 2004, Premiere Wen Jiabao approved new 'Religious Affairs Regulations', effective nationwide on 1 March 2005. These regulations serve as national guidelines for religious administration in place since 1982. The regulations continue the general scheme of state supervision and administration. The new national regulations generally codify and standardize provisions found in provincial regulations and clarify the scope of government oversight and provide some avenues of appeals for administrative decisions, though the vagueness of these rights and the uncertainty of effective legal recourse leave much to be desired. For groups outside the established registration scheme, however, the regulations provide no additional protections. In fact, unregistered religions may be worse off, as the regulations give less room for maneuvering in gray areas than the prior ambiguous rules.[23]

The government is also expanding and upgrading the Religious Affairs Bureau in anticipation of the growth of religion in China. High-ranking Politburo officials have given their blessing to the continuation of the current religious policy.[24]

In October 2007, Chinese Communist party premier Hu Jintao may have signaled a new chapter in the Communist Party's attitude towards religion, when an amendment to the Party Constitution for the first time mentioned religion. In his report to the Seventeenth National Congress of the Communist Party of China on 15 October, Hu stated:

> Promoting harmony in relations between political parties, between ethnic groups, between religions, between social strata, and between our compatriots at home and overseas plays an irreplaceable role in enhancing unity and pooling strengths. Acting on the principle of long-term coexistence, mutual oversight, sincerity, and sharing of both good and bad times, we will strengthen our cooperation with … personages without party affiliation in better performing their functions of participation in the deliberation and administration of state affairs and democratic oversight, and select and recommend a greater number of outstanding non-CPC persons for leading positions. Keeping in mind the objective of all ethnic groups working together for common prosperity and development …. We will fully implement the Party's basic principle for its work related to religious affairs and

22 Some unofficial religious groups not labeled as 'evil cults' would include, for example, followers of folk beliefs.

23 Chan and Carlson, supra note 12 at 24.

24 Chan and Carlson at 24.

> bring into play the positive role of religious personages and believers in promoting economic and social development.[25]

Although the announcement that the government seeks to incorporate religious groups into economic and social development in China was monumental, it applies only to those religious groups that are officially recognized by the government. Those groups that do not fall within the sanctioned five religions remain prohibited from providing any public service. Additionally, the government has yet to draft any detailed measures to provide an avenue through which the religious groups may play a more active role in promoting economic and social development.

The Three-Market Model Explanation of the Chinese Regulatory System

In a 2006 article, Yang Fenggang explained the current religious market in China with his 'three-market model.'[26] According to Yang, the Chinese religious market consists of three markets: the red market, the black market, and the gray market. The red market is the legal market for religious worship. This is the legal outlet for religious observance the CPC and PRC have created through the establishment of the Patriotic Religious Associations that is overseen by the Religious Affairs Bureaus, the State Administration for Religious Affairs, and the United Front Work Department.[27] The black market is the illegal market. Often referred to as 'evil cults' in CPC statements, these are the groups that are actively denounced by the CPC, and actively suppressed by the PRC's Ministry of Public Security.[28] Yang defines the gray market narrowly, as simply those members of legally recognized religious groups acting outside the law[29] – for example, members of the legally recognized Protestant church who proselytize off of church premises.[30] However, a much larger segment of religious observance ought to be categorized as existing within the gray market. This segment is comprised of those religious groups who operate without legal protection, but whose practice is tolerated by CPC and PRC officials. Examples of these groups could include some local Buddhist, Taoist, or Shamanistic temples, certain underground Protestant and Catholic churches, and religions that have no recognition in the PRC such as the Orthodox Church and the Bahá'í. These groups are correctly categorized as operating within the gray market because they operate

25 Hu Jintao's report at 17th Party Congress, Part VI. Unswervingly Developing Socialist Democracy, para. 4, available at http://www.china.org.cn/english/congress/229611.htm (accessed 4 Feburary 2013).

26 See Fenggang Yang, 'The Red, Black, and Gray Markets of Religion in China', 47 *The Sociological Quarterly* 93 (2006).

27 Fenggang Yang at 97.

28 Fenggang Yang at 97.

29 Fenggang Yang at 97.

30 Fenggang Yang at at 109.

within a zone of legal uncertainty. So long as they operate within a zone of tolerance, they are allowed to hold religious services and in some cases own land. However, they have no legal rights; they exist by the grace and tolerance of enforcing officials, making their existence tenuous at best.

In his explanation of the Chinese religious market, Yang makes three propositions. First, '[t]o the extent that religious organizations are restricted in number and in operation, a black market will emerge in spite of high costs to individuals.'[31] Second, '[t]o the extent that a red market is restricted and a black market is suppressed, a gray market will emerge.'[32] And third, '[t]he more restrictive and suppressive the regulation, the larger the gray market.'[33] Yang does well to prove each proposition. However, recent history has proved an additional proposition: To the extent that a red market is restricted, a large gray market will eventually lead to the growth of the black market.

The difficulties the CPC and PRC have had in dealing with 'evil cults' serves as proof that the current religious regulatory system has failed to meet CPC and PRC interests by contributing to a larger black market of religion. The main interest of the CPC is maintaining power.[34] The increased funding towards maintaining social stability is strong evidence that the CPC views their ability to maintain social stability as the one of the most important keys to retaining political power. In 2009 funding towards maintaining social stability nearly matched the funding of the Party military.[35] Since 2009 funding towards maintaining domestic stability has increased by 11.5 percent.[36] Traditionally, the CPC has seen religious organizations, or any social organization other than the CPC, as a threat to CPC power because these groups have the ability to indoctrinate organization members and mobilize these members for their own purposes.[37]

In an attempt to prevent religious organizations from serving as an incubator for anti-Communist ideologists to use for breeding social unrest, the CPC created the current system of control with the hope that this system would create a highly-regulated legal outlet for religious observance.[38] By creating CPC-loyal religious associations, the CPC had hoped to be able to oversee religious practice from the

31 Fenggang Yang at 98.

32 Fenggang Yang at 98.

33 Fenggang Yang at 99.

34 See R. L. Moses, 'So Much for Stability: Reality Catching Up With the Communist Party ', *China Real Time Report, Wall Street Journal* (5 November 2012), available at http://blogs.wsj.com/chinarealtime/2012/11/05/so-much-for-stability-reality-catching-up-to-the-communist-party/.

35 Cheng Li, 'The End of the CCP's Resilient Authoritarianism? A Tripartite Assessment of Shifting Power in China', 211 *China Quarterly* 595 (2012), 615–616.

36 Cheng Li at 615–616.

37 T. D. DuBois, 'Religion and the Chinese State: three crises and a solution', 64 *Australian Journal of International Affairs* 344 (2010), 347.

38 B. Leung, 'China and the Falun Gong: Party and society relations in the modern era', 33 *Journal of Contemporary China* 761 (2003), 779.

top down; by creating the PRC's State Administration for Religious Affairs and Religious Affairs Bureaus the CPC hoped to oversee religious practice from the bottom up. However, the CPC's primary method of maintaining oversight over religious groups by strictly limiting the number of religious groups and requiring CPC approval of the leadership of the groups is one of the main contributors to the failure of this system of regulation. Ultimately, the failure of this regulatory system lies the inability of the CPC and PRC to effectively regulate groups that do not fit within the narrowly-defined categories the system is meant to control.[39] Using Yang Fenggang's model, the current religious regulatory system is able to regulate groups within the red market, and structures are in place to suppress the black market organizations. However, this regulatory system has no method to regulate groups within the gray market – both those which exist as 'radical branches' of red market organizations and those which are tolerated by officials despite having no legal entity.

Ironically, while the CPC sought to regulate religious organizations to prevent radical groups from fomenting social unrest, the gray market that has been created by the current regulatory system has the effect of fomenting this exact type of social unrest. Under the current regulatory system, groups that exist within the gray market have three options: first, they can join the legal red market; second, they can continue to operate within the gray market indefinitely; or third, they can radicalize and join the black market. Currently, groups who attempt to make the transition from the gray to red market have only one choice – to submit to the leadership of a Patriotic Religious Association, and ultimately the Communist Party. Needless to say, this option is less than appealing to the vast majority of religious groups as it would require the group to accept CPC-initiated changes in their leadership and doctrine.

The majority of religious groups operating within the gray market naturally opt to attempt to continue operations within the gray market. However, the CPC and PRC's attempt to substitute tolerance of the religious group for legal recognition of the religious organization is not only theoretically problematic;[40] it is practically problematic as well. First, organizations that exist within the gray market have no legal-entity status. While this does limit the ability of the group to organize and operate, this also is very problematic for reporting and oversight. Whereas these organizations are already operating outside of the law, they rarely, if ever, conform to reporting procedures designed to assist the Religious Affairs Bureau in oversight of the religious group. Moreover, even if a group were to obtain the permission of the local Religious Affairs Bureau to assemble, there is no reporting process within the RAB or codified methods of Religious Affairs Bureau oversight.

Second, religious organizations that operate within the gray market cannot operate within the gray market indefinitely. Historically, when the CPC leadership becomes suddenly aware of a well-organized group that was previously unknown

39 Leung at 779.

40 W. C. Durham, Jr. & B. G. Scharffs, *Law and Religion: National, International, and Comparative Perspectives*, (New York: Aspen/Wolters Kluwer, 2010), 433.

their reaction has been to prosecute group members and leaders under Chinese anti-cult laws. However, these groups have only been able to expand and organize without alerting CPC authorities because of the existence of the gray market. Groups that seek to continue to operate within the gray market indefinitely will always be at risk that CPC authorities will be alerted to the group's activities and will label the group an 'evil cult', making this choice impractical.

Groups operating within the gray market also foment social unrest when group members become frustrated with their treatment under the law. As the economy has slowed, many members of the middle class, who have stopped profiting from the country's economic success, have turned to gray-market religious organizations to fulfill their basic needs.[41] However, the CPC's current system of regulation suppresses these gray-market organizations and recent studies in China show when 'middle-class Chinese begin to feel that their voices are being suppressed, that their access to information is unjustly being blocked or that their space for social action is being unduly confined, increased political dissent may begin to take shape.'[42] Studies have also shown that this political dissent within the middle class has increased in recent years as the economy has slowed.[43]

The gray market directly contributes to the social unrest the current regulatory system is intended to prevent as groups operating within the gray market transition into the black market, whether voluntarily or by edict of CPC officials. By marginalizing these groups and actively suppressing them, the CPC create the very type of opposition groups the religious regulatory system was intended to obviate. The sad irony of the situation is that these people and groups became radicalized in response to the system of regulation the CPC set up to prevent radical groups and people from disrupting public order.

Models of Constitutional, Legislative and Regulatory Change

As many would agree, the current religious regulatory system is in need of revision. One possible option for revising the regulatory system would be the passage of constitutional, legislative, or regulatory changes to bring current religious regulatory policy closer in line with Article 36 of China's Constitution, which states: 'Citizens of the People's Republic of China enjoy freedom of religious belief. No state organ, public organization or individual may compel citizens to believe in, or not to believe in, any religion; nor may they discriminate against citizens who believe in, or do not believe in, any religion. The State protects normal religious activities.' The Constitution does not define what constitutes a 'normal' religious activity.

41 Leung, supra note 38 at 771–772.

42 Cheng Li, supra note 35 at 606.

43 Cheng Li at 606.

Legislation Regarding Religion

There is a severe lack of published scholarship and research in China on the topics of legislation on religion. Except for a brief mention in the Constitution, there is no congressionally passed or nationally enforceable law that publicly announces the systematic protection of the freedom of religion and the lawful rights of religious believers.

There are few public debates over the legislative status of religions. One exception is a recent petition submitted to the National Congress by house church pastors nationwide requesting the Congress to examine the current religion regulations. This petition emerged in relation to tension between the Beijing government and the Shouwang church, a Beijing house church. However, in general, the public has not heard open discussions whether China can go on without such a basic law or comprehensive law on religions, or what this law should be like or how the rule of law should apply to religious affairs and religious problems.

In order to fully understand the contributions of grassroots groups to societal development and stability, we must look at the underlying environment and conditions enabling or inhibiting those contributions, especially the environment for the rule of law.

Diverging Views about the Purpose of Legislation Regulating Religion

One opinion emphasizes the protection of freedom of religious belief. It advocates implementing China's constitutional provision of religious freedom in form of statutory laws. This opinion regards religious belief as a fundamental right of a citizen, pointing out that religious belief involves not only ideas and abstract mental exercises, it inevitably involves outward activities for expression, and therefore it needs systematic, procedural protections that are realistic and effective. Respecting and protecting the fundamental rights of citizens are the signs of a modern and progressive nation.

From the government's perspective, the purpose of religious legislation is to 'maintain public interest in society', that is to 'maintain harmony among religious groups and social elements' and to 'regulate religious affairs'. The government's perspective seems fair, because they consider the need to protect freedom of religious belief as well as to maintain public order. However, the government perspective focuses on 'regulating religious affairs' under the banner of 'maintaining public interest in society'.

These are the issues that are dividing people: (a) whether China needs a comprehensive religious law, (b) what level and type of law China needs, and (c) the conflicting needs of protecting the fundamental rights of citizens and the government's desire to strengthen its power over civil society by way of legislation. It is only natural that all of the concerned players of a legislation process uphold their interests from their own perspectives. On the issue of religious freedom, the government and the governed are standing on the opposite sides of ideological divides. Therefore, according to the government, even after over a decade of state-sponsored feasibility studies on the introduction of a comprehensive law of religion, the overall environment for reading and passing a bill protecting religious believers is 'not ready'. The government attributes this unreadiness to lack of consensus on the issues of religious freedom, and it will 'take a very lengthy process' to reach the consensus. Therefore, before a religious legislation process takes place in China, the question of legislative purposes must be asked and answered.

The Need for a Comprehensive Law Concerning Religion

Some argue that while religious freedom should be protected and the separation of church and state should be upheld, there is no further need for a comprehensive law of religion in China. They argue that the United States, the most looked-upon nation in the world, never had such a statutory law, why should China? They point out that China's Constitution already specifically provides for freedom of religious belief, and the constitutional principle belief should be sufficient to govern matters related to religions through the implementations of regulations issued by the State Council and other administrative agencies at central and local levels and clauses related to religion scattered in laws governing various areas of society.

These arguments have some merit. However, they fail to take into account the gravity of the right to freedom of religion. The right to freedom of religious belief (right to freedom of religion to be more precise) is one of the fundamental human rights. It is an important part of human dignity. As an important right of a human being, only laws legislated by the National Congress have the authority to regulate or restrain it (see 2000's Law on Legislation). As it became obvious (in a few cases where citizens were demanding equal protection of law), although the Chinese Constitution does have provisions for freedom such as religious freedom, constitutional clauses cannot be used as court trial or appeal authority. The right of religious freedom has yet to be secured by laws enacted to enforce the constitutional provisions. The only useful authority lies in administrative regulations and rules issued by the governments at various levels.

This structure of legal authority puts administrative agencies in the advantageous position of interpreting through their rule-making process the meanings of the fundamental rights of citizens and the limitation of the scope of the protection intended for citizens. Since this process is not subject to congressional voting and vetoing procedures required of laws governing the rights of all citizens, the regulations and rules made under such a process should not be elevated to the level of governing citizens' fundamental rights. The lack of a congress-made law on religion despite years of ignored but documented needs of the religious community of China perhaps raises the question of 'non-feasance of the legislature'.

The argument that 'the United States has no comprehensive law of religion, and therefore neither should China have a law of religion' misplaces the focus. The

United States and China have followed dramatically different legal traditions. The United States follows the case law tradition. The Supreme Court has heard and decided numerous cases on religion. The decisions are legal authorities by which local governments and law enforcement agencies handle religious affairs. China follows no such case law tradition: where statutory laws are absent in certain areas of social interaction, there is simply a vacuum of legal authority to govern the area. The legal vacuum gives the perfect excuse for agencies to draft rules and regulations primarily for their regulatory convenience. Despite the existence of governmental regulations over fundamental rights of citizens in China, true legislative authority remains lacking because of the non-feasance of the legislature to draft and consider a comprehensive law of religion.

Another difference is that clauses of the United States Constitution carry full legal authority in court trial as if they were statutory provisions. The United States Constitution's First Amendment contains specific provisions on religion; it has become the basis for the separation of church and state relationship in United States. The Constitution of China is not a direct source of legal authority for court trials. The constitutional provisions on the freedom of religious belief are general principles and are of a non-binding nature. These provisions rely on a congress-made law to become effective and available to real cases.

The United States does have various generally applicable laws responding to cases and controversies related to religions. People and groups rely on these laws and the Constitution for their rights to religious freedom. Similarly, China does not have a comprehensive law of religion, and generally applicable laws touch on various aspects of religions. However, these religious provisions scattered in laws are hardly comprehensive or complete in dealing with religious practices and religious belief. The real question may be whether all the current laws and regulations added together in China are capable of dealing with the complicated religious issues and controversies presented in contemporary Chinese society.

Is a Constitutional Amendment Needed?

The purpose of such religious legislation would be to span the empty space between the Constitution and administrative regulations. This is the comprehensive law of religion currently lacking to complete the structure of religious legislation. With such a law that enables the operation of law enforcement, the constitutional provision of freedom of religious belief no longer remains a mere non-binding principle.

In addition to providing a general principle of protecting freedom of religious belief, Article 36 of the Constitution in its fourth part contains provisions for government defenses against religious influences. The political background of the provision can be traced back to 1950s when the People's Republic was newly established. The historical roots of it can even be traced back to old China back to the Opium War of the 1840s. The provisions were perhaps justifiable reactions to past grievances felt then in the 1950–60s, but after 30 years of Reform and 60 years of nationhood, they seem odd. Even judged from the internal logic and the prevailing jurisprudence, provisions as such obviously are discriminative against religion.

For example, Article 36 of the Constitution provides that 'no person is permitted to use religion to engage in activities that disturb social order, impair the health of citizens, or obstruct the state's education system.' The clause is concerned more about social and human welfare than religion itself. No one would argue otherwise, saying that religious activities that caused the provided damages ought not to be prohibited by law. If the word 'religions' is substituted in this clause with all other common and neutral terms such as politics, economy, culture, social groups, science and technology, sports, the clause still makes good sense. The singling out of religion while leaving out all other possible candidates with damaging capacity gives readers the dangerous impression that religion is more prone to be used to accomplish the prohibited activities than all others. There are numerous methods that can be used to accomplish these social evils; in most cases, religion is not the chosen method.

The Cultural Revolution resulted in the destruction of social order and people's property. It devastated human dignity and even lives, and virtually wiped out China's education system. The fervor of the Cultural Revolution was not a religion, neither was it motivated by religion. There is no evidence that the Chinese Constitution made any efforts to present a complete list of potential elements that can be used to accomplish the prohibited activities or results. Why then has it singled out religion? If the Chinese Constitution already contains clauses safeguarding social order, people's health and education system, that inevitably prohibits the obstruction of such benefits by any person with any means which logically should include all unauthorized agents and resources under the sun, and the provision in Article 36 is superfluous and should be stricken. As to disturbing the social order, etc. and the corresponding responsibilities, one only needs to insist that equal treatment before law shall be guaranteed regardless of religious belief, ethnic identity or sex (see Const. art. 5, art. 28 and art. 53).

The final clause of Article 36 prohibits foreign manipulation of Chinese religious groups and religious affairs. This clause has defects similar to those of the fourth clause. China is a sovereign nation; its internal affairs should undoubtedly be free from unwanted foreign interferences, let alone foreign manipulation. All social groups of China have the right to be free from foreign interference; religious groups are no different from any other groups in their status as independent Chinese groups, governmental or non-governmental in nature. One can easily think of virtually all government non-government groups and their affairs as never being 'subject to foreign interferences'. These include all political, business and educational associations and their affairs. It is not the job of the Constitution to list all groups that should be free from foreign interference, nor to single out religious groups or individuals for special regulations. A powerful nation that enjoys the universal recognition of the world's overwhelming majority of nations needs not emphasize the independence of its citizens' associations of any kind as long as they comply with the generally applicable laws and regulations. Article 54 of the Constitution prescribes citizens' obligations to the state to maintain the state security and dignity and to protect state interests and not to engage in activities that may threaten such state interests. This article alone implies the obligations of all social groups not to be subject to foreign interferences or manipulations. The Constitution is subject to criticism as it discriminates against religious groups and believers. The provision is one of the serious defects of the Constitution.

There is no explicit provision in the Constitution of China on the separation of church and state. Unlike the majority of nations in the world that have explicit provisions on the separation, the Chinese Constitution adopted this very different and troublesome approach to the issue. This is another defect of the Constitution when it comes to religion.

As the Constitution of China, like any constitution of the world, is the fundamental law of the land, its provisions directly affect the health of the legal system. The effort of drafting and passing a law of religion alone is not enough to fill the gap of legal authority on religious affairs. The source of power embedded in the Constitution has to be corrected before true perfection of the legal system can be seen and true protection of fundamental rights can be realized. The correction process should focus on the constitutional provisions and regulations unfit for the changed social structures. These provisions and regulations were drafted under outdated notions and can no longer meet needs under the new meanings of social stability. New provisions need to be added to the Constitution to better protect the fundamental rights of citizens. The amended Article 36 of the Constitution should be concise and precise. It is suggested here that it be amended as follows: 'China recognizes the endowed freedom of religious belief and religious practices of all citizens. Religion and State shall be separated.' Other issues related to religion may be stipulated by the legislated law of religion and other laws governing specific areas.

Without first amending Article 36 of the Constitution, there will not be sufficient protection of citizens' fundamental rights. This is because the effect of legislated law of religion will be confined by the limitations of some of the dated and shortsighted clauses of constitutional provisions. Amending Article 36 is a necessary step in the process of strengthening China's judicial system and speeding up the legislation on religion. Constitutional problems have to be dealt with if China wants to solve other problems. Constitutional amendment is the starting point for legal reform in China.

Difficulties in Legislating Religious Matters

A number of practical difficulties arise when contemplating legislation to govern religious affairs in China. These include the following:

> First is the difficulty of determing how to prevent the state from assuming the position of an arbitrator of religion, or police of religious affairs. In the case where a group of citizens claim the activities they engage in are of a religious nature, the issue arises as to who has the final say on the religious nature. There is no dispute that individuals may legally claim affiliation to certain religious faith. The question

> is whether a group of such individuals may claim rights to form an organization in the name of the religion. Should the state subject the legal existence of the group to governmental permission? If so, should the process for permission look into the substance of the religious belief? Or rather check for its format compliance only? Should the requirement for approval by a leading government agency be omitted if a group of voluntary religious believers form a group? If such an agency should be in place, what is the nature of such an agency? Where does an agency's power to judge religions find its legitimacy'?

Second, China recognizes only five religions. Does state have the obligation to provide equal protection to those believers outside the recognized five religions? Who possesses the power to judge the merits of each religion outside the scope of the recognized five? These issues are unavoidable in the process of pushing for a legislated law of religion. The drafters of the law of religion must have a general scheme to deal with such issues.

Third, should public resources be used to promote or suppress certain religions? Can individual religious believers and religious groups engage in community services in the name of their religions (i.e., education, medical and other charitable activities)? Can religious believers and non-believers enjoy equal opportunities in society (i.e., employment, military service and education opportunities)? Can religious leaders be granted political privileges? Can they be elected into congressional assemblies as religious leaders representing their religions, or can they be elected only as geographically representing individuals and non-affiliates? What should act as the impartial arbitrator when conflicts arise between the state and religious groups or individuals?

In the process of religious legislation, the state sees itself as the guardian of public interests. There is a danger of over-emphasized public interests that become the political tools of state control over religion. With such concerns, finding solutions to the following issues become some of the major tasks in Chinese legislature: (a) how to balance the relationship of state and religion that fits Chinese circumstances, and (b) how to balance the need to maintain public interests and the need to protect religious freedom. Facing the issues is the only way toward solving the issues.

In summary, rule of law is the minimum requirement to solve religious issues and promote positive contributions by grassroots groups. Rule of law does not mean simply codifying and elevating ministerial regulations and rules to the status of law. Legislating on religion will require a long journey in China.

Conclusion

The CPC has built a framework of oversight agencies and exercised influence over the legal 'red market' of religious activity through use of these agencies. The design of the CPC in creating these devices for regulation has been to ensure Communist oversight over religious organizations to prevent these groups from incubating anti-Communist groups and subverting Communist influence over the Chinese people.

This system of regulation and oversight has had success in bringing a certain segment of religious organizations under CPC regulatory control. However, a large 'gray market' of religious organizations also exists within China, outside of the boundaries of the religious regulatory system of the PRC. Because officials are unwilling or unable to enforce the harsh regulations the PRC has established for dealing with all of these groups that operate outside the religious regulatory system, this religious gray market has become extremely large. While official policy has been to suppress these groups absolutely, many groups operate within a range of tolerance established ad hoc by local enforcing officials. These groups that operate outside of the religious regulatory system often operate under limited or no supervision by PRC officials.

This status quo of allowances and tolerances cannot continue. The current religious regulatory system has no methods for groups operating within this gray market to legalize their activities. Furthermore, as can be shown by the transition of religious groups which were previously tolerated by officials and operated within the gray market, organizations that operate within the gray market cannot hope to continue within the gray market indefinitely. As gray market organizations expand, CPC officials eventually forfeit tolerance and criminalize these groups' activities. Groups that are forced into the black market contribute to social unrest, becoming the types of groups that the current religious regulatory system was intended to prevent from being formed.

CPC and PRC officials must address these problems, as the gray market continues to expand and the potential for future unrest increases. One proposed method for officials to prevent gray market religious organizations from joining the black market is to create a method for gray market religious organizations to legalize their organizations and join the red market without having to submit to regulations on doctrine and leadership. If officials implement this change into the current system, those legitimate religious organizations will enter the legal market, allowing for the religious regulatory system to properly regulate these groups, and will prevent these groups from being forced into the black market.

One avenue that Chinese officials may pursue to accomplish these means would be to enact changes of the current regulatory system. Legislative enactments and constitutional amendments each present their own advantages and disadvantages. Drafting comprehensive legislation regulating religion would prove an onerous task and may produce inequities. Constitutional amendments may not have sufficient legal effect to bring change. And there may yet be several possibilities which have not been explored in this chapter. Ultimately, it will be left to Chinese officials, who must independently determine which method best suits Chinese needs.

Chapter 15

The Constitutionalization of Freedom of Religion in the European Union: What Changes Are the Charter of Fundamental Rights Expected to Bring About?

Emma Svensson

An Evolving Approach to Fundamental Rights in the European Union

With the introduction of the Lisbon Treaty, the European Union now has a Bill of Rights of its very own. The Lisbon Treaty, signed 13 December 2007, and entered into force on 1 December 2009, has made the Charter of Fundamental Rights (CFR) a distinguished part of primary law in the European Union legal order. First proclaimed in the year 2000, the Charter is the first formal EU document to combine all the values and fundamental rights, economic and social as well as civil and political, to which EU citizens should be entitled. The main aim of the Charter is to make these rights more visible. It is important to be aware that the Charter does not establish new rights, but assembles existing rights that were previously scattered over a range of international sources.

The expanding European Union, with 27 Member States, has long been seen as having little to do with questions of religion. Although the EU does not have competence to legislate on matters of direct religious importance, such as state-church relationships, it does not hinder other areas of law to have a spill-over effect on religious issues. Labour law, media law, criminal law, free establishment and migration law are all areas in which EU has competence to legislate and which concern religious issues to a greater or lesser extent. With the aim of creating 'an ever closer Union' and a European social market, the European Union will inevitably affect the way Member States organize and handle religious phenomena.

What, if any, changes and challenges will the Charter bring to Europe, in comparison with the European Convention of Human Rights? Freedom of religion is enshrined in Article 10 of the Charter of Fundamental Rights, and shows a clear resemblance to Article 9 in the European Convention on Human Rights (ECHR). Although freedom of religion serves as a longstanding principle within the European Union it has rarely been examined how this freedom could be facilitated throughout the legal order. This chapter aims at presenting the context of the Charter, showing that even if the wordings of Article 10 CFR and Article 9

ECHR are similar, the Charter of Fundamental Rights forms an integral part of the self-standing legal order of the European Union, with constitutional aspirations and multilevel governance. Hence, the Charter is positioned in a different setting compared to the ECHR, since the latter serves as an international agreement between contracting states, though supervised by the Council of Europe and interpreted by the European Court of Human Rights (ECtHR).

What changes could be expected when religious freedom now serves as a part of European Union primary law? It must be borne in mind that freedom of religion was established already in the 1970s, by the European Court of Justice (ECJ), as a core value of the EU through the *Prais* v. *Council*[1] case. In 1976 the ECJ had before it a staff case, concerning recruitment tests for linguistic experts, filed against the Council of the European Communities. A British woman, of Jewish religion, sought annulment of the decision of the Council to refuse her complaint regarding the specific date for a recruitment test. As the test was set for Friday 16 May 1975, the first day of the Jewish Feast of *Shavuot*, Ms. Prais asked for a new possible date for the test, since she was not allowed to travel or write on this particular day. The defendant, the Council, rejected her application, and based its rejection on the principle of equal treatment, stressing that it was essential that all candidates were tested on the same day.

The applicant based her argument on Article 27, paragraph 2, of the staff regulations, which provides that officials shall be selected without reference to race, creed or sex. In addition, she claimed that prohibition of religious discrimination formed a part of the protection of fundamental rights, which the ECJ is bound to ensure. She also based her argument on Article 9 of the ECHR. She claimed that both the staff regulation and the fundamental rights in Union law, as well as Article 9 ECHR, should be interpreted in a way which enables a person to take part in a test, regardless of religious circumstances.

The Council objected to this interpretation of the staff regulation, as well as the alleged interpretation of the fundamental rights and Article 9 ECHR. It claimed that interpreting said provisions in such a manner would oblige the Council to 'set up an elaborate administrative machinery […] and it would be necessary to ascertain the details of all religions practiced in any member State in order to avoid fixing for a test a date or a time which might offend against the tenets of any such religion'.[2] The Court of Justice agreed with the Council on this matter. It stressed that the principle of equal treatment makes it necessary for a fixed date to be set, a date that is the same for all participants of the test. Any requirement for changing the date, due to religious reasons, must be balanced against this necessity. The Court stated that a Union institution does not have a duty to keep itself informed of all details of religious holidays present in the Union. However, if the participant of a test, in due time, informs the institution that a date is unfitting; there is an obligation to try to avoid such dates. Even though is it generally desirable to try

1 Case 130–75 *Prais* v. *Council*, [1976] ECR, 1589.

2 *Prais*, para. 11.

to avoid certain dates, there is no obligation under Union law to avoid conflicts with religious requirements of which an institution has not been informed.[3] Thus, in this case, the ECJ confirmed the importance of freedom of religion in the Union setting, but also stressed that this right must be balanced with the legitimate interests of the Union.

Since the 1960s, beginning with the *Stauder*[4] case establishing the right to privacy as an integral part of the general principles of Union law, the ECJ has gradually incorporated the European Convention on Human Rights into the EU legal order. Step by step the Court has advanced the integration of fundamental rights in its judgments, based on the ECHR and the constitutional traditions of the Member States. Since the Amsterdam Treaty, entering into force in 1999, these principles are enshrined in the Treaties, thus serving as primary law of the Union. The Lisbon Treaty advances the status further. It not only opens up the accession of the EU to the ECHR, but through the Charter it places freedom of religion at the core of the primary legal body in the constitutionalization process of the EU.

European Convention on Human Rights Serving as a Minimum Requirement

The European Convention on Human Rights is a European regional human rights treaty, enshrining the basic civil and political rights, such as freedom of expression, assembly and the right to a fair trail. It has been described as the most efficient human rights instrument in the world, mostly due to its enforcement mechanism. The Convention is enforced and interpreted by the European Court of Human Rights, before which individuals can bring claims when a contracting state is accused of infringing the rights enshrined in the Convention. Regarding first generation human rights in Europe, the European Convention on Human Rights is the main carrier of a state's duty to comply with a minimum human rights standard. All 27 EU Member States are, and must be according to the accession criteria of the Union, contracting states to the Convention. Freedom of thought, conscience and religion is enshrined in Article 9.[5]

3 *Prais*, paras. 13–18.

4 Case 29–69 *Stauder v. City of Ulm*, [1969] ECR, 419.

5 In addition to Article 9, the ECHR contains Article 14, which enshrines the principle of equality and prohibits unequal treatment on the grounds of religion. Article 14, however, is not a self-standing article but must be seen in conjunction with other rights under the Convention. Article 2 of the First Protocol (1952) also forms a part of the ECHR legal body, and endorses the right of parents to choose the religious or ideological orientation of their children's education.

Article 9 ECHR:

1. Everyone has the right to freedom of thought, conscience and religion; this right includes freedom to change his religion or belief and freedom, either alone or in community with others and in public or private, to manifest his religion or belief, in worship, teaching, practice and observance.
2. Freedom to manifest one's religion or belief shall be subject only to such limitations as are prescribed by law and are necessary in a democratic society in the interests of public safety, for the protection of public order, health or morals, or for the protection of the rights and freedoms of others.

It serves as an illustration of the sensitivity of religious issues that it was late as in 1993 that the Court of Human Rights first found a state to be in breach of Article 9. This was the landmark judgment *Kokkinakis*,[6] in which the Greek prohibition of proselytism was considered a violation of the right to freedom of religion.[7] The European Court of Human Rights merely creates a minimum standard of protection, something which is specifically true regarding religious freedom. Proclaiming the Convention a 'living document', the Court of Human Rights seeks common consensus among the contracting states when enhancing the level of protection and evolving the interpretation of contested concepts. The common standard when it comes to Article 9 cases is kept at a minimum, and a wide 'margin of appreciation' is left for the contracting states, due to the lack of common consensus in these matters.[8] This is particularly evident in *Leyla Şahin* v. *Turkey*,[9] a case concerning the right of a Muslim woman to wear a headscarf:

> Where questions concerning the relationship between State and religion are at stake, on which opinion in a democratic society may reasonably differ widely, the role of the national decision-making body must be given special importance [...] Rules in this sphere will consequently vary from one country to another according to national traditions.[10]

The much-debated Grand Chamber judgment in the recent *Lautsi*[11] case also awarded Italy a margin of appreciation. The case concerned crucifixes in Italian

6 *Kokkinakis* v. *Greece*, App. No. 14307/88, 25 May 1993.

7 M. W. Janis, R.S. Kay, and A.W. Bradley, *European Human Rights Law – Text and Materials*, 3rd edn. (Oxford: Oxford University Press, 2008), 323.

8 See, *inter alia*, C. Evans, *Freedom of Religion under the European Convention of Human Rights* (Oxford: Oxford University Press, 2001), 142 ff, and D. Augenstein, *The Contested Polity: Europe's Constitutional Identity between Religious and Secular Values* (University of Edinburgh, School of Law, Working Papers Series, 2009/13), 6.

9 *Leyla Şahin* v. *Turkey*, App. No. 44774/98, 10 November 2005.

10 *Leyla Şahin*, para. 109.

11 *Lautsi and Other v. Italy*, App. No. 30814/06 (Grand Chamber), 18 March 2011.

public schools, which the Grand Chamber held to be compatible with the Convention, since the basic requirement of non-indoctrination was met. Arguably, the margin of appreciation granted states under Article 9 is still wide.

The ECtHR has held that the so-called state-church systems are compatible with the Convention, if certain minimum requirements are met. Moreover, a state does not have to collaborate with all religious groups on an equal basis. However, collaboration with a certain creed cannot, as a side effect, cause unjustified harm to the freedom other groups and individuals enjoy. Furthermore, the ECtHR has not used its jurisprudence to create any sort of 'model-relationship' between church and state in Europe, nor to impose a compulsory secularism. The reason for this approach is said to be 'that the State's attitude towards religion is primarily a political issue and is the result, to a large extent, of the historical tradition and the social circumstances of each country'.[12]

Instead, Article 9 ECHR, as interpreted through the jurisprudence of the ECtHR, focuses primarily on the rights of private individuals, setting aside the broader aspects of law and religion. In other words, it emphasizes the guarantee of non-interference of the state, and protects the individual, but does not have a bearing on the structure of exactly how this is organized. Nevertheless, it does provide a safeguard, a minimum standard of protection a state has to fulfil. In that sense, Article 9 can modify the arrangement between state and church.[13] Article 9 has also been interpreted as an outer boundary of democracy and of the law-religion relationship. In *Refah Partisi v. Turkey*[14] the ECtHR stated that democracy, and public elections, cannot be used to introduce a theocratic state, *in casu* Shari'a law in Turkey. Doing so, the Court held the Turkish Highest Court's decision to dissolve the Refah Party, a quite drastic measure, as compatible with the Convention.

As for minority groups, the ECtHR has increasingly paid attention to the rights they carry. They carry the right to act upon their beliefs, not merely to be tolerated in a specific setting. Under Article 14 ECHR all discrimination is prohibited when enjoying a Convention right. In *Hoffman v. Austria*[15] the ECtHR held that differential treatment on the basis of religious conviction, when deciding a custody case, was unacceptable.[16] In addition, the equality principle has also been interpreted

12 J. Martínez-Torrón, 'European Court of Human Rights and Religion', in in R. O'Dair and A. Lewis (eds.), *Current Legal Issues Volume 4 – Law and Religion* (Oxford: Oxford University Press, 2001), 189ff.

13 S. Van Bijsterveld, 'Religion, International Law and Policy in Wider European Arena: New Dimensions and Developments', in R.J. Ahdar (ed.), *Law and Religion* (Aldershot: Ashgate, 2000), 165, 167.

14 *Refah Partisi* v. *Turkey*, App. Nos. 41340/98; 41342/98; 41343/98; 41244/98, 13 February 2003.

15 *Hoffman* v. *Austria*, App. No. 12875/87, 26 June1993.

16 Martínez-Torrón, 'European Court of Human Rights and Religion', supra note 12 at 191.

as protecting individuals from states' treating persons differently in analogous situations, without providing an objective and reasonable justification for the different treatment. The latter was the case in *Thlimmenos v. Greece*,[17] where the ECtHR found a violation of Article 14, in conjunction with Article 9 ECHR.[18]

There are a few important aspects of the freedom of religion, such as the ECtHR has interpreted it, which need to be highlighted. First of all, the ECtHR differentiates strictly between the internal and the external aspects of the freedom. The internal aspect, *forum internum*, is held to be absolute and may not be restricted in any way, whereas the external aspect, *forum externum*, is by its very nature relative and may be restricted under the specification provided in paragraph 2 of Article 9 ECHR. It is evident that a state should not compel citizens to believe, or refrain from believing, in a certain way. The ECtHR confirmed this in 1976 in *Kjeldsen, Busk Madsen and Pedersen v. Denmark*,[19] in which it stated that a state is not allowed to organize its educational system (*in casu* sexual education) in such a way as to amount to indoctrination of pupils with a certain religious or moral view which is contrary to the view of the parents.[20]

A second aspect that needs to be highlighted is the differentiation the Convention makes between 'manifestation' and 'motivation'.[21] The Convention does not contain an unrestricted right to behave according to one's religion. The right is strictly limited to manifestations of belief, not to acts motivated or influenced by religion. This approach has an important influence on the way Article 9 functions. The ECtHR has held that actions simply *permitted* by one's conscience are not protected by Article 9, something that seems plausible since permitted behaviour is different from *obliged* behaviour. Nevertheless, the ECtHR has gone one step further and stated that Article 9 does not even protect behaviour that is *required* by one's religion, belief or conscience. This seems like a strict approach, which gives no protection for religious freedom from 'neutral law', law that has a secular aim in mind. Article 9 protects from state interference strictly aimed at a religious group, but does not protect when moral obligations of an individual, or group, clash with laws that pursue a secular goal. Inevitably, the individuals concerned see their right to freedom of religion as being '*indirectly* and nonetheless unavoidably restricted'.[22]

This strict approach on 'neutral law' has been criticized, since the burden has been placed upon the individuals. Either they are required to disobey a law, leading to a secular sanction, or to disobey their own consciences, something

17 *Thlimmenos* v. *Greece*, App. No. 34369/9, 6 April 2000), para. 44.

18 Martinéz-Torrón, supra note 12 at 194.

19 *Kjeldsen, Busk Madsen and Pedersen* v. *Denmark*, App. Nos. 5095/71; 5920/72; 5926/72, 7 December 1976.

20 Martínez-Torrón, supra note 12 at 198.

21 *Arrowsmith v. United Kingdom*, App. No.7050/75 (European Commission), 12 October 1978.

22 Martínez-Torrón, supra note 12 at 199 [emphasis in original].

leading to a spiritual sanction. In addition, concern has been raised that the ECtHR has substituted the individual's conscience for its own judgment, and determines what beliefs are reasonable. Furthermore, it is stated that it does not lie upon a court to decide which thoughts and worldviews are 'true', and, hence, which are false. It is alleged that the duty to protect a right to religion is not determined by the reasonableness of a religion or worldview. In other words '[w]hat freedom of religion and belief protects is the right to choose the truths in which one is willing to believe in'.[23] State control of different worldviews must then be limited to restrictions that are 'necessary in a democratic society', to use the wording of Article 9(2) ECHR. What are considered 'neutral' laws are often the views prevailing among the majority of the population. The strict and narrow interpretation of the 'private sphere' performed by the Court of Human Rights, may then have a more severe impact on those minority groups that hold ideas that are further from the ethical consideration of the majority, than on those who are more in line with mainstream thinking.[24]

Freedom of religion carries, perhaps to a larger extent than many of the other rights, a great corporate, institutional, and collective content. As for minorities, the right to equal treatment, including prohibition of so-called indirect discrimination, often assumes an assimilationist model or approach. It is often assumed that minority groups wish to achieve the same standard of rights protection as the majority group, or simply the absence of the disadvantage it means to belong to that minority group. The assimilationist model does little to promote the existence of the minority group itself, and the protection of the specific characteristic traits they carry. In that sense, the right to freedom of religion is often linked to non-discrimination on the basis of race or ethnicity, or gender. Discrimination is rarely a single-handed phenomenon, it is important to keep in mind the intersectionality of different grounds of discrimination.[25] The problems a Muslim woman from an Arabic country living in Europe may face are different from what a British man belonging to a New Religious Movement such as the Hare Krishna may face.

When discussing freedom of religion, it is common to focus on the status of minority religions. However, due to the strong principle of secularism in most European countries, and the separation of private and public, the right to be religious, and what that entails, is often neglected in the discussion. This can be seen when discussing the alleged right to be exempted from apparently neutral law, and the right to consentious objection to state duties and obligations. These alleged rights might very well come to the forefront with the European Charter of Fundamental Rights, since national 'neutral' law often stems from Union

23 Martínez-Torrón, supra note 12 at 202.

24 Martínez-Torrón, supra note 12 at 202.

25 K. Monaghan, M. du Plessis, T. Malhi, and J. Cooper (eds.); *Race, Religion and Ethnicity Discrimination – Using International Human Rights Law* (London: Justice, 2003), 13ff.

measures, which bring to the fore possible exemptions and derogations in the implementation.

Charter of Fundamental Rights – Nothing More than a Replica of the ECHR?

Since the entering into force of the Lisbon Treaty of the European Union, on 1st of December 2009, the EU has a binding fundamental rights document of its very own. Whether the European Union needs a Human Rights Charter of its own has been thoroughly discussed. Is it not enough to have the European Convention on Human Rights? After several failed attempts to find consensus, a final successful effort was made in October 1999. Only months later the work began, with observers from the Council of Europe. The Council of Europe had earlier been reluctant to show support for a new standard of fundamental rights, and rather emphasized a succession by the Union to the ECHR. However, this time the Council of Europe agreed to be a part of the work:

> It was realized that more and more acts of the European Union affected the everyday life of the citizens of Europe, not only in an economic context, but also in a civic, social and political context. [...] Finally it was also realized in Strasbourg that the process was unavoidable and that it was in the interest of the Council of Europe to see to it that the Charter would adequately take into account the European Convention on Human Rights.[26]

The outcome is the 'Charter of Fundamental Rights of the European Union'.

As for the right of protection for freedom of thought, conscience and religion, Article 10 CFR corresponds to a great extent with Article 9 ECHR.

Article 10 CFR
Freedom of thought, conscience and religion

1. Everyone has the right to freedom of thought, conscience and religion. This right includes freedom to change religion or belief and freedom, either alone or in community with others and in public or in private, to manifest religion or belief, in worship, teaching, practice and observance.
2. The right to conscientious objection is recognized, in accordance with the national laws governing the exercise of this right.

To further emphasize the close relationship between the ECHR and the CFR, Article 52(3) CFR contains a stipulation that the meaning and the scope of the rights

---

26 H.C. Krüger, 'The European Union Charter of Fundamental Rights', in S. Peers and A. Ward (eds.), *The European Union Charter of Fundamental Rights* (Oxford and Portland, Oregon: Hart Publishing, 2004), xviii.

contained in the Charter that correspond to rights protected by the Convention shall be the same as what is laid down in the latter.

Article 10 CFR is not absolute, but the limitation clause is differently framed in comparison with Article 9(2) ECHR. Article 52 CFR serves as a limitation mechanism to all the rights enshrined in the Charter instead of being targeted towards the specific right of freedom of religion. In the CFR, exceptions are provided by Article 52(1), which states that any limitation to the rights enshrined in the Charter must be provided for by law and must respect the essence of those rights and freedoms. Subject to the principle of proportionality, limitations may be made only if they are necessary and genuinely meet the objectives of general interest recognized by the Union, or the need to protect the rights and freedoms of others. This is in substance similar to the ECHR.

The scope of CFR is not as wide as that of the ECHR. According to Article 51 of the Charter, the Charter only applies to actions of the Union institutions and their bodies, and to actions of the Member States when implementing Union law. Thus, criticism has been raised, claiming that the CFR has merely aesthetic value, since it neither provides an enhanced protection for fundamental rights nor contains symbolic value. It has been observed that the European Court of Justice has already developed a body of law relating to protection of fundamental rights within the Union legal order; hence, there is no need for the new Charter.[27] Nevertheless, the Charter is binding for the European Union institutions and the Member States when implementing Union law. The Charter does indeed open up for a more extensive protection, according to Article 52(3) CFR. In that respect, it will be interesting to investigate whether the great margin of appreciation awarded the contracting states in the Convention system, specifically concerning Article 9 ECHR, will be challenged by the interpretation given by the ECJ.

A prominent novelty in the Charter, compared to the interpretation of Article 9 ECHR, is that Article 10(2) CFR includes the right to conscientious objection, in accordance with national laws governing the exercise of this right. ECtHR has been reluctant to grant permission for exceptions of generally applicable law. On the other hand, the jurisprudence concerning Article 18 International Covenant on Civil and Political Rights (ICCPR) has moved towards including a right to conscientious objection to the extent that 'the obligation to use lethal force may seriously conflict the freedom of conscience and right to manifest one's belief or religion.'[28]

The Charter explicitly refers the question of conscientious objection back to the national laws governing the issue. This is a matter connected with the way religion is organized in a state, and is closely attached to the rights of minorities amongst a majority culture. If one is part of a majority culture, in power and in control of

---

27 U. Haltern, 'On Finality', in A. von Bogdandy and J. Bast (eds.), *Principles of European Constitutional Law*, Max Planck Institute for Comparative Public Law and International Law (Oxford and Portland, Oregon: Hart Publishing, 2006), 742ff.

28 D. McGoldrick, 'The Charter and UN Human Rights Treaties', in Peers and Ward (eds.), supra note 26 at 112.

the laws enacted, one does not need to object, to the same extent, as if one were a part of a minority. But the issue of conscientious objection also relates to the right to be religious in a predominantly secular society. During the negotiations of the Charter, the scope of Article 10(2) was discussed in relation to a suggested amendment in the Slovakian concordat with the Holy See. The Commission of the European Union drew a line at a wide right to conscientious objection for doctors and nurses, since the Slovakian provision would have enabled them to refuse to perform abortions. In a country which is 80 percent Catholic, the Commission held that this would severely infringe the rights of women.[29] Nevertheless, as Article 10(2) CFR refers the issue back to the Member State, it shows a reluctance to interfere with national culture on such a delicate matter. But the actions of the Commission also point to the sharp conflict between secularism and religion, and the question of how far religion can be allowed to influence Union law.

Article 22 CFR provides that '[t]he Union shall respect cultural, religious and linguistic diversity.' Union law concerning packaging, labelling and advertizing, naturally involves linguistic diversity, but as seen with the regulation of Genetically Modified Organisms (GMO), also religious sensitivity can play a role. Does the duty to protect religious diversity grant the Member States a greater freedom to keep measures, which may in other cases disturb free movement? Insofar as religious phenomena and peculiarities have an economic dimension, or otherwise have an established link to Union law, such as harmonization, they do fall within the scope of jurisdiction of the Court of Justice. The Charter does not seem to indicate a wider obligation to respect national religious diversity; rather it reaffirms an already existing demarcation.

Another Charter provision that refers back to national legislation on the matter is Article 14 CFR. Through this provision the right to found an educational establishment is confirmed, and the parental right to choose a child's education in line with religious convictions is stressed. Yet, again, this operates only in accordance with national laws governing the matter. Policies on private schools with a religious ethos, as well as religious teaching in public schools, differ widely throughout the Union states. The obligation for a state to respect the right of parents to choose an education for their children, in accordance with their religious conviction, is also enshrined in Article 2 of the First Additional Protocol of thBoth provisions might play an important role for minorities, but as the Charter has limited application, according to Article 51, the Charter provision might prove especially important for migrant workers and their children. But, again, this right can only be invoked insofar as national legislation permits it.

29 L. Christoffersen, 'Religion as a Factor in Multi-Layered European Union Legislation', in R. Mehdi, H. Petersen, E.R. Sand, and G.R.Woodman (eds.), *Law and Religion in Multicultural Societies* (Copenhagen: Djøf Vorlag, 2008), 115.

The Context of the Charter: Freedom of Religion in an 'Ever Closer Union'

As described above, it is not in content and/or drafting that the two human rights documents necessarily differ. Quite the opposite, they are deemed to be interpreted in the same manner. Instead, and this is the argument I would like to make, it is the context of the two documents as well as the methodology of interpretation that differs.

The Charter places the right to freedom of religion in the middle of a complex legal system, namely the EU legal order. The Member States have given over legislative competence to the European Union in various, but broad, fields, and the principle of supremacy of EU law over national (constitutional) law makes the enforcement of religious freedom very different from that available through the ECHR. The European Union is an economic union of 27 states, which *raison d'être* is the economic and social integration of European Union, with the overall aim to create peace between the Member States.

The ECtHR has established the Convention as a living document, searching for European consensus and thereby bit by bit interpreting the Convention more broadly. The *raison d'être* of the European Union makes the incentive for Article 10 CFR distinct. The Charter of Fundamental Rights is a part of 'an ever closer union', a Union in which the ECJ is interpreting the Treaties with the goal of wider and deeper harmonization, cooperation as well as integration.[30] The four fundamental freedoms of movement – namely of capital, workers, services and goods – and the freedom of establishment function as the main integrating factors. As elaborated on above, the Court of Justice has gradually incorporated fundamental rights into this equation. However, this right of the individual has to be balanced against the Union's interests as well as the rights and freedoms of others.

In several cases the ECJ has balanced the right to freedom of movement with fundamental rights. In the case of *Schmidberger*[31] the issue concerned whether Austria neglected its duty to guarantee free movement through the Brenner passage when a demonstration was held by environmentalists, the effect of which was to completely close that motorway to traffic for almost 30 hours. The ECJ held that the free movement of goods through the Brenner passage had to be balanced against the fundamental right in a democratic state to demonstrate and make one's voice heard. However, for a measure to fall under an acceptable limit of free movement, the objective must essentially be to state an opinion, in a legal and public way. In other ways, the freedom of movement is crucial albeit not absolute; only proportionate and legitimate hindrances and inconveniences are acceptable by the Court of Justice.

30 See, *inter alia*, M. Maduro Poiares, *We the Court – the European Court of Justice and the European Economic Constitution*, (Oxford: Hart Publishing, 1998).

31 Case C-112/00 *Schmidberger*, [2003] I-5659.

In line with the *Schmidberger* case law, the ECJ held in *Omega*[32] that a fundamental right, in this case the right to human dignity, does not have to be interpreted in the same manner in all member states in order to be recognised in the Union legal order. Germany could, by prohibiting laser shooting games, derogate from the fundamental freedom of providing services, in line with their specific constitutional tradition of interpreting human dignity. In *Omega*, the Court viewed the German constitutional principle of 'human dignity' as a general principle of Union law, but said that the scope of that principle could be defined in detail by the Member State in question. Germany relied on its own Constitutional principle in order to justify a restriction on the freedom to provide services, which the ECJ accepted, due to the broad discretion granted to the Member State for the purpose of specifying the content and scope of human dignity. As a result, it does not matter that another Member State would define the general principle of 'human dignity' differently; Germany still could justify a restriction in the chosen manner. The large margin of discretion given to the Member State can be viewed as an outcome of the obligation to protect national identity, *in casu* in form of a fundamental right. It seems that the Court of Justice is increasingly willing to accept national restrictions of Union fundamental freedoms, on the basis of 'cardinal constitutional principles' inherent in a particular national constitutional identity.[33]

The Charter can be seen as a factor in the context of constitutionalization of the European Union and its power-shaping tradition. The symbolic function cannot be underestimated, and since entering into force it has 'placed European actions under further legal control'.[34] It has been argued that even if the Charter does not automatically and fundamentally shift European social policy away from the market integration model and towards the social citizenship model, it does make a statement in favour of, and a positive contribution to, the latter model. To what extent this will be fulfilled remains in the hand of the Court of Justice, but the Charter indicates at least a willingness to examine Union law through the lens of fundamental rights in a more extensive manner.[35]

In addition to the interpretative differences, the Charter functions in a legal framework which differs in enforcement compared to the Convention. In order to reach the European Court of Human Rights, a single individual has to exhaust the national judicial system. Concerning the interpretation of the rights enshrined in the Charter, a national court in a Member State can, and in some cases, must, refer the case to the European Court of Justice and ask for interpretative aid. As Article 267 of the Treaty on the Functioning of the European Union (TFEU) states: 'The Court of Justice of the European Union shall have jurisdiction to

32 Case C-36/02 *Omega*, [2004] ECR I-9609.

33 Augenstein, *The Contested Polity*, supra note 8 at 27.

34 C. Möllers, 'Pouvoir Constituant – Constitution – Constitutionalism', in Bogdandy and Bast (eds.), supra note 27 at 218.

35 M. Bell, *Anti-Discrimination Law and the European Union* (Oxford: Oxford University Press, 2002), 23–27.

give preliminary rulings concerning: (a) the interpretation of the Treaties; (b) the validity and interpretation of acts of the institutions, bodies, offices or agencies of the Union.' If there is ambiguity in how to interpret Union law in a specific case before the lower national court, that court can ask for a preliminary ruling by the ECJ. Moreover, if it is a case before a court or tribunal of a Member State against whose decisions there is no judicial remedy under national law, that court or tribunal is obliged to ask for a reference if it finds it necessary to give a ruling in the case. In other words, citizens of the EU can directly invoke freedom of religion, according to EU law before the national court, which then has to ask the European Court of Justice for a preliminary ruling. In other words, the applicant does not have to exhaust all national remedies; rather, there is a back door to the higher common European norms of freedom of religion, thus, indirectly, to the European Convention on Human Rights.

Non-Discrimination as a Test-Case for the Court of Justice

As stated above, the EU does not have competence in matters directly dealing with how a member state organizes religion. However, the EU does have direct competence in the field of non-discrimination. Article 19 TFEU serves as a legal basis for the Union to take action against discrimination on the basis of, among other grounds, religion and belief. In order to pursue this aim, the Union has enacted two Directives: Council Directive 2000/43/EC[36] implementing the principle of equal treatment between persons irrespective of racial or ethnical origin ('The Equal Treatment Directive') and Council Directive 2000/78/EC[37] establishing a general framework for equal treatment in employment and occupation ('The Employment Framework Directive'). The latter contains the prohibition against discriminating on the basis of religion or belief, or lack thereof, in employment and occupation.

The Employment Framework Directive concerns, at its core, a prohibition of discrimination on the grounds of religion or belief, age, disability and sexual orientation, in employment and occupation. The Directive defines 'unlawful discrimination' as direct and indirect discrimination, harassment, and an instruction to discriminate, according to Article 2. The wide range of prohibited grounds evoked strong disagreement among the Member States, and the outcome is a Directive full of omissions, exemptions, and derogations. First of all, Article 2(5) provides for an ambiguous exception, in relation to 'measures, laid down in law which, in a democratic society, are necessary for public security, for maintenance of public order and the prevention of criminal offences, for health protection and

36 Council Directive 2000/43/EC of 29 June 2000 implementing the principle of equal treatment between persons irrespective of racial or ethnical origin, (2000) O.J. L180/22.

37 Council Directive 2000/78/EC of 27 November 2000 establishing a general framework for equal treatment in employment and occupation, (2000) O.J. L303/16.

for the rights and freedoms of others. The intended purposes for this clause are not clear-cut, and the provision was introduced late in the negotiations.[38]

For the field of religion, inspiration might be drawn from *Van Duyn*[39] and subsequent case law on public policy exceptions, which among other issues have concerned national prohibitions of the Church of Scientology. In *Van Duyn* the United Kingdom relied on public policy in its attempt to treat the Church of Scientology less favourably than other organizations, considering the organization socially harmful. In *Van Duyn*, the question of free movement in order to take up employment with a 'religious'[40] organization arose.

Ms. Van Duyn, a Dutch national, wanted to work in the United Kingdom, as a secretary in the Church of Scientology. She was refused entry into Britain, since the activities of the Church of Scientology were considered socially harmful, albeit not illegal, in the United Kingdom. British citizens were not precluded from taking up employment with the organization. The ECJ held that a Member State is entitled to take into account, as a matter of personal conduct, the involvement with an organization the state considers socially harmful. This situation would fall under the scope of a possible derogation of a directly applicable provision on the basis of 'public policy'.[41] *Van Duyn* shows that the ECJ leaves a certain amount of discretion to the Member State concerning national values and public policy. The justifications possible under public policy might well vary between the Member States, but also from time to time. Nevertheless, the scope of the exception will be for the Court of Justice to determine.

A more specific exception is provided by Article 4(2) of the Framework Directive, stating that employment 'in churches or other public or private organizations the ethos of which is based on religion or belief' is exempted. This exception is commonly understood as aiming at sexual orientation and religion. Those two issues were heavily debated during the negotiation rounds, and the terms and terminology of the provision shifted throughout the process. At the end, the outcome can be said to have three dimensions. The first dimension is access, by gays and lesbians, to employment in religious organizations. According to Article 4(2) the exception to the prohibition on discrimination on grounds of religion or belief shall not justify discrimination on any other grounds, such as sexual orientation. But one of the main reasons for the existence of this provision is the reluctance of certain religious organizations to employ homosexuals. The Directive does not allow a religious organization to automatically exclude all lesbians and gay men from employment, but might open up for more proportionate measures.[42]

38 Bell, *Anti-Discrimination Law and the European Union*, supra note 35 at 115ff.

39 Case 41/74 *Van Duyn*, [1974] ECR 1337.

40 There is no consensus on whether or not the Church of Scientology should be considered a religious organization.

41 *Van Duyn*, paras. 23–24.

42 Bell, supra note 35 at 117.

The second dimension is that, when national law or practice already permits it, religious organizations will continue to be able to take into account religion or belief when making recruitment decisions, but only insofar as it is necessary to maintain the ethos of the organization. In order to define the scope of an exception, especially regarding what constitutes an ethos, and whether a difference in treatment is necessary, one must regard the specific occupation in question.[43] To give an example, it is in accordance with the Directive to employ only Catholic teachers in religion at a Catholic school, or only Muslims as imams in Muslim congregations. But if the teacher were to teach math or physical education, a closer examination of the relationship to the ethos of the organization might have to be assessed. If all teachers at the school were to participate in daily or weekly prayers, or religious counselling, the necessary link might be established.

Third, and finally, a religious organization can require of existing employees to 'act in good faith and with loyalty to the organization's ethos', if this is in compliance with the other provisions of the Directive. The exact meaning of such 'loyalty oaths' is hard to define, and the provision was introduced late in the negotiations, so few interpretative sources exist.[44] Again, the full scope of Article 4(2) will be the difficult task of the Court of Justice to examine.

The freedom of religion considerations arising from the Directive, including individual as well as collective freedom of religion, have yet to come before the Court of Justice. Guidance, however, can be found in another case on the scope and interpretation of the Framework Directive. In *Chacon Navas*[45] the ECJ held that concepts mentioned in Article 19 TFEU, and in the Framework Directive, *in casu* disability, would be independently interpreted in the Union legal order. This definition of the protected grounds might differ from how it is used in national legislation. Will this eventually lead to an autonomous Union interpretation of religion? If so, will such an interpretation have implications for how religion is organized in the different Member States? Or, will a mere minimum definition or standard be assessed, since this is a greatly debated area and something which comes close to very core of the national identity of a Member State, the latter which the ECJ has a duty to protect?

These are questions that remain to be answered by the Court of Justice. The Framework Directive serves two somewhat contradictory purposes in relation to the question of freedom of religion within the European Union. It can be seen as a factor in an evolving framework for state-religion relationships within the European Union itself, in that it harmonizes equal treatment irrespective of religion or belief. At the same time, it keeps such a relationship as a matter for the Member States, in that the derogations are plentiful and relate to the specific measures taken by the Member States, prior to the Directive. But it is inevitably true that

---

43 Bell, supra note 35 at 117.

44 Bell, supra note 35 at 118.

45 Case C-13/05 *Chacón Navas*, [2006] ECR I-6467.

religion and the aspects of religious life concerning employment do fall within the scope of Union law, hence within the jurisdiction of the European Court of Justice.

If, or when, a case of freedom of religion in employment situations arises before the ECJ, the Court has the difficult task of interpreting religious matters in a European Union setting. As stated earlier, the European Court of Human Rights has given the contracting states a rather wide margin of appreciation to decide matters under Article 9 ECHR. Will the ECJ keep this approach, giving the Member States a margin of discretion under notions of public order and public morality derogations, or will it aim towards a harmonious interpretation, as in the case of disability? Should a margin of appreciation under the Convention system be awarded the EU as a union, and not individual Member States, in matters of EU law? This could be a possibility when the EU accedes to the European Convention on Human Rights, but it is hardly possible at present, since religious matters are so closely connected to the identity of the Member State.

Concluding Remarks

The Framework Directive serves as the most likely vehicle for actualizing freedom of religion before the European Court of Justice in the foreseeable future, but other areas of EU law could serve as potential test-cases. An example of how free movement of capital connects with questions of what counts as a religion and the interpretation, or lack thereof, of collective religious freedom, is the case of *Église de Scientolgie*.[46]

In the 1990s the French prime minister had laid down in law a system of prior authorization for certain categories of direct foreign investments. This system affected the Church of Scientology in Paris, to which the Scientology International Trust Reserve, a trust established in the United Kingdom, wanted to transfer capital. The Church of Scientology asked for a repeal of this system, submitting that it was contrary to Union law governing free movement of capital. France, on the other hand, claimed that the prohibition of all restriction on free movement of capital is without prejudice to the right of Member States to take measures, which are justified on grounds of public policy or public security.

The Court of Justice stated that the system of prior authorization is indeed a restriction, and agreed that a Member State is, in principle, free to determine the requirements of public policy and public policy in the light of national needs. However, the state must do so in accordance with Union law. The derogations from the free movement of capital must be interpreted strictly, and cannot be decided unilaterally by the Member State, without control by the Union institutions. Only if there is a genuine and sufficiently serious threat to a fundamental interest of society can a Member State rely on the public policy and public security derogation clauses. In addition, the clauses must not be misapplied, to serve a purely economic

46 Case C-54/99 *Eglise de Scientlologie*, [2000] ECR I-1335.

interest, and the persons affected must have means of legal redress. Furthermore, the measures taken by the Member State must fulfil the proportionality criteria, and must not be able to be attained by a less restrictive measure. In this case, the Court of Justice affirmed that the French system of prior authorization might very well be the least restrictive measure, and that prior declaration is an inadequate measure, due to the difficulty of tracing and identifying capital once it has entered the state. However, in the French provisions at stake there was no definition of what constitutes a threat to public policy and security; hence, French legislation did not fulfil the principle of legal certainty.[47]

The assessment of the case made by the Court of Justice lacks any discussion of whether the French provisions could infringe the collective religious freedom of the Church of Scientology. Admittedly, the religious status of the Church of Scientology is very much debated in Europe, both politically and in European courts. Nevertheless, free movement of capital could be actualized concerning other, non-contested religious organizations. Would then the Charter of Fundamental Rights provide a higher degree of protection?

Following that line of thinking, the collective freedom of religion aspects, taken together with the fundamental EU law aspects of freedom of establishment, could mean a higher degree of protection for churches and other religious organizations, including new religious movements, wanting to establish themselves in other Member States. This holds especially true for organizations that some member states regards as ‘cults’ and ‘sects’ but that have the status of religions in other member states. The critical matter concerns whether the Charter establishes a free-standing link to Union law. If that is the case, then an individual or groups of individuals can claim freedom of movement, for workers as well as goods, services and capital, in order for individuals to practice freedom of religion either in another way than in their home country, or as branches of certain religious activities – be they commercial or benevolent in nature.

At the end of the day, the impact the Charter might have lies in the hands of the European Court of Justice. The protection of freedom of religion has already been present in the European Union, through the constitutional traditions of the Member States, the ECHR, and international agreements, all serving as parts of the general principles of Union law. In that sense, the Charter does not alter the substantive legal situation. The ECJ has the opportunity to make something more out of the Charter, but it has yet to do so, specifically concerning religious freedom. On the other hand, the symbolic intention should perhaps not be underestimated. For, what signals would be sent if freedom of religion were not to be included in a Charter proclaiming fundamental rights? That would indeed amount to a speaking silence.

47 *Eglise de Scientlologie*, paras. 13–23.

Chapter 16
The Right to Religious Liberty in English Law

Julian Rivers

Religious Liberty as a Constitutional Right

In a codified constitution which states that fundamental human rights are higher law, and which protects them against all other sources of public and private power by providing legal remedies enforceable by an independent Supreme or Constitutional Court, it is very easy to identify a constitutional right. The matter becomes much more problematic if some or all of those features of constitutional design are absent. In the case of the 'unwritten' British Constitution, the highest norm is generally taken to be the supremacy of Parliament: whatever the Queen in Parliament enacts is law. There is no higher law than the latest expression of the will of Parliament found in primary legislation. It would be easy to conclude that constitutional rights are purely residual, marking out a sphere of liberty which is left to civil society by the non-exercise by Parliament of its right to legislate. Indeed, the slightly older term of 'civil liberties', which was dominant until the turn of the millennium, can be taken to reflect the supposedly residual nature of constitutional rights in the United Kingdom.[1]

However, such an account of constitutional rights is inadequate.[2] It presupposes not merely omnicompetence on the part of Parliament, but also the internal capacity to legislate regularly over the entire body of law, as well as a complete absence of moral or political constraint in doing so. In reality, the common law contains a rich and complex body of precedent, in which Parliament can only ever intervene sporadically, and only ever wants to. Both judges and parliamentarians are heirs to an historical and political tradition which contains a commitment to fundamental values, many of which are now treated as 'human rights', but which enjoy a much longer pedigree than that term suggests. Furthermore, Parliament and the courts collaborate in the protection of constitutional rights by reference

---

1 The transition can be seen in the titles of leading textbooks. Bailey, Harris & Jones (1st edn., 1980) is still called 'Civil Liberties'; Feldman (1st edn., 1993) was *avant-garde* in being called 'Civil Liberties and Human Rights'. 'Human Rights' is now widespread and the normal label.

2 From the substantial literature, see T.R.S. Allan, *Law, Liberty and Justice: The Legal Foundations of British Constitutionalism* (Oxford: Clarendon Press, 1993).

to what has become known as the 'principle of legality'. This principle takes seriously Parliament's historic function in approving the limitation of common law rights. It requires limitations of rights by public bodies to have sufficient statutory authorization, and it empowers the judiciary to interpret ambiguous legislation narrowly in accordance with those rights.[3]

As well as such features of institutional design, the British Constitution has tended to avoid grand statements of principle. A.V. Dicey made a virtue of this, by pointing out the importance of practical remedies against state power, such as habeas corpus, and the impotence of merely rhetorical commitments to rights.[4] This point is now better made by contrasting the boundaries between politics and law in different legal traditions. Where some countries might treat the codification of broad principles as part of the law, leaving their determination and application to judges and academic lawyers, the British constitution has tended to see the abstract level of discourse as more broadly social and political, with the work of lawyers being the practical one of designing and enforcing concrete practical remedies in situations of conflict.

It was for these reasons of constitutional tradition that British Governments long resisted the codification of human rights. Although an early signatory to the European Convention on Human Rights, as well as the individual right of petition,[5] it was only in 2000 that the Human Rights Act 1998 started to give general judicial protection to fundamental rights. However, here, too, Convention rights have been domesticated in a way which is sympathetic to British constitutional traditions. The judiciary are bound to interpret statute (and by implication develop the common law) compatibly with the Convention 'wherever possible' – which, however obscure the limits of judicial creativity implies that in some cases at least the law is too clear and settled to admit of reworking.[6] Where primary legislation cannot be moulded into conformity with Convention rights, the judiciary are limited to making a 'declaration of incompatibility', which triggers a new legislative procedure, but has no effect on the validity of the law.[7]

It follows that an exposition of any constitutional right in the British Constitution is not so much a systematic presentation of academic and judicial comment on the meaning of an abstract term. Rather it has to be the reconstruction

---

3 J. Rivers, 'Constitutional Rights and Statutory Limitations', in M. Klatt (ed.), *Institutionalized Reason: The Jurisprudence of Robert Alexy* (Oxford: Oxford University Press, 2012). For a clear judicial statement, see *R v. Lord Chancellor ex parte Witham* [1998] QB 575 per Laws J at 580. There is no clear example of religious liberty operating to produce a narrow statutory interpretation, but the comments of Lords Wilberforce and Fraser in *Blathwayt v. Cawley* [1976] AC 397, 425–6 and 442–3 are apposite.

4 A.V. Dicey, *Introduction to the Study of the Constitution* (ed. E.C.S. Wade), 10th edn. (London: Macmillan, 1959), 213–237.

5 Available to British subjects from 1966.

6 Human Rights Act 1998, sec.3.

7 Human Rights Act 1998, sec.4.

of a value, which is sensitive both to historic political commitments and change and as well as the expression of those commitments in the concrete detail of the law. Such an exercise is inherently interpretative. In the case of religious liberty it is made all the harder by the stability of law for much of the twentieth century. By about 1880, the place of religion in the law had become subject to a reasonable consensus, which by 1920 was normal and unquestioned.[8] Discussion of the scope and limits of religious liberty were thus subject to a threefold absence: absence of political contestation, absence of litigation, and absence of academic interest.[9] The unravelling of this constitutional settlement would only become plain as the twentieth century drew to a close. Where the 'unwritten' constitution is settled, it disappears. Only in the last decade has this situation changed, and it has done so against a background of religious commitment and political values significantly different from those dominant for much of the twentieth century. Paradoxically, there is thus both historic social stability in some aspects of religious liberty and also a vulnerability in others. In some ways religious liberty is written into the political identity of the British people, but in other ways important debates and resolutions have been forgotten, and the motivating forces behind them dissipated, leaving religious minorities – which must now include practising Christians – in a weak legal position.

The right to religious liberty can be expounded by reference to eight basic elements which underlie much of the relevant law.[10] Some of these elements are more well-rooted than others, and the final section briefly suggests some ways in which the modern law may be changing.

Eight Elements of Religious Liberty

Religion Is Voluntary

Perhaps the strongest principle of all to give shape to the British conception of religious liberty is that there should be no compulsion in matters of religion. The last serious attempt to use the law to secure 'an universal agreement in the Public Worship of Almighty God' was made in the Act of Uniformity 1662. Together

8 J. Rivers, *The Law of Organized Religions: Between Establishment and Secularism* (Oxford: Oxford University Press, 2010), ch. 1.

9 To pick two examples, old and new, Dicey (*Introduction to the Study of the Constitution*, supra note 4) only has the briefest discussion of blasphemy law in the context of freedom of expression; religion is otherwise absent. Feldman (supra note 1) still has no chapter on freedom of religion.

10 For much fuller treatments, the reader is referred to Rivers (*The Law of Organized Religions,* supra note 8), R. Ahdar & I. Leigh, *Religious Freedom in the Liberal State* (Oxford: Oxford University Press, 2005) and R. Sandberg, *Law and Religion* (Cambridge: Cambridge University Press, 2011) among others.

with associated statutes penalizing non-conformist worship it compelled regular attendance at public worship in the Church of England. When legal toleration was introduced in 1689, the obligation to attend the church could be satisfied by attendance at a licensed place of worship instead. Although such obligations had been a familiar part of reformation legislation from the mid-sixteenth century onwards, they were only ever enforced sporadically, and rarely after the Whig ascendancy from 1714.

Non-conformist churches were constituted in law as voluntary societies; any obligations were thus assumed by the willing submission of individual members to the internal law of their religion in accordance with general principles of property and contract law. Courts would regularly insist on the fundamental distinction between coercive and consensual jurisdiction.[11] This continues to apply today and is further reflected in the status of religious tribunals, which only have jurisdiction as the internal decision-taking organs of private organizations or as arbitration tribunals acting under a contract of arbitration.[12]

In order to satisfy this principle, the established church needed to be reconceived as a voluntary body. This took place in a long series of developments stretching from the mid-18th century to the early twentieth century. Already in 1736, the courts held that the canons of the church are not binding on the laity.[13] The last direct public funding given to the Church of England was for building new churches in 1824. In 1836, church tithes (local taxation) were commuted for rentcharges on property, and then in 1936 these were abolished outright.[14] Misplaced concern about the compulsory nature of the law in the case of the obligations of lay rectors to keep the chancels of their local church in good repair lay behind the decision of the Court of Appeal in *Aston Cantlow*.[15] The endpoint of such changes were the 'disestablishment' of the churches and their re-establishment as consensual bodies, which happened in the case of the Church of Ireland in 1870 and the Church in Wales in 1920.[16] For practical purposes today, the established status of the Church of England only confers benefits, not burdens, on individual parishioners.[17] In practice, if not in strict law, it is a voluntary body.

Two other major historic examples can be noted. English law showed early sensitivity to the need for accommodation of religious diversity in the swearing

---

11 *Long v. Bishop of Capetown* (1863) 1 Moo PC (NS) 411, 15 ER 756.

12 *Jivraj v. Hashwani* [2011] 1 WLR 1872.

13 *Middleton v. Crofts* (1737) Andr, 57, 95 ER 296.

14 Tithe Act 1936.

15 *Aston Cantlow and Wilmcote with Billesley PCC v. Wallbank* [2002] Ch. 51, reversed in [2004] 1 AC 546.

16 Irish Church Act 1869; Welsh Church Act 1914.

17 See the discussion in N. Doe, *The Legal Framework of the Church of England* (Oxford: Clarendon Press, 1996), 225–228.

of oaths as part of normal legal process.[18] The extension of this principle to atheists and others who wished to affirm, as well as to public office came later in a protracted series of developments throughout the second half of the nineteenth century.[19] By 1888, complete liberty in this regard had been secured.

When compulsory elementary education was introduced in 1870, the religious component was subject to parental opt-outs.[20] Religious worship and instruction had to be at the start or end of the day to make this practically possible. Attendance at a place of worship could not be made a condition of school attendance, and parents were also given the right to withdraw children from school for religious holidays. Religious education was exempt from state inspection. These concerns continue to characterize the law of religious education, with one of the most recent changes being a new right of a child of 16 to object to participation in religious education (independently from his or her parents).[21]

No Religion or Belief Is Contrary to the Policy of the Law

Until the mid-nineteenth century it was possible to argue that the only lawful religion was the Christian religion in the form established by law, and such other religions as were tolerated by law from time to time. At some indeterminate point, the legal culture shifted, and the policy was reversed: all religions and worldviews were within the policy of the law except those specifically prohibited. From this point onwards, the silence of the law meant that there was a presumption of liberty. The shift can be seen at work for the first time in the Places of Worship Registration Act 1855, which allowed for the registration of places of worship of 'any … body or denomination of persons.'[22]

This principle required a reworking of criminal offences relating to blasphemy. Whereas, in strict law from *R v. Taylor* (1676) onwards,[23] the mere expression of an opinion contrary to the established religion could constitute a criminal offence, as toleration expanded, so the limits of the offence were more tightly drawn. By the mid-nineteenth century, the courts were making explicit reference to the manner and tone of the publication,[24] and then in 1883, Lord Coleridge CJ stated that 'if the decencies of controversy are observed, even the fundamentals of religion may

---

18 Quakers Act 1695; *Omychund v. Barker* 1744 Willes 538; 125 ER 1310, referring to earlier cases in respect of Jews.

19 See generally, C. Braithwaite, *Conscientious Objection to Compulsions under the Law* (York: William Sessions Ltd., 1995), ch. 1.

20 Elementary Education Act 1870, secs.7, 74(2) and 76.

21 School Standards and Framework Act 1998, sec.71(1B).

22 The obligation to register places of worship ceased to be enforced around the same time, although it was not formally repealed until Statute Law (Repeals) Act 1977, sec.1 and sched. 1 pt. 5.

23 1 Vent. 293.

24 *R v. Hetherington* (1841) 4 St Tr NS 563.

be attacked.'[25] The offence of blasphemy lingered on to have some impact on literary and artistic censorship,[26] before being finally abolished in 2008.[27]

The protection of Christianity was also present in the civil law. Lord Eldon LC refused to issue injunctions to prevent the circulation of pirated copies of anti-Christian works,[28] and other judges refused to enforce contracts made with bodies such as the Rational Society and the Secular Society.[29] This line of reasoning died towards the end of the nineteenth century, before being overruled formally in *Bowman v. Secular Society*.[30] Similarly in the case of charity law, the courts both adopted a very wide definition of what counted as 'religion' for the purposes of the law,[31] and also gradually abandoned the old notion of 'superstitious trusts' which had operated to make Jewish and Roman Catholic foundations unenforceable.[32] The House of Lords confirmed that this idea was redundant in *Bourne v. Keen*.[33]

A relatively late example of the removal of laws hostile to religions as such could be found in the Fraudulent Mediums Act 1951 which repealed earlier offences of witchcraft and vagrancy. These had been used to secure the conviction of a well-known medium, Helen Duncan, in 1944.[34] The replacement legislation still made it an offence deceitfully to purport to act as a spiritualist medium for the sake of reward, although this in its turn has recently been replaced by consumer protection legislation.[35]

Thus no religion or belief can be said to be intrinsically contrary to the policy of the law. Any obstacles are the result of general laws operating without exception on specific instances of unconventional behaviour. It is true that this may give rise to questions of conscientious objection, but cannot be seen as an attempt to exclude or suppress the religion itself.

---

25 *R v. Ramsey and Foote* (1883) 15 Cox CC 231, 238.

26 *R v. Lemon* [1979] AC 617, *Wingrove v. United Kingdom*, App. No. 17419/90 (ECtHR), 22 October 1996.

27 Criminal Justice and Immigration Act 2008, sec.79.

28 *Murray v. Benbow* (1822) 4 St Tr NS 1409; *Lawrence v. Smith* (1822) Jac 471.

29 *Pare v. Clegg* (1861) 29 Beav 589, 54 ER 756; *Cowan v. Milbourn* (1867) LR 2 Ex 230.

30 [1917] AC 406.

31 The high-point is generally taken to be *Thornton v. Howe* (1862) 31 Beav 14, 54 ER 1042, in which Sir John Romilly MR upheld a trust to propagate the writings of a mystic who claimed to be pregnant by the Holy Spirit and give birth to a second Christ.

32 See, for example, *Da Costa v. De Paz* (1753) Amb 228, 27 ER 150; *West v. Shuttleworth* (1835) 2 My & K 684; 39 ER 1106.

33 [1919] AC 815.

34 *R v. Duncan* [1944] 1 KB 713.

35 Consumer Protection from Unfair Trading Regulations 2008, SI 2008/1277.

Public Bodies Are Non-Religious

Church and state were deeply intertwined right up to the end of the nineteenth century. Nevertheless, one can see a principle of secularity emerging more and more clearly as the century unfolded. To some extent, this was the reverse side of the principle that religious participation should be voluntary. Since the state exercised coercive power, it should not be religious. However, after 1832 this rejection of coercion was combined with a growing democratic sensibility which held as a matter of principle that participation in public bodies should not require any specific religious commitment.

The major political campaign in this regard was to secure the repeal of the Test and Corporation Acts of the 1660s which prevented those who were not willing at least occasionally to conform to the established church from standing for public office. In practice, parliament passed an annual indemnity Act from 1726 onwards to relieve protestant dissenters, whom the courts protected from malicious prosecution after 1767.[36] But the mark of second-class citizenship remained until removed in 1828. Emancipation was extended to Roman Catholics in 1829 and Jews in 1846.[37] Formal education in the ancient public schools and universities remained more closely allied to the church, and here emancipation took a little longer to achieve, taking place in a series of developments from 1850s to 1870s.[38] The swearing of oaths of office also remained an obstacle to atheists until the Bradlaugh affair brought about comprehensive reform in the Oaths Act 1888.[39]

The principle that public bodies should be non-religious required the removal of governmental functions from the church. The registration of births, marriages and deaths was transferred to the new secular office of the Registrar-General in 1836, as was a new power to conduct civil marriage. After a protracted campaign, the jurisdiction of the ecclesiastical courts over defamation suits was abolished in 1855; testamentary and matrimonial causes followed in 1857, and the final residue of their ancient criminal jurisdiction went in 1860.[40] From this time onwards, ecclesiastical courts became domestic religious tribunals, albeit strictly speaking courts of law.

The Church of England was also slowly removed from local government. The Local Government Act 1894 created secular rural parishes and 'disestablished' local charities by distinguishing between those with secular purposes (typically,

36 *Evans v. Harrison* (1762) Wilm 130, 97 ER 51; (1767) 3 Bro PC 645, 1 ER 1437.

37 Roman Catholic Relief Act 1829; Religious Disabilities Act 1846.

38 Oxford University Act 1854, secs.44–45; Cambridge University Act 1856, secs.45–46; Public Schools Act 1868, sec.12; University Tests Act 1871; Oxford and Cambridge Act 1877.

39 *Clarke v. Bradlaugh* (1881) 7 QBD 38; *AG v. Bradlaugh* (1885) 14 QBD 667.

40 R.B. Outhwaite, *The Rise and Fall of the English Ecclesiastical Courts*, 1500–1860 (Cambridge: Cambridge University Press, 2006).

the relief of the poor) and those with ecclesiastical purposes. Control of the funds for secular purposes went to the new parish councils.

Religious Groups Are Autonomous Within Their Own Sphere

There is a sense in which any private or commercial body is autonomous or self-governing within the framework of the law and free from state intervention. But in the case of religious groups the concern to secure this freedom is heightened, leaving religious group autonomy as an island of immunity in a rising tide of state regulation. A number of features of the law demonstrate this concern, although recent years have also seen a weakening of the principle.

The principle of autonomy can be seen most clearly at work in the development of the law relating to church property and employment disputes. As far as property is concerned, in cases of schism, the court will seek to determine ownership of the property so far as possible in line with the doctrinal and ecclesial identity of the body in question. The two dimensions of identity do not always coincide, as in the Free Church of Scotland case.[41] Here, the highest governing body of the church had decided to depart from a founding tenet considered minor and dispensable by the vast majority, but still of central significance by a small minority. The fact that the House of Lords found for the minority does not mean that the law always prefers doctrinal continuity over the decisions of properly constituted governing bodies. Rather, they held that in this case, the church had decided on its founding to elevate the tenet in question to constitutive status. The fundamental question in cases of schism concerns which of the parties to the litigation acted unconstitutionally according to the group's own internal law.

The principle that Government should not interfere in religious group life was seen clearly in attempts to protect religious groups from the regulatory oversight of the Charity Commission.[42] As originally conceived in 1853, the Commissioners had no jurisdiction to approve schemes for the adjustment of the terms of religious charitable foundations. When this proved an unhelpful restriction, it was cautiously removed, but only at the request of the religious group concerned and with the consent of Parliament expressed in a private Act. The Jewish United Synagogues were the first religious charity to benefit from this.[43] Other elements of the protection of autonomy remained, such as the fact that religious groups did not need to register trusts of places of worship and connected premises, and they did not need to account for their finances. By contrast, the Charities Act 2006 is based on a policy of universal accountability to Government, although the 'temporary'

41 *Free Church of Scotland v. Overtoun* [1904] AC 515.

42 The complex law is summarized in Rivers, *The Law of Organized Religions*, supra note 8 at 166–171.

43 Jewish United Synagogues Act 1870.

exemption from accounting for the major Christian denominations has recently been extended.[44]

Another example of the sensitivity towards internal autonomy can be seen in the rise of planning legislation protecting historically sensitive buildings, many of which are owned by religious groups. Internal changes are subject to systems of consent operated by the religions themselves, rather than by local government.[45]

Autonomy was continued throughout the twentieth century as employment law developed. Ministers of religion were held not to have contracts of employment, thus exempting their churches from related general legal obligations.[46] This line of case-law, which developed in almost total disregard for nineteenth century precedent, reached the point at which some courts were prepared to hold as a matter of law that there was no legal relationship between a minister and his or her church at all.[47] In recent years, this has suddenly reversed into the presumption that they are employees with all the normal rights of employees – again in ignorance of the difficulties this can give rise to.[48] There are also suggestions in the recent cases that the right to religious liberty still empowers the group to prevent the arrangements with their ministers from having legal effect, so it is not yet clear how the new law will settle down.

A concern for church autonomy lay at the heart of the Scottish establishment debates, and culminated in the Church of Scotland Act 1921. This took autonomy so seriously that it took the form of recognizing the self-constituting power of the Church and assuring to it complete non-interference in its 'doctrine, worship, government and discipline'.[49] Although the movement for autonomy was never as strong within the Church of England, it too had its impact in the creation of new internal organs of legislation and the loosening of control by Parliament and Government.[50]

A more recent version of autonomy can also be seen in some recent cases showing the extreme unwillingness of courts to get involved in questions of religious

---

44 Charities (Exception from Registration) Regulations 1996, SI 1996/180, as extended.

45 *Ecclesiastical Exemption (Listed Buildings and Conservation Areas) Order* 1994, SI 1994/1771.

46 *Davies v. Presbyterian Church of Wales* [1986] 1 WLR 323; *President of the Methodist Conference v. Parfitt* [1984] QB 368.

47 E.g. *Khan v. Oxford City Mosque*, unreported, 23 July 1998.

48 *Percy v. Church of Scotland Board of National Mission* [2006] 2 AC 28; *New Testament Church of God v. Stewart* [2008] ICR 282; *Moore v. President of the Methodist Conference* [2011] EWCA Civ 1581.

49 For historic background, see Lord Rodger of Earlsferry, *The Courts, the Church and the Constitution: Aspects of the Disruption of 1843* (Edinburgh: Edinburgh University Press, 2008).

50 Key developments are the Church of England Assembly (Powers) Act 1919; Synodical Government Measure 1969; Church of England (Worship and Doctrine) Measure 1974.

doctrine. Defamation actions have been stayed by judges on this ground,[51] and there are signs that in cases of schism and subsequent property dispute, the courts may be moving to modes of resolution which completely avoid any determination of who is 'right'.[52] Religion then becomes a 'law-free' zone, which while representing an extreme version of autonomy can result in injustices to individuals.

The Powers and Privileges of Religious Groups Are Available on Terms of Equality

English law does not have a clear distinction between more privileged 'public' or 'known' religions and less privileged 'private' ones. For example, questions of tax status, the ability to perform marriages, chaplaincies, schools and representation on public consultation bodies are treated as separate with their own criteria of inclusion. The only clear distinction in law is between the established church and all others, and it has been a clear theme of political campaigning and legal change from the mid-19th century onwards that the privileged position of the established church should either be removed or extended to other religious groups. For the most part, religious establishment is now residual and symbolic. The fact that English law does not think in terms of monolithic 'statuses' but disaggregates the various powers and privileges of religious groups itself contributes to collective liberty.[53]

The principal privilege enjoyed by religious groups is charitable status, which carries with it both tax exemptions and the right to reclaim income tax on donations. Until recently, the law presumed that a trust for the advancement of religion was publicly beneficial, although this now has to be demonstrated. While there are ongoing debates about the limits of 'religion' for these purposes, the boundaries are widely drawn. The limits are exemplified by religious purposes which are purely private such as enclosed religious orders and personal rituals,[54] as well as by worldviews or practices with barely any spiritual dimension, such as Scientology, or no discernable moral or ethical framework, such as Gnosticism.[55]

When in 1753 marriage became subject to state regulation in collaboration with the established church, Quakers and Jews were exempt from the new scheme. This was a cause of considerable grievance to other non-conformist groups, and from 1836 all religious groups have been entitled to celebrate marriages with civil effect. Both the building and the celebrant need to be licensed and registered by the

---

51 *Blake v. Associated Newspapers Ltd.* [2003] EWHC 1960 (QB); *Maharaj v. Eastern Media Group Ltd.* [2010] EWHC 1294 (QB); *Shergill v. Purewal* [2010] EWHC 3610 (QB).

52 *Varsani v. Jesani* [1999] Ch 219; *Dean v. Burne* [2009] EWHC 1250 (Ch).

53 As the ECtHR implicitly recognizes: *Religionsgemeinschaft Zeugen Jehovahs v. Austria*, App. No. 40825/98, 31 July 2008.

54 *Gilmour v. Coates* [1949] AC 426; *Re Hetherington* [1990] Ch 1.

55 See P. Luxton and N. Evans, 'Two recent decisions of the Charity Commission', *Conveyancer and Property Lawyer* (2011), 144.

Registrar-General.[56] There is considerable variation in the extent to which different religious denominations make use of this ability, with very high registration rates among Sikh gurdwaras contrasting with low rates of registration for Islamic mosques. The Government has proposed moving to a celebrant-based system after universal civil preliminaries, but this has so far not been enacted.[57]

Public and Religious Bodies Coordinate Action and Collaborate in the Areas of Education and Social Welfare

In broader historical perspective, the provision of education and social welfare has been seen as a religious responsibility. However, distinctive aspects of secularization in the UK must also be noted. Protestant individualism and voluntarism tended to produce autonomous welfare organizations capable of determining the degree to which they displayed overt religious motivation and practice independently from any large denomination with which they might be loosely associated. British welfare in the twentieth century has been indelibly moulded by the explosion of religiously-motivated social action in the previous one – sometimes by way of appropriation, sometimes by way of rejection. This context has contributed to quicker processes of secularization in some cases. Thus, although it was always normal to appoint chaplains, hospitals quickly became independent charities thought of in largely non-religious terms. When the National Health Service was formed in 1948, there were fears that the 'secular state' would stifle what protection for religious belief and practice survived, but the story has been essentially one of continuity with an already-secularized sector.

Education provides the clearest example of complex forms of coordination and collaboration between state and religious groups. For much of the nineteenth century, the state sought to achieve universal education by making grants in support of voluntary religious societies set up to establish elementary schools. When this model finally lost the support of non-Anglican Protestants, direct state involvement started in the Elementary Education Act 1870 and grant funding ceased. For a while it seemed that state schools would come to supplant the church schools, but there were too many of the latter to lose. In 1902 state funding for church schools was reintroduced. In 1944, different levels of funding and control became available. In practice, the vast majority of church schools were Anglican or Roman Catholic, with much smaller numbers of Jewish and other protestant Christian foundations. In 1998, a general framework for faith-based schools was created, and the first publicly funded schools of other faiths began to be formed. The current policy of encouraging independently governed but state-funded schools (academies) has also contributed to a rise in faith-based schools. Private education, which allows for a fuller expression of religion in the life of a school, remains an option for many parents.

56 Marriage Act 1949,secs.41–44.

57 *Civil Registration: vital change*, Cm 5355 (January 2002).

As far as other areas of social welfare are concerned, the model has been one of coordination rather than collaboration. The financial aspects of the rise of the 'welfare state' such as pensions, unemployment benefit and other forms of welfare payment have naturally been taken over by the state. However, until recently, personal services such as care for the elderly and child services have been dominated by organizations many of which have a religious foundation and ethos. By contrast, recent years have arguably seen 'welfare pluralism' becoming replaced by a greater degree of state regulation, which is sometimes hostile to distinctive religious emphases and concerns.

Personal Religious Commitments Are Accommodated in Public

The expanding law of religious liberty from the Toleration Act 1689 onwards has been motivated to a substantial extent by respect for conscience. However, the exercise of conscience has been conceived primarily in group terms. Even when the individual was the subject of legal exemption, they were treated as members of a discrete religious group. It was 'Quakers' who were relieved from taking oaths and then 'Moravians' were added in the case of military service.[58] However, from the second half of the 19th century onwards, the benefits of conscientious objection began to be available also to the non-religious person as an individual.[59]

The principal historic examples of exemption from general laws on account of conscientious objection include oath-taking in a whole range of public contexts, compulsory military service, compulsory vaccination and, more recently, compulsory trades union membership.[60] Affirmation in place of oath-taking continues to have current significance, as do exemption from religious education in schools,[61] protection for doctors refusing to take part in abortions,[62] exemptions for Sikhs wearing turbans in place of safety helmets and for carrying knives in public,[63] protection for those unwilling to act in the fields of regulated human fertilization and embryology,[64] and the refusal to provide emergency contraception services.[65] It is noteworthy that relief from the operation of general laws has been achieved by political pressure and statutory provision, not by judicial

58 See, e.g., Militia Act 1803.

59 See, e.g., Oaths Act 1888; Military Service Act 1915, sec.2(1)(d). Generally on this topic, Braithwaite, *Conscientious Objection to Compulsions under the Law*, supra note 19.

60 Industrial Relations Act 1971, sec.9(1)(b).

61 School Standards and Framework Act 1998, sec.71.

62 Abortion Act 1967, sec 4.

63 Road Traffic Act 1988, sec.16(2); Employment Act 1989, sec.11; Criminal Justice Act 1988, sec.139(5)(b).

64 Human Fertilisation and Embryology Act 1990, sec.38

65 National Health Service (General Medical Services Contracts) Regulations 2004/291.

development. Indeed, the judiciary have generally been unwilling to extend rights of conscientious objection.[66]

Personal religious commitments have also been accommodated by meeting spiritual and pastoral needs in public institutions through the provision of chaplaincies in the armed forces, prisons and hospitals, as well as in educational and industrial contexts.[67] Here, to varying degrees, the Church of England still dominates both numerically and in having a coordinating role in respect of other religions. But provision has been made for a long time for other religious minorities and in recent times this has expanded beyond the older religious minorities (Roman Catholics and Jews) to embrace Muslim, Hindu, Sikh and other chaplaincies. It is an open question whether the structural imbalance in favour of Anglican chaplains overall acts as a constraint on other denominations or secures their participation.

Generally speaking, public culture has been tolerant in matters of dress, diet and holy days as well, although a resistance towards certain more extreme forms of Islamic veiling must be noted.[68] As far as the law is concerned, special provision has been made for Jewish (and later, Islamic) ritual slaughter from the start of state regulation,[69] and Jewish shops closing on a Saturday have long enjoyed various forms of exemption from Sunday trading restrictions.[70] In many cases, public officials have been able to wear distinctive forms of dress without much difficulty. A general loosening of social conventions as the 20th century has proceeded has tended to make such questions less problematic. In many cases, casual dress codes, a wide range of special dietary needs and more flexible working time combine to mask the religious commitment behind individual behaviour.

Religious People and Places Receive Special Protection from Hostile Acts

The principle that religious people and places require specific protection from hostile acts has been a constant, albeit minor, theme within the law. In recent years the need for such protection has been questioned, but specific criminal offences remain.

It is an offence at common law to obstruct or disturb any minister performing divine service, and it is also an offence to strike any person in a church or churchyard.[71] It would seem that the protection extends beyond the Church of England to any lawful religious denomination.[72] However, the authority for these

66 *R v. Salford Area Health Authority ex parte Janaway* [1989] AC 537.

67 Rivers, *The Law of Organized Religions,* supra note 8, ch. 7

68 *R (Begum) v. Denbigh High School Governors* [2007] 1 AC 100; *Azmi v. Kirklees MBC* [2007] I.C.R. 1154.

69 See, now, Welfare of Animals (Slaughter or Killing) Regulations 1995/731.

70 See, now, Sunday Trading Act 1994, sched. 2, pt. 2.

71 *R v. Parry* (1686) Trm PC 239; *R v. Wroughton* (1765) 3 Burr. 1683; *Wilson v. Greaves* (1757) 1 Burr. 240, 243.

72 Lord Mansfield referred to disturbing Methodists and dissenters engaged in 'decent and quiet devotion', *R v. Wroughton*, 1684.

common law offences is scanty, their precise scope obscure, and there has been no prosecution for at least two centuries.

The main existing offence can be found in the Ecclesiastical Courts Jurisdiction Act 1860, Section 2 of which makes it an offence to engage in 'riotous, violent or indecent behaviour' on religious premises.[73] In 1981, the Law Commission considered whether the offence was still necessary and concluded that it was.[74] In particular the Law Commission noted the way in which the section has been used to prosecute behaviour which might not ordinarily reach the threshold of severity required for a public order offence, but which in the context is disruptive and offensive. An example from the case-law involves shouting a political message during a service.[75] It could also be used to cover acts of desecration, such as placing a pig's head in a mosque. The Law Commission recommended more tailored offences for these purposes.

Section 36 of the Offences against the Person Act 1861 contains a specific type of aggravated assault against clergymen and other ministers of religion in relation to their celebrating divine service or otherwise officiating in any church, chapel, meeting house or other place of divine worship, or performing their duty in the lawful burial of the dead. It would appear not to be used in practice, and it has been recommended for repeal by both the Criminal Law Revision Committee[76] and the Law Commission.[77] There are also other specific statutory offences in relation to disturbances in cemeteries, graveyards and burial grounds.[78]

Historically, it is questionable whether the common law offences of blasphemy and blasphemous libel were directed to protecting religious people as opposed to upholding the close association between the state and the established church. This offence survived into modern times, and continued to have an impact in areas such as film classification.[79] In spite of judicial attempts to justify its existence by reference to the avoidance of religious offence it continued to be closely connected with Christianity as maintained by the Church of England.[80] A majority of the Law Commission considered it that it should be abolished as an unjustified restriction on freedom of expression, while a minority considered that it should be reformulated to protect religious people more generally from offence. Its narrow historic formulation became a matter of grievance particularly for Muslims, but an initial attempt by the Government to introduce a more general offence of incitement to religious hatred in 2000 failed. Eventually such a law was passed,

73 Rivers, *The Law of Organized Religions,* supra note 8 at 153–155.

74 Law Commission, *Offences against Religion and Public Worship*, no. 145 (1985).

75 *Abrahams v. Cavey* [1968] 1 QB 479.

76 Fourteenth Report, *Offences against the Person*, Cmnd. 7844 (1980), paras. 179–180.

77 Fourteenth Report, *Offences against the Person*, supra note 76.

78 Cemeteries Clauses Act 1847, sec.59; Burial Laws Amendment Act 1880, sec.7.

79 See *Wingrove v. United Kingdom*, App. No. 17419/90, ECtHR, 22 October 1996.

80 *R v. Lemon* [1979] AC 617.

amid considerable public concern about its chilling effect on speech. This resulted in such a qualified offence that some commentators doubt whether it has any effect at all.[81] The old common law blasphemy offences were then quietly abolished.[82]

Finally, one should note the recent creation of 'religiously aggravated' offences,[83] brought about by expanding the existing category of racially aggravated offences. Assaults, criminal damage, lesser public order offences and harassment are aggravated, and thus attract more severe penalties, if they demonstrate or are motivated by hostility towards members of a religious group.[84]

Religious Liberty in the New Millennium

The wide-ranging constitutional reform agenda initiated by 'New Labour' after their election victory in 1997 included enhanced legal protection for human rights as well as a major extension of equality law. The European Convention on Human Rights, including its religion-relevant Articles 9, 14, as well as Article 2 First Protocol were given further effect by the Human Rights Act 1998. Protection against discrimination on grounds of religion in employment and occupation was enacted in 2003, and extended to the provision of goods and services in 2006. The rapidly growing body of equality law was codified in the Equality Act 2010, which also includes a positive duty on public authorities to promote equality including equality on grounds of religion.[85]

Even if these new rights are not expressed in a single codified document, with a status as higher law, and upheld by a Supreme Court, they do have quasi-constitutional status. The assumption that 'equality' is a human right of similar status to other civil and political rights is borne out not only by the fluid boundaries between European Convention equality cases and European Union equality cases, but also by the creation of a new single 'Equality and Human Rights Commission' with wide-ranging powers to investigate and remedy breaches of equality and human rights.

It is an open question whether the new legislation has had an impact on the historic understanding of religious liberty in English law. However, three relatively uncontentious observations may certainly be made. First, there has been a substantial increase in litigation involving questions of religion even up to

81 Public Order Act 1986, secs.29A–29N, as inserted by Racial and Religious Hatred Act 2006. See especially sec.29J.

82 Criminal Justice and Immigration Act 2008, sec.79.

83 Anti-Terrorism, Crime and Security Act 2001, sec.39.

84 Criminal Damage Act 1998, secs.28–32, as amended.

85 See L. Vickers, 'Promoting equality or fostering resentment? The public sector equality duty and religion and belief', 31 *Legal Studies* (2011), 135; J. Rivers, 'Promoting Religious Equality', 1 *Oxford Journal of Law and Religion* (2012), 386.

the highest judicial level. Recent cases have involved applications for asylum,[86] school admissions,[87] school transport,[88] school discipline,[89] school uniform requirements,[90] teacher dress codes,[91] Hindu sacred cows and funeral rites,[92] conscientious objection to same-sex partnerships,[93] faith-based welfare services,[94] foster parenting,[95] religious rest days and religious symbols in the workplace,[96] the appointment and dismissal of church ministers and workers,[97] funding and tax exemption of religious bodies,[98] noise pollution from religious services,[99] and religious arbitration.[100] Five of these cases are pending before the European Court of Human Rights.

The second observation is that religious individuals, organizations and their representatives have almost always lost when challenging secular bodies and that religious organizations have almost always lost when faced with claims by individuals. A crude hierarchy which nevertheless has good predictive power is emerging: state – individual – religion. The third observation is that judicial consideration of these problems shows a remarkable lack of historical awareness. As was pointed out in the introduction to this essay, religious litigation was rare in the period 1920–2000, and scholarship (with the partial exception of ecclesiastical law in the strict sense of the internal law of the Church of England) almost non-

86 *R (Ullah) v. Special Adjudicator* [2004] 2 AC 323.

87 *R(E) v. JFS Governing Body* [2010] 2 AC 728.

88 *R (R) v. Leeds City Council* [2005] EWHC 2495 (Admin).

89 *R (Williamson) v. Secretary of State for Education and Employment* [2005] 2 AC 246.

90 *R (Begum) v. Denbigh High School Governors* [2007] 1 AC 100; *R (Playfoot) v. Millais School Governing Body* [2007] EWHC 1698 (Admin); *R (Watkins-Singh) v. Aberdare Girls' High School Governors* [2008] EWHC 1865 (Admin).

91 *Azmi v. Kirklees MBC* [2007] I.C.R. 1154.

92 *R (Swami Suryananda) v. Welsh Ministers* [2007] EWCA Civ 893, *R (Ghai) v. Newcastle City Council [2011]* QB 591.

93 *Ladele v. Islington LBC* [2010] 1 WLR 955; *McFarlane v. Relate Avon Ltd* [2010] EWCA Civ 880.

94 *Catholic Care (Diocese of Leeds) v. Charity Commission for England and Wales* [2010] EWHC 520 (Ch).

95 *R (Johns) v. Derby City Council* [2011] EWHC 375 (Admin).

96 *Copsey v. WWB Devon Clays Ltd* [2005] ICR 1789; *Eweida v. British Airways plc* [2010] ICR 890; *Chaplin v. Royal Devon and Exeter Hospitals Trust* (unreported).

97 *R (Amicus) v. Secretary of State for Trade and Industry* [2007] ICR 1176; *Percy v. Church of Scotland Board of National Mission* [2006] 2 AC 28; *New Testament Church of God v. Stewart* [2008] ICR 282; *Reaney v. Bishop of Hereford* (unreported); *Moore v. President of the Methodist Conference* [2011] EWCA Civ 1581.

98 *Aston Cantlow and Wilmcote with Billesley PCC v. Wallbank* [2004] 1 AC 546; *Gallagher (Valuation Officer) v. The Church of Jesus Christ of Latter-day Saints* [2008] 1 AC 1852.

99 *R (Hackney LBC) v. Rottenburg* [2007] EWHC 166 (Admin).

100 *Jivraj v. Hashwani* [2011] 1 WLR 1872.

existent. In a common law jurisdiction in which the law is kept alive by litigation and academic commentary this makes the law vulnerable to fresh starts in ignorance of historic disputes and historic resolutions. It may well be that as a result religious liberty is starting to develop new contours less dominated by the tolerant and broadly even-handed extension to all religions of the legal position of established Christianity.

Particular features of these new contours would seem to be (1) a reduction in the autonomy of religious organizations as they become subject to the same regulatory oversight by the state as other private and commercial bodies. This is tangentially linked to the remarkably hostile public reaction to the Archbishop of Canterbury's suggestion that there may be some limited scope for the recognition of Islamic law.[101] There is one law, and it must apply to all. (2) An unwillingness to accommodate unconventional religious commitments in public and semi-public contexts, including the workplace. This is particularly obvious in relation to the new sexual ethic which approves of same-sex relationships. (3) The increasing subordination of religious groups working in education and welfare to a statist, rather than pluralist, conception of role and ethos. The conception of equality which is being enforced is univocal, and in cases of conflict between protected characteristics, religious liberty and equality is being subordinated to other interests.

Thus although religious liberty is still secure as a matter of private pursuit, the law may be coming to reflect an increasing intolerance of the public presence and status of religion on its own terms. Increasingly, the law seems to be trivializing the claims of religions and instead exalting its own secular ethos as a fundamental constitutional good.[102]

---

101 R. Williams, 'Civil and Religious Law in England: a Religious Perspective', 10 *Ecclesiastical Law Journal* (2008), 262. For more measured responses, see S. Bano, 'In Pursuit of Religious and Legal Diversity: A response to the Archbishop of Canterbury and the "Sharia Debate" in Britain', 10 *Ecclesiastical Law Journal* (2008), 283; and Lord Phillips of Worth Matravers, 'Equality before the Law', a speech given at the East London Muslim Centre on 3 July 2008, reproduced in various places including 161 *Law and Justice* (2008), 75; as well as many of the essays in R. Ahdar & N. Aroney (eds.), *Shari'a in the West* (Oxford: Oxford University Press, 2010).

102 For a more extended version of this argument, see J. Rivers, 'The Secularisation of the British Constitution', 14 *Ecclesiastical Law Journal* (2012), 371.

Chapter 17

Religious Equality in the Spanish Constitutional System[1]

Santiago Cañamares Arribas

Constitutional Framework

Before carrying out a case-by-case analysis of possible situations of religious discrimination that arguably are taking place in Spain, it is necessary to make a short reference to the Spanish constitutional framework of equality and religious freedom.

Article 14 of the Spanish Constitution states that all Spaniards are equal before the law, without any discrimination for reasons of birth, race, sex, religion, opinion, or any other personal or social conditions or circumstances.

It has been stated that Article 14 of the Constitution, in recognizing the equality of all before the law, contains three separate elements: First, it includes a substantial right that has a secondary or related nature, as it is always referred to when other rights are at issue; second, it includes a constitutional principle, related to the universality of the legal framework, which prohibits unequal legal treatment and demands that any exception must be subjected to a narrow interpretation; and finally, it operates as a limit to the actions of public authorities that prevents them from adopting rules or making decisions that may introduce inequalities.

Article 16 of the Spanish Constitution guarantees freedom of religion to individuals and groups, with no other restrictions on religious expression than those that may be necessary to maintain public order, as protected by law. Also, this article enshrines the principle of cooperation between religious denominations and the state, by saying that public authorities shall take into account the beliefs of the Spanish people and shall consequently maintain appropriate cooperative relations with the Catholic Church and other religious confessions. At this point, it is worth noting that although this article makes special mention of the Catholic Church, the Spanish doctrine has been largely understood, from the outset, to mean that this does not lead to religious discrimination, as it is only intended to

1 This chapter is the result of several Research Projects funded by the Spanish Ministry of Education (DER2008-05283), the Universidad Complutense funding program, and the Social, Legal and Humanistic Research Program of the Autonomous Community of Madrid P2007/HUM-0403.

show that religious minorities are able to obtain the same legal recognition as the largest religious denomination in Spain.[2]

Setting this clarification aside, the content of Article 16 of the Constitution has been developed by Organic Law 7/1980 on Religious Freedom.[3] Article 1 of this law includes a general provision regarding religious equality, stating that 'religious beliefs shall not occasion unequal or discriminatory treatment under the Law and that no one may be deprived of any occupation or activity or public positions or employment for reasons of religion.'

In analyzing the interaction of equality, as a principle, with the free exercise of religion, the Spanish Constitutional Court has stated that it is not possible to support any kind of discrimination or different legal treatment of citizens based on their ideology or belief, and that there should be an equal enjoyment of religious freedom for all citizens. Therefore, the religious attitudes of the subjects of law cannot justify different legal treatment.[4]

However, equality does not mean uniformity. As the Spanish Constitutional Court has stated, the application of this principle does not prevent public authorities from considering the different circumstances of every single situation in order to give a different legal treatment.[5]

As a consequence, it can be said that what the equality principle forbids is any different legal treatment that cannot be justified on a reasonable and objective basis. According to the doctrine established by the Spanish Constitutional Court in one of its very first decisions, 'Equality is breached only when the different treatment lacks an objective and reasonable justification'. The existence of such justification must be assessed in relation to the purpose and effect of the measure under consideration and by the application of a proportionality rule between the means employed and the aim sought to be realized.[6]

---

2 See, generally, P.-J. Viladrich and J. Ferrer, 'Los principios informadores del Derecho Eclesiástico español', in J. Ferrer (ed.), *Derecho Eclesiástico del Estado español* (Pamplona: EUNSA, 2007), 102.

3 The text of this law can be found only in Spanish in *Boletín Oficial del Estado* [hereinafter BOE] (State Official Bulletin) of 24 July 1980, available at http://www.boe.es (accessed 4 December 2012). According to Article 81 of the Spanish Constitution, organic acts are those relating to the implementation of fundamental rights and public liberties, those approving the Statutes of Autonomy and the general electoral system and other laws provided for in the Constitution. The approval, amendment or repeal of organic acts shall require the overall majority of the Members of Congress in a final vote on the bill as a whole.

4 See Constitutional Court Sentence 24/1982, 13 May 1982, at first statement as to the law.

5 See Constitutional Court Sentence 34/1981, 10 November 1981, at third statement as to the law.

6 See Constitutional Court Sentence 22/1981, 2 June 1981, at third statement as to the law. The content of this judgment follows the doctrine set out by the European Court of Human Rights in the Belgian Linguistic Cases *(Case relating to certain aspects of the laws on the use of languages in education in Belgium*, App. Nos. 1474/62, 1691/62, 1769/63, 1994/63,

Religious Discrimination Regarding the Individual Exercise of Religious Freedom

Throughout the next sections of this chapter, the principles referred to above will be applied, under a strict scrutiny standard, to some cases from the Spanish experience. These cases may be considered *prima facie* cases of discrimination. The analysis will focus separately on the cases referring to the individuals' free exercise and the cases relating to the collective dimension of religious freedom.

Accommodation of Religious Practices

Since 1980, when the Organic Law on Religious Freedom entered into force, Spanish society has undergone major social changes, which have been fostered primarily by the important role played by immigration. In fact, there have been many conflicts caused by the desire of the immigrants to exercise their religious freedom at the same level as the traditional majorities in the country.

One of the first questions that may arise when analyzing these free-exercise-of-religion conflicts from a legal perspective is whether the current Organic Law on Religious Freedom still provides an adequate solution to these new challenges. In my opinion, the answer should be in the affirmative, because of the broad character of the law itself, which allows the exercise of any religious manifestation, as long as all the limits established in Article 3 of the law are respected: the protection of public security, health, morals, and the rights and freedom of others.

In this sense, the doctrine of the Constitutional Court, according to which religious freedom 'guarantees the existence of an area of intellectual self-determination before the religious phenomenon, linked to the personality and individual dignity' is worth mentioning. Furthermore, 'this freedom ... also includes an external dimension of *agere licere* which empowers citizens to act in accordance with their own convictions and to sustain them before others'. More specifically, the external dimension of religious freedom deals with 'the possibility of exercise, without any coercion, of those activities that are manifestations or expressions of religious phenomenon'.[7]

2126/64, 23 July 1968). The European Court has subsequently upheld this doctrine in several decisions, including some regarding the free exercise of religion. See J. Martínez-Torrón, 'La Protección Internacional de la Libertad Religiosa', in *Tratado de Derecho Eclesiástico* (Pamplona: EUNSA, 1994), 229-237. For a more detailed analysis on the principle of equality in the case law of the Constitutional Court of Spain, see J. Calvo-Álvarez, *Los principios del Derecho Eclesiástico español en las sentencias del Tribunal Constitucional* (Pamplona: Navarra gráfica ediciones, 1999), 129-164; see also R. Rodríguez Chacón, *El Factor Religioso ante el Tribunal Constitucional* (Departamento de Derecho Eclesiastico del Estado de la Facultad de Derecho de la U.C. de Madrid, 1992), 33–38.

7 See Spanish Constitutional Court sentence 177/1996, 11 November 1996, at ninth statement as to the law. See also from the same Court its sentence 46/2001, 15 February 2001, at forth statement as to the law.

However, when turning to a more specific analysis, it can be observed that the Spanish administrative bodies and the judiciary have not given a uniform response concerning the conflicts regarding the individual free exercise of religion. Furthermore, they have been reluctant to apply a strict scrutiny standard in order to guarantee that any burden on religious freedom is justified in the pursuit of a compelling interest.

In order to clarify my position, some recent examples may be provided. In April 2010, the educational authorities of the Autonomous Community of Madrid had to solve a major conflict when a Muslim girl, who was attending a public secondary school, decided to cover her head with the Islamic veil. The School Council informed her that the internal rules forbade any clothes covering the head and, therefore, she was forced to choose between observing the school norms or following her religious commitments. The school's decision banning the wearing of the headscarf was appealed before the Board of Education of the Autonomous Community of Madrid. That body decided to respect the school's autonomy by transferring the Muslim girl to a second educational center, the internal rules of which had no provisions regarding the student's attire. However, once the resolution of the Board of Education was delivered, the School Council of the second secondary school decided to amend its internal regulations to prohibit the wearing of head garments. The Board of Education decided to respect the decision of this second school by providing the Muslim student with a third public school, where the use of the Islamic headscarves was allowed.

From my own perspective, there were, in this conflict, different instances of indirect and direct discrimination. There is little doubt that, in the first case, the existence of a general rule prohibiting pieces of clothing from covering the head caused an indirect burden to the girl's religious freedom. However, the second case can be regarded as a case of direct discrimination, given that the school authorities suddenly decided to modify their internal rules in order to prevent the student from attending her classes due to the use of the Islamic headscarf.

It is obvious that the Board of Education of Madrid, when it decided twice to send the student to a different public educational center, did not apply a strict scrutiny standard. Otherwise, it would have decided, after considering whether or not the decisions of the educative centers placed heavy burdens on her free exercise of religion and whether the decisions aimed to achieve compelling educational interests, to accommodate the religious tenets of the student.

When deciding on the accommodation of individual, religiously-based practices, the strict scrutiny standard has not been followed by the judiciary at all times. For instance, the Superior Court of Justice of Baleares, in its ruling of 9 September 2002, recognized that the religious beliefs of a driver from a municipal bus company in Palma de Mallorca, who started to cover his head with a cap while at work because of his Jewish convictions, should be accommodated.[8] This is one

8 See S. Cañamares Arribas, 'Religious symbols in Spain: a legal perspective', in 11 *Ecclesiastical Law Journal* 2 (2009), 181, 186. For a more detailed exposition on the use

of the few cases in which Spanish courts have applied strict scrutiny in religious matters. However, in a decision regarding the observance of religious holidays, the Constitutional Court, in its Judgment 19/1985 of 13 February, stated that the employer was not required to accommodate the beliefs of an employee belonging to the Seventh-day Adventist Church, who demanded a right to observe the Sabbath.[9] Finally, and setting aside the labor environment, the National Audience, in a 2008 ruling, denied the authorization requested by a registered religious denomination, the Church of the Holy Daime in Spain. It was denied authorization for using *ayahuasca* in its religious ceremonies, according to a general regulation that prohibited its use due to its high toxicity.[10]

Considering that the Spanish courts have not been able to state a uniform criterion to be applied across these kinds of conflicts, it might be useful to consider the inclusion of a general provision in the Spanish legal system that could serve as a guideline to protect the free exercise of religion from disparate treatments that are not justified on an objective and reasonable basis.

Arguably, a suitable reference for confronting this issue could be the EU Council Directive 2000/78/EC, November 27, which provides a general framework for equal treatment in employment and occupation.[11] Article 2 of the Directive states that the 'principle of equal treatment' shall mean that there shall be no direct or indirect discrimination on, among others, religious grounds. It is interesting to note that the Directive defines 'indirect discrimination' as an apparently neutral provision, criterion, or practice that would put persons having a particular religion or belief at a particular disadvantage when compared with other persons. The European regulation establishes that any provision of this kind should be considered illegal unless that provision is objectively justified by a legitimate aim and the means for achieving that aim are appropriate and necessary.[12]

---

of religious clothing in Spain, see generally S. Cañamares, *Libertad religiosa, simbología y laicidad del Estado* (Navarra: Thomson-Aranzadi, 2005), 56; see also J. Rossell Granados, 'Improcedencia de sanción laboral por uso de vestimenta religiosa', in 1 *Aranzadi Social* (2003), 2809–2812.

9 See third statement as to the law. The 1992 agreement between the state and the Spanish Federation of Evangelical Religious Entities and the accommodates Protestant entities, such as the Seventh-day Adventists, that celebrate Saturday as the Sabbath, by giving them Friday afternoon off from work with pay to prepare for the Sabbath.

10 For a detailed analysis on the content of this judgment form a comparative perspective, see S. Cañamares Arribas, 'La importación y uso de sustancias alucinógenas para el culto en perspectiva comparada. ¿Desfile de los horrores o libre ejercicio de la Religión?' in 25 *Anuario de derecho eclesiástico del Estado* (2009), 177–201.

11 The text of this Directive can be found in the *Official Journal of the European Communities*, 2 December 2000.

12 Moreover, a general provision of this type is also embedded in the US Religious Freedom Restoration Act, which had been passed by the Federal Congress in 1993 in order to enshrine the doctrine set out by the US Supreme Court in *Sherbert* (*Sherbert v. Verner*, 374 US 398 (1963)) and in other cases related to the free exercise of religion in which a

Religious Assistance in Public Centers

The Spanish Constitutional Court has stated on a regular basis that religious freedom encompasses an external dimension of *agere licere*, which can be exercised with full immunity from coercion, even in situations where the individual is under a state's special subjection. However, making the free exercise of religion under the special circumstances of incarceration effective certainly requires the state to enable the inmates to receive spiritual assistance from their own religious denominations.

The development, through secondary legislation, of the Organic Law of Religious Freedom has given rise to some situations of religious discrimination, as the provisions relating to religious assistance have been embedded mainly in the 1992 cooperation agreements, signed between the State and religious minorities.[13] This legal framework has led to a gross misunderstanding of the nature of religious assistance.

In my opinion, in the Spanish experience, religious assistance has been considered, to a certain extent, mainly a consequence of the cooperation principle enshrined in Article 16.3 of the Spanish Constitution. This has led to the provision of spiritual support only to those inmates who are members of a religious denomination with a cooperation agreement. However, it should be emphasized that the right to receive spiritual assistance from one's own confession is above all an inherent aspect of the free exercise of religion, which demands a cooperative attitude on the part of public authorities.

Moreover, it should be noted that the 1992 agreements have not included—strictly speaking—a system of state cooperation in this matter.[14] They have simply

---

strict scrutiny standard was applied. The text of the act is available at http://www4.law.cornell.edu/uscode/42/ch21B.html (accessed 4 December2012).

13 So far, the Spanish Government has signed three cooperation agreements with religious minorities that have been passed as ordinary laws by the Congress: Law 24/1992, 10 November, passing the Cooperation Agreement with the Spanish Federation of Evangelical Religious Entities; Law 25/1992, 10 November passing the Cooperation Agreement with the Federation of Jewish Communities; Law 26/1992, 10 November, passing the Cooperation Agreement with the Islamic Commission of Spain. All of them were published in BOE, 12 November 1992, available at http://www.boe.es (accessed 4 December 2012).

14 For instance, Article 8 of the Cooperation Agreement signed with the Islamic Commission of Spain states in relevant part: '3. Islamic religious services shall be rendered by ministers designated by the imams or persons designated on a regular basis by the Islamic Communities belonging to the Islamic Commission of Spain and authorized by Army commanders, who shall lend such aid as needed so they can perform their duties on the same footing as the clergy of other Churches, faiths or communities that have signed Co-operation Agreements with the State.' Article 9 deals with the religious assistance other public centers by saying: 'The right to spiritual support is hereby guaranteed for all persons committed to penitentiaries, hospitals, social service or other analogous public institutions, provided by imams or persons designated by the communities, subject to authorization by the corresponding administrative bodies.'

made more explicit certain aspects of religious liberty that are already protected on a constitutional and legislative basis.[15] In fact, these instruments only provide a free entry model of religious assistance in favor of religious ministers of each religious denomination. This model can hardly be labeled as a real system of state and religious cooperation since it has not been adopted by taking into consideration the needs and characters of each religious institution.

Given that religious assistance is a fundamental element of religious freedom, its individual exercise cannot be dependent upon the previous signature of a cooperation agreement with the State, as this would lead to religious discrimination.[16]

Setting this aside, it should be pointed out that the current Spanish legislation on armed forces and prisons has offered religious assistance to every individual who belongs to any registered denomination, irrespective of any other requirements. For instance, Law 39/2007, on Military Careers,[17] stipulates in its Eighth Additional Disposition that those who do not belong to a religious denomination with a cooperation agreement can also receive religious assistance in accordance with general legal provisions. The crucial issue here is that there has been no subsequent development of this provision and, therefore, from a practical perspective, it is difficult to conclude that the content of the Additional Disposition can be applied. So far, only religious assistance to Catholic members of the military, as provided for in the 1979 Agreement on Religious Assistance in the Armed Forces,[18] has been developed through the Royal Decree 1145/1990, 7 September, which established a Religious Assistance Service in the Armed Forces.[19]

At any rate, in order to avoid any possible discrimination on religious grounds in this field, it would be helpful to include a more explicit provision for religious assistance in the Spanish Organic Law on Religious Freedom. This provision would be aimed to guarantee every individual the right to receive religious assistance in situations constituting a special relationship with the State. As this regulation would be intended as a general rule, it could only envisage a free entry model for ministers of registered religious denominations, which could only be restricted for extremely important reasons relating to the proper functioning of the public institution.

---

15 See J. Martínez-Torrón, *Separatismo y cooperación en los acuerdos del Estado con las minorías religiosas* (Granada: Editorial Comares, 1994),139–159.

16 In similar terms, see M. López Alarcón, 'Asistencia religiosa', in J. Ferrer (ed.), *Derecho eclesiástico del Estado español* (Pamplona: EUNSA, 2007), 251.

17 Law 39/2007, 19 November 2007. Text in BOE, 20 November 2007, available at http://www.boe.es (accessed 4 December 2012).

18 Article I of this Agreement states as follows: 'Religious and pastoral assistance to Catholic members of the Armed Forces shall continue to be provided by the Military Vicariate.'

19 See BOE, 21 September 1990, at http://www.boe.es (accessed 4 December 2012).

Religious Discrimination Regarding the Collective Exercise of Religious Freedom

Equality and Legal Personality of Religious Entities

In my opinion, the discrimination cases that have come up in the realm of the Spanish experience are the result of the lack of harmonization between the different regulations at stake. Indeed, the Organic Law on Religious Freedom declares in its Article 5 that 'Churches, Faiths and Religious Communities and their Federations shall acquire legal personality once registered in the corresponding public Registry created for this purpose and kept in the Ministry of Justice.' Furthermore, its Article 6.2 states that 'Churches, Faiths and Religious Communities may create and promote, for the accomplishment of their purposes, Associations, Foundations and Institutions, pursuant to the provision of ordinary legislation.' This provision means that some institutions created by the Churches themselves are not ruled by the Organic Law on Religious Freedom, but by general regulations that are applicable to all different legal entities.

However, the Royal Decree 142/1981, on the Registry of Religious Entities,[20] allows the registration of Orders and Religious Congregations alongside associations that Churches may create, but it does not make any reference to religious foundations. The Agreement on Legal Affairs, signed by the Spanish Kingdom and the Holy See on 3 January 1979, on the other hand, had declared in its Article I that foundations created by the Catholic Church could acquire legal personality by registering in the corresponding State Registry. Commentators agree that this Registry could not be different from the special Registry of Religious Entities that was created later on by the Organic Law on Religious Freedom.[21]

In order to respect the content of the 1979 Church-State Agreement, the Spanish Government approved Royal Decree 589/1984, dealing with the inclusion of the religious foundations created by the Catholic Church, or its subordinate institutions, in the Registry created by the Organic Law on Religious Freedom.[22] However, for the time being, there has been no development through secondary legislation that would lead to the admission in the Registry of Religious Entities of those foundations that may be created by other religious denominations. Following the Constitutional Court doctrine, it should be born in mind that inclusion in the Registry of Religious Entities provides these groups with more organizational autonomy under the provisions of Article 6.1 of the Organic Law on Religious Freedom than the autonomy which they would have achieved in compliance with

20 Text published in BOE, 31 January 1981, available at http://www.boe.es (accessed 4 December 2012).

21 See J. Mantecón, 'Confesiones religiosas y Registro', in *La libertad religiosa en España a los veinte años de su ley orgánica* (Madrid: Ministerio de Justicia, 1992), 82.

22 See BOE 28 March 1985, available at http://www.boe.es (accessed 4 December 2012).

the General Registry of Legal Persons.[23] From this perspective, the unification of rules would be desirable, as this would contribute towards the equality of different religious bodies. All religious foundations would achieve the same level of autonomy by acquiring the same legal status. To be honest, the current legal framework implies a difference of treatment, which hardly can be justified in an objective and reasonable manner.

Religious Equality and Church Financing

As already mentioned, the Spanish Constitution enshrines in its Article 16.3 a cooperation principle between the State and religious denominations. Such cooperation can be implemented in many areas of common interest, including financial matters. In fact, the Organic Law on Religious Freedom refers to financial cooperation, saying in its Article 7.2 that 'subject to the principle of equality, the Agreements between the State and religious communities may confer upon Churches, Faiths or Religious Communities the tax benefits applied by ordinary legislation to nonprofit Entities and other charitable organizations.' From a practical perspective, however, this provision has led to limiting state economic cooperation only to those denominations that have signed a cooperation agreement.

It is worth noting that, in the Spanish system of church financing, two different models can be found. On the one hand, there is direct cooperation, which has been for a long time exclusively reserved to the Catholic Church; and, on the other hand, there is indirect cooperation, which can be enjoyed by all religious denominations, as long as it is included in their agreements.

Many Spanish commentators have emphasized that limiting direct financing to the Catholic Church is not discriminatory, since other religious denominations with cooperation agreements have rejected this model.[24] However, Protestants have recently declared their desire to join the direct funding system,[25] although other religious denominations, especially the Jewish community, remain reluctant.

23 See Constitutional Court Sentence 46/2001, 15 February 2001, at statement as to the law 7.

24 In fact, religious minorities had decided not to join this direct financing because of two reasons. First, they considered that the direct financing system established in the 1979 Economical Agreement between the Catholic Church and the State had a temporary nature, since its Article II.5 highlights the Catholic Church's intention to raise its own sufficient funds in due course. On the other hand, these religious minorities considered that the total amount they had received from the State would have been drastically reduced because of their small membership. See S. Meseguer Velasco, 'A propósito de la reforma del sistema de asignación tributaria: hacia el sostenimiento económico de las confesiones religiosas', in 22 *Revista General de Derecho Canónico y Eclesiástico del Estado* (2010), available at http://www.iustel.com/v2/revistas/detalle_revista.asp?id=2 (accessed 4 December 2012).

25 On this topic, see the documents 'Negociación del Ministerio de Justicia con evangélicos, judíos y musulmanes sobre un sistema de financiación similar a la de la Iglesia Católica' and 'Acuerdo de las Iglesias de FEREDE'. Both documents are available at the

In addition to this, it should be pointed out that, in 2004, the Spanish Government created a public foundation, 'Fundación Pluralismo y Convivencia', aimed at giving financial support to all the religious groups that have been recognized by the public administration as 'well-known roots', excluding the Catholic Church.[26]

Actually, the direct financial cooperation enjoyed by the Catholic Church and that enjoyed by religious minorities are very different from each other. For the Catholic Church, the 1979 Financial Agreement established a tax allocation model, by which taxpayers decide whether or not to support the Catholic Church by allocating a small percentage of their income tax (0.7%) to the Church. On the other hand, for religious minorities, the foundation, 'Fundación Pluralismo y Convivencia', allocates funds to support activities and projects of a cultural or educational character, in order to foster the social integration of those faiths that have been recognized as 'well-known roots'.[27]

Irrespective of this recent solution, the equality principle binds public authorities to provide religious minorities with the same tax allocation system as the Catholic Church, when there is no objective and reasonable justification that allows public authorities to act differently.[28] The model of direct financial cooperation through a public foundation, as found in the Spanish legal framework, does not resolve the inequalities of church financing, since both the Catholic Church, the largest denomination in Spain, and religious denominations that have not been recognized as 'well-known roots' are outside the scope of this framework.

In relation to indirect church financing, it should be noted that both the Catholic Church and religious minorities with a cooperation agreement enjoy the same tax benefits. All of them are acknowledged by the government through their respective agreements. Moreover, these agreement documents grant tax

---

web site of the Observatorio delle libertà ed istituzioni religiose, http://www.olir.it/news/archivio.php?id=1219 (accessed 4 December 2012).

26 See M. J. Ciáurriz, 'La fundación pluralismo y convivencia', in A.-C. Álvarez Cortina and M. Rodríguez Blanco (eds.), *Aspectos del régimen económico y patrimonial de las confesiones religiosas* (Granada: Editorial Comares SL, 2008), 105-122.

27 Until now the Spanish Government has granted the recognition of 'well-known roots' in addition to those religious denominations that have signed a cooperation agreement, to The Church of Jesus Christ of Latter-day Saints (Mormon), Jehovah's Witnesses, and the Spanish Federation of Buddhist Communities. For a more detailed analysis on this topic See S. Cañamares and R. Palomino, 'Recent development of Church financing in Spain', in M. Moravčíková and E. Valová (eds.), *Financing Churches and Religious Societies in the 21st Century* (Bratislava: Institute for State-Church Relations, 2009).

28 See *Alujer Fernández and Caballero García v. Spain,* App. No. 53072/99 (Inadmissible), 14 June 2001 (page 7), where the Court stated that 'the conclusion of agreements between the State and a particular Church establishing a special tax regime in favour of the latter does not, in principle, contravene the requirements of Articles 9 and 14 of the Convention, provided that there is an objective and reasonable justification for the difference in treatment and that similar agreements may be entered into by other churches wishing to do so.'

benefits to other charitable entities owned by the religious confessions. In this regard, it is important to emphasize that the 1992 Agreements declare, in Article 11.5, that each religious denomination and its member communities, as well as its associations and entities devoted to charitable activities, shall be entitled to all other tax benefits granted by the Spanish tax legal framework, both for non-profit organizations and for private charitable organizations.

The current regulation of this discipline is contained in Law 49/2002, 23 December, on the tax scheme of non-profit entities and tax incentives for patronage.[29] The regulation's Ninth Additional Disposition extends the fiscal benefits granted to non-profit organizations to those churches referred to above and their charitable organizations. As a result, they can enjoy a more favorable system of tax exemptions than the ones granted in their respective agreements.[30]

Spanish legal scholars have declared that the tax benefits granted to non-profit organizations are clearly justifiable, because these institutions must be compensated for their activities in fields of public interest. In similar terms, the public funding of churches is justified on a different ground: the fostering of the individual's free exercise of religion, which is the result of granting financial support to the churches to which the individuals belong.[31]

From this general perspective, it seems clear that restricting public funding to those entities that have signed a cooperation agreement is not acceptable under the equality principle. It is hardly justifiable according to an objective and reasonable standard. Therefore, in order to avoid potential harms to religious equality, it is

29 See BOE, 24 December 2002, available at http://www.boe.es (accessed 4 December 2012).

30 Furthermore, the Eighth Additional Disposition of the same law has also rendered applicable the privileged fiscal regime to those foundations of the Catholic Church which are registered in the Religious Entities Registry. Obviously, there is no discrimination at this point between the Catholic Church and other religious groups because this regime is also applicable to those foundations created by any religious denomination regardless of further requirements, as long as they had acquired legal personality through their inscription in the General Registry of Foundations.

31 See A. Motilla, 'Confesiones religiosas y entidades sin fin de lucro (Comparación de su régimen económico)', in M. Rodríguez Blanco (ed.), *Aspectos del régimen económico y patrimonial de las confesiones religiosas* (Granada: Editorial Comares, 2007, 13). Futhermore, as it has been observed, religion is appreciated as a positive social phenomenon. It is primarily considered a reality that contributes more to the improvement of society than to conflict or social concern (although, sometimes, some religions are conflictive). This perception is based on the fact that institutionalized religions, in addition to expressing the exercise of a fundamental right, actually play a positive role in society, which is visible in different domains. See J. Martínez-Torrón, 'Religious Freedom and Democratic Change in Spain', *Brigham Young University Law Review* (2006), 777, 790. See also, generally, R. Navarro-Valls, 'Justicia constitucional y factor religioso', in J. Martínez-Torrón (ed.), *La libertad religiosa y de conciencia ante la justicia constitucional* (Granada: Editorial Comares, 1998), 25–38.

advisable to modify the current framework contained in Article 7.2 of the Spanish Law on Religious Freedom.

Final Remarks

When analyzing the Spanish experiences in religious equality under a strict scrutiny standard, some instances of religious discrimination can be perceived at both levels of the free exercise of religion: individual and collective.

Considering that all public authorities are bound by the fundamental rights enshrined in the Spanish Constitution, it is obvious that the legislature must carry out amendments, which are necessary to achieve a greater equality in the free exercise of religion within the Spanish legal framework. This need to amend goes even beyond amending those laws referred to throughout these pages, which have introduced discriminatory practices. Above all, it demands the adoption of a clear criterion to solve all the conflicts related to the free exercise of religion. The adoption of such a pattern should lead both the administrative authorities and the judiciary to apply a strict scrutiny standard when resolving conflicts, in order to enable the priority of religious freedom over other interests. The only exception acceptable in those cases should be when the public authorities show a compelling interest in applying a general rule. In those cases, it must be guaranteed that the religious freedom restrictions shall have the minimum possible impairment.

There is no doubt that the Spanish Organic Law on Religious Freedom, which came into force more than thirty years ago, remains, in general terms, a valid law, but it can be improved in particular areas for the sake of religious freedom.

PART III
Open Issues

Chapter 18
Freedom of Religion and Freedom of Speech in the French Case Law: A Constitutional Dilemma

Alain Garay

> 'No one shall be disquieted on account of his opinions, including his religious views, provided their manifestation does not disturb the public order established by law.'
>
> Article 10, Declaration of the Rights of Man and of the Citizen
> Paris, 26 August 1789

Introduction

In a democratic society, the individual, at the heart of the tensions, in the name of his religious beliefs or his status as a mass media professional, claims his right to the exercise of freedoms. This claim is made in the lawsuits that take on the form of proceedings and litigation in national or international courts. The litigious logic that is initially beyond the reach of both the man of faith and the media professional constitutes an even more significant challenge in a litigious society.[1]

The legal relationships that link the 'media' and the 'religions' have been the object of few studies, and those that exist often deal only with the social status of the actors, their respective strategies of influence and the tools used to inform and communicate with the actors involved.[2] This study takes the French legal experience

---

1 Extract from the *Problématique* selected by the organizers of the National Colloquium 'Liberté des *médias* et *Liberté* de *convictions religieuses'*, Aix-en-Provence, 4–5 June 2004 (Université Paul Cézanne Aix-Marseille III).

2 See the program of the International Colloquium 'Les Eglises et les médias de masse – Ecclesiarum modus communicandi', organized 16–17 April 1993 at Université d'Aix-Marseille III, which included the 'frameworks of religious information (semiological, moral and canonical aspects)'; institutional communication in 'the Church'; religious broadcasts on public television, etc. See also the proceedings of the French-Italian Colloquium in Rome 20–21 March 1998 on the topic 'Churches and Mass Media, Doctrine and Law', published in *Année Canonique* XLI (1999). See also H. Tincq and G. Defois, *Les médias et l'Eglise. Evangélisation et information: le conflit de deux paroles* (Paris: Éditions CFPJ, 1997), which includes chapters titled 'La vérité en débat' and 'Un couple explosif' (bibliography on page

as a mere example of the great difficulty associated with ensuring a balance between democratic freedoms and obligations, even in a state under the rule of law.

There is a need for more studies on the state of the relationships in question as, when tensions arise, they may be submitted to the control of the courts, especially if statements of a defamatory or slanderous nature have been made.[3] Such situations threaten both personal and personality rights,[4] the right to respect of so-called religious beliefs or feelings, rights that are not related solely to questions of defamation or slander. Indeed, legal protection against attacks on religious beliefs is not limited merely to legal frameworks for defamation or slander.[5] Other bodies of legislation related to provocation, hatred or discrimination based on religious affiliation may also apply.

In the face of the 'Internet Revolution', the freedom of communication of opinions which, for the French Constitutional Council, is a fundamental principle recognized by the laws of the Republic (verdict of 27 July 1982), continues to the basis of protection of defamed or slandered religious beliefs, pursuant to the provisions of Article 10 of the Declaration of the Rights of Man and of the Citizen (DRMC). In fact, Article 11 of the Declaration of the Rights of Man and of the Citizen subordinates 'the free communication of ideas and opinions' to the punishment of 'abuses of this freedom as shall be defined by law'. Thus, the French Law on the Freedom of the Press of 29 July 1881 provided for legal protection, instruction and the repression of such abuses related to defamatory or slanderous statements. Moreover, the legal framework for the repression of abuses gives judges in emergency proceedings (Article 809 of the New Civil Code) powers of preservation and restoration in order to 'prevent impending harm, or to stop manifestly unlawful harassment'.[6]

An anti-clerical heritage, the struggles for democratic emancipation in a country marked by a history of a certain kind of secular and religious censure, and the satirical tradition[7] explain the contemporary popularity of defamatory or

156); J.-P. Willaime and P. Bréchon, *Médias et religions en miroir* (Paris: Presses Universitaires de France, 2000). See also the report by M. Rizzon, *La communication religieuse en France: des médias traditionnels à Internet* (Institut d'Études Politiques d'Aix-en-Provence: Travaux Universitaires Inédits de Science Politique, 2001), N° 769.

3 A. Lacabarats, 'La *juge* et la laïcité: le *droit au respect des croyances*', *Les petites affiches* (3 October 1997).

4 See *La protection de la personne face aux madias*, special edition of *Gazette du palais* (2–6 September 1994), which contains some useful reflections by specialist authorities (judges and lawyers).

5 M. Louvet, '*Liberté d'expression et respect des croyances*', *140 Légipresse* (April 1997), 49 et seq.

6 P. Bertin, 'Le *juge des référés, protecteur des croyants*', 2 *Gazette du palais* (1984), doc. 534.

7 The boom in reality television programming show that a note of mockery is an indispensable ingredient in the arenas of confrontation: rumors, furious replies, tensions expressed in the form of insults. Television has been able to establish gossip as a rule of

slanderous accusations. But the subtlety and extremely complex nature of press law considerably reduce the possibilities for action open to people who consider themselves defamed or slandered. Such restrictions are all the more regrettable considering that, as a general rule, defamation and slander of religious beliefs are inscribed in dynamics of denial of beliefs that could lead to acts characterized by antisemitism, Islamophobia,[8] and other forms of systematic intolerance.[9]

The choice of topic for this study was partly inspired by the observation that the denial of freedoms, both those of the mass media and those associated with religious beliefs, is the product of the proliferation of written texts and defamatory and slanderous language of all kinds, both punished and unpunished, all published in the name of public information.

The courtroom is the arena of confrontation between legal standards and the weighing of democratic values: on the one hand, respect for the rules of a fair trial, and on the other, respect and protection of religious feelings.[10] Is this a brick wall keeping out the democratic 'watchdogs' of the mass media, or a cardboard shield against media agendas and incisive and troublesome research journalism? It is neither one nor the other, but both at the same time, insofar as the judicial process offers very limited protection of religious beliefs, but in a way favors the structuring and legitimacy of religious beliefs in the democratic public arena.

The Judicial Framework Offers Limited Protection of Religious Beliefs from the Perspective of Process and Redress for 'Media Harassment'

The French judge Jean-Yves Monfort explains that 'press law is a balancing act between two contrary demands: one on side, the right to say anything and the right of the public to know everything; on the other side, the imperatives of public order, the legitimate right of each citizen not to have his honor or reputation attacked,

---

communication. The spiral of denigration hits rock bottom in these kinds of programs, in which betrayal is legitimized as prime-time entertainment.

8 See the report by the High Commissioner for Human Rights presented to the UN Economic and Social Council's Commission on Human Rights on 19 February 2004 (E/CN.4/2004/16), *Racism, Racial Discrimination, Xenophobia and All Forms of Discrimination – Combating Defamation of Religions*. See also the report of 23 December 2004 on the *Situation of Muslim and Arab Peoples in Various Parts of the World* presented by M. Doudou Diène, the Special Rapporteur on contemporary forms of racism, racial discrimination, xenophobia and related intolerance, UN Human Rights Commission (E/CN.4/2005/19); see especially the extensive bibliography presented in the report.

9 A. Garay, '*Quels moyens de défense et de protection des faits religieux*? La situation en France', in E. Poulat, D. Kounkou (eds.), *Les discriminations religieuses en France: situation à partir des églises* (Paris: L'Harmattan, Coll. *Théologie et vie politique de la terre*, 2004).

10 T. Massis, 'La liberté de conscience, le sentiment religieux et le droit penal', *Receuil Dalloz* (1992), 113 et seq.

the right to have his character respected.'[11] The press process, highly technical and extremely formal, is in itself a 'process within a process'.

Some people believe that the legal right of response established under Article 13 of the French Law on Freedom of the Press of 29 July 1881 should be able to be exercised before an action for defamation or slander is brought before the courts. Believers or their institutions may therefore consider it sufficient to make a simple demand to publish an article in response to an accusation. In fact, many confuse the right to demand publication of an article as a 'simple response' or a 'reaction' that is offered in exceptional conditions with the right to seek a legal remedy as provided in Article 13, which responds to legal conditions of form and substance.[12] On the one hand, the 'right of response' is part of the protection not only of the person, but also of the personality.[13] On the other hand, the exercise of the right of response does not constitute 'a free an open forum that the newspaper cannot evade'.[14] The practice of publishing a response pursuant to Article 13 does not eliminate the possibility of an action for covert defamation. Therein lies the difficulty associated with seeking such a remedy, the punishment for which would be the rejection or silence of the mass media.[15]

Suing the perpetrator of a press-related crime is never an easy task. The merits of the case are established on the basis of symbolic and technical dimensions. The symbolic dimension is the assessment of the direct and indirect effects of the attack on the victim's character, honor and reputation. But how can such an attack be assessed objectively, given that it involves an element as subjective as morality? The technical dimension involves the determination of the defamatory or slanderous nature of the attack, which does not have the same legal basis. Men and women of faith rarely have the skills necessary to answer these symbolic and technical questions on their own. When should a court action be filed? To weigh

---

11 J-Y Monfort, 'Le droit de réponse', *Gazette du palais* (23–24 May 1997), 28.

12 Along with the following conditions, among others: statute of limitations; terms and size of the response; defense of the personality and not only of the person, which 1) must have been accused specifically, and 2) for whom the desired response is limited to the defense of this personality; strictly personal exercise of this right which cannot be entrusted to a third party; the content of the response cannot exceed the strictly limited scope of the accusation (criterion of appropriateness and relevance of the response); protection of the public order and common decency, protection from attacks against the legitimate interests of third parties or the honor of the journalists. Montfort, 'Le droit de réponse', *Gazette du palais* (23–24 May 1997), 28 et seq.

13 C. Bigot, *'Protection des droits de la personnalité* et *liberté de l'information'* *Recueil Dalloz* (1998), 235 et seq.

14 Paris Trial Court, 1st Chamber, 15 January 1997. See J.-P. Lévy, '*Pratique* du *droit de réponse dans la presse écrite et la communication audiovisuelle'*, in J.-Y. Dupeux and A. Lacabarats (eds.), *Liberté de la presse et droits de la personne: Thèmes et commentaires* (Paris: Dalloz, 1997), 31–35.

15 Y. Mayaud, 'L'*abus de droit* en matière de *droit de reponse'*, in Dupeux and A. Lacabarats (eds.), *Liberté de la presse et droits de la personne*, 5–16.

up the costs and benefits is a matter of delicate evaluation, but here the uncertainty brings an element of anxiety into the equation.

To pursue a remedy pursuant to press law requires a good dose of professionalism that is often the exclusive property of press group legal specialists seasoned in the 'procedural mysteries' and familiar with the press office hearing room of the Trial Court of Paris. As a result, in this case, the choice of professional assistance is a determining factor.

The 'Press Law' System: A Framework that Enshrines the Control of the Mass Media and Journalists over Believers?

The narrowly technical and formalist aspects of press law constitute barriers of adversity for the layperson. Believers, sensitive to religious discourse on resignation, indulgence or forgiveness, may also see there instruments of ideological control. Indeed, in the best of cases, the mass media are criticized, and, in the worst, demonized in the context of the discourse of denunciation of contemporary forms of spiritual conditioning. The criticism of the *prêt-à-porter ideologique* is thus aimed at the mass media, which are determined to confuse container and contents[16] for their own benefit. It often proves extremely hard to analyze the determination of the legal definition of the attack – defamation or slander pursuant to Article 29 of the Law of 1881. For the layperson, the question of classifying the charges somehow constitutes a 'mystery', which the case law has been able to clarify only with great effort. Thus, for the 2nd Civil Division of the Court of Appeals, pursuant to Article 29, paragraph 1, and Article 32 of the Law of 1881, any statement that contains an accusation of a specific and exact nature, which attacks the honor or reputation of the person at whom it is directed, constitutes defamation, even if it is presented in a subtle or doubtful way or through insinuation.[17]

In this respect, what is an 'accusation or claim of a specific nature'? What distinction needs to be made between insulting language or pejorative, adversarial, hostile words, and defamatory or slanderous statements? It is hard to draw the line between them. Detailed and precise analysis of the content of the terms, in accordance with the context, is essential.[18]

16 See the report 'Médias et contrôle des esprits', *Le Monde Diplomatique* (*Manière de voir* no. 27). See also the studies published by A. Accardo, G. Abou, G. Balbastre and D. Marine, *Journalistes au quotidien : Outils pour une socioanalyse des pratiques journalistiques* (Bordeaux: Le Mascaret, 1995); D. Cornu, *Journalisme et vérité: L' éthique de l'information au défi du changement médiatique* (Geneva: Labor et Fides, Coll. *L'Éthique,* 1994); and A. Freund, *Journalisme et mésinformation* (Paris: *Pensée sauvage*, 1991).

17 'Les *Témoins de Jéhovah* de France c. R. *Pflimlin* et F. *Laffon' (*11 December 2003), 210 *Légipresse* (April 2004).

18 Similarly, for the 2nd Civil Division, 'the judgment should be overturned when, to dismiss an association's action for defamation, it is argued that the claim that this

The jurisprudential methodological process requires that the conditions of proof be met. First of all, it falls upon the victim of the defamation to provide proof of the defamatory statements as quickly as possible, and, ultimately, to plead good faith. The first element is objective; the second is imprecise and evolutionary. The 'good faith' of a defamer or slanderer mainly involves a combination of some of the four following elements: the legitimacy of the aim persued, the absence of personal animosity, prudence and restraint in the expression and the seriousness/reliability of the research. It is wise to measure the relative ease of pleading 'good faith' through a wide range of methods: returning to previously published articles, the existence of a local controversy or a national debate, the authority of a personality quoted, the public's right to legitimate information.[19] In such cases, the 'good faith' of journalists may offend the religious faith of believers.

Article 32, paragraph 2, and Article 33, paragraph 3, of the emblematic law of 29 July 1881 on freedom of the press offer a specific categorization of defamation and slander 'for a person or a group of people on the basis of (…) their adherence or non-adherence to … a particular religion.' But after the Law of 9 December 1905 regarding the separation of the churches and the state, what in France is a 'particular religion'? Herein lies a major challenge in terms of the consequent recognition by the court of the religious nature of a group or doctrine. Religious defamation, judged and accepted by a court, is a testament to respectability and an 'officialization' of the ideological nature of the group or individual.

On this question, the proceedings will be more effective with the repeal of press law in relation to defamation or slander of an individual or group, because Article 48 of the Law of 1881 empowers the public prosecutor to initiate a public action *ex officio*, without the need for the victim to file charges. But it is rare to see direct action by the public prosecutor in this respect.

Provocation of Beliefs: A Source of Manipulation of the Process?

A defamatory attack on beliefs may also be an effort to put them on trial at the expense of those who hold them. We thus find the emergence of different ways

association was a sect was not in itself defamatory language, even if, in public opinion, this term has a pejorative connotation, because in fact this association is cited among currently existing sects in a parliamentary report on December 20, 1995.… establishing in this way that the comparison of the association in question with an association of delinquents required evidence and a hearing of both sides, the Court of Appeals rejected the meaning and application of the allegedly slanderous language and violated Articles 29 and 32 of the Law of July 29, 1881'. (*Assoc. X v. Ms. Y.*, *Gazette du palais* (23 December 2003), 71.) See also TGI Paris, 22 October 2002, *La Ligue française pour la défense des droits de l'homme v. Michel Houellebecq et al.*, *Gazette du palais* (2 October 2003), 1422.

19 *Cronique* de jurisprudence, *Revue de Sciences Criminelles* (January–March 2004), 120–122.

of challenging beliefs, multiplying exponentially on the Internet, the purpose of which is to transfer the debate from the public arena to the courtroom.

It is worth noting that one of the ten criteria for identification of a 'sect' accepted by the First Parliamentary Survey Commission on Sects, the public report for which dates back to 10 January 1996, makes reference to 'legal disputes'. Some militants or activists, appealing to the 'tyrannie de la norme', [20] didn't hesitate to resort en masse, between 1996 and 1999, to defamation or slander proceedings in an effort to corner the 'sects' under the spotlight of the judicial stage. This resulted in a series of litigations before the courts entrusted with providing legal protection and punishing so-called press crimes, before public opinion had been able to discern the origin of the accusations or the content of the defamatory discourse common to the demonized anti-sect lobby, much less the definitive case law of the courts on the question[21]. The result could have partly been, through confirmation at the expense of the sects, of their association by Parliament with 'legal disputes'. By bringing the cases to justice, these movements have exposed themselves, but did they have any other option considering the old saying that 'silence gives consent'? The lawsuits in question have also resulted in something of a deterrent against prosecution due to the personal and financial cost of the proceedings, and in a pusillanimous case law made up of half-measures.

The Rules for Defamation and Slander Proceedings Are a Means of Structuring and Legitimating Religious Beliefs

As Gérard Defois, former secretary-general of the Catholic Conference of Bishops, explained:

> [T]to be judged in the name of Humanism, to be challenged in the name of the fears that we inspire, to be rejected due to the questions we ask, is to be made to answer for the questions we ask, is to be made to answer for our points of view and our differences and, in so doing, to engage in a debate with society on the pluralism of beliefs and the evolution of social mores. Otherwise, to stay on the level of controversy, as we are invited to do by the mass media, would be to remain trapped in the tugs of war. We must therefore explain, show,

20 Expression taken from B. Lempert in his testimonial work *Le retour de l'intolérance – Sectarisme et chasse aux sorcières* (Paris: Bayard, 2002). For another, different perspective, see the iconoclastic book by L. Hincker, *Sectes, rumeurs et tribunaux* (Strasbourg: La Nuée Bleue/DNA, 2003) (especially the chapter 'De la rumeur à la diffamation').

21 See R. Campiche and C. Depraz, *Quand les sectes affolent. Ordre du Temple Solaire, médias et fin du millénaire* (Geneva: Labor et Fides, 1995). See also the studies directed by B. Leblanc, including 'Les représentations des « sectes » dans les médias écrits en France', in G.-R. Saint-Arnaud and J. Duhaime (eds.), *La peur des sectes* (Montreal: Fides, 2001).

> give meaning to our reasons for hoping for something more and for judging in a different way (...). Thus, to be active in sharing information means to accept conflictive relationships whereby my truth is challenged, examined and expressed in a confrontation of ideas and feelings. A passive attitude ties every responsible authority down to a role of self-defense.[22]

Indeed, defamatory or slanderous accusations, apart from the pain they inflict in the moral sense of the term, may also be a means of transcending 'the boxing ring', favoring instead the search for explanations and arguments in order to prove the falsehood of the accusations. The judicial search for evidence of the defamatory statements involves a task of analysis and presentation of religious beliefs and practices. The defamatory or slanderous statement requires believers to question their relationship with society in the sense that it destabilizes and compels introspection.

By way of example, the anthropologist Malek Chebel pointed out that if Muslims are somehow 'mass media victims', it is also because they do not always contribute to the enhancement of the image of Islam. In reference to Muslims, he explains that

> We are on the front line because, in some cases, we fall into the trap of the 'lynchers'. Indeed, when a journalist calls us to ask us how we feel about the veil (...), the answers we give require long explanations before they become clear. No newspaper goes beyond the few minutes needed to fill the columns of its pages. We thus turn into the agents of our own lynching either by omission (we forget to outline the basic points) or by excessive sophistication (we bury the journalist under a mess of secondary considerations) (...) Muslims are also responsible for the disastrous image we have of them; they need to assume at least part of the responsibility that is theirs.[23]

The stringent nature of case-law criteria on questions of the truth of defamatory or slanderous statements places vital importance on the presentation of evidence. Religious 'beliefs in process' need to be explained and disseminated in order to avoid 'mirror relationships' between the mass media and religions which at worst seriously distort the facts and at best preserve the misunderstandings.[24]

---

22 See Tincq and Defois, *Les médias et l'Eglise*, supra note 2 at 54, 64.

23 See Chebel's contribution to 35 *Panoramiques* (1998).

24 J.P. Willaime and P. Bréchon, *Médias et religions en miroir* (Paris: Presses Universitaires de France, 2000).

The Choice of Some 'Emerging' Groups in France

The choice to litigate can be transformed into a means of achieving social 'recognition' of certain groups acting in defense of their beliefs who have been subjected to serious accusations by the mass media.

I refer here to the lawsuits initiated by certain controversial movements from the point of view of society, classified as 'sects' by the Parliament in 1996, which, by defending their interests step by step in the courts, were able to achieve a certain balance, however fragile. Court action performs a 'preventive' and deterrent role. It is not about intimidation or threatening the work of the mass media, but subjecting the tensions to cross-examination in a public debate in the courts, in the weighing of the values of 'freedom of the press' and 'freedom of belief'. In the long term, prosecution acts as a means of defusing the tensions of the disputes from the moment that, subjected to the constraints of the process, the parties thereto are required to do some internal and external work on their methods of exploitation of 'information' and the limits of any act of 'communication'.

Without doubt, the existence of a highly 'litigious' press process, in the context of defense of beliefs, does not in itself guarantee the pacification of the conflictive relationships resulting from courtroom confrontations. This is regrettable; nevertheless, prosecution is not the only option. The use of conciliation, overseen by the court, pursuant to Article 21 of the New Civil Code is conspicuously rare. The mechanism of conciliation would allow the parties to reach settlements that could restore a balance of rights and values, even in a press process. Of course, this option requires an agreement between the parties in order to reach a settlement. The power of the judge to propose this option, with prior indication to the parties of a potentially unfavorable judicial outcome for one of them, would facilitate this solution.[25]

---

25 By way of illustration, consider the judicial mediation that brought an end to the case against the book *La Face cachée du Monde*, which resulted in actions for defamation brought mainly by the newspaper *Le Monde*. Subsequently, after mediation accepted by the parties from the Chairman of the Court of Appeals, a settlement agreement was reached between the parties to publish a press release that would bring an end to their differences. Some extracts from the press release: 'Thanks to the dialog they established in the context of the judicial mediation process, the editor and authors have come to regret certain expressions used and the interpretation that might be given to them, as well as some excessive assertions and comments, which for some are unfounded … Sharing the belief that the proceedings brought are not conducive to a debate in the press and in the hope of ending the lawsuit brought against them with regard to the alleged defamatory accusations, and then with regard to the reactions of the directors of Le Monde during the mediation period, which were hurtful to Messrs. Péan, Cohen and Durand, the parties agree, by way of settlement, to the following reciprocal concessions … The withdrawal from the actions brought shall be announced through the publication of this agreement protocol, whereby the parties shall abstain from making any declaration or comment or engaging in any debate on the question of the disputes to which they seek to bring an end.'

The Contribution of the Case Law of the European Court of Human Rights: Dangerous or Prudent Intervention?

In Le tiers pouvoir: vers un autre justice, Denis Salas notes:

> For the first time in European history, a choice is being made to fully embrace this tradition of natural law: the old medieval idea that law is a faculty of man, *jus est facultas*, is recovering its full meaning in a Europe that has left wars and national rivalries behind. Faced with the nationalizing force of sovereignty, the law is being applied to the needs of the universal that is unique to the human. Against the dominance of the apparatuses of power, a jurisdiction is being established to provide the individual with a means of action in the public arena.[26]

Article 9 of the European Convention on Human Rights places 'religion' and 'belief' on an equal footing insofar as the freedom to change them or manifest them is concerned (paragraph 2). Article 9 provides for protection of more than just freedom of thought, conscience and religion, since it also includes a guaranteed right to all beliefs of an individual, thus covering political and philosophical opinions as well. Since no definition of religion or belief is provided either in the text or in the case law of its international regulating body, the means of regulating offenses against beliefs, whatever those beliefs may be, are left open.[27] It is important to understand here that journalists and the mass media can also avail themselves of the right to express their beliefs, including non-religious beliefs.[28] I refer here to the 'belief-based mass media'.

The question of recognition of freedom of expression of religious beliefs and their degree of conventionality was addressed in the European Court of Human Right's foundational judgment on religious matters. The 1993 judgment in the case of *Kokkinakis v. Greece* imposes precise limits on national repression of

---

26 D. Salas, *Le tiers pouvoir: vers un autre justice* (Paris: Hachette Littératures, 2000) [editor's translation].

27 In his own way, Régis Debray notes that 'the religious institution can be understood as a belief group; not the only one, but the most resilient of all... How can a belief mutate into an organization? The religious question in a broad sense puts the articulations of being and doing to work'. *Le feu sacré: Fonctions du Religieux* (Paris: Fayard, 2005), 32. A distinction is made here between collective logic and individual logic, which in terms of 'religious beliefs' raises the question of the definition of freedom as far as transmission and acquisition of 'knowledge' and 'faith' are concerned. Is a man free in his religious beliefs when subjected to the pressure of the teachings, the clergy, the monopoly on authority of institutions and groups?

28 Y. Galland, 'Les obligations des journalistes dans la jurisprudence de la Cour européenne des droits de l'homme', *Revue trimestrielle des droits de l'homme*, Brussels (2002), 853–874. The author presents a full analytical panorama of the case law of the European Court.

religious 'proselytism'.[29] Subsequently, the Court issued its 1994 judgment in the case of *Otto-Preminger-Institut v. Austria*:

> As the Court pointed out in its judgment in the case of Kokkinakis v. Greece [...], freedom of thought, conscience and religion, which is safeguarded under Article 9 of the Convention, represents one of the foundations of a 'democratic society' within the meaning of the Convention ... Those who choose to exercise the freedom to manifest their religion, irrespective of whether they do so as members of a religious majority or minority, cannot reasonably expect to be exempt from all criticism. They must tolerate and accept the denial by others of their religious beliefs and even the propagation by others of doctrines hostile to their faith. However, the manner in which religious beliefs and doctrines are opposed or denied is a matter which may engage the responsibility of the State, notably its responsibility to ensure the peaceful enjoyment of the right guaranteed under Article 9 to the holders of those beliefs and doctrines. Indeed, in extreme cases the effect of particular methods of opposing or denying religious beliefs can be such as to inhibit those who hold such beliefs from exercising their freedom to hold and express them.[30]

Thus, in accordance with the second paragraphs of Articles 9 and 10 of the European Convention, the Court exercised its control over state measures deemed to be restrictions.[31] In a judgment issued in 1980, the European Commission on Human Rights did not consider 'that a particular belief or faith could derive form the notion of freedom of religion a right that would exempt it from criticism. However, this does not preclude the possibility that criticism or "agitation" fostered against a Church or religious group may reach such an extreme that it could endanger freedom of religion, in which case, the fact that the public authorities tolerated such behavior could compromise the responsibility of the State.'[32] In the 1996 case of *Nigel Wingrove v. the United Kingdom*, the Court, confirming the precedent of Otto-Preminger-Institut, found no violation of Article 10 in the rejection of a film distribution certificate because the film in question presented the erotic dreams of a character resembling Saint Teresa of Ávila involving the crucified Christ.[33]

---

29 *Kokkinakis v. Greece*, App. No. 14307/88, 25 May 1993.

30 *Otto-Preminger-Institut v. Austria*, App. No. 13470/87, 20 September 1994, para. 47. See H. Surrel, '*La liberté religieuse devant la Cour européenne des Droits de l'Homme*', 3 *Revue française de droit administratif* (1995), 573 et seq.; F. Rigaux, 'L'incrimination *de prosélytisme face à la liberté d'expression*, observations sous arrêt *CEDH*, Kokkinakis c. Grèce', *Revue trimestrielle des droits de l'homme*, Brussels (1994), 144–150; *A. Garay, 'Liberté religieuse et prosélytisme: l'expérience européenne', Revue trimestrielle des droits de l'homme*, Brussels (1994), 7–29.

31 J. Duffar, 'Les *limites à la liberté d'expression* en matière religieuse en *Europe'*, 42 *Année Canonique*, Paris, (1999), 71–86.

32 *Church of Scientology v. Sweden*, App. No. 8282/78, 14 July 1980, para. 5.

33 *Wingrove v. the United Kingdom*, App. No. 17419/90, 7 December 1996.

The Court also established restrictions on commercial advertising, political interventions and 'abusive proselytism' represented by a corruption or distortion of 'Christian testimony' (cf. *Kokkinakis v. Greece*), carried out in the name of freedom of religion. The Court also progressively admitted that freedom of expression includes freedom of information in a broad sense and religious freedom. For Jean-François Flauss, 'the defense of freedom of expression constitutes a serious obstacle to the preservation or establishment of measures to combat excessively repressive religious defamation … '.[34] Recent developments in the case law of the Court in the area of 'defamatory' discourses against secularism (*Gundüz v. Turkey*, infra) and against Islam (*Arslan v. Turkey*, infra) should be followed closely for the increasing material distance they place between freedom of expression and freedom of religion. Indeed, here, the conflict of fundamental rights is, at its most extreme point, between Europe and the East.

The judgment issued on 20 September 1994 in the case of *Otto-Preminger-Institut v. Austria* might have given the impression that, based on the essential nature of freedom of religion as a foundation for a democratic society, following the same line as the *Kokkinakis* judgment, the European Court privileged an increased 'protection of religious feelings'.[35] The Court also directed European oversight of interference with religious beliefs to the protection of Article 10, which refers only to freedom of expression, thus seeming to divest the principle of freedom of manifestation in Article 9 of content.

By now in Strasbourg the scope of the decisions issued has broadened considerably, in the specific cases of *Refah Partisi v. Turkey*,[36] *Murphy v. Ireland*,[37] and *Gundüz v. Turkey*,[38] and the Court does not seek to enter into a logic of consent to the aggravation of religious beliefs.[39] Did it not perhaps decide to exercise its oversight of the restrictions on religious beliefs or feelings related to freedom of expression to avoid engaging in a debate on the legitimacy and degree of acceptability of beliefs in a Europe divided on questions of faith?[40]

---

34 See Flauss's article 'La *diffamation* religieuse en *droit international'*, *Les Petites Affiches*, 23 July 2002, no. 146.

35 AJDA, Paris (20 March 1995), 215; P. Wachsmann, '*La religion contre la liberté d'expression* : sur un arrêt regrettable de la Cour européenne des droits de l'homme', 6 *R.U.D.H.* (1994), 441–449; F. Rigaux, 'La *liberté d'expression et ses limites*', *Revue trimestrielle des droits de l'homme*, Brussels (10 July 1995), 401–415.

36 *Refah Partisi v. Turkey*, App. Nos. 41340/98, 41342/98, 41343/98, 41344/98, 13 February 2003 (Grand Chamber Judgment).

37 *Murphy v. Ireland*, App. No. 44179/98, 10 July 2003.

38 *Gundüz v. Turkey*, App. No. 35071/97, 4 December 2003.

39 G. Gonzalez, 'La *convention européenne des droits de l'homme* et la *liberté* des *religions*', *Economica*, Paris, (1997).

40 We will be closely following the reports of the Council of Europe's Steering Committee on the Mass Media with the aim of harmonizing national legislations and practices in the area of defamation according to European laws (Conference of Strasbourg, 17–18 October 2002).

Conclusion

Believers who find it easy to practice forgiveness have a reputation for being less suspicious and resentful than their contemporaries. Their detractors mock their reserve, basing their attacks on reciprocal rumors between the mass media and believers.[41] But have the 'thought police'[42] perhaps turned into one of the 'media lynching' mechanisms, given that 'whoever reports the lynching risks being lynched himself'?[43] On this question, the debate is open.

On the one hand, an institutional organization representing and defending the legal interests of certain groups of believers, not of the minority, is very recent. The same is true of the 'religious association'; the Catholic Church of France, with more than twenty centuries of experience, waited until the year 1996 to create the *Association Croyances et Libertés*, with the aim of 'offering Catholics a means to defend themselves'.[44] We might believe that an organization like this one would offer 'resources' and methods in keeping with the challenges.

On the other hand, as explained above, the elasticity and volatility of press law does not offer believers sufficient protection of the beliefs they express. Recourse to the court is neither a panacea nor an effective remedy given that, when intervening after the fact in the 'damages' caused, the 'harm is already done' and any compensation for the 'media harassment'[45] is highly uncertain and inadequate. Are resignation and a hope for 'better days' enough when an ethics of information

---

41 On the distrust of law with regard to 'rumor' (to which the Athenians had dedicated an altar, cult and sacrifices), see the article 'La rumeur et le droit', *Receuil Dalloz* (2 May 1996), doc. N°18. See also the excellent article by H. Madelin, 'Rumeurs et complots', *Christus*, Paris (October 2002).

42 E. Lévy, *Les Maîtres censeurs : pour en finir avec la pensée unique* (Paris: Lattès, 2002).

43 See the editorial by G. Hennebelle in 'Le *lynchage* médiatique', 35 *Panoramiques* (1998).

44 B. Lagoutte, 'L'action en justice — l'exemple de l'Association Croyances et Libertés', in *Religions, droit et société dans l'Europecommunautaire*, proceedings of the Colloquium of 19–20 May 1999, Université d'Aix-Marseille III (Presses Universitaires d'Aix-Marseille, Collection Droit et Religion, 2000). This is also an attempt to respond to the possibility, since the Law of 1 July 1972 against racism, for any association, regularly declared for at least five years since the date of the incident, to come before the court as a civil party, in support of victims of 'defamation, hatred or violence' on religious grounds. According to Article 48-1 of the aforementioned Law of 29 July1881, 'when the offense has been committed against persons considered individually, the association shall not be admitted in their action, unless it can provide proof that it has received the agreement of such persons.'

45 M.-D. Douaoui, 'La *réparation du trouble médiatique', Receuil Dalloz* (2001), doc., 1333 et seq.; see also E. Dreyer, '*Qu'est devenue la responsabilité civile en matière de presse* ?', *Receuil Dalloz* (2004), doc., 590 et seq.

has been declaimed?[46] Is it a simple question of ethics and/or freedom?[47] But without doubt, there is still much to be done to explain, educate and inform believers and mass media professionals in relation to the rights, freedoms and obligations available to avoid frustrations in a society marked by a history and a tumultuous contemporary context of secularism.[48] Thus, the notion of 'beliefs in process' could avoid the stringent rules of the 'process of beliefs' … of both the mass media and of believers.

46 The so-called 'religions of the Book' are familiar with the Imprecatory Psalm 109, which reads as follows: 'Hold not thy peace, O God of my praise! For the mouth of the wicked and the mouth of the deceitful are opened against me: They have spoken against me with a lying tongue. They compassed me about with words of hatred, and fought against me without a cause. For my love they are my adversaries (…) let Satan stand at his right hand; when he shall be judged, let him be condemned… '? (Bible, Authorized King James Version, OUP, 2008). See also E. de Montéty, 'L'Eglise devant les médias', *Liberté Politique*, Paris (Summer 2000), 13.

47 'Le Vatican demande une éthique de l'information', *Le Monde* (3 June 2000). See also '*La liberté de pensée*', 61 *Revue Géopolitique*, Paris, (Spring 1998).Salas, explains that freedom of the press can no longer continue to be confused with freedom of expression. He calls for an institutionalization of democracy of opinion 'that would open a public space for deliberation where these issues would be debated, opinions would be given and, otherwise, penalties would be imposed.' It would involve taking the lawsuits out of the courts and entrusting them to a regulatory body. Salas, *Le tiers pouvoir*, supra note 26 at 244).

48 See the work of Emile Poulat on the question of tumultuous secularism dealt with in his last book, *Notre laïcité publique* (Paris: Berg International, 2003); see also A. Garay and E. Tawil, 'Tumulte autour de la laïcité', *Recueil Dalloz*, (29 January 2004), 225 et seq. On the effects of this tumultuous history on media treatment of religious matters. see the analyses by M. Noailles, 'Una historia conflictiva', and J. Fortier, 'Ninguna escritura santa', *La Croix* (26 January 2001).

Chapter 19

Freedom of Religion, Freedom of Conscience and Education: A Nordic Example

Pamela Slotte

Introduction

At the turn of the 21st century, Finland adopted a new Constitution, which guarantees the right to freedom of religion and conscience to everyone. The paragraph on freedom of religion and conscience had changed already with the 1995 reform of the basic rights and liberties when the Finnish Constitution was worked through in respect of international law. The constitutional changes led to amendments in the Finnish legislation on religious freedom, including a new Act on Freedom of Religion in 2003. In the preparatory works concerning the new Act, it was acknowledged that the right to freedom of religion and conscience has implications for education. For this reason, changes were also made to the Basic Education Act and the Upper Secondary School Act. The changes also included a reassessment and renewal of the model of religious instruction in Finnish public schools to better respond to the demands of freedom of religion and conscience.

The purpose of this chapter is to analyse the legislative changes that took place in Finland at the turn of the new millennium and the implications of these changes for the protection of freedom of religion and of conscience in the Finnish educational setting. This will include putting the concrete legislative work into the context of the wider Finnish society and the social transformations and transformations in understanding of the issues at stake at the end of the twentieth century. Some fundamental questions are raised: What notions of freedom in religious matters, education (especially religious education), society and faith informed the decision to carry out the legal revisions? How were these notions reflected in the legislative process, the final legal outcomes as well as in the subsequent new educational model?

I do not analyse actual instruction in any detail. Though I will, for comparison, look at the aims formulated by the school authorities as a reflection of the legislation. Rather I am interested in the perceptions of such instruction articulated in law via categorizations, distinctions, and so forth, and which are discussed, for example, during the drafting process of new legislation on religious freedom.[1]

The chapter will moreover address the situation approximately ten years later. In the intervening years, education professionals, non-governmental organizations and faith communities have all engaged with the question of freedom of religion and conscience in education, so too have public officials and the government. What have been the experiences of the new legislation and educational models and how has the discussion continued as regards these issues? What problems have been identified now the scheme has been put in place? What legal and educational measures have been taken to tackle identified problems concerning freedom of religion and conscience in Finnish basic and secondary education?

Moreover, during the years 2009–2010, the Finnish government proposed amendments to the law on education, and the school curriculum. One of the proposals was the introduction of a new compulsory ethics subject. The faith communities jointly objected to this proposed change in the curricula. The proposal was dropped at the final stages of the preparations to amend the law on education. What discussion did the proposal cause and what were the objections voiced? Finally, the chapter offers some reflections on how the trends in Finland relate to the situation in other Nordic countries, as well as some tentative remarks on possible future scenarios.

In relation to Rafael Palomino's contribution to this volume that analyses a European human rights approach to religious education, this chapter can be viewed as a country study of sorts. However, through the perspective I adopt on the issue of freedom of religion, freedom of conscience and education, I also seek to exemplify the following with my chapter. In a certain sense, neutrality or impartiality is intrinsic to our image of law, to international and to national law. This then also goes for our understanding of law's relationship to religion. As a colleague of mine recently put it with reference to Paul Ricœur: it is a commonly held belief that implementing freedom of religion requires some sort of neutrality of states that could be labelled 'institutional agnosticism'. The state should not take sides in religious matters.[2] It is this that Javier Martínez-Torrón calls the only universalizable understanding of 'neutrality'.

---

1 The author approaches law (and faith) on the level of language, as a discourse. Hence, what is undertaken is an analysis of 'linguistic practice'. The analysis adopts what in theology, the 'home-discipline' of the author, is commonly called an analysis of meaning (or content), which includes analysis of texts, sentences and concepts. In relation to other ways of framing methodological considerations, it comes close to what is often called discourse analysis. The author wishes to thank Saila Poulter and Ida Koivisto for valuable comments on the manuscript.

2 P. Frilund, 'The Fragility of Religious Freedom', in 3 *Agathos. An International Review of the Humanities and Social Sciences* 1 (2012), 141–164 at 143, http://www.agathos-international-review.com/issue3_1/ Patrik%20Fridlund%20-%20The%20Fragility%20of%20 Religious%20Freedom.pdf (accessed 10 December 2012); P. Ricœur, *Critique and Conviction:*

However, agnosticism and the question of religious truth aside, we in a sense regularly hold divergent views regarding what it means for legal protection to be neutral vis-à-vis religion. When the meaning of 'neutrality' is elaborated, when 'neutrality' is given a context, and often these issues of neutrality are framed in terms of equality, we differ. While we recognize faith as important to human life, and thus worthy of protection, we differ as to what actual forms protection shall take and how far-reaching it shall be.

In this chapter, I look at what generic 'neutral' constitutional guarantees of freedom of religion and conscience come to mean when conceptualized with regard to the field of education in Finland, more specifically religious education in public (state-funded) schools.

As we shall see, international law, including European human rights law, does not decide in itself the parameters for thinking about religious education in Finland. It has a role, and an important one. However, other things also influence and guide the approach to religious education, such as the specific church-state model, majority religious sentiment, and the parameters for conceptualizing majority faith.

These and other significant variables are reflected in the national laws put in place. Legal protection of religion and conscience and the conceptualization of this task in relation to education, for example, are related to assumptions about religion, to ideas about what religion is all about, and to the role and meaning of religion in human life.

To put it more generally, despite the idea and perhaps ideal of agnosticism, and however self-consciously 'secular' the actual rule of law claims to be, when states through law regulate religion, limiting and even prohibiting certain practices, alternatively putting in place 'positive' constitutional safeguards, such regulatory exercises do seem to rely on some notion or other of world view. In this chapter, I seek to highlight how this shows itself in the Finnish legislation and organization of religious education.

Historical Background

The Law

In the Nordic context, the ties between the Evangelical Lutheran Church and the state run deep. Lutheran thinking has influenced Nordic and Finnish culture in multiple ways, for example the manner in which church-state relations have been conceptualized in law.[3] Modern Nordic societies have made an effort 'to

---

Conversations with François Azouvi and Marc de Launay (New York/Chichester: Columbia University Press, 1998), 128.

3 This section draws on views expressed in a forthcoming article co-written with Johannes Heikkonen on religion and non-discrimination law in Finland. The chapter as a

separate state and church'.[4] It is a fact, however, that the system historically put in place in Finland, while separating the spiritual and temporal realms in one sense, has simultaneously in and of itself reinforced an understanding of how to divide powers that is shared by both the state and the dominant church. Church and state have agreed on how to rule, and the system reaffirms the status of the Evangelical Lutheran Church.

The fact that Finland has historically had a state church that has left its mark on both the institutional culture and societal structures must therefore be kept in mind, in order to understand the present-day realities and how Finnish national law deals with issues of freedom of religion and conscience.

Naturally, European and international human rights law, as we shall see, today affect the perception of these issues. Finland has, among other things, ratified the International Covenant on Civil and Political Rights (ICCPR),[5] the International Covenant on Economic, Social and Cultural Rights (ICESCR),[6] the Convention on the Rights of the Child (CRC),[7] the European Convention for the Protection of Human Rights and Fundamental Freedoms (ECHR),[8] and the UNESCO Convention against Discrimination in Education.[9] In 1995, work began on reforming the Constitution thoroughly in light of international legal obligations.[10]

---

whole also draws on previous research carried out by the author and published, among other places, in P. Slotte, 'Waving the 'Freedom of Religion or Belief' Card, or Playing it Safe: Religious Instruction in the Cases of Norway and Finland', 3 *Religion and Human Rights* 1 (2008), 33–69, and P. Slotte, 'A Little Church, a Little State, and a Little Commonwealth at Once: Towards a Nordic Model of Religious Instruction in Public Schools?', in L. Christoffersen et al. (eds.), *Law & Religion in the 21st Century – Nordic Perspectives* (Denmark: Djøf Publishing, 2010), 239–273. For a new comprehensive study of historical and present-day church-state relations in the Nordic countries, see generally Christoffersen et al., *Law & Religion in the 21st Century – Nordic Perspectives.*

4 T. Kurtén and V. Päivänsalo, 'Legitimacy and Religion in a North European Perspective', in L. Hertzberg and T. Kurtén (eds.), *Legitimacy: The Treasure of Politics* (Frankfurt am Main, Berlin, Bern, Bruxelles, New York, Oxford, Wien: Peter Lang Verlag, 2011).

5 *International Covenant on Civil and Political Rights*, GA res. 2200A (XXI), UN Doc. A/6316 (1966), 999 UNTS 171, entered into force 23 March 1976.

6 *International Covenant on Economic, Social and Cultural Rights,* GA res. 2200A (XXI), UN Doc. A/6316 (1966), 993 UNTS 3, entered into force 3 January 1976.

7 Convention on the Rights of the Child (Sales No. E.94.XIV.1) (hereinafter 'CRC').

8 European Convention for the Protection of Human Rights and Fundamental Freedoms (Sales No.E.97.XIV.1) (hereinafter 'ECHR'); Protocol No. 1 to the Convention for the Protection of Human Rights and Fundamental Freedoms, securing certain rights and freedoms other than those already included in the Convention (Sales No. E.97.XIV.1).

9 Convention against Discrimination in Education, 429 UNTS 93, entered into force 22 May 1962.

10 T. Ojanen, 'Perusoikeuspluralismi kotimaisessa tuomioistuimessa', 4 *Defensor Legis* (2011), 442–455, at 444. See also T. Ojanen and M. Scheinin, 'Kansainväliset

However, as emphasized in the introduction, not only international legal considerations are important if we want to understand why religious education (hereinafter 'RE') is regulated and organized as it is in a country like Finland. Among the general issues that influence the approach to RE in a country, John M. Hull has listed the religious sentiment in the society in question, the concrete church-state relationship, the historical tradition of the country, as well as the task ascribed to RE in school and the form it takes in the school system.[11]

In the case of Finland, history explains why the legal status of churches and religious communities has been regulated in a twofold way. It also helps explain the framing of RE in Finnish public schools, how it has been understood and organized and how it has changed.

'One of the peculiar characteristics of Finland's ecclesio-political situation is the fact that two churches, Lutheran and Orthodox, have a legal and economic status which differs from that of the other churches and religious communities in Finland'.[12] The special status of these two churches has not been considered to be contrary to freedom of religion and conscience, as long as the rights of individuals are adequately guaranteed.[13] The legal status of the Evangelical Lutheran Church and the Orthodox Church are regulated in separate laws, the Church Act [*kirkkolaki* (1054/1993)] and Order of the Church [*kirkkojärjestys* (1055/1993)], as well as the Act on the Orthodox Church [*laki ortodoksisesta kirkosta* (985/2006)], respectively, and in parts one and three of the Act on Freedom of Religion [*uskonnonvapauslaki* (453/2003)].[14] The special legal status of the Evangelical Lutheran Church is referred to in Section 76 of the Finnish Constitution [*perustuslaki* (731/1999)].[15]

---

ihmisoikeussopimukset ja Suomen perusoikeusjärjestelmä', in P. Hallberg et al. (eds.), *Perusoikeudet* (Helsinki: WSLT, 2011), 171–195, at 185–191.

11 J. M. Hull, 'The Contribution of Religious Education to Religious Freedom: A Global Perspective', in *Religious Education in Schools: Ideas and Experiences from around World* (International Association for Religious Freedom, 2001), 1–8, at 1–2, as referred to in A. Kallioniemi, 'Näkökulmia eurooppalaiseen uskonnon opetukseen – oppiaineen kehittämisen haasteita Norjassa ja Suomessa', in A. Kallioniemi and E. Salmenkivi (eds.), *Katsomusaineiden kehittämishaasteita Opettajankoulutuksen tutkinnonuudistuksen virittämää keskustelua* (Helsinki: University of Helsinki, 2007) 55–76, at 56.

12 J. Seppo, 'Finland's Policy on Church and Religion', in L. Christoffersen et al., *Law & Religion*, supra note 3, 89–105, at 90.

13 T. Ojanen and M. Scheinin, 'Uskonnon ja omantunnon vapaus (PL 11 §)', in Hallberg et al., *Perusoikeudet*, supra note 10, 413–458, at 441–442.

14 It is the Greek Orthodox Church of Finland, which belongs to the Patriarchate of Constantinople, which has a special status in Finnish law alongside the Evangelical Lutheran Church.

15 However, during the work to reform the Constitution, the working group 'Constitution 2000' *(Perustuslaki 2000–työryhmä)* proposed that any references to the status of churches and other religious communities should be omitted. The Evangelical Lutheran Church opposed the suggested omission, suggesting instead that also other churches and religious communities be mentioned in the Constitution Act. J. Seppo,

Other religious communities are afforded protection under the Act of Freedom of Religion if they duly register in the manner prescribed in the Act.[16]

Before the 1995 reform of the basic rights and liberties enshrined in the Constitution Act, the Constitution Act of 1919 [*Suomen hallitusmuoto* (94/1919)] of the newly independent Finnish state (1917) enshrined the principle of religious freedom in Section 11. Freedom was guaranteed as long as it was practised within the boundaries of the law and of accepted mores [*hyvät tavat*]. In practice, this limitation was interpreted as requiring that the exercise of religious freedom could not impinge on the religious freedom of others. In addition, Section 9 of the Act stated that all citizens, independent of their religious affiliation, enjoyed equally the rights laid down in the Act. This section granted formal religious and conscientious equality to all Finnish citizens (nowadays this is granted to everyone within the Finnish jurisdiction).

The Finnish state itself became 'religiously neutral' with the Constitution of 1919.[17] The state is neither confessional nor non-confessional,[18] which means that in normal law it can support religious communities. If the negative religious freedom is guaranteed, there may also be RE and religious fostering in public schools.[19]

The Finnish legal approach could therefore be interpreted as expressing both the idea of equality and the idea of religious freedom of individuals and groups. Section 9 of the Constitutional Act granted formal equality and Section 11 freedom of religion to all citizens, and the Act on Freedom of Religion [*uskonnonvapauslaki* (267/1922)] expressed the idea of religious freedom and equality for religious communities.

The old Constitutional Act used the term 'religious freedom' (*uskonnonvapaus*). With the reform of 1995 that worked through the Finnish Constitution in respect of international law, this was replaced with 'freedom of religion and conscience' (*uskonnon ja omantunnonvapaus*). According to the Constitutional Committee, this phrasing encompassed both religious and non-religious beliefs.[20]

'Die Religionsfreiheit im Spiegel des Staat-Kirche-Verhältnisses in Finnland', 57 *Studia Theologica* 1 (2003), 20–35, at 25.

16 Act of Religious Freedom 2003, §2. See further Religionsfrihetskommittén, *Religionsfrihetskommitténs betänkande* 2001:1 (Report by the Committee on Religious Freedom) (hereinafter RK 2001), 9, 22, 29, for a discussion of the concept 'religious community'.

17 A. Kallioniemi, 'Uskonnonopetus ja uskontokasvatus uskontohistoriallisessa kontekstissaan', in A. Kallioniemi and J. Luodeslampi (eds.), *Uskonnonopetus uudella vuosituhannella* (Helsinki: Kirjapaja Oy, 2005), 14.

18 PeVL 12/1982; Ojanen and Scheinin, 'Uskonnon', supra note 13 at 414, 442.

19 Ojanen and Scheinin, 'Uskonnon', supra note 13 at 427; A. Koikkalainen, *Uskonnonopetus ja ihmisoikeudet* (Helsinki: Ihmisoikeusliitto, 2010), 30.

20 PeVM 25/1994vp (Perustuslakivaliokunnan mietintö hallituksen esityksestä perustuslakien perusoikeussäännösten muuttamisesta), Constitutional Law Committee of the Parliament, 8–9. See also Ojanen and Scheinin, 'Uskonnon', supra note 13 at 415–416.

Religious Education

However, the understanding of what the ideas of freedom and equality mean in practice, for example in education, have evolved and broadened over time. Generally speaking, revisions concerning religious protection have been the result of a change in consciousness influenced by socio-political transformations. Finnish law has historically protected religious minorities by way of acknowledging a religious group's sense of being detrimentally affected by the majority culture as an issue of religious freedom – as noted, the principle of religious freedom was enshrined in the Constitution Act of 1919 – and additionally by providing for exceptions in general law, for example in the law on education. Hence, minority groups have been granted freedoms: freedom *to* religion, such as freedom to worship in one's own home, and freedom *from* religion, such as the freedom not to take part in majority RE in public schools.

What we find here is an approach that Juha Seppo identifies as a model where the state extends rights enjoyed by the dominant Christian church to other religious communities as well. It is at present the most common state approach in Europe.[21] However, while this can be interpreted as something positive, it is also worthwhile to critically observe, as does Tuula Sakaranaho, that 'what the model of extended privileges does, in short, is to reify the status-quo of the prominent Christian church, thereby strengthening its position in society'. For this reason, she notes that this approach may not balance the scales between minority and majority religious communities.[22]

Moreover, this extension of privileges has naturally been dependent on official recognition as a religious community. Over time, such recognition has become more inclusive. Historically, it was first afforded to other Protestant communities, then other Christian churches and the Mosaic faith (Jews), and so forth. As the first Nordic country, the position of being non-religious was also acknowledged in law as a legitimate position.[23] The latest figures show that 57 religious communities are currently registered.[24]

The 1919 Constitution Act did not regulate RE. This was regulated in the Education Act (*Lag om grunderna för folkskolväsendets organisation*

---

21 J. Seppo, *Uskonnonvapaus 2000-luvun Suomessa* (Helsinki: Edita Prima Oy, 2003), 30–31.

22 T. Sakaranaho, *Religious Freedom, Multiculturalism, Islam. Cross-reading Finland and Ireland* (Leiden: Brill 2006), 117, referring to Seppo, *Uskonnonvapaus*, supra note 21 at 33.

23 Slotte, 'A Little Church', supra note 3 at 256. For a concise overview of the history of religious freedom and church-state relations in Finland, see Sakaranaho, *Religious Freedom*, supra note 22 at 123–128; J. Seppo, 'The Freedom of Religion and Conscience in Finland', 40 *Journal of Church and State* 4 (1998), 847–872.

24 It is important to remember that not all communities are allowed to register, nor do all want to register themselves as religious communities.

[18.5.1923/137]) in 1923. Until this time, the religious instruction in schools had been intimately linked to the baptismal teaching of the Evangelical Lutheran church. From 1889 on, exemption was (as indicated above) guaranteed by law to pupils belonging to other Protestant denominations, if they received teaching within their own communities. Pupils belonging to other denominations were also usually exempted.

The new system for instruction provided for in the Education Act was at that time connected to the new Act on Freedom of Religion (*Uskonnonvapauslaki* [10.11.1922/267]). It introduced alternative instruction in 'the history of religion and ethics' (*sedelära*) for those pupils who for some reason were exempted from the instruction otherwise given.[25] Moreover, if there were at least twenty pupils in a school who belonged to a belief community other than the majority (being the belief according to which RE was to be organized), the school authorities had to arrange instruction for them in their own belief.[26]

This confessional instruction had two distinguishing features. First, it was delivered in accordance with the creed of the religious denomination. Second, the teachers, with some exceptions, belonged to that specific religious community. Hans-Olof Kvist speaks here of an *objective* and a *personal* element.[27] By contrast, instruction in the general history of religion and ethics did not offer instruction *in* religion but *about* religion, and it was characterized as fact-based and objective. In a conceptual analysis of the instruction, Kvist explains 'objective' as denoting that 'anyone can ascertain that what is being taught is based on actual states of affairs.'[28]

Changes in the system took place throughout the twentieth century. In the reform of 1957, the minimum number of pupils required before alternative

25 While not mentioned explicitly in *Uskonnonvapauslaki* 10.11.1922/267, room was made for such instruction through § 3 of *Lag om grunderna för folkskolväsendets organisation* 18.5.1923/137. For an analysis of what was hereby understood, see H.-O. Kvist, *Konfessionell religionsundervisning: En begreppsanalytisk undersökning av konfessionalitetens innebörd i Finlands nu gällande lagstiftning rörande skolarnas religionsundervisning* (Åbo: Institutet för ekumenik och socialetik vid Åbo Akademi, 1973), 50–51. See further Kvist, 20–23, 44, 48–49; Religionsfrihetskommittén, *Till Hans Kejserliga Majestät Från Religionsfrihetskommittén underdånigst. Kommittébetänkande 1908:13* (Helsinki, 1908). For a more thorough analysis of the historical context, see Kvist, 13–16; M. Pyysiäinen, *Tunnustuksellinen, tunnustukseton ja objektiivinen uskonnonopetus: Opetussuunnitelma-analyysi Suomen ja Ruotsin peruskoulun uskonnonopetuksen tavoitteista ja sisällöstä* (Helsinki: Kirjapaja, 1982) 19–41, 56–62; Antti Räsänen, *Koulun uskonnonopetus: Suomalaisten käsitykset uskonnonopetuksen luonteesta ja sisällöstä* (Helsinki: Suomalainen teologinen kirjallisuusseura, 2006) 13–15; RK 2001, supra note 16, 6–7.

26 See e.g. Pyysiäinen, *Tunnustuksellinen*, supra note 25 at 19–24.

27 Kvist, *Konfessionell*, supra note 25 at 36, 44. Cf. Pyysiäinen, *Tunnustuksellinen*, supra note 25 at 58.

28 Kvist, *Konfessionell*, supra note 25 at 51 [author's translation].

religious instruction could be offered was lowered to eight pupils.[29] Moreover, the minimum number of pupils required for 'instruction in the history of religions and ethics' was fixed to five (there had been no set number before).[30] A later reform of the basic education in 1975 reduced the minimum number of pupils required for minority RE further to five. In 1991, the number was further reduced to three. Regulations were further revised so that the number of students is not counted on a school-by-school basis but with regard to the region administratively in charge of the school.[31]

However, the overall model was not fundamentally revised.[32] A system of parallel confessional instruction became the practice through a major reform of the school legislation in 1982. Nevertheless, what in fact happened was that an existing practice was extended to include new groups. The Basic School Education Act afforded Orthodox RE the same status as majority RE. Parents no longer had to request that their children receive Orthodox RE. On top of this, 'life-stance' education, or as it is also called in English, 'secular ethics and life questions' (*elämänkatsomustieto*) came to replace instruction in the history of religions and ethics.[33]

---

29 Kallioniemi, 'Näkökulmia', supra note 11 at 64; K. Lyhykäinen, 'Vähemmistön uskonnon opetusta profiloimassa', in Kallioniemi and Salmenkivi (eds.), *Katsomusaineiden*, supra note 11, 17–24, at 18; Koikkalainen, *Uskonnonopetus*, supra note 19 at 42, referring to A. Jamisto, 'Pienryhmäuskontojen opetus Suomessa ennen ja nyt', in T. Sakaranaho and A. Jamisto (eds.), *Monikulttuurisuus ja uudistuva katsomusaineiden opetus* (Helsinki: Helsingin yliopisto, uskontotieteen laitos, 2007), 32–33.

30 Koikkalainen, *Uskonnonopetus*, supra note 19 at 43, referring to Jamisto, 'Pienryhmäuskontojen', supra note 29 at 34–35; E. Salmenkivi, P. Elo, T. Tomperi and T. Ahola-Luttila, 'Elämänkatsomustiedon kehkeytyminen', in Kallioniemi and Salmenkivi, *Katsomusaineiden,* supra note 11, 125–162, at 130.

31 Kallioniemi, 'Näkökulmia', supra note 11 at 64–65.

32 For an analysis of the discussion about confessional and non-confessional instruction in Finland and Sweden during the 1970s and the changing understanding of its meaning, see Pyysiäinen, *Tunnustuksellinen*, supra note 25. For an analysis of confessional instruction in Finnish public schools in the 1990s based on the curricula, see M. Pyysiäinen, *Yksi oppiaine, seitsemän opetussuunnitelmaa. Peruskoulun ja lukin opetushallituksen 1990-luvulla vahvistamien uskonnon opetussuunnitelmien tunnustuksellinen luonne* (Helsinki: Helsigin yliopiston opettajankoulutuslaitos, 2000).

33 Slotte, 'A Little Church', supra note 3; Lyhykäinen, 'Vähemmistön', supra note 29 at 18–19. The direct translation of the Finnish word 'elämänkatsomus' would be 'worldview' or 'view of life'. In the case of *Hartikainen* v. *Finland*, the United Nations Human Rights Committee dealt with the system of RE in place in Finland in the 1970s. More specifically, it studied whether 'the history of religions and ethics-subject was compatible with the ICCPR. The committee decided that this was the case, taking into account the revisions that at the time were being made to the Finnish system. *Erkki Juhani Hartikainen et al.* v. *Finland* (Communication No. 40/1978), Report of the Human Rights Committee, UN General Assembly Official Records, Thirty-sixth Session, Suppl. No. 40 (A/36/40), 147–152. For an analysis of *Hartikainen* v. *Finland*, see e.g. M. Scheinin, 'Secular Human Rights Perspectives', in Christoffersen et al., *Law & Religion*, supra note 3 at 547–560.

With a rise in immigration, the system of parallel confessional instruction expanded. Before the 1990s, there were in practice only Evangelical Lutheran and Orthodox RE. During the 1980s and 1990s, the National Board of Education *(Opetushallitus)* also devised curricula for the teaching of Adventism, Baha'i, Catholicism, Islam, and the Christian Community. The National Board of Education set the goals, but it cooperated with the religious communities in the elaboration of the curricula. However, religious communities had no right to control the school instruction.[34]

What we encounter instead of a thoroughly changed model *per se* is a changed understanding of what the instruction was about.

However, before examining this changed understanding, I want to stress that the scheme of RE that I discuss in this chapter affects the vast majority of all Finnish children, which makes it all the more important to scrutinize it. If we study the Finnish school system, we find that the majority of all children take part in public school education. Those very few that attend private schools follow the same core curricula and have the same hours of teaching of different subjects. But of course, these schools can also include other emphases in their activities. Of the schools that have registered with the Association of private schools in Finland, only some 5 percent are Christian faith schools. There is also one Jewish school that incorporates both primary school and high school, but no private Muslim primary school or high school as of yet.[35]

Changed Understanding of Religious Education

I asserted that laws have been changed and education rearranged because of changes in consciousness influenced by socio-political transformations. In the case of Finland and the other Nordic countries, it is clear that the earlier close affiliation of the established Evangelical Lutheran churches with the educational institutions slowly unravels as a result of a changed understanding of the content and goals of RE. The instruction of Lutheran RE is increasingly understood as focusing on knowledge about Christian and other life-views. Following the terminology used

34 Koikkalainen, *Uskonnonopetus*, supra note 19 at 24; Jamisto, 'Pienryhmäuskontojen', supra note 29 at 37; Kallioniemi, 'Näkökulmia', supra note 11 at 65.

35 Some 20,000 pupils and students attend the 52 private schools that are members of the Association of private schools in Finland. The total number of private schools is 85. See http://www.yksityiskoulut.fi/ (accessed 15 November 2011); http://www.yksityiskoulut.fi/aineisto/Ykpaiva250107tiivistelmat.pdf (accessed 15 November 2011). This should be compared to the fact that in 2011, 541,931 pupils took part in basic education. Out of the 2870 primary schools, regional authorities ran 97 percent of them, http://www.stat.fi/til/pop/2011/pop_2011_2011-11-15_tie_001_fi.html (accessed 15 November 2011). As regards upper secondary schools, the latest figures are from 2010. They show that 111 780 students attended upper secondary schools, http://www.stat.fi/til/lop/2010/lop_2010_2011-06-09_tie_001_fi.html (accessed 15. November 2011).

by Palomino, it is about learning *about* and to some extent also *from* religion. The instruction is viewed as providing food for thought on existential issues and elements for identity construction without influencing in any particular direction, and as developing the pupils' capacities for ethically responsible conduct. Changes in society, among other things regarding freedom of conscience and belief (and as part of this tolerance) as well as new pedagogical ideas, contribute to the churches' loss of influence. This is not to say that the religion that historically has held a strong position in society would not still receive a great deal of attention in the actual instruction. The importance of knowing about the religious cultural heritage of the country is underscored. However, public school authorities are responsible for the curricula. RE is an ordinary school subject.[36]

I believe it is wise to exercise some caution at this point by stating explicitly that it is presumably largely the perceptions of the majority Evangelical Lutheran population that we are here talking about. From a minority point of view, and such views may have gained less publicity in the past, it may well be that RE continues to be characterized as confessional and understood as an important way of safeguarding the religious identity of the group.[37] Similar views are voiced also today.

However, even in the 1970s, majority RE (in practice Evangelical Lutheran RE) was no longer considered an expression of doctrinal teaching in Finland. In a theological sense, it had not been confessional for decades. RE was considered confessional in legal and pedagogical terms only.[38] This meant that education

---

36 See e.g. J. Alwall, 'Vart tog religionsfriheten vägen?', in P.B. Andersen et al., *Religion, skole og kulturel integration i Danmark og Sverige* (København: Museum Tusculanums Forlag, 2006) 11–20 at 64–65; R. Larsson, 'Religionsundervisning i svensk skola – en historisk exposé', in Andersen et al., *Religion, skole og kulturel integration*, 113–140, R. Larsson, 'Rätten till befrielse från skolans religionsundervisning i Sverige', in Andersen et al. at 141–163; Pyysiäinen, *Tunnustuksellinen*, supra note 25 at 41–56; J. Stenbæk, 'Religionsfrihed og religionslighet', in Andersen et al., *Religion, skole og kulturel integration*, 75–85 at 77–78; I.Thorson Plesner, 'Promoting Tolerance through Religious Education', in T. Lindholm et al. (eds.), *Facilitating Freedom of Religion or Belief: A Deskbook* (Leiden: Martinus Nijhoff Publishers, 2004), 791–812 at 802; I. Thorson Plesner, *Freedom of religion or belief – a quest for state neutrality?* (Oslo: University of Oslo, 2008), 94, 208, 210, 214, 223; as well as H. Hugason, 'A Case Study of the Evolution of a Nordic Lutheran Majority Church', in L..Christoffersen et al., *Law & Religion*, supra note 3 at 107–122.

37 Cf. Koikkalainen, *Uskonnonopetus*, supra note 19 at 45–46, referring to T. Sakaranaho, 'Katsomusaineiden opetus monikulttuurisen yhteiskunnan haasteena', in Sakaranaho and Jamisto, *Monikulttuurisuus*, supra note 29 at 23.

38 Koikkalainen, *Uskonnonopetus*, supra note 19 at 5; T. Sakaranaho, 'Pienryhmäisten uskontojen opetus ja monikulttuurisuuden haasteet', in Kallioniemi and Salmenkivi, *Katsomusaineiden*, supra note 11, 3–23 at 5, referring to E. Kähkönen, *Uskonnon opetuksen asema Suomen koulunuudistuksessa 1944–1970* (Helsinki: Suomalainen Teologinen Kirjallisuusseura, 1976), 238–242; Pyysiäinen, *Tunnustuksellinen*, supra note 25 at 66–67, 74–75; Seppo, *Uskonnonvapaus*, supra note 21at 179–181; Sakaranaho, *Religious Freedom*, supra note 22 at 332–335.

authorities were under a duty to organize RE 'according to the religious affiliation of the pupil, entitled to education of her or his own religion in school'. Sakaranaho here prefers the wording 'faith-specific' to 'confessional'. The pedagogical aspect RE 'refers to an organising principle, in pedagogic terms, with regard to the contents'. First, students familiarized themselves with the tradition that they had most affinity with, and then they would proceed to other traditions present in the own society and beyond.[39]

It is the changing understanding of the meaning of RE that has already been observed that finally led to a major revision at the beginning of the new millennium, a topic I will turn to in the next section. This finds expression in the argumentation for a change in terminology, which stands out when we study the preparatory works of the new Act on Religious Freedom. The term 'religious instruction in accordance with the confession of the pupil' is considered outdated, given present-day school realities, the actual nature and content of religious instruction, and wider societal realities.[40]

An emphasis on education in times of societal change is often viewed as symptomatic of something, and times are always changing. As part of the educational programme in public schools, RE is inevitably linked to political processes, because the way school instruction is organized mirrors societal ideals and political choices. The historically largely mono-religious Nordic societies[41] are experiencing a new form of heterogeneity because of, among other things, steadily increasing migration. Such observations, as can also be found in the preparatory work of the new Act, make clear that respect, tolerance and equal treatment, as well as knowledge of others are vital for coexistence.

Given that public schools in the Nordic countries and elsewhere reflect the increasing societal heterogeneity of these countries, it is of course valuable that this change is affirmed and contemplated in the goal-setting for education and in the values that society wants schools to echo. While some of the aims of RE are formulated in terms of the personal growth of pupils, other aims will be directed at their future status as adult members of national and international society. In the

39 Sakaranaho, *Religious Freedom*, supra note 22 at 333–334, referring to Kähkönen, *Uskonnon opetuksen asema*, supra note 38 at 238–239, 241–242; Pyysiäinen, *Tunnustuksellinen*, supra note 22 at 74, M. Pyysiäinen, 'Koulun uskonnonopetuksen luonne', in M. Pyysiäinen and J. Seppälä (eds.), Uskonnonopetuksen käsikirja (Helsinki: WSOY, 1998), 41–68 at 66–67; Seppo, *Uskonnonvapaus*, supra note 21 at 179–181.

40 See e.g. RP 170/2002 rd (Government bill RP 170/2002 rd): Regeringens proposition till Riksdagen med förslag till religionsfrihetslag och vissa lagar som har samband med den (hereinafter RP 170/2002 rd), 56.

41 However, approximately 80 per cent of the population still belongs to the Evangelical Lutheran Church. According to the Population Information System, approximately 17.7 per cent is not currently registered with any religious affiliation. This leaves 2.3 per cent for the other 57 registered religious communities. For the latest figures on religious affiliation in the Finnish population, see www.tilastokeskus.fi/til/vaerak/2009/01/vaerak_2009_01_2010-09-30_tau_008_en.html (accessed 20 September 2011)

current situation, shared knowledge entailing 'cultural or religious competence'[42] is emphasized as part of the educational goals, as is ethical growth. Moreover, we find formulations of the goals of education in the Finnish and other Nordic school curricula that envision all students coming to share a commitment to democracy, tolerance and human rights.

However, despite the identified similarities of the Nordic countries, they have drawn different practical solutions in light of societal transformations. Sweden, Norway, Denmark and Iceland have all opted for integrated non-denominational RE. RE is a public school subject for all pupils. The instruction is pluralistic in its content. The focus is on a variety of beliefs.[43]

In Denmark, RE in upper secondary schools became non-confessional in 1961 and in primary schools in 1975. Pupils can be exempted upon request.[44] Iceland only more recently began to move away from a confessional model and towards integrated RE in the public school system.[45] Norway introduced a model of integrated RE in 1997. It is coupled with a system of exemption in relation to those parts of the teaching that may be perceived by parents and pupils as religious practice of another faith.[46] Sweden introduced instruction in religious knowledge at the end of the 1960s. The possibility for exemption as a general rule was dropped in the 1990s with the consent of representatives of different faith traditions.[47]

Finland took a different route when the model of RE was renewed on the threshold of the twenty-first century, even if the government identified similar

42 Religious competence has been defined in the following way: 'Religious competence means being able to deal with one's own religiosity and its various dimensions embedded in the dynamics of life-history in a responsible way but also to appreciate the religious views of others. It includes active tolerance, competence to act in ethically oriented ways, readiness for dialogue on religious matters. It includes also the ability to deal with religious pluralism and differences in a constructive way.' H.-G. Heimbrock et al. (eds.), *Towards Religious Competence: Diversity as a Challenge for Education in Europe* (Münster/Hamburg/Berlin/London: Lit Verlag, 2001), 9.

43 Thorson Plesner, 'Promoting Tolerance', supra note 36 at 799; G. Skeie, 'Citizenship, Identity Politics and Religious Education', in Heimbrock et al., *Towards Religious Competence*, supra note 42, 237–252, at 242.

44 P. B. Andersen et al., 'Indledning', in Andersen et al., *Religion, skole og kulturel integration,* supra note 36, 11–20, at 16; Per Bregengaard, 'Kristendomskundskab eller religion? – En strid om mere end et ord', in Andersen et al., *Religion, skole og kulturel integration,* supra note 36, 87–99, at 92–93; Stenbæk, 'Religionsfrihed', supra note 36 at 77–78.

45 Skeie, 'Citizenship', supra note 43 at 244–246.

46 See e.g. Slotte, 'Waving', supra note 3; P. Slotte, 'Securing Freedom whilst Enhancing Competence: The "Knowledge about Christianity, Religions and Life stances' Subject and the Judgment of the European Court of Human Rights', 6 *Religion and Human Rights* 1 (2011), 41–73.

47 Slotte, 'A Little Church', supra note 3. See also e.g. Pyysiäinen, *Tunnustuksellinen,* supra note 25 at 58–59; Larsson, 'Rätten till befrielse', supra note 36 at 154–160.

societal challenges to those in the other Nordic countries, and set similar goals for RE. The outcome of the consultation and legislative processes was a distinct model for RE in public schools. Finland did indeed abandon a model of confessional instruction, but it chose to retain its model of parallel teaching in what was now to be called 'instruction in the pupil's own religion', with life-stance education as an alternative.

Why did Finland not adopt the model of integrated RE that other Nordic countries had opted for? In fact, the matter had been on the table over the years. During the educational reform in the 1970, for example, integrated RE was the subject of lively debate.[48] Skeie offers a realistic suggestion for why a country may proceed as Finland did:

> [O]ne gets the impression that when the historically based and structurally different types of RE-arrangements meet the multicultural questions they tend [sic] react to them in different ways. This leaves the impression of nationally based efforts to adjust an existing system to the new challenges. This may be interpreted as a tendency to understand the new challenges in terms of the old ones, rather than seeing them as really new.[49]

Indicative of this is the fact that a recent survey of attitudes of Finnish people towards RE showed that the model for organizing RE supported by the majority bore a resemblance to earlier arrangements. Irrespective of the support for multicultural education, an overwhelming majority opposed common non-confessional instruction for all pupils during the nine-year compulsory school period. This was so even though the desired instruction, while providing insights into pupils' personal religious traditions, should not be 'too confessional'. Objective, fact-based instruction about different religions and other worldviews was widely supported. However, the instruction should not amount to just a presentation of different worldviews (religious knowledge). It should also entail an element of 'life-view fostering'.[50]

I now want to move to the discussion on and renewal of that model in the context of the new Constitution Act and Act of Religious Freedom that made its way into the statute book at the turn of the twenty-first century.

---

48 Kallioniemi, 'Näkökulmia', supra note 11 at 66; Koikkalainen, *Uskonnonopetus*, supra note 19, 45. See also Seppo, 'Die Religionsfreiheit', supra note 15 at 23.

49 Skeie, 'Citizenship', supra note 43 at 246.

50 Räsänen, *Koulun uskonnonopetus*, supra note 25 at 109.

Amendments to the Legal Framework

From 'Confessional Instruction' to 'Instruction in the Pupil's Own Religion'

In 1999, Finland adopted a new Constitution (*perustuslaki* [731/1999]), which in Section 11 states that

> [e]veryone has the freedom of religion and conscience. Freedom of religion and conscience entails the right to profess and practice a religion, the right to express one's convictions and the right to be a member of or decline to be a member of a religious community. No one is under the obligation, against his or her conscience, to participate in the practice of a religion.

Together with Section 6 on equality (in the old Constitution Article 9) Section 11 form the two most important Constitutional rights with regard to RE.[51] Section 6 states, among other things, that '[c]hildren shall be treated equally and as individuals and they shall be allowed to influence matters pertaining to themselves to a degree corresponding to their level of development.' Juha Sihvola recently noted that the status of children is now regulated in more detail than was previously the case.[52]

Following these constitutional changes, the Finnish legislation on religious freedom was revised. This work resulted in the new Act on Freedom of Religion in 2003 (*uskonnon-vapauslaki* [453/2003]). Juho Seppo identifies the guiding principle of the Act as follows: the State should not interfere in religious matters apart from laying down common ground rules and making sure that these are not violated.[53]

Anu Koikkalainen has noted that both legally and structurally, no drastic changes were made to the Act on Freedom of Religion. However, what does stand out is the stress on positive freedom *to* religion (the interpretation of which I will discuss in more detail below) alongside freedom *from* religion (the freedom to neither confess religion nor be subjected to another faith) and the duty to not violate the freedom of religion or belief of others. The old Act had regulated the grounds for exempting pupils from RE. By contrast, the new legislation on education stresses the right of individuals to get teaching in 'one's own religion or a belief that shows close affinity with the own faith'.[54] The Committee of Religious

51 Koikkalainen, *Uskonnonopetus*, supra note 19 at 34.

52 Paper by Juha Sihvola, conference on religious diversity and religious freedom, Helsinki University 20.6.2011.

53 Seppo, 'Die Religionsfreiheit', supra note 15 at 28.

54 Koikkalainen, *Uskonnonopetus*, supra note 19 at 5: 'oman uskonnon tai siihen verrattavissa olevan katsomuksen opetusta'; Sakaranaho, *Religious Freedom*, supra note 22 at 336. See also Kallioniemi, 'Näkökulmia', supra note 11 at 63–64; Sakaranaho, 'Pienryhmäisten uskontojen opetus', supra note 38 at 5. Religious education is no longer regulated in the Act on Freedom of Religion, rather 6§ notes that religious education is regulated separately. Act on Freedom of Religion (453/2003). While acknowledging the

Freedom noted that since the end of World War II, the positive aspect of religious freedom has gained in importance and been specified in international law.[55]

Since it was acknowledged that the right to freedom of religion and conscience entails an aspect concerning education, the Basic Education Act (*Lag om grundläggande utbildning*) and the Act for the Upper Secondary School (*Gymnasielag*) were revised. On top of this, the model of RE in Finnish public schools was renewed in order to accommodate the demands of freedom of religion and conscience.

Noteworthy is that the special status of the Evangelical Lutheran and the Orthodox Churches was reaffirmed when legislative changes were made to the laws on education following the new Act on Religious Freedom in 2003.[56] Thus it is compulsory for public schools to organize RE in these faiths even if the number of pupils adhering to these faiths is lower than three pupils and parents and pupils have not asked for the instruction. In contrast, a prerequisite for organizing RE in other beliefs is that the adherents demand this. According to Sakaranaho, churches and religious communities are thus treated differently in law.[57]

Returning to the preparatory works, however, what stands out here is the aforementioned argumentation for changing the name of the subject to 'instruction in the pupil's own religion'. The old concept 'religious instruction in accordance with the confession of the pupil' does not reflect present-day school realities, the actual nature and content of religious instruction, or wider societal realities. The instruction is described in the following terms:

> The foundations for the curricula of the nine-year compulsory school and the upper secondary school, which the National Board of Education establishes with support of the Basic Education Act and the Act for the Upper Secondary School, state that the goal of religious instruction is that the student gets many-sided general knowledge about questions having to do with religion and life-view. This includes becoming acquainted with the pupils' own religion and its cultural heritage, so that the pupil gets impulses to shape a view of life. The instruction, furthermore, includes orientation in other religions and world views and their traditions, in order for the student to grow in tolerance in a multicultural society and develop an ethically responsible attitude to life. Greek Orthodox religious instruction also mentions the readiness to be an active member of the congregation as a goal. According to the foundations of the curriculum,

---

emphasis on positive religious freedom as something positive, Sakaranaho has critically remarked that the new Act upholds the existing power balance that favours the Evangelical Lutheran and Orthodox churches. Sakaranaho, *Religious Freedom*, supra note 22 at 162.

55 Seppo, 'Die Religionsfreiheit', supra note 15 at 28, referring to Rk 2001, supra note 16 at 5–9, 21–22.

56 Koikkalainen, *Uskonnonopetus*, supra note 19 at 31.

57 Sakaranaho, ' Pienryhmäisten uskontojen opetus', supra note 38, 6. See also Koikkalainen, *Uskonnonopetus*, supra note 19 at 63.

> preaching and devotions do not belong to the instruction. The instruction has, furthermore, for a long time not meant confession to a faith. According to the foundations of the curriculum, actual religious practice (the participation in a cult) does not belong to the instruction. The legislation and the foundations for the curriculum do not, e.g., presuppose that the school organizes worship in the school, even if the schools can organize such for their pupils and students.[58]

Whether this was the case in relation to all confessional instruction in the public schools at the time of the drafting process is open to doubt.[59] Nevertheless, a specific understanding of RE is promoted and leads to consequent re-elaboration of all curricula concerning RE in Finnish public schools. According to this understanding, there is no longer a close connection between the subject taught and the doctrine of a specific faith. There is no link made between the instructional aims in the school and, for example, a church's baptismal catechism.[60] The instruction has a broader focus.

Religious practices have no obvious place in RE, in the same way as they have no self-evident place in public schools overall. For some time the focus of the instruction has been on attaining knowledge about religions and other worldviews and giving pupils tools to deal with existential matters. RE is here seen within the framework of the overall goals of education.[61]

The lack of clear links to religious communities is further underlined by the fact that it is the Finnish National Board of Education that devises the national core curricula of the instruction. The municipalities, in turn, elaborate these foundations in their local curricula. For these reasons, the drafters conclude that RE is based

58 RP 170/2002 rd, supra note 40 at 62 [author's translation]. See also RK 2001, supra note 16 at 53. As mentioned above, the Greek Orthodox Church of Finland, which belongs to the Patriarchate of Constantinople, has a special status in Finnish law alongside the Evangelical-Lutheran Church. While I am aware of the fact that the Russian Orthodox Church is also represented in Finland, and that there are other additional distinctions that can be made among the adherents to this faith, I here use the term 'Greek Orthodox' as a generic term. The curricula in question also concern all adherents.

59 See the analysis of the confessional instruction in different religions in the Finnish public schools during the 1990s, in Pyysiäinen, *Yksi oppiaine,* supra note 32 at 76–86. As regards Orthodox RE, Kaarina Lyhykäinen does identify societal changes such as increasing diversity as a reason for why the goals of education needed to be partly revised. The teaching could not be conceptualized in the same way as it was as late as back in the 1990s when integrating children in the active life of the Church had explicitly been a primary task. Now this task of RE is, as mentioned above, reframed as to strengthen and uphold the identity of the child. Moreover, knowledge of other faiths and non-religious life-views become a learning goal already in primary school. Lyhykäinen, 'Vähemmistön', supra note 29 at 19.

60 RP 170/2002 rd, supra note 40 at 56.

61 RP 170/2002 rd, supra note 40 at 56.

on law and curricula that have been approved by public authorities.[62] (They also draw from this the somewhat misguided conclusion that the personal conviction of individual teachers does not influence the content of the instruction.[63])

As a result, the requirement that the teachers of Evangelical Lutheran and Orthodox RE must be members of these churches is dropped. There is no reason to keep this requirement. What is required of teachers is instead sufficient knowledge of the subject taught as well as pedagogical competence.[64] Teachers are no longer viewed as representatives of a certain denomination, but as professionals in their own field of expertise.

Lastly, the conclusion is reached that, in accordance with the curriculum and the aims spelled out there, this type of RE does not amount to religious practice as defined in Section 11 of the Constitution, taking into account the changes proposed in the draft.[65] This was also the conclusion of the Constitutional Law Committee of Parliament.[66]

During the drafting process, the Education and Culture Committee of the Parliament also deliberated over the aim of the instruction and its content. It was argued that the instruction could include, for example, prayers and hymns, visits to churches and mosques as well as information about different religious ceremonies, such as baptisms and funerals. This was seen as something somewhat different from what was otherwise understood by 'knowledge' (*kunskapsinslag*). Yet these features were still considered to fall within the acceptable frames of neutral and objective instruction.[67] These views of the Education and Culture Committee actualize the topic of the following section, namely those concerns about freedom of religion and conscience that were voiced when the model for RE was revised.

Notions of Religious Freedom as Frame of Reference

Apart from societal considerations and an assessment of the current state and content of the actual instruction, the changes made to the model of RE were strongly influenced by considerations of freedom of religion and conscience. As

62 RP 170/2002 rd, supra note 40 at 56.

63 RP 170/2002 rd, supra note 40 at 56. For a critique of the possibility of teachers staying completely clear of influencing the actual instruction, see Mikael Lindfelt, 'Religionsfrihet och åskådningsundervisning i teori och praxis', in Tage Kurtén, Mikael Lindfelt and Pamela Slotte (eds.), *Ratio et fides: Studia in honorem Hans-Olof Kvist* (Åbo: Åbo Akademis förlag, 2001), 229–251, at 238–239.

64 RP 170/2002 rd, supra note 40 at 56–57.

65 RP 170/2002 rd, supra note 40 at 62–63.

66 GrUB 10/2002 (Report 10/2002), Constitutional Law Committee of the Parliament (Grundlagsutskottets betänkande). See further RK 2001, supra note 16 at 21, 49, 53; Lindfelt, 'Religionsfrihet', supra note 63 at 238.

67 KuUU 14/2002 (Statement 14/2002), Education and Culture Committee of the Parliament (hereinafter KuUU 14/2002 rd).

noted above, the renewed model came about in the context of a larger revision in Finnish legislation on religious freedom.

Moreover, the new regulations emphasize, as did the Committee on Religious Freedom at the time, positive freedom *to* religion rather than mainly on a negative freedom *from* religion. Children have a right to receive some sort of instruction in their life-view.[68]

However, the meaning of Section 11 of the new Constitution Act which states that '[c]hildren shall be treated equally and as individuals and they shall be allowed to influence matters pertaining to themselves to a degree corresponding to their level of development', caused serious debate in the Committee on Religious Freedom. Eventually, committee member Martin Scheinin added a dissenting opinion to the committee report. According to Scheinin, the existing Finnish age limits pertaining to children's right to choose their religious affiliation should have been lowered in order to accord with international legal trends[69]affording the views of the child greater acknowledgement alongside that of their parents or legal guardians.[70] The existing limitations to children's autonomy were problematic from the perspective of freedom of religion and conscience.

As the committee chose a different stance, Scheinin went on to state that in order to comply with Section 11 of the Constitution Act, children belonging to a religion must as a minimum condition be allowed to abstain from participation in the RE of their own religion.[71] Scheinin was also sceptical about the change in terminology. In his view, it was a way to alter the characterization of the majority RE subject so that it could be mandatory and yet comply with international human rights law. If it is asserted that religious practice does not form part of the subject, pupils can be compelled to participate. However, Scheinin doubted whether anything would change in practice. The teaching would retain elements of religious practice. He consequently found the stance of the majority of the committee problematic, as the right to freedom of religion entails the right to decide when and how you want to participate in religious practice even while you are still a minor and even if parents and legal guardians are justified partly in making decisions for you.[72]

However, the age limits were retained. Parents or legal guardians make the decisions for children in primary school. In the case of the students in the upper secondary school, though, it is the students themselves, having reached the age of

---

68 RK 2001, supra note 16 at 7, 20–22, 25, 34, 50; Lindfelt, 'Religionsfrihet', supra note 63 at 236; Räsänen, *Koulun uskonnonopetus*, supra note 25, 15–16.

69 Koikkalainen, *Uskonnonopetus*, supra note 19, 67, referring to RK 2001, supra note 16 at 95–98. See also Martin Scheinin, 'Koulujen uskonnonopetus ihmisoikeuksien näkökulmasta', 106 *Teologinen aikakauskirja* 6 (2001), 515–517, at 516.

70 Scheinin, 'Koulujen uskonnonopetus', supra note 69 at 515.

71 Scheinin, 'Koulujen uskonnonopetus', supra note 69 at 516–617. See also Koikkalainen, *Uskonnonopetus*, supra note 19, 67, referring to RK 2001, supra note 16 at 95–98.

72 Scheinin, 'Koulujen uskonnonopetus', supra note 69 at 516.

15, that choose which RE to participate in (we shall see what the choices are in the next section).[73] We can interpret this difference at the two educational stages as an expression of the meaning of the notion of the 'evolving capacities of the child'.[74] With the permission of the legal guardian, Finnish children are, at the age of 15, free to choose their religious denomination, if any. Consequently, they may choose whether to participate in religious practice and instruction.[75]

Moreover, it was not only the freedom of religion and conscience of children that had to be considered. Human rights law also demands that the right of parents to bring up their children in accordance with their own convictions is respected in all education. During the drafting process, it is also apparent that the instruction, despite being non-confessional in nature, is seen in this light. The link with homes and parents is underlined. *If* offered in the public schools, RE should be viewed on a continuum with the religious or other upbringing a child might be getting at home.[76]

[N]o one can be enjoined to participate in 'a service or another similar event' against his conscience. On the other hand, confessional education has also been held to be part of the right to confess and practice a religion, secured in § 11 … [R]eligious freedom presupposes that the individual has the opportunity to receive instruction either in religion or life-stance, and that education and upbringing more generally shall respect the conviction of the individual, the rights of children and the right of the legal guardian to answer for the development of the child.[77]

These considerations of what religious freedom includes, thus further explain why the Finnish authorities chose the 'segregation' model they did, because in principle nothing prevented a model of integrated RE resembling that of other Nordic countries from becoming the practical consequence of the new Act. Neither the societal and legal context, nor the educational goals, nor the actual school reality make one model inevitable. As we saw earlier, the situation in Finland resembles the historical development in the other Nordic countries.

The only explanation in principle that remains in order to justify the confessional feature as a pedagogical and organizational principle, is the idea that life-view instruction at school must complement religious upbringing in the home.[78]

I would myself speak here of 'respecting' rather than 'complementing' religious upbringing, but besides that, Mikael Lindfelt here affirms the strong focus on religious freedom that was present in the deliberations. The freedom of religion and conscience of pupils and their parents or legal guardians is accommodated through a system of choice. By organizing non-confessional RE along confessional lines,

73 RP 170/2002 rd, supra note 40 at 60

74 CRC, art. 5.

75 Act of Religious Freedom [453/2003], §3; Lindfelt, 'Religionsfrihet', supra note 63 at 237; and RK 2001, supra note 16 at 11, 20–21, 23, 30–31, for the argumentation.

76 RK 2001, supra note 16 at 22; RP 170/2002 rd, supra note 40 at 61–62; Lindfelt, 'Religionsfrihet', supra note 63 at 237; ECHR, art. 9; ECHR, Protocol No. 1, art. 2.

77 RP 170/2002 rd, supra note 40 at 61–62. [author's translation].

78 Lindfelt, 'Religionsfrihet', supra note 63 at 240 [author's translation].

additional safeguards are put in place. Pupils and their parents or legal guardians may feel that even 'objective' and 'neutral' imparting of religious knowledge is coercive. They may perceive that they are forced to partake in the practice of a foreign religion, something that no one should be compelled to do.

Finally, we have also seen that at the time of reform, it was noted that the foundations of the Finnish curriculum made clear that neither 'preaching' nor 'devotions' nor any other 'actual religious practice' belongs to RE. It was further highlighted that RE has not 'for a long time meant confession to a faith'. Taking into account the changes proposed to the existing model of RE, the teaching did not amount to religious practice as defined in Section 11 of the Constitution.[79]

However, it was also observed that '[t]he legislation and the foundations for the curriculum do not, e.g., presuppose that the school organizes worship in the school, even if schools can arrange it for their pupils and students.'[80] With regard to this observation, the National Board of Education some three years later observed that the new Finnish Act does not intervene in school traditions. Singing traditional hymns at a Christmas celebration or at the end of the school year in spring, does not amount to religious practice as defined by the Finnish Act on Religious Freedom. These celebrations are instead viewed as transmitting and upholding culture.[81] The National Board of Education issued this statement in order to clarify some of the issues that were raised in the years following the new legislation.

These issues will be the topic for the last parts of this chapter, but before turning to that analysis, the next section will offer some facts about the new model that came to be called 'non-confessional instruction in the pupil's own religion' (*Regeringsproposition* 170/2002 rd).

New Model of Religious Education

Following the Act on Religious Freedom 2003, which regulates Section 11 of the Constitution in more detail, changes were made in the Basic Education Act (*Lag om grundläggande utbildning* [454/2003]) and Act for the Upper Secondary School (*Gymnasielag* [455/2003]). Pupils in the public, compulsory, nine-year school programme, and students in the upper secondary school are not automatically included in majority religion RE, which in Finland is the Evangelical-Lutheran faith. They receive instruction in their own religion or take part in life-stance education. Consequently, they do not have to ask to be exempted. If parents or legal guardians do not specifically notify the educational institution that a pupil is to accept instruction in religion, those who do not belong to any religious

79 RP 170/2002 rd, supra note 40 at 62–63 [author's translation].

80 RP 170/2002 rd, supra note 40 at 62. [author's translation]

81 Utbildningsstyrelsen, *Meddelande* 19/2006 (28 February 2006) (Utbildningsstyrelsen, Helsingfors, 2006a), 7; Utbildningsstyrelsen, *Meddelande* 28/2006 (16 August 2006) (Utbildningsstyrelsen, Helsingfors, 2006b), 6–7.

denomination automatically take part in life-stance classes.[82] As concluded in the government bill:

> The provisions about exemption from the religious instruction fit badly with the provision about religious freedom in the Constitution ... It is consistent with the principle of religious freedom that no one is, even as a point of departure, assumed to participate in such instruction, which does not correspond to that person's own religious view of life.[83]

Pupils belonging to the majority religion cannot choose life-stance education instead of instruction in their own religion. Rather, they are obliged to take part in the latter.[84] The reason this is not considered a violation of Section 11 of the Constitution Act is that the grounds for compulsory participation lies in the free choice, on the part of the child or the parents, to join the religious denomination according to which the instruction is given.[85] However, commentators have noted that this puts children in unequal positions.[86] In a sense, they end up having different freedom of religion and conscience depending on whether they belong to the majority or a minority.

As far as the instruction in other religions is concerned, it is offered if the parents of at least three pupils living in the municipality wish that such instruction be organized. Otherwise, the pupil may choose to receive instruction in the majority religion, participate in life-stance classes, or attend instruction organized by his or her own religious community. Furthermore,

> [a] pupil who does not belong to any religious community may, at the request of his or her parent/carer, also participate in religious education provided by the

---

82 *Lag om grundläggande utbildning* 21.8.1998/628, FörfS 1998, 1719, § 13, www.finlex.fi/sv/laki/kokoelma/1998/19980081.pdf (accessed 15 July 2011; *Gymnasielag* 21.8.1998/629, FörfS 1998, 1731, § 9, www.finlex.fi/sv/laki/alkup/1998/19980629 (accessed 15 July 2011); *Lag om ändring av 13§ lagen om grundläggande utbildning* 6.6.2003/454, FörfS 2003, 2091, www.finlex.fi/sv/laki/kokoelma/2003/20030077.pdf, (accessed 15 July 2011); *Lag om ändring av 9 § gymnasielagen* 6.6.2003/455,FörfS 2003, 2093, www.finlex.fi/sv/laki/kokoelma/2003/20030077.pdf (accessed 15 July 2011); RK2001, supra note 30 at 11, 50.

83 RP 170/2002rd, supra note 40 at 38 [author's translation]. See also RK 2001, supra note 16 at 34 (§8).

84 RP 170/2002rd, supra note 40 at 38; Lindfelt, 'Religionsfrihet', supra note 63 at 236–237.

85 RK 2001, supra note 16 at 53.

86 Koikkalainen, *Uskonnonopetus*, supra note 19 at 81; Sakaranaho, 'Pienryhmäisten', supra note 38 at 5–6.

> provider of basic education which, in view of his or her upbringing and cultural background, evidently corresponds to his or her religious beliefs.[87]

If a child belongs to more than one religious community, the parents can choose in which RE to enrol their child. In the Upper Secondary School, the individual student makes this choice.[88] Koikkalainen notes that the guiding principle here, both for the government and the Committee on Religious Freedom, was that the state has no right to limit the possibility of individuals to be members of multiple religious communities. This was not the case under the old Act of Religious Freedom.[89]

Moreover, the system of choice also reflects an idea in the new Act on Religious Freedom that the religious status of the child is no longer automatically determined by the status of the parent or legal guardian. Rather, parents usually at some point make a conscious decision on how to register their child. RE is given in accordance with this belonging. Religious belonging is a guiding organizational principle.[90]

In addition, we have seen that in the case of the students in the upper secondary school, it is not the parents or legal guardians but the students themselves, having reached the age of 15, who make the choice regarding participation in RE. The students are the ones who have to be informed about the alternatives, as well as of possible upcoming events that can be characterized as 'religious practice', in which they may choose not to participate. Still, the legal guardians are also informed about the possibility not to participate in religious practice.[91]

At present, there are 14 framework curricula: Adventist, Baha'i, Buddhism, Catholicism, Evangelical Lutheran faith, God's People (*Herran Kansa*), Islam, Judaism, Krishna Movement, the Christian Community, The Church of Jesus Christ of Latter-day Saints, Free Church faith, Orthodox faith, and life-stance education. In practice, however, the latest figures show that 94 percent of pupils take part in RE of the majority Evangelical Lutheran faith, 1 percent takes part in Orthodox RE, 3 percent in life-stance education and another 2 percent get other RE. Moreover, 34 percent of public schools offer teaching in Evangelical Lutheran RE and Orthodox RE, 32 percent only in Evangelical Lutheran RE, 18 percent of schools offer a combination of Evangelical Lutheran RE, Orthodox RE and Islam RE. Only 29 percent of schools offer teaching in two different religions, a mere

87 Quote from the official English translation of *Lag om grundläggande utbildning,* supra note 82 at § 13, www.finlex.fi/en/laki/kaannokset/1998/en19980628.pdf (accessed 15 July 2011). The same paragraph, with respect to the students in upper secondary school, is found in *Gymnasielag,* supra note 82 at § 9.

88 Koikkalainen, *Uskonnonopetus*, supra note 19, 37, referring to Sakaranaho, 'Katsomusaineiden', supra note 37 at 16.

89 Koikkalainen, *Uskonnonopetus*, supra note 19 at 36–37, referring to Seppo, *Uskonnonvapaus*, supra note21 at 159–160. See also RK 2001, supra note 15.

90 Koikkalainen, *Uskonnonopetus*, supra note 19 at 36, referring to Seppo, *Uskonnonvapaus*, supra note 21 at 160.

91 RP 170/2002 rd, supra note 40 at 60.

1.6 percent of schools in three religions and 0.4 percent of schools offer RE in four or more religions. For this reason, Antti Räsänen recently concluded that Finnish public schools are therefore still commonly mono-religious schools.[92]

It also has to be remembered that some parents, Jehovah's Witnesses for example, choose the option of having their children receive their religious teaching outside the public school system. Adherents to certain Christian communities, on the other hand, take part in the Evangelical Lutheran RE. This as a rule is the case with Pentecostals and Methodists. None of these communities have sought their own national curricula in RE.[93]

Experiences, Problems and Proposed Amendments

As noted in the introduction, during the last ten years, education professionals, non-governmental organizations, and faith communities have all engaged with the question of freedom of religion and conscience in education, and so too have public officials and the government. Problems have been identified, and further improvements as well as changes to the educational system and the legislation have been proposed. This section will offer an overview of these matters.

A System Modelled to Suit the Evangelical Lutheran Faith

Starting where I left it in the last section, because participation in RE as a rule is decided based on the religious affiliation of the pupil or student, this creates problems for adherents of faiths who are not registered as religious associations. Unregistered religious communities cannot apply for their own RE curriculum. The religious communities themselves may not consider registration important. It may even be that this would be contrary to the tenets of the faith in question. However, public authorities have also on occasion refused to register a community, such as Wicca or Scientology.[94]

As noted, children adhering to such faiths can naturally participate in RE given in a faith that shows cultural affinity to theirs, and they can alternatively receive teaching in their own communities. However, the symbolic impact may still be of such magnitude that the alternatives do not satisfy everyone.

Drawing on Sakaranaho's findings, we could say that the way these matters are regulated reflects a majority perspective on faith, and consequently also on religious freedom and organization of education. Sakaranaho has made critical

92 Paper by Antti Räsänen during the 11th Nordic Conference of Religious Education (NCRE), 6–9 June 2011 at the Faculty of Theology, Aarhus University.

93 Koikkalainen, *Uskonnonopetus*, supra note 19 at 50.

94 Koikkalainen, *Uskonnonopetus*, supra note 19 at 64–65; Sakaranaho, 'Pienryhmäisten', supra note 38 at 6.

observations that seem to be pertinent. Since religious rights are being based on belonging, on membership in a religious community, she says, the new Act on Religious Freedom and other consequent legislation take as a model the Finnish and more generally the Nordic mode of religious affiliation, church membership, which is conceptualized rather more frequently in terms of custom than explicit choice. The Act affirms standard practice, and privileges religious organizations rather than the rights of individuals. This being so, Sakaranaho considers the new Act out-dated at the very outset from the perspective of multiculturalism. It is institution-centred; it reflects the views of the majority culture and neglects the diversity and distinctiveness of minority beliefs. Majority Lutheran belief is still privileged, and while the rights enjoyed by the majority are afforded also to minorities, it is thus done on majority terms.[95]

An example of practice with regard to RE, which Sakaranaho views as indicative of a majority paradigm, is the following. In some regions, such as in the city of Espoo, where RE in Islam has been organized because of the demand of three pupils and their families, this subject at one point became compulsory for all pupils who were publically registered as being of Muslim faith even if they had not asked for it. This practice was incompatible with current legislation, even if it, in one sense, treats pupils of the Muslim faith in an equal manner as pupils of the majority Lutheran faith.[96]

Moreover, although various Christian denominations have their own RE, there is only one curriculum in Islam. The teaching has been characterized as being a kind of 'general Islam', perhaps in a similar fashion as Evangelical Lutheran RE is often characterized as a subject in 'general Christianity', in which children adhering to various branches of Christianity take part. Commentators find this problematic. The system glosses over the variety of interpretations of Islam in an attempt to teach something that all can accept.[97]

A further issue that has arisen is that sometimes non-religious children have automatically been directed to RE classes owing to close affinity between that religion and the culture of the region from which they originate. Such has been the case of Iraqi and Iranian children who have been made to attend classes in Islam.[98]

---

95 Koikkalainen, *Uskonnonopetus*, supra note 19 at 6–7, referring to Seppo, *Uskonnonvapaus*, supra note 21 at 30–34; Sakaranaho, *Religious Freedom*, supra note 22 at 116–119, 193–194, 339, 422–424. See also Sakaranaho, *Religious Freedom*, at 145–148, 338, 341.

96 Sakaranaho, 'Pienryhmäisten', supra note 38 at 7. See also Koikkalainen, *Uskonnonopetus*, supra note 19 at 70–71. The idea was that the subject strengthens their Muslim identity and sense of citizenship.

97 Koikkalainen, *Uskonnonopetus*, supra note 19 at 65 (and fn 129), 66, 69; Sakaranaho, 'Pienryhmäisten', supra note 38 at 10; Sakaranaho, *Religious Freedom*, supra note 22 at 368.

98 Koikkalainen, *Uskonnonopetus*, supra note 19 at 55, referring to Erkki Haapaniemi, 'Katsomusopetus puntarissa', 3 *Vapaa Ajattelija* (2008), 14–15.

Expressions of 'Secularized' Christianity

I wish to pursue some notions of how majority faith informs the debate about religious freedom in education. The new Act of Religious Freedom of 2003 and the revised model of RE has been called a 'cultural statement'. The cultural importance of religion is affirmed.[99] The intertwinement of culture and religion, and in Finland especially the majority religion, is also what is actualized when something, as I noted earlier, is framed as an expression of religion rather than merely culture.

During the process of legal revisions, as we have seen, it was repeatedly stated that the new Act of Religious Freedom does not interfere with traditions and celebrations in educational institutions. Moreover, we have seen that positive freedom to religion was a key feature and guiding principle in the legislative work. It helped shape and justify the current Finnish system of RE. However, what about other school activities, such as the reading of the Nativity story in December. For sure, it is a Finnish tradition, and as such justified on cultural grounds. Nevertheless, can it also be accommodated if viewed as a religious activity?

On examining the parliamentary debate, it becomes apparent that, following the new regulations, some school authorities have been hesitant to organize worship and other religious acts. In order to be on the safe side, some have occasionally abstained completely from organizing such events.[100] I view this as an expression of a common insecurity relating to religion in contemporary secularized Finnish society. Just as with the choice to legislate for neutral and objective instruction *in* their own religions for all children, school authorities too are playing it safe.

At the drafting stage, suggestions were made to add sections about participation in religious practice to the regulations in Act for the Upper Secondary School (§ 9) and the Basic Education Act (§ 13). The aim of the sections was to spell out in more detail how students, pupils and their parents could exercise their right not to participate in religious practice organized by the school, either as part of the general activities of the school or within the ambit of specific school subjects. The religious activities mentioned were typical, generally recognized forms of religious manifestation: various celebrations and worship practices, as well as other religious events that subsume a religious programme, like some morning assemblies. The regulations stated that school authorities had to inform children and their families well in advance of planned religious activities. They also had to tell how pupils (their parents) and students could communicate their intention to be absent from these. Alternative activities should also be offered.[101] While not

---

99 Koikkalainen, *Uskonnonopetus*, supra note 19 at 56, referring to Seppo, *Uskonnonvapaus*, supra note 21 at 289.

100 SS 724/2005 rd: Religionsfriheten i skolorna (Päivi Räsänen/kd m.fl.) (Skriftligt spörsmål), 1.

101 RP 170/2002 rd, supra note 40 at 59–60. Among such activities are excursions, discussions and alternative Christmas celebrations. Jaakko Rusama, *Religion,*

included in the final legal texts, the proposed regulations have found their way into the memoranda of the Finnish National Board of Education.[102]

In 2005, the Finnish National Board of Education, taking into consideration recent experience and issues perceived to be unclear, added to its directives the note that pupils may be exempted from participation in the religious practices of their own and other denominations for reasons of conscience, with no further justification required. In the report of the Committee on Religious Freedom in 2001, this was interpreted as an aspect of the so-called negative freedom of religion.[103]

Furthermore, pupils belonging to a denomination other than that of the majority did not even need to attend instruction in their own religion, even if such is currently being offered. Finally, if they had been taking part in majority instruction, they should now be asked whether they wished to switch.[104] This duty to inform and explain was laid at the door of the school authorities.

However, this is a recurring issue. While confessional elements throughout the twentieth and the start of the twenty-first century have been increasingly downplayed, and, both in practice and in law, room has been made for arrangements tending to the needs of religious minorities, it is always important to be critically aware that a majority culture and majority religiosity might have blind spots. Owing to the fact that the Nordic countries are largely secular, there might be large-scale ignorance among the public and public authorities as to how the majority is 'not merely a historical and cultural phenomenon' but a *religion*:

The majority religion, often in a secularized or symbolic form, may be present in the law and in public institutions to the extent that individuals not belonging to

---

livsåskådningskunskap och umgängesfostran i den grundläggande utbildningen (Helsingfors: Utbildningsstyrelsen, 2002), 32. It is conceded that different celebrations, worship and other activities that contain religious elements form part of the traditions of the Finnish school. This praxis can be upheld. Nevertheless, there is a need to secure that everyone is free to abstain from participation in religious practice. RP 170/2002 rd, supra note 40 at 59. Concerns about whether schools would be able accurately to inform pupils and guardians in advance had already been raised before the Act was enacted. KuUU 14/2002 rd, supra note 67.

102 Utbildningsstyrelsen (2006a), supra note 81 at 7–8; Utbildningsstyrelsen (2006b), supra note 81 at 6–7.

103 RK 2001, supra note 16, 53.

104 Utbildningsstyrelsen (2006a), supra note 81 at 3; 'The National Board of Education will suggest to the Ministry of Education that it also clarify, at a constitutional level, the duty of students to participate in instruction in their own religion, whether or not they have requested it. The National Board of Education recommends that only those pupils whose legal guardians have requested such instruction participate until the duty to so do has been defined at a constitutional level (decision by the Parliamentary Ombudsman 6.6.2005).' [author's translation]

the Lutheran Church may experience a lack of respect for their own freedom of thought, conscience and religion.[105]

Secularized Protestantism can be taken for neutrality. It is also with regard to this sort of blindness or ignorance that a human rights perspective has shown itself to be of importance in the Nordic context, and lately more specifically in relation to RE in public schools.[106]

The system of exemption that accompanies the Finnish educational model fulfils several functions: to safeguard freedom of religion and conscience (of course, 'conscience' is understood as more than just an 'opinion'[107]), to guarantee the formal equality of all citizens that the Constitution Act affirms, and to comply with Section 11 which among other things states that '[n]o one is under the obligation, against his or her conscience, to participate in the practice of a religion'. Students and pupils and their parents can seek exemption both for particular events and as a general exemption with regard to all school events of a religious nature.[108]

To take a recent example that confirms this stance, during winter 2010/2011, a Finnish provincial government was asked to decide whether in public schools it is acceptable to pray before meals. Such is the practice in some Finnish schools, perhaps primarily in the countryside. The provincial government found that as children could choose to stay silent while their peers prayed, or leave the room for that moment, prayer before meals is acceptable practice.[109]

Finally, the examples of religious practices mentioned above, which are partly taken from the preparatory works, represent activities that are identified as central to majority religion. However, what is or is not an expression of foreign faith, or alternatively allowed or prohibited from the perspective of one's own faith, is a fluid issue. Opinions differ. So far, Finland seems to have adopted a pragmatic approach to issues such as classes of music and visual arts. This has been a common practical problem where solutions have been found that accommodate

---

105 See Scheinin, 'Secular', supra note 33 at 548. See also Anna-Leena Riitaoja, Saila Poulter and Arniika Kuusisto, 'Worldviews and Multicultural Education in the Finnish Context – A Critical Philosophical Approach to Theory and Practices', 5 *Finnish Journal of Ethnicity and Migration* 3 (2010), 87–95, and Skeie, 'Citizenship', supra note 46 at 246; 'Seen from the point of view of immigrated minorities, the combination of nation and religion look much firmer than is perceived by the majority. To the extent that a strong system sees itself as being secularised, it may be difficult for the majority to observe the extent to which religious tradition continues to live in transformed versions as part of national self-understanding.' Skeie is here thinking about a system like that in Norway and Sweden.

106 See case of *Folgerø and others v. Norway*, App. No. 15472/02 (Grand Chamber), 29 June 2007.

107 Koikkalainen, *Uskonnonopetus*, supra note 19 at 58, referring to Seppo, *Uskonnonvapaus*, supra note 21 at 187.

108 Salmenkivi et al., 'Elämänkatsomustiedon', supra note 29 at 152–153.

109 http://www.ristinvoitto.fi/sisalto/artikkelit/lounais-suomen_aluehallintoviraston_paatos_paivakotien_ ruokarukousasiassa_1632010/ (accessed 22 November 2011)

the wishes of those Muslim parents who do not want their children to take part in such classes.[110]

I want to sum up this section by referring to certain observations of Sakaranaho. She observes that the model of parallel RE in Finland puts adherents of different faiths at a close to equal footing and enhances their positive freedom to religion. From the perspective of religious freedom, it is nevertheless a reason for concern that the school culture is so monocultural, that Finnish culture is so strongly identified with the Lutheran tradition, and that Lutheran traditions are justified as school activities in cultural terms.

Consequently, it is not farfetched to say that the indirect effect of the new Freedom of Religion Act is to strengthen the Finnish national identity coupled with Lutheranism, however vaguely the latter might be understood. The freedom of Religion Act thereby fosters, in the context of secular education, some kind of civic Christian education, where religion and national identity are closely intertwined, and where the implicit aim of the education is to enhance national identity of pupils as members of a particular nation-state. ... Positive as it may be, religious freedom in Finnish schools will be seriously limited as long as the 'public sphere' of a school remains monocultural.[111]

This is not to say that it is not important to know the 'national religio-cultural heritage'. However, while pupils and their parents of minority beliefs are treated

110 Koikkalainen, *Uskonnonopetus*, supra note 19 at 58, referring to M. Halonen, 'Islam alakoulussa: koulu kaksisuuntaisen sopeutumisen kenttänä', 3 *Nuorisotutkimus* (2009), 36–37, 44. See also Sakaranaho, *Religious Freedom*, supra note 22 at 381–382, who notes that in addition to subjects such as music and visual arts, classes of biology and especially sexual ethics also give rise to concern among some Muslim parents. It is worth noting that Finnish experts of constitutional law and human rights law hold that the second paragraph of Section 11 of the Constitution Act does not give rise to a general right to exemption from teaching on grounds of worldview, for example from biology classes because of creationist beliefs. However, they do hold that from the perspective of freedom of religion and conscience, schools should seek to solutions when school activities give rise to issues of concern to believers. Ojanen and Scheinin, 'Uskonnon', supra note 13 at 430. In 2010, the National Board of Education issued a set of general guidelines on the 'multicultural school community' and which in part deal with exactly these issues of how to accommodate religious convictions with regard to classes in music, visual arts and sports, and also with regard to other school activities such as excursions or school camps. P. Immonen-Oikkonen ja A. Leino (toim.), *Monikulttuurinen kouluyhteisö. Oppaat ja käsikirjat 2010:8* (Opetushallitus, 2010), 71–85, available at http://www.oph.fi/download/126666_Monikulttuurinen_kouluyhteiso.pdf (accessed 22 November 2011). However, as a colleague recently pointed out, the fact that solutions are sought at the level of local schools and leave much leeway to individual teachers can result in unequal treatment as the needs of the pupils are accommodated differently depending on which school they happen to go to.

111 Sakaranaho, *Religious Freedom*, supra note 22 at 350, referring to D. MacNeill. 'Religious Education and National Identity', 47 *Social Compass* 3 (2000), 343–351, for the notion 'civil Christian education'.

more or less equally as far as RE is concerned, the same is not true as regards school life in general, and there is reason to be aware of this.[112] It is good that a system of exemption that safeguards freedom from religion exists. However, it is easy to see that having to resort to this scheme on a regular basis can affect negatively the sense of belonging of children of minority beliefs.

Practical Problems as Regards Organization and Teaching

There is also another batch of problems that have been identified and that concern the actual organization of the tuition in RE. Schools have to organize RE in minority faiths if the students or the parents or legal guardians of three pupils demand this. The pupils do not have to go to the same school. It is enough that they live in the same 'administrative' area.

To organize teaching for these children, then, is sometimes difficult in practice. Pupils belonging to minority faiths and those attending life-stance classes are scattered throughout the school system. The few teachers of minority faith have to travel extensively between different schools in the region of the capital city of Helsinki, for example, in order to provide teaching. It has proved difficult for schools to coordinate this. The teaching of RE and life-stances subject has to fit with the rest of the school teaching, but also with the teaching in other schools that share the same RE teachers. It is a challenge to fulfil regulations, to ensure that teachers of minority RE get enough hours of teaching, and gap-hours for pupils (something that is prohibited in primary school) are kept to a minimum. To harmonize the schedules of everyone concerned—pupils, parents, teachers and schools—presents quite a challenge.[113]

Moreover, the pupils participating in minority RE are often of different ages and backgrounds, at different educational levels of attainment, and some may not speak the official language of instruction very well.[114] The teachers have a challenging job. Good teaching material may also not be readily available. The first student's school textbook *Salam* was published just recently.[115]

---

112 Sakaranaho, *Religous Freedom*, supra note 22 at 351.

113 Koikkalainen, *Uskonnonopetus*, supra note 19 at 68–70, 80, referring to Sari Vahtera and Ilona Kuukka, 'Kuntajärjestäjän näkökulma oman uskonnon opetukseen', in Sakaranaho and Jamisto, *Monikulttuurisuus*, supra note 29, 126–127; Lyhykäinen, 'Vähemmistön', supra note 29 at 20; Sakaranaho, 'Pienryhmäisten', supra note 38, 11–12. For an overview of challenges mentioned in this section as they arise regarding teaching of Islam RE, see Sakaranaho, *Religious Freedom*, supra note 22 at 372–382.

114 Koikkalainen, *Uskonnonopetus*, supra note 19 at 64; Lyhykäinen, 'Vähemmistön, supra note 29 at 20; Sakaranaho, 'Pienryhmäisten', supra note 38 at 12.

115 http://verkkokauppa.oph.fi/epages/OPH.sf/fi_FI/?ObjectPath=/Shops/OPH/Products/9789521347993 (accessed 22 November 2011)

Similar problems pertain to life-stance classes. The groups may be heterogeneous in several ways. On top of this, both children who belong to minority faiths and children who are expressly non-religious and whose parents are eager to ensure their right to freedom from religion may attend these classes. What then should the character of these classes be? Teaching of life-stance classes has also occasionally taken place in classrooms with religious symbols on the walls.[116]

A further practical problem with what is sometimes called 'small group RE' and life-stance classes has been to find teachers with formal pedagogical competence.[117] Schools have at times had to organize their own teacher training.[118] A further challenge is to ensure that this pedagogical competence is coupled with sufficient knowledge of the subject matter. Parents have to be able to trust that the teaching is up to standard. It can be difficult for some parents to understand that affiliation to the community in question is not a formal requirement for teachers, and thus doubts about competence arise.

Regardless of the problems identified, and critical voices, the current Finnish model of RE is seen as safeguarding freedom of religion and conscience. In a recent survey, teachers of majority Evangelical Lutheran RE expressed this opinion.[119] Teachers of minority RE also support the model.[120] The current model of RE caters to the need of religious minorities and offers pupils the chance to gain knowledge about their own religion, and to integrate into Finnish society.[121]

116 Koikkalainen, *Uskonnonopetus*, supra note 19, 80. However, to make a small comparative note with regard to an issue that has given rise to much debate elsewhere in Europe, it has been self-evident that like pupils, teachers of RE can wear head coverings. Sakaranaho, 'Pienryhmäisten', supra note 38 at 11; Sakaranaho, *Religious Freedom*, supra note 22 at 376.

117 Koikkalainen, *Uskonnonopetus*, supra note 19 at 80, referring to Rusama, 'Religion', supra note 101; Miikka Kabata and Satu Honkala, 'Elämänkatsomustiedon opetuskysely peruskouluille keväällä 2003', in Pekka Elo et al. (eds.), *Hyvän osaamisen katsomustieto* (Filosofian ja elämänkatsomustiedon opettajat (FETO) ry:n vuosikirja; Helsinki: FETO, 2004).

118 Sakaranaho, 'Pienryhmäisten', supra note 38 at 11.

119 Koikkalainen, *Uskonnonopetus*, supra note 19 at 66, 75; Liisa Odiah, 'Evankelisluterilaisen uskonnon opettajat ja uskonnon opetuksen tulevaisuus monikulttuuristuvassa yhteiskunnassa', in Kallioniemi and Salmenkivi, *Katsomusaineiden*, supra note 11, 91–109, at 95, presenting the views of a small sample of teachers of Evangelical Lutheran RE.

120 Sakaranaho, 'Pienryhmäisten', supra note 38 at 13, Sakaranaho, *Religious Freedom*, supra note 22 at 380.

121 Koikkalainen, *Uskonnonopetus*, supra note 19 at 61, 66, 75; Odiah, 'Evankelisluterlaisen', supra note 118 at 95; Sakaranaho, 'Pienryhmäisten', supra note 38 at 7–8, 13, Sakaranaho, *Religious Freedom*, supra note 22 at 380.

Religious leaders have in recent times voiced similar views.[122] The Evangelical Lutheran Church finds that the way state and church share the duties is working well. The role of the church is to offer baptismal teaching. Public schools have as their task to promote all-round general competence in religious and life-stance matters, and to help children develop a well-grounded identity, including respect for their own cultural heritage. Church and state complement each other in promoting 'religious and cultural literacy'.[123] In similar fashion, the deputy leader of the Finnish Islamic Council, Anas Hajjar, last year noted that only approximately 5,000 out of 40,000 Finnish Muslims are members of a registered Muslim community. For this reason, Islam RE plays an important role in offering unregistered Muslim pupils the possibility to learn about and 'sustain their own religion, culture and worth'.[124]

Suggested Alternative Schemes

Integrated Religious Education

However, while the system enjoys wide-ranging support, there have also been calls for an altogether new model, and researchers have analysed different possible scenarios,[125] including integrated RE. The reasons such a move would be legitimate are not surprising. They are the outcome of reflections on what we need to coexist fruitfully in a contemporary multicultural society. It is assumed that if children study together, they will grow tolerant. The segregation model instead emphasizes the need to strengthen the identity of children belonging to minority faiths. On the

122 See e.g. common statement by religious leaders, at http://evl.fi/EVLUutiset.nsf/Documents/55D1F5870A030D5EC22577C100282317?OpenDocument&lang=FI (accessed 3 November 2011); Matti Repo, 'Oman uskonnon opetus auttaa kunnioittamaan toisia', Piispainkokouksen avajaispuhe, 14 September 2010, http://evl.fi/EVLUutiset.nsf/Documents/BF426D9B2107F458C225779D0034D6CB/$file/Piispainkokous_Repo_140910.pdf (accessed 3 November 2011); Jukka Paarma, 'Uskonnonopetus on lasten ja nuorten perusoikeus', Avauspuhe Suomen ekumeenisen neuvoston syyskokouksessa, 8 October 2009, document accessible via http://evl.fi/EVLUutiset.nsf/Documents/2AD54BAFBF979C2EC2257649003A4A6C?OpenDocument&lang=FI (accessed 3 November 2011).

123 Markku Holma, 'Koulun uskonnonopetus ev.lut.kirkon näkökulmasta', 24 August 2009, http://www.oph.fi/download/118224_Koulun_uskonnonopetus_kirkon_nakokulmasta_Markku_Holma_syksy_2009.pdf (accessed 2 November 2011).

124 http://evl.fi/EVLUutiset.nsf/Documents/7207C2B5D6822CCAC22576550034036C?OpenDocument&lang=FI (accessed 3 November 2011). Latest figures from the National Statistics point to 8,230 registered Muslims, which still is a significantly low number. http://www.stat.fi/til/vaerak/2009/01/vaerak_2009_01_2010-09-30_tau_007_fi.html (accessed 20 September 2011).

125 See e.g. various contributions in Kallioniemi and Salmenkivi, *Katsomusaineiden*, supra note 11.

one hand, it can of course be asked whether integrated RE automatically furthers tolerance better than does segregated RE. On the other hand, we can question whether it is the role of schools to place divisions between children.[126]

Some of the reasons given relate to the substance of the teaching. In the recent survey of teachers of Evangelical Lutheran RE, some teachers found that it would be easy to introduce integrated RE, as their teaching already adopts the perspective on the study of religions that integrated RE would have.[127] As we have seen, the instruction in both majority and minority RE is formally non-confessional. It is not provided in accordance with the doctrine of a certain religious community. On the contrary, the subject is characterized as a knowledge subject. State organs develop the curricula; they are also the ones authorizing the schoolbooks used in teaching.

However, whether the actual instruction is perceived in this way is another question. At a seminar on religion organized by the Swedish Student Union of Finland (*Finlands Svenska Skolungdomsförbund*) in autumn 2008, which inspired a subsequent media debate, it was noted that pupils often perceive of the instruction as being, in fact, confessional. The Swedish Student Union of Finland stated that it wanted to work towards the goal of a common non-confessional instruction in religion, to replace the present model.[128]

This is possibly indicative of a generational difference. As the recent survey on the attitudes of Finnish people towards religious instruction mentioned earlier showed, irrespective of the support for multicultural education, an overwhelming majority opposed common non-confessional instruction for all pupils during the nine-year compulsory school period. (This position was predominant especially among older generations.)[129]

Moreover, for certain, the elements in the core curricula that are common to the teaching of all the different RE subjects stress religious knowledge and competence. However, the instruction of the majority faith approaches the pupils' own religion to a large extent as a way to understand religion as a cultural phenomenon and to learn *from* religion – in addition to taking a Lutheran and more general Christian approach to learning *about* one's own faith. This is not so in the other RE. Instead, the main aim is to learn about one's own faith and the curricula are formed around this main goal. In light of the teaching goals and the content of some curricula in

126 Koikkalainen, *Uskonnonopetus*, supra note 19 at 59, 75. See also Odiah, 'Evankelisluterilaisen', supra note 118 at 99–101, for an account of how these views are expressed among teachers. As I have argued elsewhere (Pamela Slotte, 'On Law, Language and Human Embeddedness', in Christoffersen et al., *Law & Religion*, supra note 3 at 181–201), identity is always formed in dialogue. Along somewhat similar lines, Koikkalainen dismisses the view that children have to have established a firm identity within their own religion before they are capable of entering into fruitful dialogue with other children with regard to the matters at hand. Rather, the dialogue itself will help them become clear about their own identity. Koikkalainen, *Uskonnonopetus*, supra note 19 at 59–60.

127 Odiah, 'Evankelisluterlaisen', supra note 118 at 101.

128 For the debate, see e.g. Slotte, 'A Little Church', supra note 3, 240–241.

129 Räsänen, *Koulun uskonnonopetus*, supra note 25.

minority RE, the RE comes across as more confessional.[130] We can interpret this as different ways of grasping what it means to strengthen the pupil's identity.

However, at the same time recent studies have also shown that to various degrees, majority RE has become the model for the 'normal', to which minority RE in non-Christian faiths, for example Islam RE, seek to accommodate itself. Researchers raise the question whether this is partly detrimental to the self-understanding of the faiths.[131]

The fact that pupils of majority and minority faith seem to be achieving different levels of general religious knowledge has also been mentioned as one reason for introducing integrated RE.[132] Other calls for a new model relate more to economic and organizational concerns.[133] The system could potentially become costly, it is argued. As noted, the educational authorities have approved 14 different curricula. While few schools presently offer teaching according to all these curricula, but only those in demand, it could potentially be the case that all curricula had to be taught.

It is the school rather than the regional authorities that take on the costs for the teaching of several RE curricula.[134] Primary and secondary public education is co-financed by the state and the municipalities. Funding is allocated in accordance with general criteria: the number of pupils and students, with the sum that has been set with regard to one student. School authorities make the decisions themselves about how to use this money[135] and meet the actual obligations of the school. We have also seen the organizational challenges that schools face when they seek to provide teaching in minority RE, and the strain it puts on teachers having to travel extensively to provide the teaching.

Taken together, these (and other) viewpoints may form the grounds for advocating the model of integrated RE that other Nordic countries have implemented. Student organizations, various teachers, civil actors, journalists and other members of the general public have expressed support for such a renewed model. With regard to the political parties, most support for integrated RE can be found among members of the Green Party and the Leftist Party. Moreover, some parents adhering to minority faiths have been found to favour integrated instruction in a subject more resembling religious studies (*uskonnontieto*). When

130 M. Kastila, 'Oppilaan oma uskonto perusopetuksen uskonnon opetussuunnitelman perusteissa' (2009), 88–89 (unpublished master's thesis).

131 Kastila, 'Oppilaan oma uskonto', supra note 129 at 90, referring to Sakaranaho, *Religious Freedom,* supra note 22, 344. See also Sakaranaho, 'Pienryhmäisten', supra note 38 at 9–10.

132 Odiah, 'Evankelisluterilainen', supra note 118 at 101–102.

133 Koikkalainen, *Uskonnonopetus*, supra note 19 at 69, 75, Odiah, 'Evankelisluterilaisen', supra note 118 at 99; Sakaranaho, *Religious Freedom*, supra note 22 at 342.

134 Koikkalainen, *Uskonnonopetus*, supra note 19 at 68.

135 http://www.minedu.fi/OPM/Koulutus/koulutuspolitiikka/rahoitus/ (accessed 20 September 2011).

the Finnish League of Human Rights interviewed twelve Muslim families in 2008, about half of these families favoured a model of integrated ethics instruction.[136]

Overall, however, the current model of RE finds more support than the alternative of integrated RE. Teachers who reject the idea of integrated RE argue, for example, that different religions and other life-views would be dealt with more schematically. The study of religions and other life-views could be largely downplayed, and the subject would develop into a study of ethics. They also point out that anxieties about offending pupils who believe differently would hamper the teaching.[137] Bishops within the Evangelical Lutheran Church have also voiced the concern that the teaching would lack depth.[138] However, the inadequacies of the current system are acknowledged. Commentators ask for more and better teacher training and that the organizational problems that have been identified are dealt with.

A New Mandatory Ethics Subject

As stated in the Introduction, in the years 2009–2010, the Finnish government proposed amendments to the Education Act, and the school curriculum. Among other things, the government proposed the introduction of a new mandatory ethics subject. During the era of independence, Finnish governments have dealt with proposals to introduce an ethics subject on various occasions. Indeed, the study of this discussion could form the topic of another article altogether. Here I merely want to offer a few remarks on the newest proposal. The ideas behind the proposal may be partly similar to those of earlier times, as may also be the responses of the religious communities.

Besides proposing the introduction of a new ethics subject, the expert group behind the proposal suggested that the RE subject should become more like religious studies.[139] The religious communities objected to the proposed amendments to the school curricula. They also opposed a suggestion to raise the number of pupils needed for schools to be obliged to offer minority RE to ten pupils.[140] This would violate the principle of equality, the communities stated.

136 http://www.minedu.fi/OPM/Koulutus/koulutuspolitiikka/rahoitus/ at 61–62.

137 Odiah, 'Evankelisluterilaisen', supra note 118 at 97–98.

138 See e.g. M. Repo, 'Oman uskonnon opetus auttaa kunnioittamaan toisia', Piispainkokouksen avajaispuhe, 14 September 2010, http://evl.fi/EVLUutiset.nsf/Documents/BF426D9B2107F458C225779D0034D6CB/$file/ Piispainkokous_Repo_140910.pdf (accessed 3 November 2011)

139 Paper by A. Räsänen during the 11th Nordic Conference of Religious Education (NCRE), 6–9 June 2011 at the Faculty of Theology, Aarhus University.

140 http://evl.fi/EVLUutiset.nsf/Documents/1647B7CE39F3040CC22577C4003ACB78?OpenDocument&lang=FI (accessed 3 November 2011)

I shall limit myself to some reflections voiced by the Finnish Evangelical Lutheran Church of Finland in official statements delivered in response to the draft proposal, and to some views voiced by the Ecumenical Council of Finland. While the views are primarily representative of the official positions of the Evangelical Lutheran Church, and of the Christian, Jewish, Muslim and other faith communities that are members to the Ecumenical Council, it is worth noting that Finnish churches and religious communities concurred in their denunciation of the draft proposal.

Faith communities feared that the redistribution of teaching hours in order to accommodate the new ethics subject would lead to a reduction of teaching in RE.[141] Freedom of religion and of conscience of both pupils and their parents was the concern here. Faith communities find that the current model functions well. The model acknowledges that state educational institutions need to safeguard the upbringing that children get at home in matters of faith. It complies with national and international legal obligations. The teaching supports the identity development of the children. It helps them develop the skills necessary for life in multi-religious and multicultural societies and offers support in children's understanding better their own religious heritage and identity and that of others.[142]

Moreover, in the current system, ethics forms an integral part of RE and the links between a person's religious life-view and his or her value notions are pointed out and explored. However, what would be the value foundations on which the new distinct ethics subject is based? Would the teaching be 'cynically relativistic'? Moreover, ethics should be emphasized as an integral part of all teaching.[143]

The proposal to introduce a new ethics subject was dropped at the final stages of the preparations to amend laws on education. The minister of education could not gather enough support for the proposal in that form, and did not want to risk the rejection of the whole law in parliament because of disagreement on some points.

Concluding Remarks: Ten Years On – A Reappraisal

My analysis in this chapter yields the following findings.

At the turn of the twenty-first century, the Finnish Constitution Act and Act of Freedom of Religion underwent changes. The law was revised to better correspond to what was viewed as Finland's international obligations. Accordingly, international legal developments affect the interpretation of the right to freedom of religion and conscience in Finland. This practically goes without saying. However, it does not provide us with nearly all the tools that are necessary when we seek to

141 See e.g. 2010–00456, *Lausunto perusopetuksen yleisten valtakunnallisten tavoitteiden sekä perusopetuksen tuntijaon uudistamista valmistelleen työryhmän ehdotuksista*, 18 August 2010, in response to *Opetus- ja kulttuuriministeriön lausuntopyyntö* 8.6.2010/20/040/2009.

142 2010–00456, supra note 141.

143 2010–00456, supra note 141.

understand the logic behind the prevailing Finnish model of RE in public schools. The picture will not be complete unless we pay due attention to how current and past ecclesio-political arrangements and parameters for conceptualizing majority faith affects the understanding and organization of RE. This is in line with Hull's observation that religious sentiments in society, the actual church-state relationship, the historical tradition of the country and notions of what RE in the school system is all about affects the actual state approach to RE.

The negotiations that took place in the debate accompanying the legislative work also reveal a political side to the matter, as does the way RE is linked to societal changes and issues of multiculturalism, minority protection, integration, and so forth. The interests of the state, religious communities, parents and pupils all figure in the discussions.

The part that the 'deep structures' play is perhaps not always acknowledged instantly in the same way as the day-to-day negotiations. However, together they make up the framework within which solutions are sought.

Finland eventually adopted a particularistic or segregation approach to RE that also seems explicable in light of the remark that new changes are regularly viewed in terms of old ones, and they will thus be addressed within the current system.

The current model of RE has its practical problems as a consequence of limited economical resources, unqualified teaching staff, the poor availability of teachers and the difficulties in coordinating the teaching of minority RE in different schools. There is, moreover, internal to the various curricula themselves, insufficient clarity about the nature of the RE subject. Nevertheless, on a formal level, the model for RE places majority faith and minority faiths – provided these are registered religious associations – on an equal footing.

Hence, in theory, the system affords the same sort of attention to minority faiths and non-faith based life-views. Their status is acknowledged and the religious identity of the adherents affirmed. In practice, however, the Evangelical Lutheran faith appears as the norm, the archetype of the kind of faith that the law seeks to accommodate and safeguard. Other faiths are accommodated in accordance with a system that suits the majority Evangelical Lutheran faith better than some other life-views. Critics point out that the Evangelical Lutheran faith is also safeguarded and privileged in other ways, for example, through specific references in law and the fact that pupils belonging to a majority faith, in practice the Evangelical Lutheran church, cannot abstain from participating in majority RE.

However, an advantage with the model, if we look at it from both a minority and a majority perspective, is the acknowledgement of the religious belonging of the pupil. A goal with RE is to strengthen the religious identity of the pupils. This may address the need of some parents for whom in religious matters the ultimate goal of education is not necessarily that their children find their own autonomous voice apart from, for example, the religious authorities.

Apart from the goal to support the personal development of pupils and strengthen their identity, RE seeks to enhance the religious competence and ethical uprightness of pupils so that they are able to function competently in contemporary society. RE, just like public school education as a whole comes accompanied by an air of citizenship education. But religious identity is not viewed as an obstacle to be overcome for there to be truly informed citizenship. I believe that this is one of the signals that religious communities fear that the introduction of an ethics subject alongside RE would send.

Moreover, while integrated RE may be favorable in a multicultural society, it seems hard to realize it in a way that does not appear abusive from a human rights and a minority perspective. What is deemed correct from the perspective of a more or less secularized majority may from a minority point of view be regarded as utterly problematic. If a common subject were to be introduced in Finland, whom would it primarily serve? Whose understanding of humankind and life would dominate? Clearly, the majority culture would be in a strong position. It would perhaps not explicitly dictate the education, but implicitly it could be highly influential.

Some teachers have noted that the alternative model of integrated RE could be seen as expressive of a Lutheran standpoint. Matters of state and church are held to be separate matters.[144] Researchers have also pointed out that integrated ethics instruction could be considered expressive of Lutheran teachings that ethics is a matter of reason.[145] These remarks are naturally entirely general but they challenge us to consider always matters at hand from both a majority and a minority perspective.

Consequently, given its present model for RE, it would seem that Finland is largely playing it safe within the specified existing legal frames. A knowledge subject is being transmitted according to group belonging, with optional life-stance education and an additional right to refrain from participation in factual religious practice of one's own religion as well as that of others.

In this model, some priority is given to 'identity politics' which, as critics point out, in certain ways may exclude an encounter with others. However, drawing on Emmanuel Levinas, freedom should not be understood as 'the reduction of the other to the same'.[146] Freedom of religion and conscience, as set out in Finnish law, shall safeguard multitude and diversity, the freedom to differ and to be different. The idea is that the same (formal and material) rights and freedoms shall facilitate the realization of individual life stories. We have seen that the ideal is not so easy to realize in practice because there are parameters that guide the Finnish discourse and which privilege majority faith-like religiosity. However, the overall sentiment in Finland still seems to be positive — the current model of RE does more good than harm.

---

144 Odiah, 'Evankelisluterilaisen', supra note 118 at 96.

145 Cf. Odiah, 'Evankelisluterilaisen', supra note 118 at 106; who refers to Arto Kallioniemi, 'Uskonnon ja elämänkatsomustiedon sisältötiedon ja tieteenalastruktuurin vertailua peruskoulun vuoden 1994 opetussuunnitelmien pohjalta' 6 *Didacta Varia* 1 (2001), 37–60.

146 E. Lévinas, 'Philosophy and the Idea of Infinity', in *Collected Philosophical Papers by Emmanuel Lévinas* (A. Lingis, trans.) (Dordrecht: Martinus Nijhoff Publishers, 1987), 48.

Chapter 20

Religion and Education in the Council of Europe: Toward a "Soft" Constitutionalization of a Model of Religious Teaching?[1]

Rafael Palomino Lozano

Introduction

The aim of this presentation is to examine models for teaching religion in public schools formulated within the Council of Europe. This examination takes into account that both the Parliamentary Assembly of the Council of Europe and the European Court of Human Rights—through Article 9 of the European Human Rights Convention and Article 2 of the First Additional Protocol—turn certain elements of religious teaching into legal paradigms.

First of all, it is important to mention an existing issue, no doubt obvious to everyone: teaching is always an area of conflict, a 'sensitive question'[2] in our societies. The source of such conflict lies in the fact that this issue involves stakeholders (states, parents, students, teachers) who bring with them claims on justice expressed in paramount social responsibilities, in duties before the community and in fundamental rights.

The convergence of these stakeholders, their rights and responsibilities, can, as we have pointed out before, frequently result in conflict and in disagreement. An example of this is the fact that educational rights were not covenanted in the text of the European Human Rights Convention (the wording, basis, etc. of which did not meet with general consensus), but rather in an additional protocol.[3]

---

1 This presentation is part of the research conducted within the 'Religion, Law and Society' research group of Universidad Complutense de Madrid, through research project DER2011-29385.

2 J. Martínez-Torrón, 'La objeción de conciencia a la enseñanza religiosa y moral en la jurisprudencia de Estrasburgo', in M. Domingo (ed.), *Educación y religión: una perspectiva de derecho comparado* Granada: Comares, 2008), 113.

3 C. Evans, *Freedom of Religion under the European Convention on Human Rights* (Oxford: Oxford University Press, 2001), 45–48.

The sensitive nature of the issue becomes even more acute when the educational content deals with beliefs, religion, and the conscience of citizens. Religious education falls within this specific field.

Religion and Education in Europe

First of all, we consider how the countries that make up the Council of Europe approach the subject of teaching religion.

In this regard, the ruling of the European Court of Human Rights in the case *Hasan and Eylem Zengin v. Turkey*[4] provides a good idea of Europe's religious education map. As is made clear in this ruling, education of this nature is closely linked to secular education. In fact 43 out of the 46 Members of the Council of Europe provide religious education in state schools. However, religious education does not follow exactly the same guideline in all countries. There are many variables which make each national model quite unique; to mention only a few: mandatory or voluntary attendance in class, denominational or non-denominational education, the provision of religious education alternatives, the opt-out system (in the case of mandatory religious education), inclusion of religious education in the state school curriculum, and the appointment and hiring of teachers.

This educational and religious plurality of the European state school system has recently attracted the attention of researchers (pedagogues, lawyers, etc.). As a result, classification criteria applied to religious education have been introduced for the different European systems.[5] It should be said, in passing, that the classification criteria necessarily come up against certain barriers which make comparison and the drafting of neat categories difficult. Thus, for example, there are countries in which some denominational schools form part of the state school system, while in others such integration would be totally unthinkable. Nevertheless, we are dealing in both cases with the state education system

A many as four different models of religious education in schools are commonly accepted. First is a minority model in which religion is not taught at all (France, Albania). Second is a denominational religious education model as followed by Austria, Belgium or Spain, among others. A third model is education organized in collaboration with religious groups (perhaps Hungary, Finland or Germany adhere to this model). And a fourth European model is that in which religious education is the

4 *Hasan and Eylem Zengin v. Turkey*, App. No. 1448/04, 9 October 2007.

5 Conferenza Episcopale Italiana, *L'insegnamento della religione risorsa per l'Europa* (Elledici, 2009); P. Schreiner, 'Religious Education in Europe – Situation and Developments', Institute of Education, University of London (March 2009), available at Comenius Institut, http://ci-muenster.de/themen/religionsunterricht/ru12.pdf (accessed 22 July 2011). J.-P. Willaime, 'Different Models for Religion and Education in Europe', in R. Jackson (ed.), *Religion and Education in Europe: Developments, Contexts and Debates* (Münster, New York, München, Berlin: Waxmann Verlag, 2007), 57–101.

exclusive responsibility of the state, and is intended to be of a non-denominational nature (this would be the case in Denmark or the United Kingdom).

From another abstract perspective—more related perhaps to pedagogy—three basic systems may be distinguished.[6] A model of 'religious education' that is denominational or serves as an introduction to a specific religious tradition; a 'study about religion'[7] model, that is, a general study of the science of different religions and their significance for believers; and finally, the 'learning from religion' model, which explores religious experience, religious life, the significance of religion in the identity and formation of the individual for the purposes of social dialogue. This is a somewhat artificial division, however, because these different approaches may often converge in one single subject.

The Council of Europe and Religious Education

Before examining the Council of Europe in relation to the topic of this chapter, a few words about this institution may be appropriate.[8]

The Council of Europe is an international, intergovernmental organization created by means of an International Treaty on 5 May 1949. Its headquarters are in Strasburg. The Council of Europe is not an organization of *integration* but one of political and legal *cooperation.* It comprises 47 European states, although originally only ten states were present to sign the founding charter. Among the objectives of the Council of Europe outlined in the charter, I would highlight 'the maintenance and further realization of human rights and fundamental freedoms' (art. 1), which has to do with the recognition both of the 'principle of the rule of Law' (art. 3) and of democracy. Included in the Council of Europe is the Committee of Ministers and its Consultative Assembly. The Assembly is a deliberative body formed from the national Parliaments of the member states and has no general power of decision. On its own initiative or when requested to do so by the Committee of Ministers, the Consultative Assembly may adopt recommendations addressed to the Committee of Ministers. Such recommendations deal with quite diverse issues, but nevertheless constitute an important body of *soft-law* which gives general guidelines on topics of sociopolitical interest within the region.

It was within the Council of Europe that the European Human Rights Convention was drawn up and ratified. The importance of the Convention of 1950 lies not only in its substance but also in the creation of a Court to supervise compliance with recognized fundamental rights. It is worth remembering that the Convention is a

6 Schreiner, 'Religious Education in Europe', 3.

7 As far as this study is concerned, the terms 'teaching about religion' and 'teaching about religions' are employed as equivalent terms, although the difference between the level of abstraction and the specific purpose of the education should be established.

8 On this subject, see A. Mangas, 'El Consejo de Europa. Estructura y Funciones', *Base del Conocimiento Juridico. Iustel*, available online by subscription (RI §911606).

regional legal instrument. In this regard, Martinez-Torrón stresses that 'regional instruments are best qualified to protect human rights in a more efficient manner, for two main reasons. First, because they are confined to a smaller territorial area, and as a result are better adapted to specific political and cultural circumstances. Second, and above all, because they possess more directly coercive mechanisms of enforcement and control which, in some cases, are strictly judicial.'[9] In the specific case of the European Convention, this strictly legal control is primarily exercised, in the absence of the original Commission, by the European Court of Human Rights.

We have therefore two relevant legal bodies inside the Council of Europe. One comprises the activity of the Parliamentary Assembly from which emanate *soft law* instruments which guide the overall actions of member countries, and a second body which comprises the activity of the European Court of Human Rights. This Court monitors, with the mandatory intervention of the Committee of Ministers, the observance by member states of the European Convention of Human Rights. I am going to deal, first of all, with the Parliamentary Assembly.

Through a series of Recommendations, the Parliamentary Assembly of the Council of Europe has since it was created continually addressed matters in the sphere of religion. Such diverse questions as incitement to religious hatred (as far back as 1966),[10] Sects and New Religious Movements,[11] the State, Secularism and Human Rights,[12] have been brought to the attention of this Council of Europe body.

Religious education also appears in the Recommendations of the Parliamentary Assembly, particularly in Recommendations 1396 (1999) 'Religion and democracy'[13] and 1720 (2005) 'Education and religion'.[14]

The former of these Recommendations states that education is the key way to combat ignorance and stereotypes. School and university curricula should be revised, as a matter of urgency, so as to promote better understanding of the various religions. Religious instruction should not be given at the expense of lessons about

---

9 J. Martínez-Torrón, 'La protección internacional de la Libertad Religiosa', *Tratado de Derecho Eclesiástico del Estado* (Pamplona: EUNSA, 1994), 165.

10 Recommendation 453 (1966) on measures to be taken against incitement to racial, national and religious hatred, text adopted by the Assembly on 27 January 1966 (22nd Sitting), available at http://assembly.coe.int/main.asp?Link=/documents/adoptedtext/ta67/erec453.htm (accessed 22 July 2011).

11 Recommendation 1178 (1992), on Sects and New Religious Movements, text adopted by the Assembly on 5 February 1992 (23rd Sitting), available at http://assembly.coe.int/mainf.asp?Link=/documents/adoptedtext/ta92/erec1178.htm (accessed 22 July 2011).

12 Recommendation 1804 (2007): State, religion, secularity and human rights, text adopted by the Assembly on 29 June 2007 (27th Sitting), available at http://assembly.coe.int/main.asp?Link=/documents/adoptedtext/ta07/erec1804.htm (accessed 22 July 2011).

13 Recommendation 1396 (1999) Religion and democracy, text adopted by the Assembly on 27 January 1999 (5th Sitting), available at http://assembly.coe.int/mainf.asp?Link=/documents/adoptedtext/ta99/erec1396.htm (accessed 22 July 2011).

14 Recommendation 1720 (2005) Education and religion, available at http://assembly.coe.int/main.asp?Link=/documents/adoptedtext/ta05/erec1720.htm (accessed 22 July 2011).

religions as an essential part of the history, culture and philosophy of humankind. At the same time, the Assembly recommends that the Council of Ministers invite the governments of member states to encourage religious studies and, specifically, the teaching about religion as a set of values towards which young people must develop a discerning approach, within the framework of education on ethics and democratic citizenship. The Assembly points out that the teaching of comparative history of religions should equally be encouraged, stressing their origins, the similarities in some of their values and the diversity of their customs, traditions, festivals, etc. The study of the history and philosophy of religions and the research into those subjects at university, in parallel with theological studies, should be encouraged, while – in the case of children – any conflict between the state-promoted education about religion and the religious faith of the families should be avoided, in order to respect the free choice of the families.

Recommendation 1720 (2005) 'Education and Religion' meanwhile, discusses directly the subject here analyzed. The Consultative Assembly here recommends that the Council of Ministers should examine possible approaches to religious studies at primary and secondary levels, for example through basic modules which would subsequently be adapted to the various educational systems. They recommend the creation of a European Institute in which to train teachers in the comparative study of religions. In accordance with this Recommendation, the aim should be to help pupils discover the religions practiced in their own and neighboring countries, to help them perceive that everyone has the same right to believe that their religion is the 'true faith' and that other people are not lesser human beings through having a different religion or not having a religion at all. It is not a question of instilling a particular faith but of helping young people understand why religions are a source of faith for millions of people, at the same time providing pedagogical tools which allow minors to understand, in safety and without danger, fanatical religious movements.

Based on these Recommendations we may deduce certain guidelines. First of all, the Consultative Assembly considers religious education as a tool for achieving certain goals. The Council of Europe considers education to be essential in combating ignorance, stereotypes and errors concerning religions. This ignorance, these errors or lack of knowledge, affect tolerance and undermine everyone's right to full enjoyment of religious freedom and are, in short, the breeding ground for discrimination and religious conflict. Religious education would be a means of mitigating these problems and has, therefore, a more general scope —that of education for citizenship and human rights.

Secondly, the Council of Europe focuses on a specific model of religious education, *teaching about religion*, thus inviting member states to adopt this model of education, without prejudging others, but making clear that *teaching of religion* and *teaching about religion* are concurrent rather than alternative forms.[15]

15 To be more specific, Recommendation 1720 (2005) reads as follows: '9. In Europe, there are various concurrent situations. Education systems generally – and especially

To what point the promotion of fundamental rights and of the underpinnings which support democracy may be achieved though a specific model, that of teaching about religion, is a question open to debate. Certainly, it implies policy choices that not all member states have adopted, and which may to some extent contradict the wishes of parents (due to their considering it to be something contrary to their religious beliefs or morals) and may not have the backing of the religious confessions themselves (due to their considering that a comparative teaching of religion should be carried out with caution). What is certain is that the Council of Europe establishes by means of a soft law an ideal, a model of religious education which, being interesting in light of the goals concerned, may turn out to be problematic when put into practice, a model which sanctifies certain subject matter trends and which, indirectly or unintentionally, demonizes other models currently being practiced.

The Jurisprudence of the European Court of Human Rights: Principles

The European Court of Human Rights analyzes religious education in a wider area, that of those conflicts which arise in schools, in which Article 9 of the Convention and Article 2 of the First Additional Protocol have a role to play.

The problems which have been raised in this ambit, more closely related to religion or convictions, basically have three patterns or themes. The first, and certainly the less frequent, has to do with school activities and behavior which give grounds for objection or rejection on the part of some members of the school community (as in the cases *Efstratiou v. Greece* and *Valsamis v. Greece*,[16] as well as *Campbell and Cosans v. United Kingdom*[17]). The second theme has to do with the broader issue of religious symbols in schools, both in how teachers (*Dahlab v. Switzerland*[18]) and pupils (*Dogru v. France*,[19] *Kervanci v. France*[20] or *Singh, R. v. France*,[21] among others) dress, and with the question of static religious

the state schools in so-called secular countries – are not devoting enough resources to teaching about religions, or – particularly in countries where there is a state religion and in denominational schools – are focusing on only one religion.' Some countries have prohibited the carrying or wearing of religious symbols in schools'. And Recommendation 1396 (1999) Religion and Democracy reads: '10. (…) religious instruction should not be given at the expense of lessons about religions as an essential part of the history, culture and philosophy of humankind.'

16 *Efstratiou v. Greece* y *Valsamis v. Greece*, App. No. 24095/94, 18 December 1996.

17 *Campbell and Consans v. United Kingdom*, App. Nos. 7511/76; 7743/76, 25 February 1982.

18 *Dahlab v. Switzerland*, App. No. 42393/98 (Inadmissible), 15 February 2001.

19 *Dogru v. France*, App. No. 27058/05, 4 December 2008.

20 *Kervanci v. France*, App. No. 31645/04, 22 July 2004.

21 *Singh, R. v. France*, App. No. 27561/08 (Inadmissible), 30 June 2009.

symbols (*Lautsi v. Italy*[22]). The third thematic pattern has to do with the subjects or the subject matter taught in school, particularly sensitive to religious and non-religious beliefs (*Kjeldsen, Busk Madsen and Pedersen v. Denmark,*[23] *Angeleni v. Sweden,*[24] *Folgerø v. Norway,*[25] *Grzelak v. Poland,*[26] *Hasan and Eylem Zengin v. Turkey,*[27] among others).

It is the latter of these groups that is of interest for the subject of this article.

Certainly, the decisions of the European Court of Human Rights, from the time elapsed since the *Kjeldsen* case of 1976 up to the *Zengin* case of 2007, have consolidated certain guiding principles on this issue.

But, before expounding on such principles, it is perhaps interesting to consider the work of the European Court of Human Rights on this and other issues which place it in what is without doubt a complex dilemma. This dilemma is made up of two imaginary lines.

In the first, the European Court of Human Rights has to deal with the double facet of fundamental rights. Indeed, the norms which recognize fundamental rights are *rules* to comply with and at the same time *principles* insofar as they are mandates to optimize the freedom of member states' citizens. In this regard, the task of the Court seems to be more that of treating fundamental rights as rules, and it delivers decisions concerning compliance with such rights.[28] But it is no less true that the Court can introduce demands to optimize, or unwittingly encourage, ideal legal habitats, in which it understands that fundamental rights are most suitably accommodated. Such optimization assertions might appear, both in the motivation behind the rulings and in the exposition of the legal interests protected by fundamental rights.[29]

The second imaginary line is the tension inherent in the interesting and disputed concept of the 'margin of appreciation' which the Court itself employs.[30] This is a tension between a unifying role of the Court insofar as the understanding of

---

22 *Lautsi v. Italy*, App. No. 30814/06 (Grand Chamber), 18 March 2011.

23 *Kjeldsen, Busk Madsen and Pedersen v. Denmark*, App. Nos. 5095/71, 5920/72, 5926/72, 7 December 1976.

24 *Angeleni v Sweden*, App. No. 10491/83 (Inadmissible), 3 December 1986.

25 *Folgerø v Norway*, App. No. 15472/02 (Grand Chamber), 29 June 2007.

26 *Grzelak v. Poland*, App. No. 7710/02, 15 May 2007.

27 *Hasan and Eylem Zengin v. Turkey*, App. No. 1448/04, 9 October 2007.

28 Article 19. 'To ensure the observance of the engagements undertaken by the High Contracting Parties in the Convention and the Protocols thereto, there shall be set up a European Court of Human Rights, hereinafter referred to as 'the Court'. It shall function on a permanent basis.'

29 Concerning the theory of Robert Alexy on Rules and Principles, see E. R. Grau, *Interpretación y aplicación del Derecho* (Madrid: Dykinson, 2007), 165–167.

30 Evans, *Freedom of Religion under the European Convention on Human Rights*, supra note 3 at 143–145; see also S. Greer, *Margin of Appreciation: Interpretation and Discretion under the European Convention of Human Rights* (Strasbourg: Council of Europe Publishing), 2000.

fundamental rights is concerned, on the one hand, and deference to the work of national authorities on the other. This tension could be clearly seen in the ruling *Lautsi v. Italy,* delivered in March 2011 by the Grand Chamber.[31]

This having been said, we can now focus on the discussion of the criteria arising from this subject matter and which turn out to be crucial for religious education in schools. This discussion follows the outline established in the *Zengin* case of 2007.[32]

The former of these criteria or principles states that the two phrases of Article 2 of the First Additional Protocol should be read not only jointly but also specifically in the light of Articles 8, 9 and 10. With regard to the demands and recognized rights, Article 2 of the First Additional Protocol does not distinguish between public and private education. The second phrase of the article, in particular, attempts to safeguard the possibility of educational pluralism, essential for the preservation of a 'democratic society' as conceived by the Convention. Due to the preeminence of the modern state in this regard, it is above all through public education that this project must be carried out.

The Court also remarks that in order to determine the scope of parents' recognized rights, Article 2 of the First Additional Protocol does not allow any distinction between religious education and other disciplines. The article requires the state to respect the beliefs of parents, both religious and philosophic, within the public educational program as a whole. This duty can be widely applied, given that it concerns both the content of the education and the way in which it is taught, and also the exercise of all the 'functions' that the state assumes. The verb 'respect' means much more than 'recognize' or 'take into account'. As well as a somewhat negative compromise, it implies for the state a certain positive obligation.

With regard to the concept 'convictions' of Article 2, the Court interprets this by indicating that it is not a synonym of the terms 'opinion" and 'ideas'. It is applied to opinions which take on a certain level of strength, seriousness, coherence and importance.

With regard to the protected legal right in Article 2 of the First Additional Protocol, the Court indicates that, when complying with the natural duty of ensuring the education and teaching of children, parents may demand that the state respect

31 'The Convention has given this Court the remit to enforce freedom of religion and of conscience, but has not empowered it to bully States into secularism or to coerce countries into schemes of religious neutrality. It is for each individual State to choose whether to be secular or not, and whether, and to what extent, to separate Church and governance. What is not for the State to do is to deny freedom of religion and of conscience to anyone. An immense, axiomatic chasm separates one prescriptive concept from the other non-prescriptive ones.' *Lautsi*, concurring opinion of Judge Bonello, para. 2.3.

32 For a more detailed review of the ruling, see Martínez-Torrón, 'La objeción de conciencia a la enseñanza religiosa y moral en la reciente jurisprudencia de Estrasburgo', supra note 2.

their religious and philosophical convictions. Their right involves, therefore, a responsibility closely linked to the enjoyment and exercise of the right to education.

However—the Court continues—defining and planning the syllabus is the responsibility of the Convention signatory states. To a large extent, it is a matter of opportunity about which the Court should not voice an opinion and whose solution may legitimately vary according to country and time. In particular, the second phrase of Article 2 of the First Additional Protocol does not prevent states from disseminating, through teaching or education, information or knowledge which, directly or otherwise, is of a religious or philosophical nature. Not even parents are permitted to object to the integration of such teaching or education in the school program, without which any institutionalized teaching would run the risk of being impracticable.

It is in fact very difficult to prevent the numerous disciplines that are taught in schools from containing, to a greater or lesser degree, a coloring or an incidence of a philosophical or religious nature. The second phrase of Article 2 implies, to the contrary, that the state, when fulfilling the functions it assumes in the area of education and teaching, must ensure that the information or knowledge included in the curriculum is presented in an objective, critical and pluralistic manner, allowing pupils to develop a critical point of view with regard to religion in a calm atmosphere, free from any misplaced proselytism. The state is prohibited—definitively—from pursuing an objective of indoctrination contrary to the religious and philosophical convictions of the parents. This is the limit which it must not pass.

The Court reminds us that, although in the past the Convention bodies have not judged as contrary to the Convention an education which disseminates information about religions, they have verified in great detail whether the pupils were obliged to participate in any way in a religious service, or whether they were exposed to any religious indoctrination. In the same context, the forms of exemption also constitute an important element worth considering. At the same time, the Court is aware that abuses in the way in which a particular school or teacher applies the texts in force may arise, and it is the duty of the corresponding authorities to ensure, with the utmost care, that the religious and philosophical convictions of parents should not be opposed at this level due to carelessness, lack of judgment or misplaced proselytism.

These are the relevant principles set forth by the European Court of Human Rights. Let us now project them onto religious education in the public system, in the light also of particular elements of the rulings which the Court has issued to date.

The Position of the Court with Regard to Religious Education: Two Elements

Two elements are of capital importance in discerning the position of the Court with regard to religious education. Both bear relation to the subject matter and appear to delimit the compatibility and congruence of religious education with Article 2 of the First Additional Protocol and Article 9 of the Convention.

One of these elements has to do with the *way* in which content matter is taught, and the other has to do with the *limit* which cannot be overstepped in education. The first element means that the state, when complying with the functions it assumes with regard to education and teaching, ensures that the information or knowledge included in the curriculum be presented in an objective, critical and pluralistic manner, allowing pupils to develop a critical point of view with regard to the religious question in a calm atmosphere, safe from any unjustified proselytism.

The second element is that the State may not indoctrinate.

At the same time, both elements fall under a necessary premise, that of the *obligatory nature* of religious education—or that of any other subject to which, on account of their convictions, parents and/or pupils might object. The obligatory nature is important because, if there were no obligation, the two elements would be open to other interpretations.

With regard to the first of these elements—objective, critical and pluralistic presentation—the Court does not describe the precise meaning of such terms. But it is a fact that this triad of terms has appeared repeatedly since the *Kjeldsen* case; we should remember that in that case it was understood that sex education in public schools was valid in accordance with the Convention, in spite of the objections of the appellants. However, in order to appreciate the content to which the Court refers in these terms, it is easier to consider recent cases in which the Court detects the absence of this requirement. Specifically, in the ruling of the *Folgerø* case, the quantitative and qualitative differences in the treatment of Christianity with respect to other religions in the context of the subject under debate implied a shortcoming.[33] Together with that, the presence of *performative* elements (adopting an attitude within the religion/s being taught) as opposed to merely *informative* elements seemed to require the need for an ample regime of exemptions.

Together with the *Folgerø* ruling, it is perhaps the *Zengin* case that most clearly shows the absence of this objective, critical and pluralistic teaching. The Court is saying in this ruling, giving priority to a specific religion in a course on religion does not make the requirements for plurality and objectivity disappear.[34] However, the total absence of any reference to a religious group which has a certain social presence, or not taking into consideration the diversity of religions in a country, are elements which impede objective, critical and pluralistic teaching. Seen from another angle, what we find in these two rulings—the *Folgerø* and *Zengin* cases—is *obligatory* religious education disguised as *teaching about religion* which lacks

33 A more detailed commentary on this ruling can be found in M. Á. Jusdado and S. Cañamares Arribas, 'La objeción de conciencia en el ámbito educativo. Comentario a la sentencia del Tribunal Europeo de Derechos Humanos Folgero v. Noruega', in M. Domingo (ed.), *Educación y religión : una perspectiva de derecho comparado* (Granada: Comares, 2008), 113–134.-

34 *Hasan and Eylem Zengin*, paras. 58–70.

the system of exemptions which would be appropriate to satisfy parents' rights as contemplated in Article 2 of the First Additional Protocol of the Convention.

Together with these notes on objective, critical and pluralistic teaching, the limit that the state must not overstep refers to indoctrination. This is a concept which has meant—in practice—a reduction in the content of Article 2 of the First Additional Protocol.[35] What does 'indoctrination' mean?

In the Spanish language, to indoctrinate means to instruct someone in the knowledge or teachings of a doctrine, to instill in him or her certain ideas or beliefs. In English, originally, 'indoctrinate' meant to instruct or teach someone or simply to instill certain doctrines. It is easy to deduce that, in line with the above meanings, the entire teaching process, indeed the entire educational process, implies indoctrination. Only recently has the term acquired a pejorative connotation, when in the twentieth century people became particularly aware that education may be employed as an element of social control.[36]

The formulation of the concept of indoctrination in the philosophy of education presupposes two elements. First, the emergence of the idea of democracy applied to the educational sphere. In fact, in a kind of direct proportionality relationship, democracy would be to dictatorship what teaching would be to indoctrination. The weight of the philosophy of John Dewey and his followers is another important premise. Dewey's educational philosophy proposed that human beings—including of course students, pupils—are rational beings potentially capable of deciding appropriately for themselves. The function of schools and of other formal or informal educational agents consists in instilling and improving this rational capacity in young people, not restricting or impeding its development. The development of this latent capacity for decision demands a situation in which education is free. The role of the teacher in the classroom would not be that of a sovereign who knows and transmits knowledge, rather more that of a companion in research, in intellectual exploration, who works in cooperation with the student to seek the best solution to the problems. To do this would be to educate[37]; the contrary would be to indoctrinate.

Following this specific school of thought, it has been understood that indoctrination is found not only in the content of what is taught; it is also present in the methods (learning by heart instead of helping to discover rationally)[38]

35 Martínez-Torrón, 'La protección internacional de la libertad religiosa', surpa note 9 at 220–221.

36 R. H. Gatchel, 'The evolution of the concept', in I. Snook (ed.), *Concepts of Indoctrination: Philosophical Essays* (London-Boston: Routledge & K. Paul, 1972), 12.

37 W. Moore, 'Indoctrination and democratic method', in Snook at 94.

38 'To focus simply upon securing a right solution without understanding the nature of mathematical operations is the mathematical equivalent of indoctrination. Indeed, when indoctrination is seen to involve a certain style of knowing or believing, we can discover the possibility of indoctrination in nearly every area of human knowledge and not simply

and in the intentions[39] (if the teacher knows that what he is teaching is false, that is indoctrination). Consequently—and only by way of example—from this pedagogical perspective, the following situations may arise:

1. Clear cases of indoctrination:
2. Teach an ideology as if it were the only possible rational option.
3. Teach something as if it were certain, although the teacher knows it is uncertain.
4. Teach propositions that are false, the teacher knowing that they are false.
5. Cases which appear to be indoctrination, but which are not, since they are unavoidable:
6. Teach small children appropriate behavior.
7. Teach facts (mathematical tables) by rote.
8. Unconsciously influence children in certain forms of behavior.
9. Problematic or doubtful cases:
10. Inculcate doctrines which the teacher believes to be true, although they are in fact disputed.
11. Teach certain subjects, such as chemistry, without due concern for understanding.[40]

This entire outline undoubtedly appears to complicate more things than it resolves. From the legal point of view, it is not easy to determine the separation between indoctrination as an intrusion in the *forum internum* and an education which helps young people in an appropriate way to develop in a society which, from the religious point of view, is frequently plural.[41]

On the other hand, to defer the problem of indoctrination to an expert pedagogical evidence, influenced by a specific philosophical-pedagogical school of thought, still means that the judge may be prey to orientations which are at

---

in those having to do with what we would more commonly call "matters of doctrine".' T. F. Green, 'Indoctrination and Beliefs', in Snook at 37.

39 '[I]indoctrination, where it is taken to be a bad thing, is a matter of trying to implant firm convictions of the truth of doctrines which are in fact either false or at least not known to be true; usually, of course, though not necessarily, the indoctrinator himself believes mistakenly that the doctrines in question are both true and known to be true. In the secondary sense indoctrination would be a matter of, in any sphere whatever, to implant beliefs, even those which are true and known to be true, by certain disfavoured methods. And the general objection to indoctrination in this sense would presumably be that such methods are in some way incompatible with the production of a proper understanding of what is taught and of a critical appreciation of its logical and epistemological status.' A. Flew, 'Indoctrination and Doctrines', in Snook at 86–87.

40 I. A. Snook, 'Indoctrination and moral responsibility', in Snook at 152.

41 Evans, *Freedom of Religion under the European Convention on Human Rights*, supra note 3 at 88; Martínez-Torrón, 'La protección internacional de la libertad religiosa', supra note 9 at 217.

the very least questionable.[42] No matter what criteria we adopt, it seems clear that some subjects are more susceptible to indoctrination (history or philosophy as opposed to mathematics) and that certain subjects which vindicate democracy (even education for citizenship, which the Council of Europe itself actively promotes) do not necessarily imply indoctrination.[43]

For this reason also (aside from the fact that there are always nuances, when abstract distinctions are being made) certain provisional criteria may provide some orientation. Teaching would be indoctrination:

1. When a subject is used as an undeclared means of transmitting values, beliefs and ideas other than those which are the actual purpose of the subject.
2. When an education which has to do with values, beliefs and ideas, changes the *informative* value for a *performative* value; that is, it submits the assessment of the pupil to his or her observance of a form of behavior which requires allegiance.
3. When an education in constitutional or political values offers an ideologically unilateral vision of such values.

The Jurisprudence of the European Court of Human Rights and Religious Education

Based on the data set out above, it is now possible to consider the general characteristics which distinguish the rulings of the European Court of Human Rights in this area.

The starting point is represented by the initial division of systems in Europe, as a result of which there is denominational religious education and teaching about religion. Is there any difference between the two, in terms of conformity with the demands of the European Convention of Human Rights?

This is an interesting question to raise because in general terms it has been supposed that, based on international instruments (fundamental rights as principles), the study of religion is congruent with human rights, while religious education is not. Furthermore, the latter would be contrary to the spirit of these

42 '[T]here can be no satisfactory treatment of at least this part of the philosophy of education which refuses to face and to come to terms with the disagreeable fact that there are fundamental differences of ideology.' Flew, 'Indoctrination and Doctrines', in Snook at 68.

43 *Council of Europe Charter on Education for Democratic Citizenship and Human Rights Education. Recommendation CM/Rec(2010)7 and explanatory memorandum* (Strasbourg: Council of Europe Publishing, 2010), available at http://www.coe.int/t/dg4/education/edc/Source/Pdf/Downloads/6898-6-ID10009-Recommendation%20on%20Charter%20EDC-HRE%20-%20assembl%C3%A9.pdf.

regulations.[44] However, the European Court of Human Rights does not make such a clear-cut distinction between the two ways of teaching religion.

With regard to religious education, or religion instruction, the European Court of Human Rights had the opportunity to analyze this model in the ruling *Grzelak v. Poland*.[45] Here the Court rules about the compatibility with the Convention not so much of a subject, which is optional, but of its specific makeup (i.e. the alternative of studying ethics and the impact on negative religious freedom, namely, the absence in the student's report of a numerical mark in the 'religion/ethics' box). That is to say: the problem is not so much the existence or absence of religious instruction as a subject, rather the practical way in which said subject is arranged. And everything seems to indicate that, in the case of this subject, there are questions which require maximum attention from academic authorities: its voluntary nature, the type of the alternative subject, marks, non-discrimination. What appears to be more complex, however, is the question of the negative religious freedom of parents and/or pupils.[46] It is more complex—and requires an analysis which, ultimately, the ruling does not enter into—because, in the end, any state action which facilitates the religious freedom of certain citizens means indirectly acknowledging the religious attitude of those who do not wish to benefit from such action and, consequently, damages their negative freedom.

Therefore, for example, religious assistance in hospitals, military establishments, prisons, immigrant internment centers, etc. would be prohibited because it would damage the religious freedom of those who do not wish to benefit from it. In this way, negative religious freedom could drown 'positive' religious freedom.[47] Ultimately, and returning to the principal theme of the ruling, teaching a religion—or denominational religious education—in the state school system is in itself permissible and requires in practice certain conditions which guarantee its voluntary nature and non-discrimination.

Nor is teaching about religion, as it couldn't be otherwise, exempt from possible problems with regard to the right of parents as recognized in Article 2 of the First Additional Protocol and Article 9 of the Convention. If one wants a course on religious studies to be compatible with those rights it is essential, first

44 J. Temperman, 'State Neutrality in Public School Education', 32 *Human Rights Quarterly* (2010), 866, 878.

45 App. No. 7710/02, 15 May 2007.

46 'Having regard to the foregoing, the Court finds that the absence of a mark for 'religion/ethics' on the successive school reports of the third applicant falls within the ambit of the negative aspect of freedom of thought, conscience and religion protected by Article 9 of the Convention as it may be read as showing his lack of religious affiliation. It follows that Article 14 taken in conjunction with Article 9 is applicable in the instant case.' *Grzelak*, para. 88.

47 K.-H. Ladeur, 'The Myth of the Neutral State and the Individualization of Religion: The Relationship Between State and Religion in the Face of Fundamentalism', 30 *Cardozo Law Review* 9 (2009), 2464.

of all, that the course should be really what it claims to be, and not a mere name which harbors a denominational religious course.

This is an issue that was illustrated by the ruling in the *Zengin* case: the absence of objective, critical and pluralistic education, specifically omitting or ignoring any reference to important minority beliefs, places this subject in an area in which it either needs to become voluntary (something which certain religions already benefit from), or should become a genuinely plural regime. It is more difficult to evaluate the boundaries and consequences of the ruling in the *Folgerø* case; first of all because the decision of the Court was adopted by the narrow margin of 9 votes to 8. Second, because it is difficult to assess to what extent this ruling may be an isolated exception to the principle set forth above, according to which prioritizing a specific religion in a general religious studies course does not make the requirements for plurality and objectivity disappear.[48] What does seem to be patently clear is that the absence of this internal balance in the course demands the articulation of an opt-out system for parents and pupils, a system which must be open (that is, not only exclusive of religions other than those which are preponderant, or even unique, in the subject that is being objected to) and that in itself does not have to go against negative religious freedom, as long as the explanation of the reasons for requesting such exemption do not end up being a 'genuine formal manifestation of religious affiliation'.[49]

Together with these requirements (perhaps the most important issues, or those that have been dealt with most directly by the European Court of Human Rights), we should be aware that religious education has other implications, many of them related to the legal protection of freedom of religion or beliefs in general, among which are (i) the sincerity of beliefs as the only element needed to recognize a breach of the rights recognized in Article 9 of the Convention and Article 2 of the First Additional Protocol; (ii) the importance of the syllabus, above and beyond the simple rule of a proportional or balanced treatment of such beliefs present in society; (iii) the extent of partial or total exemption from the subject; and (iv) the conditions which make the opt-outs discriminatory or non-discriminatory. It also seems necessary to establish to what extent the state may or may not consider itself responsible for the harassment or the physical or mental abuse which pupils may suffer when upholding their beliefs against the system. In principle, I think that recurring generically to potential harassment or abuse does not imply undisputable evidence nor does it incline the verdict one way or the other.

48 *Hasan and Eylem Zengin*, paras. 58–70.

49 Martínez-Torrón, 'La objeción de conciencia a la enseñanza religiosa y moral en la jurisprudencia de Estrasburgo', supra note 2 at 131–132.

Conclusion

In the light of the above reflections it may be concluded that the treatment of religious education in the Council of Europe calls for two separate sets of considerations. First, regarding the intervention of the Parliamentary Assembly, and second, concerning the configuration of religious education in the European Convention of Human Rights.

With regard to the first set of considerations, the programmatic interest of the Council of Europe as far as religious education is concerned is of an instrumental nature with respect to another overriding interest, that of making tolerance and the freedom of religion and beliefs possible in society. Such interest means to focus the issue preferably on teaching about religion in the context of education for a democratic citizenship. The consequence of this stance taken by the Council of Europe is that countries which maintain religious education of a denominational nature in their educational programs will find themselves in an area of suspicion or marginality.

With regard to the second set of considerations, it is necessary to make a distinction between denominational religious education and teaching about religion. As far as the former is concerned, the basic principle must be that it should be voluntary and that there should be an appropriate alternative. As far as the second is concerned, the basic principle must without doubt be based on internal aspects (critical, plural, objective education) and maximum limits which the state may not overstep (indoctrination).

The relationship between denominational religious education and teaching about religion is—in theory—indirectly proportional to the demands of freedom. That is to say: denominational religious education in the state school system appears to require maximum optionality, while teaching about religion involves maximum obligation or compulsion, as long as the conditions laid down by the European Court of Human Rights since the ruling of the *Kjeldsen* case are complied with. This does not in any way mean that religious education is not exempt from problems, as it is possible that, in spite of its neutral and impartial appearance, it may also be challenged in society by those who believe that public education should remain separate from all religions, from any religion. Although it is evident, and it is frequently recognized as such by legal experts and teachers, that it is not possible to imagine a complete or integral education of minors which does not include the knowledge of the social-religious milieu in which they live.

Chapter 21

Competing Fundamental Values: Comparing Law's Role in American and Western-European Conflicts over Abortion

Ofrit Liviatan

Introduction

Legal actions have been a prominent feature of the bitterly fought struggles over abortion in the Western World. Activists regularly turned to courts and legislatures in an attempt to entrench clashing moral views about women's right to terminate pregnancies and the protection of unborn life. Among these struggles the US Supreme Court ruling in *Roe v. Wade* (1973)[1] has often been heralded as one of the greatest legal victories for reproductive choice.[2] Declaring a judicially mandated constitutional right to abortion, this ruling stands in sharp contrast to Western European laws, which maintained a normative disapproval toward the termination of pregnancies that could go unpunished under specified circumstances.[3]

Different explanations have been offered for these diverging legal developments among countries customarily clumped together for their political, economic, and socio-cultural commonalities. One explanation identified a structural difference between the two locations, arguing that the regulation of abortion in the USA has been dominated by the US Supreme Court, compared with greater opportunities for political dialogue and bargaining as part of the European legislative processes.[4] Another view attributed the divergence to differing attitudes on rights, with the American system approaching the regulation of abortion through the prism of individual rights whereas Western Europe emphasized a communitarian vision of

---

1 410 US 113 (1973).

2 F. Kissling and D. Shannon, 'Abortion Rights in the United States: Discourse and Dissention', in E. Lee (ed.), *Abortion Law and Politics Today* (Houndmills: Macmillan Press, 1998), 145.

3 P. Sachdev (ed.), *International Handbook on Abortion* (New York: Greenwood Press, 1988), 474.

4 M.A. Glendon, *Abortion and Divorce in Western Law* (Cambridge: Harvard University Press, 1987), 24–25.

society in reconciling competing visions on abortion.[5] Although these explanations capture important dimensions of the diverging abortion politics across the two sides of the Atlantic, they do not seem to explicate the picture to its fullness. Employing a socio-legal approach, this chapter proposes an alternative hypothesis, arguing that the legal process acted in a different *social capacity* in each of the abortion debates, thus generating diverging effects on the regulation of abortion in the USA and Western Europe.

Two principal social functions have been identified for the legal process:[6] (i) *Integrative*, classifying law as a mechanism of governance that manages conflict and facilitates social order; and (ii) *Transformative*, perceiving law to be a vehicle to express values and advance social and political change. In the American context legal actions pertaining to abortion have been primarily employed ideologically in an attempt to generate *social and cultural change*. Abortion controversies have played out as a perpetual power struggle among pro-life and pro-choice activists each attempting to legally entrench a competing worldview on abortion and foreclosing possibilities for compromise. In contrast, the legal process acted as a mechanism of *social and cultural order* in Western European debates over abortion. There, legislatures and courts framed debates beyond the clash of rights and worldviews by including additional social and public policy concerns. This process resulted in resilient legislative compromises and the gradual fading away of deeply divisive cultural debates into the background of European politics.

Drawing on these comparative findings the chapter argues that socio-cultural conflicts amplify the political nature of law. In perpetual conflicts over values, legal processes possess an irresistible appeal for social activists to entrench political and moral preferences as binding in the democratic public sphere. The American experience with abortion politics demonstrates that legal arrangements remain susceptible to shifts in political power. It further reveals that the utilization of the legal process solely in its transformative capacity may result in the negation of law's integrative function. Yet, when legal processes are utilized to institutionalize compromises as demonstrated by the Western European examples, cultural-based controversies may be pacified even as ideological worldviews remained unaffected.

The chapter proceeds in three parts: (1) A brief survey of abortion politics in the USA as evolving into a perpetual tug-of-war dynamics between competing moral views; (2) Survey of the legal developments in Britain, France, Germany,

5 D.P. Kommers, 'Abortion and the Constitution: The Cases of the United States and West Germany', in E. Manier, W. Liu and D. Solomon (eds.), *Abortion: New Directions for Policy Studies* (Notre Dame: University of Notre Dame Press, 1977); D.P. Kommers, 'Liberty and Community in Constitutional Law: The Abortion Cases in Comparative Perspective', *Brigham Young University Law Review* (1986), 371–409; L.H. Tribe, *Abortion: The Clash of Absolutes* (New York: Norton, 1990); D.E. McBride, *Abortion in the United States: A Reference Handbook* (Santa Barbara: ABC-Clio, 2008).

6 S. Vago, *Law and Society*, 7th edn. (Upper Saddle River: Pearson Education, Inc., 2003), 18–21.

Italy, the Netherlands and Belgium, uncovering a contrasting dynamics where the once bitterly-fought abortion controversies have been pacified; (3) Drawing on these surveys, an analysis of the diverging role of the legal process in each of these debates and the implications of this divergence for legal resolutions of socio-cultural conflicts.

Abortion Politics in the United States

State legislation prohibiting abortions in the USA began to appear in the early nineteenth century, remaining a matter for the state level until the 1970s.[7] The motivation to criminalize abortion was multifaceted and varied from state to state: (i) medical and technological advancements enabling safer abortions generated growing opposition toward their accessibility;[8] (ii) falling birthrates relative to the newer Catholic immigrants raised fears among white Protestants;[9] finally, (iii) aggressive lobbying by the medical establishment seeking to eradicate competing abortion services (midwives, apothecaries, homeopaths, etc.) proved pivotal in generating criminalization across the country.[10] By the early twentieth century abortion was generally prohibited throughout the United States in all stages of gestation with some exceptions for therapeutic (medically-authorized) abortions.

Nonetheless, as the century progressed public opinion shifted in the direction of reform. Primary triggers for liberalization included[11] (i) widespread clandestine abortions endangering women's life and health; (ii) a growing role for women in the workforce and openness toward female sexuality; and (iii) shifting attitudes within the medical profession favoring greater accessibility to abortion. By the late 1960s approximately one-third of all US states had already repealed or were in the process of reforming their legislative prohibitions on abortion. The issue reached the federal level with *Roe*'s (seven to two) holding that the concept of personal

---

7 B.J. George Jr., 'State Legislatures Versus the Supreme Court: Abortion Legislation into the 1990s', in J.D. Butler and D.F. Walbert (eds.), *Abortion, Medicine and the Law*, 4th edn. (New York: Facts on File, 1992).

8 J.W. Dellapenna, 'The History of Abortion: Technology, Morality, and Law', 40 *University of Pittsburgh Law Review* (1979), 406–407.

9 N.J. Davis, 'Abortion and Legal Policy', 10 *Contemporary Crises* (1986), 378.

10 J.C. Mohr, *Abortion in America: The Origins and Evolution of National Policy 1800-1900* (New York: Oxford University Press, 1978), 147.

11 McBride, *Abortion in the United States,* supra note 5 at 10–16; L.C. Hillstrom, *Defining Moments: Roe v. Wade* (Detroit: Omnigraphics, 2008); L. Greenhouse and R.B. Siegel, 'Before (and After) Roe v. Wade: New Questions about Backlash', 120 *Yale Law Journal* 8 (2011), 2028-2088; L. Greenhouse and R.B. Siegel, *Before Roe v. Wade: Voices that Shaped the Abortion Debate Before the Supreme Court's Ruling* (New York: Kaplan Pub, 2010).

liberty in the Fourteenth Amendment's Due Process Clause 'is broad enough to encompass a woman's decision whether or not to terminate her pregnancy'.[12]

The ruling has been the subject of ample scholarly criticism emphasizing the Court's intervention in a hotly debated political matter as the cause of subsequent polarization over abortion.[13] A recent study questioned this premise, tracing the escalation of the conflict to the 'entanglement of abortion with party realignment not only after the [*Roe*] decision but before it, as well.'[14] Notwithstanding these academic disagreements over the precise evolution of the abortion conflict, pro-life advocates have been engaged for decades now in a continuous legal crusade to block access to abortion against an equivalent pro-choice struggle to ensure reproductive freedom. This tug-of-war dynamics has been occurring at the federal as well as the state level and typically included the following elements:[15] (a) rigorous lobbying for legislative entrenchments of the competing moral views on abortion at all levels of government; (b) initiation of judicial proceedings and amicus curiae submissions to precipitate new deliberations on the abortion issue; (c) relentless efforts to elect, appoint or defeat political candidates and justices based on their position on abortion; (d) wide ranging public campaigns and protest at times turning violent, particularly outside abortion performing facilities.

---

12 *Roe v. Wade,* 410 US at, 153.

13 J.H. Ely, 'The Wages of Crying Wolf: A Comment on Roe v. Wade', 82 *Yale Law Journal* 5 (1973), 920–949; R.A. Epstein, 'Substantive Due Process by Any Other Name: The Abortion Cases', *The Supreme Court Review* (1973), 159–185; P. Freund, 'Storms over the Supreme Court', 69 *American Bar Association Journal* (1983), 1474; R.B. Ginsburg, 'Some Thoughts on Autonomy and Equality in Relations to Roe v. Wade', 63 *North Carolina Law Review* (1985), 375–386; R.B. Ginsburg, 'Speaking in a Judicial Voice', 67 *New York University Law Review* (1992), 1185–1209; Glendon, *Abortion and Divorce in Western Law,* supra note 4; C.R. Sunstein, 'Three Civil Rights Fallacies', 79 *California Law Review* (1991), 751–774; M.J. Klarman, 'Fidelity, indeterminacy, and the Problem of Constitutional Evil', 65 *Fordham Law Review* (1997), 1739–1756; J.M. Balkin (ed.), *What Roe v. Wade Should Have Said* (New York: New York University Press, 2005); G. Silverstein, *Law's Allure: How Law Shapes, Constraints, Saves and Kills Politics* (New York: Cambridge University Press, 2009).

14 Greenhouse and Siegel, 'Before (and After) Roe v. Wade: New Questions about Backlash', supra note 11 at 2086.

15 K. Luker, *Abortion and the Politics of Motherhood* (Berkeley: University of California Press, 1984); M. McKeegan, *Abortion Politics: Mutiny in the Ranks of the Right* (New York: Free Press, 1992); K.A. Farr, 'Shaping Policy through Litigation: Abortion Law in the United States', 39 *Crime and Delinquency* 2 (1993), 167–183; L.R. Woliver, 'Rhetoric and Symbols in American Abortion Politics', in M. Githens and D. McBride (eds.), *Abortion Politics: Public Policy in Cross-Cultural Perspective* (New York: Routledge, 1996), 5–28; K. O'Connor, *No Neutral Ground? Abortion Politics in an Age of Absolutes* (Boulder: Westview Press, 1996); M.Y. Herring, *The Pro-Life/Pro-Choice Debate* (Westport: Greenwood Press, 2003); C. Francome, *Abortion in the USA and the UK* (Aldershot: Ashgate, 2004).

Over the years pro-life activists consisting of religious and anti-abortion groups achieved several successes in limiting the effects of *Roe*. Examples at the federal level include (i) the Hyde Amendment, a rider to the Health, Education and Welfare (HEW) Appropriation Act that prohibited the use of federal funds to pay for abortions except those necessary to save the life of the pregnant woman or in cases of rape and incest;[16] and (ii) gag rules prohibiting healthcare providers and employees paid by federal funds from paying for, counseling for or even mentioning the abortion option to their patients.[17]

Furthermore, the gradual reconfiguration of the Supreme Court through appointments of conservative justices accompanied by a regular stream of pro-life amicus curiae generated certain judicial limitations on the scope of the woman's constitutional right to abortion: (a) State and federal restrictions on the funding of abortions were found constitutional.[18] (b) *Roe*'s trimester framework and the 'compelling state interest' standard has been replaced with the less stringent 'undue burden' in evaluating state restrictions on abortion procedures throughout the course of the pregnancy.[19] (c) Detailed reporting, record-keeping and other requirements on abortion procedures were upheld.[20] (d) Earlier invalidations of parental consent to a minor's abortion gradually gave way to some parental involvement.[21] (e) Counseling requirements and mandatory waiting periods that were initially held unconstitutional were replaced with meticulous consultations enabling an 'informed consent' and 24-hour-waiting periods for reflection prior

16 Pub. L. 96–123, § 109, 93 Stat. 926.

17 Ex: the 1973 Church Amendment Pub. L. No. 93–45, §401, 87 Stat. 91, 95 (1973) 42 USC § 300a-7; the 1974 Church Amendment Pub. L. No. 93–348, §214, 88 Stat. 342, 353 (1974); Coats amendment to the Public Health Service Act (1996) 42 USC § 238n; and the Federal Refusal Clause (Weldon Amendment, 2004) FY'06 Departments of Labor, Health, and Human Services, and Education Appropriations Act, Pub. L. No. 109–149 (enacted 30 December 2005); Continued in the Revised Continuing Appropriations Resolution, 2007, Pub. L. No. 110–5 (enacted 15 February 2007).

18 *Beal v. Doe,* 432 US 438 (1977); *Maher v. Roe,* 432 US 464 (1977); *Poelker v. Doe,* 432 US 519 (1977); *Williams v. Sbaraz,* 448 US 358 (1980); *Harris v. McRae,* 448 US 297 (1980); *Webster v. Reproductive Health Services,* 492 US 490 (1989); *Rust v. Sullivan* ,500 US 173 (1991).

19 *Planned Parenthood v. Casey,* 505 US 833 (1992).

20 *Planned Parenthood Association of Kansas City v. Ashcroft,* 462 US 476 (1983); *Simonopoulos v. Virginia,* 462 US 506 (1983); *Webster*, 492 US 490; *Mazurek v. Armstrong* ,520 US 968 (1997).

21 *Bellotti v. Baird* 443 US 622 (1979); *H. L. v. Matheson* 450 US 398 (1981); *Planned Parenthood Association of Kansas City v. Ashcroft*, supra note 20. *Hodgson v. Minnesota,* 497 US 417 (1990); *Ohio v. Akron Center for Reproductive Health* 497 US 502 (1990); *Casey*, supra note 19; *Lambert v. Wicklund* 520 US 292.

to performing abortions.[22] Finally, (f) the federal ban on partial birth abortion was found constitutional, narrowing the scope of an earlier ruling by the Court.[23]

Pro-life activism intended to restrict the effects of *Roe* flourished at the state level as well, although many of these actions were later repealed through judicial proceedings initiated by pro-choice activists.[24] The *Right to Know* legislation currently in force in more than twenty states, is an example of a measure that survived thus far.[25] It requires that women be informed about the abortion procedure, its medical and psychological risks, anatomical and physiological characteristics of the fetus, alternatives to abortion, financial assistance available during and after childbirth, father's responsibilities and so forth. Lastly, the pro-life camp also advanced abortion 'trigger laws,' namely conditional legislation prohibiting abortions that will immediately take effect in the event that *Roe's* rationale is overturned.[26]

The pro-choice movement consisting of women's groups, medical professionals and civil rights advocates, proved comparably energized in reaffirming the constitutional right to abortion against attacks of the pro-life camp. With a growing pro-life block in the Supreme Court, pro-choice activists sought additional statutory guarantees for the parameters laid out in *Roe* at the federal and state levels.[27] With violent harassments of abortion providers peaking in the early 1990s, pro-choice organizations lobbied successfully to secure access to abortion through buffer zones and penal measures designed to protect clinics, staff and patients.[28] Other attempts, such as the Freedom of Choice Act (FOCA), have been less successful thus far with repeated legislative introductions yet to materialize.[29] Nearly four decades since the right to abortion was judicially mandated controversies have

---

22 *Casey*, supra note 19.

23 *Gonzales v. Carhart* 550 US 124 (2007).

24 Francome, *Abortion in the USA and the UK*, supra note 15; P.B. Linton, *Abortion Under State Constitutions: A State-By-State Analysis* (Durham: Carolina Academic Press, 2008).

25 Ex: Florida Bill H 1205 (1997); West Virginia Senate Bill No. 170 (2002); Georgia O.C.G.A. § 31-9A-1 (2008); South Carolina: A268, R345, H3245, 118th Session (2009–2010); Minnesota H.F. No. 669 83rd Legislative Session (2003–2004); North Carolina House Bill 854 S.L. 2011–405 (=S769) 2011–2012 Session.

26 Ex: North Dakota (H.B. 1466 §1, 2007 Leg. Sess. (N.D. 2007); Louisiana (La. R.S. 40:1299.30 (2011).

27 G.A. Halva-Neubauer, 'Abortion Policy in the Post-Webster Age', 20 *The Journal of Federalism* (1990), 27–44; G.A. Halva-Neubauer, 'The States After Roe: No "Paper Tigers", in M.M. Goggin (ed.), *Understanding the New Politics of Abortion* (Newbury Park: Sage, 1993), 167–189; Linton, *Abortion Under State Constitutions*, supra note 24.

28 Ex: Freedom to Access Clinic Entrances (FACE), 1994, 18 USCA §248(a) Pub L. No. 103–259, 108 Stat. 694.

29 Versions of the bill was introduced in 1989 (H.R. 3700, 101st Cong. (17 November 1989); Sen. 1912, 17 November 1989 101st Cong.), 1991 (H.R. 25 102nd Cong. (3 January 1991) Sen. 25, 102nd Cong. (14 January 1991) 1993 (H.R. 25 103rd Congress (5 January

not subsided. In fact, the 2010 election cycle reignited abortion politics, as newly elected Tea Party representatives initiated numerous new bills across the USA, already meeting judicial injunctions instigated by the pro-choice camp.

Abortion Law in Europe

Between the late 1960s to the late 1980s conflict-ridden abortion debates have submerged the Western-European public sphere. These debates generated new regulatory regimes that institutionalized uneasy compromises over contested norms and ultimately resulted in the substantial pacification of the abortion conflicts.

High mortality caused by abortions and the births of children with disabilities steered Britain toward reforming its century-old legislation criminalizing the induction of abortion.[30] The newly enacted 1967 Abortion Act focused on regulating the medical performance of legal abortion, refraining altogether from rights discourse or the assigning of moral weight either to the women's choice or the fetus' life.[31] Allocating decision-making authority to the medical system proved a crucial determinant in calming British abortion politics. Pro-lifers found solace in the fact that a woman's decision to abort is monitored by the medical profession inherently committed to preserving life. For pro-choicers this compromise offered a viable expansion of abortion possibilities, since bestowing doctors with medical discretion has not limited access to abortion in Britain.[32] Moreover, this 'medicalized' approach made a standard gynecological service offered in public hospitals, limiting the possibility (and mobilizing potential) of protest against private abortion facilities.[33] Since the passage of the Act abortion

---

1993) Sen. 25 103rd Cong. (21 January 1993)), 2007 (H.R. 1964 110th Cong. (19 April 2007) Sen. 1173 110th Cong. (19 April 2007).

30 E.M. Jackson, *Regulating Reproduction: Law, Technology and Autonomy* (Oxford: Hart, 2001), 77; Francome, *Abortion in the USA and the UK*, supra note 15, 53; M.D. Kandiah and G. Stareck (eds.), *The Abortion Act 1967* (ICBH Witness Seminar Program, 2001, 16.

31 J. Radcliffe-Richards, *The Sceptical Feminist: A Philosophical Enquiry* (Boston: Routlege, 1982); E. Lee, 'Reinventing Abortion as a Social Problem: 'Postabortion Syndrome' in the United States and Britain', in J. Best (ed.), *How Claims Spread: Cross-National Diffusion of Social Problems* (New York: Aldine de Gruyter, 2001), 42; M. Latham, *Regulating Reproduction: A Century of Conflict in Britain and France* (New York: Manchester University Press, 2002), 89.

32 Jackson, *Regulating Reproduction: Law, Technology and Autonomy,* supra note 30 at 83; Lee, 'Reinventing Abortion as a Social Problem: 'Postabortion Syndrome', supra note 31 at 43; J. Lovenduski, 'Parliament, Pressure Groups, Networks and the Women's Movement: The Politics of Abortion Law Reform in Britain 1967–83', in J. Lovenduski and J. Outshoorn (eds.), *The New Politics of Abortion* (London: Sage Publication, 1986).

33 A. Furedi and D. Nolan, 'Fighting a Battle of Ideas – Conflict on Abortion in the UK', 24 *Planned Parenthood in Europe* 3 (1995), 7.

has remained in the margins of British politics. Private bills to amend it have been introduced over the years but were all defeated. Similarly, attempts to challenge the abortion arrangements in courts met a reluctant judiciary ever since.[34]

The French reform was set in motion around the same time as Britain, stimulated by the changing role of women, over-population growth and harmful clandestine abortions.[35] A legislative compromise construed abortion a criminal act that can be medically authorized until the tenth week of pregnancy when a woman is 'in a state of distress.' With France's highest constitutional authority, the *Conseil Constitutionnel* clearing its enactment, the compromise became France's new legal arrangement on abortion.[36] The law refrained from providing a definition to a state of 'distress,' leaving its determination in the hands of the pregnant women. Originally perceived as degrading by pro-choice activists, the state of 'distress' nevertheless made abortion a readily available procedure for French women. By the time the law, which was originally enacted on a trial basis, was brought for reevaluation the legislative compromise has already taken hold and the law was re-enacted with minor changes.[37] One such change was the inclusion of the state's duty to actively promote the principle of respect for life and implement family-oriented policies. The 'state of distress' formula proved a fitting legislative compromise for the Netherlands as well following years of political opposition and parliamentary deadlocks. A narrowest majority (76–74 in the Lower House, 38–37 in the Senate) finally managed to clear its enactment in the early 1980s. The law came into force after additional regulations were issued designed to ensure that any decision to terminate a pregnancy was carefully balancing the protection of the fetus and the rights of the mother.[38]

---

34 Ex: *Paton* v. *British Pregnancy Advisory Service Trustees* [1979] QB 276; *R. (on the application of Axon) v. Secretary of State for Health and Another* [2006] E.W.H.C. 37 (Admin).

35 M. Allison, 'The Right to Choose: Abortion in France', 47 *Parliamentary Affairs* 2 (1994), 223–226.

36 74–54 DC, 15 January 1975.

37 M. A.Glendon, *Abortion and Divorce in Western Law*, supra note 4 at 15; D.M. Stetson, 'Abortion Policy Triads and Women's Rights in Russia, the United States, and France', in M. Githens and D.M. Stetson (eds.), *Abortion Politics: Public Policy in Cross-Cultural Perspective* (New York: Routledge, 1996), 109; Allison, 'The Right to Choose: Abortion in France', supra note 35 at 230; C. Gallard, 'France', in B. Rolston and A. Eggert (eds.), *Abortion in the New Europe: A Comparative Handbook* (Westport: Greenwood Press, 1994), 105.

38 J. Rademakers, 'The Netherlands', in P. Sachdev (ed.), *International Handbook on Abortion* (New York: Greenwood Press, 1988); J. Outshoorn, 'The Rules of the Game: Abortion Politics in the Netherlands', in J. Lovenduski and J. Outshoorn (eds.), *The New Politics of Abortion* (London: Sage Publication, 1986); J. Outshoorn, 'Policy-Making on Abortion: Arenas, Actors, and Arguments in the Netherlands', in D.M. Stetson (ed.), *Abortion Politics, Women's Movements and the Democratic State: A Comparative Study of State Feminism* (Oxford: Oxford University Press, 2001); E. Ketting, 'Netherlands', in

In Germany, lengthy and intense parliamentary debates during the 1970s generated the legalization of abortion in the first trimester, only to be annulled by the Federal Constitutional Court.[39] The Court constructed a constitutional hierarchy between the protection of the fetus and the personal choice of the mother, asserting that the state's duty to protect the fetus's right to life and human dignity exists even against its mother. Thus, the legal order must clearly express a condemnation to abortion that can only be justified in specified circumstances (Indications) stipulated by the Court under four classifications: medical, criminal, eugenic and social.[40] Political controversy continued as both sides of the abortion debate found this constitutionally mandated construction increasingly unsatisfactory.[41] The reunification of Germany in the early 1990s presented an opportunity for change as the *Indication* model of West Germany had to be reconciled with abortion on-demand available in East Germany. Following a protracted period of debates the unified Bundestag decriminalized (declared 'not-unlawful') first-trimester abortions for any reason subject to a counseling requirement, a three-day waiting period and a doctor's performance of the procedure.[42] Once again the Court annulled substantial parts of this unified legislation reaffirming its earlier rationale on the fundamental unlawfulness of abortion.[43] However, taking into account Germany's post-unification reality the Court amalgamated its original policy framework with

---

B. Rolston and A. Eggert (eds.), *Abortion in the New Europe: A Comparative Handbook* (Westport: Greenwood Press, 1994); S.L. Henderson and A.S Jeydel, *Women and Politics in a Global World*, 2nd edn. (New York: Oxford University Press, 2010).

39 39 BverfGE 1(1975). Translated in R.E. Jonas and J.D. Gorby, 'West German Abortion Decision: A Contrast to Roe V. Wade', 9 *John Marshall Journal of Practice and Procedure* 3 (1976), 605–684.

40 D.P. Kommers, *The Constitutional Jurisprudence of the Federal Republic of Germany* (Durham: Duke University Press, 1997), 347; M.M. Ferree, W.A. Gamson, J. Gerhards and D. Rucht (eds.), *Shaping Abortion Discourse: Democracy and the Public Sphere in Germany and the United States* (Cambridge: Cambridge University Press, 2002), 25–26; M.A. Case, 'Perfectionism and Fundamentalism in the Application of the German Abortion Laws', in S.H. Williams (ed.), *Constituting Equality: Gender Equality and Comparative Constitutional Law* (New York: Cambridge University Press, 2009), 95–96.

41 S. Walther, 'Thou Shalt Not (But Though Mayest): Abortion after the German Constitutional Court's 1993 Landmark Decision', 36 *German Yearbook of International Law* (1993), 386–387; G. Czarnowski, 'Abortion as a Political Conflict in the Unified Germany', 47 *Parliamentary Affairs* 2 (1994), 252–267; E. Maleck-Lewy and M.M. Ferree, 'Talking about Women and Wombs: The Discourse of Abortion and Reproductive Rights in the G.D.R. During and After the Wende', in S. Gal and G. Kligman (eds.), *Reproducing Gender: Politics, Publics and Everyday Life after Socialism* (Princeton: Princeton University Press, 2000), 94.

42 Text translated in R. Will, 'German Unification and the Reform in Abortion Law', 3 *Cardozo Women's Law Journal* (1996), 399–426, n. 86.

43 Text translated in Will, 'German Unification and the Reform in Abortion Law', 419–421; S. Michalowski and L. Woods, *German Constitutional Law: The Protection of Civil Liberties* (Aldershot: Ashgate, 1999), 145.

additional preventative measures of assistance and counseling designed to create a 'child-friendly' society and dissuade abortions. Upon the Court's specifications, the current German law includes measures providing financial and social support to pregnant women in education, housing, childcare and employment.[44]

Mirroring the German experience, in 1975 the Italian Constitutional Court declared unconstitutional the criminalization of all abortions except in strict necessity.[45] Concerned by the rise in backstreet, life-threatening abortions the Court found it unsatisfactory to give absolute priority to the fetus' constitutional right without adequate protection to the health of the woman. Speaking to a heated political atmosphere in an overwhelmingly Catholic nation the ruling contributed to the mobilization of both camps, but at the same time framed the direction of the legislative debates toward reaching an acceptable compromise over contested values.[46] A compromise between the two houses of parliament was reached in a 1978 law which kept abortion a criminal act, but established conditions – health, economic, social, or family circumstances – under which legal abortions in the first 90 days of pregnancy were permitted.[47] This enactment did not end public contestations. The heated debate culminated with the simultaneous referendum initiatives in 1981, a liberal one to expand the law and a conservative one to revoke it. Both failed the national referendum as did later judicial challenges, indicating a general consensus on the contours of abortion regulation in Italy.[48]

44 Walther, 'Thou Shalt Not (But Though Mayest)', supra note 41, 394; Michalowski and Woods, *German Constitutional Law*, supra note 43, 146; Ferree et al., *Shaping Abortion Discourse*, supra note 40 at 42; G.L Neuman, 'Casey in the Mirror: Abortion, Abuse and the Right to Protection in the USA and Germany', 43 *American Journal of Comparative Law* (1995), 273–314; C.P. Schlegel, 'Landmark in German Abortion Law: The German 1995 Compromise Compared with English Law', 11 *International Journal of Law, Policy and Family* 1 (1997), 45–48.

45 Carmosina et al. Corte costituzionale. Sentenza no. 27 of 1975, translated in M. Cappelletti and W. Cohen, *Comparative Constitutional Law: Cases and Materials* (Indianapolis: Bobbs-Merrill, 1979).

46 Glendon, *Abortion and Divorce in Western Law*, supra note 4 at 43; M. Calloni, 'Debates and Controversies on Abortion in Italy,' in D.M. Stetson (ed.), *Abortion Politics, Women's Movements and the Democratic State: A Comparative Study of State Feminism* (Oxford: Oxford University Press, 2001), 186.

47 Law no. 194 of 1978. Gazzetta Ufficiale della Repubblica Italiana, Part I, 2 May 1978, no. 140, 3642–3646. Translated in http://www.hsph.harvard.edu/population/abortion/ITALY.abo.htm.

48 I. Figà-Talamanca, 'Italy', in P. Sachdev (ed.) *International Handbook on Abortion* (New York: Greenwood Press, 1988), 281–282; M. Nijsten, *Abortion and Constitutional Law: A Comparative European-American Study* (Florence: European University Institute, 1990), 102; J. Andall, 'Abortion, Politics and Gender in Italy', 47 *Parliamentary Affairs* 2 (1994), 245; P. Hanafin, *Conceiving Life: Reproductive Politics and the Law in Contemporary Italy* (Aldershot: Ashgate, 2007), 28–33.

The tumultuous abortion politics engulfing Western Europe between the late 1960s and the late 1980s ended with the Belgian reform in 1990. An arrest of a physician performing abortions in the early 1970s mobilized intense political controversies, generating dozens of legislative proposals and a long political stalemate over reforming the criminalization of abortion.[49] The 1990 reform closely resembled the French and Dutch compromises, decriminalizing abortion in the first trimester when the pregnancy causes a 'situation of distress or emergency' for the woman. A constitutional crisis was averted when the Catholic King who refused to then sign the law and bring it into was declared 'unable to govern' for a day to allow the law to pass.[50]

To summarize, a period of turbulent Western-European abortion politics between the late 1960s and the late 1980s concluded with the emergence of relatively cohesive national legislative compromises. To maintain a normative disapproval toward the termination of pregnancies, abortion was kept criminal yet not unlawful during the first semester when grave hardship is involved, and even in later weeks when the well-being of the woman is at stake. Moreover, as part of a vital concern for the unborn life, termination of pregnancies in these states can only take place following mandatory waiting periods and counseling processes designed to discourage abortions by emphasizing social and financial possibilities for life with a child.

A Comparative Outlook on Law's Role in Abortion Politics

Abortion politics in the United States and Western Europe seemingly conform to the 'great divide' within *Political Liberalism* over the manner in which multicultural societies ought to be organized.[51] The US Supreme Court's construction of the woman's right to choose steered abortion politics in the classical liberal direction, entrenching the discourse of fundamental rights as the principal paradigm for the American debate. Termination of pregnancies became a conflict over women's rights versus the rights of the unborn. In contrast, the European discourse emphasized communitarian dimensions, interweaving rights-based arguments with

49 R. Boland, 'Recent Developments in Abortion Law in Industrial Countries: International Review', 18 *Law, Medicine and Health Care* (1990), 404–418; V. Claeys, 'Belgium', in B. Rolston and A. Eggert (eds.), *Abortion in the New Europe: A Comparative Handbook* (Westport: Greenwood Press, 1994), 19–23; K. Celis, 'The Abortion Debates in Belgium 1974–1990', in D.M. Stetson (ed.), *Abortion Politics, Women's Movements and the Democratic State: A Comparative Study of State Feminism* (Oxford: Oxford University Press, 2001).

50 J. Outshoorn, 'The Stability of Compromise, Abortion Politics in Western Europe', in M. Githens, D.M. Stetson, D.E. McBride (eds.), *Abortion Politics: Public Policy in Cross-Cultural Perspectives* (London: Routledge, 1996), 145, 158.

51 C. Taylor, 'Cross-Purposes: The Liberal-Communitarian Debate', in N.L. Rosenblum (ed.), *Liberalism and the Moral Life* (Cambridge: Harvard University Press, 1989).

economic policies, social concerns over family welfare and political objectives for the society as a whole. Accordingly analysts not only employed this philosophical prism to explain the diverging abortion politics across the Atlantic, but also to critique the legal arrangements in each of the locations. Disapproval of the 1973 Supreme Court ruling highlighted its neglect of collective tenets.[52] In comparison, echoing the liberal-constitutional justification for the need to guarantee individual rights against majority's prejudices, European legal developments were criticized as inadequate in protecting the rights of women.[53]

Yet, the general climate of abortion conflicts following the liberalization of abortion laws has been strikingly different in the two geographical locations. Abortion debates in the USA have consistently taken a morality-based and highly public confrontational path, with the competing camps utilizing the legal process ideologically. Attempts to refashion, maneuver and circumvent legal arrangements on abortion remain active components of the American political debate since the early 1970s. Contrasting the American debate, the meeting of law and politics in Western Europe evolved as a protracted search for social accord. Prompted by varying socio-political challenges, Western European legislatures and constitutional courts negotiated over a long period of time and amid great public controversy uneasy compromises. Despite these transitional hardships, the Western European compromises have shown decades-long durability and low levels of political controversy compared to that of the USA.[54]

One can argue that the American polity has been susceptible to contentious constitutional politics more than Western Europe for two main reasons:[55] (i) By definition, the American separation-of-powers doctrine induces the potential for competing actions between the state and the federal level. Moreover, its judicialized politics epitomized by *Roe*-type rulings, reinforces the perception among political actors that courts can entrench their moral preferences when the political system will not. (ii) The American public is overall more religious than its European counterpart, making morality-based debates like abortion more contentious.

Nonetheless, the surveyed data substantially weakens these two assumptions. The premise that competing legal arenas provoke structural vulnerability toward a tug-of war dynamics is countered by the British experience, where courts have

52 G. Calabresi, *Ideals, Beliefs, Attitudes and the Law: Private Perspectives on a Public Law Problem* (Syracuse: Syracuse University Press, 1985); Glendon, *Abortion and Divorce in Western Law*, supra note 4.

53 Tribe, *Abortion: The Clash of Absolutes,* supra note 5; S. Sheldon, *Beyond Control: Medical Power and Abortion Law* (Chicago: Pluto Press, 1997); Francome, *Abortion in the USA and the UK*, supra note 15 at 51; Hanafin, *Conceiving Life*, supra note 48; J. N. Erdmann, 'Moral Authority in English and Mexican Abortion Law', in S.H. Williams (ed.), *Constituting Equality: Gender Equality and Comparative Constitutional Law* (New York: Cambridge University Press, 2009).

54 Outshoorn, 'The Stability of Compromise, Abortion Politics in Western Europe', supra note 50 at 161.

55 Francome, *Abortion in the USA and the UK*, supra note 15 at 102.

shown unwavering will to keep the 'medicalized' statutory model regardless of an institutional capability to override them. Even after Britain joined the international trend of constitutional politics by enacting the Human Rights Act 1998,[56] the court continued to reject a move in the direction rights-based jurisprudence on the issue of abortion. Contemporary observers of British politics 'note with relief that abortion in Britain generates less conflict and controversy than in the United States.'[57] Notwithstanding institutional differences between the American and the European constitutional review processes,[58] the experiences of France, Germany and Italy breed additional doubts for the inevitability a tug-of-war dynamics between the different branches of government. The involvement of the European constitutional courts in abortion controversies has proven pivotal in the emergence of long-lasting and durable compromises. In the French context the referral to the *Conseil Constitutionnel* legitimized the abortion legislative compromise. In Germany, constitutional vetoes on legislative reforms were accompanied by elaborate frameworks guiding the future legislative process. Finally, by requiring the legislature to equally balance competing rights, the Italian constitutional court effectively compelled a compromise as the ultimate legislative outcome.

Explaining the difference between present-day Western European and American abortion politics by way of secularization process appears insufficient as well. Aside from the sociological debates over Europe's processes of secularization,[59] the data suggests that secularization was one of many social developments prompting legal reforms in European states. Pressing social needs, including clandestine dangerous abortions, dwindling population, the thalidomide problem, specific historical developments such as the unification of Germany and so forth, all acted as engines of reform in the reconsideration of the criminalization of abortion. Moreover, in every example examined above reform processes met fierce anti-abortion opposition, leading to protracted debates that stretched the liberalization process over many years.

Comparing existing legal rules on either side of the Atlantic suggests a process of conversion. The 1973 judicial promulgation of a constitutional right to abortion has been gradually supplemented by legislative and judicial actions modifying the scope of this right and the ease in which abortions are obtained

---

56 Incorporating the 1950 European Convention for the Protection of Human Rights and Fundamental Freedoms into English Law.

57 Erdmann, 'Moral Authority in English and Mexican Abortion Law', supra note 53 at 108; J.K. Mason, *The Troubled Pregnancy: Legal Wrongs and Rights in Reproduction* (Cambridge: Cambridge University Press, 2007), 14.

58 A. Stone Sweet, 'Why Europe Rejected American Judicial Review, and Why it May Not Matter', 101 *Michigan Law Review* (2003), 2744–2780.

59 R. Stark, 'Secularization R.I.P.', 60 *Sociology of Religion* 3 (1999), 249–273; J. Casanova, *Public Religions in the Modern World* (Chicago: University of Chicago Press, 1994); G. Davie, *Religion in Modern Britain Since 1945: Believing without Belonging* (Oxford: Blackwell, 1994).

in the USA.[60] In comparison, Western European legislation, which kept a stern rhetoric of criminalization in its laws effectively made the termination of unwanted pregnancies rather accessible as well as state-funded. Yet, in line with the hypothesis on the diverging social role of law, the legal models in each of the locations differ in the length of mandatory waiting periods and consultation processes. In Western Europe, the social goal of dissuading abortions generated longer waiting periods prior to the performance of abortions compared to the USA. Moreover, the European consultation processes placed its primary emphasis on the possibilities of life with a child, whereas the American legal arrangements have customarily included elaborate requirements on informing the woman about physical and emotional risks associated with abortion and disclosing the fetus' gestational characteristics.[61]

Attention is now turned to assessing the realization of law's goal in each of the debates, namely law's actual effect on: (i) social change and (ii) its contribution to the resolution of the socio-cultural conflict. Public opinion polls in the USA on the question of abortion reveal remarkably stable views, with a minority favoring unrestricted abortions, a minority opposing abortion altogether, and the median position agreeing that abortion needs to be available 'but that women should be able to obtain the procedure *only* for good reasons.'[62] Yet, the definition of 'good reasons' is still subject to continual alterations shaped by shifts in political power.[63] Bestowing constitutional status to women's choice should have in principle transformed the extent of protection for women seeking abortion, nevertheless observers note that access to abortion in the USA remains effectively limited.[64] Thus, with the pro-choice/pro-life dichotomy becoming the dominant prism of the American conflict, broader political compromises were effectively shelved.[65] The recent stream of pro-life legislation in Republican-dominated states encountering immediate pro-choice

---

60 M.A. Graber, *Rethinking Abortion: Equal Choice, the Constitution and Reproductive Politics* (Princeton: Princeton University Press, 1996).

61 Glendon, *Abortion and Divorce in Western Law,* supra note 4 at 20.

62 Balkin, *What Roe v. Wade Should Have Said*, supra note 13 at 4; T.G. Jelen and C. Wilcox, 'Causes and Consequences of Public Attitudes toward Abortion: A Review and Research Agenda', 56 *Political Research Quarterly* 4 (2003), 490; McBride, *Abortion in the United States*, supra note 5 at 210–216.

63 K.L. Scheppele, 'Constitutionalizing Abortion', in M. Githens and D.M. Stetson (eds.), *Abortion Politics: Public Policy in Cross-Cultural Perspective* (New York: Routledge, 1996), 46–47.

64 Graber, *Rethinking Abortion*, supra note 60 at 215; R. Solinger, *Pregnancy and Power: A Short History of Reproductive Politics in America* (New York: New York University Press, 2005); J. Novkov, 'Law and Political Ideologies', in K.E. Whittington, R.D. Kelemen and G.A. Caldeira (eds.), *The Oxford Handbook on Law and Politics* (Oxford: Oxford University Press, 2008), 637.

65 M. Deflem, 'The Boundaries of Abortion Law: Systems Theory from Parsons to Luhmann and Habermas', 76 *Social Forces* 3 (1998), 775–818.

challenges in courts have been the latest incarnation of the perpetual battle over accessibility to abortion with mixed victories (or defeats) on either side.

In comparison, keeping abortion as a criminal act in the Western European systems should have in principle worked against the entrenchment of abortion rights. Observers even suggested that the European legal compromises of codifying pro-life rhetoric with pro-choice policy were 'empty compromises,' if not 'hypocrisy' that 'can take an unacceptably high toll on confidence in the rule of law and the integrity of the legal system as a whole'.[66] Nonetheless, the availability of abortion in Europe has proved significantly higher than in the USA. According to a recent examination 'Western Europe has had a quite stable abortion environment. In contrast to the situation in the USA, access to abortion providing facilities … is substantially easier … [and] free from the extremes of violence and controversy that have characterized abortion care in the USA.'[67]

Moreover, the frequency in which US courts and legislatures have been occupied with abortion issues has been unparalleled anywhere in Western Europe. It has been suggested that tensions within constitutional systems and backlash dynamics between courts and legislatures are not necessarily negative and may even prove as an effective political method in responding to moral controversies.[68] Yet, the 'medicalized' model of Britain, the 'distress' formula of France, the Netherlands and Belgium, and the court-prescribed compromises of Germany and Italy, all seemed to have worked substantially well not only in channeling political controversies over abortion but in depoliticizing them as well. Moreover, while the American law on abortion continues to be passionately debated in federal and state legislative sessions, judicial proceedings or in executive policies, the European legal arrangements have remained unshakable over decades.

Conclusion

Moral controversies over abortion are seemingly perpetual. The history of abortion reform in the USA and Western Europe suggests that women with unwanted pregnancies resorted to abortions regardless of the legality of the procedure or its health risks. For people who are convinced that life begins at conception, the thought of voluntarily ending prenatal life remains incomprehensible regardless of decades-long pro-choice advocacy. Hence, resolving the question of abortion on a moral basis is presumably hopeless.

---

66 Tribe, *Abortion: The Clash of Absolutes*, supra note 5at 73–74; Scheppele, 'Constitutionalizing Abortion', supra note 63 at 46–47.

67 C. Joffe, 'Abortion and Medicine: A Sociopolitical History' in M. Paul, S. Lichtenberg, L. Borgatta, P.G. Stubblefield and M.D. Creinin (eds.), *Management of Unintended and Abnormal Pregnancy* (Chichester: Wiley-Blackwell, 2009), 4.

68 R. Post and R. Siegel, 'Roe Rage: Democratic Constitutionalism and Backlash', 42 *Harvard Civil Rights-Civil Liberties Law Review* (2007), 373–433.

The global trend of constitutionalism swayed scholarly deliberations toward discerning the relationship between law and social change.[69] Yet, this study highlighted the limitation of this quest in the context of abortion compared to the political potential of swinging the academic pendulum toward law's integrative social function. Morality-based socio-cultural controversies underline the political nature of the legal process.[70] Abortion politics in the USA demonstrated that moral preferences translated into law remain susceptible to shifts in the distribution of political power. However, utilizing law with the goal of generating compromises seems to offer greater promise for perpetual socio-cultural conflicts. The Western European examples demonstrated that integrative legal solutions offer more than temporary resolution to moral conflicts even if their scope of protection for the competing rights at stake (choice v. life) remains ideologically insufficient.

An argument can be made that the American legal process has been effectively functioning as a conflict-defusing mechanism, in providing orderly legal procedures to channel perpetual partisan controversies over abortion.[71] Yet, these debates also seemed to have fueled social polarization, acrimonious constitutional conflicts, a culture of evasion toward judicial edicts and periodic violent disruptions. Assessing these ongoing controversies comparatively revealed that enduring US debates over abortion rights during different trimesters, parental involvement, waiting periods, consultations, public funding and so forth, have been decades-old settled law in Western European nations. Moreover, European legal arrangements resulted in pro-choicers securing state funding for abortion procedures as pro-lifers achieved different forms of state assistance to ease motherhood.

Structural characteristics specific to Western European constitutional systems have been instrumental in realizing consensual arrangements and compromises over abortion as demonstrated by the developments in Germany, France and Italy.[72] Given the divergence in constitutional review processes in each of the

69 O. Liviatan, '*The Impact of Alternative Constitutional Regimes on Religious Freedom in Canada and England*', 32 *Boston College International and Comparative Law Review* 1 (2009), 45–82; O. Liviatan, 'Judicial Activism and Religion-Based Tensions in India and Israel', 26 *Arizona Journal of International and Comparative Law* 3 (2009), 583–621.

70 O. Liviatan, 'Faith in the Law: The Role of Legal Arrangements in Religion-Based Conflicts Involving Minorities', 34 *Boston College International and Comparative Law Review* 1 (2011), 53–89.

71 J. Ferejohn and P. Pasquino, 'Constitutional Adjudication: Lessons from Europe', 82 *Texas Law Review* (2004), 1699.

72 On these process see: A. Stone Sweet, *Governing with Judges: Constitutional Politics in Europe* (Oxford: Oxford University Press, 2000); A. Stone Sweet, 'The Politics of Constitutional Review in France and Europe', *International Journal of Constitutional Law* 1 (2007), 69–92; G. Nolte (ed.), *European and US Constitutionalism* (Cambridge: Cambridge University Press, 2005).

locations, constitutional transfer is often impossible and frequently undesirable.[73] Yet, the European models remain instructive in highlighting the absence of a systematic search within American legal proceedings of a *shared* approach as to what is constitutionally feasible in the context of abortion. Even as part of two-sided disputes American courts are still engaged in the creation of general rules, providing them with an opportunity to prescribe substantive guidance for a plausible compromise-building approach. This potential is all the more realizable as part of law-making in legislative chambers, as parliamentary deliberations remain the most acceptable democratic response to social conflicts.[74] Given that both the USA and Western Europe continue to experience qualified rights protection and persistent ideological disagreements over abortion, the Western European examples serve as a constant reminder that social and political peace remains the striking variant across the two sides of the Atlantic.

73 J.E Ferejohn, 'Constitutional Review in the Global Context', 6 *New York University Journal of Legislation and Public Policy* (2002), 59; Ferejohn and Pasquino, 'Constitutional Adjudication: Lessons from Europe', supra note 71.

74 J. Waldron, *Law and Disagreement* (Oxford: Oxford University Press, 1999).

Chapter 22
Secular Human Rights, and Religious Pluralism: The British Debate

Zachary R. Calo

A European Jurisprudence of Democratic Pluralism

The European Court of Human Rights (ECtHR) in the 1993 case *Kokkinakis v. Greece* stated that:

> As enshrined in Article 9 [of the European Convention on Human Rights], freedom of thought, conscience and religion is one of the foundations of a 'democratic society' within the meaning of the Convention. It is, in its religious dimension, one of the most vital elements that go to make up the identity of believers and their conception of life, but it is also a precious asset for atheists, agnostics, sceptics and the unconcerned. The pluralism indissociable from a democratic society, which has been dearly won over the centuries depends on it.[1]

This claim that pluralism is linked with religious freedom and democratic order has been repeated in subsequent decisions and represents one of the basic principles defining the meaning of Article 9.[2] As Françoise Tulkens observes, the 'principle of pluralism seems to be the main – the core – principle' guiding the Court's approach to religious freedom.[3] The Court has not only deemed religious pluralism to be a basic good of the liberal democratic society. It has deemed pluralism to be the proper expression of authentic religious freedom. Religious pluralism reveals the capacity of a social order to permit the flourishing of alternative loci of

1 *Kokkinakis v. Greece*, App. No. 14307/88, 25 May 1993, para. 31.

2 Article 9 of the European Convention on Human Rights provides that:

(1) Everyone has the right to freedom of thought, conscience and religion; this right includes freedom to change his religion or belief, and freedom, either alone or in community with others and in public or private, to manifest his religion or belief, in worship, teaching, practice and observance.

(2) Freedom to manifest one's religion or beliefs shall be subject only to such limitations as are prescribed by law and are necessary in a democratic society in the interests of public safety, for the protection of public order, health or morals, or the protection of the rights and freedoms of others.

3 F. Tulkens, 'The European Convention on Human Rights and Church-State Relations: Pluralism vs. Pluralism,' 30 *Cardozo Law Review* (2009), 2579.

meaning, and thus discloses patterns of cultural self-understanding that shape the relationship between law and religion more generally.

While the ECtHR has often linked religious freedom with religious pluralism, it has also rendered a number of decisions seemingly at odds with the principle in *Kokkinaks*. A series of cases concerning the right of Muslim women to wear headscarves – *Dahlab v. Switzerland* (2001), *Leyla Şahin v. Turkey* (2004/2005), and *Dogru v. France* (2008) – offers a vivid example of the difficulties the Court has had in fully actualizing the normative religious pluralism described in *Kokkinakis*. The particular circumstances at issue in these three cases differ. *Dahlab* concerned a teacher in a state primary school who had converted to Islam and began wearing a head covering.[4] *Leyla Şahin* addressed a prohibition on University of Istanbul students wearing headscarves.[5] Finally, *Dogru v. France* involved a young Muslim student disciplined for wearing a headscarf to her physical education class.[6] Yet, in each of the cases, the Court upheld headscarf bans on the ground that they were necessary to protect public order and safety, religious harmony, and democratic culture.

The concern of this chapter is with the facial discontinuity between the Court's endorsement of religious pluralism and its legal treatment of Islam. While these cases might be interpreted as mere prudential exercises in the application of Article 9 to difficult facts, or as expressions of deference to the margin of appreciation, it is argued that they more basically reveal tensions within the Court's framing of the relationship between religion, pluralism, and human rights. In particular, these cases disclose the limits of contemporary legal liberalism, particularly the challenge of actualizing religious pluralism within a normative secular order. The jurisprudential logic at operation in these cases, informed by the ontological disjuncture of law and religion at the base of legal modernity, lacks adequate internal resources for supporting the account of pluralism the Court has endorsed.

Secular Nomos and the Limits of Pluralism

The Court's approach to the headscarf issue reveals how the legal categories and culture within which it operates have become tethered to a particular mode of secularity. If only in subtle and unacknowledged ways, the ECHR's Article 9 jurisprudence advances this secular legal order by constructing religion and liberal human rights as competing moral traditions.

One factor shaping the Court's jurisprudence is its location within a secular and secularizing Europe. Along these lines, Phillip Blond and Adrian Pabst have described the tendency of 'the secular European state [to arrogate] to itself the right to control and legislate … religion and its civic influence. Legally, secularism

4 *Dahlab v. Switzerland*, App. No. 42393/98, 15 February 2001.

5 *Leyla Şahin v. Turkey*, App. No. 44774/98 (Grand Chamber), 10 November 2005.

6 *Dogru v. France*, App. No. 27058/05, 4 December 2008.

outlaws any rival source of sovereignty or legitimacy. Politically, secularism denies religion any import in public debate and decision making. Culturally, secularism enforces its own norms and standards upon all other belief systems.'[7] These patterns, in turn, shape the meaning and possibilities for pluralism. In the end, an account of human rights grounded in such a secularism cannot sustain normative religious pluralism, for religion becomes a potential problem to be managed and controlled. The secular negation of public religion is particularly intense with respect to Islam, which presents a symbolic challenge to the normative secular order, and the headscarf, which stands at odds with the conception of freedom and self-creation that find expression within the European liberal tradition.[8]

The secular character of the Court's jurisprudence also reveals how the modern moral order has shaped the relationship between law and religion. In this respect, the barriers to religious pluralism are not merely cultural or political but also ontological. At the heart of modern politics has been the ontological separation of law and religion, a conceptual development that gave full expression to the idea of secular political space. The process of political desacralization found its genesis in Christian insights concerning the limits of politics,[9] but the desacralized political order of modernity was one in which law eventually came to be defined over and against religion. Historical linkages between theology and the secular were abandoned, as the secular came to represent an autonomous political space that maintained no necessary connectedness to a theological economy.

This desacralized political order birthed an attendant secular jurisprudence. This jurisprudence took different forms. Legal secularity, at its core, meant only that law was located within an ontological sphere distinct from religion and dependent on its own internal logic. Legal secularity, as such, did not intimate that the order of law stood in fundamental opposition to the order of religion. Legal secularism, by contrast, defined law over and against the order of faith so as to segregate the public from the sacred. Both secularity and secularism are expressions of a desacralized politics. They represent two distinct expressions of modernity.

The account of law's relationship to religion that has informed recent ECHR jurisprudence reflects the tradition of legal secularism more so than that of legal secularity. Severed and divorced from a theological economy, the law of religious freedom thus represents not a neutral political space, but a political space defined by a normative secularity. One explanation for the triumph of this secularism is the logic embodied in the law and idea of human rights. Human rights has become the dominant moral vocabulary of modernity and achieved a particular preeminence

7 P. Blond and A. Pabst, 'Integrating Islam into the West', *The New York Times*, 4 November 2008.

8 See, R. Williams, 'Europe, Faith and Culture' (2008), available at http://www.archbishopofcanterbury.org/articles.php/1164/archbishops-liverpool-lecture-europe-faith-and-culture.

9 See R.A. Markus, *Saeculum: History and Society in the Theology of St. Augustine* (New York: Cambridge University Press, 1970).

within Europe, which as Janne Matlary notes, 'has become the major exponent of human rights, democracy, and the rule of law all over the world'.[10] Yet it is not simply that Europe has embraced human rights, but that it has embraced them as the foundation of a civilizational worldview. Marco Ventura makes the case more gently, yet his remarks on the civilizational role of human rights within Europe are nevertheless revealing:

> The European Convention on Human Rights (ECHR) expressed a shift towards a civil religion of human rights having the potential to develop a European common standard beyond national specificities. The ECHR did not mention Christianity as the course of rights; instead, what mattered was adherence to the specified rights regardless of the source of those rights. The civil religion of rights and freedoms fit better with an open society; secular faith in freedom and rights … had replaced religious faith in the transcendent meaning of worldly life.[11]

Viewed in this light, the rise of human rights is part of the rupture in western thought whereby the world was turned in on itself. In its strongest form, human rights challenge religion as an ordering cosmic narrative within which the nature and destiny of the human person are made sensible. Especially in the European context, human rights have achieved cultural and legal primacy in tandem with the abnegation of religious sources of meaning.

The resulting moral order does not encourage the flourishing of religious pluralism because the universal and secular nomos of human rights law grants little space to strong expressions of religious particularity. The normative secularity of legal modernity ultimately stands at odds with the cultivation of thick public religiosity. This being the case, the problematic of religious pluralism must be assessed not only on jurisprudential but moral, ontological, and finally, theological grounds, for what is at issues is the deep way in which law has been defined against religion within the late modern moral order. With this in mind, the chapter turns in its final section to discussing conceptual jurisprudential alternatives, particularly those grounded in theological insight. As a point of entry into this matter, this section considers recent arguments advanced by Rowan Williams and John Milbank.

Reconceptualizing Pluralism

If the limited capacity of liberal human rights to undergird religious pluralism is rooted in the structure of legal modernity, alternatives must then move beyond the universal and secular underpinnings of this tradition. The two arguments

10 J. Haaland Matláry, *When Might Becomes Human Right: Essays on Democracy and the Crisis of Rationality* (Leominster, UK: Gracewing, 2007), 108.

11 M. Ventura, 'The Changing Civil Religion of Secular Europe', 41 *The George Washington International Law Review* (2010), 958–959.

discussed below both aim to do this, with Williams interrogating the concept of legal universalism and Milbank legal secularity. In so doing, both thinkers move to advance an account of law within which group rights and religious pluralism might flourish more fully.

One of the most interesting contributions to recent debate about religious pluralism is Rowan Williams's lecture on 'Civil and Religious Law in England'. The initial question Williams takes up is whether there ought to be space made within English law for recognition of religious law, particularly Sharia law.[12] There is an expansive literature addressing this topic, but William's contribution is distinct in that it considers the issue on theological terms. In fact, Williams proposes that the question of legal and religious pluralism can be fully addressed only by developing a 'theology of law.'[13]

Williams proposes that constructive debate about legal pluralism has been undermined by the dominant assumptions shaping legal thought within secular modernity. He notes that, 'So much of our thinking in the modern world, dominated by European assumptions about universal rights, rests, surely, on the basis that the law is the law; that everyone stands before the public tribunal on exactly equal terms, so that recognition of corporate identities or, more seriously, of supplementary jurisdictions is simply incoherent if we want to preserve the great political and social advances of Western legality.'[14] There is a basic tension, in other words, between legal modernity and supplemental religious jurisdiction. Yet, it is precisely this tension that Williams critiques and deconstructs, because the totalizing grip that legal universalism maintains on the jurisprudential imagination has limited the capacity to think fully about the ends of law in relation to human life and community. Advancing debate about religious pluralism must therefore begin with a critical reappraisal of the idea of legal universalism within western modernity.

By opening legal universalism to critical judgment, Williams is not advancing a reactionary screed against the Enlightenment. To the contrary, he affirms much of legal modernity, noting that the universal norms of human rights are expressive of religious insights. The Enlightenment achievement, far from involving a negation of religion, affirmed 'themes consistently and strongly emphasized by the "Abrahamic faiths"'.[15] The modern world thus gave birth to an account of human dignity that drew from religion while also provoking the internal reformation of religious thought and practice. Religious legal pluralism must therefore operate within the bounds of such basic human rights, for these norms 'prevent the creation of mutually isolated communities, in which human liberties are seen in incompatible ways and individual persons are subjected to restrains or injustices

12 R. Williams, 'Civil and Religious Law in England: A Religious Perspective', 10 *Ecclesiastical Law Journal* 3 (September 2008), 262–282.

13 Williams, 'Civil and Religious Law in England', 272.

14 Williams, 'Civil and Religious Law in England', 270.

15 Williams, 'Civil and Religious Law in England', 272.

for which there is no public redress'.[16] The universal norm of human dignity stands in dialectical tension with all particular loyalties, so as to disrupt the possibility that discrete communities of meaning will claim 'finality for their own boundaries of practice and understanding'.[17]

Yet, while Williams affirms the universality of human rights, he is concerned with how a certain form of legal universality has stifled religion. No one form of law can account for the diverse loyalties that shape human life-in-community. But secular law, particularly as enshrined within human rights norms, has increasingly exhibited such totalizing meaning-making ambitions. The problem is not with legal universalism as such, but with linking such universalism to the modern state in a way that secular law acquires a 'monopoly in terms of defining public and political identity'.[18] In such a system, law assumes an either/or quality in which universality comes to be defined against other particularistic loyalties.

As an alternative, Williams defines rule of law not as 'the enshrining of priority for the universal/abstract dimension of social existence but the establishing of a space accessible to every one in which it is possible to affirm and defend a commitment to human dignity *as such*'.[19] He develops this insight by reference to the negative and positive functions of law. In particular, Williams advances the provocative claim that 'it helps to see the universalist vision of law as guaranteeing equal accountability and access primarily in a negative rather than a positive sense.'[20] By so proposing, it would appear that Williams ascribes to universal legal norms the narrow vocation of protecting 'certain elementary liberties of self-determination'.[21] The role of such basic norms, in turn, is to create and preserve space within which persons and communities might seek fulfillment according to deep and particular sources of meaning. The problem, Williams argues, is that legal universalism enacts both the negative and positive dimensions of law in a way that limits the ability of persons to cultivate and enact these deep loyalties. The 'specific community understandings' that ground pluralism have been suffocated by a universalism that claims finality over legal meaning.[22]

Perhaps the most significant contribution Williams makes is to analyze the problem of pluralism in theological terms. For Williams, the positive aspect of legal universality is ultimately a matter of theological concern because it speaks to the 'possibility for every human subject to live in conscious relation with God and in free and constructive collaboration with others'.[23] It is the universal possibilities disclosed in the theological that ground pluralistic particularity. Just as theology

16 Williams, 'Civil and Religious Law in England', 271–272.
17 Williams, 'Civil and Religious Law in England', 272.
18 Williams, 'Civil and Religious Law in England', 265.
19 Williams, 'Civil and Religious Law in England', 272.
20 Williams, 'Civil and Religious Law in England', 271.
21 Williams, 'Civil and Religious Law in England', 271.
22 Williams, 'Civil and Religious Law in England', 272.
23 Williams, 'Civil and Religious Law in England', 272–273.

made possible the emergence of Enlightenment claims about universal human dignity, so too does theology provide resources to prevent this universality from becoming allied against the particular. While theological anthropology affirms the universality of legal norms that stand outside of history, so too does it acknowledge the dynamic and contingent openness of history. The universal principle of legal right, Williams writes, 'requires both a certain valuation of the human as such and a conviction that the human subject is always endowed with some degree of freedom over against any and every actual system of human social life'.[24] Only when law is located within a theological economy can space be maintained for the possibility of divine interruption. The problem with the universal jurisprudence of secular modernity is that it bestows upon law an autonomy disconnected from theological roots and thus theological limits. By loosing universal right from the theological insight that universality also represents 'a way of recognizing what is least fathomable and controllable in the human subject,' law has become a totalizing form of meaning that subverts the particular and thus limits religious pluralism.[25] Only by interrogating this aspect of the modern legal inheritance is it possible to think constructively about the conditions needed to foster genuine religious pluralism.

The critique Williams develops can be usefully employed in analyzing the Court's jurisprudence in the headscarf cases. In particular, it might be proposed that by locating pluralism within a universal human rights framework, the Court impliedly adopts a constitutional hermeneutic that cannot ultimately account for the meaning and purposes of religious pluralism. The logic of universality overrides the possibilities of particularity, especially when tension exists between strong religiosity and normative secularity. Williams's discussion of religion, secularism, and pluralism highlights the narrow way that the Court framed the issue and the limits of the legal methodology it employed.

Like Williams, Milbank begins his contribution to the debate by asserting the need to consider 'religious group rights ... from a specifically theological position'.[26] However, an overriding concern of his essay 'Shari'a and the True Basis of Group Rights' is to examine ways in which Williams fails to develop the logic of his theological position with sufficiently critical depth. In particular, Milbank proposes that Williams remains bounded to a secular and liberal conception of the legal order that leads him to adopt an account of pluralism based on 'the "postmodern" application of liberal secular thought to the group rather than the individual'.[27] Williams fails, in other words, to fully examine how theological insights might reshape thinking about law, religious pluralism, and group rights. The theological turn Williams takes is not, for Milbank, sufficiently radical

24 Williams, 'Civil and Religious Law in England', 272.

25 Williams, 'Civil and Religious Law in England', 275.

26 J. Milbank, 'Shari'a and the True Basis of Group Rights', T. Ahdar and N. Aroney (eds.), *Shari'a in the West* (New York: Oxford University Press, 2010), 136.

27 Milbank, 135.

because the only authentic and sustainable basis for pluralism is the reconstitution of a Christian conception of the social order that stands over and against the orders of secular liberalism. As Milbank boldly proposes, 'My argument is that only a hegemonically Christian outlook, and not a secular one, can accord to Islam respect *as Islam*.'[28]

The starting point for Milbank's argument is the premise 'that liberalism is *incorrigibly* atomistic'.[29] This being the case, 'Liberal recognition of group identity must always logically give way before the recognition of individual rights.'[30] As such, the liberalism of western modernity is ultimately incompatible with true religious pluralism because it accords no recognition to the group. The inability of liberalism to recognize the group means that it cannot uphold religious freedom for, 'In not being able to tolerate group rights we end up not being able to tolerate individual freedom.'[31] In fact, liberalism not only fails to respect group rights. It actively undermines them because, 'Liberal principles, when pressed to a logical extreme, will always ensure that the rights of the individual override those of the group.'[32] In the end, liberal religious freedom collapses on itself because the public becomes nothing but unmediated space between the individual and the sovereign state. The residue of an organic Christian social order has, and continues in certain ways, to mitigate against such a totalizing collapse. But the ever increasing inability of law to uphold a principled religious pluralism against the pressures of the secular state evidences the internal weaknesses of the entire system.

A related problem Milbank identifies is that liberalism is not and cannot be neutral. Neutrality and secularism, linked as they are within the liberal framework, feed ambivalence about the rights of religious groups. [33] As such, legal neutrality must be named as a normative position, and more specifically a normative position defined against religion, for the secular grounds of neutrality mean that deep recognition cannot be given to the religious. A secular mode of neutrality is, in short, 'unable to accord the religious perspective equal protection,' thus leading liberalism to 'eventually self-deconstruct.'[34] The failure of liberalism to be genuinely neutral leaves it foundationally incapable of supporting a principled religious pluralism.

Williams, in Milbank's assessment, is correct to move from the individual to the group in discussing the problem of religious pluralism. Yet, the project Williams undertakes relies too heavily on a desiccated liberalism that lacks the resources to support group religious rights. Parallel jurisdiction aims to salvage liberalism by carving sacred space within a secular shell, when what is required is

28 Milbank, 138.
29 Milbank, 137.
30 Milbank, 137.
31 Milbank, 144.
32 Milbank, 145.
33 Milbank, 138.
34 Milbank, 144–145.

a more totalizing alternative. This 'non-liberal theory of plural sovereignty' must rest on a 'kind of religious or metaphysical dimension'[35] because recognizing 'group personality … requires a teleological ethic: one has to say that that a group is aiming for a goal, that its collective character fosters desired social ends.'[36]

Milbank's non-liberal alternative takes the form of a reconstructed Christian order. Christianity, and to a degree Judaism, constructed a model of 'corporatism' that alone could 'comprehend "the other"'.[37] This development, moreover, was not mere historical accident but the expression of theological resources within the Christian political imagination. For Christianity, a corporatist politics is grounded in Christology, particularly the idea of the church as body of Christ, an idea that eventually generated the idea of Europe as a corporation of corporations.[38]

Milbank is less concerned with the particulars of legal policy than with resetting the terms of debate over law, religion and pluralism. On one matter of legal policy, however, Milbank is clear: a Christian defense of group rights stands in basic tension with the establishment of parallel legal jurisdictions.[39] In this respect, Milbank positions himself against Williams. While Milbank acknowledges that certain areas of British law, such as marriage and finance, can already be adjudicated according to group religious principles, he nevertheless argues that these practices operate within the bounds of secular norms of Christian origin.[40] This claim is somewhat peculiar at first glance, yet it rests on Milbank's assertion that Christianity is not at odds with a certain form of secularity. In fact, he posits that Christianity has had a secularizing effect on politics and is 'uniquely' able to secularize 'the law of the land'.[41] The achievement of secular law within the West, expressed in the defining of law as distinct from the sacred, is an achievement that has happened within bounds of Christian culture.

This line of argument is one of Milbank's most significant, for it explains why a Christian account of group rights stands in tension with the notion of supplemental religious law. It is equally significant because it means that secular law, properly conceptualized, is itself a theological achievement for which it would be incoherent to demand sacral supplementation through religious law. In fact, Milbank's thought rests on the paradox that religious pluralism is not to be advanced by opening space for religious law within the civil law, but by more thoroughly and authentically secularizing the civil law. The secularization of law, though, is not to be understood in terms of a secularist framework in which law is denied any form of religious meaning. Law is instead presented as having a secular purpose whose full meaning is only disclosed within a Christian

35 Milbank, 138.
36 Milbank, 143.
37 Milbank, 147.
38 Milbank, 140.
39 Milbank, 135.
40 Milbank, 146.
41 Milbank, 146.

theological framework. As a result, Milbank's project has the simultaneous effect of elevating and diminishing the significance of secular law. These dueling aspects find resolution in a corporatist order whose logic is ultimately disclosed by the body of the Christ, within which individualism and community, universality and particularity, engage in a dynamic interplay. Whereas Williams maintains a certain sanguinity that introducing religious law into the civil law might enhance pluralism and draw law into a constructive engagement with theology, Milbank locates this possibility in the establishment of Christianity as the basis of a plural social order.

The aim of this essay is not to render judgment on whether Williams or Milbank offers a superior account of pluralism, but rather to draw legal debate about religious pluralism into a broader theological framework. It is on such terms that the limits of the jurisprudential methodology employed by the European Court of Human Rights are brought into focus and possibilities introduced for the development of constructive alternatives. In particular, Williams and Milbank offer ways for thinking about religious pluralism that move beyond inherited patterns of legal discourse. They provide a framework for interrogating secularism as the dominant paradigm within which religious human rights are conceptualized. They provoke a rethinking of the nature and foundations of pluralism as bequeathed by the liberal human rights tradition. They offer a starting point for reframing constitutional debate about religious group rights in the multicultural state. Above all, the emergence of this debate augurs the possibility of transformative developments within legal and constitutional thought, particularly as it has taken shape within the category of human rights, which has remained one of the most impregnable embodiments of the modern universal and secular project. Perhaps the most intriguing prospect is for the development of a theological jurisprudence to rival liberalism's account of the relationship of law and religion. Such an alternative would challenge András Sajó's claim that constitutionalism 'needs a considerable level of secularization'.[42] In the least, it would demand a rethinking of the form and foundations of legal secularism as it relates to the religious heritage and future of the West.

42 A. Sajó, 'Constitutionalism and Secularism: The Need for Public Reason', 30 *Cardozo Law Review* 6 (2009), 2401.

Index

For Product Safety Concerns and Information please contact our EU representative GPSR@taylorandfrancis.com
Taylor & Francis Verlag GmbH, Kaufingerstraße 24, 80331 München, Germany

www.ingramcontent.com/pod-product-compliance
Ingram Content Group UK Ltd.
Pitfield, Milton Keynes, MK11 3LW, UK
UKHW022006180926
475701UK00003B/227

* 9 7 8 0 3 6 7 6 0 1 4 7 8 *